INTERNATIONAL
FINANCE AND OPEN-ECONOMY
MACROECONOMICS

Theory, History, and Policy

INTERNATIONAL
FINANCE AND OPEN-ECONOMY
MACROECONOMICS
Theory, History, and Policy

Hendrik Van den Berg

University of Nebraska-Lincoln, USA

 **World Scientific**

NEW JERSEY · LONDON · SINGAPORE · BEIJING · SHANGHAI · HONG KONG · TAIPEI · CHENNAI

Published by

World Scientific Publishing Co. Pte. Ltd.

5 Toh Tuck Link, Singapore 596224

USA office: 27 Warren Street, Suite 401-402, Hackensack, NJ 07601

UK office: 57 Shelton Street, Covent Garden, London WC2H 9HE

British Library Cataloguing-in-Publication Data
A catalogue record for this book is available from the British Library.

First published 2010
Reprinted 2011

INTERNATIONAL FINANCE AND OPEN-ECONOMY MACROECONOMICS
Theory, History, and Policy

ISBN-13 978-981-4293-51-8 (pbk)
ISBN-10 981-4293-51-2 (pbk)

Typeset by Stallion Press
Email: enquiries@stallionpress.com

Printed in Singapore.

Preface

On this summer day in July 2009, dark clouds are passing rapidly overhead, and are moving eastward towards Mt. Washington. Against this splendid scene, stands the Mount Washington Hotel, where my wife and I can be found, seated at the veranda. The roof of the long veranda that stretches around three sides of the Mount Washington Hotel protects us, along with a small number of other hotel guests, from the rain. As we sit comfortably on soft, pillowed wicker chairs, we observe several people huddled under a small shelter on the golf course that lies between the hotel and the dark green forest at the base of Mt. Washington. Soon, the peak of the mountain disappears in the clouds, leaving visibly only the tree-covered lower sections of the highest mountain in the eastern half of the United States.

I try to imagine similar summer storms passing over the hotel 65 years earlier in July 1944, when John Maynard Keynes, Harry Dexter White, and nearly 500 other economists and government officials from the 44 Allied nations fighting World War II met here at the Mount Washington Hotel in Bretton Woods, New Hampshire. Of course, turbulent weather was probably the least of their concerns. They had come to this beautiful hotel in this peaceful natural setting as delegates to a conference organized to come up with a set of rules under which the international financial system would operate after the war. They were given three weeks to complete the task.

It is tempting to find parallels between 1944 with 2009; after all, the 2008 financial crisis and the serious global recession that followed have, in 2009, caused annual global output to decline for the first time since the end of World War II. Upon further reflection, however, it would be arrogant on our part to give our current economic problems equal billing with those in 1944.

The financial and political clouds hanging over Bretton Woods in 1944 were darker and much more threatening than anything we are experiencing in 2009. The 1944 guests at the Mount Washington Hotel were living through the most destructive and deadly war ever, which had followed closely on the heels of the Great Depression, the collapse of globalization, and World War I. Yet, despite the difficult situation, approximately 500 men and one woman who made up the delegations attending the Bretton Woods Conference managed to agree on a new set of global institutions and rules that would permit global output to grow for 65 years!

Still, it is important to ask why the growth of world GDP suddenly collapsed in 2009. Was there a flaw in the system that John Maynard Keynes, Harry Dexter White, and their fellow delegates put together 65 years ago? Or was their work undermined by subsequent changes in the rules and institutions? I cannot help but question why the Mount Washington Hotel at present is not bustling with economists, government officials, and central bankers in search of a reformed system that can restore economic health for another 65 years. However, this July of 2009, only the thunder of the passing storm disrupts the tranquility of the stately Mount Washington Hotel.

I hope that this textbook on international finance and open-economy macroeconomics will communicate an appreciation for what went on at Bretton Woods in 1944 and a concern about the shortcomings of our current international financial system. Perhaps the success of the Bretton Woods "system" over the past 65 years has reduced the urgency sensed by the 1944 Bretton Woods conference delegates. Surely the 2009 worldwide recession makes it clear that not everything is right with our current system.

More specifically, the purpose of this textbook is to describe how the international financial system operates within the set of economic, social, and natural environments that we humans inhabit. I hope that the evolutionary perspective of economic theory, combined with historical events and policy debates, succeeds in giving the reader a comprehensible and accurate view of the fascinating complexity of our human existence. Of course, I also hope that I can communicate to you the importance of the international financial system to how humanity copes with the complexity of its existence. However, the accomplishments of Keynes and the others here in Bretton Woods 65 years ago reassure us that humanity has enough knowledge and understanding to shape and improve the economic outcomes generated by these complex interactions. I hope this book gives you a comprehensible view at our human existence and the importance of the international financial system within that existence.

In closing, I would like to thank my wife Barbara for her constant and competent support in my efforts to write a relevant textbook on international finance. Without her suggestions, enthusiastic research, and critical proof-reading, this book would not have been completed. I also want to thank the several hundred students in my undergraduate and graduate international finance classes here at the University of Nebraska for their many comments and suggestions on earlier drafts of this book. Finally, I must acknowledge a huge debt to all the thinkers, teachers, and questioners who, over the centuries, provided the insights that help us make sense of our world today. Holistically, there is really no such thing as a personal accomplishment; everything we do is but a small extension of the efforts and contributions of countless others.

Hendrik Van den Berg
Bretton Woods, New Hampshire
13 July 2009

Contents

Part I

Introduction to International Finance

Chapter 1
Introduction

There is the curious notion that the protection of national interest and development of international cooperation are conflicting philosophies — that somehow other men of different nations cannot work together without sacrificing the interests of their particular nation.... Yet none of us has found any incompatibility between devotion to our own country and joint action. Indeed, we have found on the contrary that the only genuine safeguard for our national interests lies in international cooperation.

(US Treasury Secretary Henry Morgenthau,
Bretton Woods, 22 July 1944.[1])

The night of 30 June 1944 was unlike any night Loyd MacNayr had experienced as a locomotive fireman for the Boston and Maine Railroad. As he fired up the steam locomotive on a siding in Springfield, Massachusetts, Loyd read the train orders that the engineer, Charlie Murphy, held up for him to see: "Run passenger extra Springfield to White River Junction. Has right over all trains". The order meant that all other trains, even scheduled express trains, had

---

[1] From Henry Morgenthau's closing speech at the Bretton Woods Conference, Bretton Woods, New Hampshire, 22 July 1944.

to let them pass. Loyd was further surprised when the section fore-man showed up to ride with them on the locomotive. This indeed was an important train!

The foreman told Loyd that the special train had already sped past many sidelined trains along the Pennsylvania Railroad from Atlantic City, New Jersey, through the outskirts of Philadelphia, and later underneath the Hudson River into New York City. Additional passengers had come on board to fill the train during a stop at Pennsylvania Station in New York. Then the train proceeded under the East River and north onto the tracks of the New York, New Haven and Hartford Railroad to Springfield, where Loyd and his fellow crew members were now waiting to head the train. When the train arrived in Springfield, the New Haven Railroad locomotive was separated from the passenger cars, and Loyd and his fellow crew members backed their Boston and Maine Railroad locomotive up to the long string of passenger cars. As soon as the couplers joined and the yard crew attached the brake hoses, they were given the signal to proceed. They rushed the train north through the Connecticut River Valley past Holyoke and Greenfield, Massachusetts, and onto Brattleboro and Bellows Falls, Vermont. The night was too dark for the passengers to see much of the beautiful New England country-side, but after the hot and steamy weather they endured in Atlantic City and New York City, they surely must have enjoyed the cooler New England air that blew through the open windows of the speed-ing train. Loyd's stint as fireman on the special train ended when the train reached White River Junction, Vermont, where another crew boarded the train to take it further north.

Loyd read later that President Franklin D. Roosevelt and the Soviet Union's Joseph Stalin had met for confidential meetings around 30 June, so he assumed that it was them who had been on his special train. "I never realized it and I wish I'd kept the train order because Mr. Pearce [the section chief] said it was very unusual and I'd probably never see another like it", he said some years later. We now know that Loyd's train was not carrying Roosevelt and Stalin. Rather, the passengers included the British economist John Maynard Keynes and the chief international economist at the US Department of the

Treasury, Harry Dexter White. Loyd was surprised to learn many years later that the special train on 30 June 1944 carried several hundred economists and financial experts from 45 Allied nations. The passengers jokingly called the train "the Tower of Babel on wheels", in reference to the many languages spoken by the several hundred international passengers on board.

After the crew change in White River Junction, the train continued north on the Boston and Maine Railroad until Whitefield, New Hampshire, where it was turned onto a short line to the resort community of Bretton Woods, New Hampshire. The passengers were then met by a long line of taxis waiting to carry them through the last mile of their journey to the Mount Washington Hotel.

The passengers on Loyd's train during that evening of 1944 were on their way to what is simply known as *The Bretton Woods Conference*. By the time two similar special trains carried the same group of delegates back to New York and Washington three weeks later, the Conference had completed what is still considered by many as the most enlightened and effective agreement for international cooperation. Even though he wrongly guessed who his passengers were, Loyd MacNayr was quite correct in assuming his train ride on 30 June had historical significance.

1.1 From War to Depression and Back to War

To grasp the importance of the Bretton Woods Conference, transport yourself back to 1 July 1944 for a moment. World War II was still raging. The Allied invasion of Normandy was just a few weeks old. There were the concentration camps, the millions of casualties on the Russian front, and the deadly naval battles in the Pacific between the US and Japan. Looking further back in time did not provide much comfort either. In the 1930s, the Great Depression had spread unemployment, hunger, misery, and a huge loss of prosperity throughout the world. The 1930s also saw the rise of fascism and militarism in Germany, Italy, Spain, and other countries, as well as millions of deaths under Joseph Stalin's brutal regime in the Soviet Union. And, before these disturbing events there was World War I, a war so devastating that it was described as "the war to end all wars". The dismal economic and political events over the three decades before that last day of June 1944 clearly challenged the delegates of the Bretton Woods Conference to alter the course of history. The past 65 years of history suggests that they were successful.

1.1.1 *The vision of the Bretton Woods delegates*

The delegates of the Bretton Woods Conference shared a spirit of cooperation and a desire to design a new economic order that could avoid further wars and economic recessions. They knew that some international monetary and trade system had to be devised that would reverse the world's fall into poverty and conflict. Among the ideas being promoted by the United States — arguably the dominant nation at Bretton Woods given their leadership among the Allied countries fighting World War II — and their close ally Great Britain, was a system of pegged exchange rates to provide the exchange rate stability deemed necessary for the world to resume international trade. The proposed system of pegged rates was similar to a plan agreed by Britain, France, and the United States in 1937 in a belated effort to restore some of the international trade and investment flows that had been choked off in the 1930s by most countries' restrictive international trade and financial policies. That 1937 plan did not have time to have the hoped-for effect on trade before the world began another world war. The idea of pegged exchange rates had been discussed by the delegates who rode on the train directly from the meeting of financial experts in Atlantic City.

At that meeting, leaders of the US and British delegations had debated, both formally and informally, the merits of different exchange rate systems and institutional arrangements that would be appropriate for the world following the end of the war. They had discussed an international central bank to provide reserves for countries and to defend the values of their currencies in the foreign exchange markets, and a development bank for funding the reconstruction of Europe and other countries devastated by the war.

They also discussed establishing an international organization to promote the reduction of tariffs and other barriers to international trade. But there were still a number of potentially contentious issues to be decided. And, unlike the smaller meeting in Atlantic City, there were delegates from 45 Allied countries in Bretton Woods, including the exiled governments of France, the Netherlands, and several other countries still occupied by Germany or Japan. In order to maintain harmony among the countries that still had to work together to win World War II, the US hosts and the negotiators would have to carefully respect the national interests and pride of the different delegations.

Fortunately, unity of purpose prevailed in Bretton Woods. No doubt, the need to maintain unity among allies in the ongoing war helped to prevent dissention. At the same time, there was a strong desire among the delegates to avoid the mistakes made at the end of World War I, when the Paris Conference in effect planted seeds that grew into new conflicts, ultimately leading to a second world war. It was clear to many of the delegates that the attempt to restore the Gold Standard — the dominant international monetary system that had existed before the war — in the fragile post-World War I economic environment had caused substantial damage to many European economies. The rigid monetary policies mandated by the rules of the Gold Standard were also blamed for spreading the 1930 US recession quickly to other countries, thus creating the worldwide Great Depression. It was only too clear to many Bretton Woods delegates that opportunistic fascists such as Hitler in Germany and the militarists in Japan had exploited the poor economic conditions to consolidate power in their respective countries. According to Nobel laureate Robert Mundell:

> Had the price of gold been raised in the late 1920s, or, alternatively, had central banks pursued policies of price stability instead of adhering to the gold standard, there would have been no Great Depression, no Nazi revolution, and no World War II.[2]

---

[2] Robert A. Mundell (2000). p. 331.

With a predominance of such sentiments, few delegates at the Bretton Woods Conference argued for a restoration of the Gold Standard.

The lead that the United States took in organizing the conference was also significant. After World War I, the US had displayed its isolationist tendencies by withdrawing from all international organizations created after the "war to end all wars". Even though US President Woodrow Wilson was the major driving force in creating the League of Nations in 1919, US public opinion did not support his efforts, and the US Congress voted against joining the League of Nations. Between 1920 and 1932, Presidents Harding, Coolidge, and Hoover, in tandem with the Congress, further isolated the US from the global economy by raising tariff barriers to trade, reducing immigrant inflows, and blocking participation in other international organizations. The United States' isolationist tendencies did not prevent the US economy from affecting the world economy, however. The US was the world's largest economy, and after the decline of Britain after World War I, the US had become a major source of international financing. It was the 1929 crash of the US stock exchanges that triggered the worldwide financial crisis that led to the Great Depression. It was not until after Franklin D. Roosevelt became President in 1933, that the US began actively seeking adjustments to the failing international monetary order and cooperating more closely with policymakers of other countries. However, this belated and very slow retreat from the rigid and isolationist US economic policies was not only too late to prevent the Great Depression, it was also too late to stop the world from separating into distinct economic camps. The economic disputes quickly became ideological disputes, and these soon became international political disputes. Another world war, this one even more destructive than the "war to end all wars", eventually followed.

1.1.2 *1 July 1944*

When the delegates and their staff arrived at the Mount Washington Hotel in Bretton Woods on the night of 30 June 1944, the hotel had been reopened just for the occasion. Like most hotels, the Mount

Washington had closed in 1942 when US entry into the war effectively shut down the tourism industry. Hotels and guest homes nearby were also pressed into service to house the delegates and their staff, some 700 people in all, plus reporters, secretarial staff, translators, and other support staff sent by the US government from Washington. The US Army's Military Police was assigned to perform various logistical tasks, and a large contingent of local Boy Scouts camped on the premises while serving as messengers, mail carriers, and cleaners during the conference. There were more than a few emotional arguments among the delegates and staff about who got to stay in the main hotel and who was assigned to other residences. The new manager of the Hotel was so overwhelmed by the task of handling the event that he resigned on the first day of the conference (rumor has it that he drank himself into a stupor and was dismissed).

Despite the logistical confusion, the conference got off to a quick start. Within hours of arriving, the American delegation met to determine their negotiating strategy. Treasury Secretary Henry Morgenthau was the official head of the US delegation, but it was Harry Dexter White, the Chief Economist at the US Department of the Treasury, who ran that first meeting and led the subsequent negotiations. Harry Dexter White held a PhD in economics from Harvard and was a highly respected Treasury Department official. He was also a committed internationalist. According to James Boughton, the official International Monetary Fund (IMF) historian: "The core of White's thinking... was a belief that cooperation among governments was necessary for global prosperity".[3]

During the US delegation's private strategy meeting on the first day of the conference, White discussed some of the ideas that emerged from the Atlantic City meetings. He said that the ideas were purely exploratory, useful for gauging the opinions of others and to evaluate the positions the US should adopt in Bretton Woods. The truth, however, was that White had already made up his mind that the international monetary system should have pegged exchange rates that would be held constant by explicit central bank intervention in

---

[3] James M. Boughton (1994).

the foreign exchange markets. Despite some differing opinions within the US delegation and more varied opinions across the other delegations, White aggressively pushed to shape the new international monetary system and give the US dollar a central role in international finance.[4] During the three weeks in Bretton Woods, White gently but very persistently steered consensus toward pegged exchange rates and dollar dominance.

The British delegation was headed by John Maynard Keynes. Like Harry Dexter White, Keynes was an internationalist. Likewise Keynes had a strong desire to maintain his country's economic and political influence in the world. But unlike White, Keynes enjoyed universal respect as an economist and as a statesman. Keynes had been a member of the British delegation to the Paris Conference that drafted the ill-fated Versailles peace treaty after World War I. He had resigned from the British delegation halfway through the Paris Conference because he disagreed with the punishing reparations payments that the leaders of Britain, France, and Italy were demanding of Germany and Austria–Hungary in the treaty that was taking shape. After he left the Paris Conference, Keynes sat down and wrote *The Economic Consequences of the Peace*, the now classic book in which he argued that the harsh terms imposed on Germany would fuel resentment that would result in another war. His predictions had sadly come true 20 years later. Keynes also went on to write his *General Theory of Employment, Interest, and Money*, which had become the premier prescription for economic policy in an economic depression. Keynesian macroeconomics prescribed active policies to keep an economy at or near full employment.

In Bretton Woods, Keynes and his British delegation supported White's efforts to reach an international monetary agreement that would eventually be open to all countries, including Germany and Japan under new governments, after the war. Keynes also insisted on a monetary system that would give policymakers sufficient flexibility to pursue macroeconomic policies aimed at maintaining full employment.

---

[4] Boughton (1994) contains many interesting excerpts from stenographers' complete notes from the meetings at Bretton Woods.

Keynes had concluded that Britain's economic troubles after World War I stemmed from attempts to tie the pound to gold under the pre-World War I gold parities, which after a serious bout of wartime inflation implied a substantial overvaluation of the pound. He thus sought more policy flexibility for governments. Like White, he concluded that pegged exchange rates, which were fixed rates that under extreme circumstances could be re-pegged, were the appropriate replacement for the Gold Standard and the inter-war chaos that followed the Gold Standard's collapse in the Great Depression.

Harry Dexter White was a convinced Keynesian economist and agreed that countries should have the freedom to use macroeconomic policies to actively promote employment and price stability, unburdened by the need to keep their money supplies in line with historical gold stocks. Keynes and White also shared a certain distrust of financial markets and agreed that freely floating exchange rates would be too volatile for the fragile post-war economy. Even though there was close cooperation between White and Keynes on many issues, White was able to get some important provisions into the final agreement that Keynes did not agree with. Despite his reputation, Keynes could not overcome the overwhelming power that the US leadership in the war effort gave to Harry Dexter White and the US delegation at Bretton Woods. White kept the discussions focused sharply on his overall agenda.

1.1.3 *The accomplishments of Bretton Woods*

At Bretton Woods, White and Keynes ultimately settled on a system of adjustable pegs, which was a system in which exchange rates were pegged through official market intervention by each country's central bank but the pegs could be changed in the case of serious economic stress. White and Keynes saw the stable exchange rates as necessary for reviving international trade. Because the pegs could be adjusted, policymakers would have the necessary flexibility to alter monetary and fiscal policies when serious recession or deflation threatened. Keynes and White also agreed to establish the *International Monetary Fund* (IMF), the institution that would become the international central bank in the post-World War II world economy. Keynes and White had discussed this type of institution prior to the conference, but it would be decided at Bretton Woods how much capital each country would contribute and how voting rights would be allocated within the IMF. A large portion of the three weeks at Bretton Woods was spent arguing over these details.

The delegates also agreed to establish an *International Trade Organization* (ITO) to promote the reduction in the high tariffs and other protectionist trade barriers that had been put into place during the Great Depression, as well as an international bank to finance reconstruction after the war. The latter became the *Bank for Reconstruction and Development*, and it is now known simply as the *World Bank*. A permanent trade organization would have to wait 50 more years until 1994, however, when the *World Trade Organization* (WTO) was finally approved. After the war, the world's market economies only ended up negotiating the *General Agreement on Tariffs and Trade* (GATT), a set of rules under which trade negotiations would proceed in the latter half of the 20th Century. The United States and several other countries concluded that a permanent international organization that monitors and enforces trade rules, as agreed upon at Bretton Woods, would be too much of an imposition on their national sovereignty.

For three weeks the delegates discussed and negotiated, with little time for golf and the other recreational activities available on the beautiful grounds of the luxurious Mount Washington Hotel. Agreement was officially reached on all items on the agenda. On 22 July 1944, US Treasury Secretary Henry Morgenthau closed the conference with a speech in which he summarized the accomplishments:

> The actual details of a financial and monetary agreement may seem mysterious to the general public. Yet at the heart of it lie the most elementary bread and butter realities of daily life. What we have done here in Bretton Woods is to devise machinery by which men and women everywhere can exchange freely, on a fair and stable

basis, the goods which they produce through fair labor. And we have taken the initial step through which the nations of the world will be able to help one another in economic development to their mutual advantage and for the enrichment of all.

Keenly aware of the causes of the world war that was still raging, Morgenthau emphasized that the agreement marked a shift to international cooperation:

> To seek the achievement of our aims separately through the planless, senseless rivalry that divided us in the past, or through the outright economic aggression which turned neighbors into enemies would be to invite ruin again upon us all. Worse, it would be once more to start our steps irretraceably down the steep, disastrous road to war. That sort of extreme nationalism belongs to an era that is dead.
>
> Today the only enlightened form of national self-interest lies in international accord. At Bretton Woods we have taken practical steps toward putting this lesson into practice in monetary and economic fields.

Morgenthau clearly saw the Bretton Woods Agreement as more than just an agreement on the international monetary system. He presented it as a complete reversal from the predominant policies of the period between the two World Wars, when nationalism, ideological conflict, and economic isolation caused a sharp decline in international trade and investment. Morgenthau's full speech is in the Appendix to this chapter.

1.1.4 *The legacy of Bretton Woods*

When the trains departed Bretton Woods carrying the delegates back to the capitals of the world on 23rd July the end of World War II was still a year away. But the 700 officials from the 45 Allied countries, with firm prodding by White and Keynes, had created an institutional framework for an international monetary system, where a robust post-World War II economic recovery had developed. More meetings and additional agreements would be necessary of course. The first was to bring Germany, Japan, and other enemy countries into the organization. Subsequently, more members were added from among the newly independent former colonies. Later, there were more substantive adjustments to the way the international monetary system operated.

1.2 The Bigger Picture

In many ways the conference accomplished what it set out to do. To date, there has been no World War III. And rather than falling into a depression, as many economists feared would happen when wartime spending ended, the world achieved unprecedented rates of economic growth. Never before in history had standards of living grown as fast in as many economies as they did during the 1950s and 1960s under the "Bretton Woods system". The best post-war economic performances were by the newly democratic countries of Germany and Japan. Most importantly, the Bretton Woods Conference showed that governments of many different countries could constructively shape the world's complex economic environment for their mutual benefit.

In his closing speech, Morgenthau explicitly addressed a fundamental conflict that humanity has wrestled with for thousands of years:

> There is a curious notion that the protection of national interest and development of international cooperation are conflicting philosophies — that somehow or other men of different nations cannot work together without sacrificing the interests of their particular nation....Yet none of us has found any incompatibility between devotion to our own country and joint action.

This issue on the perceived dangers of dealing with strangers is, unfortunately, anything but "a curious notion". Human societies have, in fact, often behaved as if cooperation and national interest are incompatible by opting for isolationist, aggressive, and protectionist policies. It is the Bretton Woods Conference that is "curious", precisely because it represents a successful effort that built the rules and procedures under which cooperation overcame the common human suspicion of strangers. The Bretton Woods delegates were obviously motivated by the devastating consequences of the uncooperative behavior that had led to two world wars and worsened the Great Depression. But, regardless of the circumstances, Bretton Woods was an amazing accomplishment. A careful reading of history shows that the enlightened shift towards international cooperation in the midst of war was a distinctive historic accomplishment.

1.2.1 *The gains from dealing with strangers*

In general, humans are better off when they cooperate with strangers than when they isolate themselves into small groups. There are three fundamental advantages gained by an individual or a group of individuals when they expand the number of people they deal with. Specifically, by cooperating with others outside the immediate group, society, or nation, it is possible to achieve:

- Higher levels of specialization
- Reduction in uncertainty and risks from unpredictable adverse outcomes
- Faster accumulation of knowledge

Today's high standards of living could not have been achieved without extensive cooperation among strangers.

The gain from specialization was detailed by Adam Smith in his classic 1776 work entitled *An Inquiry into the Nature and Causes of the Wealth of Nations*:

> The greatest improvements in the productive powers of labour, and the greater part of the skill, dexterity, and judgement with which it is any where directed, or applied, seem to have been the effects of the division of labour.[5]

---

[5] Adam Smith (1776 [1976]). p. 7.

By splitting tasks among people within a society, the total product is increased. Smith correctly distinguished international trade as a vital component in the process of economic growth. In his analysis of the Industrial Revolution that was gaining momentum in Britain and his native Scotland at the time of his writing, Smith also recognized the phenomenon that we now call *economies of scale*. Smith observed large differences in productivity between the traditional cottage system of production and the *factory system* that characterized the Industrial Revolution. He explained that such improvements in productivity required large-scale factories; they could not be achieved by simply multiplying the number of cottage industries. Of course, he duly noted that large scale production requires people to exchange products over greater distances with people engaged in other types of specialized large scale production, people they almost certainly do not know personally. That is, economies of scale leads to more impersonal transactions.

The second advantage of expanding economic interaction to more people is that broader interaction creates better opportunities for reducing risk. To the extent that people face risks that are, at least in part, specific to them rather than to all of society, cooperation among a greater variety of people can reduce such individual risks. For example, when an isolated individual's crops fail, starvation is the likely outcome. However, people that are spread over geographic distances could find a way to agree that when some people's crops fail, others will feed them; and when other's crops fail, the former will help feed them. In this way, people who engage in such cooperative behaviors are likely to survive longer together than on their own.

Modern complex societies have developed a great variety of ways to cooperate. Institutions, markets, and organizations have been created that effectively enable distrustful individuals and groups to better cooperate and deal with misfortune. For example, we have insurance companies that will compensate people for a variety of disasters, and bond markets that permit the accumulation of wealth in assets that can be quickly converted to cash when needed. Other examples include private charities that extend personal assistance beyond traditional family units, international banking firms that let entire countries borrow from other nations to deal with emergencies, foreign trade networks that make goods and services available anywhere on earth, and international organizations that directly assist people in dealing with misfortune.

The third advantage of dealing with more strangers is the acceleration of technological progress. The source of knowledge is the human capacity to think and reason. The rate of technological progress thus directly depends on the number of people who think. Also, since new knowledge builds on existing knowledge, the more people share ideas, the more knowledge will be created. As they say, two heads are better than one. In the words of William Petty, a 17th century English intellectual: "...it is more likely that one ingenious curious man may rather be found among 4 million than among 400 persons".[6]

Most importantly, the value of new knowledge depends on how quickly it is passed from the person(s) who created it. When people are willing to communicate and deal with strangers, knowledge can be used by more people than those who remain in close proximity to the creators of such knowledge. It is no coincidence that throughout history the most advanced societies had the most contact with other societies, and the most backward regions are isolated from the rest of the world. Isolated societies literally have to "reinvent the wheel". In an integrated world, only one person has to actually invent the wheel for the innovation to become available to everyone.

1.2.2 *The three benefits of human interaction are intertwined*

Adam Smith saw a close relationship between specialization, or what he referred to as the division of labor, and the creation of knowledge:

> ...the invention of all those machines by which labour is so much
> facilitated and abridged, seems to have been originally owing to the

---

[6] William Petty (1682). Another Essay in Political Arithmetic.

division of labour. Men are much more likely to discover easier and readier methods of attaining any object, when the whole attention of their minds is directed towards the single object, than when it is dissipated among a great variety of things....[7]

Smith describes a concept that we now refer to as *learning by doing*. That is, when they concentrate on a specific task, people have a stronger incentive to learn to perform the task more efficiently than if they perform a great variety of tasks. Thus, exchange among a greater number of strangers promotes specialization, and specialization promotes learning.

There is also likely to be a close relationship between knowledge creation and risk reduction. If people are less likely to die during any given year of their lives, and people reduce the risk of starvation by establishing some mutual assistance or exchange mechanism, then they are also likely to adopt a long-term view of life. A longer time perspective enhances investment and innovation, two activities that require short-run sacrifice for future gains. In short, the three advantages of larger societies interact to enhance each of the advantages from dealing with strangers.

1.2.3 *Dependence on strangers is inherently problematic*

Interaction with strangers also has its costs and dangers. First of all, cooperating with others often implies that people must adjust their own behavior to that of others. At the personal level, working with someone else often means that you cannot do everything exactly the way you might do them on your own. At the national level, an international monetary system imposes restrictions on national policymakers and influences a nation's overall economic outcomes. Also, international economic activity and frequent contacts with foreigners may undermine the authority of national leaders. International trade opens domestic producers and consumers to

---

[7] Adam Smith (1776[1976]). p. 13.

foreign competition. Interaction with foreigners may also cause cultural clashes and conflicts among institutions.

There are more fundamental reasons why, throughout human history, people have avoided cooperating with strangers. People have often found it convenient and less costly to steal than to exchange. And it may be advantageous to force others to do the least desirable work, which is why slavery and oppression have been common features of human societies for tens of thousands of years. In general, individuals, groups, and entire nations often have strong incentives to exploit, oppress, rob, pillage, and murder. Human survival has always depended on a careful balance between closer interaction and "keeping one's distance".

Interaction with others was mostly limited to family, clan, and other small groups during nearly all of human history. Matt Ridley (1996) details how the evolutionary process over the past several million years gave hunters/gatherers practical instincts for cooperating within small groups of individuals. Furthermore, Paul Seabright (2004) points out that the social conditions of hunter/gatherer societies, in which humans and their ancestors evolved, did not favor the development of those human behavioral instincts necessary for engaging in complex transactions with total strangers. Seabright points out, however, that the growth of economic and social interaction between strangers and the observed globalization of economic activity suggest that humans have found ways to reduce their propensity to exploit, steal, and kill:

> To manage the hazards imposed on us by the actions of strangers has required us to deploy a different skill bequeathed to us by evolution for quite different purposes, the capacity for abstract symbolic thought.[8]

The exceptional capacity to engage in *abstract reasoning* has, in turn, enabled humans to design social and economic institutions that

---

[8] Paul Seabright (2004). p. 257.

effectively induce strangers to behave in a cooperative manner required for more complex societies to function and survive.

1.2.4 *The crucial role of institutions*

Institutions are the cultural norms, social customs, formal laws, and explicit government regulations that shape individual human behavior. Institutions are needed because humans' "hard-wired" behavioral instincts, evolved when social and natural environments were different, are not appropriate for dealing with the complexity of modern societies. Somehow, humans have managed to create these necessary institutions, albeit haltingly and imperfectly, as evidenced by the prevalence of war, oppression, crime, and deprivation throughout human history.

Bretton Woods is an impressive example of humans' ability to create complex social organizations that induce individuals and small groups to effectively cooperate with strangers from the far corners of the world. In the middle of war, when emotions and instinct, the so-called evolved human "hardware", normally dictate people to concentrate on defeating their enemies, the leaders of the Allied countries engaged in abstract reasoning that is necessary to understand complex processes, draw lessons from the past, and put together measures that would have positive effects well beyond the most pressing issues. The Bretton Woods system stands out because it is very difficult to create institutions that successfully induce selfish and poorly-prepared human beings to cooperate with strangers. The cruel and deadly Crusades, the Inquisition's oppression of human thought, slavery, the World Wars, the Holocaust, the Soviet Gulags, and an endless list of other atrocities right up to present-day global society serve to remind us that humanity often fails to manage its complex society.

Douglass North (2005) reminds us appropriately that the real improvement in human existence "has been a trial and error process of change with lots of errors, endless losers, and no guarantee that we will continue to get it right in spite of the enormous accretion of knowledge over those centuries".[9] According to North, the frequent inconsistencies between people's objectives and society's actual outcomes are caused, first of all, by the lack of information and understanding on how their economic, social, and natural environments function and interact. Second, even when they understand the circumstances, people and groups often resist change because they prefer the status quo. The latter cause of failure is consistent with humans' instinctive desire to preserve one's current status. The former cause, namely the lack of understanding of our natural and social environments, is a more daunting problem.

Knowledge about our natural and social environments is incomplete, which means that the ability to accurately apply our capacity for reason and abstract thought is limited as well. Again, in the words of North:

> Throughout human history there has always been a large residual that defied rational explanation — a residual to be explained partly by non-rational explanations embodied in witchcraft, magic, religions; but partly by more prosaic non-rational behavior characterized by dogmas, prejudices, "half-baked" theories. Indeed despite the...assertion by eminent theorists that it is not possible to theorize in the face of uncertainty, humans do it all the time; their efforts range from ad-hoc assertions and loosely structured beliefs such as those encompassed in the labels "conservative" and "liberal" to elegant systematic ideologies such as Marxism or organized religions.[10]

Humans therefore face life in their complex social and natural environments with their evolved instincts, bits of rational knowledge, and a whole set of non-rational beliefs we can best describe as *culture*. On the positive side, today's high levels of material wealth, longer life

---

[9] Douglass C. North (2005). p. 15.

[10] Douglass C. North (2005). pp. 15–16. Deepak Lal (1999) makes a very similar argument but calls the non-rational portion of our overall belief system cosmological beliefs.

spans, and more complex societies suggest that, in recent centuries, humans have, over the generations, substantially expanded their knowledge and understanding of their environment.

1.2.5 *The importance of learning*

Expanding knowledge may not be enough for human survival, however. Ironically, the fact that humans have used their expanded knowledge to sustain ever more complex social arrangements among even larger numbers of people means that they have effectively created new social complexities and expanded interactions with the natural environment. That is, more knowledge enables more complexity, but that additional complexity creates new problems that humans must learn to deal with. It is not clear if we understand our complex social and economic environment better today than our distant ancestors understood their much smaller social hunter/gatherer environment 50,000 years ago. It is safe to say that most people today do not understand how the international financial system and the global economy work, despite the fact that their very existence depends on these systems. The 2008 financial collapse reminds us, once again, that even our world leaders do not fully understand how to make our global economic and social environment consistently work to our greatest benefit. How do we accelerate the growth of understanding our social environment in general, and the economic environment in particular?

1.3 How Humans Advance Knowledge

The acceleration in learning over the past several centuries has been attributed, in part, to the widespread adoption of the *scientific method*. This method of thinking and accumulating knowledge has enabled humans to get more out of their expanded interaction with more people. That is, humans have *learned to learn* more effectively.

1.3.1 *The scientific method*

The scientific method is a straightforward and logical approach to research and learning. The method is difficult to apply, however, because it requires strict discipline on the part of the "scientist". But without strict adherence to the scientific method, inquisitive human minds are more likely to reach unwarranted conclusions, accept falsehoods as truths, ignore or misinterpret evidence, and lose valuable knowledge accumulated by others in the past.

The scientific method is a process that requires a thinking person to follow these steps rigorously:

1. Observe some phenomenon or event.
2. Use reason to invent a *hypothesis*, which is an untested idea that clearly and logically explains something about the facts observed.
3. Confront the hypothesis' predictions with evidence of real outcomes or the outcomes of controlled experiments that simulate real events.
4. Perform many experiments or observe large amounts of real world outcomes under a variety of circumstances in order to avoid "spurious" outcomes driven by forces that are not considered in your hypothesis.
5. Record everything observed and tested, as well as the methods used.
6. Objectively examine whether all the observed outcomes consistently conform to the hypothesis.
7. If these "tests" of the hypothesis are not consistent with observed real world outcomes or experimental outcomes, modify the hypothesis and return to step 2.
8. If observations and experiments consistently confirm the hypothesis, the hypothesis becomes a *theory* (a confirmed hypothesis). At this point, the scientist publishes the results, accompanied by all the details of the tests that confirm the hypothesis so that others can verify the methods and results.

Note that when the scientific method is followed, unsupported hypotheses are abandoned and only proven hypotheses are maintained. As Albert Einstein wrote:

> Creating a new theory is not like destroying an old bar and erecting a skyscraper in its place. It is rather like climbing a mountain, gaining new and wider views, discovering unexpected connections between our starting point and its rich environment. But the point from which we started out still exists and can be seen, although it appears smaller and forms a tiny part of our broad view gained by the mastery of the obstacles on our adventurous way up.[11]

In summary, the scientific method is a systematic step-by-step process that builds knowledge, prevents losses of previous knowledge, and reduces the need to keep "rediscovering" what others before us had already known.

The scientific method provides a precise definition for the term *theory*. Unlike the popular use of the word "theory" that refers to a "vague" or "fuzzy idea", in science a theory means "confirmed hypothesis". A theory is a conceptual framework that consistently and accurately explains observed facts. The scientific method also implies that a hypothesis can become a theory only if it is *falsifiable*. That is, only in the case where we can collect evidence to prove or disprove a hypothesis can we arrive at a scientific theory. Something that is not falsifiable may become a *belief*, but it cannot serve as a hypothesis nor become a theory. For example, in the field of economics, the prediction that an expansion of the money supply in excess of growth of economic activity will cause inflation is sometimes referred to as an economic *theory* because we have observed large amounts of evidence across many countries and time periods that confirm this predicted result of excessive monetary expansion. However, the hypothesis that money growth causes inflation has also been falsified when observed under certain economic circumstances, such as when there is excess

---

[11] Albert Einstein, quoted in Wikipedia in the entry "Scientific Method".

capacity in the economy or open borders that permit domestic demand for goods and services to spill over into the global economy. Clearly, the hypothesis needs to be reformulated or qualified if it is to become a theory.

1.3.2 *The scientific method and absolute truth*

The repeated verification of a hypothesis, and its designation as a theory, often tempts us to conclude that we have uncovered *truth*. Realistically, all theories based on solid evidence and objective experimentation may still be falsified as we learn more and engage in further scientific activity. An interesting example is Isaac Newton's theory that the gravitational force between two objects is directly proportional to the objects' mass and inversely proportional to the square of the distance separating them. This was confirmed repeatedly by large amounts of evidence. In fact, the basic formula continues to be very useful for most practical applications. However, in the 19th century, more accurate instruments found some discrepancies, such as the observed fact that the planet Mercury did not orbit the way Newton's theory suggested. Albert Einstein's theory of relativity did a better job of explaining the universe, and his hypothesis was accepted by most scientists as a theory, effectively replacing Newton's hypothesis. However, recent experiments using a set of satellites orbiting the Earth uncovered some slight variations in their predicted orbits that were not envisioned by either Newton's theory of gravity or Einstein's theory of relativity. There seem to be more forces in the universe than previous theories could explain. As a result, we are back to testing new hypotheses.

Recall Douglass North's (2005) words, "throughout human history there has always been a large residual that defied rational explanation...", this is discouraging given humans' evolutionary development of intelligence and their ability to find creative solutions to life's problems. We humans, therefore, have to be content with our ability to think, reason, and organize our lives so that we can continue gaining knowledge, one step at a time. On further thought, our grossly incomplete knowledge provides us an exciting future. Would we, a species with an exceptional ability to think, want to figure everything out now and leave us with nothing left to learn and discover? Fortunately, this book will argue clearly that in the field of international finance, we still have much to learn.

1.3.3 *Economic models and the scientific method*

In the social science of economics, economists often put their hypotheses in the form of *models*, which are simplified representations of real world phenomena. That models are simplifications should not, per se, disqualify them from being used as hypotheses or from becoming theories. All theories are probably simplifications of reality in some way.

The *principle of Occam's razor* is often cited as a justification for the use of simplified models. The principle states: "One should not increase, beyond what is necessary, the number of entities required to explain anything". That is, we should use Occam's razor to shave away all those variables and relationships that are not necessary, to explain or predict a given economic phenomenon. This principle effectively advises us to first choose the simplest model of economic activity among a set of equally promising ones. The simplest model is usually the easiest to test. And, further enhancements can be introduced incrementally if tests fail to confirm the simplest hypothesized model.

Social scientists are always faced with what seems to be an infinite number of possible hypothetical constructs. For example, supposing we have observed the three points in Fig. 1.1, we now seek to hypothesize the relationship between X and Y. The principle of Occam's razor suggests that we hypothesize a simple inverse linear relationship between X and Y. However, the true relationship could be nonlinear, possibly one of the curves shown in Fig. 1.2. Further evidence (additional points) will be needed to definitively justify or reject the hypothesis of an inverse linear relationship.

One of the common errors humans commit is to base their beliefs on individual cases or a single observation. Case studies and individual examples represent isolated events. They are, effectively, a sample

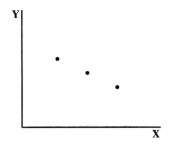

Figure 1.1   How are X and Y related?

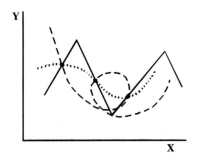

Figure 1.2   Alternative functions containing the observed points.

of one. A single point in Fig. 1.1 would have given us no clue whatsoever about the relationship between X and Y because a single point would have been compatible with just about any hypothesis about the relationship between X and Y. In general, case studies are not very useful for testing hypotheses about complex economic phenomena.

It is common in economics to represent economic models in mathematical form. For example, the linear relationship between X and Y shown in Fig. 1.1 can also be stated as a linear equation $Y = a + bX$, where Y is the dependent (endogenous) variable, X is the explanatory (exogenous) variable, a is the constant, and b is the slope variable. Models can, of course, be represented verbally or graphically. Most early economic models were presented without mathematical equations or diagrams. It was not until the late 1800s that graphic illustrations became popular; mathematical models became the common choice for economic theorists after the middle of the 20th century. Often, in order to make the logic of the model as clear as possible, this textbook will represent the same model using words, graphs, and mathematics.

1.3.4 *Holism*

As social scientists, economists should be suspicious of Occam's razor and the fact that our simple models omit things that can vary across space and time. Economic activity occurs within complex economic, social, and natural environments. Given the complexity of the international monetary system, the broader economic system, and the overall social and natural environments that we live in, economists should expect any simple model to fail, at least occasionally, as it is tested under varying circumstances. Economists may not, in fact, be able to always uncover meaningful hypotheses that hold under general conditions. The growing appreciation for complexity has led many social scientists to reduce their reliance on the principle of Occam's razor and, instead, embrace a perspective called *holism*.

The root of the term *holism* is the Greek word *holos*, meaning *entire, total, whole*. The term is usually attributed to Jan Christiaan Smuts, who in his 1926 book entitled *Holism and Evolution* used the term to describe dynamic theories in the physical sciences such as Charles Darwin's theory of evolution, Henri Becquerel's theory of radioactivity, and Albert Einstein's theory of relativity. These theories described the world as evolving dynamic systems, in which the parts are related to all other parts in complex ways that condition how each observed part functions. Holism is the recognition that the components cannot be understood in isolation and their functions cannot be predicted without knowing the environment in which they exist.

A good example of the necessity of a holistic approach to understand human action is the Three Mile Island nuclear power plant in Pennsylvania. On 28 March 1979, the second reactor of the Three

Mile Island nuclear plant released radioactive water. Soon after, radioactive gas was detected near the plant. Everyone could see that something was wrong at the plant, but no one seemed to know what the problem was. "I think it's safe to say chaos was the best way to describe it", wrote Samuel Walker, the US Nuclear Regulatory Commission's historian.[12] Later, it was apparent that the plant had come very close to a critical meltdown that would have devastated the entire region, including Washington D.C. One scientist in the US Nuclear Regulatory Commission, which oversees all US nuclear power plants, later admitted that although many experts had been consulted in an attempt to understand what had gone wrong, not one of them fully understood the whole Three Mile Island plant. No one was able to grasp why the separate parts of the plant, each performing as expected, could interact in a way that collapsed the whole system.

The example of Three Mile Island reminds us that it is true complex systems cannot work well if each component is below par, but even when each of the components in the complex system are managed well, the whole system may still fail. The linkages between the parts of the system must be understood and managed well. "This is true for atomic power plants, large enterprises operating in many countries and sectors, and the international financial system", according to international economist Vito Tanzi.[13]

1.3.5 *Economics and holism*

The failures of the international monetary system during the Great Depression or the recent financial crisis have caused huge economic damage. Clearly, economists and policymakers should have been more holistic in describing and overseeing our complex international

---

[12] Quoted in "Three Mile Nuclear Fears Revealed", *BBC News Website*, 17 June 2006.
[13] Vito Tanzi (2006). "Things Will Fall Apart But It Is the Aftermath that Matters", *Financial Times*, 24 February 2006.

financial system. Yet, economics may actually be lagging other social sciences and natural sciences in embracing holism.

In sociology, Emile Durkheim argued against the notion that society is nothing more than a collection of individuals. He showed that a *community* can take on many different forms, depending on how individuals, who make up society, organize themselves and behave within that organization. In medicine, the holistic approach to healing recognizes that the emotional, mental, and physical elements of each person work together. Most psychologists recognize that a person's relationship to society shapes behavior. The International Electrical Engineering Association has published guidelines suggesting engineers should take a holistic approach to their work in order to avoid incompatibilities between specific projects and the societies in which the projects are carried out. And, of course, holism is fundamental to the field of ecology. For example, the biologist E. O. Wilson (2002) describes the apparent hundred-fold increase in the rate of extinction of living species that we have experienced this century. Humanity appears to have triggered an ecological collapse of major proportions, the consequences of which can only be understood from an holistic perspective that bridges our natural and social environments.

Economists, therefore, are in good company when they embrace holism. In fact, it was one of their own, the economist Kenneth Boulding, who very appropriately described holism half a century ago as the approach that links "the specific that has no meaning and the general that has no content".[14]

1.3.6 *Holism and science*

Holism has been described as a diametric opposite to *scientific reductionism*, which in the minds of some people leaves the impression that it is in some way "unscientific". Scientific reductionism refers to the strategy of gaining understanding about the *whole* by learning about its *parts*. To the extent that there is a clear relationship

---

[14] Kenneth Boulding (1956). p. 197.

between the whole and its component parts, there is no conflict between scientific reductionism and holism. However, an understanding of a complex process or system also requires an understanding of how the parts *interact*. Focusing only on the parts, as scientific reductionism prescribes, is clearly not *scientific*. This is a critical point for international economists who study the international financial system because there is overwhelming evidence that the performance of the overall system has huge consequences for individual consumers, workers, firms, banks, investors, and all other distinct groups in the economy. Just imagine the different job markets an individual faced in 1929 as compared to 1933. To avoid confusion about holism, we might better describe the perspective of this textbook as *scientific holism*.

1.4 The Field of International Finance

The discussion of the Bretton Woods Conference, the financial system it established, and its significance within the broader perspective of our human history provides an appropriate introduction to our study of international finance. International finance studies the "system" within which people, businesses, governments, and other groups interact in the global economy. Specifically, international finance describes and explains the flows of payments between countries, but, in explaining those payments, international finance inevitably examines how these payments are related to the overall performance of economies and the human societies they inhabit.

1.4.1 *Defining the field*

Specifically, international finance focuses on many types of international transactions between individuals, firms, banks, governments, groups, and organizations in the global economy. These financial flows therefore provide an indication of how dependent we are on foreigners for our daily are existence. The study of international finance examines how institutions, such as those that were designed at the Bretton Woods Conference, enable the international monetary system to effectively advance international specialization, risk sharing, and technological progress. And more fundamentally, international finance uses models from open-economy macroeconomics to examine how the international financial system affects all macroeconomic variables that economists normally use to evaluate, explain, and influence the performance of the economic system.

Before setting out on our journey through the field of international finance, recall Douglass North's distinction between the rational and non-rational components of the overall belief system, or *culture*, within which intelligent human beings must try to explain their social and natural environments. We have relatively few proven theories that can be applied to numerous outcomes and problems in international finance. Harry Dexter White, John Maynard Keynes, and other policymakers at Bretton Woods offered their best answers to address the economic, political, and social circumstances that drove the world into the Great Depression and World War II.

As it turned out, White, Keynes, and other delegates at Bretton Woods got many things right in 1944. The financial system that emerged after World War II worked well enough to permit the world economy to recover from the war, and allowed many economies to enter a long and sustained period of rapid economic growth. However, the pegged exchange rates that distinguished the system ultimately proved to be unworkable, and the Bretton Woods system was replaced with another system in 1973. Economists continued to learn, and policymakers amended their economic policies. Yet, the new system was not able to establish conditions that led to consistent improvements in people's lives. Income disparities across countries grew, and even within most national economies, income distributions became less equal. The mixture of floating and managed exchange rates that characterized the post-Bretton Woods system caused numerous financial crises and deep recessions in many developing countries. Subsequently in 2008, a severe financial crisis and recession spread throughout the entire world, creating the fear of another Great Depression. Economists today face as many difficult questions as

Harry Dexter White, John Maynard Keynes, and other delegates did at Bretton Woods.

1.4.2 *The topics to be covered*

Among the topics to be covered in the remainder of the book are the balance of payments, foreign exchange markets, futures markets, international banking, international equity and bond markets, foreign direct investment, multinational firms, central bank intervention in the foreign exchange market, open-economy macroeconomics, the history of the international monetary system, and recent developments such as the euro, the imbalances between the world's major economies, and the 2008 financial crisis. In covering these topics, we will address these issues:

- Are international capital flows disruptive or stabilizing?
- Should exchange rates be controlled or should they be permitted to "float"?
- Should we abandon individual currencies and create a single money for the entire world, much like how the euro replaced national currencies?
- Should governments surrender national sovereignty and coordinate economic policies or should governments address only domestic economic goals and let the international financial system deal with the global consequences?
- Do we need more international institutions to regulate accounting standards, banking, bond markets, and corporate disclosure?
- Are national governments weakened by globalization?
- Should we reform or abolish the international institutions, such as the IMF and the World Bank that were created at Bretton Woods?
- What are the roles of Europe, China, and the US in the international monetary system today?
- Will the euro supplant the US dollar as the world's vehicle currency, or will the Chinese yuan play that role in the future?
- How could the entire world economy be so adversely impacted by the collapse of the housing market in the US in 2007?

- Will the huge US trade deficit cause the value of the US dollar to fall against other currencies, and if so, by how much?
- Holistically, how does the international financial system interact with the social and natural systems and affect the "whole"?

This list of questions is far from complete. The field of international finance is inherently broad. This textbook will take the international financial system out of the shadows and reveal the important role it has played in human history.

1.5 Back to Bretton Woods: Some Additional Introductory Comments

The Bretton Woods Conference vividly illustrates humanity's ability to shape its economic and social environments. However, the complete story of the Bretton Woods Conference also reveals the difficulty humans have in dealing with the complexity of their economic and social environments. The latter difficulty is clearly brought out by how Harry Dexter White was treated after the war. You might think that after successfully pushing the negotiations at Bretton Woods towards the outcome the United States sought, Harry Dexter White would be widely applauded. On the contrary, despite his central role in establishing the US dollar as the world's major currency and placing the United States solidly at the center of the post-war international monetary financial system, Harry Dexter White was publicly accused of treason.

1.5.1 *Is talking to foreigners treason?*

In August 1948, Harry Dexter White, the leader of the US delegation to the Bretton Woods Conference, was called before the US House of Representatives' Committee on Un-American Activities. He was accused by several prominent politicians of spying for the Soviet Union. Apparently, White had met Soviet officials after the war, when the US and the Soviet Union were in the beginning stages of what was to develop into the Cold War. White's contacts with Soviet officials were interpreted by some Congressmen as treason. There had been other allegations that White worked for foreign communist regimes. For example, after World War II, White held the Nationalist government in China closely accountable for hundreds of millions of dollars of US aid for fighting the Japanese occupation. Consequently, some interpreted this as an intentional effort by White to undermine the Nationalists in favor of the Communist Mao Tse Tung in China's civil war. White also supported a US$10 billion loan by the United States to aid postwar reconstruction in the Soviet Union. White argued that such a loan was necessary for the economic recovery in Europe, but as the Cold War began to develop in 1947, many people in the US viewed any aid to the Soviet Union as nothing other than active support of communism.

Three days after his appearance before Congress in 1948, White died from a heart attack. White's death was interpreted by some as proof of his guilt. White, in fact, had been suffering from a serious heart condition, and his emotional defense of his reputation most likely led to the heart attack. Among the most memorable moments of the hearing was his response to a question about his loyalty to the United States:

> I believe in freedom of religion, freedom of speech, freedom of thought, freedom of the press, freedom of criticism, and freedom of movement. I believe in the goal of equality of opportunity, and the right of each individual to follow the calling of his or her own choice, and the right of every individual to have an opportunity to develop his or her capacity to the fullest.... I consider these principles sacred. I regard them as the basic fabric of our American way of life, and I believe in them as living realities, and not mere words on paper. This is my creed.[15]

When he finished these words, White received thunderous applause from the majority of those in attendance. His conservative critics in the Congress and elsewhere in the government were undeterred, however.

---

[15] Quoted in J. Bruce Craig (2004).

After Harry Dexter White's death, the Director of the Federal Bureau of Investigation (FBI), J. Edgar Hoover, continued investigations into White's alleged treason. In 1953, nearly five years after White's death, Wisconsin's Senator Joseph McCarthy again accused White of having aided the Soviet Union and Communist China, and he held him up as an example of the many foreign agents he claimed had infiltrated the US government. At the same time, President Eisenhower's Attorney General, Herbert Brownell, even accused former President Harry Truman of knowing that White was a Soviet spy but still appointed him to the Executive Board of the new International Monetary Fund in 1947. President Truman successfully fought a subpoena to testify before Senator McCarthy's committee, but in the process White's reputation was further damaged.

The attacks on White's national loyalty were never substantiated, and Senator McCarthy, Hoover, and Brownell never presented the evidence they claimed they had. This episode of personal destruction leaves the question of why prominent politicians and members of the US government, including the Attorney General and the Director of the Federal Bureau of Investigation, would viciously attack Harry Dexter White years after his death, just when his biggest accomplishment, the Bretton Woods system, was beginning to meet the stated goals of the US delegation.

Simple politics is the most probable reason for the attacks on White, as Congressmen and Senators from the Republican Party took advantage of the distrust among conservative Americans of the internationalism and international cooperation that the Democratic administrations of Presidents Roosevelt and Truman actively and openly advocated. Even though leaders of many Western nations had little interest in dealing with Joseph Stalin, White had favored doing everything possible to convince the Soviet Union to remain part of the international financial system. Perhaps White's mistake was to openly lament the Soviet decision to withdraw behind its *iron curtain*; or maybe it was his refusal to join the anti-communist rhetoric that was becoming the norm at the beginning of the Cold

War.[16] The apparent political points to be gained from attacking White suggest that many American voters were still not comfortable with dealing with people they perceived as hostile strangers.

Interestingly, even today, textbooks and historical accounts of the Bretton Woods Conference still minimize White's role. Why are people so inclined to distrust the efforts of those who seek cooperation over isolation and conflict?

1.5.2 *Do we need another Bretton Woods conference?*

Today, 65 years after the Bretton Woods Conference, the international financial system is once again on the front page. The 2008 worldwide recession that made 2009 the first year of negative world economic growth since the end of World War II has led to an increase in international discussions on reforming international financial institutions and regulations. In addition to the immediate global economic recession, the world faces the need to eliminate extreme poverty of over one billion people and reduce economic volatility. The debate on how to address these issues often centers on the question of whether further economic gains can be best achieved through uncoordinated action by individual governments and multinational firms, or with more cooperative action through international organizations and governing institutions. In short, do we need to reform the international financial system, and is another meeting of national financial leaders like the one at Bretton Woods the best way to further human welfare?

Many political leaders and a number of economists claim that a coordinated reform of the international monetary system is not needed. After all, there have been no more world wars, and many international institutions are already in place. The IMF and the World Bank are fully operational and the World Trade Organization was

---

[16] In a very interesting book, J. Bruce Craig (2004) describes the meager evidence against White. White apparently had contact with Soviet operatives in the US, but it is not clear if he passed them secret information to the detriment of the US.

finally created in 1994 to replace the General Agreement on Trade and Tariffs and is now actively promoting free trade. Numerous other international organizations and institutions are working to harmonize accounting regulations, banking regulations, and providing other forms of oversight throughout the world. In April 2009, the leaders of the 20 largest economies, the G20 group, decided to deal with the global recession by providing the IMF with hundreds of billions of dollars in additional funds.

Despite the weaknesses of the current system, international economic activity has been growing more rapidly than overall economic activity, so we seem to be dealing with strangers more successfully. International trade accounted for over 25 percent of world output in 2007, international investment has blurred distinctions between national and foreign ownership in most economies, and nearly four percent of the world's population is living outside their country of birth. The two largest developing economies, China and India, which together account for over one-third of the world's population, have been growing at very rapid rates.

Those who call for more international cooperation emphasize areas where the global economy is not performing well. Poverty remains a problem in today's global economy, with about one billion people existing on an income of just US$1 per day. Ominously, the AIDS epidemic has substantially reduced human welfare in about twenty countries in Africa, a continent where many countries have experienced no growth in real per capita income over the past several decades. This problem is spreading to India, China, and other developing economies. The Bretton Woods goal of increasing international trade has been substantially met, but the benefits of trade and other global economic activity have not spread across all countries. The world economy is dependent on sources of energy supplied by a few countries, some of which teeter precariously on the verge of political and social collapse.

More worrisome is the tendency for the current international financial order to undergo repeated exchange rate crises, financial crises, and economic imbalances. Financial crises in 1982 were followed by prolonged economic recessions in some 40 countries. New exchange rate crises, financial crises, and deep economic declines occurred in Mexico, Brazil, Argentina, Southeast Asia, Russia, Turkey, and many other developing countries over the past 15 years. Each of these financial crises began with overvalued exchange rates, followed by speculative attacks on currencies, reversals of capital flows, declines in investment, bankruptcies, and deep recessions. Clearly, the current international financial order does not guarantee economic stability or consistent economic development policies.

Much criticism of the Bretton Woods institutions still remains. The IMF has been unable to prevent the numerous international financial crises that caused sharp income declines in many developing economies and some developed economies. The World Bank has also been ineffective in promoting economic growth where most help is needed. Recent reports on the World Bank have focused mainly on corruption within the institution. The development success stories in East Asia, China, and India occurred without much or any assistance from the World Bank. The World Trade Organization, envisioned at Bretton Woods but only created in 1994, is still not trusted or fully supported by leaders in the largest economies of the world. Overall, cooperation among countries is still far from complete.

Most worrying is the 2008–2009 international financial crisis and the deep worldwide recession, already being referred to as the *Great Recession*. For the first time since World War II, overall world GDP declined in 2009. The causes of this recession are unfettered financial innovation, the breakdown of national banking regulation, and, yes, widespread corruption and unethical behavior in the US financial industry. The globalization of finance and the international spread of large private financial firms increased the speed at which the contamination of "toxic" US assets spread throughout the global financial system. Economists are seriously debating whether international financial integration has gone too far.

John Maynard Keynes had anticipated these difficulties, which is why he argued for rules in the Bretton Woods agreement that would limit the free flow of capital across borders, keep international debt at a minimum, and prevent the development of large trade deficits. Keynes was overruled by Harry Dexter White at Bretton Woods. White and the US government sought to establish open international financial markets where the US dollar would be able to reign as the world's premier and reserve currency. This observation does not imply that the 2008 world financial crisis is the final legacy of Harry Dexter White. And, it is difficult to say whether the world economy would have performed better if Keynes had gotten his way at Bretton Woods to establish rules to limit capital mobility and force the balance of international trade.

Therefore, should we call the world's financial policymakers together for another meeting and create a new international monetary order that can address the world's economic problems? There is a lot of international finance, macroeconomics, and financial history to cover before we can answer this question. Keep the question in mind as you read the next 16 chapters, though. Then, in the final chapter, we can discuss this question again.

1.6 Summary and Conclusions

The intention of this chapter is to set the tone for the next 17 chapters that will take you through the field of international finance and open-economy macroeconomics. The purpose of this chapter is to:

1. Introduce the 1944 Bretton Woods Conference.
2. Highlight some of the events that led up to the Conference.
3. Place the Bretton Woods Conference within the broader context of how we manage our complex global society.
4. Explain the importance of abstract thinking for understanding complex economic and social arrangements.
5. Discuss the role of institutions in translating individual actions into optimal social outcomes.
6. Explain that "dealing with strangers" potentially enhances well-being by increasing specialization, reducing risks, and advancing knowledge.

7. Explain the scientific method and how it advances knowledge.
8. Introduce holism and explain its importance for understanding the relationships among the component parts of a complex system such as an economy or human society.
9. Explain that the international financial system is a complex one that must be studied from a holistic perspective that focuses on the parts, the overall system, and the linkages between the parts and the system.
10. Point out the inevitable failures of economic modeling and scientific reductionism within the complex, holistic environments humans inhabit.
11. Introduce international finance as the study of the international movement of money, the institutions that govern this movement, and the macroeconomic consequences of alternative systems.

More generally, this chapter makes it clear that, despite achievements such as the Bretton Woods Conference, today's international financial system still has many shortcomings. The current set of national and international institutions that shape our international financial system reflects many conflicts between evolved instinctive human behaviors, culture, unscientific beliefs, and occasional applications of forward-looking abstract reasoning. The attacks on Harry Dexter White by some prominent political leaders and government officials after World War II are further evidence of the complexity of our human existence. We have built complex economies that provide unprecedented levels of material well-being, but we still struggle to deal with the large number of strangers on whom we depend for our existence in our global economy and society.

The holistic and scientific approach embraced in this textbook will make it very clear that we inhabit a global society in which the international financial system affects the existence and welfare of every human being on Earth. If we want to improve our economic and social situations, we must deal with strangers and scientifically apply our capacity for abstract and scientific thinking. The Bretton Woods Conference shows that humans are capable of doing this.

Key Terms and Concepts

Bretton Woods Conference

Complexity

Floating exchange rates

General Agreement on Tariffs
  and Trade

Gold standard

Great Depression

Holism

Institutions

International Monetary Fund (IMF)

Models

Macroeconomics

Occam's razor

Pegged exchange rates

Scientific method

Scientific reductionism

Specialization

World Bank

Chapter Questions and Problems

1. What are the three main benefits that humanity gains from expanding human interaction by dealing with more "strangers"? Why do people often shun what Paul Seabright (2004) refers to as "the company of strangers"?

2. Discuss the role of institutions in a modern economy. Specifically, explain why institutions are needed to translate individual actions into outcomes that optimize outcomes for the entire group and society as a whole. Also, provide some examples of institutions that have enabled people to benefit from dealing with strangers.

3. Explain exactly what we mean by the scientific method. What are the precise steps that come under the scientific method? Why has this method been so instrumental in accelerating the process of technological progress? Also, why do people behave "unscientifically" so often?

4. Can the scientific method uncover absolute truth? Please explain why or why not.

5. Discuss the legacy of Bretton Woods. Was it successful? Was it a step forward for humanity?

Appendix

Henry Morgentau's closing speech, Bretton Woods, July 22, 1944.[17]

I am gratified to announce that the Conference at Bretton Woods has completed successfully the task before it.

It was, as we knew when we began, a difficult task, involving complicated technical problems. We came to work out methods which would do away with the economic evils — the competitive currency devaluation and destructive impediments to trade — which preceded the present war. We have succeeded in that effort.

The actual details of a financial and monetary agreement may seem mysterious to the general public. Yet at the heart of it lie the most elementary bread and butter realities of daily life. What we have done here in Bretton Woods is to devise machinery by which men and women everywhere can exchange freely, on a fair and stable basis, the goods which they produce through fair labor. And we have taken the initial step through which the nations of the world will be able to help one another in economic development to their mutual advantage and for the enrichment of all.

The representatives of the forty five nations faced differences of opinion frankly, and reached an agreement which is rooted in genuine understanding. None of the nations represented here has had altogether its own way. We have had to yield to one another not in respect to principles or essentials but in respect to methods and procedural details. The fact that we have done it in a spirit of good will and mutual trust, is, I believe, one of the hopeful and heartening portents of our time. Here is a sign blazoned upon the horizon, written large upon the threshold of the future — a sign for men in battle, for men at work in mines, and mills, and in the fields, and a sign for women whose hearts have been burdened and anxious lest the cancer of war assail yet another generation — a sign that the people of the earth are learning how to join hands and work in unity.

---

[17] Downloaded from the International Monetary Fund's website, http://www.imf.org, 20 August 2005.

There is a curious notion that the protection of national interest and development of international cooperation are conflicting philosophies — that somehow or other men of different nations cannot work together without sacrificing the interests of their particular nation. There has been talk of this sort — and from people who ought to know better — concerning the international cooperative nature of the undertaking just completed at Bretton Woods. I am perfectly certain that no delegation to this Conference has lost sight for a moment of the particular national interest it was sent here to represent. The American delegation which I have the honor of leading has been, at all times, conscious of its primary obligation — the protection of American interests. And the other representatives here have been no less loyal or devoted to the welfare of their own people.

Yet none of us has found any incompatibility between devotion to our own country and joint action. Indeed, we have found on the contrary that the only genuine safeguard for our national interests lies in international cooperation. We have to recognize that the wisest and most effective way to protect our national interests is through international cooperation — that is to say, through united effort for the attainment of common goals. This has been the great lesson taught by the war, and is, I think, the great lesson of contemporary life — that the people of the earth are inseparably linked to one another by a deep, underlying community of purpose. This community of purpose is no less real and vital in peace than in war, and cooperation is no less essential to its fulfillment.

To seek the achievement of our aims separately through the planless, senseless rivalry that divided us in the past, or through the outright economic aggression which turned neighbors into enemies would be to invite ruin again upon us all. Worse, it would be once more to start our steps irretraceably down the steep, disastrous road to war. That sort of extreme nationalism belongs to an era that is dead.

Today the only enlightened form of national self interest lies in international accord. At Bretton Woods we have taken practical steps toward putting this lesson into practice in monetary and economic fields.

I take it as an axiom that this war is ended; no people — therefore no government of the people — will again tolerate prolonged or wide-spread unemployment. A revival of international trade is indispensable if full employment is to be achieved in a peaceful world and with standards of living which will permit the realization of man's reasonable hopes.

What are the fundamental conditions under which the commerce among nations can once more flourish?

First, there must be a reasonable stable standard of international exchange to which all countries can adhere without sacrificing the freedom of action necessary to meet their internal economic problems.

This is the alternative to the desperate tactics of the past — competitive currency depreciation, excessive tariff barriers, uneconomic barter deals, multiple currency practices, and unnecessary exchange restrictions — by which governments vainly sought to maintain employment and uphold living standards. In the final analysis, these tactics only succeeded in contributing to worldwide depression and even war. The International Monetary Fund agreed upon at Bretton Woods will help remedy this situation.

Second, long-term financial aid must be made available at reasonable rates to those countries whose industry and agriculture have been destroyed by the ruthless torch of an invader or by the heroic scorched earth policy of their defenders.

Long-term funds must be made available to promote sound industry and increase industrial and agricultural production in nations whose economic potentialities have not yet been developed. It is essential to us all that these nations play their full part in the exchange of goods throughout the world.

They must be enabled to produce and to sell if they are to be able to purchase and consume. The International Bank for Reconstruction and Development is designed to meet this need.

Objections to this Bank have been raised by some bankers and a few economists. The institution proposed by the Bretton Woods Conference would indeed limit the control which certain private bankers have in the past exercised over international finance. It would by no means restrict the investment sphere in which bankers could engage. On the contrary, it would expand greatly this sphere by enlarging the volume of international investment and would act as an enormously effective stabilizer and guarantor of loans which they might make. The chief purpose of the International Bank for Reconstruction and Development is to guarantee private loans made through the usual investment channels. It would make loans only when these could not be floated through the normal channels at reasonable rates. The effect would be to provide capital for those who need it at lower interest rates than in the past, and to drive only the usurious money lenders from the temple of international finance. For my own part, I cannot look upon the outcome with any sense of dismay. Capital, like any other commodity, should be free from monopoly control and available upon reasonable terms to those who would put it to use for the general welfare.

The delegates and technical staff at Bretton Woods have completed their portion of their job. They have sat down together and talked as friends, and have perfected plans to cope with the international monetary and financial problems which all their countries face in common. These proposals now must be submitted to the legislatures and the peoples of the participating nations. They will pass upon what has been accomplished here.

The results will be of vital importance to everyone in every country. In the last analysis, it will help determine whether or not people will have jobs and the amount of money they are to find in their weekly pay envelope. More important still, it concerns the kind of world in which our children are to grow to maturity. It concerns the opportunities which will await millions of young men when at last they can take off their uniforms and can come home to civilian jobs.

This monetary agreement is but one step, of course, in the broad program of international action necessary for the shaping of a free future. But it is an indispensable step in the vital test of our intentions. We are at a crossroad, and we must go one way or the other. The Conference at Bretton Woods has erected a signpost — a signpost pointing down a highway broad enough for all men to walk in step and side by side. If they will set out together, there is nothing on earth that need stop them.

References

Boughton, JM (1994). Harry Dexter White and the International Monetary Fund, downloaded from the IMF website [20 August, 2005].

Boulding, K (1956). General systems theory, the skeleton of science. *Management Science*, 2(3), 197–208.

Craig, JB (2004). *Treasonable Doubt: The Harry Dexter White Spy Case.* Lawrence, KS: University of Kansas Press.

Keynes. JM (1921). *The Economic Consequences of Peace.* London: Harcourt, Brace and Howe, Inc.

Keynes, JM (1936). *The General Theory of Employment, Interest, and Money.* London: Harcourt and Brace.

Lal, D (1999). Unintended Consequences: *The Impact of Factor Endowments, Culture, and Politics on Long-Run Economic Performance.* Cambridge MA: MIT Press.

North, DC (2005). *Understanding the Process of Economic Change.* Princeton, NJ: Princeton University Press.

Mundell, RA (2000). A reconsideration of the twentieth Century. *American Economic Review*, 90(3), 327–340.

Ridley, M (1996). *The Origins of Virtue.* London: Penguin Books.

Seabright, P (2004). *The Company of Strangers: A Natural History of Economic Life.* Princeton, NJ: Princeton University Press.

Smith, A (1776 [1976]). *An Inquiry into the Nature and Causes of the Wealth of Nations.* Chicago: University of Chicago Press.

Tanzi, V (2006). Things will fall apart but it is the aftermath that matters. *Financial Times.* (24 February 2006).

Wilson, EO (2002). *The Future of Life.* New York: Alfred A. Knopf, Inc.

Chapter 2

The Balance of Payments and the Macroeconomy

The present path is unsustainable, since both the current account deficit and external liabilities are on an explosive upward trajectory.

(Martin Wolf.[1])

We begin this textbook on international finance with a discussion of the balance of payments (BoP). Because the BoP account records the international transactions that link one economy to other national economies in the rest of the world, they are an important source of data for open-economy macroeconomic analysis. The data also provide insight into the process of globalization.

The BoP is a balance sheet, drawn up in a similar manner by all countries. By international agreement, all countries follow the same standard double-entry accounting procedures when they compile the international transactions carried out by their citizens, businesses, organizations, and government agencies. Among other things, the BoP shows a country's exports and imports of goods and services, its private and public transfer payments to foreign individuals and

---

[1] Martin Wolf (2004). "Why America Is Switching to a Weak Dollar Policy", *Financial Times*, 1 December 2004.

governments, foreign direct investment inflows and outflows, domestic investors' stock and bonds purchases overseas and foreigners' purchases of stocks and bonds in the domestic economy, and the interest, dividends, profits, and other earnings on foreign assets.

This chapter also discusses some of the fundamentals of macroeconomics. It is impossible to understand the logic of the BoP accounts without also discussing how macroeconomists model an open economy. While accounting conjures up thoughts of tedium and technicality, you will find that a brief investment in grasping the logic of the procedures quickly enables you to engage in serious discussion about globalization.

Chapter Goals

1. Explain link between Keynesian macroeconomic analysis and the *balance of payments* accounts.
2. Use the circular flow diagram of an open economy to illustrate the macroeconomic logic of the balance of payments account.
3. Focus on the US balance of payments as an example.
4. Explain the net investment position account and its relationship to the balance of payments.
5. Discuss the concerns about the sustainability of the large trade deficit and the large accumulation of foreign debt by the United States.

2.1 Introduction

The balance of payments (BoP) account is compatible with other national accounts routinely compiled for economies, such as the national income accounts and gross domestic product (GDP). This compatibility between national economic data and the balance of payments is an obvious necessity since the BoP provides the details on how each national economy fits into the global economy. In fact, once you grasp how the BoP fits into the national accounts you are already familiar with, you will have few difficulties in understanding the new accounts detailed below.

2.1.1 *Some observations on macroeconomics*

Macroeconomics is holistic in the sense that it looks at the economy as a *system* within which the parts interact. But, an economy literally has millions of parts, namely all the consumers, producers, government agencies, savers, investors, corporations, banks, employees, owners, debtors, creditors, etc. that transact, interact, compete, cooperate, oversee, and otherwise deal with all others in a great variety of ways. To make a *holistic* analysis of such a complex system possible, macro-economics *aggregates* individuals, firms, or organizations that can reasonably be assumed to behave in similar ways into groups, and each of these groups is then hypothesized to interact in consistent and predictable ways with the other aggregate groups within the structural system we call the economy. For example, macroeconomics hypothesizes that *consumers* behave according to a uniform consumption function. Similarly, *producers* are a group of firms that employ labor, capital, and other resources in order to produce goods and services according to a production function that links output to a set of inputs and the level of technology. By aggregating, the system consists of just a few units, and it can be modeled with just a few equations.

The macroeconomic approach to modeling an economy is a simplification of reality in the tradition of Occam's razor. As discussed in Chapter 1, simplification always risks omitting relevant variables and relationships. However, by modeling the complex economy as a small and manageable number of relationships among aggregate groups rather than a realistic, but much more complex, system of relationships linking the millions of consumers, firms, agencies, and organizations, it becomes possible to actually make some sense of the complexity. Equally important, a practical simplification, if proven to be reasonably accurate, helps policymakers design economic policies.

2.1.2   *The legacy of Keynes*

John Maynard Keynes, who you already know from the first chapter as a participant in the Bretton Woods Conference, is credited with establishing the distinct field of macroeconomics. He developed a macroeconomic model during the Great Depression of the 1930s that proved to be useful for explaining how an economy gets stuck in a lengthy depression. By breaking the economy down into its key aggregate components, Keynes (1936) explained how consumers, workers, firms, investors, government agencies, banks, and other groups can each act in ways that they see as promoting their own best interests, but which result in total output well below levels at which all resources and workers are fully employed. That is, by using a practical model of how well-defined group in the economy interact, Keynes concluded that the "invisible hand" of self-interest did not necessarily maximize total output in the economy.

Keynes' legacy is greater than his analysis of the Great Depression, however. His macroeconomic model has proven to be useful more generally for designing economic policies in many economic environments. Keynes' macroeconomic approach showed policymakers how to design broad economic policies aimed at entire groups and sectors of the economy in order to effectively maintain economic stability and keep an economy near its full employment level of output.

Since the 1980s, the field of macroeconomics moved away from Keynes' prescriptions for economic stability and full employment. A more *laissez faire*, rational expectations view of economic policy gained popularity, especially in the United States, although more recent macroeconomists still embraced Keynes' pioneering approach of analyzing how aggregate categories of consumers, firms, financial intermediaries, and governments interact within an economic system. The financial crisis and recession of 2008 undermined the more recent macroeconomic models based on rational expectations and the so-called efficient markets hypothesis. Arguably, the financial crisis would not have happened if the wisdom of Keynes' *General Theory* and his analysis of the financial sector had not been forgotten. In fact, the speed with which most governments enacted Keynesian fiscal expansions to prevent their economies from falling into recession makes it clear that the Keynesian model remains relevant in 2009.

After Keynes' model became the standard framework for macro-economic analysis in the 1940s, the aggregate categories of economic activities suggested by Keynes were used to design the economic data and the national income accounts policymakers used to judge the performance of the economy and to shape their monetary, fiscal, and regulatory policies. To illustrate the basic logic of Keynesian macro-economic aggregation, it is convenient to represent the economy with a *circular flow diagram*. This diagram shows the main flows of payments among aggregate groups of people and organizations, and it reveals how the various aggregate groups interact in an economy. That same circular flow diagram also explains the logic of the BoP accounts.

2.2 The Circular Flow Diagram

You may already have encountered the circular flow diagram in a macroeconomics course. But, a brief discussion here will, hopefully, help to give the circular flow a broader meaning. And, for those of you who are not fully familiar with the circular flow method of classifying payments within an economy, this introduction will quickly bring you up to speed. This section explains the circular flow model of a single-closed economy. The next section then adds the international payments flows detailed in the BoP, which show how an economy is linked to the rest of the world.

2.2.1 *The simple circular flow between consumers and producers*

Figure 2.1 shows a circular flow diagram of an economy that consists of (1) individual consumers, (2) producers, (3) banks and other financial organizations, and (4) the government. The most basic elements of the circular flow of an economy are, on the one hand, the wage-payments, dividend payments, interest payments, and other

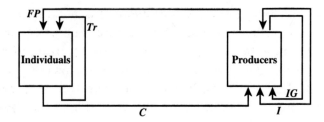

Figure 2.1   The simple circular flow between individuals and producers.

factor payments, from producers to individuals, labeled as *FP*, and, on the other hand, the flow of payments by individuals to producers to acquire *consumption goods*, which is labeled as *C*. Because individuals spend their income to acquire products, producers can afford to pay them for their labor and the other factors they own. And, because they sell their labor and other factors of production to producers, individuals have income with which to acquire producers' goods and services. Note that the direction of the flows in the diagram follows the payments, not the direction of the flow of goods or services. The *payment flows C* and *FP* measure the *value* of the consumption goods and factors' income, respectively.

An economy's production does not consist entirely of consumption goods, of course. Its producers also supply *capital goods* and *intermediate products*. Investment in capital is shown in Fig. 2.1 as the flow labeled *I*. These payments flow between producers of capital goods to producers who purchase the capital goods for use in production.

Producers also supply *intermediate inputs* to other producers. They are labeled *IG* in Fig. 2.1. Business management theory calls for firms to focus on their core competencies and to outsource more stages of production to other producers. This means that exchanges of intermediate goods and services among producers are growing in proportion to final production. For the group of producers as a whole in a closed economy, intermediate inputs cancel out, which is why we show the *IG* (intermediate goods) payments leaving and returning to the producers box in Fig. 2.1. The total value of production, such as

GDP, is estimated by summing the *value added* of all producers. Value added is the difference between the final price of the product and the cost of the raw materials, parts, components, and other inputs acquired from other producers. Economics textbooks commonly assume that the flow of payments for intermediate goods occurs within the Producers box; we show the *IG* curve explicitly here, however, because in an open economy some of the intermediate transactions by producers spill across the border and show up in the BoP.

Just as there are transactions among producers, namely *I* and *IG*, there are transfer payments among individuals. Transfers, denoted as *Tr* in Fig. 2.1, are gifts, as opposed to FP for productive activity. Depending on an individual's personal situation and the society he or she lives in, social norms call for variety of interpersonal transfers, such as the care of children, elders, and the unfortunate, compensation for social activities, the maintenance of social institutions, and the maintenance of common assets. Theft and extortion are also transfers, although most societies try hard to prevent such types of *involuntary* transfers. People also transfer income to relatives, friends, and to unrelated people as simple acts of personal kindness.

2.2.2 *The financial sector*

The financial sector serves to allocate resources in the economy by channeling funds from savers to investors and innovators. When it performs this function well, it channels savings to the most productive investments, permits individuals and producers to earn high returns even though they are not able to carry out the high-return projects themselves, and permits those individuals and firms with high return projects to carry them out even though they do not possess the funds to fully pay for their current costs. A well-functioning financial sector is critical for an economy to provide a high standard of living for its residents.

If people are unable to borrow money or acquire assets in which to store (save) purchasing power for future use, each individual in the economy must exactly balance income and expenditures. In such a case, producers can only invest an amount exactly equal to total earnings minus FP to individuals, and individual consumption exactly equals FP received. The financial sector lets producers borrow in order to acquire capital in excess of their income minus FP. Consumers can borrow to consume more than they earn, or they can accumulate wealth by consuming less than they earn. The financial sector normally consists of the banks, pension funds, venture capitalists, stock markets, bond markets, and other organizations that provide intermediary financial services and maintain the markets, where financial assets are bought and sold.

A circular flow model of a modern economy, therefore, must explicitly include a *financial sector*. In Fig. 2.2, the savings flows between individuals and the financial sector and producers and the financial sector, S_I and S_P, respectively, normally flow in both directions. While some individuals save part of their income, others borrow in order to consume more than they earn during the year. Producers save or borrow, depending on whether their earnings exceed their expenditures or not. The payment flows S_I and S_P shown in Fig. 2.2 are *net* amounts that can be positive or negative.

Savings flows result in flows of *returns* to assets, which are labeled r_I and r_P. The letter r is used to represent these returns on assets. Depending on the type of asset, returns include such things as interest, rents, profits, and dividends. These flows are also shown as net flows that can be positive or negative. Figure 2.2 also shows

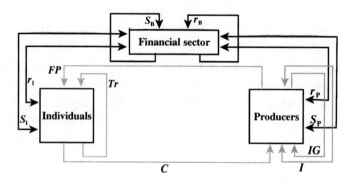

Figure 2.2   The circular flow with the financial sector added.

savings S_B and returns r_B flowing within the banking and financial sector. Some of the banks, pension funds, and insurance companies in the financial sector may also acquire or sell assets and earn or pay returns on assets. The financial sector is not just a conduit through which savings flow; the individual units in the financial sector lend and borrow too.

Before moving on, note that by including more sectors in the circular flow diagram, we add to the complexity of the relationships between the individual units in the model. While it is easy to envision how the simple circular flow in Fig. 2.1 maintains a stable equilibrium, you can, no doubt, envision where the smooth circular flow could be interrupted or disturbed in Fig. 2.2. In Chapter 7, we will examine the Keynesian macroeconomic model, and it will become clear why flows through the financial sector may stall and, therefore, destabilize the whole economic system.

2.2.3 Government

The fourth aggregate component of an economy consists of the various levels of government and the economy's various public agencies. A complex modern economy cannot function without a government to carry out collective actions, transfer income between individuals, groups, and households, operate institutions to moderate individual and firm behavior, and provide public goods and services.

Public goods provided by the government are acquired from producers, sometimes government-owned and -managed but often in the private sector. These payments are labeled G in Fig. 2.3. Government may pay producers out of revenue from taxing individuals and producers, TX_I and TX_P, respectively. Transfer payments to individuals and producers, TR_I and TR_P, respectively, may also be paid for out of tax revenue. Governments seldom exactly balance tax revenue TX_I and TX_P and expenditures on G, TR_I, and TR_P. If, for example, the government is a net borrower, the *net* flow of government saving, S_G in Fig. 2.3, is negative. Also, accumulated debt means government must pay interest, and *net* interest payments to the government, r_G, will be negative.

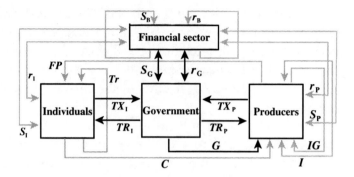

Figure 2.3   The circular flow with the government included.

2.2.4 *The circular flow and economic interdependence*

In the *closed* economy depicted in the circular flow diagram in Fig. 2.3, total payments by consumers, producers, and government to the banks and other financial intermediaries in the financial sector must equal total receipts from the financial sector. What one person borrows, another must lend, and one person's receipt of a return on an asset is another person's payment. Therefore, the following condition must hold in a closed economy:

$$S_I + S_P + S_G + S_F + r_I + r_P + r_G + r_F = 0 \qquad (2.1)$$

The circular flow of payments shows that each economic activity in an economy is linked to many other economic activities in the economy. Any change in activity by one individual, firm, bank, or government agency has effects on others throughout the economy because the circular flow must balance. This interdependence of all economic activities means that people's choices are dependent on what others do. Consumers cannot consume more than producers produce. Producers are limited by how much labor people are willing to supply. Government tax revenue depends on others' incomes, sales, and accumulation of wealth. Borrowers depend on others to save. Individual choices depend on the choices others make. Equally important is how the many individual choices affect the overall flows in the circular flow of the economy. Some of the greatest controversies in macroeconomics revolve around how individual choices affect the overall economic outcomes, and how the resulting aggregate flows impact the individual units. Of special concern is how those choices are made. Macroeconomics requires holistic analysis of system and parts.

2.3 Opening Up the Economy

According to the circular flow diagram for a closed economy in Fig. 2.3, total aggregate demand for output, Y, is divided among consumption demand, C, investment demand, I, and government demand for goods and services, G:

$$Y = C + I + G \tag{2.2}$$

If all the economy's resources are being used efficiently, then the only way to increase one of the three components of aggregate demand is to decrease one of the other two components. For example, for investment to rise, consumers and government must acquire less of the economy's output. If consumers demand more of the economy's production capacity, then there is less left to produce capital goods or products for the government.

An open economy does not have to satisfy the relationships given in equations (2.1) and (2.2). An open economy can use more products than it produces, or it can use less than it produces. An open economy can also be a net saver or borrower. When we link the domestic circular flow diagram shown in Fig. 2.3 to the rest of the world, it becomes clear how the constraints given by equations (2.1) and (2.2) can be relaxed and replaced by a looser set of constraints. Figure 2.4 shows a circular flow diagram for an open economy, in which each of the economy's four sectors are linked to the rest of the world, or what we label as "Abroad" in the diagram.

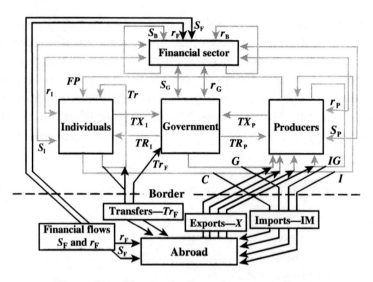

Figure 2.4   The circular flow of an open economy.

2.3.1 *Extending the circular flow across the border*

Figure 2.4 makes it clear that in an open economy everyone's choices are affected not only by what others do in the domestic economy, but also by what others do throughout the rest of the world. The linkages between the domestic circular flow and the rest of the global economy imply that everyone's choices are, in some ways, more restricted in an open economy. On the other hand, an open economy provides additional freedoms because international transactions make available choices that are out of reach in a closed economy. Each of the links between the domestic economy and the rest of the world deserves a detailed explanation.

2.3.2 *Exports and imports*

The open economy illustrated in Fig. 2.4 differs from the closed economy illustrated in Fig. 2.3 in several ways. For one thing, consumers, investors, and governments import goods and services from foreign producers. *Imports*, denoted as IM, are the payments for foreign consumption goods, foreign capital goods, foreign intermediate goods, and foreign goods and services purchased by government.[2] Also, foreign consumers, producers, and governments acquire goods and services from the domestic economy's producers. These goods and services sold to foreigners are *exports*, denoted as *X*. Figure 2.2 shows how domestic demand for *C, IG, I*, and *G* spills over into demand for imports, and how foreign demand for *C, IG, I*, and *G* results in exports. Aggregate demand for output from domestic producers is therefore:

$$Y = C + I + G + X - IM \qquad (2.3)$$

2.3.3 *Outsourcing, vertical specialization, and international trade*

Note that unlike the closed economy circular flow model (2.3), in which intermediate goods and services, IG, never really left the aggregate producers box, in an open economy some of the sales and purchases of intermediate products do leave the domestic producer box and cross the border. Also, in an open economy the flow of intermediate goods does not generally cancel out. In the BoP, sales of intermediate goods and services to foreign producers are tallied as exports, and purchases by domestic producers of intermediate goods and services from foreign producers are recorded as imports.

Outsourcing, which is the contracting to other firms for the production of some portion of a firm's output, explains a large part of the international trade in intermediate goods and services. This rapid growth of international trade in intermediate products is also referred to as the growth of *vertical specialization*. Vertical specialization occurs when producers in a country import foreign materials, parts, components, etc. in order to produce goods that are then again exported to other countries. That is, they carry out just one stage in the complex series of production stages that eventually result in a final

---

[2] *IM* is used to represent imports because the letter *I* has already been designated to represent *investment*. Similarly, the letter *M* is already taken to denote *money*.

product. Typical of vertical integration are the so-called *maquiladora* firms located in Northern Mexico along the US border. These firms import all types of raw materials, semifinished products, and all types of parts and components, use relatively inexpensive Mexican labor to further transform the products, and then re-export them to the United States and other countries.

The inclusion of intermediate goods in the BoP can cause the total value of goods and services traded internationally to overstate the true value of goods and services traded across borders. The true value of a country's exports is the value-added exports. If exports contain intermediate goods or services imported from abroad, then the value of exports exceed domestic value added. Intermediate products get counted in international trade twice, first as imports and then as exports.

An extreme example of this is Hong Kong, a trade center located on the coast of China. A former colony that was imposed on China by Britain for over a century, Hong Kong continues to be a vibrant intermediary through which China trades with the rest of the world. Vertical integration and intermediate goods dominate Hong Kong's international trade, and its total value of exports exceeds its total GDP. Hong Kong's main production is transforming imports, mostly from mainland China, and sending the goods on the rest of the world. Such vertical specialization generates enough GDP to give its citizens one of the highest standards of living in the world. But Hong Kong cannot, of course, export more than its entire national product. Hong Kong's true exports are mostly reprocessing, repackaging, marketing, wholesaling, and other distribution activities that ultimately channel Chinese exports to global markets. This value added is just a fraction of the value of the exports recorded in the BoP.

2.3.4 *International transfers*

While international trade gets most of the attention in international economics, people make payments across borders for many reasons other than to pay for imports and exports. Some payments across borders are not in direct payment for any particular product, service, factor input, or asset. As discussed above, just as there are domestic transfers between individuals and between the government and domestic individuals and producers, there are also international transfers. For one thing, governments make transfers to foreign governments and organizations. Government transfers are often referred to as *foreign aid*. Private individuals and organizations also make cross-border transfers. In fact, private transfers have grown very rapidly in recent decades while government-to-government foreign aid has stagnated.

The growth of private transfers is largely the result of the rapidly increasing number of immigrants, who often remit income back to family in their native countries. Today, close to four percent of all people in the world live outside the countries where they were born. Immigrant transfers, or *remittances* as they are usually called, are estimated to have exceeded $200 billion in 2008. Transfers are shown in Fig. 2.4 as *net* inflows to a country's individuals and government. They are labeled Tr_F. Such net transfers are usually negative for high income countries with large immigrant populations.

2.3.5 *Asset trade*

A unique characteristic of today's global economy is the volume and variety of the assets that are exchanged by individuals, producers, financial firms, and governments in different countries. For example, individuals and firms store savings in overseas banks, hold shares in foreign firms, and own foreign property. Domestic firms borrow from foreign banks, sell bonds to foreigners, and accept credit from foreign suppliers. Governments cover budget deficits by selling bonds to foreign investors or borrowing directly from foreign banks. As we did for domestic assets, purchases and sales of foreign assets are summed together into *net* flows. The net purchases of domestic assets by foreigners is labeled as S_F (net foreign saving) in Fig. 2.4. Note the direction of the payments related to the purchase and sale of assets. For example, a foreigners' purchases of domestic assets, such as bonds, checking accounts, or houses, involve payment inflows and imply a positive addition to S_F. The purchase of foreign assets by domestic investors results in a payment *outflow*. A country's BoP shows a positive value for S_F if the value of domestic assets that foreigners are purchasing in the country exceeds the value of foreign assets that domestic savers are purchasing abroad. A negative S_F means that domestic citizens, firms, and government agencies are buying more assets overseas than foreigners are acquiring in the domestic economy.

Finally, the stock of foreign assets held by domestic individuals, producers, and government generates inflows of interest, profits, rents, and dividends from abroad. Foreign holdings of domestic financial assets will result in interest, profits, and dividends flowing abroad. The net *inflow* of returns to assets is denoted as r_F. The accumulation of foreign assets eventually affects the flows of returns. It seems likely that the accumulation of foreign assets will eventually increase in net inflows of interest, dividends, profits, rents, etc.

2.3.6 *Summarizing Foreign Transactions*

The open-economy circular flow diagram in Fig. 2.4 highlights four main categories of international payments:

- An open economy exports goods and services, X, to foreign consumers, producers, and governments, and domestic consumers, producers, and governments import goods and services, *IM*, from abroad.
- The *net* inflow of international transfers between governments, individuals, and organizations of individuals, Tr_F, can be positive or negative.
- An open economy sends savings abroad and receives an inflow of foreign savings, and the *net* inflow, S_F, may be positive or negative.
- Past inflows and outflows of savings result in both payments of returns to foreigners and receipt of returns from abroad in the form of interest, dividends, rents, profits, etc., and the *net* inflow of these returns on assets, r_F, may be negative or positive.

To sustain the circular flow of payments, all payments leaving the domestic economy must be balanced by payments entering the country. Total payments *to* the rest of the world must be equal to the total receipts *from* the rest of the world. Balance occurs quite automatically because any receipt from abroad not used to explicitly purchase something becomes a *de facto* acquisition of an asset (currency or a bank balance). Therefore, the *net* inflows of payments for goods and services, or exports minus imports, plus net asset purchases, net returns on accumulated foreign assets, and net transfer payments must sum to zero. That is

$$(X - IM) + S_F + r_F + Tr_F = 0 \qquad (2.4)$$

Each of the four different subcategories of foreign payments may have a net positive or negative value, however.

2.4 The BoP

The reason we have taken so much time to detail an open economy's circular flow diagram and, specifically, the international flows that enter and leave the circular flow is that the balance of payments accounts exactly match the circular flow. Specifically, the BoP reports the foreign payments and receipts described in the open-economy circular flow diagram in Fig. 2.4. The BoP was designed to be compatible with the domestic flows, which underlie the typical national accounts compiled by most countries, such as GDP, national income, and aggregate demand.

2.4.1 *History of the BoP accounts*

Countries throughout the world compile BoP accounts according to guidelines originally set after World War II by a group of economists at the United Nations. These rules are periodically updated by the International Monetary Fund (IMF), which now oversees the BoP accounting practices. In 1996, the IMF issued the fifth edition of its

Balance of Payments Manual, which introduced some minor changes in the accounting rules. The discussion below follows these latest revisions.[3] The IMF conveniently publishes all countries' BoP accounts in its quarterly *Balance of Payments Statistics* under the IMF's standard format.

The BoP of a country for, say, the year 2006 measures the payments by people, firms, organizations, and government agencies in that country *to* people, firms, organizations, and government agencies in other countries on the one hand and payments *from* people, firms, organizations, and government agencies in other countries to people, firms, organizations, and government agencies located in the country during the entire year of 2006.

The term *credits* is used for those transactions that involve payment *inflows*, and *debits* describes the international transactions that lead to payment *outflows*. For example, the export of a product from China to the United States would show up as a credit in the Chinese BoP equal to the yuan value of the export. This same transaction would show up as a debit in the US BoP as the US dollar value of the same transaction. The purchase of 100 shares of stock on the New York Stock Exchange by a Japanese investor would also show up as a credit in the US BoP, since the payment is from Japan to the United States. This same purchase of 100 shares of US stock by a Japanese citizen shows up as a debit in the Japanese BoP.

It is common practice to use a "+" for a credit and a "−" for a debit in the BoP. These signs are intended only to show the *direction* of a payment flow; they do not in any way imply that inflows are "good" and outflows are "bad". Be careful to avoid judgment of individual items in the BoP according to their sign. The circular flow diagram made it amply clear that all flows are related; each individual flow is just one component of the overall global economic system. It is certainly possible, and appropriate, to judge the performance of the overall economic system, but every economy, whether rich or poor,

---

[3] Some of the terminology in this book may clash with that of other older books based on earlier balance of payments accounting conventions; we will point out one such clash below.

will generate both debits *and* credits on their BoP. What ultimately matters is whether an open economy makes its residents better off than if the borders were closed.

2.4.2 The split between the current account and the financial account

The BoP account is divided into two main parts, the first is called the *current account* and the second is the *financial account*. The current account contains all transactions related to the trade of goods and services. In the current account, portions of the BoP are items such as merchandise exports and tourism expenditures abroad (service imports). The current account also contains payments to factors of production and earnings on assets. In terms of the notation used earlier:

$$\text{Current account balance} = (X - IM) + Tr_F + r_F \qquad (2.5)$$

The current account thus includes all payments except those for the purchase and sale of assets.

The *financial account* contains all international payments associated with the sale and purchase of assets. In terms of the notation above:

$$\text{Financial account balance} = S_F \qquad (2.6)$$

Detailed BoP accounts distinguish between short- and long-term assets, as well as between private asset transactions and transactions undertaken by the government and its various agencies. The financial account registers transactions such as net purchases of government bonds by foreigners (credit) and the net increase in overseas bank accounts held by domestic residents (debit). The current account and the financial account must sum to zero:

$$(X - IM) + Tr_F + r_F = -S_F \qquad (2.7)$$

Therefore, a deficit (surplus) on a country's current account must be balanced by a surplus (deficit) of the same absolute value on the financial account. Also, any change in one item of the current account must be offset by changes in one or more other items elsewhere in the BoP. For example, an increase in exports must be offset by reductions in one or more components of IM, S_F, r_F, or Tr_F. Any number of combinations of changes in the items of the BoP can end up offsetting a change in any one item. In the end, however, total outflows must always equal total inflows.

The division of the BoP into *current* and *financial* accounts dates from the early post-World War II period, when most activity on a country's BoP was related to trade in goods and services. At that time, most countries restricted the acquisition of foreign assets. For example, citizens of many European countries and Japan were not permitted to open foreign bank accounts or acquire stock in foreign companies. Much of the activity recorded in the financial account consisted of intentional ("official") transactions by central banks for the exclusive purpose of compensating for deficits or surpluses in the current account. Today, most countries no longer restrict the sale and purchase of foreign assets, and the activity recorded in the financial account is determined by economic factors just as are the international transactions recorded in the current account. Because it is still useful to distinguish international investment from other international transactions, the separation of international transactions into current and financial accounts continues. The special nature of assets plays a critical role in our discussion of financial crises in later chapters, for example.

2.5 The BoP of the United States

The discussion in this section focuses on the United States' BoP in order to provide an example familiar to many readers of this book. The BoP of the United States for 2000 through 2009 is shown in Table 2.1.

We focus on the US BoP for several reasons. First, the international flows recorded in the US BoP help determine the value of the US dollar, the central currency in the global economy since the end of World War II. Second, the United States is the largest economy in

Table 2.1 The US BoP: 2000–2009 (billions US$)

	2000	2002	2004	2006	2008	2009
Current account						
Exports of Goods	$771.9	682.4	807.5	1,023.1	1,277.0	1,045.5
Exports of Services	299.5	294.9	343.9	422.6	545.2	509.2
Asset Returns from Abroad	350.9	281.2	401.9	650.5	764.6	561.2
Imports of Goods	−1,224.4	1,167.4	−1,477.1	−1,861.4	−2,117.2	−1,562.6
Imports of Services	−225.3	−250.4	−292.2	342.8	−405.3	−370.8
Asset Returns to Foreigners	−329.9	−253.5	−345.6	−613.8	−646.4	−472.2
Unilateral Transfers (net)	−58.8	−63.6	−84.4	−89.6	−128.4	−130.2
Financial account						
Change in U.S. assets abroad	−$560.5	−294.0	−905.0	−1,055.2	−1.1	−237.5
Official assets	−0.3	−3.7	2.8	2.3	−4.8	−52.3
Other U.S. Gov't assets	−0.9	.3	1.7	5.3	−529.6	541.8
Direct investment	−159.2	−154.5	−279.1	−235.4	−332.0	−221.0
Foreign stocks & bonds	−127.9	−48.6	−146.5	−289.4	60.8	−288.7
Bank loans to foreigners	−133.4	−38.3	−359.8	−454.6	443.4	−424.3
Other claims on foreigners	−138.8	−50.0	−124.1	−83.5	−0.7	283.8
Change in foreign assets in U.S.	1,046.9	797.8	1,461.8	1,859.6	534.1	435.2
Official assets	42.8	115.9	397.8	440.3	487.0	447.6
Direct Investment	321.3	84.4	145.8	180.6	319.7	152.1
U.S. Treasury bonds	−70.0	100.4	93.6	−35.9	196.6	37.6
Private stocks & bonds	459.9	283.3	381.5	592.0	−126.7	−6.6
Foreign bank borrowing	117.0	96.4	334.7	434.4	−326.6	−235.0
Other claims by foreigners	170.7	95.9	93.5	235.8	−45.3	26.9
Statistical discrepancy	−69.4	−42.1	85.8	−17.8	200.1	224.9
Capital account	0.8	−1.5	−2.4	−3.9	1.0	−2.9
Merchandise trade balance	−452.4	−485.0	−669.6	−838.3	−840.3	−517.0
Balance on services	74.1	61.2	57.5	79.7	144.3	138.4
Balance on goods and services	−378.3	−423.7	−612.1	−758.5	−696.0	−378.6
Current account balance	−416.0	−459.6	−640.2	−811.5	−706.1	−419.9

Source: U.S. Department of Commerce, Bureau of Economic Analysis; downloaded May 25, 2010 from www.bea.doc.gov.

the world, and it therefore has a large economic impact on the rest of the world. Third, the US BoP is characterized by very large imbalances among the individual items. Note in Table 2.1 that the US BoP shows very large imbalances between imports and exports, the current and financial accounts, and the inflows and outflows of the categories of assets. Finally, even though we detail the US BoP, this example will familiarize you with the overall logic of every BoP account; all countries use the same classifications and accounting methods.

2.5.1 *The current account*

Exports and imports of physical goods, like shoes, aircraft, soybeans, and computers (merchandise), are the two largest items in the US current account. The net of merchandise exports and imports is called the *merchandise trade balance*, and it is given at the bottom of Table 2.1. In the calendar year 2009, US consumers, governments, and producers imported $517 billion more stuff than they exported.

The deficit between total US exports of goods *and* services and total US imports of goods *and* services is not as large as the merchandise trade balance because the United States ran a substantial services trade surplus of $138 billion in 2009. When both services and goods are included in exports and imports, the 2009 total trade balance is −$379 billion versus −$517 billion for the merchandise trade balance. Traditionally, few services were traded across borders, and, since goods are easier to track, most countries focused on compiling the merchandise trade balance. In a modern economy, however, services are the largest category of output, and increasingly services are entering into international trade. The balance on both goods and services is thus a more accurate estimate of the US *trade balance*. Be aware of the difference as you read newspaper accounts of the latest trade data.

The current account balance also includes factor payments, returns on assets, and net unilateral transfers. In 2009, US owners of foreign assets received $561 billion in interest, rent, profits, royalties, dividends, wages, and salaries from their overseas investments and labor services, while foreign-owned assets and labor used toward production in the

United States were paid $472 billion. Thus, the United States had a surplus of $89 billion on factor payments and returns to foreign assets. Net US unilateral transfers were −$130 billion in 2009. These payments included military and other forms of foreign aid by the US government to foreign governments, humanitarian aid by nonprofit organizations, and gifts sent by immigrants to their families in their home countries. This item has almost always been negative for the United States not just because it is a relatively wealthy country, but also because its relative wealth has in recent years attracted a large number of immigrants who still have close ties to overseas family.

Summing the $517 billion deficit on trade in goods, the $138 billion surplus on services trade, the $89 billion surplus on asset returns and factor income, and the $130 billion net unilateral transfers to foreigners leaves an overall current account balance of $420 billion for 2009. In dollar terms, this is not the largest current account deficit that the United States has ever registered for a calendar year, but, despite the share fall in overall international trade during the recession it is still the third largest ever. Only the 2007 and 2006 deficits were larger. As a percentage of GDP, other countries have had larger deficits than the United States has had in recent years. Nevertheless, there is some concern about whether the US current account deficit is sustainable. US consumers, producers, and governments can continue buying more goods and services from foreigners than they sell to foreigners only if foreigners remain willing to buy large amounts of US assets. That is, the United States can sustain huge current account deficits only if there are equally-large surpluses on its financial account.

2.5.2 *The financial account*

The financial account covers a variety of asset sales and purchases. *Foreign direct investment* (FDI) is defined as the acquisition of a controlling interest in foreign firms and enterprises. The general rule of thumb is that any acquisition of more than 10 percent of a company's shares falls into this category. Included in FDI would be the construction of a new factory or the acquisition of full ownership in a foreign manufacturer. Notice that in 2008 and 2009 foreign firms and investors acquired a controlling interest in US firms and enterprises at about the amount that American firms and investors acquired foreign business facilities and businesses. In 2009, new FDI overseas by US firms, investors, and financial firms was $222 billion, a high amount by historical standards. Foreigners invested $152 billion to acquire direct ownership in US firms and enterprises. Table 2.1 also makes it clear that net US FDI abroad has fluctuated quite a bit from year to year.

Foreigners acquired a very large amount of US stocks and bonds. Such acquisitions of foreign securities are called international *portfolio investment* in order to differentiate it from FDI. Portfolio investment is defined as investment that does not lead to any influence in the management of the firms and enterprises who issue the stock and the bonds. On a practical level, for example, stock purchases of less than 10 percent of a company's shares are normally considered to be a portfolio investment. Private foreigners acquired almost $200 billion more US Treasury bonds than they sold in 2009, but foreigners' purchases of bonds and stock issued by US private firms, financial institutions, and state and local governments fell sharply. Also, foreign banks reduced their loans to US borrowers by $327 and $235 billion in 2008 and 2009, respectively. American investors also sold more foreign stocks and bonds than they acquired in 2008. Over the past decade, American investors tended to purchase fewer stocks and bonds overseas than foreigners purchased in the United States. Worldwide, such international portfolio investment has been the fastest growing category of international investment over the past decade.

Also included in the financial account are purchases and sales of *official assets*. Official assets are currencies and assets bought and sold by central banks for the purpose of influencing the foreign exchange rate. For example, when the Bank of China seeks to raise the price of dollars relative to the Chinese yuan, it *intervenes* in the foreign exchange market by using yuan to purchase US dollars in the foreign exchange market. Rather than just hold the dollars it acquires, the Bank of China often uses the dollars to purchase US Treasury bonds or other *liquid* assets that pay interest but which can be converted back to dollars if necessary. A net change in the amount of dollars and dollar-denominated assets held by foreign central banks or the change in foreign-denominated assets held by the US central bank, the Federal Reserve Bank appears in the BoP under as a net change in official assets.

In each of the past five years, foreign central banks have acquired about $400 billion additional US dollars and dollar-denominated liquid assets for the purpose of keeping the value of the dollar high or preventing their own currencies from rising in value relative to the dollar. The central bank of the United States, the Federal Reserve Bank, engaged in very little foreign exchange market intervention during the period 2000–2009. The official assets item was just a net $4.8 billion in 2008, although the Fed purchased an exceptionally high $52 billion in foreign currencies in 2009 as it made dollars available to foreign central banks to support their private banks' foreign losses as a result of the 2008 financial meltdown. Note that with $448 billion in purchases of dollars and dollar assets by foreign central banks, well over half of the US current account deficit was effectively financed by foreign central banks. This suggests that the value of the dollar would have been substantially lower if there had not been such massive central bank *intervention* in the foreign exchange markets.

2.5.3 *The capital account*

You may have wondered about the −$2.9 billion debit in what is called the *capital account* for 2009. This account contains various capital transfers, including debt forgiveness, goods and financial assets accompanying immigrants, gift and inheritance taxes, and uninsured damages to fixed assets. Also included in this account are the sales and purchases of nonproduced, nonfinancial assets such as the rights to natural resources and the sales and purchases of intangible assets such as patents, copyrights, trademarks, and franchises. As you can tell from Table 2.1, the capital account is very small relative to the rest of the BoP.

The use of the term *capital account* for this assortment of minor international transactions is very confusing, however, because the account we now call the *financial account* used to be called the *capital account*. When you look up BoP data published before 1996, you will see that the BoP was then split between the *current* account and the *capital* account. It makes sense to change the name to financial account, since the account records mostly transactions accompanying the sale and purchase of financial assets. It is rather strange, however, that the old term was continued as the heading for a new subaccount in the new format of the BoP.

2.5.4 *Statistical discrepancies*

There is one more item in the financial account of the US BoP that needs some explanation: the *statistical discrepancy*. This is a balancing item that is equal to the difference between the sum of the estimated current account, the small capital account, and the estimated asset sales and purchases in the financial account. The statistical discrepancy was $225 billion in the preliminary 2009 account. This is a large number. Clearly, data collectors miss many international payments.

The variations in the statistical discrepancy indicate how difficult it is to measure all of the international transactions that occur over the course of a year. The numbers in the BoP are derived from a great variety of sources, including customs information about imports and exports, surveys of exporters and importers, records on international transactions from banks and other financial institutions, and tax records. In most countries today, individuals and firms engaged in international transactions are not required to report all of the transactions estimated in the BoP. The customs services of most countries only spot check imports and exports, so even those supposedly solid data are really based only on a sample, not the full flow, of imports and exports. In general, government agencies charged with compiling the BoP must use surveys, take small samples, and make estimates using indirect infor-mation on the many categories of international transactions. Such estimation methods are subject to many errors. Complicating matters further is the fact that importers and exporters sometimes intentionally fail to report transactions in order to evade taxes and tariffs.

Interestingly, when the IMF carried out a study to estimate the reliability of BoP data some years ago, it found that the sum of all countries' current account deficits during the 1990s averaged about

$100 billion per year.[4] Such a deficit is impossible, of course. One country's exports are another's imports. Technically, trade must balance across all countries of the world. In a more recent study, two IMF economists compared all countries' trade data and found that the world's merchandise trade deficit had apparently grown to nearly $300 billion by 2000.[5] What were the BoP accounts missing for them to sum to such a large net deficit?

Some portion of the discrepancy is due to smuggling by exporters and importers who want to evade import tariffs and quotas. For example, Fisman and Wei (2001) noted that Hong Kong reported much greater exports to China than China reported as imports from Hong Kong. Fisman and Wei found that the discrepancy across different product categories varied in direct proportion with the level of Chinese tariff rates. On the other hand, in the financial account, there may be a connection between the deregulation of international financial activities and the poor reliability of the data on international financial flows. Whatever the sources of the discrepancies in the estimates of international transactions, the impossible $300 billion world trade deficit in 2000 makes it clear that many international transactions are not being counted by the agencies charged with compiling BoP accounts.

Despite the obvious shortcomings, it is generally accepted that the BoP accounts provide a reasonably accurate picture of how international activity has grown over the years. If it is reasonable to assume that the BoP accounts are likely to suffer from similar errors year after year, then the year-to-year changes in the BoP probably give an accurate picture of the changes in foreign payments flows, even if the absolute amounts may be somewhat inaccurate. On the other hand, the sudden major shifts in the components of the US BoP estimates for 2008 and 2009, years when the US and most other world economies fell into deep recessions, may not be a very accurate indicators of long-run shifts in the US BoP.

---

[4] John Motala (1997).
[5] Jaime Marquez and Lisa Workman (2001).

Despite the inaccuracies, however, the BoP accounts are our most complete source of information on the globalization of economic activity. Perhaps the return to greater regulation of financial activities and international financial flows that has been suggested by many government officials following the 2008 financial crisis will have as a welcome by-product the improvement in the our BoP data.

2.6 Evaluating the Recent Trends in the US BoP

One of the major issues in international finance over the past 30 years has been the growing trade deficits of the United States. The US current account was near balance throughout the 1950s, 1960s, and 1970s. But then after 1980, the United States began running increasingly large trade deficits, and by 2006 the US balance of trade in goods and services reached $800 billion, about six percent of US GDP. That is, the United States was spending 106 percent of its national income. As a result, the United States was increasing its debt to foreigners at a rate that most economists described as "unsustainable" in the long run.

The US BoP is important for the world economy, given the size of the US economy and the US dollar's role in the international monetary system. We will, therefore, discuss the trade deficit, and the accompanying need for the US to accumulate international debt, throughout the upcoming chapters. In this section, we merely suggest some of the reasons for the unsustainable trend in the US current account.

2.6.1 *What happened in the 1980s?*

A sharp shift in the path of the US trade balance occurred in the early 1980s. This shift was driven by several factors: (1) the US dollar gained value relative to the other major currencies of the world as a result of tight monetary policies to combat inflation, (2) the US economy recovered rapidly from its 1980–1982 recession, (3) many countries liberalized their financial account transactions, (4) US deregulation of its financial markets made US assets easy to acquire, and (5) the shifts in US economic policy raised the returns to US assets. The first factor, an appreciation of the dollar in the foreign exchange markets, caused imports to increase rapidly and exports to grow slowly, if at all.

The 1981 tax cuts and increased defense expenditures initiated by President Reagan stimulated a quick recovery from the 1980–1982 recession. But, this fiscal stimulus coincided with a very tight monetary regime engineered by Federal Reserve Bank Chair Paul Volcker to reduce the high inflation that took hold in the 1970s. The tight monetary policies raised interest rates in the United States, which made US assets more attractive to foreigners, just when foreigners were permitted to acquire more foreign assets by their own governments. The demand for US assets increased the value of the dollar relative to other currencies, which caused a further deterioration in the trade balance.

The 1980s are often used as an example of how independently motivated financial account transactions can influence current account transactions, contrary to the common belief that financial account transactions largely react to current account transactions. Recall our earlier comment about why borrowing and lending were relegated to a separate account. In the 1980s, it can be argued that it was the borrowing and lending that was driving the trade flows in the current account!

After 1987, the current account deficit began to shrink, and by 1991 it was virtually zero. There are several reasons for the rise in the current account in the late 1980s. First of all, the US dollar fell in value after 1985, when the foreign exchange markets became concerned about the huge US trade deficit. Several major countries also adjusted their macroeconomic policies in ways that made people, firms, financial intermediaries, and other wealth holders more reluctant to hold their wealth in assets priced in dollars. In 1991, the US economy entered a brief recession that reduced US demand for imports. Excess capacity led US firms to market more aggressively overseas, which helped exports to rise. Also, there were one-time large transfers from foreign governments to the US government to cover the cost of the war against Iraq, the so-called Operation Desert Storm, in 1991.

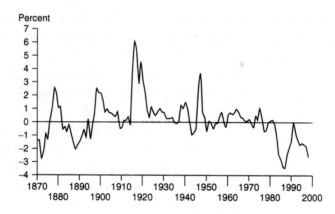

Figure 2.5   The long-term history of the US current account balance.

Figure 2.5 shows that the balanced current account was short-lived. Growing current account deficits over the remainder of the 1990s have been attributed to a number of factors, including (1) the increased growth of the US economy, (2) the increase in US productivity reflecting the rapid growth of technology, and (3) the slowdowns in Europe, Japan, and several other economies around the world. There was also a growing demand for US assets because (4) the US economy was seen as a growing economy where returns to investments were already higher than in many other slower-growing economies and likely to continue to be higher, and (5) more countries permitted domestic savers to invest in foreign assets. A sixth factor that also played a large role in pushing the US current account deeper into deficit was the growing desire of emerging economies to accumulate dollar reserves to protect against the types of speculation that caused several financial crises in the 1980s and 1990s. We will discuss these issues in later chapters. Whatever the reasons for the downward trend in the US current account, the question on everyone's mind was: Is the current account deficit sustainable?

2.6.2 *How long can the United States run large current account deficits?*

Through 2006, the current account deficit of the United States continued to grow. The current account deficit exceeded half a trillion dollars in 2003 and in 2006 it exceeded $800 billion. Never before had a country run such large deficits, certainly not the world's largest economy. When Great Britain was the leading economy during the 19th century and the pound was the currency against which all others were measured, Britain was a net saver that usually lent to the rest of the world.

Herbert Stein, the former head of the Council of Economic Advisors under President Nixon, once remarked: "If something cannot be sustained forever, it will stop". Since a current account deficit of over five percent of GDP cannot continue forever, the obvious question is: When will it stop growing?

Figure 2.5 suggests that, eventually, deficits turn into surpluses. Note that between 1870 and 2000, the US fluctuated between surpluses and deficits. Technically, the current account deficit will stop growing when foreigners stop buying US assets in quantities large enough to cover the current account deficit. We have no way of knowing exactly when that will occur, however. What economists can predict is that when the foreign demand for US assets does finally begin to decline, (1) US interest rates will rise and (2) the value of the US dollar (the exchange rate) will fall. Both of these changes will tend to improve the trade balance. The change in the value of the dollar relative to other currencies should make US products cheaper overseas, thus enhancing exports, and it should make foreign goods more expensive in the United States and, thus, reduce imports. The change in the exchange rate and the rise in interest rates will bring about another critical change: they will reduce domestic demand for goods, services, and investment goods. This reduction in demand is necessary because the economy must make more capacity available to produce exports. In the short run, these changes will reduce the welfare of US residents, and there is no way to avoid this welfare decline. After all, the problem is precisely the unsustainable trade deficit and foreigners' accumulation of US assets that permit US residents to consume and invest much more than the US economy has the capacity to supply them. Essentially, the United States will have to save more. At the same time, the countries that have been running large trade surpluses will have to increase their imports and stop acquiring so many foreign assets.

One way for the United States to increase savings is for the government to reduce or even reverse its budget deficit. It is more difficult to change the saving behavior of US citizens and firms, even with a sharp increase in the interest rate, to quickly close the trade deficit. As Quiggin (2004) explains:

> At the moment, roughly 40 percent of each marginal consumption dollar in the United States is currently allocated to imports, so the restoration of balance through increased household saving alone would require an increase in national saving equal to something like 12 percent of GDP. As such an individual saving increase is unlikely, a return to substantial government surpluses would be needed.

Obstfeld and Rogoff (2004) similarly explain that the elasticities of demand and supply of exports and imports are such that very large changes in exchange rates would be necessary to bring about the needed current account shifts. Thus, only changes in the government budget can bring about the required shifts in trade flows between countries to eliminate the US trade deficits. In 2009, US government policy took a perverse turn, at least in terms of the current account deficit: as the economic recession and the financial crisis pushed Americans to sharply increase their saving, the aggressive financial bailout and fiscal stimulus measures by the government caused the US government deficits to rise to $1.8 trillion, which was over 12 percent of GDP.

This relationship between the current account and the government budget deficit, the so-called *twin deficits*, have been discussed for decades. Indeed, if domestic households and private firms do not change their saving behavior, less government saving must be offset by increased foreign saving; that is, a rising government budget deficit must be matched by a larger trade deficit. In 2009, however, because household saving rose, the current account deficit shrank even though the government deficit surged.

2.6.3 Updating the BoP

Table 2.1 will be quickly outdated. Fortunately, BoP data are easily available on the Internet. You can always update Table 2.1 by accessing the convenient Web site at the Bureau of Economic Analysis of the US Department of Commerce: www.bea.gov. The Bureau of Economic Analysis of the US Department of Commerce publishes a preliminary version of the previous year's BoP every April, a first definitive version every July, and then it usually revises the numbers over the next several years as more information becomes available.

The OECD provides data on the BoP of all its members as well as a few other emerging economies. And the IMF combines all BoP data into a vast data base that can be accessed online. Most individual countries also make BoP data available on line.

2.7 The International Investment Position

Another frequently reported international account is the *international investment position*. Whereas the BoP is a compilation of *flows* of payments over some period of time (usually one calendar year), the international investment position is a measure of a country's net *stock* of foreign assets at one given moment in time (customarily midnight, December 31st). A country's international investment position measures how many foreign assets are owned by private citizens, firms, and government agencies of the country versus how many of its private and public assets are owned by foreign citizens, foreign firms, and foreign governments. The value of total assets recorded in a country's international investment position reflects (1) past purchases of assets as recorded on the financial account and (2) adjustments to the accumulated assets for depreciation and changes in the assets' values.

2.7.1 The international investment position of the United States

Table 2.2 presents the United States international investment position through 2008. The amount of foreign assets owned by US citizens

Table 2.2 The International Investment Position of the United States (US$ Billions, Current Cost Basis).

International	US-owned assets abroad	Foreign-owned assets in United States	US Net investment position
1982	$961.0	$725.1	$235.9
1983	1,129.7	872.3	257.4
1984	1,127.1	993.0	134.1
1985	1,302.7	1,205.8	96.9
1986	1,594.7	1,493.9	100.8
1987	1,758.7	1,708.2	50.5
1988	2,008.4	1,997.9	10.5
1989	2,350.2	2,397.2	−47.0
1990	2,294.1	2,458.6	−164.5
1991	2,470.6	2,731.5	−260.8
1992	2,466.5	2,918.8	−452.3
1993	3,081.4	3,235.7	−144.3
1994	3,326.7	3,450.4	−135.3
1995	3,930.3	4,270.4	−305.8
1996	4,631.3	5,010.9	−360.0
1997	5,379.1	6,201.9	−822.7
1998	6,179.1	7,249.9	−1,070.7
1999	7,399.7	8,437.1	−1,037.4
2000	7,401.2	8,982.2	−1,581.0
2001	6,930.5	9,269.9	−2,339.4
2002	6,807.8	9,263.0	−2,455.1
2003	8,296.6	10,669.0	−2,372.6
2004	9,972.8	12,515.0	−2,542.2
2005	11,576.4	13,814.7	−2,238.4
2006	14,225.8	16,607.1	−2,225.8
2007	18,278.8	20,418.8	−2,139.9
2008	19,888.2	23,357.4	−3.469.2

Source: Nguyen (2005). The International Investment Position of the United States at Year end 2004, Survey of Current Business, US Department of Commerce, July, 2005, Table 2, pp. 38–39; EL. BEA (2009). The International Investment Position. Downloaded from the BEA website. http://www.bea.gov/international on 10 January 2010.

and firms and the US assets owned by foreigners have both grown rapidly. But because foreign ownership of US assets has grown more rapidly, the net investment position of the United States has turned sharply negative.

The table shows the clear trend over the past 20 years: the United States went from being a net creditor to a net debtor to the rest of the world. In fact, the United States is today the largest net debtor in the world. The year-to-year changes in the numbers in Table 2.1 in large part reflect the United States' large current account deficits beginning in the early 1980s. Large current account deficits are balanced by large financial account surpluses, which mean that US citizens, businesses, corporations, and governments sell more real estate, stocks, bonds, entire businesses, and US dollars to foreign citizens, firms, corporations, and governments than they purchase from foreign citizens, firms, corporations, and governments. Table 2.2 shows that the United States was a net creditor to the rest of the world until some time between 1988 and 1989, even though the United States began running large financial account surpluses early in the 1980s. The United States had accumulated foreign assets over the previous six decades, when, more often than not, it ran current account surpluses and financial account deficits. Large current account deficits since the 1980s have pushed the US net investment position into deficit, however, and by the beginning of 2009, foreign citizens, firms, organizations, and governments owned almost $3.5 trillion more assets in the United States than American citizens, firms, organizations, and governments-owned abroad.

Table 2.2 also shows that the increasingly negative net investment position of the United States is not the result of declining overseas investment by US individuals, firms, government agencies, banks, and other organizations. International investment grew in both directions. Where US investors owned nearly $1 trillion worth of assets abroad in 1982, by the end of 2008, the value of foreign assets owned by US individuals, firms, government agencies, banks, and other organizations had grown to nearly $20 trillion. Granted, prices have about doubled over the period covered in Table 2.2, but that still leaves a real five fold increase in the real value of foreign assets owned by Americans. The growth of foreign-owned assets in the United States was even faster. In 1982, foreigners owned about $0.725 trillion worth of US assets; by the beginning of 2009 this total had grown to over $23.4 trillion, nearly twice the average annual percentage increase in US investment abroad over the same 25-year period.

2.7.2 *The BoP and the net investment position*

The BoP and the international investment position are, of course, related. The BoP records the *flows* of payments for foreign investment, the international investment position measures the *stock* of foreign assets. The latter should change roughly in line with the annual net flows recorded in the financial account of the BoP, adjusted for asset price changes and depreciation. Specifically:

Net Investment Position of the United States at the end of 2008
  + Net Purchases of Foreign Assets by Americans
  − Depreciation of Foreign Assets Owned by Americans
  + Net Change in the Value of Foreign Assets Owned by Americans
  − Net Purchases of US Assets by Foreigners
  + Depreciation of US Assets Owned by Foreigners
  − Net Change in the Value of US Assets Owned by Foreigners
  _____
Net Investment Position of the United States at the end of 2009

In most years, there are substantial changes in the values of assets over the course of the year, which can offset the net payments for the purchase of assets over the course of the year. The net international investment position, therefore, does not change exactly in line with the recorded international investment flows recorded in the BoP. In the long run, the annual flows in the BoP and the stocks of assets in the net investment position are related. For example, the US net international investment position turned negative after the US current account turned negative in the early 1980s.

2.7.3 *The effect of growing foreign debt on the current account*

The rapid increase in foreign ownership of US assets suggests that there should also have been a shift in *net* interest, rent, profit, and dividend payments recorded in the current account. Despite the large and growing deficit in its net international investment position, however, the United States has continued to record positive net asset returns. Table 2.1 shows that in 2008 earnings by American individuals, firms, banks, etc. on their foreign assets were $755.5 billion while payments to foreigners for returns on their US assets were $627.9 billion, a surplus of $127 billion. Given the net negative international investment position of the United States, equal to about $3.5 trillion in 2008, shouldn't the net returns to foreign assets have been a negative number?

One possible explanation for this contradiction is that US investors earn higher returns on their foreign investments than foreigners earn on US investments. Indeed, much of the foreign portfolio and official investment in the United States consists of government bonds, which are a less risky and lower return investment. Foreign investors in the United States may also not be sending all of their earnings back home, in which case their earnings on US assets do not appear in the BoP. It has also been suggested that, because FDI in the United States is newer on average than US FDI abroad, foreign investment in the United States is not as profitable; new investments often take time to mature and generate cash flows. Finally, some have suggested that foreigners' rush to acquire US assets after their governments removed restrictions on overseas investment during the 1980s led them to invest carelessly. The *Financial Times* reported in 2004 that research by Alan Gregory, professor of corporate finance at Exeter University in Great Britain, "...shows that on average that UK companies make disastrous acquisitions in the United States".[6]

2.7.4 Dark matter

Some economists have interpreted the reported net debt of the United States not as a serious problem, but rather as a failure of

---

[6] Quoted in Kate Burgess (2004). "Acquisitions in US 'Disastrous' for British Companies", *Financial Times*, 11 October 2004.

international accounting. For example, Hausman and Sturzenegger (2006) perform an interesting form of reverse engineering. They begin with the data on international income flows that show the United States earns more on its overseas investments than foreigners earn on their US investments. They capitalize the recorded flows of returns to assets, assuming a five percent average annual return, and conclude that US net wealth in 2004 was not the huge negative number reported in the net international investment position, but a positive $724 billion. They refer to the unrecorded wealth as "dark matter", a term physicists use to refer to the unknown forces in the universe whose existence has been hypothesized based on observed movements of planets, stars, comets, and other objects in space.

What could this financial "dark matter" be? For one thing, the hidden wealth could consist of accumulated know-how that gives US firms operating abroad higher returns to its productive and innovative activities. Or, perhaps, it reflects the better marketing abilities of US firms. Others have suggested that US wealth should include the value of US brands and reputations, which gives US firms some degree of market power that they can exploit in the future. It has long been argued that savings flow to the United States in part because of the country's superior institutions, which reduces investors' risk compared to potential investments in other countries. Another explanation for the dark matter is the observation that foreign immigrants bring substantial amounts of money with them when they move to the United States; the United States receives more immigrants than any other country in the world.

The dark matter calculated by Hausman and Sturzenegger is not nearly enough to keep the net wealth positive given the rate at which the United States is accumulating new debt, however. Just in 2008, a year when the US current account deficit was somewhat smaller than it had been recently, it was still about equal to the total estimated value of dark matter for 2004. If future dark matter grows according to Hausman and Sturzenegger's long-run 1970–2004 estimate of $125 billion per year, then current trade deficits indicate that the United States is still headed for a large, and unsustainable, level of net foreign debt.

There are many other reasons why the United States current account deficit remains a concern. If many foreigners have indeed kept their returns in the US financial markets, there could be a sudden crunch if foreigners eventually decide to invest the earnings at home or in a third country. The recession and slowdown in US innovation and market power may reduce the profits, and investors may decide the US market no longer promises higher returns in the future. There is also the frequent suggestion that the net investment position of the United States may actually be worse than the numbers suggest because foreign companies intentionally manipulate transfer prices and expenses so as to lower the profits in the United States and avoid US corporate profits taxes. Time will tell whether these explanations hold up to scrutiny.

2.8 Summary and Conclusions

This chapter introduced the BoP account, where countries record their international transactions. It also reviewed the circular flow diagram, which reflects the logic of the Keynesian macroeconomic model. Among the main points emphasized in this chapter are:

1. An open economy is directly linked to the world economy through international trade and international investment, the value of which are recorded in the country's BoP account.
2. The circular flow details all the flows among major sectors of the economy.
3. The circular flow clearly illustrates how households, producers, financial firms, and the government are linked.
4. The BoP is designed to be consistent with the circular flow diagram of an economy, and once you understand the circular flow, it is easy to remember the logic of the BoP account.
5. The circular flow of an open economy is stable only if the maze of internal and foreign outflows and inflows remain stable.
6. By linking the BoP to the circular flow, it is clear that changes in a country's international economic activities impact all sectors of an open economy.

7. Alternatively, any major changes in the performance of an economy will impact international trade and international investment.
8. Macroeconomic models, therefore, must recognize an economy's links to the rest of the world.

In addition to these general conclusions derived from the discussion in this chapter, the description of the BoP account and the net international investment position account pointed out that:

9. International transactions are classified into two major subaccounts, the current account and the financial account.
10. While these two subaccounts must sum to zero, either can take on negative or positive values.
11. A country's net investment position nets the stock of domestic assets owned by foreigners and foreign assets owned by domestic investors.
12. The *stocks* of assets in the net investment position account change with the *flows* in the financial account of the BoP.

This chapter's focus on the US BoP also showed that:

13. The United States has run unprecedented current account deficits since 1980.
14. Correspondingly, the United States has had large financial account surpluses and net investment position deficits.
15. The US current account deficits imply that the United States, as a country, has in recent years absorbed five percent more products than it produces.
16. The United States has, therefore, become the largest net debtor in the world.

US deficits are troublesome because the US dollar is widely used for international transactions, as the unit of account for valuing assets and commodities throughout the world, and as the principal reserve currency held by central banks. The Bretton Woods Conference, under the astute leadership of Harry Dexter White and against the wishes of

John Maynard Keynes, created a system that placed the dollar at the center of the international financial system. But can the currency of the largest global debtor remain in this position?

In early 2009, the US trade deficit declined as a result of the global financial crisis and recession. But, the fact that the financial crisis began with the breakdown of the US financial system seemed likely to further undermine the long-term position of the dollar. Much will depend on how the United States and the rest of the world adjust to the new economic realities after the deep recession and the financial crisis that caused it work themselves out in the coming years.

Now that you have familiarized yourself with the international accounts that record international payments and how those international payments interact with the systemic macroeconomic flows illustrated by the open-economy circular flow diagram in Fig. 2.4, you are ready to begin your study of international finance. The remaining chapters will describe and explain those payments in greater detail, and more importantly, the study of international finance and open-economy macroeconomics will provide a holistic perspective of how the whole international economic system functions.

Key Terms and Concepts

Aggregate demand	Financial account	Outsourcing
BoP	Financial flows	Remittances
Capital account	Foreign aid	Returns to assets
Circular flow diagram	Intermediate products	Statistical discrepancy
Current account	Macroeconomics	Trade balance
Dark matter	Merchandise trade	Transfers
Economic	Net investment	Twin deficits
interdependence	position	Value added
FP	Open economy	

Chapter Questions and Problems

1. The following items are from a hypothetical country's BoP ($billions):

   a. Imports of services: $91.6
   b. Borrowing from private foreigners: $85.9
   c. Merchandise exports: $213.2
   d. Net outflow of transfer payments: $8.9
   e. Exports of services: $119.2
   f. Private lending to foreigners: $48.2
   g. Merchandise imports: $273.5
   h. Borrowing from foreign central banks: $5.1
   i. Increase in official reserve assets: $1.2

   (a) Assume that there are no other payments and these payments cover all of the country's international payments. Place each item where it belongs in the current account or in the financial account, and designate each as a credit or a debit.
   (b) Do the debits and credits sum to zero?
   (c) What exactly are the current account and financial account balances?

2. Why include a line for statistical discrepancy in the BoP?

3. Brief Essay: Econoland runs a current account deficit of $100 billion in a given year. Explain what must have happened to the financial account and Econoland's international investment position. Specifically explain how the financial account and Econoland's international investment position are related.

4. Discuss why the United States may be able to continue running current account deficits for a long time, and then present reasons why the United States will have to adjust soon. (Hint: Use the discussion in the chapter, and also focus on the individual items in the BoP and the incentives that determine each of those categories of foreign and domestic expenditure flows.)

5. Describe how a country's international investment position is related to its BoP. Make use of the information on the US BoP and the US net investment position to support your verbal description. Why is there not a perfect relationship between the flows in the BoP and the subsequent changes in the net investment position?

6. Explain the meaning of the relationship (2–5), $(X - IM) + Tr_F + r_F = -S_F$. Define each term of the equation and explain the relationship between the terms.

7. Section 2.2.4 concludes with the following sentences:

"Some of the greatest controversies in macroeconomics revolve around how individual choices affect the overall economic outcomes, and how the resulting aggregate flows impact the individual units. Of special concern is how those choices are made. Macroeconomics requires holistic analysis of system and parts".

Discuss and provide examples of how choices by individuals, firms, organizations, government agencies, etc. affect other parts of the economy. Specifically, discuss how these decisions affect the circular flow.

References

Fisman, R and S-J Wei (2001). Tax rates and tax evasion: Evidence from 'Missing Imports' in China. *NBER Working Paper w8551*, October.

Hausman, R and F Sturzenegger (2006). US and global imbalances: Can dark matter prevent a big bang? *Working Paper*, Harvard University.

Hummels, D, J Ishii and K-M Yi (2000). The nature and growth of vertical specialization in world trade. *Journal of International Economics*, 54, 75–96.

Marquez, J and L Workman (2001). Modeling the IMFs statistical discrepancy in the global current account. *IMF Staff Papers*, 48(3), 499–521.

Motala, J (1997). Statistical discrepancies in the world current account. *Finance & Development*, March.

Obstfeld, M and K Rogoff (2003). The unsustainable US current account position revisited. *NBER Working Paper 10869*, October, 2004.

Quiggin, J (2004). The unsustainability of US trade deficits. *The Economists' Voice*, 1(3), article 2, www.bepress.com/ev.

Part II

The Foreign Exchange Market

Chapter 3

The Foreign Exchange Market

The puzzling thing is that despite the obvious gain from the use of
one money, it appears to be quite difficult to introduce one money
in the international economy which will be acceptable to everyone.

(Paul De Grauwe, 1989, p. 1)

If you have traveled overseas, you are already familiar with *exchange
rates*, the prices at which one country's money is exchanged for another
country's money. In your travels, you were probably intrigued by the
different currencies in countries you traveled to, viewing it as part of
the "international experience". Importers, exporters, and international
investors generally do not view the coexistence of many different currencies throughout the world as a positive experience, however. They
are more likely to see the many different moneys as a complication
that adds to the cost of international transactions. Evidence suggests
that there would be more international trade and international investment if importers, exporters, and investors did not face the cost of
having to exchange currencies every time they exchanged products or
assets across borders.

Foreign exchange markets are one of the distinguishing characteristics of the global economy. It is difficult to avoid the foreign exchange
markets when conducting international business. One way would be
to avoid dealing with foreigners, but in today's global environment

that would severely limit business opportunities. Another way to eliminate the need for dealing with foreign exchange markets would be for governments to abandon their national moneys for a single world currency. Despite some recent efforts to move in that direction, as in the case of the 16 European countries who, by 2009, had jointly adopted the euro as their shared money, most governments are not yet willing to surrender their national currencies and adopt an international currency. The global economy will in all likelihood have multiple currencies for the foreseeable future, and cross-border transactions will continue to require the exchange of currencies.

Chapter Goals

1. Familiarize the reader with foreign exchange markets.
2. Present a brief history of foreign exchange markets.
3. Explain the sources of supply and demand in the foreign exchange market.
4. Illustrate how shifts in supply and demand cause currency *appreciation* or *depreciation*.
5. Introduce the concept of *arbitrage*, and explain its role in modern foreign exchange markets.
6. Explain how *geographic* (spatial) arbitrage creates an integrated global foreign exchange market even though trades are carried out over the counter in separate geographic locations.
7. Explain how *triangular* (cross-currency) arbitrage links all exchange rates among n currencies to $n-1$ fundamental exchange rates.
8. Introduce and illustrate the *effective* exchange rates.

3.1 Overview of Foreign Exchange Markets

The existence of different national currencies effectively gives all products that are traded between countries many prices rather than just one. For every traded product, there is the price in the currency of the country where the product is produced, and then there are the prices in terms of other countries' currencies. There are many reasons why prices differ from one country to another, but the main long-run determinant of the price differences are the exchange rates between the world's many different currencies. Exchange rates are, therefore, very important for international trade because the attractiveness of buying foreign goods or selling domestic goods overseas depends on how exchange rates translate foreign currency prices into prices denominated in the domestic currency.

Exchange rates also impact international investment. Potential buyers of foreign assets must take into consideration both the current prices and expected future returns of foreign assets compared to domestic assets. Prices and returns of foreign assets must be translated into domestic currencies before they can be compared to domestic assets and returns. In the case of assets, decisions to buy or sell are based on both known current exchange rates and expected future exchange rates. Foreign investment decisions, therefore, face not only the usual risks and uncertainty of long-run investment, but, because the exchange rates at which the future selling prices and returns are translated back into the investor's home currency cannot be predicted with certainty, foreign investment is subject to an additional *foreign exchange risk*.

Foreign exchange markets are not mere inconveniences. The exchange rates set in foreign exchange markets have a direct bearing on economic activities in the global economy. As will be detailed later in this chapter, by determining the relative prices of products and assets across different economies, the exchange rate plays a critical role in balancing the flow of payments between countries described in the previous chapter.

3.1.1 *The basics of exchange rates*

Major newspapers report foreign exchange rates every day. Exchange rates between the major currencies are also continuously available on Internet sites of major newspapers. Table 3.1 reports the values of each of the world's currencies in terms of the world's two major currencies, the US dollar and the euro reported by the *Financial Times* on

Table 3.1   Exchange Rates, 26 May 2009.

Country	Currency per		Country	Currency per	
	Dollar	Euro		Dollar	Euro
Argentina (peso)	3.7413	5.2327	Poland (zloty)	3.1567	4.4150
Australia (dollar)	1.2802	1.7905	Romania (new leu)	2.9876	4.1786
Bahrain (dinar)	0.3770	0.5273	Russia (rouble)	31.3265	43.8148
Bolivia (boliviano)	7.0200	9.8185	Saudi Arabia (SR)	3.7502	5.2453
Brazil (real)	2.0353	2.8467	Singapore (dollar)	1.4484	2.0257
Canada (dollar)	1.1216	1.5687	South Africa (rand)	8.2900	11.5947
Chile (peso)	562.95	787.37	S. Korea (won)	1262.90	1766.36
China (yuan)	6.8306	9.5536	Sweden (kroner)	7.5687	10.586
Colombia (peso)	2210.6	3091.9	Switzerland (franc)	1.0837	1.5156
Costa Rica (colon)	576.395	806.176	Taiwan (dollar)	32.655	45.6729
Czech R. (koruna)	19.0877	26.697	Thailand (baht)	34.475	48.2185
Denmark (kroner)	5.3227	7.4446	Tunisia (dinar)	1.3502	1.8885
Egypt (pound)	5.6235	7.8653	Turkey (lira)	1.5545	2.1742
Estonia (kroon)	11.1869	15.6465	U.A.E. (dirham)	3.6727	5.1368
Hong Kong ($)	7.7520	10.8423	UK (pound)*	1.5943	0.8773
Hungary (Forint)	201.301	281.550	1 mo. forward	1.5941	0.8771
India (rupee)	47.930	67.037	3 mo. forward	1.5937	0.8769
Indonesia (rupiah)	10335.0	14455.1	1 yr. forward	1.5924	0.8766
Israel (sheckel)	3.9666	5.5479	Ukraine (hrywnja)	7.6575	10.7102

(Continued)

Table 3.1 (*Continued*)

Country	Currency per		Country	Currency per	
	Dollar	Euro		Dollar	Euro
Japan (yen)	94.7750	132.557	Uruguay (peso)	23.5500	32.9382
1 mo. forward	94.7417	132.467	The United States (dollar)	—	1.3987
3 mo. forward	94.6824	132.316	1 mo. forward	—	1.3982
1 yr. forward	94.1988	131.490	3. mo. forward	—	1.3975
Kenya (shilling)	78.150	109.305	1 yr. forward	—	1.3959
Kuwait (dinar)	0.2879	0.4027	Venezuela (bolivar)	2.1473	3.0033
Malaysia (dollar)	3.5125	4.9128	Vietnam (dong)	17781	24869
Mexico (peso)	13.1380	18.3755	Euro*	1.3987	—
New Zealand ($)	1.6138	2.2572	1 mo. forward	1.3982	—
Nigeria (naira)	148.00	207.00	3 mo. forward	1.3975	—
Norway (krona)	6.4008	8.9525	1 yr. forward	1.3959	—
Pakistan (rupee)	80.615	112.752	SDR	0.6479	0.9062
Peru (new sol)	2.9993	4.1950			
The Philippines (peso)	47.355	66.2331			

Source: Closing rates, 16:00 Greenwich Mean Time, published in the *Financial Times*, May 27, Marketing and Investing Section, p. 20. Also, see www.ft.com/markets/data.

* Exchange rates for the British pound and the euro are from the dollar perspective; all other rates are local currency per dollar.

13 May 2009. The *Financial Times* reported the values of 216 national currencies. Many of the reported exchange rates listed are determined on active markets where the forces of supply and demand determine the price of a currency in terms of other currencies. These markets are referred to as *foreign exchange markets*, or collectively as the *foreign exchange market*. In markets where the forces of supply and demand are free to drive the prices of currencies, the exchange rates are said to *float*. The foreign exchange market is not a true free market, however. The uncertainty associated with floating exchange rates and the potential negative effects on international trade and investment have often led governments to interfere in the foreign exchange market. Governments often influence the price of their currencies by selling or buying currencies to offset shifts in supply and demand that would otherwise cause the exchange rate to change. We will show in later chapters that it is not easy to keep an exchange rate from changing when the fundamental forces of supply and demand shift. Governments nevertheless actively interfere in the foreign exchange market, and some even attempt to rigidly *fix* the values of their currencies by constantly intervening in the market or directly restricting supply and demand.

The foreign exchange market plays a prominent role in the national economies that make up the global economy. These markets are driven by a complex set of variables, as the remainder of this textbook will explain. Given the critical role they play in the global economy, we need to explain how the foreign exchange markets evolved, how they operate today, and how they are likely to evolve in the future. That is the purpose of this and the next three chapters.

3.1.2 *Why foreign exchange markets matter*

The daily business news constantly reminds us of how important exchange rates are. For example, in 2001 you would have read that the Honda Motor Company of Japan had to take a large one-time accounting charge because of the decline in the value of the euro. Honda manufactures cars for the European market in a factory located in the United Kingdom, and it uses parts imported from

Japan and the United States. In 2000, the value of the euro had depreciated (fallen in value) relative to the British pound, the US dollar, and the Japanese yen. Therefore, Honda's profits from selling British-made cars, for which it incurred pound costs, were reduced in the rest of Europe. British-made Hondas had to compete with autos manufactured in France, Germany, and Italy, where costs were almost entirely in euros, and for competitive reasons, Honda could not raise euro prices to cover its pound, yen, and dollar costs.[1]

The year before, exchange rates were a hot topic of conversation at the 2000 Cannes Film Festival. According to one movie producer, "the exchange rate is something that comes up every minute of every discussion".[2] Were filmmakers really discussing exchange rates? The market for films has become global, and US film producers no longer target only the United States when they plan upcoming productions. Europe, with its high per capita incomes, has become a very important market for US film producers. But in 2000, the fall in the value of the euro relative to the US dollar threatened to reduce revenues by millions of US dollars. Also, because foreign movie distributors often put up money toward the production of US movies, the fall of the euro meant that that source of financing had been substantially reduced.

One US film producer took the exchange rate in stride, however. It turns out that he had found a convenient way to mitigate the negative effects of the falling euro by shifting the filming of his movie, *Affair with a Necklace*, from Hollywood, where his costs were in dollars, to France, where his costs would be in depreciated euros. He boasted the rare accomplishment of completing his film under (dollar) budget.

By 2005, however, the exchange rates had again shifted. The euro cost about $0.80 in 2001, but by 2005 the tables had turned and it

---

[1] Todd Zaun (2001). "Honda Takes Currency Hit in Europe", *Wall Street Journal*, March 28.

[2] Charles Goldsmith (2000). "Moguls Rewrite Script at Cannes As Euro Tanks", *Wall Street Journal*, May 19.

cost over $1.30. That is about a 60 percent appreciation of the euro relative to the dollar. Therefore, in 2005 it was European manufacturers who were complaining about the difficulties of selling in the United States and competing with "cheap" American imports.

An interesting 2005 example was Superior Products Inc., a manufacturer of gas fittings and assemblies in Cleveland, Ohio. Superior Products had begun importing some parts and components from Germany in 2000, when the dollar was expensive relative to the euro. But, when the euro began rising in value after 2002, "the Germans just kept raising their prices", according to Superior's vice president. Superior, therefore, began making the parts and components themselves in the United States. In early 2005, the company was asked by an Italian firm if Superior Products could manufacture gas fittings for export. By 2008 the US dollar had depreciated to where it took $1.50 to buy a euro, and after further fluctuation it remained above the 2005 value of $1.30 midway in 2009.

The decline in the value of the dollar since 2001, and reciprocal rise in the value of the euro, is obviously related to the US trade deficit discussed in the previous chapter. However, the earlier appreciation of the dollar in 2000, when the current account deficit was already clearly growing larger, suggests that the relationship between the balance of payments and exchange rates is complex. The trade balance is apparently not the only variable that comes into play in the foreign exchange market. The fact is that exchange rates are very difficult to predict. Filmmakers had better not book their locations too far in advance!

3.2 The Evolution of the Foreign Exchange Market

Markets for foreign exchange have operated for over 2000 years, ever since there have been distinct national moneys. In ancient times, gold and silver coins from different parts of the world were used by the merchants who carried goods from one region to another. Even though coins were made of the same precious metals, the actual coins varied greatly in weight and purity. Professional moneychangers became experts in measuring the relative worth of coins minted by the many different regions, empires, and city-states.

3.2.1 *The early moneychangers*

The origin of money is not known with certainty. Coins minted in the region of Lydia (located in modern-day Turkey) about 650 BCE were among the very earliest coins. The practice of minting coins spread from the cities of ancient Greece to other regions in the Middle East, Asia, and the Mediterranean.[3] Most coins in circulation in ancient times were made of bronze (for small transactions) and silver (for larger and foreign transactions). Because of their scarcity and high value relative to the prices of most goods at that time, gold and gold coins served mostly as a store of value rather than a medium of exchange.

The ancient moneychangers effectively operated the first foreign exchange markets, and these moneychangers plus the growing supplies of coins comprised the ancient *international monetary system*. By the 5th century BCE, moneychangers were active in Greece, Persia, and throughout the Middle East. The job of the 5th century BCE Greek moneychanger was:

> ... to know the value of foreign coins and the proper exchange rates and to make the exchanges. There were, after all, a great many different coinages in circulation in Greece and they were on several different standards.... While the coins of some cities were sound, those of others were more or less debased. On the simplest level exchanges would be freely made and, allowing for the moneychanger's commission, such exchanges should have reflected the metallic contents, weights, and relative purity of the gold, silver, and bronze in the coins.[4]

The ancient moneychanger's job was complicated by the variety and unreliability of the coinage in circulation. Coins lacked uniformity in terms of weight and purity. Minters of coins sometimes cheated on how much gold and silver they actually put into their coins, passing

---

[3] See, for example, Davisson and Harper (1972), Davies (1996), and Cameron (1993).
[4] Davisson and Harper (1972). p. 157.

them off at some greater value than the actual gold and silver they contained. As time passed, emperors, kings, queens, pharaohs, and other heads of states increasingly monopolized coinage for themselves. With the supply restricted, coins gained value over and above the implicit value of the gold or silver in them because they served as a constant and known measure. That is, merchants were usually willing to accept for payment a standard coin rather than gold or silver of unknown purity and weight. The difference between the value of the gold or silver in a coin and the actual value at which the coin circulates is called *seignorage*, which is effectively the gain that the "seignor", or the monarch, derives from the monopoly right to mint coins. The ancient gold and silver coins were often *debased* by intentional scraping of some of a coin's gold or silver from its edges. Moneychangers therefore carefully weighed and analyzed coins in order to determine their true content of gold, silver, or other precious metals. The risks involved in exchanging coins was high, and money changers extracted much higher margins between buying and selling prices than the miniscule margins that we observe in modern foreign exchange markets.

3.2.2 *The development of banking*

Foreign exchange markets became more complicated after the development of banking and the introduction of new types of payments to supplement the traditional use of coins made from precious metals. In the Middle Ages, merchants in the major European trading centers increasingly made payments using *bills of exchange* that were linked to deposits of gold or silver coins or bullion in banks, a procedure very similar to the current practice of writing checks on money deposited in a checking account. Bills of exchange were a welcome financial innovation because merchants no longer needed to carry gold or silver over long distances under the risk of loss or theft. The claims on gold or silver deposited in distant but known banks were exchanged among merchants multiple times before being redeemed. A merchant from one country might sell goods in another country and pay for the goods with a bill of exchange drawn on a bank in his home country. The merchant who sold the goods could sell the bill to a moneychanger in exchange for local money, and the moneychanger could then sell the bill to someone going to the country where the bank is located. Or, the merchant could use the bill to pay for goods purchased from another merchant, who could then sell the bill to a moneychanger or use it to yet again buy goods.

The banks that provided the bills of exchange were usually the same banks that financed merchants and their trade costs. These banks enjoyed good reputations among merchants, and they naturally came to dominate the exchange of bills of exchange from banks in other kingdoms and cities. In effect, the most reputable commercial banks became not only suppliers of foreign exchange and bills of exchange, but they also effectively became wholesale moneychangers, exchanging the new negotiable financial claims denominated in different currencies. The financing of foreign trade and the exchange of currencies went hand in hand. Today, foreign exchange markets are still operated by the world's largest commercial banks.

3.2.3 *Fiat money and exchange rates*

Paper money was allegedly invented in China, and the practice later spread to Europe. Gold and silver were known commodities that had value all over the world, but paper money's value depended only on the expectation that it could be used to purchase some quantity of goods or assets some time in the future. Paper money is a *fiat* money, which has value only if people trust they will be able to exchange it for something of value in the future. With paper or *fiat* money, the job of the moneychanger became much more difficult. Now the price of one fiat money in terms of other fiat moneys reflected not the value of some well-known precious metal, but only an expectation of the fiat money's future *purchasing power*. That is, the relative value of each paper money depended on what it, and all other currencies, could buy currently and, most importantly, what it was expected to be able to buy in terms of real goods and services in the future.

This fundamental difference between using gold or silver coins and bullion to back financial instruments, such as the bills of exchange mentioned above, and using fiat money should be obvious. In the former case, the relative values of instruments denominated in different currencies can never deviate very much from the values of gold and silver that backs the instruments. But, if paper money and bills of exchange backed by fiat paper money are exchanged in the foreign exchange markets, then it is the perceived relative values of the paper money that determine the exchange rates. Bills of exchange drawn on accounts containing deposits of fiat money will be accepted in payment for goods so long as people expect the fiat money can be used to acquire goods or assets of the stated value. If people suspect, for example, that the government may abuse its privilege to print money by printing much more than is needed for the exchange of goods, services, and assets, then people will expect inflation to rise and the purchasing power of the fiat money to diminish over time. Sellers of goods will then demand to be paid in other currencies, thus reducing the value of the diminished money ever further. And, those who hold the currency or bills drawn on accounts denominated in that currency may begin to exchange those bills for other currencies or assets denominated in other currencies. In the end, demand for a currency that is expected to lose purchasing power will decline, and there will be growing demand for currencies whose value is expected to rise in the future. The exchange rate at which the currencies are traded reflects these shifts in supply and demand.

Specifically, expectations of fiat money exchange rates depend on a variety of information about current economic conditions and policies, as well as people's understanding of how economic and political conditions are likely to evolve in the future. Demand for fiat currencies issued by governments less likely to engage in inflationary money creation will tend to rise. Exchange rates among fiat moneys tend to be subject to continual changes as news about political and economic events becomes known and people's understanding of the world changes. Given that today's moneys are nearly all fiat moneys, backed only by the monetary policies of the issuing government agency or designated central bank, it should not be surprising that exchange rates are often volatile.

This brief discussion of the history of money and foreign exchange markets has, hopefully, served to distinguish several important relationships that help explain how foreign exchange markets work today. The role of expectations about future purchasing power is key to understanding exchange rates among modern fiat moneys. Now let us add some more details about today's moneychangers, or what we call the foreign exchange market.

3.3 Foreign Exchange Markets Today

When you travel overseas and exchange dollars for foreign money at an airport foreign exchange counter, you are dealing in what is called the retail foreign exchange market. The retail market accounts for a very small part of the world's foreign exchange transactions, however. Nearly all of the \$3–\$4 trillion worth of currencies that are exchanged every working day are traded through a worldwide network of dealers that are collectively referred to as *the over-the-counter foreign exchange market*. The term "over-the-counter" implies that the dealers maintain stocks of currencies and they are open to buy and sell to whoever "steps up to the counter". The details of each query, offer, and actual exchange are known only to the customer and dealer, although most market participants have some knowledge of recent prices at other counters.

Another distinguishing feature of modern foreign exchange dealers is that they are more like wholesalers, dealing only with large sales and purchases. A \$1 million deal is referred to as "thin" in the foreign exchange market. Dealers are located mostly in the offices of large banking organizations, linked by the most sophisticated electronic communications network available. The dealers make a market for international businesses, financial firms, pension funds, insurance companies, hedge funds, and other large investors.[5] The dealers both sell to and buy from the same group of customers, and the dealers also trade for themselves in order to balance their inventories of currencies,

---

[5] BIS (2007).

to exploit arbitrage opportunities, and occasionally to take speculative positions. The dealers buy and sell foreign exchange to customers on demand.

Foreign exchange dealers are exposed to the risk of changing exchange rates by holding foreign exchange because they are what we call *market makers*, which are dealers who are willing to quote both bids and offers for one or more currencies and stand ready to commit the firm's capital to complete transactions at those quoted prices. The market makers provide the price information that guides the market and permits trades upon demand. These foreign exchange dealers, trading on behalf of their customers and for their own accounts, make up what is the single largest financial market in the world.

3.3.1 *The over-the-counter market*

Today's over-the-counter foreign exchange market evolved from the banks that provided trade credit and dealt in foreign bills of exchange centuries ago. The over-the-counter market is located throughout the world, wherever commercial banks and other financial organizations have gone into the business of dealing in foreign exchange. It is known that traders located in the United States accounted for 16.8 percent of the world's foreign exchange transactions in 2007. The United Kingdom, primarily London, accounts for over one-third of the world's foreign exchange transactions. London has a long history of financial dealings, and its current prominence in foreign exchange dealings is the result of centuries of banking experience. The deregulation of international financial transactions in London has also helped to solidify London's current position in the world financial markets. Worldwide, over 1,200 active dealers reported to the Bank of International Settlements (BIS) in 2007.[6]

Most foreign exchange transactions, nearly 90 percent, involve the US dollar as one of the currencies exchanged. This percentage seems rather high given that the United States accounts for less than

---

[6] BIS (2007).

20 percent of world trade in goods and services. But, many international transactions are denominated in dollars even when they are by people, firms, agencies, banks, or other organizations from countries that do not use the dollar as their currency. Commodities such as oil, coffee, copper, and most others are usually priced in dollars, regardless of who is supplying or buying the commodities. Also, most international loans by large commercial banks to firms and governments of developing economies are denominated in US dollars, and many foreign firms and governments issue bonds in dollars. The dollar's prominence in the foreign exchange market also reflects the fact that it serves as a *vehicle currency* for many trades of less common currencies. For example, if you want to exchange Uruguayan pesos for Malaysian ringgit, you will have to first trade pesos for dollars and then dollars for ringgit. Such roundabout trades may appear to be cumbersome, but they are actually more efficient than trading pesos directly. A peso/ringgit market would be very "thin", which means it would not clear very frequently and its price would tend to fluctuate excessively because small random shocks would easily overwhelm the market. The peso–dollar and ringgit–dollar markets are much larger than the missing peso–ringgit market would be, and the peso–dollar and ringgit–dollar markets therefore provide more accurate information and greater *liquidity* to market participants. Greater *market liquidity* means market participants can more often close trades in precisely the quantities of currencies desired. Costs are also often lower with two trades through larger markets than one trade through a small illiquid market. Economies of scale substantially come into play because with a smaller number of markets, dealers and other market participants need to hold fewer working balances in different currencies.

3.3.2 *A 24-h worldwide market*

Modern communications have created an integrated world market for foreign exchange that essentially functions 24-h per day. There are major financial centers where large dealers are located in nearly every time zone of the world. When it is late afternoon in San Francisco and financial markets close there, markets in Auckland, New Zealand, in Sydney, Australia, and in Tokyo, Japan are just opening. And, before those markets close, other markets in Singapore in Southeast Asia and Bahrain in the Middle East will have opened, followed by the foreign exchange dealers in the financial centers of Europe. Then, as the London, Paris, and Frankfurt markets are in their afternoon trading, dealers in New York open, followed by dealers in Chicago and San Francisco, at which point the whole cycle starts over again.

The foreign exchange market is, by far, the largest financial market in the world. Table 3.2 provides some estimates of the size of the foreign exchange market compiled by the Bank for International Settlements (BIS). According to the latest BIS data, the overall volume of the spot, forward, and swap markets exceeds $US3 trillion per day. Notice from Table 3.2 that that the overall 2001 volume declined relative to 1998. This contraction in trading volume was caused by the introduction of the euro, the new currency that replaced 12 separate European currencies. The single currency eliminated the large volume of currency trades that had occurred between German marks, French francs, Dutch guilders, Spanish pesetas, Italian lira, Belgian francs, and the other national currencies that the euro replaced. But, after that adjustment, worldwide currency trading resumed its growth, and by 2004 the total market reached a new daily turnover

Table 3.2   Global Foreign Exchange Market Turnover (Daily Averages on 1 April, $US Billions).

	1989	1992	1995	1998	2001	2004	2007
Spot transactions	317	394	494	568	387	621	1,005
Forward transactions	27	58	97	128	131	208	362
Foreign exchange swaps	190	324	546	734	656	944	1,714
Total turnover*	590	820	1,190	1,490	1,200	1,800	3,210

Source: BIS (2007), Trennial Central Bank Survey of Foreign Exchange and Derivatives Market Activity in April 2007, Basel: Bank for International Settlements, September (downloaded from www.bis.org).

* Note: The total turnover includes some items not includes in the above three categories, and there is some double counting across the three categories; hence, the total is not the simple sum of the three categories of foreign exchange transactions.

of about $1.8 trillion. Before the international financial crisis slowed international transactions at the end of 2008, daily volume was edging toward $4 trillion per day.

Table 3.2 shows that trading on the foreign exchange market falls into several categories of trades. There are *spot* transactions that consist of exchanges of currencies immediately at current exchange rates. There are also *forward* transactions, which consist of contractual arrangements closed today for an exchange of currencies to be carried out at some future date. In actual practice, spot and forward market transactions are settled two days after the actual exchange in order to give banks ample time to confirm the agreement and arrange for the necessary crediting and debiting of accounts in different business locations, but the prices and volumes are determined at the moment they are agreed to. As will be explained in the next two chapters, forward transactions are an important method by which international traders and investors reduce uncertainty about the future value of currencies.

A growing proportion of foreign market transactions are *swaps*. These are contractual arrangements, where a party buys (sells) foreign exchange for delivery on one date and agrees to sell (buy) it back at some later date. Some swaps combine a spot and a forward transaction that reverses the spot transaction. Many *swaps* involve two offsetting forward transactions for distinct future dates. Table 3.2 shows the growth of swaps as a proportion of total foreign exchange transactions. Swaps permit investors to temporarily acquire foreign assets without incurring the risk of future exchange rate changes, an important attribute for short-term investors, speculators, and the financial managers of international businesses.

3.3.3 *Arbitrage*

Foreign exchange markets are characterized by several forms of *arbitrage*. Arbitrage is any process that causes distinct markets to effectively merge into a single integrated market. Such a process occurs when profit-seeking *arbitrageurs* buy goods or assets in those segments of a general market where prices are low and sell where prices are high; these arbitrageurs cause the price differences to diminish between the market segments. A simple example illustrates the concept of arbitrage.

Suppose that there are two separate markets for cucumbers, one in Toronto, Canada, and the other in Chicago, in the United States. Suppose also that there are a large number of cucumber producers in the regions around each city and millions of consumers interested in buying the cucumbers. Of course, the producers around Toronto and Chicago are not identical. Labor costs differ in the two locations, land rents may be different, and perhaps technology or management may be different as well. Consumers of cucumbers are not the same in the two cities either. Differences in tastes, culture, income, and the total number of people make the demand curves different in Chicago and Toronto. Suppose the two isolated markets for cucumbers are as shown by the supply and demand curves in Fig. 3.1. Note that the price of cucumbers is much higher in Toronto.

The large price difference between the two cities is likely to come to the attention of buyers in Toronto and producers in Chicago, who see opportunities for gains. Some smart merchants from Toronto might decide to go to Chicago and buy cheaper cucumbers to haul back to Toronto. Some equally observant merchants in Chicago might also decide to load a truck with cucumbers and drive to Toronto to sell them there. This shift of demand from high-priced markets to low-priced markets and supply from low-priced to high-priced markets is precisely what economists call *arbitrage*.

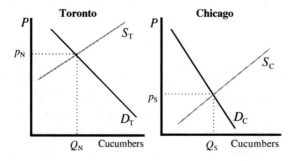

Figure 3.1   Two isolated markets for cucumbers.

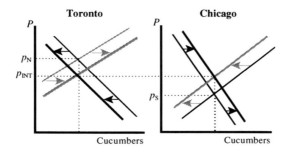

Figure 3.2 Price equalization with complete arbitrage.

The arbitrage effectively reduces demand for cucumbers in Toronto and increases demand in Chicago. When the Chicago merchants load their trucks with cucumbers and drive to Toronto, they reduce supply in Chicago and increase it in Toronto. Figure 3.2 illustrates the shifts of supply and demand in the two markets as a result of the arbitrage in cucumbers. The final effect of the arbitrage is to make prices more similar. In fact, if there are no costs to moving cucumbers from Chicago to Toronto, then prices will equalize at the international price of p_{INT}. At that point, there are no further arbitrage opportunities, and the shifts in the demand and supply curves define the level of trade in cucumbers between Chicago and Toronto.

This simple example of cucumbers and the assumption of zero transportation costs is not very realistic. It is costly to ship a perishable product like cucumbers from Chicago to Toronto. However, the example of complete arbitrage is quite realistic for the foreign exchange markets located around the world. Transport costs for money are virtually nil, and communications about prices in all the foreign exchange markets around the world are instantaneously available in all other locations. There should be no differences in exchange rates across geographic locations. Indeed, the low transaction costs of the foreign exchange market imply that even differences in exchange rate of one ten-thousandth of one cent provide a profitable arbitrage opportunity. The electronic communications also imply that these small arbitrage opportunities cause large amounts of money to move almost instantaneously. The result of this large and lightning-quick arbitrage implies that at any moment in time there is effectively just one worldwide exchange rate for every pair of currencies in the world.

3.3.4 *Geographic arbitrage in the foreign exchange market*

The world's many far-flung foreign exchange dealers are in practice very tightly linked by a state-of-the-art electronic network. Furthermore, the several hundred major commercial banks who house foreign exchange dealers nearly all have branches in each of the world's major financial centers, so many of the global communications are, in a sense, in house. Dealers from the different banks are in continuous contact to manage their foreign exchange exposures, always seeking to balance assets and liabilities in each currency so that they do not suddenly find themselves carrying excessive foreign exchange risk. Dealers also continuously trade foreign currencies in order to take advantage of differences in prices across the different geographic locations of foreign exchange dealers. This continuous arbitrage by foreign exchange dealers effectively keeps exchange rates the same in all locations. This latter arbitrage activity is referred to as *geographic arbitrage* or *spatial arbitrage*.

As an example of how *geographic arbitrage* in the foreign exchange markets works, suppose that dealers in the New York trading room of Citicorp are trading US dollars at 90 yen per dollar. Suppose also that, at that same moment, dealers at Barclays Bank in London are exchanging yen and dollars at 91 yen per dollar. In such a case, there is an obvious arbitrage profit to be made. The New York dealers would immediately begin selling the dollars in London for 91 yen rather than selling dollars for 90 yen in New York. On the other hand, Barclays' traders in London would sell yen in New York rather than in London. A huge amount of yen would be supplied to New York, while dollars moved to London. This trading activity would very quickly lower the price of yen in New York and raise the price of yen in London. Or, seen from the alternative perspective, the huge volume of transactions would raise the price of dollar in New York and lower its price in London. In the end, the price of a dollar will fall somewhere between 90 and 91 yen in both location.

Such geographic arbitrage would take a matter of seconds with modern online communications, and the process would quickly end when the exchange rate became the same, perhaps somewhere around 90.5 yen per dollar, in both locations. In fact, such a large differential as we used above in our example would never occur in today's world of electronic transactions; the low costs of trading between geographic locations means that even differences in exchange rates of one-thousandth of one percent are quickly erased by arbitrage activity.

Geographic arbitrage did not always work so well. Before modern communications permitted continuous contacts between different parts of the world, geographic arbitrage was very slow and exchange rates often varied substantially from one part of the world to another. Sailing ships and horses took a long time to carry price information from one part of the world to another. Dealers in foreign exchange therefore required much larger spreads between bid and offer prices to cover potential risks of unknowingly buying or selling currencies at prices that differed from those in the rest of the world. The potential profits from being the first to discover discrepancies and exploit arbitrage opportunities were greater, of course, since prices could diverge more than they ever do in today's electronic trading system.

The potential gains from being the "first to know" of course motivated foreign exchange dealers to quickly adopt new channels of communications as they became available. For example, among the very first commercial messages on the trans-Atlantic telegraph cable in the mid-19th century were foreign exchange trades. Similarly, the first commercial messages on the trans-Atlantic telephone cable involved currency trades. Today, online communications link all dealers. They can instantaneously exchange information, bids and offers, and take advantage of any geographic arbitrage opportunities within seconds.

3.3.5 *The shift to online trading*

Today, two rival foreign exchange trading systems for dealers are in operation. These networks are generally not open to the dealers' customers, however. While they use the Internet technology for trading with each other, the foreign exchange dealers do not normally provide their retail customers with the same online services. However, large customers such as hedge funds have pressured the dealers for better and less expensive service, and some banks offer proprietary electronic systems that link clients directly to the dealers. These proprietary systems lowered costs, but clients cannot easily engage in shop comparison without logging into several different dealer systems. Dealers continue to be linked with each other through the two dealer trading systems.

There are now several new online trading websites open to individuals and firms. The first opened in 2000, a small multibank website called Currenex, operated by a former America Online executive. Shortly thereafter, a small firm launched FXTrade, which directly trades currencies for retail customers, mostly small exporters and importers. Its computer system could handle 100 trades per second, and all trades were taken regardless of size.[7] This entrance of "outsiders" into the foreign exchange trading business prompted the major trading banks to begin offering electronic trading to their customers. In June of 2000, seven of the largest foreign exchange banks — Bank of America, Goldman Sachs, J.P. Morgan, Morgan Stanley Dean Witter, HSBC, Credit Suisse First Boston, and UBS Warburg — inaugurated an online foreign exchange trading service named FXall.com. Together, these seven firms already accounted for slightly over 30 percent of all foreign exchange transactions. In August of 2000, the three largest foreign exchange banks that controlled about 28 percent of all foreign exchange business — Citibank, Chase Manhattan, and Deutsche Bank — announced a linkup with Reuters to create a competing foreign exchange trading service over the Internet called Atraix. Reuters already operated one of the worldwide interbank systems.

Another new online trading platform opened in 2005 called Hotspot FX, and it quickly gained market share because its procedures maintained the anonymity of clients, a feature that hedge funds in particular liked. As hedge funds increasingly traded currencies

---

[7] *The Economist*, "Enter the Little Guy", 12 April 2001.

directly to earn profits or indirectly from trading other foreign assets, they increasingly suspected that their trades through dealers generated market gossip that revealed their trading strategies and reduced their earnings. Another major step toward online trading occurred in late 2004, when EBS, the largest of the interbank communications networks used by dealers, began a pilot program to let some outsiders have direct access to the network. This meant that some pension funds, large multinational firms, and other large customers could begin directly requesting quotes and then acting on those quotes without the active involvement of the traditional dealers.

It is still early to predict the full consequences of the technology developments and changes in the foreign exchange markets. It is clear that direct online trading is replacing the telephone business that has been the norm for 100 years. While the great bulk of foreign exchange trading still passes through the traditional dealers or their online platforms, competition among online platforms has already caused the margins of dealers to fall, reducing the transaction costs for exporters, importers, and international investors. This represents a huge loss of profits for the dealer banks, however. Chapter 6 examines the profitability of foreign exchange trading in greater detail.

3.4 A Supply and Demand Model of Foreign Exchange

The market for foreign exchange can be represented by supply and demand curves, just like any competitive market. Figure 3.3 provides an example of the hypothetical market, where Swiss francs and US dollars are exchanged. The horizontal axis shows the quantity of francs, and the vertical axis shows the dollar price of francs. In Fig. 3.3, the demand curve intersects the supply curve at the price $0.50. That is, the dollar price of the foreign currency, the Swiss franc in this case, is 50 US cents. At this exchange rate, 500 million francs are exchanged. The letter e is often used to represent the *foreign exchange rate*. Therefore, the equilibrium in Fig. 3.3 is written as $e = \$0.50$.

Our depiction of the equilibrium exchange rate between dollars and francs as $e = \$0.50$ is somewhat arbitrary. The equilibrium could

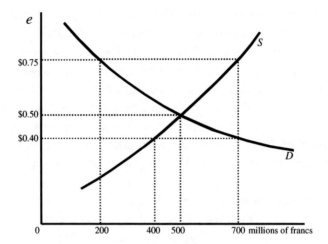

Figure 3.3   The foreign exchange market.

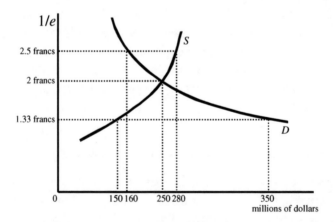

Figure 3.4   The alternative view of the foreign exchange market.

equally well have been represented as $e = 2.00$ francs, the price if the market is viewed as the market for dollars in terms of francs. Figure 3.4 illustrates this alternative view of the market: The quantity of dollars traded is shown along the horizontal axis and the franc price of dollars along the vertical axis.

The *supply* curve for dollars in Fig. 3.4 is simply the *demand* curve for francs from Fig. 3.3 multiplied by $1/e$, and the *demand* curve for dollars is the franc *supply* curve multiplied by $1/e$. The intersection of the curves, or the equilibrium exchange rate, in Fig. 3.4 is $1/e = 1/0.5 = 2$. The equilibrium exchange rate of $e = 0.5$ in Fig. 3.3, where 500 million francs are exchanged, is equivalent to the equilibrium franc price of dollars $1/e = 2$ at which $500/2 = 250$ million dollars are exchanged. The two alternative, but equally appropriate, views of the same dollar/franc foreign exchange market reflects the fact that when holders of dollars demand francs, perhaps to acquire some goods or assets priced in francs, they simultaneously supply dollars to the foreign exchange market. Similarly, francs are supplied when dollars are demanded.

Since either e or $1/e$ represent the same foreign exchange rate, you need to be clear about how you define e. Economists commonly adopt the rule that the symbol "e" represents the home country currency price of the foreign currency; it is referred to as the *foreign* exchange rate, after all. If you are in the United States, you would, therefore, reply with the answer "0.5" if you were asked for the equilibrium exchange rate between dollars and francs. But, since this does not help us much in deciding how to depict, say, the yen/euro exchange rate in London, we usually respect long-standing traditions. For example, London's traditional dominance in international finance gives it the privilege of representing exchange rates between pounds and other currencies as pound prices. Nevertheless, there is always potential for confusion. You are well advised to always carefully and explicitly define in which currency you are setting your exchange rates.

3.5 Triangular Arbitrage

There are close to 200 different countries in the world. That many currencies imply that there is a very large number of exchange rates. Not only are there exchange rates between US dollars and the Japanese yen, dollars and British pounds, dollars and Mexican pesos, and US dollars and Canadian dollars, but there are also exchange rates linking yen and pounds, yen and pesos, yen and Canadian dollars, pounds and pesos, and pesos and Canadian dollars. With

200 currencies, there must be an awful lot of different foreign exchange markets.

3.5.1 *How many foreign exchange rates are there?*

In a world of 200 currencies that all trade for each other, you could set up a 200×200 grid containing 40,000 currency combinations. Of course, when you square the total number of countries, you actually count each exchange rate twice. As shown in the previous section, the amount of dollars per Swiss franc and the amount of francs per dollar are two sides of the same rate, e versus $1/e$. Are there 20,000 exchange rates then? Well, nearly that many.

Table 3.3 illustrates the case of four countries, say A through D, each with its own currency, say α, β, γ, and δ, respectively. There are markets for exchanging α for β, α for γ, and α for δ. Furthermore, there must be markets to trade β for γ, β for δ, and γ for δ. The exchange rate between currencies α and β can be expressed as either the amount of β per unit of α that is β/α, or as the amount of α per unit of β, α/β. The grid in Table 3.3 has a diagonal set of 1s; these trivial cases of α/α, β/β, etc. are not foreign exchange rates because one currency is priced in terms of itself.

In the case of four currencies, there are only 10 different foreign exchange markets and exchange rates. The total size of the grid is $4 \times 4 = 16$, but after subtracting the four diagonal values of one and half of the remaining exchange rates, there are six actual exchange rates. In general, for n different currencies, there are $[n(n-1)]/2$

Table 3.3   Example: Four Countries and Four Currencies.

Countries	Currencies			
	α	β	γ	δ
Country A	1	α/β	α/γ	α/δ
Country B	β/α	1	β/γ	β/δ
Country C	γ/α	γ/β	1	γ/δ
Country D	δ/α	δ/β	δ/γ	1

different foreign exchange markets. In the real world of 200 countries and moneys, there are thus $[200(199)]/2 = 19,900$ foreign exchange rates. This is still a very large number of exchange rates.

Arbitrage links all of these exchange rates. In fact, the 19,900 exchange rates can be reduced to only 199 fundamental foreign exchange rates when foreign exchange dealers and their customers engage in another form of arbitrage known as *triangular arbitrage*. That is, when people are free to move money across borders and shift their wealth from one currency to another, the world's 19,900 exchange rates are not set in 19,900 independent currency markets with their own supply and demand. The overall forces of supply and demand for all the world's currencies can be reduced down to a set of 199 out of the 19,900 exchange rate rates. The next section explains why.

3.5.2 *Triangular arbitrage*

To keep things very simple, suppose there are just three countries A, B, and C, with currencies a, b, and c, respectively. Suppose, also, that the exchange rates are as given in Table 3.4. That is, suppose that a costs two units of b in country B (or, what is the same thing, b equals one half unit of a in country A), a is worth four units of c, and b trades for one unit of c.

A foreign exchange trader, seeing these exchange rates on her terminal, would immediately detect an arbitrage opportunity. For example, she could sell one million a's and acquire four million c's (since $a = 4c$), then exchange the c's for an equal amount of b's (since

Table 3.4   Arbitrage with Incompatible Exchange Rates.

	Price of		
	a	b	c
Country A	1	0.5b	0.25b
Country B	2a	1	1b
Country C	4c	1c	1

$1b = 1c$), and, finally, exchange the four million b's for 2 million a's (since $a = 2b$). She would end up with one million more a's than she started out with by just making three quick online trades! Many other attentive traders will do the same thing. There will be a large increase in supply of a in the c/a market, an increase in supply of c in the b/c market, and then an increase in the supply of b in the a/b market. This would cause the price of c to rise relative to a, the price of b to rise relative to c, and the price of a to rise relative to b. *Triangular arbitrage* will result in a price of $c > 0.25a$, a price of $b > 1c$, and the price of $a > 2b$. Arbitrage will continue until the exchange rates have moved to where there is no longer any way of making a few trades and ending up with more money than you started out with.

One possible final outcome of the arbitrage and the exchange rate changes that it caused is given in Table 3.5. Note that in Table 3.5 there are no longer any arbitrage profits to be made. If the foreign exchange trader now carries out the trades that made her a lot of money at the original exchange rates, she will have to pay 0.29 a per unit of c, in which case one million a's would buy 3.5 million c's, not four million as before. She could then use the c's to buy $3.5(0.71) = 2.5$ million b's, and then use the 2.5 million b's to get exactly one million a's again. You can now try any series of trades at these new exchange rates, and you will find that you neither gain or lose money in the process. Thus, the forces of supply and demand, fueled by triangular arbitrage profits, moved exchange rates in directions that restored consistency across all currencies. Notice that now you only need to know the exchange rates between a and b and a and c to find the exchange rate between b and c. That is, $(b/a)/(c/a) = b/c = 2.5/3.5 = 0.71$. Triangular

Table 3.5 Compatible Exchange Rates After Arbitrage.

	Price of		
	a	b	c
Country A	1	0.4a	0.29a
Country B	2.5b	1b	0.71b
Country C	3.5c	1.4c	1c

arbitrage ensures us that in the general case of n currencies, you only need to know the rates of exchange between one of the n currencies and the other $(n - 1)$ currencies to calculate the remainder of the $[n(n - 1)]/2$ exchange rates.

You can easily confirm that triangular arbitrage works in the real world. Every day, the *Financial Times* presents the exchange cross rates for nine currencies. The *Wall Street Journal* and all other business/financial newspapers present similar tables daily, as do most business sections of major general newspapers. In the published tables, you can see that (1) rates in the southwest half of the table are reciprocals of corresponding rates in the northeast half of the table and (2) all rates can be derived from the $n - 1$ rates in one column or row.

Triangular arbitrage has an important implication, which is that if any one exchange rate changes, then arbitrage will cause all other exchange rates to change. This implication makes it difficult to fix the value of an exchange rate. Because it is very difficult to keep *each and every* one of the $n - 1$ exchange rates constant, it is difficult to keep *any* one of the $n - 1$ exchange rates constant.

3.5.3 *Where to find exchange rates*

Daily information about exchange rates can be found on the websites of the *Wall Street Journal,* www.wsj.com and the *Financial Times,* www.ft.com. Long-run series of exchange rates can be found on the Federal Reserve Bank, Board of Governors website or from one of the regional Federal Reserve Banks. The central banks of most countries also provide exchange rate series; your best bet is to use the search engine www.google.com to find the central bank home pages, and then click to find exchange rate data. Also, the Bank for International Settlements (BIS) provides exchange rate data at www.bis.org.

3.6 Effective Exchange Rates

With about 200 currencies in the world, on any particular day, an individual currency could depreciate against some foreign currencies and appreciate against others. For example, a change in the exchange rate between the US dollar and the Canadian dollar tells us little about how the overall competitive position of US exporters has changed. Similarly, investors interested in knowing how their portfolio of many different foreign investments is affected by a depreciation or appreciation of their currency need more than a single exchange rate. To provide better information about a currency's appreciation or depreciation, several government agencies, banks, and international organizations now routinely compile broader exchange rate measures called *effective exchange rates*, which are weighted averages of sets of foreign exchange rates.

3.6.1 *The effective value of a currency*

In the United States, the Federal Reserve Bank compiles the *Broad Dollar Index*, which is a weighted average of 26 exchange rates between the US dollar and other currencies, weighted for each country's share of US exports plus imports. The *Major Currencies Index* just weights the exchange rates of Australia, Canada, Japan, Sweden, Switzerland, and the euro area, and *The Other Important Trading Partner Index* is a weighted average of the remaining 19 exchange rates in the Broad Index but not included in the Major Currencies Index. The weights are summarized in Table 3.6. Because Canada is the US's largest trade partner, the Canadian dollar exchange rate has the highest weight in both the Broad Index and the Major Currencies Index. The weights are continually changed to match the United States' changing trade patterns. Table 3.6 gives the weights for the Broad Index in 1997 and 2003 published in a recent issue of the *Federal Reserve Bulletin*.

3.6.2 *Recent behavior of effective exchange rates*

Figures 3.5 and 3.6 graph the Broad Dollar Index and the Major Currencies Index described above, the former for 1974–2009 and the latter for 1994–2009, the time periods for which the Federal Reserve Bank published these indexes. Note that two indexes trace similar but

Table 3.6   Broad Dollar Index: Trade Weights.

	1997	2003		1997	2003
Canada	17.49	18.80	Thailand	1.59	1.43
Euro Area	16.92	16.43	Australia	1.31	1.25
China	6.58	11.35	Sweden	1.22	1.16
Japan	14.27	10.58	India	0.88	1.14
Mexico	8.50	10.04	The Philippines	1.18	1.06
UK	5.73	5.17	Israel	0.84	1.00
Korea	3.68	3.86	Indonesia	1.25	0.95
Taiwan	3.77	2.87	Russia	0.78	0.74
Hong Kong	2.65	2.33	Saudi Arabia	0.80	0.61
Malaysia	2.25	2.24	Chile	0.53	0.49
Singapore	2.87	2.12	Argentina	0.61	0.44
Brazil	1.82	1.79	Colombia	0.49	0.41
Switzerland	1.43	1.44	Venezuela	0.58	0.30
			Total	100.0	100.0

Source: Mico Loretan (2005). "Indexes of the Foreign Exchange Value of the Dollar", Federal Reserve Bulletin, Winter, 2005, Table 3, p. 5.
Note: Bold colored countries make up the Federal Reserve's Major Currencies Index.

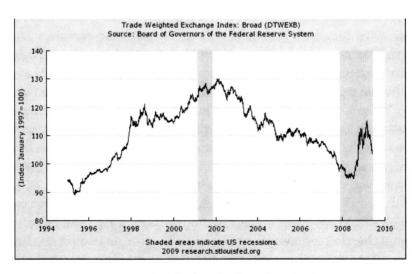

Figure 3.5   The broad index, 1994–2009.
Note: The shaded areas denote periods of economic recession.

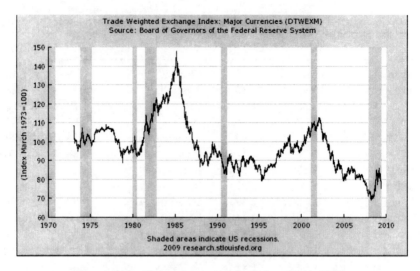

Figure 3.6　The major currencies index, 1974–2009.

Note: The shaded areas denote periods of economic recession.

not identical paths. It makes a big difference which exchange rates are included in an effective exchange rate index. As you can see from comparing the ups and downs with the index on the vertical axis, the US dollar fluctuated more against the seven major currencies than it did against the broader index. Market forces seem to have kept these latter currencies more closely aligned to the dollar. This means that when the dollar depreciated rapidly against the major currencies after 2001, many of the currencies in the broader index, such as those of Asian economies like Taiwan, Hong Kong, and China, as well as other developing economies, generally depreciated against those same major currencies in tandem with the dollar. As a result, the US dollar depreciate much less against the Asian currencies. This may help to explain the continued growth of the trade deficit vis-a-vis the Asian economies.

Figure 3.5 also shows how volatile exchange rates have been over the past 25 years. As an average of individual exchange rates, an effective exchange rate should be less volatile than individual exchange rates. But notice that even the effective exchange rates of the US dollar have fluctuated widely, changing by more than ten percent in many years. The decline of the Major Currencies Index from nearly 150 to under 100 between early 1985 and the middle of 1986 stands out. Only a bit less surprising is the equally sharp increase in the effective value of the dollar during the first half of the 1980s.

3.7 Summary and Conclusions

This chapter introduces the foreign exchange rate, which is set in the foreign exchange market. This variable is one of the most important prices in our global economy, as it has a substantial long-run influence on the flows of payments between countries.

Among the many points emphasized in the chapter are

1. The foreign exchange market is the largest financial market in the world; over $3.5 trillion in currencies are exchanged each working day.
2. Foreign exchange markets have existed ever since money came into use and there was trade between regions with different moneys.
3. In today's global economy, the foreign exchange market is characterized by several forms of arbitrage.
4. The process of arbitrage, when carried out to its conclusion, equalizes prices across separate markets.
5. This chapter detailed two specific forms of arbitrage in the foreign exchange market: geographic arbitrage and triangular arbitrage.
6. Modern global communications have made geographic arbitrage nearly perfect, so that for each pair of currencies, the exchange rate is virtually identical in every financial center of the world.
7. Triangular arbitrage means that all exchange rates are related to all others, and if the fundamental forces of supply and demand change one exchange rate, all others tend to change as well unless they are explicitly pegged or fixed.
8. Triangular arbitrage also means that in a world of n different currencies, one only needs to know the exchange rates between one currency and the other $n-1$ currencies to know all the $[n(n-1)]/2$ cross rates.
9. The true value of any one currency depends on its exchange rates with all other currencies, which is why economists often rely on

effective exchange rates, which are weighted averages of exchange rates.

10. Effective exchange rate indexes are usually made up of some subset of exchange rates, weighted by each currency's share of bilateral trade and/or investment flows.

Perhaps the most important point above is that, in a global economy where there are few if any restrictions on where people, firms, and financial groups buy and sell products and assets, triangular arbitrage will make it difficult to keep exchange rates steady in the face of policy changes, economic trends, and other shocks to the world economy. If any one exchange rate changes, all exchange rates will be affected. And all economies will be affected by how the exchange rate changes affect the other variables that determine the macroeconomic output.

Our story of the foreign exchange market is not yet complete, however. The next chapter examines a third important type of arbitrage that characterizes the foreign exchange market.

Key Terms and Concepts

Appreciation	Foreign exchange	Major Currencies
Arbitrage	market	Index
Bill of exchange	Foreign exchange	Market liquidity
Broad Dollar Index	rate	Market maker
Depreciation	Foreign exchange risk	Over-the-counter
Effective exchange rate	Foreign exchange	market
Exchange rate	swap	Seignorage
Fiat money	Fundamental exchange	Spot transactions
Fixed exchange rate	rate	Triangular arbitrage
Floating exchange rate	Geographic arbitrage	Vehicle currency

Chapter Questions and Problems

1. Below, you are given four exchange rates between US dollars, Japanese yen, Argentinean pesos, Taiwanese dollars, and Turkish lira. Complete

the grid by filling in all the blanks, assuming triangular arbitrage is complete:

	US$	Yen	Pesos	T$	Lira
US$ per	—	—	—	—	—
Yen per	100	—	—	—	—
Pesos per	2	—	—	—	—
T$'s per	25	—	—	—	—
Lira per	50	—	—	—	—

2. If the world consists of 127 countries, each with their own money, how many exchange rates are there? How many fundamental exchange rates are there?

3. What are the implications of complete geographic arbitrage and complete triangular arbitrage in the foreign exchange markets?

4. Define an effective exchange rate. Why may an effective exchange rate be more useful than an individual exchange rate that links two specific currencies?

5. If the dollar–euro exchange rate as seen from France is €0.80, what is the rate from the US perspective? Which is the more appropriate rate to use? Why?

6. Suppose the exchange rate between Mexican pesos and US dollars is 10 pesos per dollar, and the rate between Japanese yen and dollars is 100 yen per dollar. Assuming perfect triangular arbitrage, what is the yen–peso exchange rate?

7. New technology has shifted a large amount of foreign exchange trading among dealers to the online trading platforms. Technically, online market platforms could be opened directly to outside buyers and sellers of foreign exchange. Why do you think that there are still only a few relatively small online markets where the general public can trade directly, and foreign exchange dealers continue to limit outside access to their interbank trading infrastructure?

8. Discuss the quote at the start of this chapter by Paul De Grauwe. Are separate moneys in each economy really necessary? Why or why not?

References

BIS (2007). *Trennial Central Bank Survey of Foreign Exchange and Derivatives Market Activity in April 2007.* Basel: Bank for International Settlements, September.

Cameron, R (1993). *A Concise Economic History of the World*, 2nd Edn. Oxford: Oxford University Press.

Cross, SY (1998). *All About the Foreign Exchange Market in the United States.* New York: Federal Reserve Bank of New York.

Davies, G (1996). *A History of Money*, rev.ed. Cardiff: University of Wales Press.

Davisson, WL and JE Harper (1972). *European Economic History*, Vol. I, The Ancient World. New York: Appleton-Century-Crofts.

Fisman, R and S-J Wei (2001). Tax rates and tax evasion: Evidence from 'missing imports' in China, NBER Working Paper w8551, October.

Chapter 4

The Interest Parity Condition

...our existing knowledge does not provide a sufficient basis for a calculated mathematical expectation.

(John Maynard Keynes, 1936, p. 152)

Over half of all transactions on the world's foreign exchange markets are *forward* transactions, which are current contracts to exchange currencies at some future date. Forward contracts set a firm price *today* for the delivery of currencies at some future date. The forward markets for foreign exchange are similar to the *futures* markets for commodities, where corn, sugar, pork bellies, petroleum, etc. are bought and sold for delivery and payment at a specific future date. And, the same way that futures markets for corn enable farmers to *hedge* by setting the price they will receive for their crops before they plant their seeds, the forward market for foreign exchange permits exporters, importers, and international investors to *hedge* their *foreign exchange risk* by contractually fixing the future exchange rate for expected future foreign currency receipts or payments.[1]

The forward markets for foreign currencies are operated by the same dealers who operate the spot markets. The forward markets

---

[1] The term "hedge" suggests the "hedging in" or strict delineation of the area within which the effects of future exchange rate shifts will be confined.

131

grew quickly after 1973, when the Bretton Woods system of pegged exchange rates was abandoned in favor of letting the exchange rates *float* in response to the continually shifting forces of supply and demand. These floating exchange rates were quite volatile after 1973, so exporters, importers, and foreign investors immediately sought ways to hedge their foreign exchange risk in the new floating rate regime. This chapter explains in detail what the forward markets mean for exchange rates and the firms, individuals, investment funds, banks, and government agencies who engage in international transactions.

Chapter Goals

1. Describe the *forward* foreign exchange markets.
2. Explain the third type of arbitrage within the foreign exchange market: *intertemporal arbitrage.*
3. Derive the *interest parity condition*, and clarify the assumptions on which it is based.
4. Explain the difference between *risk* and *uncertainty.*
5. Examine the meaning of "expectations" when there is risk compared to when the future is uncertain.
6. Discuss the implications of the interest parity condition under alternative assumptions about expectations and uncertainty.
7. Explain what the interest parity condition implies about the predictability of exchange rates.
8. Examine the empirical support for the interest parity condition.

4.1 Intertemporal Arbitrage

The spot and forward exchange rates are determined by supply and demand for currencies today and for purchase/sale in the future, respectively. In general, the supply and demand for currencies delivered/purchased today will not result in the same exchange rate as the equilibrium between supply and demand for currencies to be delivered at a future date. A lot is expected to happen between now and the future. Price levels change, economies grow at different rates, and many other things that influence international trade and international investment will change. The forward exchange rate will reflect how people, firms, and international investors expect all of these things to change over time. In general, their supply and demand for currencies at some future date will tend to be different from their current supply and demand for currencies.

The spot and forward exchange rates are not determined independently of each other, however. Wealth and obligations can be held over from one period to another, and when exchange rates in the spot and forward markets differ a lot, foreign exchange purchases and sales will be shifted forward or backward. In fact, when buyers and sellers of foreign exchange are not restricted from transacting in either the spot or forward markets, the spot and forward rates will tend to be related by a type of arbitrage we refer to as *intertemporal arbitrage*. The term "intertemporal" means "over time". This intertemporal arbitrage process does not, in general, cause the spot and forward exchange rates to be equal. However, the spot and forward exchange rates will be related in a way that reflects the differences in returns to holding the assets denominated in the different currencies and the perceived risk of not hedging.

4.1.1 *A simple example of intertemporal arbitrage*

A simple hypothetical exercise will suffice to clarify this intertemporal arbitrage process. Suppose that you have the option to store your wealth in assets denominated in your domestic currency or in a foreign currency. That is, you can deposit your savings in a bank in your hometown, buy a bond from your government, or buy stock in a company in your country, all denominated in your country's currency. Or, you can shift your savings overseas to buy foreign currency and then open a deposit in a foreign bank, buy a foreign government's bond, or buy stock in a foreign corporation. Your choice between foreign and domestic assets normally depends on the expected risk and return on the domestic and foreign assets. For the time being, let us assume the problem of risk away. Suppose, therefore, that you are not concerned about the risk of holding the foreign versus domestic assets and that you only care about the relative rates of return on potential investments at home and abroad. In making your decision as to where to store your wealth, you therefore compare only the expected returns on domestic and foreign assets. Suppose, finally, that the domestic country is the United States and the foreign country where you are contemplating the purchase of assets is the United Kingdom.

Say your wealth consists of $100, and you seek to buy the highest return asset you can find for that $100. We denote this $100 of wealth as $w(\$)_t$, where the subscript stands for the time, and the dollar sign denotes that the wealth is denoted in US dollars. Suppose that a dollar-denominated asset in the United States will earn a return of r, which means that over the period of one year your wealth would grow to

$$w(\$)_{t+1} = w(\$)_t(1 + r) = \$100(1 + r) \qquad (4.1)$$

where r is the annual return on US dollar assets and t denotes the current year, so that $t + 1$ represents the next year. Alternatively, you could invest in a British asset denominated in British pounds (designated by the symbol "£"). To purchase British assets, you would first need to exchange the $100 for pounds. The amount you actually invest in Britain is the pound equivalent of $100, or

$$w(£)_t = w(\$)_t/e_t = \$100/e_t \qquad (4.2)$$

That is, your current wealth in pounds, $w(£)_t$, is equal to the $100 divided by the spot exchange rate, e_t, which is defined here as the dollar price of a British pound. For example, if the spot rate $e_t = \$2$, then your wealth in pounds will be equal to $\$100/\$2 = £50$. If r^* is the rate of return on foreign (British) assets, then after one year your wealth in British pounds will be

$$w(£)_{t+1} = w(£)_t(1 + r^*) = (\$100/e_t)(1 + r^*) \qquad (4.3)$$

Before you can make your final decision about which assets to buy, you must convert the future pound value of your investment back to dollars at next year's exchange rate, e_{t+1}. You do not know e_{t+1} with certainty, but if you have reason to believe that the exchange rate will change between now and next year, you can eliminate this uncertainty by contracting today for the sale of your pounds one year from now on the forward market at the forward exchange rate f_t^{t+1}. In writing the forward exchange rate, we let the subscript stand for the point in time when the forward exchange is contractually agreed to, and we let the superscript stand for the time when the exchange of currencies actually occurs.

To get next year's dollar value of your British investment, multiply next year's pound value of your British asset by the forward exchange rate:

$$w(\$)_{t+1} = w(\pounds)_{t+1}(f_t^{t+1}) = (\$100/e_t)(1 + r^*)(f_t^{t+1}) \qquad (4.4)$$

Now you can compare this dollar value of the British investment to the dollar value of the US investment:

$$\$100(1 + r) \leftarrow ? \rightarrow (\$100/e_t)(1 + r^*)(f_t^{t+1}) \qquad (4.5)$$

Note that the forward foreign exchange market eliminates exchange rate risk, and if it is possible to assume that the returns r and r^* are also riskless in that they can be contractually established today, your choices on each side of relationship (4.5) are both said to be *covered* against risk. Your best investment strategy is thus the side of the relationship (4.5) that has the greater value.

4.1.2 *The covered interest parity condition*

To understand the process of *intertemporal arbitrage*, suppose that the relationship between the right-hand and the left-hand terms in (4.5) is

$$\$100(1 + r) < (\$100/e_t)(1 + r^*)(f_t^{t+1}) \qquad (4.6)$$

In this case, US wealth holders will elect to shift their wealth to British assets, and if British investors had their wealth invested in dollar assets, they will shift funds back toward pound assets. Thus, holders of dollars and dollar-denominated assets will purchase pounds and pound assets. If a lot of people do this, e_t will rise (provided we continue to define the exchange rate from the US perspective as the dollar price of pounds). The dollar therefore falls in value relative to the pound. American purchasers of pound assets will simultaneously want to buy dollars with their pounds next year after they gain their asset values and returns, which will increase the demand for dollars and the supply of pounds on the forward market and, therefore, cause the forward exchange rate to fall. Notice that the rise in e_t and the fall in f_t^{t+1} cause the right hand side of inequality (4.6) to diminish. Of course, if the shift in wealth from the US to Britain is very large, it will also affect the rates of return on assets in the two countries, r and r^*. With more being invested in British pound assets, their returns r^* would fall, thus decreasing the right side of (4.6), and with savings leaving the United States, rates of return would rise there, thus increasing the left hand side of (4.6).

In a perfect world devoid of transfer costs and other frictions, the process of international investment arbitrage will cause international transfers of wealth to expand until the inequality (4.6) becomes an equality:

$$\$100(1 + r) = (\$100/e_t)(1 + r^*)(f_t^{t+1}) \qquad (4.7)$$

This equation is the *intertemporal arbitrage* condition that links the present spot rate to the future. It is more commonly known as the *covered interest parity condition*, where the "covered" refers to the use of the forward market to eliminate all exchange risk from storing wealth in foreign assets.

A little mathematical manipulation of equation (4.7) will reveal a convenient equation that also reveals the logic of the relationship between the spot and forward exchange rates. First, divide each side by $100, which leaves

$$(1 + r) = (1/e_t)(1 + r^*)(f_t^{t+1}) \qquad (4.8)$$

Then divide each side of (4.8) by $(1 + r)$ and multiply each side by e_t:

$$e_t = [(1 + r^\star)/(1 + r)](f_t^{t+1}) \tag{4.9}$$

This equation says that the spot exchange rate is related to the forward exchange rate by the factor $[(1 + r^\star)/(1 + r)]$, which reflects the relative rates of return for pound and dollar assets. Note that the spot rate e_t is equal to the forward rate f_t^{t+1} only if $r = r^\star$. If, for example, $r > r^\star$, then $[(1 + r^\star)/(1 + r)] < 1$ and $e_t < f_t^{t+1}$.

4.1.3 *A more general form of the interest parity condition*

Forward foreign exchange markets exist only for the currencies of the world's larger economies, and then only for up to one or two years into the future. Unless a market processes some minimum amount of transactions, the banks who run the foreign exchange markets cannot afford to maintain the inventories of currencies, employ the dealers, and operate the sophisticated communications systems to make a market. If you are contemplating purchasing the assets in Egypt or Chile or debating whether to build a factory in a foreign country that will generate returns for the next 50 years, you will not be able to eliminate your exchange rate risk by using the forward market; the market for Chilean pesos or for delivery of even the major currencies 50 years from now are said to be "too thin".

The next chapter will describe some other methods for hedging exchange rate risk when there are no forward markets. These methods require hedgers to base their decisions on their expectations of the future. For example, in the absence of a forward market to quote you a price for future foreign exchange transactions, you will have to compare returns on domestic and foreign assets based on your *expectations* about exchange rates in the future. That is, you must effectively alter equation (4.5) by entering your expectation of the spot rate one year from now in place of the forward rate f_t^{t+1}.

The expectation at time t of the exchange rate at time $t + 1$ is denoted as $E_t(e_{t+1})$. To evaluate the expected earnings from, say, a Chilean asset, you must use the expected future exchange rate, $E_t(e_{t+1})$, to convert the future value of your Chilean assets from

Chilean pesos to dollars. This dollar value of the Chilean investment can then be compared to the dollar value of the alternative US investment:

$$\$100(1 + r) \;\leftarrow\; ? \;\rightarrow\; (\$100/e_t)(1 + r^*)(E_t e_{t+1}) \qquad (4.10)$$

Intertemporal arbitrage will still tend to occur so long as the difference between the right-hand and left-hand sides of (4.10) is large enough to overcome the perceived risk associated with the exchange rate uncertainty. There will be a tendency for the following relationship to hold approximately:

$$\$100(1 + r) \cong (\$100/e_t)(1 + r^*)(E_t e_{t+1}) \qquad (4.11)$$

The sign $\cong$ stands for "approximately equals". Manipulating the terms just as we did above for the covered interest parity condition then shows that the spot exchange rate is directly related to the expected future exchange rate:

$$e_t \cong [(1 + r^*)/(1 + r)](E_t e_{t+1}) \qquad (4.12)$$

Equation (4.12) is known as the *uncovered interest parity condition* or simply as the *interest parity condition*. This is one of the most important relationships in international economics. The *covered interest parity condition* is thus a special case of the more general interest parity condition, one in which there is a formal market, where expectations are effectively revealed in the form of a forward exchange rate through market participants' willingness to buy and sell the currencies in the future.

Equation (4.12) effectively tells us that, if people are relatively free to store their wealth where and how they want, so that intertemporal arbitrage can freely occur, then the spot exchange rate is a function of expectations about the future exchange rate and the relative rates of return on assets at home and abroad. Hence, in today's global economy, in which people in most countries can move their wealth across borders without restrictions, it is not so much current economic conditions that explain the spot exchange rate. Rather, the spot exchange rate effectively depends on expected future exchange rates, which depend on the expected future supply and demand for currencies and, therefore, expected future economic conditions.

This conclusion should not be a surprise to someone familiar with large asset markets such as stock markets, bond markets, and property markets. The current prices of stocks, bonds, houses, and land generally reflect expectations about the future value of those assets. Currency is also an asset, and Eq. (4.12) simply verifies that the spot price of foreign exchange depends on the expected future price of foreign exchange.

4.1.4 *A simplified version of the interest parity condition*

The logic behind the interest parity condition can be clearly distinguished with a few more simple mathematical manipulations of Eq. (4.12). First, divide each side of Eq. (4.12) by $(1 + r^*)$, then divide by e_t, and you get

$$(1 + r)/(1 + r^*) = (E_t e_{t+1}/e_t) \tag{4.13}$$

The equality in Eq. (4.13) is maintained if 1 is subtracted from each side. In this case, subtract $1 = [(1 + r^*)/(1 + r^*)]$ from the left-hand side of the equation and subtract $1 = e_t/e_t$ from the right-hand side of the equation:

$$(1 + r)/(1 + r^*) - (1 + r^*)/(1 + r^*) = E_t e_{t+1}/e_t - e_t/e_t \tag{4.14}$$

This equation can be simplified to

$$(r - r^*)/(1 + r^*) = (E_t e_{t+1} - e_t)/e_t \tag{4.15}$$

To reveal the intuitive explanation for the interest parity condition, only two more adjustments to Eq. (4.15) are needed. First, write $(E_t e_{t+1} - e_t)$ as $E_t(\Delta e)$, where the symbol "Δ" stands for "the change in". That is, the difference between the expected exchange rate one period ahead and the current spot rate at time t is written as the expected "change in" the exchange rate. Second, when inflation is low and interest rates are very small numbers, $(1 + r^*)$ is very close to 1. Thus, it is reasonable to assume $(1 + r^*)$ is *approximately* equal to 1, in which case you can ignore the denominator on the left-hand side of (4.15) and write the equation as

$$(r - r^*) \cong E_t(\Delta e)/e_t \qquad (4.16)$$

The right-hand side of Eq. (4.16) consists of the *change* in the exchange rate divided by the *level* of the exchange rate. Since a change divided by the level defines the proportional or percentage *rate* of change, $E_t(^a e)/e_t$ represents the expected percentage rate of change in the exchange rate. Therefore, the interest parity condition effectively states that when arbitrage has run its course, the difference between the rates of return on the assets in the two countries is exactly offset by the expected percentage change in the exchange rate over the period that investors expect to hold those assets. When, for example, the rate of return abroad is higher, the spot and expected future exchange rate will diverge just enough so that the investor's gains from the higher foreign rate of return are exactly offset by the expected depreciation of the foreign currency over the time the foreign assets are held. In terms of the home currency, what the investor expects to gain for investing overseas is about equal to the expected earnings from investing at home at the domestic rate of return.

4.1.5 *An exercise in interest parity*

The interest parity condition rests on a number of assumptions, namely that wealth holders act rationally in their self-interest, that there are no barriers to moving wealth between countries, that investors are not highly risk averse, and that investors objectively examine and analyze all available information on assets and the economic conditions likely to affect the asset returns. These are not trivial assumptions, and many have argued that they are unlikely to hold under any realistic circumstances. The predictive value of the interest parity condition thus comes down to whether it offers a reasonable approximation to what really happens in the global economy. Economists have, therefore, carried out extensive empirical tests of the interest parity condition using data on forward and spot exchange rates from many countries over many time periods.

We first present a simple test using readily available information published every day in the *Financial Times*. Table 4.1 presents interest rates in the *eurocurrency* market as well as the spot and 1-year-forward exchange rates for the arbitrarily-selected day of 12 January 2005, as reported by the *Financial Times* on the following morning, 13 January 2005. The eurocurrency market will be discussed in Chapter 17, where we detail international banking. For now, it is enough to know that eurocurrency markets are the worldwide wholesale markets, where the world's major commercial banks lend and accept deposits in most of the major currencies. The eurocurrency interest rates are often stated in terms of the London interbank offered rates, or LIBOR. These are the interest rates at which the large London banks lend the currencies to each other. Bank customers would pay slightly above LIBOR to borrow, and they would receive slightly below LIBOR on deposits in each of the currencies shown. Table 4.1 also includes the relevant foreign exchange rates that we will need to test the interest parity condition.

Let us look at the dollar and pound first. Table 4.1 tells us that on 12 January 2005, the rate of return on a 1-year dollar deposit in the

Table 4.1   Interest Rates and Exchange Rates on 12 January 2005.

	1-Year libor	Spot	1-Year forward
US dollar	3.22000	—	—
British pound	4.89500	1.8932	1.8642
Euro	2.32450	1.3286	1.3346
Swiss franc	0.97167	0.8595	0.8790
Japanese yen	0.09313	0.00977	0.0101

As reported in the *Financial Times*, 13 January 2005.

eurocurrency market was 3.22 percent, and a similar pound deposit in the eurocurrency market was 4.895 percent. At the end of the normal trading day in London on 12 January, the spot exchange rate was 1.8932 dollars per pound, and the one-year forward exchange rate was 1.8642 dollars per pound. Using Eq. (4.9):

$$e_t = [(1 + r^*)/(1 + r)](f_t^{t+1}) = [(1.04895/1.0322)]1.8642$$
$$= 1.01623(1.8642) = 1.8945 \quad (4.17)$$

The calculated spot rate is almost exactly the actual spot rate of 1.8932 of reported by the *Financial Times* for the same day. Thus, the interest parity condition seems to hold almost exactly. The small difference could easily be explained by the fact that the exchange rates reported are from 4:00 p.m. the previous day and the reported interest rates were those observed at 11:00 a.m.

Similarly, the reported forward rate and the interest rates for dollars and euros can be used to "predict" the spot rate at 4:00 p.m. on 12 January 2005:

$$e_t = [(1 + r^*)/(1 + r)](f_t^{t+1}) = [(1.023245/1.0322)]1.3346$$
$$= 0.99132(1.3366) = 1.3250 \quad (4.18)$$

The spot rate implied by the reported interest rates and the forward exchange rate is 1.3246, which is almost exactly the reported spot exchange rate of 1.3250.

Note how well the covered interest parity condition holds for dollars/pounds and dollars/euros. As an exercise, you should calculate the spot dollar–franc and dollar–yen rates from the given information on interest rates and forward exchange rates in Table 4.1. How well does the covered interest parity condition hold for those currency combinations? By the way, be sure that all your exchange rates are given from the same perspective; in the examples above the rates were all from the US perspective, that is, dollars per unit of foreign currency. Also, be sure to match one-year forward exchange rates with the differences in the one-year interest rates;

newspapers typically report forward rates for 90 days, 180 days, and one year forward.

4.2 Extending the Basic Interest Parity Model

The interest parity condition and intertemporal arbitrage are very important concepts in international finance. The exposition thus far has painted a simplified picture. This section introduces several logical extensions of the model. In a later section, we will challenge some of the interest parity model's assumptions.

4.2.1 *The risk premium*

Economists have recently favored defining the expected value of an economic variable as the weighted average of all possible outcomes. This is the common statistical definition of an expected value. Most people who "expect" a certain outcome also recognize that the actual future value of a variable like an exchange rate is likely to differ from the expected outcome, but it is common to assume that the possible values of the variable will fall along some known distribution of possible outcomes. In this case, the magnitude of exchange rate risk depends on the width of the spread of possible future exchange rate values around the expected value. Depending on how wide the distribution of outcomes is, a risk-averse investor may well opt to store wealth in a domestic asset even though the *expected* return on foreign assets is higher than the certain return on domestic assets. On the other hand, if the distribution of possible exchange rate values is "tightly" bunched around the expected value, it becomes easier to decide between domestic and foreign assets.

Individuals, multinational firms, financial firms, and most other investors are said to be *risk averse* when, all other things equal, they prefer a less risky asset to a more risky one. One practical implication of risk aversion is that there will not be enough arbitrage activity to bring the inequality in Eq. (4.6) to equality as in equation (4.9). For example, if potential arbitragers are risk averse, the condition

$$(1 + r) < (1 + r^*) \left[(E_t e_{t+1})/e_t \right] \tag{4.19}$$

may prevail despite people's freedom to engage in arbitrage and move their wealth between different countries' assets. In fact, the evidence on interest rate parity is that in the absence of forward markets, the interest parity condition does not hold precisely. Risk aversion may help to explain the commonly observed phenomenon of *home bias* in investment, which is the name given to the observed fact that investors favor domestic assets over foreign assets, all other things equal.

In Eq. (4.19), the difference between the left-hand and right-hand sides of the equation is the *risk premium p*:

$$(1 + r) = \left[(1 + r^*) \left[(E_t e_{t+1})/e_t \right] \right] \tag{4.20}$$

This risk premium is the extra reward that wealth holders require before they will bear the foreign exchange rate risk. The risk premium can be positive or negative from the perspective of one currency, depending on which of the two currencies has the larger stock of wealth denominated in it and which wealth holders are more risk averse.

In the real world, corporations and financial firms are often required to be risk averse by their directors or by regulatory agencies. For example, in most countries, regulatory agencies require banks to diversify risk and avoid excessively risky investment strategies; after all, banks are managing other people's money. Multinational firms are usually in the business of providing goods or services rather than seeking profits from risky investment strategies. Corporate boards of directors usually mandate that managers concentrate on the firm's core competencies rather than risking the firm's future by exposing it to excessive amounts of exchange risk. For this reason, the risk premium is usually positive, and the uncovered interest parity condition is unlikely to be strictly satisfied. This is not to say that firms and banks do not sometimes take on too much risk. During the years just before the 2008 financial crisis, the financial markets displayed decreasing risk premiums, which should have warned investors and regulators that corporate and financial managers were underestimating risk.

There may be some additional uncertainties that drive a wedge between the spot and expected future exchange rates in the real world. Assets in two different countries are never exactly the same because taxes may differ, the risk of default may vary, institutions governing individual and firm behavior may differ, and foreign investors may not have the same rights as domestic investors across the different countries.

Nevertheless, even if the interest parity condition only holds approximately, it still is true that expectations about future exchange rates are a major determinant of spot exchange rates. For a constant risk premium p, changes in future expectations still cause the spot exchange rate to change in a predictable direction. By shuffling the terms in Eq. (4.20), the spot rate can be written as follows:

$$e_t = [(1 + r^*)/(1 + r)](E_t e_{t+1}) - p \qquad (4.21)$$

This equation shows that, all other things equal, a change in the risk premium can also cause a change in the spot exchange rate. For example, if a change of government increases uncertainty about the future, p will change and the spot rate exchange rate changes even if there is no change in the expected value of future exchange rates.

4.2.2 *There are many future exchange rates*

The analysis above represented the expected future exchange rate as if there was just one at one specific point in time in the future. There are, of course, an infinite number of future exchange rates, one for each future point in time. The logic of the interest parity condition still means that each of these expected future exchange rates is systematically linked to the spot exchange rate. In addition, the expected future exchange rates at each point in the future are systematically linked to every other expected future exchange rate by intertemporal arbitrage in accordance with the interest parity condition.

For example, if the rates of return in the United States and Britain are expected to be r and r^*, respectively, for the next two periods, then in the case of perfect arbitrage, the following two-period interest parity condition will hold:

$$\$100(1 + r)^2 = (\$100/e_t)(1 + r^*)^2(E_t e_{t+2}) \qquad (4.22)$$

The spot rate is thus a function of the expected exchange rate two periods from now:

$$e_t = [(1 + r^*)/(1 + r)]^2 \, E_t e_{t+2} \qquad (4.23)$$

In general, for n periods into the future:

$$e_t = [(1 + r^*)/(1 + r)]^n \, E_t e_{t+n} \qquad (4.24)$$

This is an exponential function, which implies that e_t is expected to rise or fall over time at an exponential rate.

If there is perfect arbitrage, then it must also be true that the exchange rates between any two periods must reflect the interest parity condition. That is, for any periods $t + n$ and $t + n + 1$:

$$E_t e_{t+n} = [(1 + r^*)/(1 + r)] \, E_t e_{t+n+1} \qquad (4.25)$$

Thus, in the case of constant but different rates of return across countries, the exchange rate is expected to follow an exponential path that must be compatible with both Eqs. (4.24) and (4.25). Suppose, for example, that the exchange rate is expected to depreciate in the future because the domestic rate of return is higher than the foreign rate of return, the time path of expected exchange rates over the next five periods will look like the upward-sloping curve in Fig. 4.1. If the exchange rate is expected to appreciate, then the exchange rate will follow a downward sloping path.

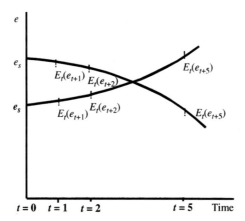

Figure 4.1 Intertemporal arbitrage and the expected path of future exchange rates.

In the general multiperiod case illustrated here, arbitrage between each period results in a smooth path of exchange rates over time, from the future expected exchange rates, or the forward exchange rates when there is enough liquidity to establish forward markets, back to the current spot exchange rate. The intertemporal relationships among the points on the curves in Fig. 4.1 reflect exactly the same logic that lies behind the simple two-period interest parity condition. The only difference is that Eqs. (4.24) and (4.25) suggest that the spot exchange rate is a function of the entire path of future exchange rates that people expect will balance the economic transactions between countries over the long term. The spot rate and the future expected exchange rates thus trace out a continuous path because intertemporal arbitrage smoothes out expected deviations from the expected continuous path in a way that best satisfies the long-run expectations about future supply and demand in the foreign exchange market.

This multiperiod, or long-run, view of exchange rates is not fundamentally different from the two-period case examined earlier. The spot rate is still a function of expectations about the future, only now the spot rate reflects a continuous set of future-expected exchange rates. And changes in an expected future exchange rate will still tend to change the spot rate, but now, of course, changes in any one or few future exchange rates will change the entire path from the spot rate to the future rates. That is, changes in expectations about any period or periods in the future will tend to change the exchange rates in all periods, not only the spot rate.

4.2.3 *Foreign exchange swaps*

Spot and forward transactions are often bundled together in what are called *swaps*, or more precisely foreign exchange swaps. A *foreign exchange swap* is the simultaneous closing of spot and forward foreign exchange contracts. These are arrangements where someone buys foreign exchange today and agrees to sell it back at some later date. Swaps are a very large portion of all foreign exchange market activity. Swaps permit investors to temporarily acquire foreign assets without incurring the risk of future exchange rate changes. Intertemporal arbitrage is a major driving force behind the demand for swap arrangements. Most forward transactions are part of swap arrangements, which suggests that intertemporal arbitrage is responsible for a very substantial portion of the high volume of forward transactions.[2]

4.2.4 *Exchange rate futures*

When you peruse the *Financial Times* or the financial pages of other newspapers, you may catch information on *foreign exchange futures*. These are contracts traded on several exchanges located in the United States and elsewhere. These *futures markets* for foreign exchange are similar to, but completely distinct from, the forward markets discussed in this chapter.

In the United States, there are organized exchanges in Chicago, Philadelphia, and New York that trade foreign exchange futures

---

[2] Do not confuse *foreign exchange swaps* with *currency swaps*, which are contracts to exchange future streams of cash flows denominated in different currencies. These will be discussed in the next chapter on hedging strategies.

contracts to buy or sell fixed amounts of foreign exchange, usually in multiples of $10,000, at standard times in the future. Because they deal in uniform contracts, these futures markets can provide foreign exchange hedges to small foreign traders, investors, and speculators at a reasonable cost. However, restricting the market to contracts of uniform length and value means that they do not offer hedgers contracts that meet their precise needs. Also, these futures contracts are available only for certain major currencies. But, because they are relatively inexpensive, futures markets permit smaller players to at least partially hedge their foreign exchange risk or to speculate on future foreign exchange rates. Overall, these futures exchanges are a very small market segment that accounts for less than one percent of the turnover on all the foreign exchange markets.

4.3 Predicting Changes in the Exchange Rate

The expected path of exchange rates effectively provides a prediction of future exchange rate changes. When rates of return on assets differ across countries and currencies, the multiperiod interest parity condition as defined by equation (4.24) predicts that a country's exchange rate will either appreciate or depreciate along a time path. For example, if $r^* < r$, then $(1 + r^*)/(1 + r) < 1$ and $e_t < E_t e_{t+n}$, which implies that e is expected to gradually increase over time, provided, of course, that r and r^* do not change.

4.3.1 *The path of expected future exchange rates*

The usefulness of the expected time path of the exchange rate for predicting the future changes in the exchange rates is limited, however. Observations of floating exchange rates for the world's major currencies suggest that exchange rates change much more than the slow gradual increases or decreases illustrated by the smooth curves in Fig. 4.1. Exchange rate changes of as much as five or ten percent in one month are not uncommon for the major currencies. Exchange rates also often fluctuate drastically from one day to the next, sometimes as much as one percent or more. Recall the 40 percent fall in the value of the US dollar in less than two years in 1985 and 1986 described in the previous chapter. The small differences in interest rates across countries cannot explain such exchange rate movements. Recall the interest rates given in Table 4.1; they ranged from about one percent to about five percent per year, which means differences between the returns on assets account for at most about a four percent (the difference between five and one percent) annual change in exchange rates.

Only fluctuating shifts in long-run expectations, which imply up and down shifts in the whole long-run time path of exchange rates, can explain the large changes in spot exchange rates that we actually observe. Figure 4.2 illustrates how a shift in expectations, which shifts the entire curve, can cause a sudden large change in the spot exchange rate.

Accurate predictions of exchange rate changes therefore require accurate predictions of the changes in long-run expectations that shift the intertemporal exchange rate paths. That is an impossible task, however. To understand why, it is necessary to understand how people set their expectations. Expectations have been widely debated in the field of macroeconomics, and we begin here with the rational expectations hypothesis that recently has, since the 1980s, been built

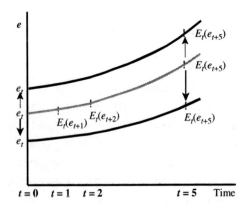

Figure 4.2   A shift in the expected path of future exchange rates changes the spot rate.

into many macroeconomic and financial models. Later in the chapter, after examining the evidence on the interest parity condition, we will discuss John Maynard Keynes' view of expectations.

4.3.2 *Rational expectations*

Economists commonly assume that people have *rational expectations*. To apply this concept to economic analysis and modeling, rationality has to be precisely defined. Economists have most often defined a rational expectation as a prediction based on logical reasoning and the objective use of all relevant information, which is assumed to consist of

1. The most accurate available explanation, or model, of how foreign exchange rates are determined.
2. All available facts and evidence that help to put values on the variables in the model of exchange rate determination.

Economists define items 1 and 2 as the *information set*. This focus on information derives from the traditional economics literature on *efficient markets*, which are markets whose prices and quantities reflect all relevant available information, including all opportunity costs.

Using standard notation from the field of finance, the expected exchange rate at time $t = n$ (n years into the future), given the information set $\Omega_{t=0}$ available today (where today is denoted as $t = 0$), is written as

$$E_{t=0}(e_{t=n} \mid \Omega_{t=0}) \tag{4.26}$$

The symbol "|" in equation (4.26) stands for "given", so that the rationally expected exchange rate for period $t = n$ is conditional on today's information set.

The information set Ω is not a constant over time. It continuously changes as new information about economic conditions, the political situation, government policies, etc. becomes available. Our understanding of what determines the exchange rate also changes over time as the application of the scientific method, hopefully, improves our understanding and models of exchange rates. Thus, the expected exchange rate for the time period $t = n$ at $t = 0$ ($n > 0$) will generally not be the same as the expected $t = n$ exchange rate at $t = 1$. Because $\Omega_{t=0} \neq \Omega_{t=1}$,

$$E_{t=0}[(e_{t=n}) \mid \Omega_{t=0}] \neq E_{t=1}[(e_{t=n}) \mid \Omega_{t=1}] \qquad (4.27)$$

Changes to the information set are called *news*, which is new information and knowledge that was not previously known or predictable.

4.3.3 *Expectations as weighted averages of possible outcomes*

The rational expectations literature in economics highlights other assumptions that must be satisfied for market outcomes to generate "rational" outcomes. The most important of these additional assumptions is that a rational expectation must be an *unbiased* predictor of actual outcomes. That is, on average, rational expectations turn out to be correct. Note that the rational expectations hypothesis does not say that expectations always turn out to be accurate, only that they are not biased, that is, consistently wrong. Rational expectations are like an *expected value* in statistics, which is the weighted average of all possible outcomes.

An alternative statement of rational expectations is that differences between expectations and actual outcomes are completely random. That is, there should be no information in the discrepancies between predictions and actual outcomes that could have been known at the time of the forecast. This is the same as saying that rational expectations are unbiased and efficient predictors of future events. Therefore, in terms of Fama's (1970) efficient market hypothesis, the foreign exchange market and the forward market are said to be *efficient* if evidence shows that, *on average*, the forward exchange rate correctly predicts actual future spot exchange rates.

4.3.4 *Future changes in exchange rates are unpredictable*

The logical application of the rational expectations hypothesis to the foreign exchange markets leads to an interesting conclusion: future changes in exchange rates are unpredictable! The reasoning is straightforward. If the interest parity hypothesis is accurate and people rationally use their full information sets to quantify their expectations about the future in accordance with Fama's (1970) efficient market hypothesis, then the spot exchange rate and the expected time path that links the future to the present must already reflect everything that we now know about future exchange rates. Therefore, the only thing that can change the spot exchange rate is new information and knowledge that changes the information set, that is, news. News is, by definition, information and knowledge that were not previously known or predictable. Hence, when expectations are rationally set and the interest parity condition holds (international investment is not restricted), future *changes* in the exchange rates are effectively unpredictable.

Alan Greenspan implied this when in 2003 he said: "My experience is that exchange markets have become so efficient that virtually all relevant information is embedded almost instantaneously in exchange rates to the point that anticipating movements in major currencies is rarely possible".[3] Was Greenspan right?

4.3.5 *Testing the "news" model*

One of the earliest tests of the "news" model was by Frenkel (1983). Frenkel used a simple statistical equation in which the current spot exchange rate e_t depends on the previous period's forward rate f_{t-1}^t plus current "news". Specifically, Frenkel used a linear regression equation:

$$e_t = a_0 + a_1 \left(f_{t-1}^t \right) + a_2(\text{news}) + u_t \qquad (4.28)$$

---

[3] From Alan Greenspan's remarks at the 21st Annual Monetary conference, co-sponsored by the Cato Institute and *The Economist*, Washington DC, 20 November 2003 (downloaded from www.federalreserve.gov).

The problem, of course, is how to quantify the variable called "news". What exactly is the new information that arrives in period t to alter expectations about the future and, hence, the spot rate? Frenkel reasoned that any news that would affect the exchange rate would also show up immediately in interest rates at home and abroad. After all, money markets are known to be very efficient in that they react extremely quickly to new information. Frenkel therefore defined "news" as the actual difference between domestic and foreign interest rates, $(r - r^*)$, at time t minus the interest rate differential that was expected to exist at time $t - 1$, or $E_{t1}(r - r^*)$. To see if news has the expected effect on the spot exchange rate, Frenkel thus estimated the regression equation:

$$e_t = a_0 + a_1 f_{t-1}^t + a_2[(r - r^*)_t - E_{t1}(r - r^*)_t] + u_t \quad (4.29)$$

Frenkel computed the term $E_{t1}(r - r^*)_t$ from a separate regression of the interest differential on a constant and two-lagged values of the differential, which implies that expectations were assumed to effectively reflect recent interest rate trends. Applying data for the late 1970s, Frenkel's regression estimates of the coefficient a_1 were very close to 1 and statistically significant, and the coefficient a_2 was positive and, usually, statistically significant as well. Frankel interpreted these results as confirming that the spot rate depended on the forward exchange rate in the previous period plus "news".

Also supporting the "news" model was Meese and Rogoff's (1983) well-known study, which found that in the 1970s a simple random walk model explained the exchange rate changes one month forward better than interest rate differentials. A variable is said to follow a random walk when at each point in time, regardless of what happened before, it may move up or down in an unpredictable fashion. Meese and Rogoff repeated their empirical exercise several times using 1980s data, and still they could not find any models, including interest parity, that did a better job explaining the exchange rate movements more accurately than the random walk model. Meese and Rogoff's studies were taken by many as proof that news model was accurate, that indeed expectations were set by rationally using the full information set, and that the interest parity condition then translated those expectations into the spot exchange rate. How else could the remaining variation in exchange rates be random?

One study provides an interesting test of Alan Greenspan's statement, namely how quickly news moves the foreign exchange rate. Evans and Lyons (2005) use continuous trading data to estimate how quickly the exchange rate moves to a new equilibrium following the arrival of news. They find that trading is affected by news for hours, even days, beyond the arrival of news; the adjustment is not instantaneous as Greenspan suggested. They do confirm the adjustment is in the expected direction, however, although the adjustment is small. As all studies of exchange rates find, hypothesized factors explain a very small part of the variations in exchange rates.

4.3.6 *Directly testing the interest parity condition*

The news model can also be indirectly tested by testing the interest parity condition on which the model is based. The interest parity condition has often been tested using a statistical regression equation such as

$$(e_t/f_t^{t+1}) = a_0 + a_1[(1 + r^*)/(1 + r)] + v \qquad (4.30)$$

in which v is assumed to be randomly distributed around zero so that least squares estimates of a_0 and a_1 will be unbiased. If data on actual observed values for e_t, f_t^{t+1}, r, and r^* result in least squares estimates of a_0 and a_1 about equal to 0 and 1, respectively, then (4.30) looks just like (4.9), and the interest parity condition is confirmed.

An alternative approach to testing the interest parity hypothesis is to use a regression equation based on the simplified version of the interest parity condition given in Eq. (4.16). We can use the forward exchange rate to serve as a measure of expectations, in which case

$$(f_t^{t+1} - e_t)/e_t = (\Delta e)/e_t = [(r - r^*)/(1 + r^*)] \qquad (4.31)$$

Note that $(\Delta e)/e_t$ is the percentage change in the exchange rate. The relevant regression equation that tests whether the percentage change in the exchange rate actually equals the difference between domestic and foreign interest rates is therefore

$$(\Delta e)/e_t = a_0 + a_1[(r - r^*)/(1 + r^*)] + \upsilon \qquad (4.32)$$

Interest parity is statistically confirmed if estimated values of the coefficients are $a_0 = 0$ and $a_1 = 1$ at a sufficiently high level of statistical significance.

The regression equation (4.30) will fail to properly test the interest parity hypothesis if interest rates r and r^* are not properly measured. Inaccurate data on interest rates r and r^* are likely because it is not clear which interest rates investors take into consideration when they make their decisions. Different assets offer different returns depending on their risk, maturity, liquidity, and size. Should researchers use the interest rates for short-term bank deposits, short-term government bonds, longer certificates of deposit, or some weighted average of asset returns? Another problem that plagues statistical tests of interest parity is that assets located in different countries are never quite comparable, if for no other reason than that they are denominated in different currencies and therefore subject to the economic policies of different governments.

Statistical tests often confirm the covered interest parity condition when data from the eurocurrency markets are used. The eurocurrency market is the global network of large private banks that offer accounts and loans in a variety of currencies in the major money market centers of the world. Because interest rates are for loans in different currencies from the same banks in the same political jurisdiction, there are fewer differences among the assets that could distort the comparability of competing assets. Tests using eurocurrency interest rates and short-term forward exchange rates for the major currencies are therefore likely to offer the least biased tests of regressions such as (4.29) and (4.31). The results of such short-term tests of the interest parity condition are similar to the single-observation "test" we performed earlier in the chapter when we compared spot and forward exchange rates and interest rates for the pound and dollar. When assumptions of free capital movements, similar assets, and the absence of tax and regulatory distortions are satisfied, interest parity is often confirmed by such tests.

The interest parity hypothesis has also been tested over longer time horizons. Such tests effectively mean testing of the *uncovered* rather than the *covered* interest parity condition because forward markets only extend out one year in most cases. The relationship does not hold up well for these tests. Nor does the relationship hold up well when tests do not involve interest rates on deposits in eurocurrency banks. In fact, in their survey of 75 studies that compared interest differentials and subsequent exchange rate movements, Froot and Thaler (1990) find that more often than not exchange rates moved in the opposite direction from what the interest parity condition predicts!

Chinn and Meredith (2004) argue that studies using short-horizon data are plagued by the excessive "noise" that influences short-term interest rates and exchange rate movements. They use long-run data covering two decades to test the uncovered interest parity condition, and they find that in the long run, interest differentials indeed do explain a substantial portion of the variation in exchange rate changes. Their regression results still leave a lot of the variation in exchange rates unexplained, however. Chinn and Meredith's test results of course depend critically on how they generate estimates of expected future exchange rates. Other studies find different levels of support for the uncovered interest parity hypothesis because they calculate expected future exchange rates differently, so it is not at all clear that these statistical tests actually reflect the interest parity condition or the variation in estimates of exchange rate expectations.

4.3.7 *Summarizing the evidence*

Frankel (2008) summarizes the evidence on the forward exchange rate as follows:

> The forward rate is not just a poor predictor of the future exchange rate, but a biased predictor. Only in developing countries with high

inflation rates do currencies with high inflation rates or high forward discounts tend to point in the right direction (toward depreciation) — and even then, the bias does not fully disappear.[4]

In short, the interest parity condition does not, in general, accurately describe the exchange rate movements. The precise reasons for the poor performance of the interest parity condition as a predictor of future exchange rates are not clear. On the one hand, Evans and Lyons (2005) found that quantifiable news events explained only a very small part, less than three percent, of the immediate and subsequent variation in exchange rates, which calls into question the efficiency of foreign exchange markets. Also, many studies of the interest parity hypothesis find persistent bias in forward exchange rates and expected future exchange rates.

The finding that the estimated risk premium varies greatly over time and across foreign exchange markets suggests that the foreign exchange market is influenced by variations in confidence, enthusiasm, and asset bubbles. Technical factors may also play a role. Finally, the foreign exchange market may simply not be fully rational, at least not as rationality is defined in macroeconomics.

Isard (2006) observes that many open-economy macroeconomic models continue to incorporate the interest parity assumption, which leads him to suggest, somewhat provocatively, that the reason such open-economy macroeconomic models have performed so poorly in predicting the macroeconomic outcomes is that the interest parity condition is just not an accurate model of how foreign exchange markets work. Isard also notes that there is some indication that open-economy macroeconomic models are beginning to more often incorporate exchange rate models that specify expectations as both forward-looking and backward-looking.

Isard bases his argument on the work of John Maynard Keynes. Isard writes: "Keynes was well aware that investor choices between foreign and domestic assets do not depend on interest rates and

---

[4] Jeffrey Frankel (2008). p. 41.

exchange rates alone".[5] In his 1923 *Tract on Monetary Reform*, Keynes recognized that economic conditions in many countries in the early 1920s were precarious and political conditions were unstable and difficult to predict. Keynes also emphasized the complex relationship between exchange risks and credit risks, a problem that persists today, as we will describe in later chapters on recent financial and exchange rate crises. Isard calls for more "sophisticated behavioral hypotheses". Isard accurately observes that "economists have not yet provided a well-specified replacement for the uncovered interest parity assumption".[6]

4.4 Reassessing Rational Expectations

The 2008 financial crisis brought the notion of rational expectations further into question. The crisis has been traced to the failure of financial models that were, like uncovered interest parity, based on the assumption of rational expectations. By 2008, valuations of assets using these "rational" financial models were dangerously wrong and had undermined the solvency of the world's financial industry. The asset markets had also greatly underpriced risk, a clear indication that not all available information had been used.

Further reflection since 2008 has led many economists to conclude that the rational expectations hypothesis is seriously flawed. In this section, we examine some of the weaknesses of the hypothesis, and we conclude with some conjectures on where this leaves our understanding of exchange rates.

4.4.1 *Risk and uncertainty*

The widespread acceptance of the rational expectations hypothesis in mainstream macroeconomics since 1980 coincided with the gradual erasing from economists' memories Keynes' (1936) insightful discussion of how expectations influence economic behavior in his work entitled *General Theory of Employment, Interest, and Money.*

---

[5] Walter Isard (2006). p. 5.
[6] Walter Isard (2006). p. 5.

Even though Keynes discussed expectations as they related to investment and the financial markets that supported real investment, his observations apply very well to foreign exchange markets. Keynes argued that investors, traders, and other participants in large financial markets, like buyers and sellers in the foreign exchange market, have very limited information on which to base their decisions. Inevitably, investors, traders, and everyone else set their expectations selectively using partial information, not complete information as the rational expectations and efficient market hypotheses suggest:

> It is reasonable...to be guided to a considerable degree by the facts about which we feel somewhat confident, even though they may be less decisively relevant to the issue than other facts about which our knowledge is vague and scanty.[7]

That is, we use what we know and remember, but that is not the complete information set the rational expectations assumes.

Keynes also observed that investors, lenders, and other market participants tend to focus on the near past rather than the distant past in shaping their expectations of the future, a human tendency that has been confirmed by psychological studies. This research reveals that people discount the past, just as they discount the future. In short, people use recent experience to project the future. People tend to attribute low probabilities to outcomes that have not occurred recently, even though, fundamentally, they are as likely to occur as more familiar outcomes. In short, we do not know everything we need to know, and what we do know and remember is relatively recent.

Second, Keynes disputed the notion that expectations are an objectively calculated weighted average of possible future outcomes. Keynes effectively argues that no future economic outcome can ever be determined with certainty, and, therefore, the expected future

---

[7] John Maynard Keynes (1936). p. 148.

exchange rate, $E_t e_{t+1}$, is not a number that is known with certainty. In the words of Keynes (1936):

> The actual results of an investment over a long term of years very seldom agree with the initial expectations. Nor can we rationalize our behavior by arguing that to a man in a state of ignorance errors in either direction are equally probable, so that there remains a mean actuarial expectation based on equi-probabilities. For it can easily be shown that the assumption of arithmetically equal probabilities based on a state of ignorance leads to absurdities....our existing knowledge does not provide a sufficient basis for a calculated mathematical expectation.[8]

In short, exchange rates are nothing more than poorly formulated guesses because we simply do not fully understand the complex economic and social processes, nor do they fully understand all the conceivable economic outcomes those processes generate.

Keynes effectively viewed the future as *uncertain*, not risky. *Risk* describes the distribution of a set of outcomes with known probabilities. Uncertainty, on the other hand, describes an unknown distribution of possible known and unknown outcomes. Under uncertainty, people have insufficient knowledge and information to attach specific probabilities to all possible outcomes. In the case of uncertainty, it is impossible to arrive at a single predicted outcome or expected value. Note how the concept of uncertainty clashes with the rational expectations models. Keynes argued that financial markets are characterized by uncertainty, not risk.

4.4.2 *The tenuous nature of expectations*

If financial markets are biased by an emphasis on recent events over more distant events and the lack of information for establishing the distribution of possible outcomes, how are spot exchange rates determined? Keynes (1936) argued that people's expectations depend on

---

[8] John Maynard Keynes (1936[1964]). p. 152.

confidence and *convention*. The latter term refers to our understanding of how things normally work out. In economics and finance, convention can be a popular model that guides thinking and analysis. Investors remain confident, and are willing to invest in foreign assets despite their inherently uncertain outcomes, as long as the outcomes from the investments seem to pan out in ways that they have come to view as normal or "conventional". That is, supply and demand in the foreign exchange market remain relatively stable as long as expectations are validated, in which case people keep doing the same things they were doing. Note that people's short memories reinforce such conventional thinking.

Paul De Grauwe (1989) follows Keynes' reasoning when he presents what he calls "near-rational" exchange rates. He specifically draws on Akerlof and Yellen (1987), who found that, in extremely uncertain environments, people are strongly guided by the initial values of prices in deciding on what price to charge or pay. De Grauwe thus argues that, in the absence of overwhelming evidence suggesting some other exchange rate clearly reflects future values more accurately, exchange rates tend to remain relatively stable around some initial "anchor" price that people are familiar with.

The problem with using an *anchor*, or what Keynes called *convention*, to guide decisions is that the anchor comes loose when something upsets the conventional world as we know it. Unexpected shifts in the supply or demand for foreign exchange can thus cause exchange rates to suddenly change. If convention was far from the new reality, then exchange rates will suddenly change a lot. When confidence is eroded, the exchange rate may collapse or surge. And if there is little consensus on what the long-run value of a currency is, a period of extreme exchange rate volatility may ensue. It may take a long time before new conventions take hold and confidence in those conventions grows.

Given Keynes' understanding of expectations, you can surely fathom why he argued for pegged exchange rates at Bretton Woods. Since expectations are based on partial information and little consensus on the future economic environment, Keynes reasoned that exchange rates, if left to themselves, were likely to be unstable during the unpredictable economic and political environment after World War II. In later chapters, we will examine whether Keynes' prescriptions for the international monetary system, namely pegged rates, balanced trade, and restricted financial account transactions could have worked out in the long run. Keynes' ideas were not fully embraced at Bretton Woods, and even the Bretton Woods system was eventually abandoned in favor of floating exchange rates after trade imbalances and growing financial account transactions made it impossible to sustain pegged exchange rates.

4.4.3 *A modern case study of expectations: the carry trade*

The interest parity condition tells us that if the rate of return is the only thing that matters, it should make little difference to investors whether they put their savings in an account overseas or at home. Any difference in interest rates will, on average, be exactly compensated by currency appreciation or depreciation. Despite this insight from international finance, people routinely exploit the interest rate differences and borrow money in low-interest countries in order to invest in high-interest ones. This practice is known as the *carry trade*, in which people "carry" assets denominated in currencies with high interest rates and pay for them by borrowing the currencies with low interest rates. The carry trade is really a bet against the interest parity hypothesis, which states that any interest differential will be fully compensated by subsequent changes in the exchange rate. More accurately, carry traders really bet that the hypothesis will not hold in the short run, and that they can exit before the prescribed depreciation of the high-interest currency occurs. The carry trade has been described as a "free lunch in front of a steamroller".[9] If you eat fast, you may do very well.

One example of the carry trade occurred during the 1990s, when Japanese savers sought alternatives to the near-zero interest rate yen accounts. The lengthy recession in Japan that began in 1989 led the

---

[9] Editorial in the *Financial Times* (2007). "Carry on Trading: Free lunches — Queue in Front of the Steamroller", 24 February.

Bank of Japan to drive interest rates to zero for many years thereafter, with little macroeconomic success. Japanese savers began seeking higher returns, and they found them overseas. Japanese savers deposited their savings in accounts in the United States, Brazil, Australia, New Zealand, and other countries where interest rates were high. For quite a few years, these Japanese carry traders enjoyed what was, literally, a free lunch as the Bank of Japan kept interest rates in Japan low. During this time, the Bank of Japan also intervened in the foreign exchange market to keep the value of the yen low in order to stimulate exports, which it saw as another tool for fighting the recession in Japan. Thus, the yen did not appreciate against any of the other currencies as the interest parity condition predicted.

More recently, homebuyers in high-interest Poland and Hungary have taken out low interest loans in Switzerland, confident that the Polish sloty and the Hungarian forint would not depreciate because their countries, which had just become members of the European Union, were poised to adopt the euro. The 2008 financial crisis has now caused the sloty and forint to depreciate sharply, and many poles and Hungarians now have to pay much more local currency to pay off their Swiss franc loans.

Frankel (2008, p. 5) points out that the carry trade is not irrational. His evidence shows that:

> When one currency pays a high interest rate, it does not later, on average, depreciate correspondingly. If anything, the markets seem to behave perversely, with currencies that can be borrowed at low interest rates more often than not depreciating with respect to high-interest rate currencies!

Frankel is, of course, referring to the same violations of the interest parity hypothesis that others have found and we reported above.

Still, the carry trade is risky. Many times the carry trade becomes a self-fulfilling prophecy early on as more and more people buying assets in the high-interest currency directly cause the foreign currency to appreciate. But this fortunate correlation of appreciation and high returns will eventually come to an end. If confidence in the foreign currency begins to erode and investors begin unwinding their carry trades, the sale of the high-interest currencies cause it to begin the depreciating. The depreciation can turn into a crash if the depreciation triggers further desperate attempts to unwind the carry trades, and thus an even faster depreciation of the foreign currency. Some investors may not be able to get out of the way of the steamroller in time, and they are crushed by the loss of the value of their overseas investments. The past 25 years suggest, however, that the interest parity hypothesis does not hold well enough in the short run to prevent the renewed interest in carry trades.

4.5 Conclusions

This chapter has introduced the forward foreign exchange market and a third type of arbitrage alleged to characterize the foreign exchange market. Intertemporal arbitrage is unlikely to be complete, which means the implications of the interest parity hypothesis are not necessarily entirely accurate. Because some of the important controversies in international finance center around the interest parity hypothesis, this chapter is rather important for later understanding of international finance and open-economy macroeconomics. This relationship reflects the intertemporal arbitrage and links the spot exchange rate to expectations of future exchange rates. The interest parity condition is important because it can help explain why exchange rates are likely to be both volatile and unpredictable.

This chapter has detailed how:

1. The unrestricted movement of money across borders to purchase foreign assets results in *intertemporal arbitrage*.
2. Intertemporal arbitrage links the spot exchange rate to expected future exchange rates in accordance with the interest parity condition.
3. The interest parity condition predicts that the future exchange rate between two currencies will reflect the relative rates of return on investment and assets denominated in the two currencies.

4. The interest parity condition, if it holds, implies that the spot exchange rate depends on expectations about how future international trade and investment flows will determine the future exchange rates.
5. This latter conclusion, in turn, implies that exchange rates remain stable only if expectations about economic policies and economic performance *in all countries* remain stable.
6. In a world where political events, economic growth, technological progress, and many other types of "news" continually alter the economic landscape, expectations will inevitably have to be revised, however.
7. The inherent unpredictability of "news" means that the inevitable changes in expectations will cause exchange rates to change in unpredictable ways.

Evidence does not consistently support the interest parity condition, however. It is preferable to refer to the suggested relationship as the interest parity hypothesis since it remains to be confirmed. Some would contend that it has been clearly rejected.

8. Failure of the interest parity hypothesis means that the underlying assumptions of efficient markets, full use of available information sets, and rational expectations do not generally hold.
9. Keynes argues that expectations are inevitably inaccurate because people favor familiar, but partial, information.
10. Exchange rates change not only because of news, but also because of shifts in confidence and shifts in beliefs that, for lack of information, are based on convention.

Volatile exchange rates mean that firms, consumers, workers, investors, and governments have to learn to live with exchange rate risk. Fortunately, recent financial innovation seems to have made it easier to live with exchange rate volatility. The next chapter will discuss how to hedge the foreign exchange rate risk.

Key Terms and Concepts

Carry trade
Covered interest
 parity
Efficient market
Exchange rate futures
Expectation
Expected returns
Foreign exchange
 risk

Foreign exchange swap
Forward transactions
Futures market
Hedge
Information set
Intertemporal
 arbitrage
Interest parity
 condition

Mathematical
 expectation
News
Rational expectations
Risk
Risk premium
Uncertainty
Uncovered interest
 parity

Chapter Questions and Problems

1. Suppose that the spot exchange rate between Canadian dollars and US dollars is e = US$0.90, the return on high-quality long-term Canadian financial assets is ten percent per year, while the interest rate in the United States for comparable assets is seven percent per year. Assuming the interest parity condition holds, calculate what "the market" expects the exchange rate to be five years from now.

2. Suppose that the market expects that next year the exchange rate between Mexican pesos and US dollars will be e_{t+1} = US$0.12. The current return on high-quality Mexican financial assets is ten percent while the interest rate in the United States for comparable assets is 20 percent. Given this information, what does the interest parity condition say the spot exchange rate e must be?

3. Suppose that the spot exchange rate between euros and British pounds is £1.00 = €0.50, the current return on high-quality euro financial assets is 13 percent while the interest rate for comparable pound assets is nine percent. Assuming the interest parity condition is satisfied, calculate the 360-day forward exchange rate.

4. Explain precisely why, under the assumption that the interest parity condition holds and people set their expectations rationally, it is impossible to accurately predict the changes in the exchange rate.

5. Explain precisely, what is the difference between the covered interest parity condition and the uncovered interest condition?

6. Why does the evidence not consistently support the interest parity hypothesis?

7. Examine the actual interest rates and exchange rates from today's newspaper and test the interest parity condition. Does it hold?

8. Using the simplified version of the interest parity condition given in equation (4.16), namely, $(r - r^*) \cong (E_t e_f - e_s)/e_s = E_t(\Delta e)/e_s$, explain the intuition behind the interest parity condition.

9. Describe the three forms of arbitrage that characterize today's foreign exchange markets, and explain the broader implications of each.

10. Explain the carry trade. Why would anyone engage in an investment that can only profit if the interest parity condition is violated?

11. Precisely state the assumptions behind the interest parity hypotheses. Under what circumstances will the spot rate indeed be related to the expected future values of the exchange rate as equation (4.12) states?

12. Contrast rational expectations with expectations as they were described by Keynes. Which form of expectations is more accurate? Which is more useful as a guide for decisions?

References

Akerlof, GA and JL Yellen (1987). Rational models of irrational behaviour. *American Economic Review*, 77(2), 197–217.

Chinn, MD and G Merideth (2004). Monetary policy and long-horizon uncovered interest parity. *IMF Staff Papers*, 51(3), 409–430.

DeGrauwe, P (1989). *International Money. Postwar Trends and Theories.* Oxford: Oxford University Press.

Evans, MDD (2005). Do currency markets absorb news quickly? *Journal of International Money and Finance*, 24(2), 197–217.

Fama, EF (1970). Efficient capital markets: A review of theory and empirical work. *Journal of Finance*, 25(2), 383–417.

Flood, RP and AK Rose (2002). Uncovered interest parity in crisis. *IMF Staff Papers*, 49(2), 252–266.

Frenkel, J (1983). Flexible exchange rates, prices, and the role of 'news': Lessons from the 1970s. In *Economic Interdependence and Flexible Exchange Rates* Chap. 1, Bhandari JS and BH Putnam (eds.), pp. 3, 4. Cambridge, MA: MIT Press.

Frenkel, J (2008). Everything you always wanted to know about the carry trade, and perhaps much more. *The Milken Institute Review*, First Quarter, 2008.

Isard, W (2006). Uncovered Interest Parity. IMF Working Paper WP/06/96, April.

Keynes, JM (1923). *A Tract on Monetary Reform*. London: MacMillan.

——— (1936). *General Theory of Employment, Interest, and Money*. London: MacMillan.

Meese, R and K Rogoff (1983). Empirical exchange rate models of the seventies. *Journal of International Economics*, 14, 3–24.

Chapter 5

Dealing with Exchange Rate Volatility: Hedging Foreign Exchange Exposure

It is the business of the future to be dangerous.

(Alfred North Whitehead.[1])

Exchange rates are always subject to change. History shows that even when central banks intervene in the foreign exchange market to off-set shifts in supply or demand, or policymakers impose exchange restrictions to block demand or supply shocks, exchange rates often still end up changing. The analysis of the previous chapter shows that it is difficult to predict these inevitable future exchange rate changes. Therefore, individuals, businesses, banks, investors, and all other participants in the global economy are exposed to *exchange rate risk*.

Exchange rate risk is not a trivial matter. Exchange rate changes can undermine the competitiveness of exporters in foreign markets, or they can create welcome export opportunities. Domestic firms may suddenly face foreign competition where there was none before. Changing exchange rates also cause domestic consumers to

---

[1] Alfred North Whitehead (1933[1967]), *Adventures of Ideas*. New York: Free Press.

gain or lose purchasing power, owners of overseas assets to experience capital gains or losses, and multinational firms to experience gains or losses in the profitability of their overseas operations. With international business activity spreading across countries with different currencies, everyone is increasingly influenced by the exchange rates that translate worldwide asset values, sales, costs, taxes, commodity prices, asset returns, etc. into to domestic currency values. Since there is no question that exchange rates are going to change, and those changes are difficult to predict, the relevant question becomes: What can firms, investors, consumers, banks, and their governments do to mitigate the exchange rate risk? This chapter addresses this question.

Chapter Goals

1. Explain exchange rate exposure.
2. Define hedging.
3. Detail a forwarded exchange market hedge.
4. Contrast the forward market hedge with a money market hedge.
5. Detail exchange rate options, and explain the unique advantage of option.
6. Compare forward, money market, and options hedges, clarifying the distinct advantages and disadvantages of each.
7. Introduce currency swaps, a new customized exchange rate hedge offered by international financial firms.
8. Discuss the effects of hedging in the foreign exchange markets.
9. Contrast hedging undertaken by individual traders and investors with government policies to stabilize exchange rates.

5.1 Exchange Rate Exposure

Foreign exchange risk depends on the *exposure* of people, organizations, businesses, financial intermediaries, investors, debtors, and governments to the consequences of exchange rate volatility.

5.1.1 *The forms of exchange rate exposure*

The field of international business finance measures the exchange rate exposure in several different ways. Each type of exposure highlights a specific way in which a firm or organization can be impacted financially by changes in exchange rates. This business perspective provides good insight into the exchange rate exposure everyone faces in the global economy.

First, there is the *economic exposure* to exchange rate volatility, which is sometimes also referred to as *operating exposure*. Economic exposure measures how exchange rate changes may affect a firm's expected future sales volumes, prices, and costs. Effectively, economic exposure measures how exchange rate volatility affects the profitability of a firm operating in the global economy. More generally, economic exposure consists of the potential effects of exchange rate changes on the present value of a firm or organization.

Second, international accountants often calculate how a firm's short-term outstanding debt and credit would be affected by exchange rate volatility. At any moment in time, an international business organization has pending receipts and payments in different currencies. This exposure is referred to as *transaction exposure*. Unless a firm or organization does all its foreign business on a cash-and-carry basis, it inevitably faces some transactions exposure.

Third, when a firm operates in the global economy, accountants continually track the effect of exchange rate changes on a firm's consolidated worldwide balance sheet. The exposure of the firm's consolidated balance sheet of worldwide activities is called *translation exposure* or *accounting exposure*.

Finally, accountants sometimes also explicitly calculate a firm's *tax exposure*, which measures how a firm's first three exposures, economic exposure, transaction exposure, and translation exposure specifically affect its tax liabilities. If the tax exposure of exchange rate volatility substantially offsets the effects of the three other exposures, the need for the firm to engage in costly hedging of its foreign exchange exposure is reduced.

The wealth of an international organization or a multinational firm continually rises and falls with exchange rates, all other things equal, and its balance sheet is affected in complex ways. Exchange rate changes often confuse the picture that standard financial accounts present about a business firm's financial performance. Management's response to, say, a fall in the sales of a specific product will generally differ depending on whether the fall in sales is due to an exchange rate change or the growing obsolescence of the product line. A firm's accountants, therefore, have to distinguish between the various effects of exchange rate volatility. The firm can hedge against exchange rate changes, but it will have to take very different measures if the fall in overseas sales is due to product obsolescence or a new foreign competitor.

The exchange rate exposure of a country's business firms, government organizations, banks, investors, and borrowers has played a central role in nearly all of the international financial crises over the past 30 years. As Chapters 10 and 11 will detail, it is exchange rate exposure that turns sudden changes in exchange rates into bankruptcies, loan defaults, and, sometimes, economy-wide financial crises. Therefore, exchange rate exposure is not just a business or banking issue. Open-economy macroeconomics cannot explain the economic events of the past 30 years without including exchange rate exposure in its analysis.

5.1.2 *Exchange rate volatility vs. exchange rate exposure*

Overall foreign exchange risk is the combination of exchange rate volatility and foreign exchange rate exposure. Hence, foreign exchange risk can be diminished by either reducing exchange rate volatility or by reducing a firm's or investor's exposure to the consequences of exchange rate volatility. There have been many attempts to reduce the exchange rate volatility. Delegates of the U.K. and US delegations at the 1944 Bretton Woods Conference were concerned that volatile exchange rates would discourage international trade, and Keynes and White addressed the issue by proposing a system of pegged exchange rates. More recently, 12 European nations adopted a single currency, the euro, in large part to reduce the uncertainties that volatile exchange rates impose on European businesses operating in the increasingly integrated European market. Most currencies continue to float, however.

Fortunately, individuals and businesses can reduce their exposure to exchange rate volatility. The deepening of financial markets and the creation of new financial instruments has made it easier to hedge the exchange rate exposure. This chapter discusses a number of strategies that savers, investors, exporters, importers, financial intermediaries, and business managers can follow to reduce their exchange rate exposures and thus protect themselves against the foreign exchange rate risk.

5.1.3 *Hedging strategies*

The strategies that people, firms, investors, financial institutions, and others use to reduce or eliminate the exchange rate risk are referred to as foreign exchange risk *hedging*. In general, hedging refers to any action to be taken to protect income, assets, debt, present value, income, commodity prices, or wealth from the consequences of potential future price changes. Think of hedging as building a "hedge" around a specific price so that the price can no longer roam freely. In most developed economies, farmers routinely use futures markets to lock in the price they will receive for their crops. Specifically, they contract to deliver their crop before they even put seeds in the ground so that they will be assured of the price they will receive for their work. The futures market similarly permits buyers of the crops, such as food processors, to plan ahead knowing the price they will pay. In our global economy, *forward* foreign exchange markets serve a similar role.

There are actually many different ways to hedge exchange rate exposure. In addition to buying and selling foreign exchange in the forward market for foreign exchange, there are also markets where foreign exchange *options* are purchased and sold. A traditional method for hedging the foreign exchange risk exposure is to use the money markets in different countries to create obligations and earnings that offset foreign exchange exposure. Recently, currency swaps have been increasingly used to protect continuous cash flows in different currencies from unexpected foreign exchange fluctuations.

Many of the available currency hedges involve derivatives, which are financial instruments derived from other financial instruments or real assets. Options and forward exchange rates are derivatives because their value is explicitly related to actual spot exchange rates in the future. In the case of the forward markets for foreign exchange, exchange rate risk is eliminated for both future sellers and future buyers. In the case of options, the foreign exchange risk exposure is effectively transferred to others better able or more willing to bear risk or better able to diversify away the risks. The ability to hedge foreign exchange exposure reduces the costs of international activity, and globalization is probably greater than it would be if all exporters, importers, and international investors had to bear the full foreign exchange risk associated with the international transactions.

The various foreign exchange hedging strategies are not always available. For example, forward markets do not exist for all combinations of currencies, nor do they exist for any currencies for distant times in the future. Supply and demand for forward transactions in the distant future or even near-term forward exchanges between lesser-used currencies are simply not large enough for a dealer to profitably make a market. In these cases, exporters, importers, and international investors must rely on alternative strategies to deal with exchange rate risk. For example, multinational enterprises (MNEs) routinely hedge the exchange rate risk by (1) shifting the production across the borders in response to exchange rate changes and (2) spreading production and marketing across the countries in order to create more closely matched earnings and expenditures flows in each different currency.

The next several sections of this chapter detail the principal foreign exchange hedging strategies. The growth of international financial markets and the creation of new financial derivatives have made more hedging strategies available. The delegates at Bretton Woods would be surprised by how well the financial markets have enabled the global economy to deal with the volatility of exchange rates and expand international trade and investment under a system of floating exchange rates. That does not imply that, were he alive today, John Maynard Keynes would now agree to substitute floating exchange rates for the pegged exchange rates he advocated at Bretton Woods. Foreign exchange rate volatility has done more than its share of economic damage in recent years. But hedging certainly has mitigated some of the costs of floating exchange rates.

5.2 Hedging in the Forward Market

The most straightforward way to hedge foreign exchange rate exposure is to use the forward foreign exchange market. The forward market was discussed in the previous chapter from the perspective of intertemporal arbitrage. The fundamental reason why the market exists, however, is its role in hedging foreign exchange exposure. As we will do for each form of hedging, we begin with a simple example.

5.2.1 *An example*

Suppose that a US manufacturer sells custom-built machine tools to a German firm, to be delivered and paid for exactly one year from now. Suppose, also, that for competitive reasons the US firm quoted a price in euros, rather than US dollars. This implies the US firm assumes the foreign exchange risk associated with the transaction. Suppose that price is 10 million euros, or €10 million. Presumably, the US firm made the offer knowing that it could hedge its exchange rate risk.

The US firm can hedge its exchange rate exposure on the future payment of €10 million by selling the euros forward. This would guarantee the US firm a precise amount of dollars to which the €10 million will be converted into US dollars one year from now.

Table 5.1 shows the gains and losses from selling euros forward as compared to taking an unhedged, or open, position. Suppose that the forward exchange rate quoted today for delivery one year in the future happens to be exactly $1.30. This guarantees the exporter $13 million

Table 5.1   The Gains/Losses from a Forward Contract to Sell Euros at $1.30.

Spot rate at future sale	Deviation of spot from future spot $E(e_t - e_{t+1})$	$ Revenue at time of future receipt of €10 million	$ Revenue with unhedged position	Gain/loss from hedging ($'s)
$1.24	−0.06	$13,000,000	$12,400,000	+600,000
$1.25	−0.05	$13,000,000	$12,500,000	+500,000
$1.26	−0.04	$13,000,000	$12,600,000	+400,000
$1.27	−0.03	$13,000,000	$12,700,000	+300,000
$1.28	−0.02	$13,000,000	$12,800,000	+200,000
$1.29	−0.01	$13,000,000	$12,900,000	+100,000
$1.30	0.00	$13,000,000	$13,000,000	0
$1.31	+0.01	$13,000,000	$13,100,000	−100,000
$1.32	+0.02	$13,000,000	$13,200,000	−200,000
$1.33	+0.03	$13,000,000	$13,300,000	−300,000
$1.34	+0.04	$13,000,000	$13,400,000	−400,000
$1.35	+0.05	$13,000,000	$13,500,000	−500,000
$1.36	+0.06	$13,000,000	$13,600,000	−600,000

in exchange for the €10 million. The actual spot rate that will prevail in the foreign exchange market one year from now may, of course, vary above or below $1.30. For example, if the spot rate settles at $1.35 one year from now, the €10 million the exporter will receive could be converted on the spot market into $13,500,000. This is $500,000 more than the $1.30 forward contract provides the hedged exporter. On the other hand, if the spot rate is $1.24 one year from now, the €10 million could be converted on the spot market into $12,400,000. This is $600,000 less than the $1.30 forward contract provides. By signing the forward contract, the exporter eliminates risk, but takes away the possibility of a gain if the spot market moves in a favorable direction.

Figure 5.1 illustrates the results from Table 5.1. The upward-sloping dark line represents the revenues in US dollars if the 10 million is not hedged and simply converted one year from now at each of the possible future exchange rates between $1.24 and $1.36. This is not to say that even higher or lower exchange rates will not occur, but we stay in this range to keep the table and graphs from getting too large. The thinner horizontal line represents the revenues

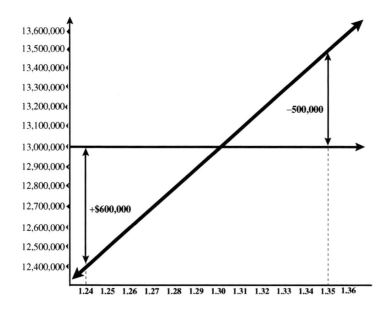

Figure 5.1 The payoff profile for a forward contract to sell €10 million at $1.30.

under the forward hedge at $1.30. The vertical difference between the two lines gives the losses or gains at each future spot exchange rate from taking an open position rather than a hedged position. For example, at the future spot rate of $1.24 the horizontal line lies above the upward-sloping line, and the distance between the two is $600,000. This is exactly the loss from not hedging noted for this case above. Alternatively, as noted above, if the spot rate rises to $1.35, the forward contract still converts the €10 million into $13,000,000, but an open position gives the exporter €10 million × $1.35, or $13,500,000. Hence, the distance between the two lines is $500,000.

5.2.2 *Hedging with foreign exchange futures*

The markets for foreign exchange futures are similar to, but distinct from, the forward foreign exchange markets. Foreign exchange futures are traded on exchanges, not in the decentralized dealer network that spot and forward contracts are traded. In the United States, there are organized exchanges in Chicago, Philadelphia, and New York that trade contracts to buy or sell fixed amounts of foreign exchange, usually in multiples of round numbers, such as $10,000, and at specified times in the future. Because they deal in uniform contracts, futures markets do not offer the hedger the opportunity to tailor the length and size of the contracts to their particular needs. Also, futures contracts only exist for a few major currencies. However, because they are inexpensive, futures markets permit smaller players to at least partially hedge their foreign exchange risk. Arbitrage between the forward and futures markets keeps the futures rates nearly identical with the corresponding forward exchange rates.

5.3 Hedging in the Money Market

It is possible to use the spot foreign exchange market in combination with traditional forms of borrowing and lending to hedge the foreign exchange risk associated with the future receipt of €10 million described in the previous example. Because it involves borrowing and lending in the money markets for the two currencies described by the exchange rate, this alternative hedging strategy is called a money market hedge. A money market hedge is especially useful for hedging the exchange rate exposure for currencies and over time horizons not covered by forward foreign exchange markets.

5.3.1 *An example*

In the case of a future receipt of €10 million, the exporter can hedge by using the receivable as collateral for borrowing an amount of euros that, one year from now, will require a total payment of principal plus interest equal to €10 million. That is, the exporter should borrow:

$$€10,000,000/(1 + r^*) \tag{5.1}$$

where r^* is the one-year interest rate for a euro loan. If, say, the euro interest rate is four percent per year, the exporter should borrow:

$$€10,000,000/(1.04) = €9,615,385 \tag{5.2}$$

When this loan comes due one year from now, the exporter will have to pay

$$€9,615,385(1.04) = €10,000,000 \tag{5.3}$$

which exactly equals the euro payment by the German importer. The euro borrowing of €9,615,385 is, therefore, fully covered by the future receipt from the German importer.

To complete the hedge, the exporter should immediately use the borrowed €9,615,385 to buy US dollars in the spot market. Suppose the spot rate is $1.325. In this case, exchanging the €9,615,385 to US dollars in the spot market gives the exporter:

$$€9,615,385(1.325) = \$12,745,098 \tag{5.4}$$

Suppose that the US interest rate is two percent. Then, depositing the $12,745,098 in a US dollar bank account one year at the US interest rate of two percent will give the exporter after one year:

$$\$12,745,098(1.02) = \$13,000,000 \tag{5.5}$$

The exporter thus ends up with exactly the same amount of dollars in one year that the exporter ended up with in the previous example in which an efficient forward market permitted him to sell the euros forward.

5.3.2 *Comparing the forward and money market hedges*

In the earlier example of a forward hedge, we assumed the forward market exchange rate to be $1.30. The interest parity condition shows that our assumption here of a spot rate of $1.325 is perfectly compatible with that earlier assumption of a forward rate of $1.30, given the assumed euro and dollar interest rates of four percent and two percent, respectively:

$$e_t = [(1 + r^*)/(1 + r)](f_t^{t+1}) = [1.04/1.02]1.30$$
$$= (1.0196)1.30 = \$1.325 \tag{5.6}$$

Table 5.2   The Gains/Losses From Hedging Future Receipt of €10 Million Using Money Markets, When Current Spot Rate = $1.30 and $i = i^*$.

Spot rate at future sale	Deviation of spot from future spot $E(e_t - e_{t+1})$	$ revenue at time of future receipt of €10 Million	$ revenue with unhedged position	Gain/loss from hedging ($'s)
$1.24	−0.06	$13,000,000	$12,400,000	+600,000
$1.25	−0.05	$13,000,000	$12,500,000	+500,000
$1.26	−0.04	$13,000,000	$12,600,000	+400,000
$1.27	−0.03	$13,000,000	$12,700,000	+300,000
$1.28	−0.02	$13,000,000	$12,800,000	+200,000
$1.29	−0.01	$13,000,000	$12,900,000	+100,000
$1.30	0.00	$13,000,000	$13,000,000	0
$1.31	+0.01	$13,000,000	$13,100,000	−100,000
$1.32	+0.02	$13,000,000	$13,200,000	−200,000
$1.33	+0.03	$13,000,000	$13,300,000	−300,000
$1.34	+0.04	$13,000,000	$13,400,000	−400,000
$1.35	+0.05	$13,000,000	$13,500,000	−500,000
$1.36	+0.06	$13,000,000	$13,600,000	−600,000

Table 5.2 presents the gains/losses from hedging in the money markets. Note that the numbers are identical to Table 5.1. This shows that, in principle, it is possible to use the money markets to achieve the same reduction in exchange rate risk that can be achieved using a forward hedge. Why do we have forward markets then? In practice, forward markets are more convenient and much less expensive. Figure 5.2 shows that a money market hedge requires three transactions. In contrast, a forward market hedge requires only one current contract and one future transaction. Also, each of the three transactions for a money market hedge must be completed in different markets, and the two money market transactions are usually much more expensive than the foreign exchange market transactions. In the money markets, the difference between the interest rate on loans and the interest rate on deposits can often exceed two percentage points even for the most reputable borrowers.

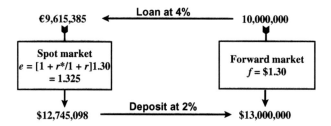

Figure 5.2 Future receipt of €10 million: Comparing forward market and money market hedges.

The eurocurrency markets operate on smaller margins than do domestic commercial banks in most countries, but the margins in these very efficient wholesale money markets are still very large compared to the margins in the forward foreign exchange market. The US firm could issue a bond to keep its borrowing costs down. In this case, however, the US firm would have to issue a bond in a foreign currency, which is likely to be very costly unless it is a very well known and a very large multinational firm. In general, however, the US exporter will normally have to pay more than the four percent money market interest rate on its euro loan, and it probably will earn less than the two percent money market interest rate on its dollar deposit. The money market hedge is thus not likely to be exactly equal to a forward hedge.

5.4 Hedging with Options

The foreign exchange markets offer *foreign exchange options* as well as actual spot and forward sales of currencies. In general, an option gives the purchaser the right to buy or sell an asset at a future date, but there is no obligation to complete the future transaction if the buyer of the option finds it in her interest to not exercise the option. However, the seller of an option must exercise the future sale or purchase of the asset if the buyer decides to exercise the option.

5.4.1 *Options contracts*

A *call option* gives the buyer the opportunity to *buy* a specified asset or set of assets at a specified price by a specified date, called the *strike price* and the *strike date*, respectively. A *put option* gives the opportunity to *sell* a specified set of assets on or before a specific strike date. If the buyer does not exercise the option by the strike date, the option expires. There are two types of options: an *American option*, which lets the buyer exercise the option on or before the strike date, and a *European option*, which lets the buyer exercise the option only on the strike date. The price of an option, called the *premium*, is the price the seller demands for assuming the one-sided foreign exchange risk from giving the buyer the opportunity, but not the obligation, to buy or sell assets at a specified price on or before the strike date. An option is a type of insurance against the unfavorable exchange rate movements. The premium is the price of this insurance.

Foreign exchange options are sold on a number of markets throughout the world. In 2009, the Philadelphia Stock Exchange was the largest exchange in the United States for exchange rate options. Foreign currency options are available for only a few currency pairs, such as the US dollar price of euros, Japanese yen, Swiss francs, and Canadian and Australian dollars. Most options traded in Philadelphia expire on the third Wednesday of each month. A smaller number of options expire at the end of the month. The Philadelphia Exchange trades both American and European options. The variety of options is small because trading volume is not large enough to provide the liquidity for a greater variety of options.

Table 5.3 shows a typical table of foreign exchange options that you can find in financial sections of business newspapers. This specific example happens to be from the 11 January 2005 *Financial Times*. The reported prices are for January 7. The first column shows the strike price. In the case of the dollar/euro options, the strike price for the exchange rate $1.31 is printed as 13,100. For Japanese yen, the strike price $.94 is shown as 9,400, and for British pounds the strike price $1.86 is given as 1,860. A call option (the option to buy euros) at the strike price of $1.31 per euro for March costs 1.88

Table 5.3   An Example of Currency Options as Reported in the Press.

US$/€ options (CME)

Strike price Jan. 7	Calls			Puts		
	Jan.	Feb.	Mar.	Jan.	Feb.	Mar.
13,100	0.08	1.29	1.88	0.35	1.58	2.15
13,200	0.01	0.86	1.36	1.37	2.18	2.81
13,300	0.01	0.55	1.12	2.32	2.81	3.42
13,400	0.01	0.38	0.81	3.32	3.64	4.08

Previous day's data: volume, 5,897; calls 14,188; puts, 20,065; open interest, 173, 132.

US$/YEN options (CME)

Strike price Jan. 7	Calls			Puts		
	Jan.	Feb.	Mar.	Jan.	Feb.	Mar.
9,400	1.64	2.09	2.44	0.04	0.36	0.50
9,500	0.75	1.46	1.86	0.06	0.70	1.03
9,600	0.04	0.98	1.42	0.26	1.16	1.58
9,700	0.10	0.64	0.96	1.22	2.03	1.60

Previous day's data: volume, 775; calls 686; puts, 1,481; open interest, 66, 722.

US$/UK£ options (CME)

Strike price Jan. 7	Calls			Puts		
	Jan.	Feb.	Mar.	Jan.	Feb.	Mar.
1,860	0.35	—	3.05	0.46	1.20	2.10
1,870	0.70	1.90	2.44	0.66	2.25	2.40
1,880	0.16	1.66	2.46	1.50	2.84	3.10
1,890	0.06	1.30	1.73	2.41	3.49	4.07

Previous day's data: volume, 144; calls 271; puts, 415; open interest, 10, 638.
Source: reported in the 11 January 2005 *Financial Times* based on data from Reuters/CME.

cents per euro, and a call option at the strike price of $1.31 at the end of January costs just 0.08 cents. Clearly, on January 7, the market did not consider it very likely that the euro would rise above $1.31 by the third Wednesday of that same month. The perceived probability that the euro would rise by the third Wednesday of March was much greater given the higher premium demanded for that more distant date.

5.4.2 *An example*

Table 5.4 presents a hypothetical case for evaluating the gains and losses from foreign exchange options, and Fig. 5.3 illustrates the case. The upward-sloping thick line shows the unhedged US dollar revenue for each future exchange rate, the thinner line represents US dollar revenues including the cost of an option to purchase the US dollars with euros at the strike price of $1.30. Assuming an option premium of $0.02 per euro at that strike price, a dollar appreciation means smaller gains than was the case for forward and money market hedges. The option premium thus costs $200,000 for the €10 million exchange. For example, in the case of a dollar appreciation to $1.24, the premium reduces the vertical distance between the two lines to $400,000 compared to the $600,000 for the forward hedge in Fig. 5.1. But, if the

Table 5.4   The Gains/Losses from an Option to Sell Euros at $1.30, Premium = 0.02.

Spot rate at exercise date	Deviation of spot from strike rate	Net proceeds from sale of euros	Unhedged position	Gain/loss ($'s)
$1.24	−0.06	$12,800,000	$12,400,000	+400,000
$1.25	−0.05	$12,800,000	$12,500,000	+300,000
$1.26	−0.04	$12,800,000	$12,600,000	+200,000
$1.27	−0.03	$12,800,000	$12,700,000	+100,000
$1.28	−0.02	$12,800,000	$12,800,000	0
$1.29	−0.01	$12,800,000	$12,900,000	−100,000
$1.30	0.00	$12,800,000	$13,000,000	−200,000
$1.31	+0.01	$12,900,000	$13,100,000	−200,000
$1.32	+0.02	$13,000,000	$13,200,000	−200,000
$1.33	+0.03	$13,100,000	$13,300,000	−200,000
$1.34	+0.04	$13,200,000	$13,400,000	−200,000
$1.35	+0.05	$13,300,000	$13,500,000	−200,000
$1.36	+0.06	$13,400,000	$13,600,000	−200,000

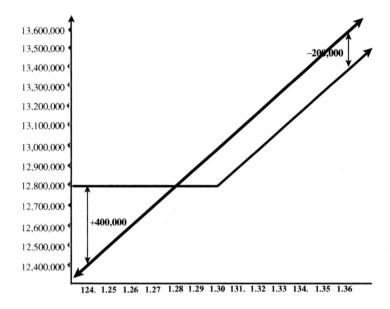

Figure 5.3 The payoff profile with an option to sell €10 million at a premium of 0.02.

dollar depreciates, the purchaser of the option only loses the cost of the option, which is $200,000. For example, if the dollar depreciates to $1.36, the holder of the option gains $200,000 less than the unhedged position, but a forward hedge would leave the hedger with $600,000 less than the unhedged position. Options set a floor on potential losses from adverse exchange rate changes while leaving most of the potential gains from favorable exchange rate movements.

5.4.3 *The advantages of an option*

Options are especially useful when future foreign currency payments or receipts are not certain. Suppose, for example, that your firm is bidding on a contract to supply equipment to a foreign government agency, and the winning bid will be announced three months from now. Delivery and payment will take place one year from today, or nine months after you learn whether you have won the bid. You want to minimize the exchange rate risk. Since you do not know if you will win the bid, you do not want to hedge by selling foreign exchange one year forward. If you do not win the bid, then, with a forward contract, you will be left with a commitment to sell foreign currency even though you will not have any to sell. If, instead of selling forward, you could wait to hear whether you won the bid and then, if you win, you can buy a nine-month forward contract to sell the foreign exchange. However, the exchange rate will probably change over the next three months, and your competitive bid could end up being unprofitable if the exchange rate moves a lot.

An option to sell foreign exchange one year from now may be a good hedge in this situation. If you win the bid, then your option protects you against a fall in the value of the foreign currency over the next three months. If you do not win the bid, you simply let the option expire. In this case, the option premium is the cost of avoiding the chance of suffering a large exchange rate loss. Of course, if you win the bid and the currency rises, then you also let the option expire and use the spot market to take advantage of the better than expected exchange rate.

Options can also be used in combination with the less expensive forward hedges in the case of uncertainty about future events. For example, if a Japanese firm expects to sell between US$15 and $25 million in the US next year, it can use the forward market to hedge the nearly certain $15 million and a additional option contracts to hedge the less certain $10 million in dollar income.

Compared to traditional forms of hedging, such as using the forward market or engaging in offsetting borrowing and lending, options have two important advantages. First, companies can profit from unexpected favorable exchange rate movements. Second, American options give the added flexibility of exercising the option when the time is most appropriate for the option buyer. If the timing of future foreign receipts or payments is subject to uncertainty, then the American option, which allows the buyer to exercise any time up to the strike date, offers more protection against unexpected losses than a forward contract with specified maturity dates.

5.4.4 *Comparing the three hedges*

There are important differences between options, forward hedges, and money market hedges:

- A forward hedge is nearly identical to a money market hedge, except that the money market hedge is more costly because of the spread between interest rates on borrowing and lending.
- For dates far into the future or for minor currencies, money market hedging may be the only practical hedging strategy.
- Options imply a fixed cost (the premium), but they have the advantage of insuring against an adverse currency movement while not eliminating the potential gains from a favorable currency movement.
- Options are useful for hedging uncertain future payments or receipts because they do not have to be exercised.
- Options are much less widely available than forward contracts.

The traditional forward market, money market, and options hedges are not the only financial market hedges available. The next section describes a recent new hedging tool: The currency swap.

5.5 Currency Swaps

International firms, investors, and financial institutions often have continual, and fairly predictable, flows of foreign payments and earnings that are subject to exchange rate risk. In our increasingly global economy, most international economic transactions are part of ongoing payment flows, not one-time isolated transactions. The great majority of exports and imports are either carried out under long-term supplier contracts, are part of the supply networks of multinational firms or occur under permanent wholesale distribution arrangements. Also, international investment normally involves not only the initial purchase or sale of an asset, but it normally also involves later flows of profits, rents, dividends, royalties, and interest payments, not to mention the future reverse flow when the asset matures or is liquidated. Therefore, when planning for the future, exporters, importers, investors, and financial institutions often need to hedge the exchange rate risk of a whole series of future foreign payments or receipts rather than just one single future payment or receipt.

A *currency swap* is a formal agreement or contract to exchange the currencies at predetermined exchange rates on a series of future dates. Effectively, a currency swap is a whole set of forward transactions with a variety of maturities. Do not confuse *currency swaps* with the *foreign exchange swaps* discussed in Chapter 4. The latter consist of a simultaneous spot purchase (sale) and forward sale (purchase) of a currency or a simultaneous purchases and sale of two forward contracts at different dates. Recall that foreign exchange swaps are usually used to carry out the intertemporal arbitrage that validates the interest parity condition. *Currency swaps*, on the other hand, are more complex contracts that consist of long series of currency exchanges. Two examples below will help to clarify what currency swaps are.

5.5.1 *A first simple example of a currency swap*

Suppose that the German automobile manufacturer BMW signs a contract with the Japanese manufacturer of industrial robots, Kawasaki, to buy 48 robots over a period of two years, or 2 per month for 24 months. These purchases are part of BMW's plan to upgrade its German automobile assembly lines and reduce labor costs. Suppose that BMW agrees to pay Kawasaki ¥50 million for each robot. BMW effectively assumes the exchange rate risk because its earnings are mostly in euros and other currencies, not yen. BMW would like to hedge this exposure to future exchange rate fluctuations.

One hedging strategy would be for BMW to enter into a series of forward contracts to buy ¥100 million each month for the next two years. In general, the forward exchange rates for each of the 24 forward contracts would not be the same. Recall our discussion of forward exchange rates in Chapter 4 and Fig. 4.1. In general, forward rates will be increasingly higher or lower the farther into the future you look; the curves in Fig. 4.1 sloped gradually upward or downward, depending on whether interest rates are higher or lower abroad than they are at home.

5.5.2 *A more sophisticated example of a currency swap*

In the above example, BMW can hedge its exchange rate exposure consisting of a series of future payments in a foreign currency with a series of forward contracts. In many cases, however, firms seek to hedge the series of payments that extend beyond the period for which forward markets exist. Increasingly, firms are finding ways to design the currency swaps that avoid the foreign exchange markets altogether. What most financial firms today describe as currency swaps consist of the exchange of two series of foreign-currency-denominated obligations or receipts by organizations in two different countries.

Suppose, for example, that a US firm, General Widgets, wants to build a factory in Japan at a cost of ¥5 billion to manufacture widgets for the Japanese market. The project is expected to generate sufficient revenue to cover its cost in about ten years. General Widgets could borrow the ¥5 billion for ten years in Japan. However, because it is not a traditional customer of any Japanese bank, it would have to pay an interest rate above the yen prime rate of two percent, perhaps three percent, on its yen loans. Alternatively, General Widgets could borrow dollars in the United States, where it has a long-standing relationship with a US bank that will lend to it at the dollar prime rate of six percent. However, borrowing in dollars to fund an investment that generates income in yen will expose General Widgets to foreign exchange rate risk. The main risk is that the yen will depreciate in the future and General Widgets' Japanese yen earnings will not be sufficient to cover its dollar debt service obligations. The project's ten-year horizon rules out a forward market hedge; forward markets do not extend that far into the future. A money market hedge may be possible, but General Widgets would face high borrowing cost in Japan. General Widgets' bank suggests a less expensive hedge: a currency swap.

Suppose that there is a Japanese firm, Sakura Gizmo Co. that is in the process of arranging financing to cover the $50,000,000 cost of building a new factory to make gizmos in the United States. This new factory will generate dollar revenues to cover its cost in about ten years. Like General Widgets, Sakura is not well known outside its home country, and it has no long-term banking relations in the US. It would have to pay seven percent on a dollar loan instead of the current prime rate of six percent on US dollar loans. Sakura could, of course, take out a two percent loan with its own bank in Japan, but then it would face foreign exchange rate exposure because it would have to meet its yen obligations with dollar earnings. Dollar depreciation would cause a cash flow problem.

General Widgets' US bank, with the help of a broker that specializes in swaps, arranges a currency swap between General Widgets and Sakura Gizmo Co. The Japanese firm is known as General Widgets' *counter party* in the swap. The two firms are matched by the swap broker because at the current dollar/yen exchange rate of $1 = ¥100, the two projects have about the same value. General Widgets takes out a $50 million loan at the six percent prime rate, which it can obtain at the prime rate, and Sakura takes out a ¥5 billion loan at the prime rate of two percent. Under the swap, General Widgets agrees to meet Sakura's ten annual interest payments plus the principal repayment in ten years on the yen loan out of its expected yen earnings from operating its Japanese plant. Sakura, on the other hand, agrees to use its dollar earnings in the United States to cover General Widgets' interest and principal payments over the next ten years. Notice that under this arrangement, both firms hedge their exchange rate exposure because they have debt payments and earnings in the same currencies. And, both firms effectively borrow at their own currencies' prime interest rates.

This currency swap arrangement may appear to provide unequal benefits. Doesn't General Widgets get the better deal here since it only has to pay two percent interest to Sakura's six percent? Closer analysis reveals that, if everything works out, General Widgets effectively pays six percent when it services Sakura's two percent loan in Japan, and Sakura really pays two percent interest covering General

Widgets' six percent US loan. The reason for this surprising result is the interest parity condition.

Recall that the interest parity condition links the spot exchange rate to the expected future exchange rates in such a way that the difference between the domestic and foreign interest rates is reflected in the differences between the spot and expected future exchange rates. With the yen interest rate equal to two percent and the dollar interest rate equal to six percent, a current exchange rate of $e = 0.0100$ (that is, $1 = ¥100$) implies that the market expects the exchange rate ten years from now to be about $0.01[(1.06)/(1.02)]^{10} = 0.0147$ (that is, $1 = ¥68$). If the dollar depreciated as the markets expects it will, then as the years pass the yen interest payments and the principal repayment will increasingly cost more in terms of dollars. Since the interest parity condition states that the dollar will depreciate at exactly the difference between the dollar and yen interest rates, the dollars expected depreciation makes the interest payments on the yen loan grow in dollar terms just enough to eliminate the seemingly lower cost of the yen loan. Table 5.5 illustrates.

Rows 1 and 2 in Table 5.5 lay out the cash flows of the ¥5 billion loan in Japan and the $50 million loan in the United States, respectively. Rows 3 and 4 show the expected future exchange rates that conform to the known spot exchange rate of $e = 0.01$ and the interest rates of two and six percent in Japan and the United States, respectively. Row 3 gives the exchange rates from the US perspective, row 4 from the Japanese perspective. Row 5 shows the dollar equivalents of the yen cash flow, converted at the expected exchange rates in each period. Similarly, row 6 shows the yen value of the dollar loan cash flow, converted at the expected exchange rates in each period. You can easily see, using a financial calculator, that the dollar cash flows in rows 2 and 5 have the same present value when you use the dollar interest rate of six percent to discount them. Similarly, the cash flows in rows 1 and 6 have the identical present value when they are discounted using the two percent yen interest rate. Thus, as suggested two paragraphs earlier, the swap implies that General Widgets effectively pays six percent when it services Sakura's two percent loan in Japan, and Sakura really pays two percent interest covering the General Widgets' US loan.

Table 5.5   Cash Flows for a Currency Swap Example (All Figures in Millions).

Year of cash flow	0	1	2	3	4	...	7	8	9	10
1. ¥ cash flow	+¥5,000	¥100	¥100	¥100	¥100	...	¥100	¥100	¥100	¥5,100
2. $ cash Flow	+$50	$3	$3	$3	$3	...	$3	$3	$3	$53
3. Expected $1/e$	100.0	96.23	92.23	89.10	85.74	...	76.39	73.51	70.74	68.07
4. Expected e	0.0100	0.0104	0.0108	0.0112	0.0117	...	0.0131	0.0136	0.0141	0.0147
5. Exp. $ flow Row 1/row 3	+$50.0	$1.04	$1.08	$1.12	$1.17	...	$1.31	$1.36	$1.41	$74.92
6. Exp. ¥ flow Row 2/row 4	+¥5,000	¥288	¥277	¥268	¥256	...	¥229	¥221	¥213	¥3,605

From a present value perspective, each firm is effectively indifferent between borrowing at home or abroad. Realistically, however, neither firm can borrow overseas at the prime rate, which makes domestic loans preferable to foreign currency loans. Domestic borrowing to build an overseas project creates exchange rate exposure, however. Therein lies the advantage of the swap! The currency swap effectively lets General Widgets borrow at the prime rate in Japan and Sakura Gizmo Co. at the prime rate in the United States, and both companies enjoy their domestic prime rates while also eliminating their exchange rate exposure. Sakura Gizmo Co. and General Widgets make future foreign loan service payments in the foreign currency as they receive the revenue from their foreign export sales, and again there is no need to exchange the currencies at forward rates or, when there is no forward market, at the unknown future spot exchange rates.

It should be clear from the details in Table 5.5 that the ultimate attractiveness of the swap depends on future exchange rates. If, for example, the dollar appreciates unexpectedly, then Sakura may regret having acquired the dollar obligations that exhaust its overseas cash flow over the first ten years of the project. Of course, in this case General Widgets will be very thankful for having entered into this hedge because the rising dollar would have eroded its overseas cash flow to where it would not have covered the servicing of its $50 million loan. These opposing views of the currency swap reflect the usual result that a foreign exchange rate hedge does not guarantee the best outcome, it only locks in an expected result. A swap is a hedge, not an investment.

In summary, swaps are equivalent to a series of forward contracts, except that a swap can usually be arranged for periods well beyond the time span over which forward markets offer contracts. Also, swaps improve on money market hedges because they bring together borrowers that are likely to have favorable access to their own national financial markets.

5.5.3 *Difficulties associated with currency swaps*

Currency swaps hedge the foreign exchange exposure, but they introduce another potential risk: *counter-party risk*. This is the risk that the other firm engaged in the swap fails to complete its side of the deal. In the example above, the counter-party risk to General Widgets is that Sakura Gizmo Company's US project runs into problems and the US subsidiary of the Japanese firm fails to make its scheduled interest and/or principal payments. In such a case, General Widgets could retaliate and stop paying the yen interest payments on Sakura's Japanese loan, for which Sakura is responsible, but General Widgets would then lose its currency hedge on its foreign receipts and is left having to meet dollar interest payments on the US loan that Sakura was servicing. General Widgets could, of course, ask a broker to find another Japanese firm with US income to assume its dollar interest payments in exchange for assuming yen interest payments. But if the dollar/yen exchange rate has changed since the start of the swap with Sakura, General Widgets may have to make some payments to get its new swap partner to accept the deal; with a different series of spot and expected future exchange rates, the swap will call for different initial loans and different principal repayments. The risk of default by the counter parties may have to be covered before firms enter the swap arrangement, perhaps by acquiring insurance in the form of another new type of option called a credit default swap.

Our example above is also not very realistic in that the two firms perfectly match their cash flows and project maturities. In general, swap brokers seldom find such a perfect match equating two future cash flows. Most actual swaps only partially hedge exchange rate exposure. However, given the difficulty of finding other exchange rate hedges for payment flows into the distant future, a partial hedge is a great improvement over no hedge at all. And, of course, firms facing long-term exchange rate risk can arrange several swaps with a diverse set of counter parties to come closer to hedging their entire foreign exchange risk.

Currency swaps also face *sovereign risk*, which refers to the possibility that governments will impose restrictions on financial transactions. Not only is there always the potential for foreign exchange market interruptions such as bans on foreign exchange transactions and bank holidays, but even minor changes in tax policies and bank regulations can cancel out the gains from carefully tuned currency swaps. Sovereign risk explains why currency swaps are most common for exchange rate exposures between currencies from countries that maintain transparent and predictable economic and financial policies. At least until the financial crisis of 2008, improvements in economic institutions in many countries seemed to be supporting the use of currency swaps. It will be interesting to see how the market for currency swaps develops after financial firms and hedge funds aggressively unwind many of their most complex financial arrangements in the aftermath of the 2008 financial crisis.

5.6 Net Exposure Versus Total Exposure

In the simple example at the start of the previous section, BMW's string of 24 future payments is likely to overstate the company's true exposure to foreign exchange rate risk. At the same time that BMW buys four robots each month from Kawasaki in Japan, it is selling automobiles in Japan. Japan does not import many automobiles from the rest of the world, but BMW has over the years succeeded at gaining a very nice niche in the Japanese market. Therefore, BMW not only makes yen payments in Japan, but it also receives yen payments from Japan each month. BMW's true exchange rate exposure is not ¥100 million per month, but rather the net difference between its yen payments and yen receipts. It is *net exposure* that contributes to foreign exchange risk.

5.6.1 *Only net exposure needs to be hedged*

To illustrate the concept of *net exposure*, suppose for a moment that BMW's plant management does not talk to BMW's overseas sales group and each goes out and hedges its foreign exchange exposure in the forward market. Suppose furthermore that BMW's monthly sales in Japan are also about ¥100 million, on average. Finally, suppose that the overseas sales group deals with the same dealer bank that the plant management group deals with when they arrange their forward hedge; however, internal communications within BMW fail, and the overseas marketing division enters into a currency swap contract to sell ¥100 million each month for the next five years in order to hedge its perceived exchange rate exposure. In this case, BMW's plant management group each month ends up buying the yen that its overseas sales group sells each month.

BMW's bank loves this arrangement, of course. They collect the spread between the rate the plant management group pays for the yen each month and what the overseas sales group receives for selling yen. Spreads are very small in today's foreign exchange markets, but they do add up. BMW is likely to pay the bank a margin of about three "pips", or three thousandths of a euro, between the purchase and selling price of yen. The 2008 exchange rate of about €1.00 = ¥150 implies a transaction cost of ¥100 million/150/3,000 = €2,000 per month, or about €48,000 over two years. That is a lot of money for unnecessary hedges. Clearly, a financial department of a multinational firm must organize themselves to take account of net exposure, not individual gross exposures, to exchange the fluctuations.

The BMW example suggests that large international businesses can hedge foreign exchange rate exposure in many different ways. Firms can explicitly organize themselves in order to balance assets and liabilities on a currency-by-currency basis. For example, a *Financial Times* article by Amy Yee describes how the cruise ship operator Carnival shifted foreign exchange risk to the Italian shipyard Fincantieri, which is building four new large cruise ships for Carnival.[2] Since Carnival serves both the European and U. S. cruise markets, the firm placed two of the orders in US dollars and two in euros in order to better align its currency liabilities and its future currency earnings. Later in this textbook, when we deal with multinational firms and international banking, we will discuss how international businesses and financial organizations shape their presence in many different national markets in ways that reduce the foreign exchange exposure.

---

[2] Amy Yee (2005). "Liners in Contest for Supremacy of Seas". *Financial Times,* 17 June 2005.

5.6.2 *Managing cash flows in different currencies*

In general, a firm or organization's foreign payments and foreign receipts do not exactly offset each other as they do in the BMW example above. You can imagine that a company like BMW generates a rather complex set of payment flows into and out of Japan. Not only does the firm purchase robots in Japan, but it also purchases a variety of components from Japan's many very efficient parts manufacturers for its assembly plants in Germany, South Africa, and the United States. BMW also incurs sales costs, like advertising, printing of manuals and brochures, and the salaries of its Japanese sales staff. BMW may also have additional receipts in Japan, such as sales of parts, accessories, and the interest earnings from consumer loans to autopurchasers. BMW only needs to hedge the net between payments and receipts in Japan for it to fully cover its yen exposure. It is also impossible for BMW to determine precisely what all of the payments flows into and out of Japan will be over the next five years. Future earnings from selling cars in Japan depend on unforeseen factors, as do future purchases in Japan. Nevertheless, when both future purchase of yen and future sales of yen are substantial, then BMW should only hedge the estimated *net* flow of total payments, not the sum of all the expected individual payment flows into and out of Japan. Foreign exchange options may be in order.

5.7 Hedging and Exchange Rate Pass-Through

A little-appreciated side effect of hedging is that it is likely to reduce the influence of exchange rates on international economic behavior, at least in the short run. In general, when, say, the dollar appreciates in value, domestic US prices of imported goods do not change in proportion to the dollar appreciation. Similarly, when the dollar depreciates, we seldom see an immediate rise in the domestic dollar prices of imports. This leads to the question: Who effectively absorbs the costs of the changes in exchange rates?

5.7.1 *Exchange rate pass-through is often low*

The diminished price effects of depreciations and appreciations observed across all countries have led economists to study what they call *exchange-rate pass-through*. Specifically, the exchange rate pass-through is the percentage change in an imported good's local currency price relative to the percentage change in the nominal exchange rate. For example, if the exchange rate depreciates by ten percent but domestic prices of imports only rise by five percent, the exchange rate pass-through is 50 percent. Observing the exchange rate pass-through helps us to measure how much producers, importers, retailers, consumers, the tax collector, and other groups are ultimately affected by exchange rate fluctuations.

In an interesting study of the worldwide beer industry, Hellerstein (2004) looks at how the wholesale and retail prices of domestic and imported beers change when the exchange rate changes. She finds that the effects of an exchange rate change are large and unevenly distributed across domestic and foreign beer makers and domestic consumers. In the case of currency depreciation in an importing country, for example, Hellerstein finds that foreign manufacturers absorb the greater part of exchange rate changes by keeping price increases well below the rate of depreciation. However, because they do not absorb all the costs and prices do rise somewhat, domestic producers tend to gain some market share after a currency depreciation. Domestic manufacturers are even able to raise their prices somewhat. Interestingly, premium domestic beers, which closely compete with imports, also lose market share as consumers switch away from imports to the cheaper high-volume domestic manufacturers. Finally, because it raises the prices of some domestic beers and all imports, depreciation squeezes the welfare of consumers and retailers. In sum, strategic behavior by beer manufacturers and retailers is an example of why the exchange rate pass-through of an exchange rate change is less than complete and why the effects of exchange rate changes on the balance of payments are relatively modest in the short run.

Krugman (1989) pointed out that exchange rates were much more volatile than the underlying economic fundamentals that were hypothesized to determine the exchange rates. Krugman further observed that the high volatility in exchange rates did not seem to have much of an effect on the economic fundamentals. Detailed studies confirmed that over the period of floating exchange rates after 1973, high exchange rate volatility is not reflected in a high volatility of other macroeconomic variables. In short, they saw exchange rates as fluctuating somewhat loosely, neither tightly driven by nor directly driving, proportionate changes in the real economy.[3]

Devereux and Engel (2002) attribute the high exchange rate volatility and that volatility's lack of consequences for the real economy to the local currency pricing described above. They also point to the heterogeneity in international marketing arrangements, which include wholly owned subsidiaries, joint ventures, distributors, wholesalers, etc. as dissipating the effects of exchange rate changes across many different groups in different countries. Duarte and Stockman (2001) suggest that the "disconnect" between exchange rate volatility and macroeconomic fundamentals is related to transport costs, which are far from trivial and are often a substantial barrier to the price arbitrage that otherwise would quickly adjust local prices in response to exchange rate changes.

5.7.2 *Hedging and exchange rate volatility*

The observed small pass-through of exchange rate changes may be largely due to the increased hedging of exchange rate exposure. It seems that in the absence of hedging, producers, importers, distributors, and retailers would not be able to protect themselves against exchange rate changes as easily, and they would have to adjust their prices more quickly. With hedging, producers, importers, distributors, exporters, investors, debtors, and retailers do not immediately change their behaviors, and consequently they do not cause the real variables in the economy to change. The foreign exchange markets must maintain equilibrium between supply and demand, however. Therefore, the adjustments in the real variables that are required for the economy

---

[3] For example, Marianne Baxter and Alan Stockman (1989) and Robert Flood and Andrew Rose (1995).

to adjust to the shifts in supply and demand in the foreign exchange market require greater adjustments from those who are not hedged. Hence, in the short run, exchange rates must fluctuate much more than in the long run, when all participants in the economy must adjust to exchange the rate changes. In short, those who do not hedge thus face greater uncertainty because others hedge their exchange rate exposure.

This discussion suggests that foreign exchange rate hedging is both a solution to, and a cause of, exchange rate volatility. Of course, there are many causes of the seemingly excessive volatility of exchange rates, and the hedging strategies described in this chapter are just several of many possible ways of dealing with foreign exchange risk. Later chapters will describe how macroeconomic policies can reduce the exchange rate volatility. The fact that hedging may do little more than protect some while increasing the foreign exchange risk for others may justify using macroeconomic policy to reduce the exchange rate volatility.

Keep this discussion in mind when, in later chapters, we discuss macroeconomic policies and international arrangements to reduce exchange rate volatility. Broad macroeconomic policies to reduce exchange rate volatility may be preferable to hedging that protects some at the expense of increasing exchange rate volatility for others.

5.8 Summary and Conclusions

This chapter describes foreign exchange risk and hedging strategies. The main points made in the chapter are

1. When savers, investors, financial firms, governments, and other organizations are exposed to foreign exchange rate risk, they have several alternative hedging strategies available.
2. A forward hedge involves buying or selling currency on the forward foreign exchange market.
3. Forward hedges eliminate the uncertainty about the future nominal exchange rate, but depending on how the spot rate moves in the future, they may leave the hedger better off or worse off compared to an unhedged position.

4. Forward markets for foreign exchange, like spot markets, operate on very small margins, and so they offer hedges at a very low transaction cost.
5. Forward hedges are possible only if forward markets exist; they exist only for major currencies and relative short-time horizons for which there is enough supply and demand to make a market.
6. Money market hedges are, fundamentally, similar to forward hedges because both reflect the interest parity condition.
7. Because they involve borrowing and lending, money market hedges are costlier than forward hedges.
8. A money market hedge uses the spot market and asset markets to implicitly fix a future exchange rate, as demonstrated in Fig. 5.2.
9. Options are a form of insurance that permit purchasers to exercise the option of exchanging currency at a predetermined rate at some time in the future.
10. Options require the payment of a premium to compensate the counter party for assuming the risk of an unfavorable exchange rate movement.
11. Options are especially attractive if future exchange exposure is not certain because, unlike forward and money market hedges, options do not have to be exercised.
12. Options also permit the option holder to benefit if exchange rate movements are favorable in the future.
13. Each of these three hedging strategies has advantages and disadvantages, which is why all three forms of hedging are used by international traders, investors, and wealth holders.
14. Currency swaps are a more recent development that involves the matching of future cash flows by organizations and firms.
15. Long-term currency swaps reduce the exchange rate exposure, but they add sovereign and counter-party risks.

From the individual firm or organization perspective, hedging is advisable given the inevitable exchange rate volatility in the global economy. In later chapters, further ways for international traders and investors to hedge exchange rate exposure will become apparent. Also, new hedging strategies may be developed by the global financial industry, which is always looking for ways to exploit the increasing complexity of the global economic system to sell innovative new financial services.

The 2008 financial crisis has demonstrated that increasingly complex financial derivatives that purport to reduce risk often shift risk in ways that are not fully understood even by the financial groups that originate the derivatives. If counter-party risk is spread widely through over-the-counter markets and through undisclosed individually tailored contracts, financial shocks could undermine a substantial portion of the world's hedging arrangements. The uncertainty created by such a "hedging crisis" could seriously worsen a financial crisis.

If the world does not move to an international financial order with fewer national currencies or a solid commitment on the part of individual governments to support pegged exchange rates, demand for foreign exchange hedges is likely to grow in the future. Economists need to further investigate the consequences of hedging on exchange rates, however. This chapter has brought up the possibility that the increased use of hedging strategies by business and international investors reduces the exchange rate pass-through. We observe that international trade and investment react very sluggishly to exchange rate movements. It often takes two years or longer before international trade flows react to even very large exchange rate changes and a country's trade balance actually begins to change. This sluggish reaction of exporters, importers, and investors to exchange rate changes means that it takes larger exchange rate changes to push an economy to adjust to a balance of payments disequilibrium. The resulting increase in the volatility of exchange rates leads international businesses and international investors to hedge more often, and this increased hedging then causes the economy's reaction to exchange rate changes to be even more sluggish, requiring even greater exchange rate changes, and so forth. Instability increases, and because some groups can hedge their exposure to this instability better than others, there are real transfers of welfare from one group to another. As the 2008 financial crisis made very clear, financial innovation does not necessarily make the world more stable.

We are not suggesting that people and businesses should stop hedging their exposure to foreign exchange risk. It is nevertheless interesting how individually responsible behavior may not be globally optimal: The increased use of hedging strategies tends to increase the exchange rate volatility. More worrisome is the conclusion that those who hedge their risk effectively increase exchange rate risk for those who do not hedge. This conclusion, together with the conclusion from the last chapter that the uncertainty of exchange rates creates a role for government policy to target or peg exchange rates, strengthens the case against a world order of floating exchange rates. John Maynard Keynes and the other delegates at Bretton Woods may have been very astute in seeking a system of pegged exchange rates. It may be that younger economists who were educated during the current era of floating exchange rates do not fully grasp the system's inherent costs and instabilities. In any case, upcoming chapters on open-economy macroeconomics will delve further into the implications of pegged and floating exchange rate systems.

Key Terms and Concepts

Accounting exposure	European option	Money market hedge
American option	Exchange rate pass-	Net exposure
Call option	through	Put option
Counter party	Exchange rate risk	Strike price
risk	Exchange rate	Transaction
Currency swap	exposure	exposure
Economic	Forward market	Translation
exposure	hedge	exposure

Chapter Questions and Problems

1. Suppose that you have ordered a large piece of equipment from a manufacturer in Japan, and you are committed to make a ¥200,000,000 payment upon delivery of the equipment exactly two years from now. Suppose also that the spot dollar/yen exchange rate is $.0100, the interest rate in Japan is 2%, and the interest rate in the United States is 6%.

a. Describe how you can hedge your exchange rate exposure using the forward market. Describe precisely what transactions you will make, how many dollars you will receive in two years, and what the exact costs of this hedging strategy are.

b. Alternatively, describe how you could hedge using the traditional money market hedge. Again, calculate exactly what transactions you will make, how many dollars you will end up with, and what other costs you incur.

c. Finally, describe exactly how you could hedge your exchange rate exposure using an exchange rate option.

2. Describe the advantages and disadvantages of

   a. A money market hedge
   b. A forward hedge
   c. An option

3. Suppose that you are bidding on a tender to provide a foreign government with earth-moving equipment. The bid is due next week, the government will announce the winning bid four months later, and the equipment is to be delivered exactly one year from now. You offer to supply the equipment at 412,500,000 euros, a price which you think stands a reasonably good chance of winning. However, there is no certainty of winning the bid. You have set your dollar price based on your estimated cost plus transportation and the one-year-forward exchange rate currently being quoted of 0.86 euros per US dollar. Describe how you would hedge your possible exchange rate exposure for your bid.

4. Could all foreign exchange exposure in the entire world ever be hedged?

5. Toyota continues to increase its sales in the United States, which implies increased dollar earnings for the Japanese firm. Explain what hedging strategies Toyota could use to reduce its dollar exposure. How many of these do you think Toyota might already be using?

6. Use Table 4.1 in Chapter 4 and look at the spot and one-year forward exchange rates for the British pound and US dollar.

   a. Suppose you know that the US dollar interest rate is 4% per year, show how the interest parity condition, the spot rate, and the forward rate enable you to find the pound interest rate.

b. Once you have the pound interest rate, explain how a US firm can use a money market hedge to eliminate the exchange risk of a 1 million pound tax payment to the British government one year from now.

7. Suppose that a US airline orders eight regional jets from Embraer of Brazil. Embraer charges US$15,000,000 for each of the aircraft, and payment will be received when the aircraft is delivered in three years. The spot exchange rate between the US dollar and the Brazilian real is US$1.00 = R$3.00, and there is no forward market for the two currencies. Explain how Embraer could hedge its foreign exchange exposure. Are there any possible hedging strategies that do not involve financial markets?

8. Currency swaps are touted by some financial experts as the solution to the "missing hedge" for long-term international investment. It has always proven difficult to hedge the exchange rate exposure for direct foreign investment and other very long-term commitments in foreign currencies. Explain how currency swaps can hedge long-run streams of payments or revenues. Then discuss whether currency swaps can really substantially reduce the long-term exchange rate exposure.

References

Baxter, M and A Stockman (1989). Business cycles and the exchange rate system. *Journal of Monetary Economics*, 23, 377–400.

Devereux, MB and C Engel (2002). Exchange rate pass-through, exchange rate volatility, and exchange rate disconnect. NBER Working Paper 7665.

Duarte, M and A Stockman (2001). Rational speculation and exchange rates. NBER Working Paper 8362.

Flood, R and AK Rose (1995). Fixing exchange rates: A virtual quest for fundamentals. *Journal of Monetary Economics*, 36, 3–37.

Hellerstein, R (2004). Who bears the cost of a change in the exchange rate? The case of imported beer. Federal Reserve Bank of New York Staff Report No. 179, February.

Krugman, P (1989). *Exchange Rate Instability*. Cambridge, MA: MIT Press.

Chapter 6

The Microstructure of
Foreign Exchange Markets

Our results suggest that, in foreign exchange, trading begets trading. The trading begotten is relatively uninformative, arising from repeated passage of inventory imbalance among dealers.

(Richard Lyons.[1])

The Bank for International Settlements (BIS) reports that the volume of the global foreign exchange markets is approaching $4 trillion per day. That daily level of foreign exchange transactions implies that the total currency trades needed to pay for one year's exports would be concluded in a couple of days. What purpose do all the currency trades serve for the rest of the time then?

The quote by Richard Lyons above provides some insight into why the foreign exchange markets are so very large in terms of the value of money exchanged compared to annual value of international trade and investment flows. Lyons is one of a growing number of financial economists who study the microstructure of the foreign exchange markets. By *microstructure*, we mean all the details, including the technology, management, and minute-to-minute trading flows, of the

---

[1] Lyons, Richard K. (1996). p. 198.

over-the-counter foreign exchange markets around the world. Traditional exchange rate models link foreign exchange rates to macro-economic variables such as price levels, interest rates, trade flows, and asset demand. But if most of the daily trades on the foreign exchange market are driven by something other than international trade and investment, those models are not accurate. The evidence shows that those models have not explained or predicted exchange rates accurately. This chapter describes the microstructure of the foreign exchange markets. Perhaps a better understanding of exactly how these markets function will enable financial economists to improve their models.

Chapter Goals

1. Provide more details on the foreign exchange markets.
2. Present the Bank for International Settlements (BIS) 2007 survey results, which show that the US dollar dominates foreign exchange transactions, London increased its geographic leadership, and trading volume grew to $3.2 trillion daily volume in 2007.
3. Discuss the shift to electronic communications and how technological change is affecting the foreign exchange market.
4. Explain how the $3 trillion-plus daily trading volume is largely the result of arbitrage and inventory adjustment trades, not fundamental demand and speculation.
5. Present and explain the evidence of fraud in the foreign exchange market.
6. Discuss the importance of fundamentals versus technical analysis in the foreign exchange market, and what this means for customers.

6.1 Overview of Today's Foreign Exchange Market

Over-the-counter dealers buy and sell foreign exchange to customers on demand. These dealers will accept temporary exposure to the risk of changing exchange rates by holding foreign exchange, unlike independent brokers, who match buyers and sellers but do not themselves ever hold foreign exchange. Not all of the dealers are what we call *market makers*, which are dealers who regularly quote both bids and offers for one or more currencies and stand ready to commit the firm's capital to complete the transactions at those quoted prices. It is the market makers who provide the price information that guides the market and permits trades upon demand.

Table 6.1 shows that in 2007, dealers located in the United States accounted for 16.6 percent of the world's foreign exchange transactions, down from 19.2 percent three years earlier. The United Kingdom, which has been the dominant location for foreign exchange transactions for as long as the Bank for International Settlements has compiled its series of triennial surveys of the foreign exchange market, increased its market-leading position over the past three years to 34.1 percent of the total worldwide value of foreign exchange transactions.

6.1.1 *Geographic concentration is increasing*

There are approximately 200 major foreign exchange dealers in London, compared to about 100 in the United States. London has a long history of financial dealings, and its current prominence in foreign exchange dealings is the result of centuries of banking

Table 6.1 Geographical Location of Foreign Exchange Trading, 1 April 2007.

	1989	1992	1995	1998	2001	2004	2007
United Kingdom	25.6%	27.0%	29.5%	32.5%	31.2%	31.3%	34.1%
United States	16.0	15.5	15.5	17.9	15.7	19.2	16.6
Japan	15.5	11.2	10.2	6.9	9.1	8.3	6.0
Singapore	7.7	6.9	6.7	7.1	6.2	5.2	5.8
Germany	—	5.1	4.8	4.8	5.5	4.9	2.5
Switzerland	7.8	6.1	5.5	4.2	4.4	3.3	6.1
Hong Kong	6.8	5.6	5.7	4.0	4.1	4.2	4.4

Source: BIS (2007).

experience. The London-based dealers are not all British banks, however. London branches of US banks account for about half of London's foreign exchange transactions. In terms of volume, about 85 percent of all trades in London are carried out by non-British financial firms.

Worldwide, over 2,000 banks and other financial institutions reported to the Bank of International Settlements (BIS) that they were active in the foreign exchange markets in 2007.[2] Just 100–200 of these institutions are active *market makers* that stand ready to buy or sell in all amounts to all takers, and just a small number of these account for the great majority of foreign exchange transactions. According to the Federal Reserve Bank of New York, of the 93 major foreign exchange dealers operating in the United States in 1998, 82 were large commercial banks. Over the past decade, there has been a slow but persistent decline in the number of market makers in the foreign exchange market.

Table 6.2 shows that in 2007, over 86 percent of foreign exchange transactions involved the US dollar as one of the currencies exchanged. This percentage seems rather high given that the United States accounts for less than 20 percent of world trade in goods and services, but there are several reasons why the dollar dominates the worldwide foreign exchange market.

6.1.2 *Dominance of the US dollar*

Many international transactions are denominated in dollars even when they are not between countries that use the dollar as their currencies. For example, commodities such as oil, coffee, and copper are priced in dollars. Many international loans by large commercial banks to firms and governments of developing economies are set in US dollars. Finally, central banks around the world hold about 65–75 percent of their reserves in dollars and use dollars to intervene in the foreign exchange markets. Government intervention in the

---

[2] BIS (2007).

Table 6.2   Currencies Exchanged in the Foreign Exchange Market.

Currency (%)	1989	1992	1995	1998	2001	2004	2007
US dollar	90%	82.0%	83.3%	87.3%	90.4%	88.7%	86.3%
Euro	—	—	—	—	37.6	37.2	37.0
Deusche mark	27	39.6	36.1	30.1	—	—	—
Japanese yen	27	23.4	24.1	20.2	22.7	20.3	16.5
British pound	15	13.6	9.4	11.0	13.2	16.9	15.0
Swiss franc	10	8.4	7.3	7.1	6.1	6.1	6.8
French franc	2	3.8	7.9	5.1	—	—	—
Australian dollar	2	2.5	2.7	3.1	4.2	5.5	6.7
Canadian dollar	1	3.3	3.4	3.6	4.5	4.2	4.2
All others	26	23.4	25.8	32.5	21.3	21.7	27.5
Total*	200%	200%	200%	200%	200%	200%	200%

Source: BIS (2007).
*Total percentage shares sum to 200% because every transaction involves two currencies.

foreign exchange markets has been a normal occurrence since World War II. Foreign exchange reserves and intervention have increased in recent years.

A second reason for the prominence of the US dollar in foreign exchange transactions is that the dollar serves as a *vehicle currency* for many trades of less common currencies. For example, if you want to exchange the Uruguayan pesos for Malaysian ringgit, you will have to first trade pesos for dollars and then dollars for ringgit. Such round-about trades are actually more efficient than trading pesos directly for ringgit because the peso–dollar and ringgit–dollar markets are much larger than a peso–ringgit market would be. The peso–dollar and ringgit–dollar markets therefore provide more accurate information and greater *liquidity* to market participants. *Market liquidity* refers to the promptness with which market participants can close trades in precisely the quantities of currencies desired. Also, with a smaller number of markets, dealers and other market participants do not need to hold working balances in as many different currencies. This implies economies of scale. Table 6.3 provides further details on the specific currency pairs that are most often traded.

Table 6.3   Foreign Exchange Turnover by Currency Pairs.

	1992	1995	1998	2001	2004	2007
$US/€	—	—	—	30%	28%	27%
$US/DM	25%	22%	20%	—	—	—
$US/JP¥	20	21	18	20	17	13
$US/UK£	10	7	8	11	14	12
$US/SFr	6	5	5	5	4	5
$US/FFr	2	4	4	—	—	—
$US/$CAN	3	3	3	4	4	4
$US/$AUS	2	3	3	4	5	6
$US/Other Europe	8	11	13	—	—	—
$US/others	6	6	12	17	17	21
€/JP¥	—	—	—	3	3	2
€/others	—	—	—	5	5	8
Euro pairs	8	9	5	—	—	—
All others	12%	9%	11%	1%	7%	4%
Total	100%	100%	100%	100%	100%	100%

Source: BIS (2007).

There is, of course, no guarantee that the dollar will always continue to play the role of unit of account for commodities and financial instruments or that it will continue to serve as the principal vehicle currency in the growing foreign exchange market. Nevertheless, the economies of scale that the dollar has attained as a vehicle currency cannot so easily be taken over by another currency, although the new euro may challenge the hegemony of the US dollar in the foreign exchange markets. In 2005 and 2006, there were more bonds issued in euros than dollars, for example, and in early 2008, the European Union had become a bigger financial market than the United States.[3]

6.1.3 *A 24-h worldwide market*

Modern communications have created an integrated world market for foreign exchange that essentially functions 24-h per day. There

---

[3] Gillian Tett (2008). "US May Have Lost Financial Lead to Europe, Says Report", *Financial Times*, January 16.

are major financial centers where large dealers are located in nearly every time zone of the world. When it is late afternoon in San Francisco and its financial markets are closing, markets in Auckland, New Zealand, in Sydney, Australia, and in Tokyo, Japan are just opening. And, before those markets close, other markets in Singapore in Southeast Asia and Bahrain in the Middle East will have opened, followed by the foreign exchange dealers in the financial centers of Europe. Then, as the European markets enter their afternoon trading, dealers in New York open, followed by dealers in Chicago and San Francisco, at which point the whole cycle starts over again.

The foreign exchange market is, far and away, the largest financial market in the world. The overall volume of the spot, forward, and swap markets in 2007 exceeded U$S3.2 trillion per day.

Table 6.4 shows how the volume of foreign exchange transactions has been rising rapidly over the past two decades. Notice, however, that the overall volume of foreign exchange transactions briefly contracted in 2001. This blip in the otherwise consistent growth of foreign exchange transactions was due to the introduction of a single currency in Europe, the euro, which suddenly eliminated the large amount of currency trades between 12 European currencies. By the time the Bank for International Settlements did its 2004 survey, however, the market had already reached a new record average daily turnover level of about $1.8 trillion. The remainder of this chapter will help you understand why there are so many spot, forward, and swap transactions.

Table 6.4   Global Foreign Exchange Market Turnover (US$ Billions).

	1989	1992	1995	1998	2001	2004	2007
Spot transactions	317	394	494	568	387	621	1,005
Forward transactions	27	58	97	128	131	208	362
Foreign exchange swaps	190	324	546	734	656	944	1,714
Total turnover[1]	590	820	1,190	1,490	1,200	1,800	3,210

Source: BIS (2007).

6.2 The Evolving Foreign Exchange Market

Ten years ago, the trading rooms of the major foreign exchange dealers located in the major financial centers around the world consisted of rows of desks covered with computers, screens, telephones, and other modern communications equipment. State-of-the-art equipment, worth millions of dollars, provided the dealers with direct links to customers, other dealers, other dealer institutions, information services, electronic brokering systems, and "back offices" that performed the paperwork supporting the trades carried out, and other support staff. But, despite the sophistication of the equipment, a deal was only completed when someone yelled "done" into the telephone. "It was bloody noisy and bloody good fun", says an ex-dealer disenchanted with life in today's foreign exchange market.[4]

6.2.1 *Recent evolution of the market*

The past ten years have witnessed radical changes in the way foreign exchange markets operate. The recent changes have been revolutionary, not only for the people working in the market, but in how the market functions.

The foreign exchange market has always been evolving. The nature of currency trading gives the market participants strong economic incentives to innovate and apply the new technologies. The importance of speed for exploiting arbitrage opportunities and covering risk means that the trading rooms have a strong incentive to use the very latest in communications technology. Just as currency dealers were the first users of the transatlantic cable back in the 19th century, dealer institutions today invest large amounts of money in upgrading their equipment.

Competition among the dealer institutions, and the resulting pressure on margins, has accelerated management changes. Dealer institutions have improved the overall organization of currency

---

[4] Jennifer Hughes (2004). "The Mouse Takes Over the Floor", *Financial Times*, 27 May 2004.

trading. The much higher trading volumes and the decreasing competitive margins on each transaction combine to make mistakes more costly. Dealers face various risks. Price risk is, of course, a given: according to the Federal Reserve Bank of New York's description of the foreign exchange market, "a gap of a few moments or less can be long enough to see what was thought to be a profitable transactions changed to a costly loss".[5] There are further risks, however, such as credit risk if borrowed funds are being used to buy currencies, settlement risk if contracts are not all settled at the same moment, and sovereign risk if transactions are taking place in different political jurisdictions. Dealer institutions put a considerable portion of their capital at risk for extended periods of time. They thus devote a large amount of resources to managing risk.

One of the ways in which dealer institutions have reduced the risk has been to add a layer of management. Many banks who deal in foreign exchange have created "mid offices" that support the actual online dealers. The dealer banks have always had "back offices" that performed the paperwork required to complete the transactions initiated by the traders. The mid-office serves another function, however, namely the support and supervision of the traders as they work. The mid-office keeps centralized information on what all of its dealers are doing in the various foreign exchange markets in order to properly assess the risk, apply the risk-reducing hedging strategies, and keep the track of specific currency and time exposures. The mid-office staff in most dealer institutions also checks on the validity of the prices and quantities quoted, analyzes the risks involved in each transaction, and prescribes the supplementary transactions required to minimize the exposure to risk. The mid-office thus continuously modifies the trading strategy pursued by the institution's traders, and it gives traders explicit instructions to buy or sell the currency or options when it discovers imbalances and excessive risks. The growth of mid-offices is undermining the independence of the traders, but the managers of the dealers feel that in today's foreign exchange markets, completely

---

[5] Sam Y. Cross (1998). p. 77.

independent traders cannot perform as efficiently, or as profitably, as traders supported by a mid-office.

The changes in technology now threaten the very existence of individual traders. Computerized trading is becoming more common, and many jobs at the major dealers will be lost as more customers trade directly. Also, the dealer institutions continue to expand their use of computers to perform routine arbitrage. The number of "voice" brokers left in the market may continue to decline further, especially if computers begin to do more of the mid-office work as well.

6.2.2 *Rankings of dealer institutions*

Market concentration among dealer institutions has been increasing for the past few years, contrary to the predictions some years back that the new electronic communications platforms that link the dealers would lead to more competitors to enter the market. Instead, the improved communications has increased the competition, and margins have become very tight. The spread between buy and sell prices can be as little as two "pips", that is, two one-hundredths of a cent. Profits can still be high in the foreign exchange market, but they depend on volume. Given the fixed costs associated with entering the market, which are in the form of equipment, building a customer base, and keeping scarce and expensive, highly qualified labor, the industry is characterized by economies of scale. Thus, concentration has been increasing.

Table 6.5 shows the ten largest dealers in the market for foreign exchange for 2009. For comparison, the rankings from five years earlier, 2004, are also shown. In the main over-the-counter market for foreign exchange, three banks handle nearly one-half of the total value of foreign exchange transactions, Deutsche Bank, UBS (Union Bank Switzerland), and Barclays Capital. The top ten dealer institutions are all large private international banking firms. The market shares are based on 2004 and 2009 surveys by *Euromoney* magazine.

Table 6.5   Top Ten Dealer Banks Market Shares.

2009		2004	
Company	Share (%)	Company	Share (%)
Deutsche Bank	21.0	UBS	12.4
UBS	14.6	Deutsche Bank	12.2
Barclays capital	10.5	Citigroup	9.4
RBS	8.2	J.P. Morgan	5.8
Citigroup	7.3	HSBC	4.9
J.P. Morgan	5.4	Goldman Sachs	4.5
HSBC	4.1	Barclays	4.1
Goldman Sachs	3.4	CSFB/Credit Suisse	3.8
Credit Suisse	3.1	RBS	3.5
BNP Paribas	2.3	Merrill Lynch	3.5

Source: Euromoney, as published in the *Financial Times*, 27 May 2004; Euromoney (2009). "FX Poll 2009: Emabattled Banks boosted by Performance in Booming FX Markets", www.euromoneyfix.com.

Since the foreign exchange market is largely unregulated and open for any firm to enter, the increased concentration and the decline in the overall number of dealers over the past decade suggest that there are economies of scale to dealing in foreign exchange. A firm that wants to begin dealing in foreign exchange needs only to connect to one or both of the interbank communications platforms, Reuters and EBS, hire a competent staff, and attract customers who want to buy and sell foreign exchange. To make a profit, however, a foreign exchange dealer must gain a large enough volume of business to be able to offer clients the liquidity they demand and to make the money at the small margins between buy and sell prices.

In 2009, the top dealer institution, Deutsche Bank, handled 21 percent of the total market's volume, five years ago the largest dealer, Union Bank Switzerland, handled just over 12 percent of a much smaller total volume. Twenty years ago, the largest dealer had just over 4 percent market share. There was also some repositioning among the top ten dealers. The US financial giants Citigroup,

Goldman Sachs, and J.P. Morgan all fell two rungs and lost market share. Ten years earlier, Citigroup led the market. Another US financial group, Merrill Lynch, fell out of the top ten altogether; it ranked 20th among dealers in 2009. The British HSBC also lost ground, but Barclays and RBS (Royal Bank of Scotland) moved up sharply in volume and the ranking.

Many smaller dealers in the market concentrate on just one segment of the total foreign exchange market. UBS, Deutsche Bank, Citibank, and other large players make markets in most or all of the major currencies, but smaller dealers handle just one or a few currencies. By focusing on one currency, they can still generate the volume to offer customers the liquidity they demand to quickly close deals for exactly the volume and timing they need, but they do not have to build a worldwide presence like the major dealers have. These smaller dealers usually also offer their clients exchanges of other currencies through other dealer institutions.

6.2.3 *Foreign exchange brokers*

Brokers differ from dealers in that they do not take any side of a transaction. Their task is to bring buyers and sellers together. Where dealers commit their own capital to buy or sell the currencies in order to subsequently earn a spread by concluding the opposite side of a trade with another customer, brokers earn predetermined commissions from their match-making service. Brokers offer their customers anonymity, and because they are not bound to any one particular dealer, they provide greater liquidity as well. But there is a price for this service. Brokers still have to go through the dealer-operated over-the-counter market, which means the customer pays the dealer spread in addition to the brokers' commissions. The decline in the number of brokers in recent years is no doubt due to the shrinking margins that customers are willing to pay for brokers' services. Dealing directly with dealers is cheaper. The new electronic brokering systems automate many of the match-making functions brokers have traditionally performed, which means these technological advances will further cut into brokers' market share, as these systems provide degrees of confidentiality similar to brokers.

Brokers were involved in about one-quarter of all foreign exchange transactions in the over-the-counter market in 2000. This share was down sharply from about 50 percent of all transactions some 15 years earlier, and by 2005 brokers handled only a very small proportion of all foreign exchange trades. Electronic brokering systems have replaced the live brokers.

6.3 Electronic Trading

In the late 1800s, the telephone replaced the telegraph as the main form of communication in the foreign exchange markets. For 100 years, foreign exchange dealers communicated among each other and with their customers using the telephone. Then, in the early 1980s, Reuters introduced the first electronic trading system, the Monitor Dealing Service. This system allowed communications between two dealers at the initiative of one of the two. The information on the computer screens included the details of the bid–offer spread, and the two dealers could then adjust and close the deal with several more simple computer messages. In 1989, Reuters introduced an improved version of the system, called Reuters Dealing 2000-1. While they permitted quicker communications, the systems were not really much different from the traditional telephone calls.

6.3.1 *The introduction of electronic communications*

In 1992, Reuters introduced a much more sophisticated system, called Reuters Dealing 2000-2, that matched the buy-and-sell quotes from a set of preselected dealers. Rather than just a replacement for the telephone, this new system effectively began replacing the foreign exchange brokers, whose personal communications took much longer to find matches than the automated system. A group of Japanese foreign exchange brokers and dealer banks set up its own electronic brokering system called Minex in early 1993. Later that year, a group of large dealing banks set up another competitor to Reuters called

Electronic Brokering Service, or EBS. In 1996, Minex transferred its business over to EBS, leaving two major interdealer electronic brokering systems handling the most electronic dealer-to-dealer trades. Telephone trades continued to account for a substantial proportion of foreign exchange trades, especially for trades involving very large sums of money, but gradually more and more of the dealer-to-dealer trades were carried out electronically. In 1992, less than five percent of dealer-to-dealer trades were handled electronically, but by 1998 the share of electronic trades had reached 40 percent of the total. By 2004, about two-thirds of all dealer-to-dealer trades were done through the two electronic brokering platforms, although in terms of money volume, over half of all foreign exchange traded was still done by telephone.

6.3.2 *Electronic dealer-to-customer platforms*

In 2006, most dealer-to-customer trades were still carried out by phone, but electronic dealer-to-customer platforms were beginning to make inroads. Proprietary platforms operated by individual dealers and some multibank platforms now permit some customers to deal directly with dealers in the foreign exchange market. There is a major difference between the proprietary platforms, which only give customers' access to one foreign exchange dealer, and the so-called multibank platforms that effectively let the customers' trade with each other directly.

Initially, the major dealer banks gave certain large customers immediate access to the dealer's price quotes. Customers usually acquired the access to several of these single-bank platforms so they could compare prices from different dealers, much as they had always done by telephone. Since the advent of new direct customer-brokering platforms that gather dealer quotes from many banks and provide access to many customers, price comparisons have become even easier. As a result, the margins enjoyed by dealers have diminished to where the number of market makers, which are those banks that always stand ready to quote the buy-and-sell prices, has fallen. Recall that above we mentioned the apparent consolidation of the industry.

Electronic trading may have contributed to this trend even though in some ways entry has become easier.

Table 6.5 shows that in 2004, two dealer-to-customer platforms accounted for the majority of computerized dealer–customer transactions. FXAll and FXConnect account for over 80 percent of all computerized dealer-to-customer transactions. The remaining platforms cater to smaller groups of customers with special requirements or cover small groups of banks. According to one 2005 report, for example, HotspotFX caters mostly to hedge funds.[6] The dealer-to-customer market is still very small, in large part because dealers do not want to relinquish their control over currency trading. Most large customers continue to just call the dealers. Much of the growth in the customer accessible computerized brokering services is driven by hedge funds, which increasingly use the foreign exchange markets as part of their investment strategies. Hedge funds are large enough to pressure the dealers into giving them direct access.

6.3.3 *Retail currency exchange*

The over-the-counter market never served the retail foreign exchange market. A separate retail market developed in the form of booths at airports, border crossings, and tourist destinations. Currency exchange offices can also be found in major cities and in certain retail businesses. For example, Marks & Spencer department stores in Britain exchange currencies on a cash basis. These retail exchanges are very expensive, often charging as much as a ten percent premium above the over-the-counter exchange rates plus, in many instances additional fees. Your author is, at the time of writing, still carrying around a 20 pound note from a trip to Britain a year earlier because he refused to pay the $5 fee plus a 12 percent premium charged in the cash market at the airport!

In 2009, financial newspapers like the *Financial Times* and *Wall Street Journal* contained many advertisements for online foreign

---

[6] Jennifer Hughes (2005). "FX Platforms See Volumes Shoot Up", *Financial Times*, 17 March.

exchange trading. These advertisements were aimed at individual investors and small businesses to entice them to become hedgers and speculators. These online systems are linked to the trading systems of the over-the-counter market.

These online systems are set up mainly to attract the individual speculators or, better said, the gamblers. Typically, speculative online foreign currency trades exploit small short-term market movements, which provide large gains only if they are highly leveraged. The online systems therefore offer leverage as high as 100:1, in some cases even 200:1.[7] That is, speculators can buy or sell currencies in amounts 100 times the amount of capital they deposit with the system. For example, a speculator with $10,000 deposited with the system can bet that the dollar will appreciate the next day relative to the one-day forward exchange rate by committing to buy $1 million in dollars forward one day. If the dollar indeed becomes one percent more expensive the next day, the speculator simultaneously buys the $1 million as contracted and sells them on the spot market for one percent more to earn $10,000 (one percent of $1 million), exactly 100 percent of the $10,000 on deposit with the trading system. Hence, 100:1 leverage converts a one percent change in the exchange rate into a 100 percent profit on the actual money deposited.

Of course, if the one percent change is in the wrong direction, and the dollar depreciated the next day, then the speculator can only sell the dollars she is committed to buy at 99 percent of the purchase price, a $10,000 loss that completely wipes out the bettor's deposit. It is worth noting that currency traders for banks and hedge funds seldom leverage more than 10:1.

The National Futures Association, the self-regulatory organization for the US futures markets, offers this legalistic cautionary message:

Like many other investments, off-exchange foreign currency trading caries a high level of risk and may not be suitable for all investors. In

---

[7] Jack Egan (2005). "Check the Currency Risk. Then Multiply by 100", *New York Times*, 19 June.

fact, you could lose all of your initial investment and may be liable for additional losses. Therefore, you need to understand the risks associated with this product so you may make an informed investment decision. This ... does not suggest that you should or should not participate in the retail off-exchange foreign currency market. You should make that decision after consulting with your own financial advisor and considering your own financial situation and objectives.[8]

This weak warning in a booklet promoting online foreign exchange speculation does not reassure us that self-regulation can work. In fact, much stronger warnings are in order, such as on average, participants will lose the money. Just like in Las Vegas or Macao, these online casinos (online trading platforms) take a small fraction of every transaction. Leveraging adds further borrowing costs and fees. Therefore, what may seem like a zero-sum game because foreign exchange rates fluctuate near-randomly in the short run, once transaction costs and fees are added in, foreign exchange speculation becomes a negative-sum game.

Quite aside from the buy–sell spread, interest costs for leveraging, and additional fees, there is still the problem of "gambler's ruin". In a repeated fair (zero-sum) game in which gains and losses occur randomly in each stage of the game, the participant with the least capital to draw on will tend to go bankrupt first. In the foreign exchange market, participants forget that they effectively play against the entire market, which collectively has nearly infinite amounts of capital. Hence, any individual participant with some limited amount of capital to devote to foreign exchange speculation (gambling) will eventually lose everything. It is only a matter time.

The large dealers (banks) in the over-the-counter market have welcomed the growth of online retail trading because they see it as an addition to their business. The over-the-counter dealers ultimately carry out the trades placed in the online retail market. Some financial economists have argued that the added volume from the speculative

---

[8] National Futures Association (2004). p. 1.

trading in the online retail market has indirectly helped all foreign currency traders by increasing the liquidity and lowering the transactions costs. Evidence of this is sparse and unconvincing, however. On the other hand, the online speculation may make foreign exchange markets, and exchange rates, more volatile, and thus, less useful, for those who use the foreign exchange market for international trade and investment. We'll return to this issue in Section 6.8 below, as well as in later chapters dealing with the international financial industry and the recent financial crisis.

6.4 The Changing Microstructure of the Over-the-Counter Market

Many economists have noted that while the foreign exchange market seems to respond largely to economic fundamentals in the long run, over short-term horizons of minutes, hours, days, and even weeks, the market seems to be driven by other forces. Some analysts have suggested that the structure of the foreign exchange market may help to explain short run market behavior. According to Flood and Taylor (1996), "It is apparent that there are important influences, not on the list of standard macrofundamentals, that affect short-run exchange rate behavior...".[9]

One issue that especially concerned economists was how the structure affected exchange rate volatility. Also, many economists and dealers have asked how costs and competition are being affected by the advances in computerized brokening and direct-dealer-to-customer trading.

6.4.1 *Centralization of the market*

The foreign exchange market has, for 100 years, been characterized by its decentralized structure. Foreign exchange trades have been carried out by dealers who are physically separated and communicated by telephone. Research on market structure in general suggests that the

---

[9] Flood and Taylor (1996). p. 285.

degree of centralization of a market influences its performance. Centralized markets more quickly eliminate arbitrage opportunities, and they do a better job of executing trades in accordance to traders' specific requirements. Information is disseminated much more slowly in decentralized markets than in centralized exchanges, where everyone can observe the price movements immediately. Flood (1994) specifically found that there are significant inefficiencies in the foreign exchange markets related to inventory imbalances inherent in a decentralized market. Dealers must engage in frequent and large transactions to keep the inventories in balance, and such transactions are costly. Bid–ask price margins tend to be larger in decentralized markets because of the higher costs, but, of course, dealers can demand higher margins because they have greater market power due to the fact that customers have less information about competing prices. Overall, therefore, decentralized over-the-counter markets are costlier than centralized exchanges.

Decentralized markets are different from centralized exchanges because dealer quotes are not observable to all market participants. Market fragmentation implies that different deals may be closed with different prices at the same time. A centralized foreign exchange market would be more transparent because one price applies to all deals and every participant could observe the bids and offers of other participants. The foreign exchange markets in most countries have no disclosure requirements, and trades are observed only by the buyer and seller. Outside customers can only observe those bid and ask prices they are offered directly and at which they actually trade currencies.

The brokered portion of the foreign exchange market has always been a little more transparent than the dealer-to-dealer portion of the market because brokers accumulate sets of orders. However, brokers do not often reveal the range of prices they observe, and even brokers see a very small portion of the total market.

6.4.2 *Do electronic systems imply more transparency and efficiency?*

Although they are viewed by some as nothing more than lower-cost replacements for the traditional telephones and brokers, the electronic brokering systems have changed the process of price discovery and the way price information is disseminated among the dealers and to the public. The electronic brokering systems like Reuters and EBS are open only to dealers, who account for about 95 percent of the foreign exchange market volume. These electronic systems have been referred to as "virtual centralization" because they effectively communicate with all market participants at once. There may be more price transparency now as prices are set more accurately and more quickly, dealers have instant access to current prices, and an increasing number of outside customers have demanded direct access to the same systems the dealers use.

When the foreign exchange market consisted of decentralized two-way telephone conversations, the "market price" was actually a small range of prices being quoted at that moment by dealers across the globe. In order to be continuously informed about market prices, dealers would regularly execute small trades throughout the day.

In sum, increased transparency makes it easier for new dealers to enter the market because the learning costs have been reduced as the process has become easier. On the other hand, established dealers may increasingly leave the market because past learning and experience no longer enhance the profits as much with the convenient electronic brokering systems. The profitability of foreign exchange dealing appears to have declined, in large part due to the competition from new electronic dealer–customer systems.

6.5 Explaining the $3 Trillion Per Day Volume

As noted at the start of this chapter, the huge volume of trade on the foreign exchange market cannot be explained by the underlying international trade, international investment, immigrant remittances, and other international payments categorized in the balance of payments of the world's 200-plus economies. International trade of goods and services plus total international investment in real and financial assets by private citizens and business account for just a couple of percentage points, certainly less than five percent, of the daily volume of the foreign exchange markets around the world. So why are the other 95 percent or more of the more than $3 trillion in currency trades carried out each day?

6.5.1 *Arbitrage*

A very substantial portion of currency trades are motivated by arbitrage opportunities. Recall the three types of arbitrage that keep exchange rates unified across the distinct geographic locations of the market, across the many cross-currency rates, and between the current spot and expected future spot rates. Arbitrage opportunities develop every time an exchange rate changes in one location, between one pair of currencies, or at one point in time. That is, every time there is a trade initiated because someone exports or imports a good, acquires or sells a foreign asset, or transfers a payment from one currency to another, additional arbitrage trades are triggered.

For example, suppose an Indian call center signs a contract for $5 million to provide customer service calls for an American firm, with payment for the services to be made in one month. The Indian firm calls its bank in India to purchase $5 million worth of rupees forward one month, an act that increases the supply of dollars and the demand for rupees in the forward market. Thus, all other things equal, the forward price of rupees will tend to rise relative to the price of dollars in the forward foreign exchange market in India. This may well result in arbitrage opportunities between forward and spot markets, and these trades will tend to also raise the spot market price of rupees in terms of dollars to where the spot rate is again compatible with the new forward rate as prescribed by the interest parity condition. The shift in the spot and forward rates will generate opportunities for geographic arbitrage, resulting in one or probably several trades between dealers in India and other parts of the world to reunify the exchange rates throughout the world. There may also be a variety of triangular arbitrage opportunities when the rupee/dollar exchange rate changes, thus spreading the change in one exchange rate to exchange rates between other currency pairs. Thus, it is clear that a currency trade directly related to one of the fundamental international transactions recorded on the balance of payments triggers a whole series of subsequent dealer-to-dealer currency trades to exploit the arbitrage opportunities created by the initial currency trade.

6.5.2 *Hot potato process*

Arbitrage is not the only reason why the volume of foreign exchange trades swamps the volume of fundamental trade and investment-driven trades. Also important is the continual management of currency inventories by dealers, increasingly directed by mid-offices. Any trade carried out by a market-making dealer in one institution with a dealer in another institution immediately alters the inventories of currencies in the possession of each market-making institution. Dealers have a strong incentive to carefully manage their currency inventories because the impact of exchange rate changes on total value of a dealer institution's inventory depends on the mix of currencies in the inventory. Lyons (1996, 1998) and Neely and Weller (2001) examined the detailed data on intraday trading and found that most dealers close their positions at the end of each trading day; that is, they conduct currency trades to eliminate the speculative positions in any particular currency. Therefore, customer-initiated trades trigger further interdealer trades to correct the inventory imbalance.

A simple example illustrates how inventory adjustments by dealers can trigger a whole series of follow-up currency trades. Suppose that foreign exchange dealers are risk-averse, and each dealer currently has the mix of currencies deemed optimal. If a customer then purchases $10 million worth of Canadian dollars from one of the market-making dealers, that dealer's inventory is no longer optimal. Not wanting to carry $10 million extra US dollars and so few Canadian dollars, the dealer begins to adjust its inventory. Suppose, specifically, that the mid-office calculates it only wants to hold on to ten percent of the newly acquired US dollars. We assume here that the dealer's bank is willing to increase its holdings of US dollars a little because the previous sale may have pushed the price of the dollars slightly below its long-run value, suggesting the dollars may appreciate soon). The mid-office therefore instructs one of its traders to call another dealer and unload $9 million worth of US dollars in exchange for Canadian dollars. Suppose that this other dealer similarly seeks to adjust its inventory after making a market for the first dealer. This second dealer thus calls yet another dealer to sell $8.1 million. In the limit, the total interdealer volume generated from the $10 million customer trade is ($9 million)/(1 − 0.9) = $90 million. Thus, the example produces a tenfold increase in foreign exchange transactions. Notice also that international trade accounted for just ten percent of the total increase in foreign exchange transactions. Lyons (1996) calls this inventory adjustment process among dealers the *hot potato process*.

6.5.3 *Speculation*

Speculators have been accused of disrupting markets in general, and the foreign exchange markets in particular. The former Prime Minister of Malaysia once called short-term investors and currency speculators the "highwaymen of the global economy".[10] Speculators are often described as producing nothing of value and profiting at the expense of hard-working people.

In the discussion of retail online foreign exchange trading, we, too, brought up some concerns about speculative trading. Nevertheless, speculators play an important role in foreign exchange markets. It is speculators who, along with the exporters, importers, international investors, and immigrants sending their income home, move foreign exchange rates. Recall the interest parity condition and the result that spot exchange rates are linked to expectations and speculative forecasts of future spot exchange rates.

Arbitrage does not change the exchange rates so much as it equalizes them across regions, currencies, and time. That is, arbitrage eliminates the differences in prices and equalizes sets of exchange rates. Speculation, on the other hand, changes entire sets of exchange rates. Speculators react to "news" by buying more of a currency or selling off a currency. An interesting case of arbitrage combined with speculation

---

[10] Mahatir Bin Mohamad (1997).

is the uncovered interest parity condition, where the arbitrager speculates about future exchange rates and arbitrages the difference between that expectation and the spot rate. Of course, speculators can also push the market far away from its long-run equilibrium.

6.5.4 *Why the foreign exchange market volume is so large?*

We have now essentially answered the question about why the foreign exchange market volume is so much larger than the fundamental transactions of the global economy, such as exporting, importing, lending, borrowing, and sending the remittances to overseas relatives. Shifts in supply and demand are also initiated by changes in expectations, which can induce both outside customers and the dealers themselves to become speculators by taking open positions in the market. But most activity in the foreign exchange market consists of arbitrage and inventory adjustments. Lyons (1998) estimates that less than ten percent of dealer-to-dealer trades can be considered speculative. And according to Neely and Weller (2001), "... there is little doubt that a much greater volume of transaction is accounted for by traders who close their positions at the end of the day than by those who take open positions with horizons of weeks or months".[11]

In sum, given the arbitrage triggered by a trade initiated by a customer-requested trade plus the *hot potato process* to adjust inventories, it is clear why the fundamental international transactions related to international trade and international investment recorded in the balance of payments account for a tiny fraction, certainly less than five percent, of all foreign exchange market transactions.

6.6 Corruption in the Foreign Exchange Market

The foreign exchange markets are almost entirely unregulated. Their decentralized structure contributes to the lack of regulation and government oversight; if any one government were to seek control or

---

[11] Neely and Weller (2001). p. 22.

tighter supervision of foreign exchange transactions, the business would simply shift to other less regulated locations. The potential for corruption is only mitigated by the self-regulation of the market by its participants. Dealer institutions have to manage their own traders, and market forces must then be relied on to effectively keep the dealers interested in maintaining their reputations as honest brokers. Occasionally there are problems, however.

6.6.1 *Allied Irish banks lost $750 million in 2002*

A famous example of what can happen when a foreign exchange dealer does not monitor the activities of one of its traders is the 1992 case of John Rusnak of Allied Irish Banks. Actually, Rusnak worked for Allfirst, a Maryland bank that had been acquired by Allied Irish Banks in 1989. Like many traders, Rusnak had permission to engage in some amount of speculative currency trading on behalf of his bank. So in early 2001, he began to bet that the Japanese yen would appreciate against the dollar. When the yen began to depreciate instead, Rusnak ran up large paper losses from speculative commitments to buy yen in the forward yen/dollar market. Traders routinely use options contracts to hedge the risk of aggressive positions, and according to Allied Irish Banks' internal controls, Rusnak seemed to be doing just that. In 2002, however, Allied Irish Banks found that Rusnak had not constructed his hedges, namely options to sell yen at his expected high prices in the future. In a statement issued in February of 2002, the bank stated that "... the foreign exchange deals were transacted in the normal manner. However, the offsetting currency options contracts were fictitious".[12]

Looking back, there obviously should have been more concern over the consistently wrong speculative positions taken in the yen/dollar market and a closer verification of the options contracts. But forged documents suggesting the existence of options contracts to

---

[12] From a statement issued by Allied Irish Banks and reported in the *Financial Times*, 7 February 2002.

offset the forward market losses enabled Rusnak to avoid closer scrutiny for about a year. Exactly how did Rusnak lose $750 million? The process went something like this:

1. In 2001, Rusnak began selling dollars forward at ¥123, hoping that the dollar would fall against the yen. Instead, the dollar rose to ¥130, leaving him with a loss of 5.6 percent.
2. Rusnak claimed he purchased dollar call options at ¥123, which would have covered the losses. The bank's back office received forged documents confirming the hedging contracts within a day.
3. When the forward contracts came due, the option contracts were found to be bogus. Allied Irish Banks were liable for a net payment of about $750 million, the difference between the contracted forward exchange rates and the actual spot exchange rates.

Many people were surprised that a relatively unimportant trader could have run up such huge losses. After all, at losses of less than six percent, an absolute loss of $750 million meant Rusnak must have accumulated an open position on currency trades of $12.5 billion! "Clearly, controls broke down and we don't wholly understand how those broke down", said Susan Keating, Allfirst's chief executive shortly after the news first broke about the losses.[13] The bank's system for measuring the performance had even singled out Mr. Rusnak for a bonus of $220,000 in 2001.

Foreign exchange traders were not the only ones out of control at Allied Irish Banks. Two years later in 2004, Allied Irish Banks revealed that it had "inadvertently" overcharged its customers by €14 million over eight years by levying a one percent charge on non-cash foreign exchange transactions instead of the stated 0.5 percent. The bank set aside €25 million to reimburse the customers. It

---

[13] Reported in John Murray Brown (2002). "Internal Controls To Be Scrutinized", *Financial Times*, 7 February.

claimed the error was caused by a software error.[14] It is clearly not easy to manage a complex modern bank.

6.6.2 *Fraud in New York in 2003*[15]

In 2003, an 18-month investigation by the F.B.I. led to the discovery of rigged currency trading by a group of 47 brokers from several currency brokerage houses and a smaller number of traders at five New York currency dealers, J.P. Morgan, UBS, Dresdner Kleinwort Wasserstein, and Société Générale. The brokers rigged prices and provided kickbacks to the traders carrying out the rigged trades. Over the course of the day, traders would engage in trades that would cause small losses for their banks, not unlike the small losses that normally occur over the course of a trader's day. Only, these losses were programed to occur across banks where fellow conspiring traders were located, and in each case the losses were designed so that the offsetting profits would end up in one account. At the end of the day, the profits accumulated in the account would be split among the conspirators.

The conspiracy was uncovered by having an F.B.I. agent posing as "a bad guy with money looking for bad things to do". The US Attorney in Manhattan, James Comey, said that the undercover F.B.I. agent "had more criminal schemes thrown at him than he could imagine". A number of the conspirators were found to have been involved in many fraudulent schemes, some amounting to over $100 million. Several of the conspirators had been defrauding their employers for over 20 years. According to the *Wall Street Journal*:

> ... the fact that so many individuals could apparently pull off the rigged trading and get caught only after an F.B.I. agent became involved may serve as a warning: the largely unregulated foreign

---

[14] Erik Portanger (2004). "AIB Encounters Fresh Worries Over Currencies", *Wall Street Journal*, 12 May.

[15] From Jonathan Fuerbringer and William K. Rashbaum (2003). "Currency Fraud ran Deep, Officials Say", *Wall Street Journal*, 20 November 2003.

exchange market, with trading volume of $1 trillion a day, is vulnerable, and banks' internal controls may not be strict enough.[16]

The *Wall Street Journal* quoted David Gilmore, a foreign exchange analyst: "What is astounding is that you have so many people involved. That is a lot of ducks to line up to commit fraud".

You might wonder what happened to those arrested in 2003. A brief search of the news media uncovers the conviction of one Anthony Iannuzzi in a Manhattan Federal District Court on 17 March 2005 for exactly the scheme described above. On 16 August of the same year, six more people plead guilty for the fraud.[17]

It is not clear whether foreign exchange markets are more or less honest than other financial markets. But John Rusnak and the 47 traders and employees of currency brokers were not the first to get caught abusing their freedom to trade large sums of money in an unregulated market. A few years earlier, in 1994, Nick Leeson brought down the centuries-old British financial firm Barings with losses of $1.38 billion from unauthorized currency trading in Asia. Barings no longer exists, its customer base having been absorbed by the Dutch financial firm ING in 1995 after the currency trading losses. From the examples above, the difficulty banks have in managing their own operations, the absence of oversight by government agencies, and the sheer amounts of money being traded almost guarantee that there will be more fraud in the future.

6.7 Technical Analysis vs. Fundamentals

Exchange rate models developed by economists invariably hypothesize that the exchange rate is some function of economic variables, or what we might call *fundamentals*. Chapter 4 pointed out how poorly such models have performed. At the end of that chapter, there was also a discussion of John Maynard Keynes' interpretation of expectations as

---

[16] Jonathan Fuerbringer and Wiliam K. Rashbaum (2003), *op. cit.*
[17] New York Times (2005). "6 Plead Guilty to Fraud in Currency Trading Case", 16 August, News Release, US Attorney, Southern District of New York, "Manhattan Federal Jury Convicts Former Police Officer in Trading Scandal", 17 March 2005.

depending on *convention*, which he defined as a set of beliefs that have been largely validated by recent experience. The adherence to convention creates some degree of certainty in the face of uncertainty. Now, research on the microfoundations of foreign exchange markets, in which researchers observe actual behavior of traders, suggests that traders often use simple rules based on past market patterns rather than fundamental economic variables.[18] Such reliance on market patterns is called *technical analysis*.

6.7.1 *How prominent is technical analysis in the foreign exchange market?*

Technical analysis, or *chartism* as it is sometimes called, consists of techniques that exclusively use information from past price movements in a financial market to forecast future price movements. In their thorough survey of research on technical analysis of foreign exchange markets, Menkhoff and Taylor (2007) summarize the research findings as follows:

1. Most foreign exchange traders and analysts use some combination of technical analysis and fundamental analysis.
2. Technical analysis tends to dominate the fundamental analysis as the forecast horizon becomes shorter.
3. Technical analysis is a profitable trading strategy, even when the risk premium is taken into consideration.
4. Technical analysis is more profitable when the market is exceptionally volatile.
5. However, the profitability of specific technical rules varies greatly over time and levels of market volatility.

At the end of their survey, Menkhoff and Taylor conclude that:

> ... technical analysis remains a passionate obsession of many foreign exchange market professionals; it is clearly an intrinsic part of this

---

[18] See, for example, Goodhart (1988) and Frankel and Froot (1986, 1990) and the broad survey of the literature by Menkhoff and Taylor (2007).

market. For academic researchers, this means that technical analysis must be understood and integrated into economic reasoning at both the macroeconomic and the microstructural levels".[19]

Indeed, the finding that a substantial amount of foreign exchange transactions are not driven by quantifiable fundamentals presents some serious problems for policymakers.

6.7.2 *Some macroeconomic implications of technical analysis*

The apparent success of technical analysis seems to undermine Fama's (1970) efficient markets hypothesis, which is that current asset prices already incorporate all available information. Under this hypothesis, there should be no technical rule based on readily available information on past exchange rates that consistently gives foreign exchange traders positive returns. Rational traders should, therefore, focus only on shifts in fundamental information, or news, which is not predictable with simple technical rules.

The fact that the foreign exchange market does not provide efficient prices of national currencies is problematic because the foreign exchange rate is supposed to provide the information that guides international trade and investment decisions. Inaccurate exchange rates generate inefficient trade and investment flows, all other things equal.

6.8 Further Observations on the Efficiency of the Foreign Exchange Market

The prominence of technical analysis as a trading strategy in the foreign exchange market no doubt reflects the lack of more accurate practical exchange rate models. There are no reliable models for predicting the future exchange rates that are based exclusively on

---

[19] Menkhoff and Taylor (2007). p. 967.

economic fundamentals. The discussion of the interest parity condition, or should we say hypothesis, in Chapter 4 suggested that it is impossible to predict the future exchange rate changes because exchange rates are driven by expectations that change only with the arrival of unpredictable news. But, even if this hypothesis were always correct, it should still be possible to find a theory that can explain past changes in the exchange rate by linking it to specific types of news. In fact, there is only one model that has been able to explain even past exchange rate movements with any degree of accuracy: the *purchasing power parity (PPP) model*.[20]

6.8.1 *Purchasing power parity*

The PPP model dates back to the 1500s, when it was clearly derived by scholars at the University of Salamanca in Spain. Specifically, the model is based on the "law of one price", which assumes that arbitrage equalizes the prices of individual goods and services everywhere. For example, if the price of a widget at home in terms of the domestic currency is p, the price of widgets abroad in terms of the foreign currency is p^*, then the law of one price states that the exchange rate e must satisfy

$$p = ep^* \tag{6.1}$$

Or, stated another way, the exchange rate reflects the law of one price if

$$e = p/p^* \tag{6.2}$$

For example, if a widget in the United States costs US$1.00 and an identical widget costs CAN$2.00 in Canada, the law of one price is satisfied if the exchange rate is e = US$.50 from the US perspective or $1/e$ = CAN$2.00 from the Canadian perspective.

---

[20] Descriptions and analysis of the PPP model are provided by Lawrence H. Officer (1982), Kenneth Rogoff (1995), and Alan M. Taylor (2000).

The PPP exchange rate model looks at the law of one price more broadly and hypothesizes that the exchange rate reflects the *overall* price levels in each country. Specifically, if *P* represents a general price index for the home economy, say the familiar wholesale price index compiled by most countries, and *P** is a similar general price index overseas, then the PPP model predicts that

$$e = P/P^* \tag{6.3}$$

Because price levels theoretically apply to goods and services, the purchasing power panty hypothesis effectively assumes that only international trade influences the exchange rate. There are other sources of supply and demand in the foreign exchange market, of course, such as international investment, earnings flows from accumulated foreign assets, and the international transfers. PPP is therefore unlikely to hold exactly. History suggests that trade imbalances tend to be temporary in nature, however. For example, Taylor (2002) presents long-run evidence showing that countries do tend to balance trade in the long run. In the long run investors tend to cash in their assets, and debtors eventually have to settle their debts. There are also limits to how much a country can borrow, or how much it is willing to lend to other countries. Therefore, it is likely that PPP will tend to hold in the long run.

The PPP hypothesis has been thoroughly tested using the actual data on exchange rates and price levels across many different countries and over different time periods. In the short run, deviations from PPP are common. Differences in price levels and rates of inflation do not seem to explain short-run fluctuations in exchange rates. However, over long periods of time, such as five or ten years, exchange rates do reflect relative price levels across the countries very closely. Lothian and Taylor (1996) found, for example, that over the past 200 years PPP explains the long-run exchange rates between the US dollar, French franc, and British pound very precisely. Other studies by Officer (1982), Ghoshroy-Saha and Van den Berg (1996) and Taylor (2000) examined other available data going back to the 1870s, and they similarly found that relative price levels explain nearly all the variation in exchange rates from the time of the gold standard in the late 19th century through the current period of floating exchange rates.

In sum, the purchasing power parity model is the only exchange rate model that explains past exchange rates with any degree of consistency over long periods of time. Even this model does not explain month-to-month or even year-to-year fluctuations in exchange rates very well at all. And, like all other exchange rate models, PPP does not predict future exchange rates more accurately than a random walk model that simply assumes next month's exchange rate will be the same as the current rate plus or minus some unpredictable random variation. Therefore, given the inability of economic models to predict the exchange rates better than a random walk, we should not be surprised that foreign exchange traders resort to technical analysis. But how can simplistic technical rules based on past price behavior deliver better results than models based on fundamental economic relationships?

6.8.2 *The dynamics of financial markets*

A rule that is followed by a significant number of market participants will have some predictive power for the simple reason that the market outcomes will be influenced by the transactions of those who follow the rule. The rule thus becomes a self-fulfilling prophecy! But even if the rule works for traders in the foreign exchange market, note that there is no reason why such a rule would take the market closer to the exchange rate that provides exporters, importers, and investors with the accurate and complete information they need to make good long-run decisions. The evidence on purchasing power parity suggests that the foreign exchange market often deviates from its long-run trend for extended periods of time.

The deviation of prices from efficient prices is common in financial markets. Keynes (1936) pointed out the inherent conflict between market liquidity and the accuracy of asset prices in financial markets. Market liquidity is normally viewed as a good thing by financial economists. For one thing, liquidity reduces the risk for buyers and sellers because they can more easily reverse or revise previous transactions. But an increase in number of market participants does not necessarily improve the accuracy with which the market prices an asset. When the increased market participation brings in more outside speculators rather than participants who purchase foreign exchange to carry out fundamental international activities such as foreign trade or foreign investment, the percentage of market participants who have direct interest in the asset being traded shrinks, and more participants concern themselves with short-run fluctuations and the technical analysis of such market behavior. And this is what has happened in the foreign exchange markets. Recall the brief description of the retail online foreign exchange markets earlier in this chapter; these markets cater to small speculators who look at the market as a casino, not as exporters or investors in overseas businesses who seek foreign exchange to engage in those fundamental international economic activities.

Keynes would argue that as a result of the outside speculators, international trade and foreign investment "are governed by the average expectation of those who deal in the [foreign exchange market] rather than by the genuine expectations of professional [exporters, importers, and foreign investors]".[21] Keynes famously warned that when financial markets become larger and less expensive, and the fundamental purpose of a financial market "becomes a by-product of the activities of a casino, the job is likely to be ill-done".[22] Specifically, with ever greater amounts of money held by speculators and gamblers who have no direct interest in the international economic activities that the exchange rate influences, the exchange rate is increasingly less likely to correctly value the long-run value of each currency's purchasing power.

---

[21] Keynes' (1936, p. 151) words were directed at the stock market, where he observed market participants with no direct interest in business investment influencing the stock prices that had a great effect on fundamental business investment, but his words are certainly equally appropriate for describing how speculators corrupt the fundamental purpose of foreign exchange markets.
[22] Keynes (1936). p. 159.

Keynes correctly pointed out that the fact that the market is largely controlled by professional traders, does not necessarily improve the market performance:

> It might have been supposed that competition between expert professionals, possessing judgment and knowledge beyond that of the average private investor, would correct the vagaries of the ignorant individual left to himself. It happens, however, that the energies and skill of the professional [financial] investor and speculator are mainly occupied otherwise. For most of these persons are, in fact, largely concerned, not with making superior long-term forecasts..., but with foreseeing changes ... a short time ahead of the general public. They are concerned, not with what an investment is really worth to a man who buys it "for keeps", but with what the market will value it at, under the influence of mass psychology, three months or a year hence .... For it is not sensible to pay 25 for an investment of which you believe the prospective yield to justify a value of 30, if you also believe that the market will value it at 20 three months hence.[23]

So, if technical analysis is believed to drive the market, then that is how professionals as well as amateurs will set their expectations. Keynes also added that "there is no clear evidence from experience that the investment policy which is socially advantageous coincides with that which is most profitable". To the contrary, taking positions in the market that reflect informed long-run expectation is much costlier than going with the short-run flows traders are familiar with. Ironically, such long-run commitments must be done with one's own money, while short-run bets can often be leveraged with borrowed money, as with the 100:1 leverage in the retail online markets.

In conclusion, foreign exchange markets are unlikely to provide us with accurate long-term values of the world's currencies. Market participants have neither the information nor the motivation to bring about such a market outcome. This is not to say that government officials, central bankers, or a monopolistic private currency dealer will

---

[23] Keynes (1936). pp. 154, 155.

necessarily do better. But it is important to be aware of the failures of financial markets when we compare alternative international financial systems.

6.9 Summary and Conclusions

This chapter presented a lot of details about the foreign exchange market. We refer to these details as the *microstructure* of the foreign exchange market. Overall, what we know about the microstructure of the foreign exchange markets forces us to alter somewhat the impressions from earlier chapters. Among the important details are

1. The US dollar still dominates the foreign exchange markets, just as it has ever since the Bretton Woods system began operating.
2. The city of London is the largest foreign exchange center, accounting for over one-third of all trades and twice as many as New York.
3. The overall volume of the foreign exchange markets has grown from a little over one-half trillion dollars per day just 20 years ago to over $3 trillion in 2007.
4. After communicating by telephone for about 100 years, foreign exchange dealers today communicate electronically with each other and their largest customers.
5. Profit margins have fallen in the foreign exchange market, and there has been a consolidation to where the top three dealer banks now account for nearly half of all foreign exchange transactions throughout the world.
6. Electronic retail currency exchanges have enabled individuals to engage in speculative foreign exchange transactions, a dangerous activity given the near-random fluctuations of exchange rates in the short run.
7. Details about who transacts in the foreign exchange market reveals that about 90 percent of the trades are dealer-to-dealer trades.
8. The $3 trillion daily volume of the foreign exchange market seems out of proportion given the daily volumes of international

trade and asset trades, but studies of the microstructure reveal how each fundamental trade triggers a whole series of arbitrage and inventory adjustment transactions by dealers known as the "hot potato process".

9. Trades driven by arbitrage and inventory adjustment do not move prices; only outside customer demand related to international trade, international investment, speculation, or other international economic activities to drive the prices.

10. The foreign exchange markets are huge but largely unregulated, and it should not be surprising that corruption and fraud occur.

11. Exchange rate models have been notoriously unsuccessful in predicting and explaining observed exchange rates, with the exception of the purchasing power parity model.

12. While still unable to predict, purchasing power parity explains past long-run exchange rate trends and shifts quite accurately because the exchange rate must balance long-run international trade.

13. In the short run, the opening of the foreign exchange market to more participants has turned it more into a casino than a market where exporters, importers, savers, and investors buy foreign exchange to carry out their international transactions, and exchange rates routinely deviate from fundamental values for extended periods of time.

14. The lack of transparency of the over-the-counter market process undermines the efficiency of the foreign exchange market.

In general, the global foreign exchange market does a poor job of pricing currencies in the short and medium term. Recall that purchasing power parity does not hold in the short run, which means that exchange rates do not accurately reflect that portion of the supply and demand for currencies derived from international trade. There is not much evidence that anything else, especially asset trade, explains much of the day-to-day or even month-to-month variation in exchange rates either. On the other hand, this chapter's examination of the microstructure of the foreign exchange market suggests the supply and demand model presented in Chapter 3 is a reasonable representation of the market in the long run. The finding that purchasing power parity closely characterizes the exchange rates over extended periods of years means that, in the very long run at least, exchange rates do serve to balance international trade that reflects countries' comparative advantages.

Studies of the microstructure of the foreign exchange markets show that the geographic and triangular arbitrage discussed in Chapters 3 are indeed carried out. However, as argued in Chapter 4, the conclusion that the spot exchange rate is a function of expectations of future exchange rates remains only as good as the assumption that people set their expectations objectively using all available information. The evidence is not reassuring in this regard, and there are many violations of the hypothesized intertemporal arbitrage suggested by the interest parity condition. The lack of evidence on what drives the market in the short and medium terms plus the precarious state of expectations highlighted at the end of Chapter 4 make it clear that the foreign exchange market lacks an "anchor" to long-term fundamentals.

Research into the microstructure of the foreign exchange market reveals new insights about foreign exchange rates not discussed in earlier chapters. Specifically, the decentralized nature of the market makes it possible that information does not disseminate throughout the market immediately, thus giving exceptional profits to those who hear the "news" first. The decentralized nature of the market also creates arbitrage opportunities that would not be available in a centralized exchange, where everyone trades at the same price. Decentralization, therefore, enhances profits for the dealers who have the first shot at finding and arbitraging the little price discrepancies across the locations, currency combinations, and between spot and forward markets. It is quite likely that the dealers will continue to resist technological or regulatory changes that would centralize the market, even if this would clearly be advantageous for the users of the foreign exchange markets.

Technological change is likely to change the market regardless of what the traditional dealer institutions may try to do to prevent it, however. Electronic trading is gradually creating a (slightly) more centralized market in which traders not only gain a greater amount of information about supply and demand, but in which more trades are concluded at identical prices. As a result, the margins between bid and offer prices are shrinking and profits from arbitrage opportunities are likely to continue to shrink as well. It is still too early to gauge all the consequences of electric brokering and the growth of direct online customer trading, but the direction of change seems clear. So far, other financial intermediaries like hedge funds seem to have gained from the lower margins in the foreign exchange markets.

In conclusion, we must admit that our understanding of the foreign exchange markets remains spotty because little data on trading, order flow, and actual prices is available to researchers. The private dealers that operate in the market do not reveal the details of their trading activity. The few studies reported in this chapter are rare cases, where researchers were allowed to enter the secret world of the currency trader. The lack of data have made it difficult to judge to what extent the foreign exchange market's current structure deviates from an efficient market in terms of volatility, the absorption of information, and the accuracy of exchange rates as incentives for fundamental international prices. We will, hopefully, learn more about the foreign exchange market as more outside customers gain direct access to electronic brokering platforms and the market effectively becomes more centralized and more information about trades become available. Also, because they are a central component of the international financial system, future discussions on reforming the international financial system will have to take into consideration the organization and efficiency of foreign exchange markets.

Key Terms and Concepts

Arbitrage	Gambler's ruin	Market transparency
Back office	Hot potato process	Microstructure
Bid–ask margins	Interbank platform	Mid office
Broker	Inventory adjustment	Off-exchange trading
Centralized exchange	Law of one price	Online dealer
Chartism	Leveraged trades	platforms
Efficient market	Market liquidity	Over-the-counter
Dealers	Market maker	market

Proprietary platforms   Random walk model   Spot market
Purchasing power   Settlement risk   Vehicle currency
  parity   Speculation   Zero-sum game

Chapter Questions and Problems

1. According to the information shown in Table 6.1, describe how the geographic location of foreign exchange trades has shifted over the past 15 years. What might be the reasons for the changes? What are the possible consequences of these changes?

2. The US dollar dominates the foreign exchange markets, as shown in Tables 6.2 and 6.3. Explain to what extent the dollar dominates, and discuss the likely reasons for the large share of dollars in total foreign exchange transactions.

3. Table 6.4 shows how large the daily volume of the foreign exchange markets is and how fast foreign exchange markets have grown over the past 15 years. What could explain the nearly $3.2 trillion daily turnover in 2007 and the rapid growth of this turnover over the past decades?

4. The communications revolution is transforming the foreign exchange market. Explain briefly how electronic trading is likely to change the market and how that will affect the market's customers.

5. Explain the role of the speculator in the foreign exchange market. Who are these speculators?

6. What does the evidence on purchasing power parity suggest about the US trade deficit in the long run? Explain precisely by first stating the assumptions behind the purchasing power parity, and then linking the concept to future trade flows.

7. Answer the question at the end of Section 6.8.1: How can simplistic technical rules based on past price behavior deliver better results than models based on fundamental economic relationships?

8. Discuss Keynes' observation that more market participants do not necessarily improve the accuracy with which an asset market prices the assets. Review the discussion on expectations in Chapter 4 and add the information on the microstructure of foreign exchange markets to answer this question.

References

BIS (2004). Triennial Central Bank Survey of Foreign Exchange and Derivatives Market Activity in April 2004, Preliminary Global Results. September, 2004; available at www.bis.org.

Chaboud, A and S Weinberg (2002). Foreign exchange markets in the late 1990s: Intraday market volatility and the growth of electronic trading. In *Market Functioning and Central Bank Policy*, No. 12 in BIS Papers, Bank of International Settlements (ed.), pp. 138–147. Basel, Switzerland: Bank for International Settlements (available at www.bis.org).

Cross, SY (1998). *All About the Foreign Exchange Market in the United States*. New York: Federal Reserve Bank of New York.

Fama, EF (1970). Efficient capital markets: A review of theory and empirical work. *Journal of Finance*, 25(2), 383–417.

Flood, RP and MP Taylor (1996). Exchange rate economics: What's wrong with the conventional macro approach? In *The Microstructure of Foreign Exchange Markets*, Frankel JA, G Galli, and A Giovannini (eds.), pp. 261–301. Chicago: University of Chicago Press.

Frankel, JA and KA Froot (1986). Understanding the US dollar in the eighties: The expectations of chartists and fundamentalists. *Economic Record*, 24–38.

Frankel, JA and KA Froot (1990). Chartists fundamentalists, and trading in the foreign exchange market. *American Economic Review*, 80(2), 181–185.

Frankel, JA, G Galli and A Giovannini (eds.), (1996). *The Microstructure of Foreign Exchange Markets*. Chicago: University of Chicago Press.

Frankel, J, L Sarno and MP Taylor (2002). *The Economics of Exchange Rates*. Cambridge: Cambridge University Press.

Ghoshroy-Saha and H Van den Berg (1996). Mexico's futile attempt to defy purchasing power parity. *Applied Economics letters*, 3(3), 395–399.

Hakkio, CS (1992). Is purchasing power parity a useful guide to the dollar? *Economic Review*, Federal Reserve Bank of Kansas City, Third Quarter.

Lothian, JR and MP Taylor (1996). Real exchange rate behavior: The recent float from the perspective of the past two centuries. *Journal of Political Economy*, 104(3), 488–509.

Lyons, RK (1996). Foreign exchange volume: Sound and fury signifying nothing? In *The Microstructure of Foreign Exchange Markets*, Frankel JA,

G Galli and A Giovannini (eds.), pp. 183–206. Chicago: University of Chicago Press.

Lyons, RK (1998). Profits and position control: A week of FX dealing. *Journal of International Money and Finance*, 17, 97–115.

Lyons, RK (2001). *The Microstructure Approach to Exchange Rates.* Cambridge, MA: MIT Press.

Mahatir, BM (1997). Highwaymen of the global economy. *Wall Street Journal*, September 23.

Menkhoff, L and M Taylor (2007). The Obstinate passion of foreign exchange professionals: Technical analysis. *Journal of Economic Literature*, 45(4), 936–972.

National Futures Association (2004). *Trading in the Retail Off-Exchange Foreign Xcurrency Market: What Investors Need to Know.* Chicago: NFA.

Neely, CJ and PA Weller (2001). Intraday technical trading in the foreign exchange market. Working Paper, Federal Reserve Bank of St. Louis, January 10.

Officer, LH (1982). *Purchasing Power Parity and Exchange Rates: Theory, Evidence and Relevance.* Greenwich, CT: JAI Press.

Rime, D (2003). New electronic trading systems in foreign exchange markets. Chapter 21 in *The New Economy Handbook.* Amsterdam: Elsevier Science.

Rogoff, K (1995). The purchasing power parity puzzle. *Journal of Economic Literature*, 34(2), 647–668.

Taylor, AM (2000). A century of purchasing-power parity. NBER Working Paper No. 8012, November.

Taylor, AM (2002). A century of current account dynamics. NBER Working Paper w8927, May.

Part III

Open-Economy Macroeconomics

Chapter 7

The Mundell–Fleming Open-Economy Model

> The classical theorists resemble Euclidean geometers in a non-Euclidean world who, discovering that in experience straight lines apparently parallel often meet, rebuke the lines for not keeping straight — as the only remedy for the unfortunate collisions which are occurring. Yet, in truth, there is no remedy except to throw over the axiom of parallels and to work out a non-Euclidean geometry.
>
> (John Maynard Keynes.[1])

Our impression of a complex phenomenon like an economy is influenced by our perspective. The conclusions we reach when we examine individual consumers, industries, or financial institutions in their immediate surroundings tend to be different from the conclusions we reach when we observe the collective economic outcomes from afar. Economists have, over the past three centuries, looked at economic activity from both perspectives, and the field of economics has divided itself into microeconomics and macroeconomics. The former analyzes the economic activities of consumers, firms, and other small groups and organizations, while macroeconomists focus on how the whole

---

[1] John Maynard Keynes (1936). p. 16.

"system" generates overall outcomes. Microeconomics looks at prices and quantities in individual markets and sectors of the economy, macroeconomics looks at gross domestic product (GDP) and total employment.

Our discussion of holism and scientific reductionism in Chapter 1 is relevant to this issue of perspective. Holism, of course, demands that economists understand the actions of the individuals and firms that make up human society. But holism also reminds us that the collective whole is not a simple sum of its parts. Or, as Keynes states in the quote above, the economic system is clearly not "Euclidean" or linear. This chapter details an open-economy macroeconomic model based on Keynes' well-known 1936 non-linear model from his *General Theory of Employment, Interest, and Money.*

Chapter Goals

1. Describe Keynes' revolutionary approach to analyzing the economy.
2. Detail how, in his 1936 model, Keynes broke the economy into separate aggregate sectors in order to build an economic model in which both the parts and the system could be analyzed.
3. Explain the simple graphic model of the product market from Keynes' complete model.
4. Extend this graphic approach to Hicks' interpretation of the Keynesian model, known as the IS-LM model.
5. Introduce Fleming and Mundell's extensions that turned the IS-LM model into an open-economy Keynesian model.
6. Compare the effects of fiscal and monetary policies in the closed-economy and open-economy versions of the model.

7.1 Keynes' Revolutionary Macroeconomic Model

To understand Keynes' criticism of the "classical theorists", one has to go back to the economic thinking of the late 19th century. At that time, mainstream economists effectively embraced the unsound strategy of *scientific reductionism* by concentrating on individual markets and resource allocation, while ignoring the overall economic system within which those markets functioned. Most economists implicitly assumed that a good understanding of the system's component parts would be sufficient for designing the policies and institutions necessary to support the economic system. Economics textbooks by Alfred Marshall and other economists in the late 19th and early 20th centuries reflected the belief, and it was really a belief rather than a sound hypothesis, that an economy automatically tends to move toward a stable equilibrium.

7.1.1 *Walras' general equilibrium model*

Of special interest from a holistic macroeconomic perspective is the model of a complete economic system by the French-born, Swiss-based economist Léon Walras in the late 19th century. Walras' mathematical model specified the economy as a huge system of equations representing the product markets, factor markets, asset markets, and the market for money. In this system, prices and quantities of products, factors of production, assets, and money are all determined simultaneously. Although he was never able to actually solve his model mathematically, he intuitively reasoned that if all markets automatically tend to move toward their respective equilibria, then the entire system would also automatically move toward a stable overall systemic equilibrium.

From one perspective, Walras' model looks deceivingly holistic because everything is related to everything else. But, Walras' elaborate model does not leave open the possibility that the whole was greater than or less than its component parts. His system of linear equations with fixed parameters does not permit the relationships among the component parts to vary. The impossibility of actually solving Walras' system of equations further encouraged economists to focus on the system's individual markets and to refrain from trying to analyze how the overall economic system performed. Interestingly, it was only much later in the 20th century that mathematical economists proved that a solution to Walras' rigid system even existed, and then only under rather extreme assumptions about how markets function. Ironically, the complex Walrasian model seems to have encouraged *scientific reductionism* and the focus on individual markets rather than the interconnections and the overall system.

7.1.2 *The Great Depression and Keynes' more holistic model*

It was only when the world economy plunged into the Great Depression during the 1930s that economic thought again began to recognize that a system of individual product markets, factor markets, asset markets, and money markets does not generally result in a general equilibrium that maximizes human welfare. The Great Depression made it all too clear that the economy's equilibrium could change quickly and drastically even though most of the component parts, such as the number of workers, the capital stock, technology, natural resource availability, etc. changed hardly at all over the short run. The Great Depression of the 1930s shifted economists' priorities away from the component parts to how the overall system performed. Keynes, effectively created the field that we know today as macroeconomics when in 1936 he published *The General Theory of Employment, Interest, and Money*. In it, he presented a model that explicitly showed how the major components of the economy interacted to affect economic aggregates such as gross domestic product and the level of employment. Keynes' model explained the failure of most of the world's major economies to achieve market-cleaning equilibria in the product and labour markets.

7.2 The Basic Keynesian Macroeconomic Model

The urgency of finding a solution to the very high levels of unemployment that plagued most economies during the Great Depression made Keynes' book an instant success. The *General Theory* pointed to clear policy prescriptions for dealing with economic recession and high unemployment. Fundamentally, Keynes disputed the conventional wisdom that the whole economy always moves promptly toward a full-employment equilibrium. Keynes admitted that if we wait long enough, full employment might eventually be restored. But, "in the long run, we are all dead", he added. He used his model to show that the long run could be very long. Also, he showed that policymakers could do more than wait for markets to slowly adjust back toward full employment.

A weakness of early versions of the Keynesian model was its focus on an individual, closed economy. This may have been appropriate in 1936, but the post-World War II economy was characterized by what we now refer to as globalization. The world economy recovered from World War II, and by 1960 international trade and investment were growing more than twice the rate of the equally impressive growth in real per capita GDP in most countries. This weakness of the Keynesian model was corrected by Fleming (1962) and Mundell (1963). Their expanded Keynesian model is now known as the Mundell–Fleming open-economy macroeconomic model. Since the latter is a straightforward extension of the closed-economy Keynesian model, this section begins with the latter, and subsequent sections then "open" the Keynesian model.

7.2.1 *Basic elements of the closed economy Keynesian model*

Keynes' key contribution to macroeconomics was to separate aggregate demand into a few aggregate categories of activity that could reasonably be described as functions of specific sets of explanatory variables peculiar to each category of activity. This was a more practical approach than Walras' huge model of countless equations representing all the microunits of an economy. Keynes then used his system of aggregate categories of economic activity to prescribe the broad macroeconomic policies to increase production and employment. Among the macroeconomic policies that Keynes suggested for stimulating economic activity at the depth of the Great Depression were increased government spending, tax reductions, and money supply expansion.

Keynes first specified total output, Y, as the sum of three categories of products:

$$Y = C + I + G \tag{7.1}$$

The variable C represents consumption goods, I represents investment (capital) goods, and G represents the government purchases. Keynes then specified functions that determined each of these three components of aggregate demand.

7.2.2 The consumption function

Central to Keynes model is his *consumption function*. He reasoned that consumption is not only a component of aggregate demand, but because aggregate demand translates into aggregate income, it is itself a function of aggregate demand. But, an increase in income raises consumption by only a fraction of the increase in income.

Keynes defined the consumption function as $C = C(Y)$ in general, but in his book he specified a linear relationship

$$C = a + bY \tag{7.2}$$

in which $a > 0$ and $0 < b < 1$. Keynes called the variable b, the slope of the line, the *marginal propensity to consume*, which is the percentage of each additional dollar of income spent on consumption. Figure 7.1 illustrates the consumption function $C = a + bY$. When income is zero, consumption is equal to a. Keynes also hypothesized that an increase in income raises consumption by only a fraction of the increase in income.

7.2.3 The I and G functions

The demand for investment goods and services is usually assumed to be a decreasing function of the interest rate, i. That is, $I = I(i)$, and the derivative of I with respect to i is $I'(i) < 0$. The causal variable i is not shown on the axes in the two dimensional diagram in Fig. 7.2, and therefore the investment function appears as a straight line, unrelated to the level of income. The level of the I line reflects a

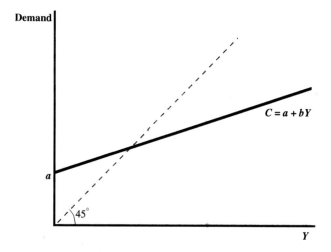

Figure 7.1 The simple Keynesian consumption function.

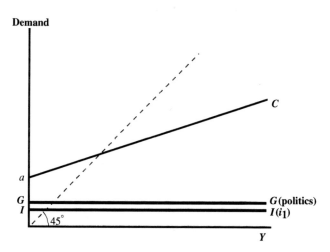

Figure 7.2 The demand for investment goods and government goods and services.

particular interest rate, say i_1. A rise in the interest rate to $i_2 > i_1$ would shift the investment function downward.

The demand for government goods and services is assumed to be a function of the complex political process, and here we accordingly specify the government purchases function as $G = G(\text{politics})$.

In Fig. 7.2, G is drawn as a straight line, unresponsive to Y but responsive to variables that lie in other dimensions.

The economy is in equilibrium when aggregate demand, $C(Y) + I(i) + G$, equals aggregate production, Y. In Fig. 7.3, equilibrium Y^* occurs at the level of output, where aggregate demand intersects the 45° line, which represents all the points that are equidistant from each axis. This diagram illustrates what is commonly referred to as the *Keynesian cross.*

The equilibrium level of output Y^* in Fig. 7.3 is a *stable equilibrium* in the sense that whenever the economy is not in equilibrium, variables will adjust so as to move the economy back to equilibrium. For example, when $Y < C + I + G$ and the aggregate demand curve lies above the 45° line, aggregate demand exceeds aggregate income and supply, and there will be shortages of goods and services. Keynes reasoned that such shortages will induce profit-seeking producers to employ available resources to increase production, and they will continue to increase production until the economy reaches Y^* and excess demand disappears. Similarly, if $Y > C + I + G$, aggregate demand is less than income and aggregate supply, and there will be an

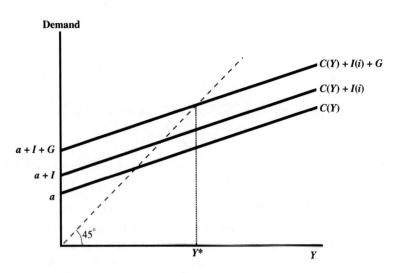

Figure 7.3   The Keynesian equilibrium, where $Y = C + I + G$.

unintended accumulation of inventory. Hence, producers will reduce output until the excess inventory is cleared.

By letting aggregate demand determine the equilibrium level of output in the economy, Keynes effectively assumed that there is no scarcity of resources and that producers can expand output at will and at constant marginal costs. This assumption of no supply constraints is what has led some critics of the Keynesian model to label it a "depression model". Clearly, in the Great Depression, there were few supply constraints when unemployment exceeded 20 percent of the labor force. In the long run, of course, economies are very much constrained by both the availability of resources and the prevailing level of technology. These issues are addressed in another model, the aggregate demand/aggregate supply model, discussed in Chapter 9.

7.3 Opening the Product Market to International Trade

An open economy differs from a closed economy in that goods and services can cross the border. That is, foreigners demand part of the economy's output, which results in exports. And, part of aggregate demand is satisfied by foreign production, that is, imports. The demand for imports consists of some mixture of consumption, investment, and government products, and it therefore depends on the level of income, the interest rate, and the other determinants of C, I, and G. Mundell and Fleming pointed out that in an open economy, foreign demand for exports and domestic demand for imports depend on the exchange rate, as well as foreign and domestic income, because the exchange rate translates the foreign currency prices of foreign products into domestic currency prices.

The Mundell–Fleming model assumes that, given the level of income and the interest rate, domestic demand for imported goods and services increases with a depreciation of the domestic currency. Hence, the import demand function is specified as $IM = IM(\Upsilon, i, e)$. In a two-dimensional diagram that relates only the level of domestic income, Υ, to aggregate demand, the import demand function IM slopes upward, like the consumption function. The curve IM

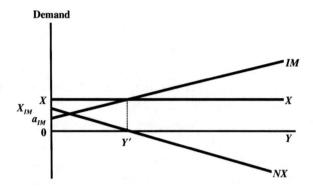

Figure 7.4   The demand for net exports: $NX = X \cdot IM$.

shifts downward with an increase in the interest rate, i, and it shifts up when the exchange rate appreciates. Figure 7.4 illustrates the IM curve.

Exports, X, depend on foreign income, the foreign interest rate, and the exchange rate. That is, $X = X(Y^*, i^*, e)$, where the starred variables Y^* and i^* are the foreign equivalents of Y and i in earlier equations. Thus, the export function is a straight line in the Keynesian cross diagram. The X curve shifts down with an increase in i^* and up with an increase in Y^* or e.

The net export function, NX, represents the difference between the horizontal X function and the upward sloping IM function:

$$NX = X(Y^*, i^*, e) - IM(Y, i, e) = NX(Y, Y^*, i, i^*, e) \qquad (7.3)$$

The NX function is the downward sloping NX line shown in Fig. 7.4. Imports grow as income rises while exports are unaffected by domestic income; hence, net exports accordingly decreases with domestic income Y. NX crosses the horizontal axis at Y' where $X - IM = 0$. Technically, the exchange rate should be depicted as the real exchange rate, or eP^*/P, but because the simple Keynesian model assumes prices remain constant in the short run, changes in the real exchange rate are

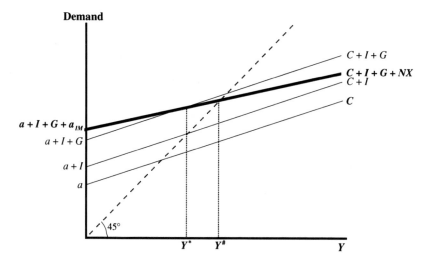

Figure 7.5 Aggregate demand in an open economy: $Y = C + I + G + NX$.

caused by only changes in e; hence, we show only e in equation (7.3). In an open economy, therefore, total product demand is equal to

$$Y = C(Y) + I(i) + G + NX(Y, i, Y^*, i^*, e) \qquad (7.4)$$

The open-economy Keynesian cross diagram in Fig. 7.5 shows that the product market is in equilibrium at $Y^\#$, where the $C + I + G + NX$ curve intersects the 45° line. The open-economy aggregate demand curve, $C + I + G + NX$, crosses the closed economy $C + I + G$ curve at Y', where NX is equal to zero.

7.4 The Mundell–Fleming Open-Economy Keynesian Model

The "Keynesian cross" diagram does not represent the complete macroeconomic model developed by Keynes. Rather, it depicts only the product market in the macroeconomic model Keynes developed in *The General Theory of Employment, Interest and Money*. In his complete model, Keynes specified the economy as consisting of three aggregate markets: (1) the *product market* of the economy, (2) the *money market,* and (3) the *asset market.* Mundell and Fleming added the *foreign market,* which is represented by the balance of payments.

7.4.1 *The product market and the IS curve*

It is inaccurate to talk about an equilibrium in the Keynesian cross diagram, which illustrates only the *product market,* without also taking into consideration the money market, the asset market, and the foreign market. Each of these markets tends toward its respective equilibrium, subject to its peculiar shocks and the determining variables. All four markets are interrelated, and equilibrium in one market depends on the equilibria in the other three markets. Figure 7.6 illustrates how, for example, changes in the interest rate, caused by shifts in the asset market and the money market, shift the equilibrium in the product market.

Figure 7.6 depicts three levels of aggregate demand, each related to one of three interest rates: $i_1 < i_2 < i_3$. For example, where i_1 is associated with the equilibrium level of output/income Y_3, the higher

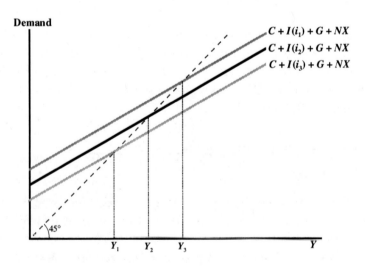

Figure 7.6   Aggregate product demand under different interest rates.

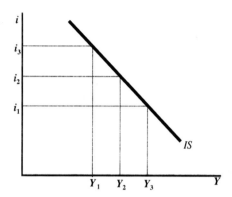

Figure 7.7   The IS curve.

interest rate i_2 implies lower investment, and thus lower aggregate demand and a lower equilibrium level of income Y_2. The highest interest rate i_3 is related to the lowest of the three levels of output/income Y_1. The relationship between interest rates and output in the product market is depicted in Fig. 7.7 as the *IS* curve, whose name is derived from the equality of saving and investment that implicitly holds at the level of output where the aggregate demand curve intersects the 45° line.

For example, suppose the domestic currency depreciates. All other things equal, this shifts the *NX* function from *NX* to *NX'*, which, in turn, shifts up aggregate demand in the Keynesian cross diagram. That is, the rise in the *NX* component of aggregate demand increases the equilibrium level of output at each interest rate. In Fig. 7.8, currency depreciation means each of the three interest rates $i_1 < i_2 < i_3$ now corresponds to the equilibrium output levels Y'_3, Y'_2, and Y'_1, respectively, where $Y'_3 > Y_3$, $Y'_2 > Y_2$, and $Y'_1 > Y_1$.

Figure 7.9 details the effect a currency depreciation on the IS curve. A depreciation changes the sets of matching pairs of interest rates and equilibrium output levels. After the depreciation, the foreign trade balance function *NX'* traces out the *IS'* curve, which lies to the right of the original *IS* curve, as illustrated in Fig. 7.9. That is, a depreciation of the domestic currency shifts the *IS* curve to the right. An appreciation would, of course, shift the *IS* curve to the left.

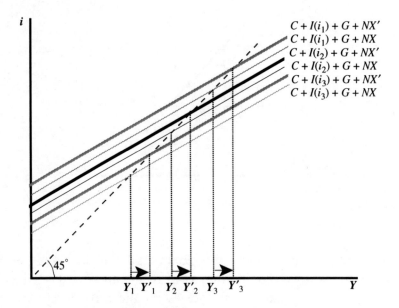

Figure 7.8   An increase in the trade balance.

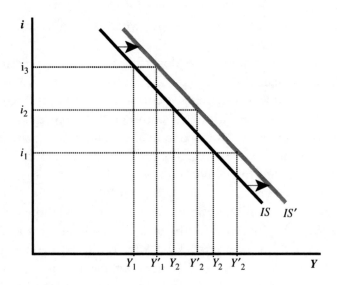

Figure 7.9   The IS curve after a shift in the consumption function.

7.4.2 *The money market and the LM curve*

The money market is in equilibrium when the supply of money, M, is equal to the demand for money, L. The supply of nominal money, M, is a policy decision, put into effect by the central bank. Here, the demand for money is assumed to reflect two principal motives for holding money: the *transactions motive* for holding money and the *store of wealth motive* for holding money.

The transactions motive for holding money means that the demand for money rises with the level of output Y. The store of wealth motive for holding money is more complex. People store wealth because there are welfare gains from satisfying wants as they actually occur rather than only when income happens to arrive. A store of wealth allows people to engage in what is often referred to as *consumption smoothing*, but this requires the transfer of purchasing power from one period of time to another. Money is unique in satisfying the transactions motive (assuming barter is not a viable option), but it competes with other assets as a store of wealth. Holding money has an opportunity cost, namely the rate of return paid by other assets that also serve as a store of wealth. The demand for money is thus inversely related to the rate of return paid by other assets. The demand for money is thus specified by the function $L(Y, i)$; demand rises with income and falls with the interest rate (the return to other assets).

Figure 7.10 relates money demand and the interest rate. The demand curve for money is downward-sloping with respect to the interest rate i, and the entire curve shifts up as Y increases from Y_1 to Y_2 to Y_3.

Combining the interest rates and output levels at which the money market is shown to be in equilibrium in Fig. 7.10 gives us the *LM* curve in Fig. 7.11. All other things equal, higher output levels require more money to carry out the increased level of transactions. If the real money supply, M/P, is held constant by the central bank, the price of assets falls (the interest rate rises) as individuals attempt to sell the assets to increase their money holdings. The interest rate must rise until the opportunity cost of holding money has increased

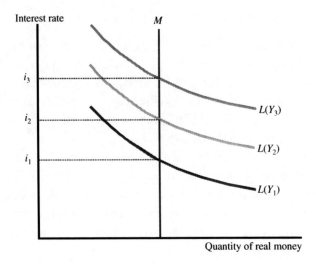

Figure 7.10   Equilibrium in the money market.

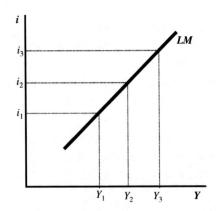

Figure 7.11   The *LM* curve: balancing the opportunity cost of holding money with transactions motive for holding money.

enough to raise the velocity of money to where the larger number of transactions can be carried out with the fixed stock of real money.

Monetary policy determines the supply of money, *M*. If prices remain unchanged, then a shift in *M* changes the real money supply

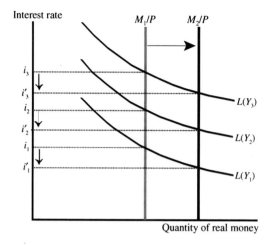

Figure 7.12 An expansion of the money supply.

M/P, and this will, in turn, cause the *LM* curve to shift. For example, an increase in the nominal money supply from M_1 to M_2 will establish a new set of combinations of output and interest rates where the money market is in equilibrium. This case is illustrated in Fig. 7.12. At the real money supply M_1/P, the money market will be in equilibrium at interest rates $i_1 < i_2 < i_3$ when equilibrium output in the product market is Y_1, Y_2, and Y_3, respectively. But if the central bank increases the real money supply to M_2, the money market will be in equilibrium when interest rates $i'_1 < i_1$, $i'_2 < i_2$, and $i'_3 < i_3$ are matched with equilibrium output levels Y_1, Y_2, and Y_3.

By matching the pairs of interest rates and equilibrium output levels when the real money supply is M_2/P, we define an *LM* curve that lies to the right of the *LM* curve that represents the equilibrium combinations of interest rates and output levels when the real money supply is M_1/P. As shown in Fig. 7.13, an increase in the supply of real money shifts the *LM* curve to the right. Specifically, at each level of output, an increase in the money supply lowers the interest rate required to balance the money demand and money supply.

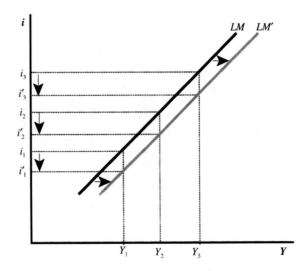

Figure 7.13   Expanding the money supply shifts the *LM* curve to the right.

7.4.3 *The financial account balance*

At this point, we begin applying the innovations brought into the model by Mundell and Fleming. Specifically, we introduce the foreign exchange market into the model. Supply and demand in the foreign exchange market is generated by the international transactions detailed in the balance of payments account. The Mundell–Fleming model focuses on two broad categories of international payments: (1) the trade balance in the current account and (2) the net international exchange of assets in the financial account. The Mundell–Fleming model simplifies by ignoring the smaller flows of international transfers, factor income payments, and asset returns.

Investors seeking to maximize the returns on their wealth are assumed to weigh the relative returns at home and abroad. Asset purchases and sales are part of the process of intertemporal arbitrage, which clearly reflects the variables in the interest parity condition, including the spot, forward, and/or expected future exchange rates. Therefore, the asset purchases and sales registered in the financial account (*FAB*) of the balance of payments depend on the domestic

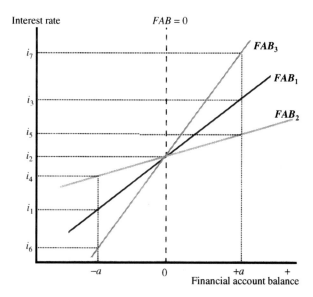

Figure 7.14 The financial account balance (*FAB*) depends on capital mobility.

and foreign interest rates (rates of return) as well as the spot and the expected future exchange rate:

$$FAB = FAB(i, i^*, e_t, E_t e_{t+n}) \qquad (7.4)$$

Figure 7.14 depicts alternative graphic representations of the financial account balance, *FAB*, in a two-dimensional diagram relating the *FAB* to the domestic interest rate. In general, the *FAB* curve slopes up in relation to the interest rate, and the steepness of the slope depends on how strongly capital flows are influenced by changes in interest rates. If it only takes slight increases in the interest rate to induce the large new inflows of foreign capital or the repatriation of domestic capital previously sent abroad, then the *FAB* curve will be relatively flat, like FAB_2 in Fig. 7.14. On the other hand, if there are many restrictions on international capital flows, such as restrictions of foreign ownership, poor protection of property rights, foreign restrictions on capital outflows, etc., then the *FAB* curve may look more like FAB_3. FAB_1 represents the intermediate case. When capital is *mobile*, the financial account increases from a to $+a$ with an interest rate rise from i_4 to i_5. However, if capital flows are relatively *immobile*, it takes the much larger increase in the interest rate from i_6 to i_7 to achieve the same increase in the financial account balance from a to $+a$.

The vertical dotted line in Fig. 7.14, $FAB = 0$, depicts the extreme case of complete capital immobility. This implies the case where a country or countries do not permit asset trade to vary and respond to changes in relative rates of return. Later chapters will detail cases where financial account transactions were tightly controlled. There is also the case of perfect capital mobility; such a case implies a near-horizontal FAB curve so that a very small rise in the interest rate generates a seemingly unlimited capital inflow. Such a case is only relevant to a small economy whose capital inflows or outflows have no discernable affect on world interest rates. For large economies like China, Japan, Germany, or the United States, changes in international capital inflows or outflows will almost always have some noticeable effect on interest rates elsewhere in the world. This is not to say that capital flows do not temper the effect of domestic imbalances on interest rates; for example, many studies have shown that US interest rates have remained surprisingly low despite the huge gap between savings and investment. But neither do these studies show that interest rates did not rise at all; some interest rate increases were likely to have been necessary to induce the net capital inflows shown on the US financial account over the past two decades.

7.4.4 *The current account balance*

The Mundell–Fleming model assumes the current account balance is equivalent to the trade balance, defined as NX in the aggregate demand equation (7.4). The model specifies the current account balance as a direct function of the level of domestic output, Y, and the exchange rate, e, and a negative function of foreign income, Y^*. All other things equal, the higher the level of domestic output, the smaller is the current account balance.

Figure 7.15 depicts the current account *deficit*, CAB, as an increasing function of the level of Y. The slope of this function

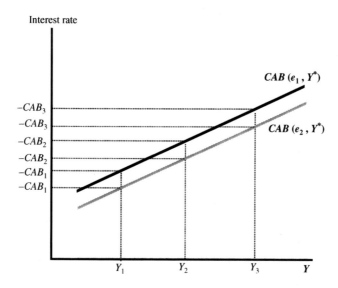

Figure 7.15 The *CAB* curve: The higher Y, the greater the *CAB* deficit.

depends on how imports react to domestic income changes. All other things equal, the greater the propensity to consume imports, the steeper the slope of the *CAB* curve. Other variables behind the *CAB* curve affect the position of the curve in the i/Y space. For example, a depreciation of the exchange rate will shift the entire *CAB* curve downward and to the right because depreciation is assumed to cause exports to rise and imports to fall, all other things equal, thus causing the current account deficit to shrink. Figure 7.15 depicts the case of a rise in e from e_1 to e_2. Such a depreciation shifts the *CAB* curve down, so that the current account deficit is smaller for each level of output/income Y.

7.4.5 *The BOP curve*

Having now specified both the financial account balance and current account balance functions, it is possible to derive a full balance of payments (*BOP*) function to represent the fourth market, the *foreign market*, in the Mundell–Fleming open-economy

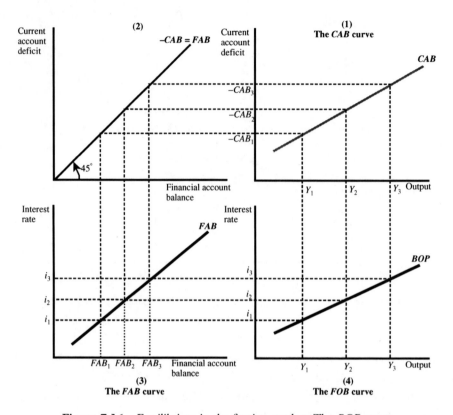

Figure 7.16   Equilibrium in the foreign market: The *BOP* curve.

macroeconomic model. The four diagrams in Fig. 7.16 show how the *BOP* function is related to the *CAB* and *FAB* curves. The *CAB* function in diagram (1), the accounting identity *CAB* = *FAB* in diagram (2), and the *FAB* function in diagram (3) combine to trace out the *BOP* curve in diagram (4). The *BOP* curve relates the levels of output *Y* and interest rates *i* compatible with the balance of payments where *BOP* = *CAB* + *FAB* = 0.

The slope of the *BOP* curve depends on how capital flows react to interest rate changes and how net exports react to changes in income. Figure 7.17 presents three alternative scenarios. All other things equal, if capital does not move easily between countries so that it takes a large change in interest rates to induce a change in the financial

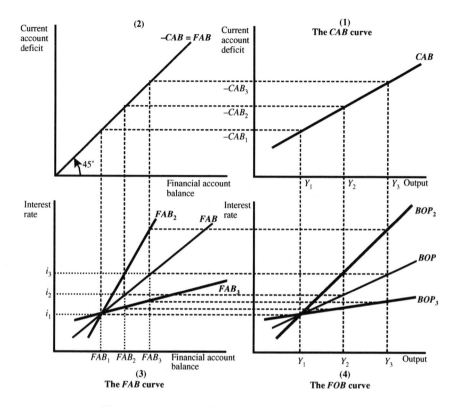

Figure 7.17 Capital mobility and the *FAB* curve.

account balance, then the *FAB* curve will tend to be relatively steep. This case is represented by the relatively steep curve *FAB₂* in Fig. 7.17 and the corresponding relatively steep *BOP₂* curve. On the other hand, if capital moves easily between countries, then a small change in interest rates induces a large enough change in the financial account balance to offset the effects on the current account of a rise in Y. This case is represented in Fig. 7.17; a flatter *FAB₃* curve translates into the flatter *BOP₃* curve.

Different slopes of the *CAB* curve similarly translate into changes in the steepness of the *BOP* curve. As shown in Fig. 7.18, a country that is open to trade and spends a high proportion of its marginal income abroad will tend to have a steep *BOP* curve, all other things equal.

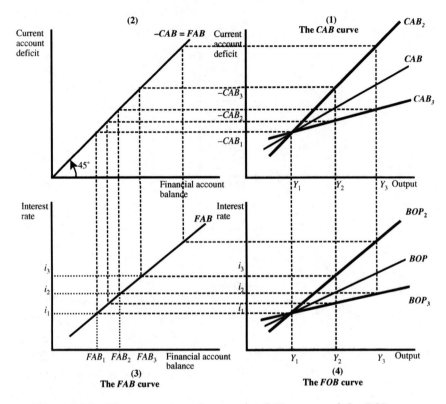

Figure 7.18   The propensity to import, the *CAB* curve, and the *BOP* curve.

The slope of the *BOP* curve is important because it helps to determine how an economy adjusts to shifts in economic circumstances. For example, when output rises from Y_1 to the full employment level Y_3 in Fig. 7.19, a relatively flat BOP_M curve implies that a modest rise in the interest rate from i_2 to i_4 is enough to offset the declining current account balance caused by the rise in income. But, if capital is immobile and the steeper BOP_{IM} curve applies, it takes a large increase in the interest rate from i_1 to i_5 to offset the same decline in the current account balance when income rises to Y_3.

In the extreme case when there are rigid capital controls on capital flows or there is a state monopoly on asset trade, changes in the interest rate cannot cause changes in the financial account to offset

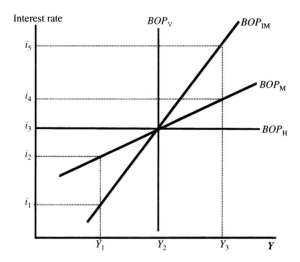

Figure 7.19 How steep is the *BOP* curve?

changes in the current account. When the *BOP* curve is perfectly vertical, as *BOP*$_V$ in Fig. 7.19, any increase in output/income that increases the trade deficit necessarily pushes the overall *BOP* into a deficit. Contrast this with perfectly mobile capital represented by the horizontal *BOP*$_H$ curve; in this case, a minuscule increase in the interest rate generates sufficient additional capital inflows to offset any decline in the current account caused by an increase in *Y*.

Note that points not on the *BOP* curve represent the combinations of *i* and *Y* that result in imbalances in international payments flows. A point above the *BOP* curve, such as the point a in Fig. 7.20, implies a balance of payments surplus because the interest rate is higher than what is necessary to generate the net financial account balance necessary to offset the current account balance related to the level of output/income *Y*$_2$. Under a regime of floating exchange rates, point a will cause the exchange rate to appreciate. A point below the *BOP* curve triggers an exchange rate depreciation. Under a fixed exchange rate regime, policies to stop such changes in the exchange rate will be called for.

Recall that the exchange rate *e* determines the height of the *CAB* curve, which in turn determines the height of the *BOP* curve.

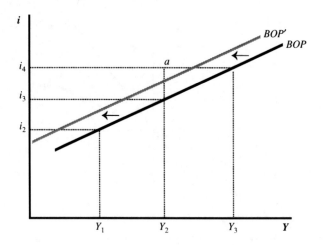

Figure 7.20   The *BOP* curve: adjustment to disequilibrium.

Appreciation changes the relationship between the interest rate and the output level by reducing the net exports at every level of income, thus shifting the *BOP* curve. Specifically, currency appreciation shifts the *BOP* curve to the left, as in the case of *BOP'* in Fig. 7.20, toward the disequilibrium point *a*. But will the exchange rate change enough to restore equilibrium in the foreign exchange market and the balance of payments? It may not have to.

The currency appreciation does more than shift the *BOP* curve. The *IS* curve also shifts because net exports, *NX*, are part of aggregate demand. Therefore, appreciation shifts both the *BOP* and *IS* curves. But now we are getting a bit ahead of the development of the model. To determine the complete set of adjustments necessary to restore the equilibrium in the economy when the product market undergoes a change, we must combine the money market, the asset market, and the foreign market into one model.

7.5 The Complete Mundell–Fleming Model

Figure 7.21 depicts the Mundell–Fleming model in its usual graphic form. Only three of the Keynesian model's four aggregate markets are

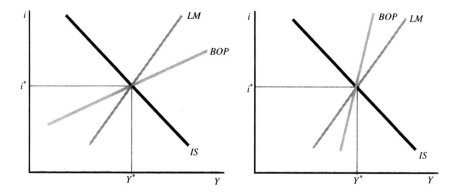

Figure 7.21 The full *IS*, *LM*, and *BOP* model: the two cases of mobile and immobile capital flows.

shown: (1) the goods market, (2) the money market, and (3) the *BOP* curve representing the foreign market. The fourth market distinguished by Keynes, the asset market, is not explicitly shown in the Mundell–Fleming model. The justification for this omission is *Walras' law* (named in honor of the 19th century French economist whom we earlier pointed out as having pioneered the use of mathematics for building large-scale economic models), which states that if $n-1$ interrelated markets are in equilibrium, then it must be the case that the nth market is also in equilibrium. The Keynesian model developed here thus leaves the asset market unobserved in the background. The asset market influences the other three markets by effectively providing the opportunity cost for holding money, which determines the demand for money in the money market and, therefore, the interest rate that influences the financial account in the foreign market and investment in the product market.

Recall that the slope of the *BOP* curve depends, in large part, on how easily money flows across borders in order to buy and sell foreign assets. Hence, Fig. 7.21 depicts two diagrams: the one on the left shows the Mundell–Fleming model when capital is relatively mobile, the other on the right shows a steep *BOP* curve representing the immobile capital. The analysis that follows will make it clear that an economy's adjustment to certain policy shifts depends on the steepness of the *BOP* curve. In other words, the mobility of capital has important consequences for the effectiveness of economic policy.

Figure 7.21 shows all of the economy's markets in equilibrium at the interest rate i^* and the level of output/income Y^*. Is the intersection of three curves at the identical combination of interest rate i^* and output level Y^* just a fortuitous coincidence, or are there economic forces at work to maintain an overall equilibrium across all four markets? Further analysis shows that the Mundell–Fleming model is indeed stable in the sense that every disequilibrium triggers forces that shift one or more curves to make them all again intersect at a common point like the ones at i^* and Y^* in Fig. 7.21.

7.5.1 *The adjustment process*

For example, suppose that the interest rate is i^* and the level of output is Y^* in Fig. 7.22. Assume, also, that exchange rates are permitted to float. Notice that the product and money markets are in equilibrium at i^* and Y^*, but the balance of payments is in surplus. Recall that a combination of i and Y above the *BOP* curve causes the domestic currency to appreciate. As Fig. 7.20 showed, appreciation

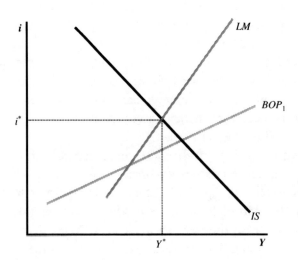

Figure 7.22 When the *BOP* is not in equilibrium.

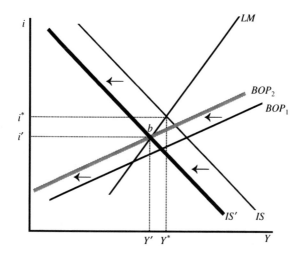

Figure 7.23 Returning to equilibrium by letting the exchange rate change.

shifts the *BOP* curve to the left because, for at every level of income, exports will be smaller and imports larger than before the appreciation. The *IS* curve also shifts because appreciation causes a decline in $X - IM = NX$, and this reduction in aggregate demand shifts the *IS* curve to the left.

The exchange rate appreciation caused by the disequilibrium in Fig. 7.22 shifts the *BOP* curve from BOP_1 curve to BOP_2 and the *IS* curve to *IS'* in Fig. 7.23. Currency appreciation continues until the *BOP* and *IS* curves have shifted far enough to restore equilibrium in all markets. Such equilibrium occurs at a lower interest rate and level of output/income than the unsustainable combination of i^* and Y^*. In the process, the lower interest rate causes investment to increase, but that decline only partially offsets the decline in net exports caused by the currency appreciation. Therefore, Y falls.

7.5.2 Adjustment with pegged exchange rates

The adjustment described in the previous paragraph assumed that exchange rates were allowed to float freely in response to changes in the supply and demand for foreign exchange. Suppose instead that the government keeps the exchange rate pegged to a specific value by intervening in the foreign exchange market. Such currency market intervention was standard operating procedure for 25 years after the Bretton Woods Conference, when countries agreed to keep their currencies pegged to all other currencies. In this case, there is a different adjustment process.

Now, the central bank responds to the tendency for the currency to appreciate by buying the excess foreign exchange. In the process, the central bank supplies its own currency in the foreign exchange market to purchase the foreign currency. This intervention effectively increases the domestic money supply, and the *LM* curve shifts to the right, as in Fig. 7.24. The *IS* and *BOP* curves remain unchanged because the foreign exchange market intervention keeps the exchange rate the same. Note in Fig. 7.24 that, with only the *LM* curve shifting to correct the imbalance in the foreign market, the interest rate declines and the level of output/income increases. Output increases because the expansion of the money supply lowers the interest rate and stimulates investment activity, which is reflected by the economy's movement down along the stationary *IS* curve. The *IS* curve does not shift, however, because the other potential driver of aggregate demand, net exports, remains unchanged with the constant exchange rate.

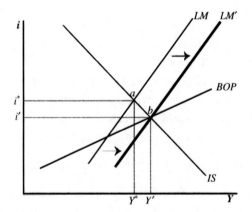

Figure 7.24   Adjustment under a fixed exchange rate.

In sum, the Mundell–Fleming model shows that an economy's adjustment to a disequilibrium depends on the type of exchange rate regime in which policymakers operate. In general, traditional macroeconomic policy tools such as fiscal and monetary policy had different effects on interest rates, output, and employment under the Bretton Woods-pegged exchange rate regime than they do in today's floating exchange rate environment. In the next section, we use the model to neatly categorize these different policy effects.

7.6 Fiscal and Monetary Policies in an Open Economy

The Mundell–Fleming open-economy macroeconomic model provides for a convenient analysis of how the two principal types of macroeconomic policy, *fiscal policy* and *monetary policy*, influence an open economy. The former encompasses the government's spending and taxation. The latter refers to the central bank's management of the economy's money supply. The analysis that follows shows that the macroeconomic consequences of fiscal and monetary policies depend critically on whether (1) exchange rates are permitted to float or the central bank intervenes to keep the exchange rate fixed and (2) the degree of international capital mobility. The two macroeconomic policies, fiscal policy, and monetary policy are analyzed across all combinations of floating exchange rates, fixed exchange rates, mobile capital, and immobile capital. There are, therefore, eight cases in all.

7.6.1 *Foreign exchange market intervention*

The Bretton Woods Agreement at the end of World War II mandated that every country's central bank carry out *foreign exchange market intervention* to keep the exchange rates fixed. Under the Bretton Woods system, as it actually came into practice, each of the world's central banks bought or sold US dollars in order to keep their currency within one percent of their currency's agreed-to target exchange rate with the dollar. Recall from Chapter 3 that when there are *n* currencies, there are only *n*–1 "fundamental" exchange rates, and triangular arbitrage keeps all other exchange rates compatible with these $n-1$ rates. Under the Bretton Woods system, the dollar was designated as the nth currency; the US Federal Reserve Bank remained inactive, thus effectively letting the remaining central banks peg their currencies to the dollar. The Bretton Woods system was able to keep the exchange rates more or less constant among all major world currencies for the 25 years between 1946 and 1971.

A simple example illustrates market intervention. Recall the example of US dollars and Swiss francs from Chapter 3, illustrated here in Fig. 7.25. Suppose that instead of the equilibrium exchange rate of $.50 shown in Fig. 7.25, policymakers in the United States and Switzerland want to keep the exchange rate at $.40 per franc. This can be accomplished by having the Swiss central bank create 300 million francs and use them to buy the dollars. Figure 7.25 shows how such an increase in the supply of francs in the foreign exchange market drives the exchange rate down to $.40.

Figure 7.26 shows the intervention from the Swiss perspective, with the exchange rate stated in terms of francs per dollar. The free market equilibrium exchange rate without intervention would take the exchange rate to $1/e = 1/0.50 = $ SFr2.00 per dollar in the market for dollars. The sale of francs by the Swiss central bank appears in Fig. 7.26 as an increase in demand for dollars, which keeps the demand curve intersecting supply at the target rate of SFr2.50.

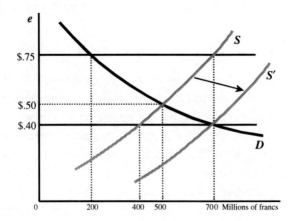

Figure 7.25   The foreign exchange market.

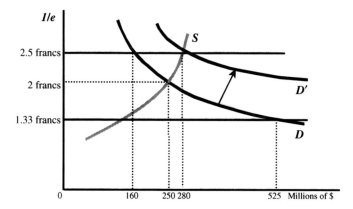

Figure 7.26 Foreign exchange market intervention from the Swiss perspective.

Intervention may not be as straightforward as the above example suggest, however. First of all, the required intervention may require the use of foreign exchange reserves rather than the creation of domestic currency. For example, if the target exchange rate in the example above is $0.75 instead of $0.40, the Swiss central bank would have to use reserves of dollars to buy francs. What if it runs out of dollars? The Swiss central bank cannot print dollars. In such a case, the Swiss central Bank would have to stop intervening and let the exchange rate deviate from the target-pegged rate.

The Swiss central bank does have another option for keeping the exchange rate from changing; however, it can tighten its monetary policy. A tighter monetary policy affects the spot exchange rate by raising Swiss interest rates and, possibly, lowering the rate of Swiss inflation. For example, by tightening the money supply and increasing interest rates, the Swiss central bank alters the ratio $(1 + r^*)/(1 + r)$ that links the spot exchange rate to expected future exchange rates. A higher r^* increases the ratio $[(1 + r^*)/(1 + r)]$ in the interest parity equation and thus, all other things equal, translates a given $E_t e_{t+n}$ into a higher spot rate e like $0.75. Furthermore, the tighter monetary policy may convince people that there will be less inflation in Switzerland in the future and that they should therefore change their expectations about the future competitiveness of Swiss producers in the world market and, hence, $E_t e_{t+n}$. Both the change in $[(1 + r^*)/(1 + r)]$ and $E_t e_{t+n}$ will tend to offset people's decreased supply of dollars and demand for francs and may keep the exchange rate at $0.75.

7.6.2 *The equivalence of monetary policy and exchange market intervention*

Actually, foreign exchange market intervention and monetary policy are fundamentally similar. Central banks normally manage the money supply by means of *open market operations*, which are purchases and sales of assets such as government bonds. In the example above, the Swiss central bank would reduce its money supply by selling bonds to the public, which are paid for by drawing down the purchasers' checking accounts and, therefore, reduces the amount of francs in circulation. There is nothing unique about government bonds when it comes to changing the amount of money in circulation, however. A central bank can decrease the amount of money in circulation by selling anything in its possession, not just bonds. The central bank could just as easily reduce the money supply by selling its headquarters building in Bern; the buyer would write a check on his or her account just as does the buyer of government bonds and thus trigger the same contraction in the amount of money in circulation. Or, the central bank could sell foreign exchange to the public!

Foreign exchange market intervention, therefore, *is* a form of monetary policy that alters the money supply. And, just like bond purchases under the typical open market operations, the central bank's selling of dollars to buy francs tends to raise the Swiss interest rates and reduces the expected inflation, thus helping to drive the franc price of dollars downs (or the dollar price of francs up).

The equivalence of exchange rate intervention and monetary policy makes it clear that a commitment to a pegged exchange rate can clash with a central bank's other goals, such as full employment, rapid economic growth, and price stability. The intervention required to maintain a fixed exchange rate may increase the inflation or raise the unemployment. This is not to say that there are no important advantages to keep the exchange rates *fixed*. The volatility and uncertainty of *floating* exchange rates makes international trade and investment more risky and, therefore, less attractive. Also, changing exchange rates can have very large wealth effects when people own assets or owe debt denominated on currencies other than their own, and these wealth effects can have recessionary or inflationary macroeconomic effects. As will be discussed in the later chapters, efforts to keep the exchange rates from changing can cause financial crises and prolonged recessions that greatly diminish the human welfare. However, there is no avoiding the fact that the goal of keeping exchange rates fixed often results in specific monetary policies that clash with other macroeconomic goals. The analysis that follows further details how macroeconomic policies are restricted under a regime of fixed exchange rates maintained through foreign exchange market intervention.

7.6.3 *Monetary policy while pegging the exchange rates*

Figure 7.27 presents the case of expansionary monetary policy, say by means of open market operations in which it purchases Treasury bonds from the public, while exchange rates are fixed. The diagram shows both the case of immobile capital and mobile capital, as represented, respectively, by BOP_1 and BOP_2. In either case, when the

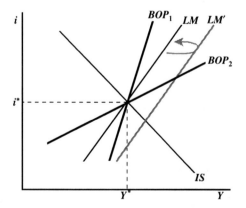

Figure 7.27 Monetary policy under a pegged exchange rate regime.

central bank carries out open market operations and increases the real money supply, the *LM* curve shifts to the right. Such a shift lowers the interest rate and raises the output to a combination below and to the right of the *BOP* curve. This causes the supply of the national currency to exceed its demand, and the exchange rate will depreciate. With instructions to prevent the exchange rate from changing, the central bank then has to intervene in the foreign exchange market by using foreign reserves to buy its national currency. This reduces the amount of currency in the hands of the public and shifts the *LM* curve back to the left. Intervention stops only when the *LM* curve is back where it started, exactly offsetting the monetary expansion. Specifically, the same amount of dollars that the central bank put into circulation when it purchased Treasury bonds are withdrawn from circulation when it sells foreign exchange to buy dollars in the foreign exchange market. The only difference is that now the central bank has more Treasury bonds and fewer foreign exchange reserves. Notice also that these results do not depend at all on whether the *BOP* curve is steep or flat.

Therefore, in both the mobile capital and immobile capital cases, if the central bank is instructed to keep the exchange rates fixed, it no longer has the freedom to carry out monetary policy to stimulate or contract output or to address other domestic policy objectives. The commitment to fix exchange rates takes away the central bank's freedom to carry out the monetary policy to address other policy goals such as full employment, low inflation, or output stability.

7.6.4 *Fiscal policy with pegged exchange rates*

Expansionary fiscal policy, say an increase in government expenditures, shifts the *IS* curve to the right. Like the shift in the *LM* curve under monetary policy, a fiscal policy shift moves the economy away from balance in its foreign payments, and the exchange rate will change. If the central bank is committed to keeping the exchange rate fixed, it will have to intervene in the foreign exchange market to compensate for the induced disequilibrium in foreign payments. Such intervention causes a de facto change in the money supply and, hence,

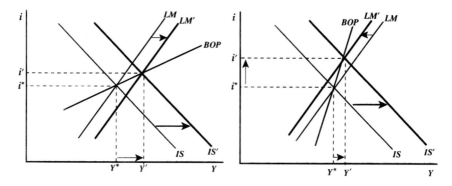

Figure 7.28 Fiscal policy under fixed exchange rates, comparing mobile and immobile capital.

a shift in the *LM* curve. In this case, the direction of the shift in the *LM* curve depends on how mobile capital is, how steep the *BOP* curve is relative to the *LM* curve.

As illustrated in the left-hand diagram in Fig. 7.28, if capital is mobile and the *BOP* curve is relatively flat, an initial shift to the right of the *IS* curve pushes the economy's interest rate/output combination above the *BOP* curve and the exchange rate begins to appreciate. To prevent the appreciation, the central bank begins buying foreign exchange and thus selling its currency on the foreign exchange market, and this increases the amount of dollars in circulation and, therefore, shifts the *LM* curve to the right. The amount of intervention required consists of selling enough currency to maintain equilibrium in the balance of payments and keep the economy on the *BOP*, which remains unchanged when the exchange rate is not allowed to change. Thus, the economy returns to equilibrium in all three markets shown in the diagram (and thus the fourth too), and the *BOP*, *LM'*, and *IS'* curves again intersect at one common point. The interest rate ends up having increased, and output also rises.

Compared to the case of mobile capital above, fiscal policy has a somewhat different effect on output and the interest rate when capital is immobile. The right-hand side of Fig. 7.28 shows that when the *BOP* curve is steeper than the *LM* curve, expansionary fiscal policy moves the economy to a combination of output and interest rate to the right of the *BOP* curve, where the supply of the domestic currency exceeds the demand in the foreign exchange market and the currency begins to depreciate. Thus, to keep the exchange rate constant, the central bank must buy its currency in the foreign exchange market, which reduces the money supply and shifts the *LM* curve to the left. Because expansionary fiscal policy forces the central bank to contract the money supply when capital is immobile, output rises less and interest rates rise more than in the case of mobile capital.

In sum, in an international monetary system of fixed exchange rates, fiscal policy shifts affect the output less when capital is immobile than when capital is mobile, but, not surprisingly, interest rates are more volatile in the case of immobile capital. The analysis also shows clearly that in an open economy, fiscal policy has different effects than in a closed economy.

7.6.5 *Monetary policy with floating exchange rates*

When exchange rates are allowed to float freely and the central bank does not have to intervene in the foreign exchange market to keep the exchange rate fixed, the central bank can focus its monetary policy on other goals, such as full employment, price stability, and economic growth. Suppose that the central bank judges the level of unemployment to be too high and it undertakes open market purchases of government bonds to expand the money supply in the expectation that this will cause total aggregate demand, and hence output, to expand. Such an expansionary monetary policy causes a rightward shift of the *LM* curve, and as both diagrams in Fig. 7.29 show, the economy moves toward a new domestic equilibrium below and to the right of the initial *BOP* curve.

With the decision to let the exchange rates float freely, the central bank does not have to react to the depreciation of the national currency; it simply lets the currency depreciate. The case of expansionary monetary policy under floating exchange rates and mobile capital is presented in the left-hand diagram of Fig. 7.29. The rightward shift of the *LM* curve pushes the economy away from the *BOP* curve, and because the depreciation of the currency increases net exports, *NX*, in

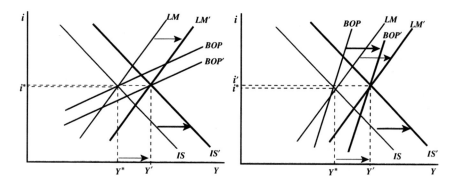

Figure 7.29 Monetary policy under floating exchange rates and immobile capital.

aggregate demand, the *IS* curve shifts to the right. The depreciation's effect on *NX* also shifts the *BOP* curve to the right. The relative shifts in the *IS* and *BOP* curves may depend on whether the monetary expansion is seen as permanent, so that the exchange rate is likely to remain depreciated for a long time, or temporary. If permanent, the *BOP* curve is likely to shift relatively less than the *IS* curve because the expected future depreciations will discourage capital inflows and at least partially offset the improvement in the trade balance. Since the *IS* curve is affected only by the growth in net exports, it will shift further than the *BOP* curve. Note from the left-hand diagram in Fig. 7.29 that if the *IS* curve shifts more than the *BOP* curve, expansionary monetary policy increase the equilibrium level of Y more.

The case of immobile capital illustrated in the right-hand diagram of Fig. 7.29 is similar to the mobile capital case. The monetary expansion shifts the *LM* curve from *LM* to *LM'*, which induces a currency depreciation that, in turn, causes net exports to increase and both the *IS* and *BOP* curves to shift to the right. The issue of whether the *IS* curve shifts more than the *BOP* curve is less important in the case of immobile capital, because the immobility implies that expectations about the permanence of expansionary monetary policy are likely to have little effect on capital movements. In any case, the new equilibrium where all three curves again intersect will involve an increase in Y. Note that the interest rate may increase or decrease.

The specific examples in Fig. 7.29 show the interest rate remaining about the same. Actually, depending on the strength of the shifts in the *BOP* and *IS* curves, the interest rate could increase or decrease modestly. However, output clearly expands in both cases. Also, compared to the case of fixed exchange rates, monetary policy is clearly more potent in raising output in the case of floating exchange rates because the expansionary monetary policy tends to keep the interest rates from rising when output increases.

7.6.6 *Fiscal policy with floating exchange rates*

To complete our analysis of macroeconomic policy in an open economy, we analyze fiscal policy in a regime of floating exchange rates. The left-hand and right-hand sides of Fig. 7.30 describe the cases when capital is mobile and immobile, respectively. Note that fiscal policy does not affect the *LM* curve because the central bank does not have to intervene in the foreign exchange market. Since we seek to isolate the effect of a shift in fiscal policy, we assume central bank monetary policy remains unchanged when fiscal policy changes.

In the case of mobile capital, illustrated in the left-hand diagram of Fig. 7.30, an expansionary fiscal policy that shifts the *IS* curve to *IS'* pushes the economy's equilibrium above and to the left of the relatively flat *BOP* curve. Therefore, the exchange rate appreciates and

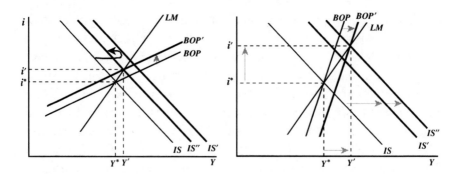

Figure 7.30 Fiscal policy under floating exchange rates, mobile and immobile capital.

the trade balance *NX* declines, which partially offsets the initial policy-mandated shift in the *IS* curve. The *IS* curve therefore only shifts to, say, *IS″*. Also, the *BOP* curve shifts upward when the currency appreciates. The economy establishes a new equilibrium at a point like Y' and i' in the left-hand side diagram. Output and employment are higher.

The case of immobile capital is illustrated in the right-hand side of Fig. 7.30. When expansionary fiscal policy shifts the *IS* curve to the right, the balance of payments goes into deficit and the currency depreciates. As a result, net exports increase and the *IS* shifts further to the right to *IS″*. The depreciation also causes the *BOP* curve to shift down and to the right. The new equilibrium is at Y' and i' in the right-hand side diagram.

A comparison of the two cases in Fig. 7.30 shows that fiscal policy is relatively more powerful in increasing output and employment when capital is immobile. In the case of mobile capital, expansionary fiscal policy causes the currency to appreciate, reducing the trade balance and, thus, aggregate demand, which offsets the initial fiscal expansion. In the case of immobile capital, expansionary fiscal policy causes a currency depreciation that further stimulates aggregate demand by improving the trade balance.

7.6.7 *Comparing macroeconomic policy in closed and open economies*

It is interesting to compare monetary and fiscal policy in open and closed economies to see whether globalization reduces or increases the strength of policymakers' traditional macroeconomic tools. Policymakers often deflect criticism of their management of their economies by claiming that the globalization has reduced their ability to influence the output and employment.

Table 7.1 compares the effect on equilibrium output of expansionary fiscal and monetary policies in closed and open economies under the eight cases discussed above. For each case, the comparable closed economy effect is the simple shift to the new intersection of the *IS* and *LM* curves, ignoring the follow-on effects of the shift in the

Table 7.1   Comparing the Fiscal and Monetary Policy in Closed and Open Economies.

	Fixed Exchange Rates		Floating Exchange Rates	
	Immobile capital	Mobile capital	Immobile capital	Mobile capital
Fiscal policy	Less effective	More effective	More effective	Less effective
Monetary policy	Completely ineffective	Completely ineffective	More effective	More effective

BOP curve or the mandated foreign exchange market intervention to avoid the *BOP* shift.

Table 7.1 shows that Mundell and Fleming's addition of the trade balance and financial account to the basic Keynesian model, in the form of the *BOP* curve and the augmented *IS* relationship, changes the potency of fiscal and monetary policy to pursue the policy goals such as increasing the economy's output and reducing the unemployment. But the differences vary across the policies and circumstances. Several results of the analysis stand out. First, in the case of fixed exchange rates, fiscal policy is more effective in changing the output than monetary policy. In fact, monetary policy is completely ineffective in changing either output or interest rates when the central bank is obligated to peg the exchange rate by intervening in the foreign exchange market. This result helps to explain the complaints from many central bankers in the 1960s, when the Bretton Woods system of pegged exchange rates was in effect, that they were powerless to respond to unemployment and inflation. Second, fiscal policy is more effective in managing the economy's level of output when the *BOP* curve is flat, that is, when capital is mobile and international trade is large relative to the individual economy. This helps to explain why fiscal policy is today seen as the main tool for managing the individual economies within the European Union, where the introduction of a single currency managed by a regional central bank has effectively eliminated monetary policy as a national policy option. Third, in the case of floating exchange rates and mobile capital, the case most relevant for most policymakers operating in today's global economy, monetary policy is the more potent policy tool for maintaining full employment and price stability.

7.7 Does a Depreciation Improve the Trade Balance?

The Mundell–Fleming model assumes that the depreciation of a country's currency increases net exports and an appreciation decreases net exports. This assumption is what justifies shifting the *IS* and *BOP* curves to the right in the case of a depreciation, for example. This assumption seems reasonable to most people, but is it accurate? The legitimacy of this assumption depends critically on the elasticities of the import and export supply and demand curves.

For example, if foreign demand for a country's exports is very price inelastic, a depreciation of the country's currency will actually result in lower earnings of foreign exchange from exports. Then, if the domestic demand for imports is also very inelastic, so that the foreign currency cost of imports remains nearly unchanged after the depreciation, the balance of payments actually declines (the *BOP* curve may shift to the left) with a depreciation!

7.7.1 The Marshall–Lerner condition

If we also suppose that the foreign exchange value of exports is about equal to the foreign exchange value of imports, so that $X^* = IM^*$, then the following relationship must hold for a depreciation to increase a country's net exports:

$$(h_x + h_{im} - 1) > 0 \qquad (7.6)$$

Equation (7.6) defines what is known as the *Marshall–Lerner condition*, which states that the sum of the elasticities of demand for exports, h_x, and imports, h_{im}, must be greater than one. This relationship is named for two prominent early 20th century economists, Alfred Marshall and Abba P. Lerner, who contributed to its derivation. When the Marshall–Lerner condition is satisfied, depreciation of its currency improves a country's balance of trade.

In the open-economy macroeconomics literature, economists often precede analysis that uses the Mundell–Fleming model by stating explicitly that "the Marshall–Lerner condition is assumed to be satisfied". They are effectively assuming that a currency depreciation increases net exports, or more specifically, that a depreciation shifts the *BOP* curve to the right and an appreciation shifts the *BOP* curve to the left. We implicitly made that assumption throughout this chapter. Were we justified in making that assumption?

7.7.2 *Evidence on the Marshall–Lerner condition*

In the 1950s, when international investment was very small and the balance of payments consisted mostly of international trade flows, some economists argued that low demand elasticities made the exchange rate a useless tool for correcting balance of payments deficits and surpluses. These economists were referred to as "elasticity pessimists" because they argued that elasticities of demand for exports and imports were very low. They argued against floating exchange rates, insisting that balance of payments problems required macroeconomic policies that changed aggregate demand. Other economists, known as "elasticity optimists", countered with estimates of demand elasticities that suggested a depreciation would indeed correct the trade deficits, and, therefore, floating exchange rates would be a stabilizing force in the world economy.

A popular study by Houthakker and Magee (1969) used data for the years 1951 through 1966 to estimate the export and import demand elasticities. They estimated that $h_x = 1.51$ and $h_{im} = 1.03$, which implied that the Marshall–Lerner condition was satisfied:

$$(h_x + h_{im} - 1) = (1.51 + 1.03 - 1) = 1.54 > 0 \qquad (7.7)$$

Equation (7.7) has been used to estimate how much the trade balance changes with a depreciation. For example, given that US exports were equal to about $59.7 billion in 1971, the year when the US dollar was devalued by an 8.57 percent against other world currencies, equation (7.7) and the estimate of the Marshall–Lerner condition from

Table 7.2　The US Trade Balance ($ Billions): 1971–1975.

	1971	1972	1973	1974	1975
Exports	59.7	67.2	91.2	120.9	132.6
Imports	−61.0	−72.7	−89.3	−125.2	−120.2
Balance (NX)	−1.3	−5.4	1.9	−4.3	12.4

Houthakker and Magee suggests that the trade balance should have improved by

$$NX^\star = X^\star(h_x + h_{im} - 1)\Delta e/e$$
$$= \$59.7(1.54)\ .0857 = \$7.9 \text{ billion} \tag{7.8}$$

Did this happen?

Table 7.2 shows the actual changes in the balance of trade from 1971 through 1975. The 1972 trade balance did not improve by $8 billion compared to 1971. Interestingly, it did improve by nearly that amount from 1972 to 1973. Then, when the US dollar depreciated further in 1973, the trade balance declined by over $6 billion in 1974, only to improve again by over $16 billion from 1974 to 1975.

7.7.3　Why the Marshall-Lerner condition is inaccurate

The analysis using the Mundell–Fleming model suggests why it is not really correct to use the Marshall–Lerner condition to predict the change in the trade balance following a currency depreciation or appreciation. In general, other things seldom remain the same. The elasticities approach to the balance of payments unrealistically assumes that all other things remain equal when the exchange rate changes. For one thing, the Mundell–Fleming model shows that a change in the exchange rate may shift other curves. The actual change in the balance of trade depends on how all the other shifts and adjustments described in the Mundell–Fleming model work themselves out.

Another weakness of the *elasticities approach* to the balance of payments is that demand and supply elasticities are not constants.

Elasticities are generally much smaller in the short run than they are in the long run. In the short run, it is difficult for importers and exporters to change their behavior, but in the long run, price changes tend to change the behavior quite substantially. Exports require marketing activities, and these take time to put into effect. It takes time to establish the distribution channels, to develop an advertising campaign, to establish a reputation, and to develop customer loyalty. Much international trade is conducted under long-term contracts and agreements. On the supply side, it takes time to increase output when the exchange rate improves international competitiveness. Increased exports may require new factories and changes in product characteristics.

There is evidence suggesting that the Marshall–Lerner condition changes gradually following a sharp change in the exchange rate. For example, the US dollar depreciated sharply in the first half of 1985, but the US trade deficit continued to grow throughout 1985 and 1986. Only in 1987 did the US trade deficit begin to shrink. Similar delayed effects of devaluations and depreciation had been observed in the 1970s following the oil price increases, with trade deficits initially increasing before beginning to shrink some two years later. This phenomenon was termed the *J*-Curve effect, for reasons that should be obvious from Fig. 7.31.

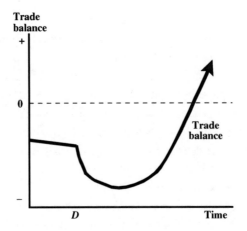

Figure 7.31   The *J*-curve.

Figure 7.31 graphs a trade balance that is negative and becoming more negative. Suppose that at the point in time denoted by the letter *D*, the government devalues the currency by changing its intervention in the foreign exchange market or it triggers a depreciation by suddenly altering its monetary and fiscal policies. If the Marshall–Lerner condition is not satisfied in the short run because short-run elasticities are small, the trade balance will actually grow larger after the depreciation. As time passes, however, importers and exporters at home and abroad begin to adjust to the new currency values. Demand and supply become more elastic as time passes, and the Marshall–Lerner condition is eventually satisfied, at which point the trade deficit begins to shrink. The deficit may even turn into a surplus in the long run if elasticities change enough.

7.8 Summary and Conclusions

This chapter detailed the popular Mundell–Fleming open-economy macroeconomic model. The Mundell–Fleming model is the open-economy version of the textbook Keynesian macroeconomic model, often called the *IS-LM* model. Among the important points to remember are

1. Keynes developed the first modern macroeconomic model during the Great Depression.
2. His model describes how the main sectors of the model interact within the overall economic system to determine the total output and the level of employment.
3. Mundell and Fleming added international trade and international investment to the Keynesian model.
4. The graphic Mundell–Fleming model shows how the exchange rate interacts with the other variables in the Keynesian model, such as income, the interest rate, the money supply, investment, consumption, and government fiscal policy to determine the economic equilibrium.
5. Like the Keynesian model, the Mundell–Fleming model shows that the economy's equilibrium is not always at or even near its full employment level.

6. Comparing the closed-economy and open-economy versions of the Keynesian model shows that globalization changes the effects of monetary and fiscal policies; Table 7.1 details the changes.

7. Overall, the Mundell–Fleming model reinforces the conclusions of Keynesian macroeconomic analysis, namely that the government has a role in keeping the economy operating near the full employment.

8. Like all models, the Mundell–Fleming model makes certain assumptions, among which is the satisfaction of the Marshall–Lerner condition.

Extending the *IS-LM* model to include international trade and investment certainly makes the model more relevant for analyzing today's global economy. However, the Mundell–Fleming model suffers from the several weaknesses that also plague the popular *IS-LM* model. First of all, the Keynesian model focuses on the demand side of the economy. It lacks a formal supply side, which is why the model was not very helpful for explaining the oil supply shock of the 1970s and the inflationary episodes that followed.

A second shortcoming of the graphic Keynesian and Mundell–Fleming models is that investment is specified to be a stable function of the interest rate. Keynes never assumed that the investment was driven by such a simple, or simplistic, function, however. He certainly never intended such a simplistic relationship to occupy the center of his model. In his 1936 *General Theory of Employment, Interest, and Money*, Keynes offered a very insightful and sophisticated discussion of investment, not at all like the investment function presented in the graphic model of this chapter.

We have to remember that the graphic model presented in this chapter is due not to Keynes, but to other economists who sought a simple graphic way to teach Keynes' most important ideas from his *General Theory*. The graphic model in this chapter clearly brings out the roles of monetary and fiscal policies in stabilizing the economy, as Keynes intended. Unfortunately, the simplified model loses Keynes' explanation of why economies are volatile and require continual stabilization policies in the first place. In short, the textbook version of the Keynesian model explains why an economy can settle into a high unemployment equilibrium. But it cannot explain the other concern of economists during the Great Depression, which was to figure out the cause of the large decline in aggregate demand that pushed the economy to its depression equilibrium. Fortunately, Keynes provides a very lucid and insightful explanation of the causes of the collapse in lending and investment in the 1930s but those insights were not included in the graphic model by those Keynesians who designed it. Chapter 18 returns to Keynes' (1936) insight in order to explain the 2008 global economic recession.

The next chapter moves beyond the Mundell–Fleming model to introduce the supply side of the economy. Then, in Chapter 9, the demand side from this chapter and the supply side from the next chapter will be combined to provide a richer macroeconomic model, in which, by the way, it is possible to more accurately bring out Keynes' investment model and his dynamic analysis that reveals the sources of instability in a modern economic system.

Key Terms and Concepts

Aggregate demand	Elasticity	Money market
Asset market	*IS-LM* model	Mundell–Fleming
Consumption function	*J*-curve	model
Crowding out effect	Keynesian cross	Product market
Export demand	Marginal propensity	Scientific reductionism
elasticity	Marshall–Lerner	Store-of-wealth motive
Fiscal policy	condition	Transactions demand
Holism	Mobile capital	Walras' law
Immobile capital	Monetary policy	Walrasian model

Chapter Questions and Problems

1. Explain under which conditions the following statement is true: "The central bank can control either the exchange rate or the money supply, but not both".

2. Explain precisely how the exchange rate affects the curves in the graphic Mundell–Fleming model. As an illustration, explain how an appreciation of the currency affects the economy's equilibrium level of GDP.

3. In the early 1980s, US macroeconomic policy combined a tight monetary policy to combat high inflation and very expansionary fiscal policy resulting from a reduction in taxes and an expansion of military expenditures. Use the Mundell–Fleming model to illustrate the effects of this combination of policies on the exchange rate. Specifically, set up the model by stating your exact assumptions about the shapes of the curves and why those assumptions are appropriate for 1980, and then show how the curves shift as a direct result of the macroeconomic shifts. Finally, describe exactly how the shifts in the curves move the economy to a new macroeconomic equilibrium.

4. In the 1960s, US macroeconomic policy combined a monetary policy that tried to keep the interest rate constant while the Lyndon Johnson administration and Congress allocated increasing amounts of money toward the Vietnam War and the social programs of the "Great Society", all without increasing taxes. Use the Mundell–Fleming model to illustrate the effects of this combination of policies on the exchange rate. Specifically, set up the model by stating your exact assumptions about the shapes of the curves and why those assumptions are appropriate for 1965, and then show how the curves shift as a direct result of the macroeconomic policy shifts. Finally, describe exactly how the shifts in the curves move the economy to a new macroeconomic equilibrium.

5. Use the Mundell–Fleming model to analyze how the deep economic recession in the major economies in 2009 would affect the economy of China, a major exporter of goods and capital to the major economies of North America and Europe. Discuss how international trade and international investment flows affect China. Does what you know about macroeconomic performance in China in 2010 match what the model suggests? Discuss.

6. Use the Mundell–Fleming model to explain precisely why in an open economy, the share of trade in the economy and the mobility of international capital are important for determining the overall effects of fiscal policies (Hint: review the explanation for the steepness of the *BOP* curve).

7. Explain how the Mundell–Fleming model depends on the Marshall–Lerner condition. Specifically, explain why the elasticities of import and export demand matter for the adjustment of the model to a stable equilibrium.

8. Read the following short mystery story entitled "The Fatal Equilibrium" below and use the Mundell–Fleming model to explain precisely how the inspector figured out who the murderer was. In your answer, you should draw an appropriate model that reflects the economic conditions in Europe in 1963, especially with regard to the exchange rate regime (Bretton Woods is still in effect) and the degree of capital mobility in Europe the early 1960s.

The Fatal Equilibrium

It was a cold Tuesday morning in January of 1963, the Minister of Economic Affairs, Dr. Henri Boulanger, was found dead on the floor of the study of his country mansion in a small village in the outskirts of the capital city. The minister was apparently killed by a single shot from a small hand weapon, and judging by the burn in his clothes near the wound, the shot had been at very close range. The newspaper delivery man, known to the whole village only as Marcel, said he had found the body at about 8:20 a.m. Marcel had called the police from the Minister's telephone in the study.

Because the murder involved a government Minister, the local police immediately called in the National Police. The National Police brought in their top investigators, who began scouring the house for clues. By mid-morning, there were about two dozen vehicles parked outside the Boulanger mansion. The local police had been relegated to directing the traffic and keeping the reporters away from the house.

This was the biggest murder case in years. Boulanger was a very popular public official, perhaps the most popular official in the country given that most people seemed to have little regard for the politicians who occupied the positions of President, Prime Minister, and Speaker of the Assembly. Boulanger was a competent economist and had been a popular professor at School of Economics at the National University. He had the ability to actually make economics understandable to the average person on the street. The country's position in the new European Common Market, the limits of monetary policy under the rules of the Bretton Woods system, the maintenance of tight controls on capital movements into and out of the country despite the commitment to liberalize the trade, the increased expenditures on education to improve the employment and productivity, and many other policy issues the

Minister had explained in entertaining radio talks listened to by surprisingly large numbers of people. The trust Boulanger inspired helped to elevate him to a prominent position in what was otherwise a very weak and undistinguished government. He had come to assume a key role in the government's attempt to introduce new economic measures to restore the economic growth and price stability after several years of political confusion and policy reversals.

Marcel was questioned by a team of investigators. He nervously explained that, over the past 30 years, he had been accustomed to entering the front door and bringing the copies of the capital's three major newspapers into Boulanger's study.

"Dr. Boulanger always left the front door unlocked for me. He couldn't wait to get his newspapers", Marcel explained. "No matter how early I came, he'd look at me as if to say: "Why are you so late? But he was a nice man", continued Marcel. "I made him the first stop on my route".

"Did anything in the house look different this morning?" asked Hercule Cognac, the renowned detective of the National Police who had been called on to head the investigation of this very sensitive case.

"It was very cold in the house; the fire had gone out in the fireplace. I knew something was wrong", continued Marcel. "I was disappointed because I had been looking forward to the little glass of brandy that the Minister usually offered me on a cold morning like this. This is terrible!" exclaimed Marcel.

"Thank you very much", said Cognac in a business-like manner. Please let us know if you think of anything else that seemed different this morning", continued Cognac, pointing Marcel toward one of the other inspectors from the National Police.

One of the investigators soon found a small handgun on a bookshelf near the front door, carelessly squeezed between Adam Smith's *Wealth of Nations* and Keynes' *General Theory*. The gun had been fired once.

"Ah, a careless amateur!" exclaimed Hercule Cognac as he eyed every detail at the crime scene.

"But not entirely stupid", replied Wilson, Cognac's long-time assistant who had accompanied him to the mansion that morning. "The fingerprints were thoroughly cleaned off".

Cognac's thoughts were already elsewhere. "You have, of course, contacted the neighbors?"

"Yes, but we learned nothing. No one heard a shot or any other suspicious activity", replied Wilson.

The minister lived alone in the large mansion that had belonged to his family for generations. The grounds were extensive, and the mansion sat far from the road and even farther from the neighbors' homes. The cold weather meant that the mansion's windows and curtains had all been tightly closed. Cognac was not surprised that the shot had not reached the ears of the distant neighbors, who were similarly enclosed in their warm homes.

The phone rang, and Wilson answered. He looked toward Cognac and said: "The preliminary autopsy suggests that the murder took place between 21:00 and 23:00".

"Ah, that gives us three suspects", replied Cognac, looking at the minister's agenda on the massive oak desk in the corner of the study. "He was expecting visits from the Central Bank Director, Louis Fabricant d'Argent, Jan Van Noord, the Minister of Economic Affairs from our neighbor Belgium, and Jean Domage, the President of the National Real Estate Association".

"In that order?" asked Wilson.

"There are no times written in the agenda, just that they were going to visit last night", replied Cognac.

"Fabricant d'Argent is the one who went through the long confirmation hearings in the Assembly, isn't he?" asked Wilson.

"Yes, of course", replied Cognac. "He's the former financial columnist from that second-rate newspaper that the Prime Minister insisted on putting in charge of the Central Bank. Rumor has it that he got the job because he was the Prime Minister's nephew. Silly sentiments always get people in trouble! I stopped reading his financial column a long time ago", Cognac went on. "For years he has been advocating rapid money creation as the solution to all economic problems. That's what his political party always pushes for".

"But then during his confirmation hearing, he swore that he would be a conservative Central Bank Director, entirely dedicated to preventing inflation", chipped in Wilson. "Few people believe him to this day. Do you suppose he had some sort of argument with the Minister of Economic Affairs?"

"It's possible", replied Cognac. "Of course, under the Bretton Woods arrangement, the Central Bank has few choices about monetary policy".

"What do you mean?" asked Wilson.

Cognac did not feel the urge to explain the international finance to Wilson, so he simply continued looking around the room. "Don't forget Jean Domage and the Belgian". Cognac said, changing the subject. "The Belgian Minister of Economic Affairs has often been criticized for his handling of economic policy. Their economy is not doing well, and unemployment is nearly 12 percent! Rumors have it that Van Noord is not a very good economist. I did read, though, that his new economic plan was praised by several leading Belgian economists."

"But, why would the economic situation in Belgium lead him to shoot our Minister of Economic Affairs?" asked Wilson.

"Borders mean little today, Wilson. We are living in an increasingly global economy!" exclaimed Cognac. "What we do in this country matters a lot to whether his new economic plan works in Belgium. Of course, our own economy has been a little lifeless lately too", continued Cognac. "What is our unemployment rate now?"

"It is a bit higher than normal, the newspaper said yesterday, the fifth straight month of above average unemployment", replied Wilson.

"But it is not very high compared to Belgium", replied Cognac, now digging through the drawers of the Minister's desk.

"I don't trust that real estate guy", said Wilson, anxious to switch the subject away from economics.

"That goes without saying", replied Cognac without looking up. "I'd rather buy a used car than a house!"

Wilson smiled at Cognac and then continued looking around the room while they talked. "Domage has been making speeches calling on the government to lower interest rates so that housing loans would be more affordable. He openly criticized the Minister of Economic Affairs. I saw the remarks in the paper just the other day".

"Yes, I read that too", replied Cognac. "But this is a case of murder, not a policy argument. We need more information. A murder requires a strong motive. We need to use our brains, Wilson. We must not jump to unsubstantiated conclusions!"

Wilson had heard these little lectures many times. He could see that Cognac was getting excited about the new case, and he just looked down while leafing through a pile of papers on the minister's desk.

The following day, the three suspects were discretely brought to police headquarters for questioning. Protests from the Belgian Embassy required the personal attention of the Foreign Minister, but the Belgian Economics Minister finally agreed to waive his diplomatic status and answer questions. Each suspect claimed to have visited the murdered minister around 21:00 and to have parted on the friendliest terms with the minister very much alive.

"Of course", said Hercule Cognac. "What else would they say? These political characters will not confess easily. We need to look for motives!"

Cognac's questioning of the Minister of Economic Affairs' secretary the previous afternoon had given him very useful information. The Minister of Economic Affairs had been given the authority by the Prime Minister to draw up the new government budget. It was entirely up to Minister Boulanger to decide the final numbers for all of the government's taxes and expenditures. The large majority that the Prime Minister controlled in the Assembly meant that the budget would probably pass without difficulty when it came up for a vote. However, getting a budget ready for the vote had proven especially difficult. Endless bickering within the party ranks had prevented the committee in charge from completing the budget. According to the secretary, "The Prime Minister was so frustrated that he decided to just let an objective financial expert like the Minister of Economic Affairs make the decisions". Cognac learned that the Prime Minister had earlier that week confirmed to several important political allies that the Minister of Economic Affairs' budget decisions would be final. Equally frustrated leaders of the party's many factions had guaranteed full support for the budget in the National Assembly, whatever the budget was to be. The agreement signaled the high regard that the Minister of Economic Affairs enjoyed throughout the party and the Assembly. It also was a recognition of a political reality: the public was losing confidence in the politicians that led the political coalition in control of the Assembly and wanted action.

The Minister of Economic Affairs was to have presented his budget decisions in a speech to the Assembly at 10:00 that cold morning of his murder. No one at the Ministry or the Assembly had any idea about what the Minister was going to say. The Minister had met with many people, but, according to those involved, he had asked all the questions and said nothing himself.

According to Boulanger's secretary, Boulanger had become annoyed at the lack of economic understanding among government leaders. "He tended more and more to make his own decisions", the secretary had told Cognac. "He often said how he missed discussing economics with his students at the University", she had added.

"We need to find his speech. That speech can tell us who the murderer is", exclaimed Cognac. "Wilson, do you remember seeing a copy of a speech anywhere in the Minister's mansion?"

"No, but I wasn't looking for a speech to solve a murder", Wilson replied.

Cognac had Wilson drive him back to the Minister's mansion. When they finally arrived at the mansion, the door was tightly locked. The investigators had apparently finished their work and left. Cognac had brought one of the keys his office had made for those on the case. He unlocked the door, and he and Wilson began searching the house.

Cognac and Wilson looked through the many file cabinets, drawers, and closets, but the speech and budget proposals were nowhere be found. The longer he searched, the more Hercule Cognac became convinced that the speech held the key to the mystery.

"If only we knew whether the budget was to have been expansionary or contractionary", thought Cognac, "That would neatly eliminate one or two of the suspects".

"Contractionary or expansionary?" exclaimed Wilson. "What on earth do you mean by that?"

Few people knew that the renowned detective and national hero Cognac had a Ph.D. in economics. He never mentioned it to anyone, perhaps for fear of undermining his social reputation. Cognac had become known as something of a bonvivant, which often served to open doors among the rich and famous of the capital city. Few people would trust him as readily if they knew he was an economist.

After looking in, under, and behind everything in the mansion, Cognac was ready to quit and go to dinner at one of his favorite restaurants in the capital. On his way out, he noticed an envelope with some scribbling sticking out from under the blotter on the Minister's large mahogany desk. He grabbed the envelope and as he began to read the scribbled words as he exclaimed: "Just like an economist, he never wasted anything".

Cognac continued to read the scribbled words on the envelope. Then he looked at Wilson and exclaimed: "Case Solved!"

"Oh, just like that?" replied Wilson skeptically.

"Listen to this, Wilson! This explains everything", continued Cognac, as he read from the envelope. "...and therefore I have become convinced that the country must have a budget that raises expenditures but does not increase taxes".

"How in the world does that statement tell you who murdered the minister?", asked Wilson, clearly puzzled by Cognac's confidence.

"Some friends of mine at the IMF, Mundell and Fleming, they gave me an interesting model some time ago. It is most helpful".

References

Fleming, MJ (1962). Domestic financial policies under fixed and under floating exchange rates. *International Monetary Fund Staff Papers*, 9, 369–379.

Houthakker, HS and SP Magee (1969). Income and price elasticities in world trade. *Review of Economics and Statistics*, 51, 111–125.

Keynes, JM (1936). *The General Theory of Employment, Interest and Money*. London: MacMillan.

Mundell, RA (1963). Capital mobility and stabilizing policy under fixed and flexible exchange rates. *Canadian Journal of Economics and Political Science*, 29, 475–485.

Chapter 8

The Supply Side of the Economy

> Knowledge is the only instrument of production not subject to diminishing returns.

> (J. M. Clark[1])

In the 1970s, policymakers in many countries faced a strange combination of declining employment and rising inflation, or what came to be called *stagflation*. The basic Keynesian macroeconomic model provided contradictory advice; expansionary fiscal and monetary policies were called for to increase employment, but contractionary fiscal and monetary policies were needed to reduce inflation. The standard demand-side Keynesian model elaborated in the previous chapter has trouble explaining stagflation.

The Mundell–Fleming open-economy macroeconomic model, like the basic Keynesain model, focuses entirely on the demand side of the economy. It implicitly assumes that the economy has the capacity to produce whatever quantity of goods and services is demanded. In the real world, however, productive resources do not exist in unlimited quantities, nor can technologies extend our limited

---

[1] J. M. Clark was an early 20th century American institutional economist, whose work contributed to the development of modern macroeconomics.

resources into infinite supplies of goods and services. There is a supply side to the economy, and that is the focus of this chapter.

First of all, this chapter examines the supply of labor. The labor market is central to macroeconomics because it determines the level of employment, a critical measure of economic performance. This chapter also discusses economic growth and the dual role of investment as both a source of aggregate demand and the source of capital on the supply side of the economy. The fundamental purpose of this chapter is to explain an economy's *aggregate supply*. We develop an aggregate supply function that incorporates modern macroeconomic concepts such as expectations, the dynamics of price adjustments in the economy, and economic growth.

Chapter Goals

1. Explain the determinants of aggregate supply.
2. Detail the traditional short-run labor supply explanation of the economy's supply side.
3. Clarify the difference between investment and technological change in determining the long-run aggregate supply.
4. Explain Solow's model of economic growth.
5. Explain why Solow's model concludes that technological change is necessary for continued economic growth.
6. Outline Schumpeter's model of technological change.
7. Explain the current state of understanding of the relationship between globalization and economic growth.
8. Relate the economic growth and technological change specifically to the international financial system.

8.1 Introduction to the Supply Side of the Economy

The economy's capacity to produce goods and services depends on the amount of resources and the level of technology or know-how that producers apply to transform the resources into welfare enhancing goods and services. Since there is a finite stock of resources and technology improves only gradually over time, there is clearly some limit to how much an economy can produce. This limit may not be absolutely rigid, however, because an economy can change the intensity with which it employs its resources or the efficiency with which it allocates its resources across alternative economic activities. Aggregate supply therefore depends on (1) resources, (2) technology, and (3) economic decisions regarding how the resources are employed and technology is applied.

8.1.1 *The microfoundations of aggregate supply*

Before deriving a general aggregate supply function, it is useful to begin by recognizing what kind of aggregate supply function we implicitly assumed for the Mundell–Fleming model. With its Keynesian assumption of constant prices, the Mundell–Fleming model effectively assumes that aggregate supply is the perfectly horizontal line AS shown in Fig. 8.1. As output increases from Υ^* to Υ', the horizontal aggregate supply curve implies that the overall price level remains unchanged at P^*. Such an aggregate supply function reflects a situation in which (1) inputs and factors of production are available in unlimited quantities at constant prices and (2) production is subject to constant returns to scale. These conditions are not generally satisfied.

In the absence of technological progress that enables an economy to produce more output from the same quantity of inputs, increases in demand for output will sooner or later cause the overall price level to rise as the economy's capacity is approached. Even if only a few resources are in limited supply, there will be diminishing returns to the increased use of other inputs, which causes the overall marginal cost of goods and services to rise. When additional supply is forthcoming only if prices rise to cover the higher costs of production, the aggregate supply curve will be upward sloping, not horizontal as the Mundell–Fleming model implicitly assumes. That is, aggregate supply is upward-sloping, as in the case of the curve AS' in Fig. 8.1.

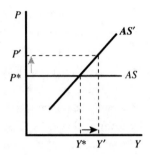

Figure 8.1   Aggregate supply and prices: perfectly elastic supply versus rising costs.

8.1.2 *The 'sticky' labor market*

Macroeconomics textbooks often explain the upward-sloping aggregate supply curve by focusing on a hypothetical model of the market for labor. The nominal wage is set in the labor market, but workers and employers are often more concerned with the *real wage*. The real wage is just the nominal wage, w, divided by the general price level, P. In effect, the real wage, w/P, reflects the actual purchasing power of the nominal wage. Rational workers are often hypothesized to be interested in the real wage, not their nominal wage. They notice what their wage can actually buy. Employers are also often assumed to focus on the cost of labor relative to the prices of the goods that labor produces; hence they also care about the real wage w/P. Workers and employers directly observe only nominal wages, and judging the real purchasing power of wages is difficult.

The market for labor is illustrated in the left-hand diagram of Fig. 8.2. Real wages are shown on the vertical axis, and the quantity of labor is given along the horizontal axis. The standard labor market model assumes that the demand for labor, D_L, is downward sloping with the real wage because there are diminishing marginal returns to labor when it is combined with society's limited set of other factors in the production process. According to the demand for labor curve, a decline in the real wage is needed to induce employers to add workers. The supply of labor, S_L, is assumed to be upward sloping

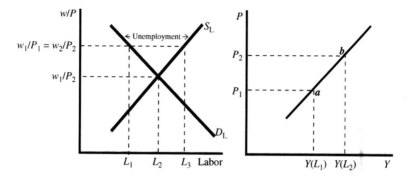

Figure 8.2 The labor market and the aggregate supply curve.

under the assumption that people demand a higher real wage to induce them to substitute work for leisure.

Note that for a given nominal wage, w_1, if $P_2 > P_1$, then $w_1/P_2 < w_1/P_1$. In the left-hand diagram of Fig. 8.2, at the real wage w_1/P_1 the quantity of labor supplied exceeds the quantity demanded by the amount labeled "unemployment". But if the general price level rises to P_2, where $P_2 > P_1$, while the nominal wage remains the same at w_1, the real wage falls to w_1/P_2. All other things equal, total employment then expands from L_1 to L_2.

The two price levels P_1 and P_2 are shown on the vertical axis of the right hand-side diagram of Fig. 8.2. The supply of real output, which is a function of the amount of labor employed, is shown on the horizontal axis. The economy's production increases when more labor is employed at the higher price level P_2 if the economy's production function $Y = f(L)$ is an increasing function in labor. In this case, $Y_2 = f(L_2) > Y_1 = f(L_1)$. The points **a** and **b**, which relate price levels P_1 and P_2 to output levels Y_1 and Y_2, respectively, trace out the economy's upward-sloping aggregate supply (AS) curve.

8.1.3 *Wage rigidity*

The analysis above suggests that upwards slope of the aggregate supply curve depends on the 'stickiness' of nominal wages. Note in the left-hand diagram of Fig. 8.2 that if the nominal wage rises in tandem with the overall price level, so that $w_1/P_1 = w_2/P_2$, then a price increase does not alter the level of unemployment. Prices have often been observed to adjust very slowly or not at all when economic conditions change. The question of why nominal wages are rigid or 'sticky' is still the object of much research. One obvious source of wage rigidity is the presence of long-term wage contracts. Two-year and three-year contracts are common in unionized sectors of the economy. Such contracts usually fix nominal wages and permit employers to adjust the quantity of labor employed by varying hours or laying off workers. Such contracts imply that nominal wages remain constant even when rates of inflation change and price levels alter real wages unexpectedly.

Nominal wages are also sticky even when there are no explicit labor contracts involved. Employers are often reluctant to change nominal wages even when there is unemployment because they fear wage reductions may have a negative effect on worker performance. Psychological research shows that workers change their behavior when their wages change. When forced to work for less, workers validate their lower wages by reducing their effort and thoroughness. In such a case, employers may not increase profit by lowering wages; in fact, they may gain by *raising* wages if higher wages increase output by a greater percentage! The economics literature refers to such wages, set to maximize the worker performance rather than to clear the labor market, as *efficiency wages*.

Labor is not the only input into the production process, and the AS curve also depends on the quantity and quality of the other factors of production supplied at each price level. In most developed economies, labor accounts for more than three-fourths of the total factor input costs, and even if the other factor prices adjust quickly, sticky wages will be enough to cause the AS curve to be upward-sloping in the short run. Even in the United States, which is said to have flexible labor markets, nominal wages react slowly to changing market conditions.

There are two important implications of sticky wages. First, sticky wages can cause unemployment if prices change or the demand for labor shifts, as illustrated in Fig. 8.2. Second, it appears that, in the short run, price increases can expand the demand for, and employment of, society's productive resources.

8.1.4 Economic growth and aggregate supply

There are limits to how much a price rise can increase the supply of labor and, therefore, the level of output when there is a fixed quantity of workers available for work. In the long run, the supply side of the economy depends on *economic growth* that effectively shifts the aggregate supply curve to the right, as from AS' to AS'' in Fig. 8.3. Notice how the shift in aggregate supply lets output increase from Y^* to Y' while the price level remains at P^*. An increase in aggregate supply can, therefore, mitigate the inflationary pressures in the economy. Or looked at another way, unless the economy is characterized by a excess supplies of factors and resources, economic growth is needed for output to grow without inflationary consequences.

A possible solution to the stagflation problem of the 1970s discussed in the opening paragraph of the chapter is the combination of expansionary fiscal and monetary policy to boost aggregate demand with other policies to promote economic growth to shift the supply curves of the economy's productive factors. Indeed, in the late 1970s, policymakers in the United States, the United Kingdom, and elsewhere began to focus more on expanding the economy's capacity, or what came to be called the economy's supply side. Practical *supply side*

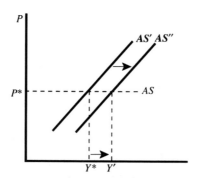

Figure 8.3 Aggregate supply and economic growth.

policies that would successfully shift the aggregate supply curve proved to be difficult. It is sobering to note that, despite the greater focus on the supply side by US policymakers after the 1970s, the US rate of technological progress actually slowed from its 1950 to 1975 trend.

Recall that there are two sources of supply side growth. Supply-side policies aimed at increasing the accumulation of productive factors are very different from the policies needed to develop and apply new technologies. Traditional policies to increase investment can boost both aggregate demand and increase the capital stock, thus expanding the supply side of the economy. But, contrary to popular belief, these familiar measures to boost investment are not sufficient for generating the growth in the long run. The next section's analysis of Robert Solow's model of economic growth shows that persistent technological change is neccessary to expand the economy's productive capacity in the long run.

8.2 The Solow Growth Model

Solow (1956, 1957) developed what is arguably the most popular model of economic growth today. Solow won the Nobel Prize in economics largely on the basis of this model, which has come to be known simply as the *Solow model*. The Solow model reaches several basic conclusions that help us understand the long-run development of the economy's supply side.

8.2.1 *Technological progress and factor accumulation*

Economic growth, or a rightward shift of the aggregate supply curve described earlier, occurs either when there is *technological progress*, which is the improvement in society's ability to transform the existing resources into output, or when there is *factor accumulation*, which is an increase in the quantity of the factors of production used to produce the output. There are fundamental differences in growth generated by technological progress and growth generated by factor accumulation, however. A simple model illustrates these differences. We first use it to illustrate factor accumulation.

Suppose that output is a function of two factors, labor, and capital. The economy's aggregate production function can, therefore, be represented by

$$Y = f(K, L) \tag{8.1}$$

where Y is total output, K is the economy's stock of capital, and L is the number of workers. Suppose also that each of the inputs has a positive effect on output, which implies that the partial derivatives of Y with respect to K and L are both positive. That is, additional doses of K, all other things equal, increases output. For example, if $K_2 > K_1$, then:

$$f(K_2, L_1) > f(K_1, L_1) \tag{8.2}$$

The Solow model makes an important assumption about the production function, which is that when only one input is increased, holding the others constant, the expansion of the variable input is subject to *diminishing returns*. Diminishing returns imply that additional amounts of one input lead to ever-smaller increases in output if the other quantities of inputs remain constant. Diminishing returns is illustrated in Fig. 8.4, which shows the technical relationship between Y and K, assuming L and all other factors of production remain fixed. The curved production function in Fig. 8.4 depicts diminishing returns to capital; notice that each equal addition to the amount of capital increases output by smaller and smaller amounts.

The logic of diminishing returns to capital is that as each additional unit of capital provides the fixed labor force with more identical tools and machines, it becomes increasingly difficult for the other factor of production, labor, to use those additional tools and machines to increase the output. Clearly, a gardener can get more work done with a shovel and a rake than she can with her bare hands. A hoe would further improve her productivity. But a second shovel of a different size would add less to her productivity than did the addition of the first shovel. And how much would a third shovel do for the worker's digging capacity? Clearly, when the quantity of workers is fixed, capital is subject to diminishing returns.

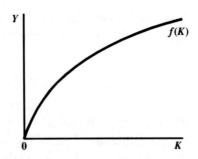

Figure 8.4   Diminishing returns to capital.

At first glance, diminishing returns seems to suggest that economic growth slows down even if investment continues at a constant pace. Solow showed, however, that diminishing returns causes output to stop growing altogether, even if investment continues at the same level, long before the marginal product of capital approaches the zero. The fundamental reason that factor accumulation ends up generating no economic growth watsoever is that capital *depreciates*. That is, capital wears out, and some portion of the capital stock must be continually replaced just to keep the total stock of capital from decreasing. The greater the capital stock, the greater the amount of capital that needs to be replaced each year. In his model, Solow assumed that the rate of depreciation, defined as the proportion of the stock of capital that wears out each year, is a constant fraction, δ, of the stock of capital, ΔK. In this case, the change in the stock of capital over the course of the year, denoted as ΔK, is equal to the difference between total new investment, I, and the amount of existing capital that depreciates, δK:

$$\Delta K = I - \delta K \tag{8.3}$$

If the capital stock K is large or the depreciation rate δ is high, then δK may be greater than I, in which case ΔK will be negative even though I is positive.

Investment depends on the economy's willingness to refrain from consuming and save instead. Solow assumed that people save a constant fraction, σ, of income Y so that total saving, S, and investment are

$$I = S = \sigma Y = \sigma f(K) \tag{8.4}$$

Combining equations (8.4) and (8.5), and assuming the amount of other fators like labor remain constant, equation (8.3) can be written as

$$\Delta K = I - \delta K = \sigma Y - \delta K = \sigma f(K) - \delta K \tag{8.5}$$

When $\sigma f(K)$ is greater than δK, and total investment exceeds what is needed to replace the portion of the capital stock that wears out, the total stock of capital K increases, and so does total output $Y = f(K)$. If, on the other hand, $\sigma f(K)$ is less than K, total savings is not large enough to fund the investment necessary to replace the capital that depreciates, and the total stock of K and output $Y = f(K)$ decreases. Note that in this latter case, investment is still positive; it is just not large enough to offset the depreciation. Hence, the conclusion that output growth stops despite positive rates of saving and investment.

The Solow model is often represented graphically. Because depreciation, investment, and output are all functions of the capital stock K, the three functions can all be included in a single diagram in which capital is shown on the horizontal axis and the values of Y, I, and depreciation are measured along the vertical axis. In addition to assuming that output was subject to diminishing returns to capital, as in Fig. 8.4, Solow also assumed the savings rate was a constant σ, so that total savings was a constant percentage of output, or $\sigma Y = \sigma f(K)$. Finally, assuming savings, and thus investment, is a constant fraction of income, the investment function $\sigma f(K)$ is therefore proportional to the production function $f(K)$. Thus $\sigma f(K)$ also slopes upward at a decreasing slope. The constant rate of depreciation, on the other hand, implies that total depreciation can be conveniently represented by a straight line function of capital, δK. Figure 8.5 combines all three functions.

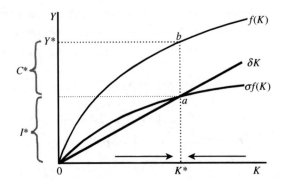

Figure 8.5   The Solow equilibrium.

Another important conclusion of Solow's model is that, given the economy's production function, savings rate, and depreciation rate, the size of the economy's capital stock automatically adjusts toward a stable equilibrium level K^*. That is, if K is not equal to K^*, it will adjust toward K^*, and if it is equal to K^*, it will stay at K^*. As shown above, when investment is greater than depreciation, or $\sigma f(K) > K$, the stock of capital grows. In Fig. 8.5, this occurs to the left of K^*, where the investment curve $\sigma f(K)$ lies above the depreciation line δK. Because diminishing returns causes the slope of $f(K)$ to diminish, the growth of savings and investment, $\sigma f(K)$, also diminishes; eventually investment only adds just enough to income and saving to cover the depreciation of the ever-increasing stock of capital. At that point there is no further growth of K. To the right of K^*, the situation is reversed; investment is less than depreciation and K declines back toward K^*.

As a direct function of capital, K, output also moves toward a stable equilibrium level $Y^* = f(K^*)$. At Y^*, consumption and investment are C^* and $I^* = \sigma Y^*$, respectively. Solow called these stable equilibrium levels of the capital stock and output the economy's *steady state equilibrium*. When not in equilibrium, the capital stock and output move toward their equilibrium levels. But once the economy reaches its steady state, there will be no further changes in K, Y, C, or I.

But, what if there is a change in one of the variables that determines the levels of the production function $f(K)$, the savings/investment function $\sigma f(K)$, or the depreciation function δK? We now examine those possibilities, while continuing to follow Solow model's basic logic.

8.2.2 *Increased investment causes only temporary growth in output*

Solow's model contradicts the common belief that increasing the rate of saving and investment, that is, *factor accumulation*, can permanently increase an economy's rate of growth. To grasp why that belief is inaccurate, suppose that there is a sudden change in the economy-wide rate of saving from σ_1 to σ_2, and, as illustrated in Fig. 8.6, the saving function shifts up from $\sigma_1 f(K)$ to $\sigma_2 f(K)$. Note that at the initial steady state level of capital and output, $K_1 \delta$ and $Y_1 \delta$ saving now exceeds depreciation. The capital stock and output, therefore, start growing. But as the capital stock grows, the amount of saving required to cover the cost of replacing depreciating capital increases, and because of diminishing returns to capital income and saving does not grow in proportion to the capital stock. The economy approaches a new steady state equilibrium, where the capital stock and output are equal to $K_2 \delta$ and $Y_2 \delta$, respectively.

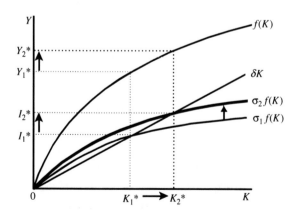

Figure 8.6 Increasing the rate of saving creates a new steady state, not permanent growth.

The shift from $\Upsilon_1\delta$ to $\Upsilon_2\delta$ is best described as *medium-run* or *transitional* economic growth. It is clearly not *permanent* economic growth because after the shift in saving, growth of output gradually slows and eventually stops when the steady state is reached. Of course, a further increase in the rate of saving could spur another round of transitional growth. However, the rate of saving cannot be raised forever; the savings/investment rate can never increase to anywhere near 100 percent of output because in the absence of any consumption, people would literally starve. The most frugal countries in the world today do not save and invest more than 30–40 percent of their income.

8.2.3 *How can an economy achieve permanent growth?*

The Solow model thus appears to be not so much a model of economic growth as a model of *short-run adjustment to a changing steady state*. The continuous rapid economic growth that occurred in today's high-income countries over the past two centuries makes it clear that the world has indeed experienced something more than a transition from one steady state to another. Maddison (2003) estimates that average real income per capita in the world as a whole increased about ten fold between 1820 and 2000, and in today's most developed economies, real income per capita increased about 20- to 30-fold over that same period. But, if Solow is right and this continuous growth could not have been the result of increased saving and investment, where did it come from? The Solow model makes it clear what caused the spectacular growth of the past two centuries: technological progress.

8.2.4 *Technological progress*

Technological progress is defined as an improvement in the efficiency with which an economy uses its resources and factors of production to produce welfare-enhancing output. In terms of the production function $\Upsilon = f(.)$, which specifies how inputs, like capital and labor, listed inside the parentheses are transformed into output, *technological change* is effectively a shift to a new production function that translates the given set of inputs into a different amount of output. For given amounts of capital, K_1, and labor, L_1, *technological progress* takes the economy to the new production function $g(K, L)$ so that

$$Y_2 = g(K_1, L_1) > Y_1 = f(K_1, L_1) \qquad (8.6)$$

Figure 8.7 illustrates. If society's technology is represented by the production function $f_1(K)$, the first unit of capital added to a given amount of other productive resources results in 100 units of output being produced. Then, because of diminishing returns, the second unit adds only 40 units of output. On the other hand, if the doubling of capital is combined with the upward shift in the production function from $f_1(K)$ to $f_2(K)$, then output also doubles to 200. Technological progress enables the economy to avoid the diminishing returns.

Permanent economic growth becomes possible provided there is permanent technological progress. Figure 8.8 illustrates how repeated shifts in the production function change the economy's steady states from points *a* to *b* and then to *c*, which represent the steady state combinations of K^* and Y^*, K^{**} and Y^{**}, and K^{***} and Y^{***}, respectively. Technological progress effectively ends up shifting the

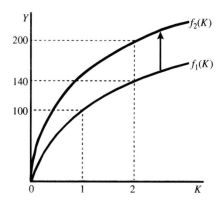

Figure 8.7   Technological progress shifts the production function.

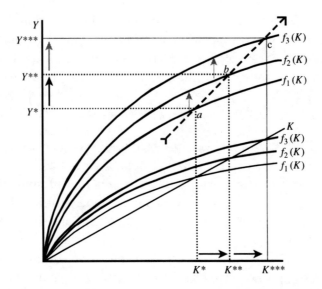

Figure 8.8   The shifting steady state with technological progress.

economy's production points along the dashed line in Fig. 8.8, not along a single production function with diminishing returns, as would be the result of capital accumulation without technological progress.

Note that by shifting the production function, technological progress results in additional investment and a rise in the capital stock from K^* to K^{**} and K^{***}. It is technological progress, therefore, that leads to an increase in the stock of capital, it is not the investment in capital that directly drives the growth in output. It may be true that, for example, for a bookkeeper to make use of computer technology, he must invest in a computer. But it is the invention of the technology that permits us to build the computer and raise the production that induces the investment in the new computer. In general, the Solow model suggests that the rising standards of living that most societies have experienced over the past 200 years have been the result of both *more* tools and machines and *better* tools and machines.

If you doubt that technological progress is really necessary for economic growth, try imagining what our standard of living would be like today if, after, 1800, we had only increased the number of horses rather than inventing the motorized farm tractors, we had used only larger doses of cod liver oil rather than developing antibiotics to fight infections, and we had only raised more carrier pigeons rather than inventing the Internet to expand communications. Or, to put it in a more contemporary setting, do you suppose that continued economic growth will be possible if we continue to increase output using the same amount of energy to power the machinery as we use now? Do you think the earth can support twice as much electricity generation using coal and today's technology, twice as many cars putting twice as much exhaust into the air, and twice as many acres for growing food for the 12 billion or so humans that will likely inhabit the earth in 100 years? For continued growth of output to be possible, we need to learn how to get more output from our exiting resources. Fortunately, humanity has been very good at improving technology over the past 200 years, as evidenced by the widespread growth of industrial output, agricultural productivity, and improved communications. However, growing resource scarcities, environmental disasters like climate change, and accelerated species extinctions make it clear that we have not yet generated nearly enough new knowledge and technology to permanently avoid the diminishing returns.

Unfortunately, the Solow model does not tell us anything about how to achieve the continued technological progress. To understand technological progress, we need another model.

8.3 Technological Progress as Creative Destruction

Economic historians who have studied technology have found that nearly all new ideas, inventions, quality improvements, design improvements, production cost reductions, improved management practices, more efficient plant layouts, etc. were the result of *intentional* efforts to improve the productivity or ease the burden of physical labor. Innovation seldom occurs in the form of an unexpected and unplanned discovery. Innovation generally requires time, effort, and resources. Even transfers of technology from other industries or countries require costly efforts to understand, adapt, and apply those ideas. In short, the acceleration of technological progress over the past 200 years was not an accident. People intentionally invested, researched, experimented, tested, learned, and worked to change the way the economy produces goods and services.

This section introduces a very insightful model that explains why individuals, firms, and other research organizations undertake the costly creation of new ideas and knowledge. In effect, this model clarifies what can be done to bring about the supply side expansion policymakers sought after the stagflationary 1970s.

8.3.1 *Jopseph Schumpeter's creative destruction*

Early in the 20th century, the Austrian economist Joseph Schumpeter (1934) criticized his contemporary neoclassical economists for being overly concerned with how the economy allocates resources and ignoring how an economy expands its productive capacity. 'The important issue is not 'how capitalism administers existing structures', he wrote, '...the relevant problem is how it creates and destroys them.'[2] Schumpeter ventured outside the box of contemporary economic theory and presented a truly dynamic model of technological change. Recent models of technological progress have built on Schumpeter's insights.

First of all, Schumpeter recognized that it takes resources to create new ideas, work out new technologies, install new methods, and teach new knowledge. Someone must bear the costs of innovation. Schumpeter noticed that private entrepreneurs and corporations willingly bear the costs of innovation because they are hopeful that successful innovations will generate a profit that exceeds the costs of innovation. Schumpeter thus saw profit in a very different light from the way it was depicted in traditional neoclassical economics. He did not view profit as a market failure that needed to be corrected, but as the incentive that rewards innovative activity. Schumpeter argued that efforts to reduce firms' profits by breaking up large firms and promoting traditional price competition would likely slow down innovation and economic growth. According to traditional

---

[2] Joseph Schumpeter (1912[1934]). p. 84.

microeconomic analysis, in the extreme case of perfect competition the market price exactly covers the cost of the resources used in *production*. This allegedly efficient market outcome leaves no income to cover the up-front cost of *innovation*. Innovation, according to Schumpeter, was the effort to gain a competitive advantage in the market and thus gain market power and, hopefully, monopoly profits that, more than cover the up-front costs of developing a new product, make a product more appealing, or reduce the costs of production.

Schumpeter was not oblivious to the dangers of letting large firms gain market power. He pointed out, however, that the key to long-run economic growth and rising living standards was to make sure that the market power gained through innovation would be only temporary and not permanent. Government regulators therefore need to make sure that there are no barriers that prevent others from innovating. As long as those innovators who are currently reaping profits from their earlier innovations are prevented from stifling innovation by others, new innovations will, sooner or later, destroy their monopoly profits. Every time an innovator *creates* a new business opportunity, it *destroys* the market power and profits that its competitors had gained as a result of their earlier innovations. Schumpeter described the capitalist economy as a "perennial gale of *creative destruction*". In short, continual creation and destruction prevents monopolies from permanently reaping the profits, yet society enjoys constant technological progress.

Schumpeter's concept of *creative destruction* captures another important characteristic of economic growth, which is that the creation of something new requires that something old be eliminated. New activities require resources, which, in the absence of unemployment or excess capacity, must be transferred from existing activities. Growing economies are characterized by *structural change* as old economic activities are replaced by new economic activities.

Finally, Schumpeter recognized the importance of the economic and social climate for innovation in which innovators, or *entrepreneurs* as Schumpeter liked to call them, had to operate. He argued that an economy's rate of technological progress depends in large part on the incentives and barriers that entrepreneurs face. Interestingly, Smith (1776[1976], pp. 13, 14) had discussed the important role played by entrepreneurs at the start of the Industrial Revolution:

> All the improvements in machinery, however, have by no means been the invention of those who had occasion to use the machines. Many improvements have been made by the ingenuity of the makers of machines, when to make them became the business of a peculiar trade; and some by that of those who are called philosophers or men of speculation, whose trade is not to do any thing, but to observe every thing; and who, upon that account, are often capable of combining together the powers of the most distant and dissimilar objects. In the progress of society, philosophy or speculation becomes, like every other employment, the principal or sole trade and occupation of a particular class of citizens ... and the quantity of science is considerably increased by it.[3]

Smith's "philosophers and speculators" and Schumpeter's *entrepreneurs* are an explicit recognition that innovation does not just happen by itself; someone must organize and manage it.

8.3.2 *Generalizing Schumpeter's ideas*

The agricultural sector is often used as an example of a highly competitive industry. In an industry with thousands or even millions of small farmers, each farmer is effectively a *price taker*. A strict interpretation of Schumpeter's model of innovation would lead one to conclude that the agricultural sector must engage in very little innovation because individual farmers have no market power to exploit their innovations, and even if they did, they are too small to reap enough profits to cover the cost of innovation. Yet, in countries like the United States, agriculture is noted for its high level of technology. Did individual farmers generate this technology?

---

[3] Adam Smith (1776[1976]). pp. 13, 14.

US farmers applied new technology rapidly, but they did not themselves develop most of the new technologies. Most innovation was carried out in the imperfectly competitive, profit-seeking firms in the chemical, equipment, and food processing industries that supplied new products to the farm sector. There has also been a well-funded program of public universities and agricultural extension services to develop and disseminate new technologies.

Justin Smith Morrill, a member of the US House of Representatives, introduced the *Morrill Act of 1862*, which established a system that allocated large amounts of government-owned land (confiscated earlier from native Americans) to each state for the establishment of universities to provide advanced education to large numbers of people who would not normally attend the universities. Many states sold the land and used the revenues to establish universities, and these universities became centers for agricultural research. They also trained large numbers of people who directly or indirectly spread the new technologies being developed at the publicly funded *land-grant universities*. In the US today, the small number of remaining farmers are, on average, more highly educated than industrial workers.

The 1887 Hatch Act provided funds for the establishment of agricultural experiment stations at each of the land-grant universities. These stations conducted extensive research and employed people to spread the new technologies among farmers throughout each state. Additional legislation in later years further expanded this program.

The land-grant universities of the United States carry out a role that is somewhat unique in the world. Unlike universities in most other countries, the US land-grant state universities consider the outreach to all citizens, farmers, and businesses in their state to be their major responsibility. Faculty members, especially in the sciences and agricultural fields, often devote as much of their time to research and serving the general public as they do teaching at the university. Growth economists, like Romer (1993), have pointed to the US land-grant university as one of the most important institutions created to stimulate technological change. The tax-funded land-grant universities have effectively operated as the US agricultural industry's R&D department. They now provide basic research to many other industries, and, increasingly, they are subsidizing and assist the entrepreneurs in setting up new businesses, in line with Schumpeter's creative destruction model of technological change.

8.3.3 Recent 'Schumpeterian' models of technological progress

Aghion and Howitt (1992), Grossman and Helpman (1991), and Romer (1990) are among those who have developed the economic models of technological progress based on the Schumpeterian assumption that technological progress is carried out by entrepreneurs, corporate managers, and government and university researchers who are motivated to employ the costly resources to develop better products, reduce the production costs, improve the organization of firms, or use the resources more efficiently. These models are called *Schumpeterian growth models* because they generalize on Schumpeter's hypothesis that profit seeking entrepreneurs engage in costly research and development (R&D) activities in order to *creatively destroy* their competition and capture the monopoly profits their innovations will make available to them.

In general, Schumpeterian innovation models specify that innovators engage in costly R&D activity as long as expected future marginal gains exceed the marginal costs of employing resources in some process that generates innovation. The level of research and development activity and the resulting rate of technological progress are, therefore, the solution to a profit maximization problem that depends on

1. The productivity of R&D activity in generating innovations
2. The (opportunity) costs of acquiring resources to carry out R&D
3. The benefits that entrepreneurs expect to reap from an innovation

The first two items above determine the *cost* of innovation. The latter item reflects the expected future *gains* from innovation. In general, the maximization problem is the same for individual entrepreneurs, corporate research departments, public research laboratories, and universities.

The above distinctions between productivity of R&D, opportunity costs, and future benefits are straightforward. However, note that each of those terms are very difficult to quantify or estimate. The productivity of R&D activities is uncertain, as are the future gains from innovation. Even the opportunity costs are uncertain. The Keynesian caveats about investment, already noted in the previous chapter, apply even more strongly to innovation. It is important to note, once again, the difference between *risk* and *uncertainty*; the former implies a known set of probabilities for alternative outcomes, the latter admits some degree of ignorance of the probabilities of specific outcomes and even of the existence of all possible outcomes. Keynes use of the term 'animal spirits' and his reference to an expedition to the South Pole are useful reminders of the uncertainty surrounding innovation and entrepreneurial activity:

> Enterprise only pretends to itself to be mainly actuated by the statements in its own prospectus, however candid and sincere. Only a little more than an expedition to the South Pole, is it based on an exact calculation of benefits to come. Thus if the animal spirits are dimmed and the spontaneous optimism falters, leaving it to depend on nothing but a mathematical expectation, enterprise will fade and die; though fears of loss may have a basis no more reasonable than hopes of profit had before.[4]

In sum, the costs and gains of innovation are uncertain and their estimates are potentially volatile as sentiments and partial information sets vary. Yet, decisions to undertake costly innovative activities must somehow be made.

8.3.4 *The cost of innovation*

Innovation requires engineers, scientists, laboratory assistants, test pilots, agronomists, computer programmers, marketing consultants, cost experts, and a great number of other people to create new

---

[4] John Maynard Keynes (1936). pp. 161, 162.

products, lower costs, improve quality, and, in general, improve the efficiency with which resources are transformed into welfare-enhancing products. These people also need time, equipment, laboratories, offices, raw materials, and many other things to help them innovate. The resources for product innovation, like all productive resources, have an opportunity cost, which is the value of the welfare-enhancing products that can no longer be produced when the economy's scarce resources are allocated to R&D activity. The quantity of resources used in R&D activity is, therefore, limited by the economy's total stock of factors of production. The cost of those resources depends on total demand for those resources by producers, investors, and innovators.

An increase in R&D activity, all other thing equal, increases total demand for factors and resources and thus increases the price of productive resources. Hence, for a given quantity of resources the cost of innovation will be an increasing function of the amount of resources applied to R&D activity. The price of productive factors and resources also depends on their total supply. The price of resources is lower, all other things equal, the greater the amount of factors and resources available to both producers and innovators.

To estimate the actual cost of generating an innovation, one also needs to know how *many* resources it is likely to take to generate new knowledge, ideas, and innovations. That is, we need some perception of the *production function* for knowledge and technology even though innovators never know exactly when, or even if, their research and development activities will actually bear fruit and deliver a breakthrough. Such a function will be directly related to the amount of resources. Its level will also reflect the society's institutions and culture, and Schumpeter discussed at great length how a society's tolerance of change, of 'deviant' behavior by entrepreneurs, and resistance by vested interests raise or lower the production function of innovative activity.

8.3.5 *The expected gains from innovation*

The gains from innovation depend not only on how much better some new product is or how much cheaper some new production technology is, but also on *how long* a successful innovation is applied and used. Think of a private innovation, say a new and better product for example. The eventual gains to the entrepreneurs depend, in part, on how much of a premium price the new product commands in the market. Second, the eventual gains depend on *how long* that new product can command a premium price. The length of time that an innovator enjoys monopoly profits from her innovation depends on how soon another innovator *creatively destroys* that profit by introducing an even better product or a more efficient production method. Thus, the gains from innovation depend on the rate at which new innovations are generated. Specifically, the length of time that an innovation generates profit is thus an inverse function of the rate of technological progress.

From society's perspective, exactly the same trade-off applies; for a costly innovation to be socially worthwhile, the improvement in human welfare brought about by the innovation must (a) be large enough and (b) generate these benefits long enough to more than cover the up-front cost of that innovation. Note that it is quite possible that innovation occurs too rapidly, with no single improvement ever recouping its costs of innovation.

Finally, because there is a time delay between when costly R&D activity is undertaken and when the gains from the innovation are earned, the value of an innovation depends on the rate at which we discount the future. Therefore, the present value of an innovation is a negative function of the rate of interest, r, with which future profit is discounted.

All other things equal, an increase in the marginal welfare improvement generated by an innovation increases the value of innovation, a decrease in the cost of innovation as represented by the production function of new technology lowers the gain from any one innovation, and a rise in the interest rate decreases the value of the future gains from innovation. The result that a decrease in the cost of innovation decreases the gains from innovation seems counterintuitive, but remember that here we focus on the present value of innovation, which reflects future gains, not costs. The gains from innovation depend on how long the successful innovator enjoys the profit and society reaps the benefits of the innovation; a decrease in the cost of innovation increases the number of innovations generated, and each innovation has less time to provide the humanity with its benefits and cover the resource costs of generating the innovation.

An illustration of the conflict between the cost of innovation and the gains from innovation is the suggestion by the chief technology officer of Taiwan Semiconductor Manufacturing Co., Calvin Chenming Hu, that computer chip makers should slow their pace of technological development. "The industry would be better off if we paid more attention to the bottom line and less attention to the beauty contest of technology introduction", said Mr. Hu.[5] Mr. Hu blamed the losses of chip makers during the early 2000s on the rapid rate of change in the industry. Of course, Mr. Hu was equally quick to point out that his firm would not fall behind others in the industry, and the speech in which he called for a slowdown in introducing new products also described the new generation of chips that his firm would shortly introduce. In short, he was not about to abandon the innovative competition his firm was in, but he sure would enjoy having less innovative competition and a longer product life for his innovations.

8.3.6 *The equilibrium level of innovative activity*

Putting together the gains from innovation and the costs of innovation, it becomes possible to conclude that Schumpeter's framework suggests that the rate of technological change is determined by the function

$$TECH = f(\pi, r, R, \beta) \tag{8.7}$$

in which π represents the increase in a product's services to humanity or the cost reduction in a productive process, r represents the society's discount rate of the future, R represents the society's stock of resources, and the β represents the efficiency of the innovation

---

[5] Don Clark (2002). "One Executive Suggests It's Time for Chip Makers to Slow Down", *Wall Street Journal*, April 9, 2002.

production function. As all other things are equal, innovation will tend to be higher in a society:

1. The larger are the potential gains from a successful innovation (the greater is π);
2. The more highly society values future gains relative to current costs (the lower is r);
3. The greater is the supply of resources (R) and, hence the lower is the opportunity cost of innovation in terms of lost current output;
4. The more efficient is R&D activity in using resources to generate new innovations (the greater is innovative efficiency β).

The latter outcome effectively assumes that the net result of shorter periods of profitable use of a new innovation is outweighed by positive effect of lower costs in innovation on the cost side of the maximization problem.

Supply side policies to promote the economic growth might include linking society's expected gains from innovation more closely to entrepreneurs' profits from innovation, building institutions that prevent vested interests from blocking the creative destruction process in order to stretch out the gains from past innovations, promoting society's tolerance for change and entrepreneurship, creating the productive resources that are critical to innovation, advancing education and communications infrastructure to spread the knowledge, and creating public institutions to undertake the most uncertain types of innovation like basic scientific research. In sum, economic growth requires much more complex policies than a simple increase in saving.

8.3.7 *Summarizing the effects of growth on aggregate supply*

The Solow model concludes that, in the absence of technological progress, the economy settles at the *steady state* equilibrium, where saving/investment is just sufficient to cover the depreciation of capital. Thus, given the economy's level of technology as represented by the production function $\Upsilon = f(K, L, ...)$, the steady state level of output depends on the rate of depreciation, δ, and the rate of saving, σ. In the long run, however, the supply side of the economy depends on economic growth, which is driven by technological progress.

The Schumpeterian model of technological progress highlighs the things that drive technological progress. Included were the payoff (profit) to innovation, π, the rate of interest, r, the efficiency of innovative activity, β, and the availability of resources necessary for creating new ideas and knowledge, R. Aggregate supply, Υ_S, is a function of both the short-run variables of the Solow model and the long-run variables of the Schumpeterian model:

$$\Upsilon_S = g(K, L, \delta, \sigma, \pi, \beta, r, R) \qquad (8.8)$$

Given the importance of technological progress in the long run, any overall prediction of an economy's long-run productive capacity would focus on the Schumpeterian variables, of course.

8.4 Globalization and Economic Growth

It is time to return to the basic theme of this textbook and ask how the international financial system impacts the supply side of the economy. Most obvious is the influence of the international financial system on globalization. Recall that the delegates at the Bretton Woods Conference in 1944 agreed that the economic recovery after World War II should include the expansion of international trade. They selected a system of pegged exchange rates because they thought that would prove less disruptive of international trade than a system of floating exchange rates or a return to the Gold Standard. The delegates also authorized the creation of the International Trade Organization to stimulate negotiations on eliminating trade barriers. Some delegations, most notably the US delegation, also promoted the idea of liberalizing international capital movements. In short, the Bretton Woods Conference foresaw the restoration of some form of economic globalization, a process that had been interrupted by the nationalism and protectionism of the interwar period.

There were, no doubt, various motivations that led the Bretton Woods delegates to favor various forms of globalization, among them the idea that improved economic relations among countries would act as a brake on future hostilities and wars. The main motivation was the belief that economies that are open to international trade and investment are likely to grow faster than closed economies. However, despite being one of the most actively researched questions in economics, there is no clear consensus on whether and how much globalization influences an economy's growth and development. Economists are still trying to determine whether open economies grow faster than closed ones.

This is a very relevant question for us to address now that we have added the supply side to our macroeconomic model. The Mundell–Fleming model has already made it clear that economic policies can have very different effects when an economy is open as opposed to when it is isolated from the rest of the world. If the openness of the economy also influences the growth of productive resources and technology, then it is clear that the supply side of the economy is also likely to evolve differently depending on whether the economy is open than when it is closed.

8.4.1 *Economic openness and economic growth*

Equation (8.8) above suggests that the amount of innovation depends on the total amount of resources. The higher the supply of resources, the lower is the opportunity cost of employing resources for R&D activity and, all other things equal, the less costly it is to innovate. This suggests that higher income societies will, all other things equal, experience relatively faster technological change. The creative destruction model furthermore suggests that large countries will generate faster technological change than small countries. In short, the model predicts that China will grow faster than Bolivia and the United States will grow faster than New Zealand.

There is no clear evidence that confirms such a direct relationship between population size and economic development or between population size and per capita output, however. Many small countries have grown very rapidly, and many very large countries have had below-average growth performances. Luxembourg's per capita real income is 20 times that of India, and the city states of Hong Kong and Singapore have grown faster than the larger countries surrounding them. One possible reason why small countries can grow rapidly despite having a small stock of entrepreneurs and thinkers is that technology moves across the borders. A country does not need to invent the wheel in order to have wagons or water wheels. The Schumpeter model may also not capture all aspects of technological change or the broader process of economic development.

Over the past several decades, economists have carried out a very large number of statistical studies of the relationship between trade and growth. Each successive study sought to improve on previous studies by using better statistical methods, a better data set, or a new data set for countries or time periods not previously covered by researchers. The most popular statistical regression models have used the growth of trade, measured either by exports or the sum of imports and exports, along with other 'control' variables deemed to be important for growth, to explain the rate of economic growth. Lewer and Van den Berg (2004) and Van den Berg and Lewer (2007) compiled the results of nearly 1,000 statistical regressions relating the growth of trade to economic growth, and they find that, on average, an economy grows by about 0.15 to 0.2 percent per year faster for every additional one point increase in the growth of international trade. That is, for two otherwise identical economies, if international trade in one economy grows by seven percent per year, compared to two percent per year in the other, the former economy will grow at about one percent per year faster than the latter. The power of compounding is such that a one percent annual growth difference over the past two centuries explains the entire difference in living standards between the United States and Mexico, for example.

8.4.2 *The robustness of the trade-growth relationship*

Any given statistical study can always be criticized for using one particular regression equation and not some other, a particular data set, or a particular statistical method. No regression model can capture all the influences of all possible variables on economic growth, data sets are wrought with inaccuracies, and statisticians continue to improve their methods. In short, a statistically significant finding in one statistical study does not imply that a true relationship has been found. However, Srinivasan (1997) argues that

> [T]he fact that a number of studies using different data sets, countries and methodologies happened to arrive at similar conclusions ... that are also consistent with a priori reasoning, suggests that they deserve serious consideration, with due allowances being made for their conceptual and statistical deficiencies.

The statistical results from the many different studies have not yet definitively decided the matter of how international trade and economic growth are related, however.

There are many problems with the existing studies. Florax *et al.* (2002) explain that there are a very large number of potential models that can reasonably explain any observed economic behavior, and in the case of globalization and international trade there are many hypothesized models that have not yet been tested adequately. Also, a positive relationship does not prove causality, and explicit tests to prove that trade causes growth have, so far, given us no clear insights. Furthermore, some economists claim that there are still too many weaknesses in the statistical methodology, the data sets, and the statistical models to definitively conclude that trade and growth are positively related. Rodriguez and Rodrik (2001) show that international trade policy is closely correlated with other economic policies, and that therefore it is impossible to differentiate between the effects of trade and those other policies on economic growth. They argue that economic growth depends more on 'those other policies' than trade policy.

At the end of his survey of individual country case studies and recent empirical studies dealing with the relationship between international trade and growth, Baldwin (2003) sums up the situation well:

> It is true developing countries are often given the advice that decreasing trade barriers is a more effective way of achieving higher

sustainable rates of growth than tightening trade restrictions. But ... those giving such advice also emphasize the need, as a minimum, for a stable and non-discriminatory exchange-rate system and usually also the need for prudent monetary and fiscal policies and corruption-free administration of economic policies for trade liberalization to be effective in the long-run. It seems to me that the various country studies do support this type of policy advice and the cross-country statistical studies do not overturn this conclusion. But the recent critiques of the latter studies demonstrate that we must be careful in attributing any single economic policy, such as the lowering of trade barriers, as being a sufficient government action for accelerating the rate of economic growth.

There are many developing countries that engaged in international trade but nevertheless failed to escape poverty. Developing countries that exported predominantly natural resources often experienced government corruption and actual declines in per capita income.

8.4.3 *International trade and the Schumpeter model*

Research has not adequately focused on the Schumpeterian model of technological innovation, even though the Solow growth model shows that long-run economic growth cannot be maintained by means of factor accumulation alone and several statistical studies have showed that international trade's effect on economic growth operates through technological progress.[6] The Schumpeterian model of technological progress is, therefore, the appropriate model for analyzing the international trade's long-run effect on economic growth.

A convenient way to illustrate the growth effects of international trade in the Shumpeterian model is to assume that trade integrates separate economies into a single economy. This approach may be reasonable because international trade is a form of arbitrage that effectively integrates previously distinct markets into a single market.

---

[6] See, for example, Ross Levine and David Renelt (1992). Sebastian Edwards (1998), Jeffrey Frankel and David Romer (1999), and Romain Wacziarg (2001).

Trade lets the products and machines that emerge from the innovative process cross borders and, therefore, benefit more users. An integrated economy also increases the supply of resources that are available for production and innovative activity and, therefore, a given absolute increase in innovation has less effect on the price of productive resources than would an identical increase in innovative activity in a single isolated economy. Finally, the principle of comparative advantage implies that international trade causes a more efficient allocation of the world's resources, which, in turn, effectively implies an increase in each country's resources.

The latter point merits further discussion. The principle of comparative advantage applies to innovative activity as well as productive activities. Given that countries have different endowments of resources and that different activities have different production functions, some countries will have a comparative advantage in innovative activity while others have a comparative advantage in producing the goods. The percentage of highly educated people, the number of engineers, and the conditions that inspire entrepreneurial activity vary greatly from one country to another. Thus, by having countries specializing in either production or innovation, unlike an isolated economy that has to *both* produce *and* innovate, worldwide production and innovation may both increase more rapidly.

Innovative activity is in fact centered in a small number of developed economies, and very little new technology is developed in developing economies. Research and development expenditures as a percentage of GDP vary greatly across countries.[7] Consistent with the concentration of R&D activity are the findings by Lewer and Van den Berg (2001, 2003) that developed countries that are relatively abundant in human capital tend to be net exporters of capital goods, whereas developing countries with their relatively lower levels of human capital tend to be net importers of capital goods.

---

[7] See, for example, the data on R&D expenditures as a percentage of GDP given in UNESCO (2002), *Statistical Yearbook*, Geneva: UNESCO, or in World Bank (2002), *World Development Indicators*, Washington, DC: World Bank, Table 5.11. pp. 320–322.

The concentration of innovative activity in a small number of countries suggests that innovation may be subject to economies of scale. If so, there are further gains from integrating the world economy and permitting countries to specialize in innovation and production. On the other hand, the concentration of innovative activity in a small number of countries of the world has led some economists to question whether such specialization is good for the world as a whole. It is often observed that cities, regions, and countries where innovative activity abounds are also relatively wealthy. In other words, letting countries specialize in either innovation or production according to their comparative advantages may be more beneficial for the innovation specialists than the production specialists. However, Bayoumi and Haacker (2002) show that most of the gains from innovation accrue to the users of the technology, not the creators of the technology. Hence, it may not matter much where the innovation takes place, provided, of course, the products and services provided by the new technologies become available everywhere.

Samuelson (2004) looks at the static welfare effects in a rich country when its poorer trading partner improves its technology. He suggests that, all other things equal, as the economy with less technology acquires more technology and "catches up" to the high tech economy, the two economies become more similar and the gains from trade are reduced. Samuelson goes one step further, however, by linking international trade directly to the transfer of technology from the technology leader to the technology follower. Samuelson suggests that because international trade effectively transfers technology, international trade can cause a loss of welfare in a high-income economy.

Samuelson's argument is relevant to the recent discussions about outsourcing of production to low wage countries. Critics of outsourcing have often claimed that the shift in production stimulates movements of capital and technology. Technology transfers appear to be especially likely when the shift in production abroad also involves foreign direct investment. By shifting production to take advantage of low wages and manufacturing the products demanded in the high-income economics, multinational enterprises supply the capital and the technology that effectively makes the poorer economies more similar to high income economies. Samuelson describes how this foreign direct investment and transfer of technology by US firms to China "gives to China some of the comparative advantage that had belonged to the United States".[8]

In short, the location of innovation in certain countries may bene-fit those countries because the returns to innovative activity are greater than the returns to productive activity. International trade clearly enables such international specialization. But international trade also spreads knowledge, which dilutes the gains from innovation. Therefore, there is considerable ambiguity about who ultimately gains from the specialization in innovative activity in an integrated world economy.

8.4.4 *Immigration and economic growth*

Globalization has also increased the immigration of people across bor-ders. At the start of the 21st century, nearly four percent of the world's population was living outside their country of birth. Immigrants have also been shown to directly contribute to innovation as entrepreneurs and workers in innovative activities. Secondly, the international move-ment of people facilitates the transfer of technology because much knowledge is embedded in human beings. Thirdly, immigration changes the size of economies, which permits economies of scale to enhance the output in the countries receiving the immigrants. Immigration can increase innovative competition by reducing the ability of vested interests to take protectionist measures to slow the process of creative destruction. On the other hand, immigration changes labor supplies and, hence, wages within and across countries. And, because the movement of people also implies the movement of cultures, immigration can be socially disruptive or socially invigorating.

The most obvious change introduced by immigration is a change in a country's resources. Rosenberg (1994) attributes the rapid eco-nomic growth of the United States in the 1800s to "rapid growth in demand and circumstances conducive to a high degree of product standardization".[9] That is, the United States was able to exploit the

---

[8] Paul A. Samuelson (2004). p. 137.
[9] Nathan Rosenberg (1994). p. 113.

economies of scale because its market grew rapidly and, because of the country's large middle class, the market was very uniform. What caused this growth of the market? "Probably the most pervasive force of all was the extremely rapid rate of population growth ... with immigration assuming a role of some significance in the 1840s".[10] Thus, the United States was able to grow despite rather protectionist trade policies in the 19th century because it became large enough to avoid, at least in part, the constraints of national borders on the division of labor. By 1870, the United States overtook England as the world's biggest economy, and by 1900 its residents enjoyed the highest per capita incomes in the world. The United States used immigration rather than international trade to achieve economies of scale.[11]

The movement of people may also change the resource cost of generating innovations. Immigrants inevitably carry ideas with them, and the arrival of ideas from abroad through immigration is likely to be much less costly than arriving at those ideas from scratch through original research. For example, the economic historian Cipolla (1978) describes the clock-and-watch industry from several hundred years ago, in which immigration greatly affected technological development and subsequent economic growth. The clock and watch industry played a particularly important leadership role in developing the technology of precision engineering. Many early clock makers were French, but a large percentage of the early French clock makers, who were highly literate and often interested in various aspects of science, were also active in the Reformation movement. When France expelled them, some went to Geneva, Switzerland, at the invitation of John Calvin, the Calvinist leader of that Swiss city. The future Swiss watch industry was founded by 'the inflow of a handful of refugees — to the injection of a small but precious amount of human skills'.[12]

---

[10] Rosenberg (1994). p. 113.

[11] Other economic historians who reach similar conclusions about 19th century US immigration and economic growth include Douglas A. Irwin (2000), Peter J. Hill (1971), and Nicholas Crafts and Anthony J. Venables (2001).

[12] Carlo M. Cipolla (1978). p. 64.

8.4.5 *Globalization, competition, and creative destruction*

Globalization can increase innovative competition by reducing the ability of vested interests to take protectionist measures to slow the process of creative destruction. For the process of *creative destruction* to work, there must be *destruction* as well as *creation*. If an initial creation is not followed by a second creation, which necessarily *destroys* the first creation's advantage, then there can be no continued technological progress and economic growth. Lee and McKenzie (1993) point out that innovators have a strong incentive to try to prevent others from *destroying* their temporary advantage in the market. The negative relationship between protecting vested interests and technological progress is discussed by Mokyr (1990): "[T]he enemies of technological progress were not the lack of useful new ideas, but social forces that for one reason or another tried to preserve the status quo".[13] Mokyr distinguished the growth of international competition in an increasingly globalized economy as a particularly favorable development for continued technological progress:

> As long as some segment of the world economy is creative, the human race will not sink into the technological stasis that could eventually put an end to economic growth.[14]

Holmes and Schmitz (1995) provide an especially insightful variation of Schumpeter's model to show how international competition limits vested interests' ability to block the innovation. The intuition underlying their model is straightforward: A technological leader can more easily block or discourage other innovators from destroying its monopoly position in a protected market closed to potential foreign competitors. In a closed economy, domestic innovators can also resort to simple collusion by agreeing to delay new innovations. In an open

---

[13] Joel Mokyr (1990). p. 301.
[14] Mokyr (1990). p. 304.

economy, worldwide competition would have to be obstructed, and that is much more difficult and costly. Hence, in an open economy, innovators find it easier to just continue the innovating than to expend resources obstructing the domestic competitor. The open economy, and the whole world, thus gains a more rapid rate of technological progress.

Open borders to investment and immigration can have a similar effect on innovative competition. Schumpeter actually wrote extensively about the role of immigrants in the process of creative destruction. Recall that he emphasized the importance of entrepreneurs. His view of the entrepreneur was complex, however. He described the entrepreneur as a 'social deviant' because his or her attitude was different from the average member of society:

> ...The reaction of the social environment against one who wishes to do something new ... manifests itself first of all in the existence of legal and political impediments. But neglecting this, any deviating conduct by a member of a social group is condemned, though in greatly varying degrees according as the social group is used to such conduct or not.[15]

Schumpeter argued that immigrants often became entrepeneurs because they were less attached to the traditions of society and, therefore, less reluctant to violate social norms and innovate. Also, Immigrants' lack of social capital and personal relationships makes it difficult for them to collude with native vested interests to stop the creative destruction.

8.4.6 *Globalization, economic growth, and international finance*

Overall, there is a substantial amount of evidence suggesting that an economy open to international trade, international investment, and immigration grows faster than a closed one. Hence, the aggregate

---

[15] Joseph Schumpeter (1934). p. 155.

supply function is likely to shift out more rapidly in an open economy than in a closed economy. We can, therefore, also conclude that the international financial system affects the macroeconomic performance of an economy. The delegates at Bretton Woods sought to expedite the economic recovery after World War II, which is why they sought a financial system that would help to revive international trade and, possibly, international investment.

In later chapters, we will detail how various international financial systems have succeeded or failed in promoting economic growth. For now, however, note that the international financial system affects both the supply and demand sides of the economy. Most obviously, the way exchange rates are determined affects trade and capital flows on the demand side, and the extent to which the international financial system facilitates the globalization affects the investment and innovation that drives the growth of productive capacity.

8.5 Summary and Conclusions

This chapter discusses the supply side of the economy. The main conclusions, concepts, and points are:

1. Where the basic Keynesian demand side model effectively assumes supply of goods and services are always forthcoming if there is demand, in fact there are limits to output because productive resources and technology are not infinite.
2. In the short run, labor supply varies in response to perceived changes in nominal wages.
3. In the long run, the supply side of the economy only increases if there are increases in productive resources and improvements in technology.
4. The Solow growth model shows that when investment is subject to diminishing returns and depreciation, growth in productive capacity can only continue indefinitely if there is technological change.
5. Schumpeter's creative destruction model provides a useful framework for designing the supply side economic policies.

6. Specifically, permanent long-run growth in productive capacity requires satisfaction of a maximization calculation that recognizes the gains and costs of innovation.
7. In this Schumpeterian framework, innovation requires the employment of scarce resources in an uncertain process carried out in the hope of generating the technological change that benefits human welfare.
8. The international financial system affects the pace of long-run technological change by setting some of the critical parameters under which international trade, international investment, and immigration occur.

The Solow and Schumpeterian models help to explain the long-run increases in standards of living that we observed in the world over the past 200 years. The growth models do not explain the short-run fluctuations in economic output that we observe in most economies, however. Short run fluctuations in output may be the result of variations in aggregate demand, as suggested by the Keynesian model in the previous chapter, or they may be the result of variations in the supply of productive factors.

The last two sections of the chapter suggest that in the long run, economic growth causes the entire aggregate supply curve to continually shift out. Therefore, it is appropriate to represent aggregate supply as a series of shifting, upward-sloping

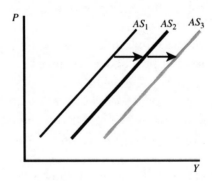

Figure 8.9   Economic growth shifts the aggregate supply curve.

short-run curves, as in Fig. 8.9. Growth theory helps us to understand what determines the long-run movement of the aggregate supply curve.

The next chapter builds an open-economy macroeconomic model that combines the aggregate demand function from the Mundell–Fleming model and the aggregate supply function from this chapter. The next chapter also incorporates into the model several other ideas that have been influential in macroeconomic analysis in recent years. Together, all of these changes lead us to a model that complements Keynes' innovative macroeconomic model outlined in the last chapter.

Key Terms and Concepts

Aggregate supply	Immigration	Short-run growth
Animal spirits	Innovation	Solow model
Creative destruction	International trade	Stagflation
Depreciation	Land grant university	Steady state
Diminishing returns	Long-run growth	Stickey prices/wages
Economic growth	Price competition	Supply side
Efficiency wages	Price taker	Technological change
Entrepreneur	Production function	Technological
Factor accumulation	Profit	competition
Factors of production	Real wages	Technology
Flexible labor	Risk	Uncertainty
market	Schumpeterian	Vested interests
Globalization	model	Wage rigidity

Chapter Questions and Problems

1. Describe why the supply of labor might vary with the price level in the economy. (Hint: Use Figs. 8.1 and 8.2 to frame your discussion.)
2. In the long run, what determines the capacity of the economy to produce the goods and services, or what we call the supply side of the economy? Your answer should refer to the discussion of the

two sources of economic growth, namely factor accumulation and technological change.

3. Describe Solow's growth model in detail, listing the assumptions behind the model and explaining the model's equilibrium condition. (Hint: Detail the relationships between the production function, the saving rate, and depreciation.)

4. Discuss what the Solow model reveals, and does not reveal, about technological change. Does the Solow model provide a useful, if simplified, picture of the process of economic growth?

5. Using both a diagram and words, discuss what the Solow model concludes would be the result of an increase in the rate of depreciation rate. (Hint: Begin by setting up the Solow model, clearly stating the assumptions made about the key variables and relationships, finding the equilibrium before the change in the depreciations rate, and then introducing the change in the depreciation rate to derive the new equilibrium.)

6. Describe Schumpeter's model of technological progress, carefully detailing how each of the model's key variables influence the gains or costs of innovation.

7. Briefly contrast the insights provided by (1) the Solow growth model and (2) the Schumpeterian model of technological progress. Specifically explain whether the two models are complementary or conflicting in their conclusions.

8. Use the insights provided by the Solow and Schumpeter models to describe what you would look for when predicting the long-run growth of productive capacity (the supply side) of an economy.

9. Explain how the level of globalization, which refers to international trade, international investment, and immigration, affects an economy's rate of growth.

10. Summarize the variables that influence an economy's supply side. Select several variables and detail how they influence and shift aggregate supply.

11. Using the Keynesian model from the previous chapter and the growth models by Solow and Schumpeterian in this chapter to compare economic policies that address the demand side and policies that address the supply side economic policies. Do these policies operate in isolation, or do policies have both demand and supply side effects?

12. Discuss Schumpeter's pespective on profit. Why was it controversial?

References

Aghion, P and P Howitt (1992). A model of growth through creative destruction. *Econometrica*, 60, 323–351.

Baldwin, RE (2003). Openness and growth: What's the empirical relationship? *Challenges to Globalization*, Baldwin RE and L Alan Winters (eds.). Chicago: University of Chicago Press.

Cipolla, CM (1978). *Clocks and Culture, 1300–1700*. New York: Norton.

Crafts, N and AJ Venables (2001). Globalization and geography: An historical perspective. *Working Paper*, April 12.

Edwards, S (1998). Openness, productivity and growth: What do we really know? *The Economic Journal*, 108, 383–398

Florax, RJGM, HLF de Groot and R Heijungs (2002). The empirical economic growth literature. *Tinbergen Institute Discussion Paper* TI 2002-040/3.

Frankel, JA and D Romer (1999). Does trade cause growth? *American Economic Review*, 89(3), 379–399.

Grossman, GM and E Helpman (1991). *Innovation and Growth in the Global Economy*. Cambridge, MA: MIT Press.

Hill, PJ (1971). The economic impact of immigration into the United States. *Journal of Economic History*, 31(1), 260–263.

Holmes, TJ and JA Schmitz (1995). Resistance to new technology and trade between areas. *Federal reserve Bank of Minneapolis Quarterly Review*, 19(1), 2–17.

Irwin, DA (2000). Tariffs and growth in late nineteenth century America. *NBER Working Paper* 7639.

Levine, R and D Renelt (1992). A sensitivity analysis of cross-country growth. *American Economic Review*, 82(4), 942–963.

Lewer, J and H Van den Berg (2001). Do capital-importing countries really grow faster? An empirical test using panel data for 27 countries. *Global Economy Quarterly*, 2(1), 1–36.

Lewer, J and H Van den Berg (2003). Does trade composition matter for medium-run growth? Time series evidence for 28 countries. *Journal of International Trade and Economic Growth*, 12(1), 39–96.

Lewer, J and H Van den Berg (2004). How large is international trade's effect on economic growth? *Surveys in Economic Growth*, George, DAR,

L Oxley, and KI Carlaw (eds.), pp. 137–170. Oxford, U.K.: Blackwell Publishing.

Mokyr, J (1990). *The Lever of Riches.* Oxford, U.K.: Oxford University Press.

Rodriguez, F and D Rodrik (2001). Trade policy and economic growth: A skeptics guide to the cross-national evidence. *NBER Macroeconomics Annual 2000*, Bernanke B and KS Rogoff (eds.). Cambridge, MA: MIT Press.

Romer, PM (1990). Endogenous technological change. *Journal of Political Economy*, 98(5), S71–S102.

Romer, PM (1993). Idea gaps and object gaps in economic development. *Journal of Monetary Economics*, 32, 543–573.

Romer, PM (1994). The origins of endogenous growth. *Journal of Economic Perspectives*, 8(1), 3–22.

Rosenberg, N (1994). *Exploring the Black Box, Technology, Economics, and History.* Cambridge, U.K.: Cambridge University Press,

Samuelson, PA (2004). Where Ricardo and Mill rebut and confirm arguments of mainstream economists supporting globalization. *Journal of Economic Perspectives*, 18(3), 135–146.

Schumpeter, J (1934). *The Theory of Economic Development.* Cambridge, MA: Harvard University Press.

Smith, A (1776[1976]). *An Inquiry into the Nature and Causes of the Wealth of Nations.* Chicago: University of Chicago Press.

Solow, R (1956). A contribution to the theory of economic growth. *Quarterly Journal of Economics*, 70(1), 65–94.

Solow, R (1957). Technical change and the aggregate production function. *Review of Economics and Statistics*, 39, 312–320.

Srinivasan, TN (1997). As the century turns: Analytics, empirics, and politics of development. *Yale Working Paper*, Economic Growth Center, Yale University, December.

Van den Berg, H and JJ Lewer (2007). *International Trade and Economic Growth.* Armonk, NY: M.E. Sharpe.

Wacziarg, R (2001). Measuring the dynamic gains from trade. *World Bank Economic Review*, 15(3), 393–429.

Chapter 9

The Aggregate Demand/Aggregate Supply Model

The basic error of modern macroeconomics is the belief that the economy is simply the sum of microeconomic decisions of rational agents. But the economy is more than that. The interactions of these decisions create collective movements that are not visible at the micro level.... It will remain difficult to model these collective movements. There is much resistance. Too many macroeconomists are attached to their models because they want to live in the comfort of what they understand — the behaviour of rational and superbly informed individuals.

(Paul De Grauwe, 2009)

The field of macroeconomics has experienced several major paradigm shifts over the past century. The Great Depression convinced policy-makers and economists to reject the scientific reductionism of microeocnomics in favor of John Maynard Keynes' macroeconomic model, which we detailed in Chapter 7. During the early 1970s, however, economic events and a shift in economic thinking led many macroeconomists to embrace new models.

Among the reasons for the Keynesian model's falling out of favor after 1970 was the demand-side model's inability to clearly diagnose the dual problems of inflation and slow growth, or *stagflation*, after the oil price increase in 1973. More important, the Keynesian model was confronted by a *New Classical* philosophy (also often referred to as *neoliberalism*) emphasizing individual welfare over collective social outcomes. The appeal to individuality struck a sympathetic cord in many countries. Of course, individual and collective perspectives are not really alternatives; individual welfare and producer profits depend on overall economic outcomes, and individual people and firms generate aggregate outcomes. Macroeconomists responded to the neoliberal challenge by seeking more mathematically rigorous *microfoundations* that related aggregate outcomes directly to the hypothesized behavior of individual consumers, workers, firms, banks, investors, and government agencies. The Keynesian model was accused of lacking clear microfoundations.

Economists' efforts to construct a logically coherent aggregate macroeconomic model based on well-defined *microfoundations* proved to be extremely difficult, however. Macroeconomists ended up going back to the standard microeconomic hypotheses about individual behavior, namely that consumers maximized utility subject to income and firms maximized profits subject to well-defined cost functions. To make the mathematical analysis manageable, macroeconomic models assumed that consumers and firms acted in accordance with stable preferences and profit functions, respectively.

Some new concepts were also introduced. For one thing, economists also began to base their macroeconomic analysis on the assumption that individuals are guided by *rational expectations*, which were conveniently defined making use of all available information to objectively make choices and determine the consequences of individual actions. Also underlying most recent macroeconomic analysis is the implicit assumption that product, labor, and financial markets exist and are efficient in setting prices that reflect true opportunity costs. These assumptions are unrealistic, but it was impossible to design practical models linking individuals and firms to aggregate outcomes without these assumptions.

Recall the discussion of Leon Walras' general equilibrium model in Chapter 7, which pointed out that, a century ago, economists were content to *assume* that the Walrasian system of equations represented a stable economic system and that they could safely focus entirely on the individual parts. Modern macroeconomists apparently felt obligated to *explain why* the parts interacted to form a stable economic system. Unfortunately, the mathematical elegance of their explanations based on unrealistic assumptions such as rational expectations and efficient markets led many macroeconomists to advocate policies to remake economies to where they more closely matched their mathematically convenient assumptions. This circular reasoning convinced many economists to advocate "market solutions" and less government involvement in the economy.

Research from psychology, behavioral economics, and some independent economists not blinded by the neoliberal culture of their profession shows that the assumptions of efficient markets and the rationality of human behavior are dangerously inaccurate. The 2008 global financial crisis, which was caused by precisely the policies prescribed by the macroeconomic models based on rational expectations and unregulated markets, may convince more economists that their models were inaccurate. It is interesting that in late 2008, the conservative Bush administration in the United States quickly implemented "collective" Keynesian macroeconomic policies to reverse the steep economic recession.

To analyze the paradigm shifts from the Keynesian model to the neoliberal models during the 1980s and now, after the 2008 financial crisis, back to a Keynesian perspective, this chapter introduces the aggregate demand/aggregate supply (*AD/AS*) model. This model combines the Keynesian Mundell–Fleming model from Chapter 7 and the supply side model from the previous chapter. The supply side was not explicitly part of the Keynesian model presented in Chapter 7, but the processes of innovation and economic growth, critical to the supply side, are fully compatible with the Keynes' insightful discussion of expectations.

Chapter Goals

1. Discuss the main criticisms of the Keynesian macroeconomic model.
2. Generalize the Keynesian demand side model before adding it to the aggregate demand/aggregate supply (*AD/ AS*) model.
3. Describe how the Keynesian demand side fits into the *AD/AS* model.
4. Add the supply side under both rational and Keynesian expectations.
5. Provide the examples of how adding the supply side modifies the effect of macroeconomic policy.
6. Illustrate the cases of stagflation and long-run economic growth using the *AD/AS* model.

9.1 The Critics of the Keynesian Model

There were several different schools of thought that questioned the Keynesian macroeconomic model. We have already discussed the need for adding a *supply side* to the model in the previous chapter. In this section, we explain the challenges to the Keynesian macroeconomic model by Milton Friedman and the *monetarists* who trusted in the efficiency of markets, Robert Lucas and other proponents of the *rational expectations* hypothesis, and finally the research from industrial organization, microeconomics, psychology, and behavioral economics that refutes the *rational expectations* and *efficient markets* hypotheses.

9.1.1 *The dissent of the monetarists*

Milton Friedman of the University of Chicago was one of the few dissenting voices when the Keynesians reigned supreme in macroeconomics during the 1950s and 1960s. Friedman was known as a *monetarist* because he emphasized the importance of a steady and consistent monetary policy rather than the Keynesian prescription of continual adjustments of fiscal and monetary to counter the year-to-year fluctuations in employment and output. A noted work was Friedman and Anna Schwartz's *A Monetary History of the United States 1867–1960*, in which they showed that the macroeconomic performance of the US economy closely tracked movements in the money supply.[1] Friedman also argued that fiscal policy was not only ineffective but often perverse because of the long lag time between policy decisions and economic effects. Friedman therefore suggested that the US Federal Reserve Bank should steadily expand the monetary base at exactly the long-run rate of real growth of the US economy, which in the 1960s was about three percent per year. Friedman's prescription for a *passive* rather than an *active* macroeconomic policy clashed with the dominant Keynesian policy approach. Friedman also became an instant favorite of those who opposed a strong government role in the economy.

Friedman (1968) and the labor economist Phelps (1968) provided a further justification for more passive macroeconomic policies by contesting the conventional wisdom that there was a tradeoff between unemployment and inflation. The evidence of an inverse relationship between unemployment and inflation had become known as the *Phillips curve*, in honor of Phillips (1958), who first uncovered an inverse relationship between unemployment and prices for Britain for the extended period 1861–1957. If true, such a tradeoff between inflation and employment could be exploited by policymakers to raise employment by means of faster money growth. Friedman claimed, however, that even though "...there is always a temporary trade-off between inflation and unemployment; there is no permanent trade-off".[2]

Friedman argued that producers might at first produce more when expansionary monetary policy causes prices to rise, but they would soon realize that their workers' wages and suppliers' prices also rise, thus leaving real profits no greater than before. Persistent

---

[1] Milton Friedman and Anna Jacobson Schwartz (1963).
[2] Milton Friedman (1968). p. 1.

inflation leads producers and workers to anticipate, or "rationally expect", further price increases, and they will then vary their output and supply of labor in accordance with their perception of real prices and wages, not nominal prices and wages. Excessively rapid monetary expansion, therefore, cannot permanently raise employment above the "natural rate" where everyone is working about as much as they want to work at the expected long-run real level of wages.

The embrace of the natural rate of employment by the monetarists suggested that a key fundamental disagreement between Keynesians and monetarists' was about how quickly markets clear and how well prices reflect true economic conditions and objective expectations. Friedman (1968) and Phelps' (1968) findings of a vertical Phillips curve suggested that labor market worked sufficiently well to balance supply and demand for labor. Their finding was widely used by commentators and many economists to argue that expansionary macroeconomic policies were futile and that, during the stagflationary 1970s, they produced more inflation but no gain in employment. By the start of the 1980s, policymakers in the US, Britain, and many other countries increasingly accepted the monetarist assumption that free labor markets would take care of unemployment. They shifted their focus to reducing inflation, assured by their economic advisors that the rational expectations hypothesis predicted that tight monetary policy would quickly reduce inflation without generating more unemployment. The monetarists and rational expectationists seemed to have successfully carried out a revolution in the field of economics. Unfortunately, the prescribed tight monetary policies plunged much of the world economy into a severe recession and triggered a debt crisis that brought economic growth to a ten-year halt in most developing countries.

9.1.2 *Deceptive microfoundations*

Economic policymakers' shift away from focusing on unemployment was facilitated by the focus on microfoundations and the adoption of convenient microeconomic models of competitive markets. As mentioned in the introduction to this chapter, simplifying assumptions were necessary to build practical macroeconomic models that were logically compatible with individual and firm behavior. Unfortunately, the microeconomic models used to represent individuals and firms were neither realistic nor general. Notable was the modeling of the labor market as a competitive market where labor was paid its marginal product. Even more inaccurate was the routine assumption that product markets are inhabited by rising-cost producers, and that there is no tendency for market power to become concentrated in oligopolies or monopolies. In reality, labor and product markets are seldom fully competitive, and prices routinely fail to accurately reflect true opportunity costs. Also notable was the widespread acceptance of the *Coase theorem*, due to Coase (1960). This theorem states that *externalities* will not, in general, cause markets to fail because people and firms are motivated to find ways to negotiate the mutually beneficial sharing of the external costs or benefits. The Coase theorem is arguably the greatest leap in faith to be found in mainstream economics, yet it has been seriously invoked in many scholarly articles and books. It is safe to say that in most cases few market participants are even aware of the existence of externalities, much less able to seriously negotiate some way to share them.

In the area of finance, the microfoundations literature has come to accept as practical approximations of reality several other highly questionable models: Fama's (1970) model of efficient markets that built all available information into asset prices, Friedman's (1953) hypothesis that speculation always stabilizes financial markets, and Jensen and Meckling's (1976) model of managers of private firms as faithful servants of the stockholders. There has also been an almost blind faith in the efficiency of financial markets, a faith that the 2008 financial crisis has now severely punished. The microfoundations for this trust was found in the work of Kenneth Arrow and Gerard Debreu (1954) and Debreu (1959), who constructed elaborate general equilibrium models reminiscent of Walras' late-19th century model.

Arrow and Debreu showed that uncertainty is eliminated when there are competitive markets in *contingent commodities*, which are commodities that are transacted only when certain pre-specified conditions are met. Wrote Debreu: "This new definition of a commodity allows one to obtain a theory of uncertainty free from any probability concept and formally identical with the theory of certainty....".[3] While a modern financial industry does indeed provide insurance against contingencies such as fire, theft, automobile accidents, and other predictable events, the 2008 financial crisis and the massive government bailouts of financial firms suggest that the financial sector has been unable to create viable insurance instruments that cover more complex contingencies. Arrow and Debreu's contingent markets are a theoretical fantasy that assumes outcomes are subject to risk rather than uncertainty. In truth, we often operate in ignorance of the full set of possible outcomes and their probabilities. Arrow and Debreu's model also seemed to suggest that financial innovation was always a positive development because it created contingent markets that reduced risk and, therefore, made the international financial system more stable and efficient.

9.1.3 *Rational expectations*

Friedman's refutation of the Phillips curve stimulated the growing acceptance of the rational expectations hypothesis. In the early 1970s, a University of Chicago colleague of Friedman, Lucas (1972, 1973), used an aggregate demand/aggregate supply model similar to the one developed in this chapter to show why rational expectations prevents accelerating inflation from reducing unemployment. Lucas drew on earlier work by John Muth (1961), who first defined rational expectations as the understanding of the future derived by rational individuals objectively using all available facts and models. Muth and Lucas argued that it is not logical to assume that when experience contradicts prior beliefs, rational people take no action to change their expectations. The hypothesis of rational expectations thus provides a precise explanation for Friedman's argument that producers and workers will anticipate future price increases and, therefore, not increase output and labor when prices rise.

---

[3] Gerard Debreu (1959). p. 98.

The concept of rational expectations was explained earlier in Chapter 4, where it was used to define the expected future exchange rate in the interest parity condition. Recall that the interest parity condition linked the spot exchange rate to future exchange rates under the assumption that people set their expectations *rationally* by reasoning logically and making use of all relevant information. In the case of exchange rates, the information set consists of:

1. People's understanding of how foreign exchange rates are determined, that is, their model of exchange rate determination.
2. All available information that helps to put values on the variables in their model of exchange rate determination.

Muth (1961, p. 316) then pointed out that the inclusion of models in the information set along with the relevant facts implies that:

> Expectations, since they are informed predictions of future events using the most trusted economic models, are essentially the same as the predictions of the relevant economic theory.

Thus, if the rational expectations hypothesis is correct, people's expectations are determined by the same models that economists and policymakers use to design economic policies. Since the final outcomes of economic policies depend on people's expectations of how future policies will affect them, it would not be "rational" for economists to use a model to predict an outcome or to decide on a policy under the assumption that people will not adjust their behavior in anticipation of the likely effect of the policies as predicted by the model. In short, rational expectations proponents argued that policymakers could not repeatedly fool people into behaving in ways that are not compatible with the expected long-term outcomes of economic policies. This conclusion was often cited to argue against Keynesian macroeconomic policies.

Muth's (1961) model of rational expectations proved very convenient for macroeconomists because he gave it a specific formulation.

Muth explicitly defined rational expectations as the mathematical expected value of all possible outcomes. Recall that we used the expected value notation when we defined the expected future exchange rate in Chapter 4. Such a mathematical expectation is justified if people know the true process (model) that generates future outcomes.

9.1.4 *Keynes' deeper understanding of expectations*

The rational expectations hypothesis has many weaknesses. First of all, people do not know all the facts. They also generally do not understand the process (or the model of the process) that generates the future outcomes well enough to be able to establish the probabilities of all possible future outcomes. Finally, people are not entirely rational because the human evolution did not design the human brain to function precisely according to the rules of mathematical logic. This latter point should not be taken as a criticism of the human brain; rather, it is a criticism of the rational expectations model of human economic behavior.

It is interesting to note that when the rational expectations revolution gained momentum during the 1970s and 1980s, there was seldom any reference to Keynes' very insightful writing on long-term expectations. As pointed out earlier in the textbook, Keynes' devoted an entire chapter of his *General Theory* to expectations. Keynes was concerned that investment, and therefore the IS curve, was unstable because the expectations that drive investment are volatile:

> Most, probably, of our decisions to do something positive, the full consequences of which will be drawn out over many days to come, can only be taken as a result of animal spirits — of a spontaneous urge to action rather than inaction, and not as the outcome of a weighted average of quantitative benefits multiplied by quantitative probabilities.[4]

---

[4] John Maynard Keynes (1936). pp. 161–162.

By broadening investment to include innovation, invention, research, and development activities, Keynes' description of investment as being driven by animal spirits rather than precise mathematical calculations of probable economic outcomes is further validated.

In the quote above, Keynes explicitly rejects Muth's assumption that expectations are "a weighted average" of possible outcomes. Keynes understood that for events in the distant future, no one has enough facts and certainly no reliable model with which to specify the probabilities associated with the many possible outcomes. Recall that when it comes to long-term investment and innovation, we face uncertainty, not calculable risk. If Keynes' is correct in that expectations are anchored in convention based on relatively recent experience and a limited understanding of the true process that generated the recent results, then the economy will inevitably be subject to occasional revisions of expectations that can severely change overall economic outcomes.

Critics of Keynesian macroeconomic policies are correct in asserting that Keynes assumes behavior that is not entirely rational, at least not as Muth (1960) defined rationality. Keynes (1936) argued that macroeconomic policy must continually adapt to economic fluctuations caused by shifts in expectations that are based on very partial information about the future and recent economic events. He furthermore showed that at times like the Great Depression or a severe recession, monetary policy would have little effect on macroeconomic outcomes, either as a stabilizing force or a corrective measure because the lowering of interest rates has little impact when there is unemployment and excess industrial capacity.

The assumption that people have accurate information and efficiently predict the future is critical to Lucas and Friedman's prescription for clear and predictable macroeconomic policies that permit people to accurately anticipate future economic policies. Lucas (1972, 1973) effectively provided a formal confirmation of Friedman's prescription of a steady pre-announced growth of the money supply. With people looking forward to determine their behavior, economic stability can be achieved only if policymakers clearly signal their intent to keep policies stable. Note, however, that Lucas' confirmation is based on the assumption of rational expectations.

The period from 1983 through 2007, when US unemployment and output levels appeared to be more stable than they had been during the earlier post-World War II period, is often held up as a validation of Friedman and Lucas' prescription for predictable and steady monetary and fiscal policies. After all, policymakers and economists in positions of power in the United States, Britain, and the International Monetary Fund during this period publicly supported largely passive economic policies based on the assumptions of rational expectations and efficient markets. The evidence suggests that actual policy did not follow the political rhetoric, however.

First of all, the US Federal Reserve Bank never applied Friedman's three percent per year money growth rule. Nor did policymakers manage government budgets conservatively and in accordance with transparent and predictable rules. The reality is that the Federal Reserve continually shifted monetary policy in response to economic events. For example, a sudden 25 percent decline in the stock market in late 1987 was immediately countered by a huge expansion of the money supply, a policy shift that Keynesians advised. Similarly, the 2000 stock market decline was addressed by an expansionary monetary stance that lowered interest rates to one percent. And, when the economy expanded rapidly afterward, the Federal Reserve tightened the money supply and consistently pushed interest rates gradually back up to over five percent. Nor was US fiscal policy steady during this period. Tax rates were lowered in 1981 when the US economy was deep in recession, they were increased in 1986 when the economy had recovered, they were adjusted in 1991 and 1994 to balance the US government budget, and they were lowered again in the early 2000s when the US economy was hit by the stock market crash. A surge in expenditures to conduct wars in the Middle East further drove the government budget sharply from surplus to deficit after 2001. There were, no doubt, many motivations for these policy shifts, but they were anything but the steady, predictable policies advocated by rational expectationists like Robert Lucas.

While U.S. policymarkers did not follow Friedman and Lucas by carrying out mechanical pre-determined and transparent macroeconomic policies, they did embrace the free-market philosophy of the neoliberal economic paradigm to justify the dismantling of regulatory structures and the privatization of many traditional government functions. That is, the emphasis on microfoundations and the unsubstantiated assumptions of market efficiency and rational expectations were effectively rejected by policymakers and central banks when they carried out their *macroeconomic* management, yet these same assumptions were implicitly accepted to reject *microeconomic* regulation of the economy. The speed with which the US government provided monetary and fiscal stimuli to the US economy to reverse the 2008 financial collapse, while it refused to press for reform of the failed regulatory structure that permitted the risky behavior that caused the crisis in the first place, suggests that this selective adherence to the microfoundations approach continues to influence policy in the US.

These issues can be better discussed using the aggregate demand/aggregate supply model. The next section begins developing this model by reviewing and generalizing the Keynesian demand side model introduced in Chapter 7.

9.2 Generalizing Keynes' Demand Side of the Economy

In the Mundell–Fleming model, the economy's demand for output, Y, is split into (1) consumer demand, C, (2) investment, I, (3) government goods and services, G, and (4) net exports, $NX = X - IM$. That is

$$Y = C + I + G + NX \tag{9.1}$$

The introductory Keynesian model in Chapter 7 included rather simple functions to represent each of the components of aggregate demand for goods. Consumption was assumed to be a function of income, investment a function of the interest rate, government expenditures exclusively a policy variable, and net exports the result of those same determinants of domestic and foreign consumption, investment, and government expenditures. More complete theoretical functions for C, I, G, and NX than were presented in Chapter 7 make it clear why the curves in the

Mundell-Fleming model are likely to shift and cause the equilibrium output and employment levels in the economy to fluctuate.

9.2.1 *The consumption function*

The Keynesian consumption function can be more accurately stated as relating consumer demand and *disposable income*. That is, consumer expenditures depend on overall output Y, taxes T, and transfers Tr. The real interest rate r also plays a role in how people allocate their incomes between savings and consumption over time. All other things equal, the lower the interest rate, the more people consume today rather than in the future. A low interest rate means there will be more credit card debt, larger mortgages, and more auto loans, all other things equal.

Modigliani and Brumberg (1954) further hypothesized that consumption also depends on accumulated wealth, W. For example, if the stock market rises, people's wealth increases and consumer expenditures rise. Friedman (1957) provided a related hypothesis that consumption depends on one's permanent income, Y_P, not current income, and that people smooth out their consumption over time. Friedman's *permanent income hypothesis*, developed in the 1950s, came to fit well with the rational expectations hypothesis later adopted by macroeconomics in the 1970s and 1980s. It seems perfectly rational for people to spend in accordance with their expected lifetime incomes rather than their actual incomes at any point in time. For example, many people buy a house on credit when they first enter the labor force, even though they do not have enough income to buy that house at that moment in time. Rational expectations and the permanent income hypothesis predict that when people change their expectations about their permanent lifetime income, their current consumption changes even though their current income may not change. For example, if you learn that you have been included in a 90-year old very rich but still living aunt's will, the permanent income hypothesis predicts a sharp increase in current consumption even though you will not receive your inheritance for some years. Keynes' basic formulation of the consumption function predicts no change in current consumption in such a case.

Akerlof (2007) lists the permanent income hypothesis as one of several popular microfoundations assumptions that US economists introduced in place of Keynesian analysis in the 1970s and 1980s. Akerlof argues that like rational expectations, the rejection of inflation-unemployment trade-off, and the efficient markets hypothesis, the permanent income hypothesis has failed to gather empirical support. There is substantial evidence that current income has a very substantial influence on current consumption, just as Keynes posited.[5] But Akerlof (2007) does not rely only on the empirical refutation of the permanent income hypothesis to salvage Keynes' hypothesized link between current income and current consumption. Akerlof also appeals to psychological and sociological factors that influence consumption behavior:

> A major determinant of consumption is what people think they *should* consume. Second, what people think they should consume can often be viewed either as entitlements or obligations. Finally, in turn, current income is one of the major determinants of these entitlements, and obligations.[6]

Akerlof's reasoning reflects the work of Max Weber (1905) and the more recent French sociologist, Pierre Bourdieu (1984), who studied how consumption patterns were influenced by people's social status and how people's income in turn influenced how they evaluated their status. Thus, people tend to consume at levels compatible with their current incomes, which they use to identify their social status and professional status.

It is often forgotten that Keynes directly appealed to psychology, and not some simple model of welfare maximization, when he specified his consumption function:

> The fundamental psychological law, upon which we are entitled to depend with great confidence both *a priori* from our knowledge of

---

[5] See, for example, studies by John Campbell and Gregory Mankiw (1989), Jonathan Parker (1999), Nicholes Souleles (1999), and David Wilcox (1989).

[6] George Akerlof (2007). p. 15.

human nature and from the detailed facts of experience, is that men are disposed, as a rule and on the average, to increase their consumption as their income increases, but not by as much as the increase in their income.[7]

Research in psychology reveals that people indeed tend to be heavily focused on the present, and they highly discount both the future and the past, which suggests that current income may still greatly influence current consumption. Friedman's permanent income hypothesis adds an important explanatory variable to the consumption function, but by itself Friedman's hypothesis provides only a partial, and thus inaccurate, description of consumption behavior.

Putting all of the potential determinants of consumption together, it is reasonable to specify the consumption function as not just $C = C(Y)$, but as

$$C = C(Y, T, Tr, r, Y_P, W) \qquad (9.2)$$

Consumption is usually hypothesized to be positively related to current income, permanent income (expected lifetime wealth), current wealth, and transfers, and negatively related to taxes and the real interest rate, all other things equal.[8]

9.2.2 *Investment demand*

The traditional Keynesian model hypothesizes that the demand for investment (capital) goods depends on the interest rates at home and abroad, r and r^*, respectively. Interest rates r and r^* represent the opportunity cost of alternative uses of the resources used for investment. The use of monetary policy to change the interest rate and

---

[7] John Maynard Keynes (1936). p. 96.

[8] In the language of calculus, the signs of the partial derivatives of this consumption function are: $\partial C / \partial Y > 0$, $\partial C / \partial T < 0$, $\partial C / \partial Tr > 0$, $\partial C / \partial r < 0$, $\partial C / \partial Y_P > 0$, and $\partial C / \partial W > 0$.

investment is referred to as the *Keynesian monetary mechanism*, which predicts that an increase in the real money supply, denoted as the nominal money supply divided by the price index, or M/P, reduces the real interest rate for loanable funds, which in turn causes investment to increase.

There may be several other monetary mechanisms that translate increased money supply into greater investment demand. For example, the demand for investment goods is also likely to be related to the overall level of output Y that it helps to produce. Given the discussion above, expectations need to be included among the determinants of investment and innovation. But to what extent are expectations "rational"? To what extent are they based on "animal spirits" or "conventions" established by recent experience? What is in the information set of rational investors? What is in the partial information set of real investors? We will return to these questions later in the chapter.

The economy's investment function can, therefore, be specified as follows[9]:

$$I = I(Y, r, r^*, M/P, M^*/P^*, \text{Expectations}) \qquad (9.3)$$

In light of the discussion above, the variable "expectations" include the variables that affect investors' and innovators' expectations of future returns as well as the myriad sociological, psychological, - cultural, and other variables that affect people's views of the future.

9.2.3 *Government expenditures*

In Chapter 7, government expenditures G were taken as a given, determined outside the model by political forces. However, for a given set of political factors, government expenditures also depend on taxes collected T, and taxes in turn depend on overall income and

---

[9] The signs of the partial derivatives of the investment function are thus hypothesized to be $\partial I/\partial Y > 0$, $\partial I/\partial r < 0$, $\partial I/\partial r^* < 0$, $\partial I/\partial(\partial/P) > 0$, and $\partial I/\partial(M^*/P^*) > 0$.

output Y. Government can, and often does, borrow domestically and overseas to finance its purchases, which means that interest rates and monetary policies at home and abroad may influence G. Government transfers Tr may have a negative effect on government demand for the economy's output because they compete with G for government tax revenue and borrowing. Transfers such as unemployment benefits, social security payments, and farm subsidies are influenced by other variables, such as income, unemployment, and product prices. The government demand function can thus be represented as:

$$G = G(POL, Y, T, Tr, r, r^*, M/P, M^*/P^*) \qquad (9.4)$$

The variable *POL* represents the complex set of political factors that influence government budget decisions.[10] The discussion of the shift in economic policy from a Keynesian perspective to the neoliberal perspective in the 1970s and 1980s suggests that *POL* is not a fixed set of influences. Over the past half century, the discussion of macroeconomic policy has shifted from favoring the activist macroeconomic posture suggested by Keynes (1936) to a more passive, albeit a very selectively passive, policy approach. The 2008 financial crisis and the rehabilitation of the Keynesian model suggest we may see another shift in macroeconomic policy in the near future.

9.2.4 *Net exports*

In an open economy, exports and imports depend on all of the domestic and foreign variables that influence the components of domestic and foreign aggregate demand, such as C, I, G, C^*, I^*, and G^*. For example, when domestic consumers increase demand, they increase demand for imports. When foreigners increase their demand for consumption goods, however, some of that foreign demand spills across the border and raises the demand for the open economy's

---

[10] The signs of the partial derivatives of this function are likely to be $\partial G/\partial Y > 0$, $\partial G/\partial T > 0$, $\partial G/\partial Tr < 0$, $\partial G/\partial r < 0$, $\partial G/\partial r^* < 0$, $\partial G/\partial(M/P) > 0$, and $\partial G/\partial(M^*/P^*) > 0$.

exports. Net foreign demand also depends on international variables such as the nominal exchange rate, e, the ratio of domestic to foreign price levels, P/P^*, and the sets of domestic and foreign trade policies that restrict and regulate international trade, *TPOL* and *TPOL**.

Net exports are therefore a function of all the variables in the domestic and overseas C, I, and G equations plus specific trade-related variables:

$$X - IM = NX(C, C^*, I, I^*, G, G^*; e, P/P^*, TPOL, TPOL^*)$$
$$(9.5)$$

The relationship between *NX* and the exchange rate is positive if the Marshall-Lerner condition is satisfied, as you may recall from Chapter 7.[11]

9.2.5 *Aggregate demand*

Aggregate demand for the economy's output, $\Upsilon_D = C + I + G + NX$, is a function consisting of all the explanatory variables in equations (9.2) through (9.5):

$$\Upsilon_D = \Upsilon_D(\Upsilon, \Upsilon^*, \Upsilon_p, \Upsilon^*_p, W, W^*, T, T^*, Tr, Tr^*, r, r^*,$$
$$M/P, M^*/P^*, POL, POL^*, e, M/P^*,$$
$$TPOL, TPOL^*, \text{Expectations}) \qquad (9.6)$$

Even this complex function is still a gross simplification of the real world, of course. You can no doubt come up with more factors that influence consumption, investment, government expenditures, and imports and exports.

---

[11] The partial derivatives between C, I, G, C^*, I^*, and G^* are given in earlier footnotes, and the partial derivatives for NX with respect to those variables should be multiplied by, respectively, $\partial NX/\partial C$ through $\partial NX/\partial G^*$. The trade-related variables influence NX according to the partial derivatives $\partial NX/\partial e > 0$ (provided the Marshall-Lerner condition holds) and $\partial NX/\partial(P/P^*) < 0$.

Specifying the directions of influence of each of the explanatory variables in equation (9.6) is difficult. The partial derivatives of some of the variables are ambiguous. For example, the sign of $\partial Y_D/\partial T$ is not obvious because taxes affect both consumption and government expenditures but in opposite directions because $\partial C/\partial T < 0$ and $\partial G/\partial T > 0$. Consumers and investors who receive government transfers will spend more, all other things equal, but budgetary pressures may force the government to reduce G. And, if real rates of return on investment increase, the demand for investment goods, and imports, increases; on the other hand, higher rates of return on investment will raise interest rates that "crowd out" demand for durable consumption goods. Similarly, increased government expenditures G financed through borrowing will also tend to raise interest rates and, therefore, crowd out investment and consumer expenditures, offsetting in part the increase in aggregate demand from the increase in G.

In short, there are many complex relationships among the variables on the right hand side of equation (9.6), and this means policymakers cannot simply multiply the projected change in a target variable by its partial derivative. Partial derivatives are "all other things equal" values, but in a real economy nothing ever remains equal. Policymakers are almost always surprised by "unintended consequences". The likelihood of such a fate can be reduced if policymakers take a holistic approach by explicitly recognizing how the parts work within the complexity that characterizes a modern economy. But, even an enthusiastic embrace of holism may not be enough to accurately predict the effects of macroeconomic policies. Some economists would argue that holism mandates that policymakers remain open to adjusting their policies.

The above functions are complicated further by the fact that human behavior depends on expectations and what Keynes would call "animal spirits". In the equations above, investment I and I^* clearly depend on expectations. The exchange rate is also an expectational variable, as explained in Chapter 4. And you have just read the discussion on consumption expenditures as dependent on long-run wealth or permanent income, both of which are clearly expectational variables. What this means, of course, is that these variables can take on very different values depending on the "mood" or "confidence level" in the economy. As Keynes explained, confidence depends on how well people's expectations have been met in the recent past. The system thus has multiple equilibria, depending on the particular state of animal spirits. That is, the same set of productive factors, state of technology, and institutions can generate very different overall levels of aggregate demand.

9.3 The Aggregate Demand Curve

Recall that in the previous chapter the aggregate supply curve is depicted as a function relating output Y and the price level P. In the Keynesian model, aggregate demand was illustrated in the *IS-LM-BOP* diagram, the Mundell–Fleming model, that related output and the interest rate, with all other variables relegated to other dimensions and, therefore, "shift" variables in the income-interest rate plane. The followers of Keynes who developed the *IS-LM* model believed focusing on the interest rate was appropriate because Keynes had argued that investment was the component most likely to shift aggregate demand. The aggregate demand/aggregate supply (*AD/AS*) model focuses on the relationship between real output Y and the price level P, reflecting the concern by macroeconomists with both unemployment and inflation after the stagflationary economic environment of the 1970s. To combine aggregate demand and aggregate supply, it is necessary to translate the Keynesian model into the output-price plane.

9.3.1 *Prices and aggregate demand*

It is not immediately obvious how we should draw an *aggregate demand (AD) curve* for an entire national economy in the price-output plane. Clearly, in a single market the quantity demanded depends critically on the price of the good in question. This is because the demanders of the specific good can substitute other products for the specific good in question and price changes have income effects

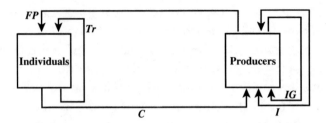

Figure 9.1   The simple circular flow: one person's payment is another's receipt.

that increase or decrease total real income remaining to spend on the good in question or on alternate products. In the aggregate economy the substitution between products largely nets out, however, and there is only substitution between consumption and saving (not consuming). Nor does a price change cause an obvious income effect because changes in the overall price level of the economy increase the income accruing to the economy's factors of production in tandem with the prices of overall output. Recall the discussion in Chapter 2 of the circular flow and illustrated in Fig. 9.1. One person's payment is another's receipt, so if prices rise, the value of the flows increase but in the aggregate, it would seem as though the flows will continue as before.

There are several subtle reasons why changes in the overall price level *do* influence the overall circular flow and, therefore, aggregate demand, however. These price effects on aggregate demand are (1) *the monetary effect*, (2) *the real-balance effect*, and (3) *the foreign trade effect*.

9.3.2 *The monetary effect*

A change in the price level changes the real money supply M/P. There are several ways that an increase in the money supply might affect total demand and output in the economy. Recall from the discussion of the LM curve in Chapter 7 that the Keynesian *monetary mechanism* consists of a sequence where an increase in the real money supply lowered the real interest rate, which in turn shifted up the investment function. Specifically, the Keynesian monetary mechanism can be summarized as follows:

$$(M/P)\uparrow \Rightarrow r\downarrow \Rightarrow I\uparrow \Rightarrow Y\uparrow \qquad (9.7)$$

The *credit view* of the monetary effect hypothesizes that an increase in the money supply that adds reserves to the banking system directly leads to an expansion of bank loans even in the absence of interest rate changes because many potential investors are credit constrained and restricted to borrowing in the banking sector. This mechanism can be summarized as follows:

$$(M/P)\uparrow \Rightarrow \text{loans}\uparrow \Rightarrow I\uparrow \Rightarrow Y\uparrow \qquad (9.8)$$

The credit view assumes that banks and other financial firms play a unique role in the financial sector because they are well placed to deal with the problems of moral hazard and adverse selection caused by information asymmetries. The credit view can be generalized to cover all financial intermediaries and markets, each of which presumably has some comparative advantage in channeling credit from savers to prospective credit-constrained borrowers.

The current chair of the US Federal Reserve Bank, Bernanke (1983, 1993), is a proponent of the credit view of the monetary mechanism. Bernanke helped to design the US government's response to the 2008 financial crisis, which has consisted of providing several trillion US dollars directly to banks and indirectly to guarantee asset values in the hope of reviving financial markets. Other countries have followed similar policies. The total cost of this strategy will ultimately depend on whether the banks and asset values recover.

Both the Keynesian monetary mechanism and the credit view can be illustrated as a shift in the *LM* curve and a downward movement along the *IS* curve in the Keynesian model. Figure 9.2 shows how, all other things equal, the monetary effect increases the equilibrium level of output from Y_0 to Y_1 when the real money supply increases due to a fall in the price level from P_0 to P_1.

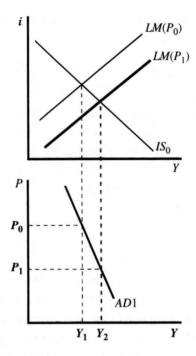

Figure 9.2   The monetary effect of a price decline

9.3.3 *The real-balance effect*

If consumption depends on accumulated wealth in addition to current income, a reduction in prices can raise aggregate demand. An economy's stock of wealth consists of the nominal money stock and the stock of real assets. Financial assets do not normally add to the economy's wealth because they tend to net out; one group's assets is another's liabilities. Private bonds do not constitute net national wealth unless they involve international borrowing and lending.

Government bonds are private net wealth only if government liabilities are not seen as, ultimately, a private liability. The concept of *Ricardian equivalence* refers to the equivalence of current government debt to the present value of future taxes to service the debt. If Ricardian equivalence holds, government bonds should not be seen as net wealth. Note also that if Ricardian equivalence holds and the permanent income hypothesis also holds, then there is no point to expansionary fiscal policy in the form of increased government expenditure funded by government borrowing. The continued use of fiscal stimulus to deal with unemployment suggests that policymakers agree that Ricardian equivalence and the permanent income hypothesis do not fully hold.

Finally, the stock of money is a store of value that does not have an obvious offsetting private liability. Net wealth, W, is therefore equal to either $W = [M + B(r)]/P$ or $W = M/P$, depending on whether the government bonds, B, are viewed as net wealth by consumers. Note that the value of government bonds is written as a function of the interest rate r because the present value of a given stock of bonds is inversely related to nominal interest rates.

The important characteristic of the net wealth represented by nominal money is that it is inversely related to the price level. A decline in overall prices increases the real value of the money in the hands of the public, all other things equal. Because the idea that the stock of real money influences the demand for goods and services is often attributed to Arthur Pigou (1917–1918), the effect of a change in prices on the real stock of money is alternatively referred to as the *real-balance effect* or *the Pigou effect*.

The real-balance effect shifts the IS curve to the right, as shown in Fig. 9.3. The shift from IS_0 to IS_1 implies that aggregate demand curve is the curve AD_2 in the bottom diagram of Fig. 9.3, sloped less steeply than the aggregate demand curve AD_1, which reflects only the monetary effect of a price decline.

9.3.4 *The foreign trade effect*

The price level also has an effect on international trade through the price ratio P/P^*, as already specified in the net foreign demand equation (9.5). Prices affect foreign trade because they determine the real exchange rate, which is defined as

$$q = eP^*/P = e/(P/P^*) \tag{9.9}$$

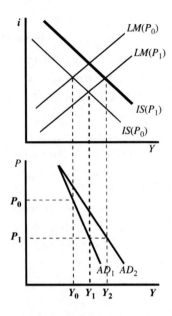

Figure 9.3   The real balance effect of a price decline.

The reason we included the nominal exchange rate e along with the domestic and foreign price levels P and P^* in the net exports equation (9.5) is that it is the real exchange rate that determines imports and exports.

The real exchange rate is closely related to the concept of purchasing power parity (PPP). Indeed, equation (9.9) makes it clear that the real exchange rate is equal to the nominal exchange rate, e, divided by the exchange rate that would satisfy purchasing power parity. A rise in q means exports become less expensive overseas and imports become more costly in terms of the domestic currency, and net exports will tend to increase.

Figure 9.4 illustrates the case of a decline in P, which raises the real exchange rate q. Therefore, a price decline shifts out the IS curve because NX increases. An increase in NX also shifts the BOP curve because it improves the current account balance, all other things equal. Chapter 7 showed that a change in e shifted both the IS and BOP curves, and the net effect on Υ may be tampered depending on the exchange rate regime and the mobility of capital, but the direction of

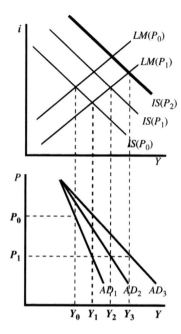

Figure 9.4   The foreign trade effect of a price decline.

influence remains as shown in Figure 9.4. The foreign trade effect, therefore, causes the aggregate demand curve to slope downward even less steeply when it is added to the monetary effect and the real-balance effects. When the foreign trade effect is added to the monetary effect and the real balance effect, the aggregate demand curve is clearly a downward-sloping curve, and a decline in the price level raises aggregate demand for output.

9.3.5 *Economic policies shift aggregate demand*

Chapter 9 described precisely how changes in fiscal and monetary policies trigger a variety of shifts in the *LM*, *IS*, and/or *BOP* curves of the Mundell–Fleming model under specific assumptions about the mobility of capital and the exchange rate regime. For example, the top diagram of Fig. 9.5, illustrates the effect of expansionary monetary policy with high capital mobility and floating exchange rates. If we assume, for the moment, that the price level remains unchanged, then

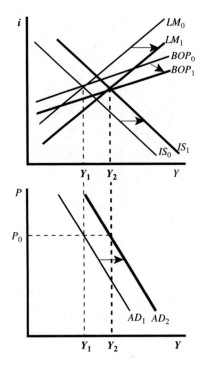

Figure 9.5   Monetary expansion and the aggregate demand curve.

the expansionary monetary policy shifts the *LM* curve from LM_0 to LM_1, which depreciates the real exchange rate, and, therefore, the *IS* curve shifts to the right from IS_0 to IS_1 and the *BOP* curve shifts from BOP_0 to BOP_1. Aggregate demand increases from Y_1 to Y_2. This change in aggregate demand is represented in the lower diagram by a shift to the right of the aggregate demand curve by exactly that same distance at the constant price level P_0. That is, an increase in aggregate demand brought about by some combination of shifts in the Mundell-Fleming model, all other things equal, shifts the aggregate demand curve drawn in the price-output plane to the right.

In general, when we take into consideration the supply side of the economy the price level does not stay the same after policies shift and other variables change. Prices may rise when aggregate demand increases. To continue our analysis, we need to bring the supply side of the economy into the model. As described in the next section of the chapter, the final effect on output, and thus employment, of macroeconomic policies must be reassessed when the supply side of the economy is taken into consideration. Among other things, the aggregate demand/aggregate supply model will enable us to understand the causes of, and solutions to, stagflation.

9.4 Combining the Demand and Supply Sides

We are now ready to combine the aggregate demand curve from Fig. 9.5 with the upward-sloping aggregate supply curve from the previous chapter. The first sub-section of this chapter illustrates how the model works by focusing on how economic policy can be used to increase total output. Further cases and examples follow in the remainder of the chapter.

9.4.1 *Analyzing policy using the AD/AS Model*

If the economy suffers from unemployment, presumably because the real wage is too high, the Mundell–Fleming model suggests that an increase in aggregate demand will, all other things equal, increase output and raise prices. Figure 9.6 illustrates the case where a shift in aggregate demand from AD to AD' causes real output to rise from Υ_1 to the full employment level of output Υ^* and the price level to rise from P_1 to P_2. This outcome reflects a trade-off between inflation and unemployment. The higher level of employment associated with the full employment level of output Υ^* can be reached only if society is willing to tolerate the inflation caused by the increase in prices from P_1 to P_2.

Figure 9.6 also illustrates the case where the aggregate supply curve shifts to the right, perhaps because the economy increases its supply of productive factors or it improves its productivity. Supply side policies may help to achieve this outcome. In this case, the economy moves to the point b, where output also rises to Υ^* but the price level falls to P_3. This latter case also illustrates the hypothesized outcome of passive macroeconomic policies proposed by Friedman,

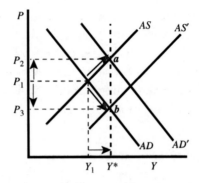

Figure 9.6 Increasing *Y*: A shift in aggregate demand or aggregate supply?

Lucas, and other neoliberal economists. If, instead of aggressively expanding the money supply or having the government borrow and spend to stimulate aggregate demand, policymakers would just let nominal wages and prices adjust to bring labor supply and labor demand back into balance, full employment can be restored without inflation. If workers and producers know expansionary macroeconomic policies will not be forthcoming, they will adjust wages and prices quickly. Keynesians argue that labor market rigidities, institutional factors, and psychological forces prevent wages from adjusting quickly.

While full employment can be achieved by moving the economy to either point a or point b in Fig. 9.6, these are not identical economic outcomes. In addition to the obvious differences in how price levels change, there are differences in many other variables as well. There may also be different long-term consequences.

9.4.2 *The demand side effects of moving to a or b*

To distinguish the full effects of an active fiscal or monetary expansion that shifts the economy to a, compared to a passive policy to let economy move itself to b, it is useful to link the aggregate demand/aggregate supply model back to the Mundell–Fleming model. For example, the bottom diagram in Fig. 9.7 details the

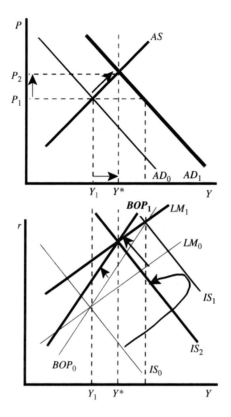

Figure 9.7 Expansionary fiscal policy to achieve full employment.

changes that occur in the Mundell–Fleming model in the case of an expansionary fiscal policy that shifts the AD curve as shown in the top diagram of Fig. 9.7. We assume immobile capital and a fixed exchange rate regime. Figure 9.7 thus draws the BOP curve steeper than the LM curve. To maintain the fixed exchange rate, the central bank must intervene in the foreign exchange market when the demand and supply of the nation's currency no longer balances after the expansionary fiscal policy pushes the IS curve to a new equilibrium that does not lie on the BOP curve.

In the bottom diagram of Fig. 9.7, the economy's initial equilibrium at the initial price level P_1 and output level Y_1 is given by the intersection of IS_0, LM_0, and BOP_0. This equilibrium is disturbed by the expansionary fiscal policy, which intends to shift the IS curve to IS_1. Recall from Chapter 7 that, with a fixed exchange rate regime and immobile capital, the BOP curve remains stationary but the foreign exchange market intervention by the central bank begins to shift the LM curve. Since the IS and LM curves intersect to the right of the steep BOP curve after the fiscal expansion, the currency will tend to depreciate, and the central bank must buy its currency. This reduction in the amount of currency in the hands of the public and the banking system shifts the LM curve to the left. In a Mundell–Fleming and Keynesian world of constant prices, the economy eventually settles at a higher output/income level where IS_1, LM_1, and BOP_0 intersect. But, the supply side of the economy tells us that an increase in output will increase the price level.

The tendency for the economy to shift after the expansionary fiscal policy, which is some combination of higher government expenditures and/or lower taxes, shifts the aggregate demand curve in the top part of Figure 9.7 to the right at the price level P1 by the amount given in the lower Mundell-Fleming diagram. But now, because we assume an upward-sloping aggregate supply curve, the price level rises. Consequently, the actual rise in output will not be as large as the constant-price Mundell-Fleming model predicts because rising prices shift the curves in the lower diagram of Figure 9.7. All other things equal, the price increase shifts the BOP curve to the left because the real exchange rate $q = e(P^*/P)$ appreciates. Hence, net exports decline as long as the Marshall-Lerner condition holds. The price increase also causes a leftward shift in the IS curve due to the effect of currency appreciation on the net exports component of product market demand. Finally, the price increase shrinks the real money supply, M/P, which causes the LM curve to shift to the left. Thus, the final shift in the LM curve in Figure 9.7 is the joint result of exchange rate intervention to keep the *nominal* exchange rate constant and the price-induced fall in the real money supply. The economy's equilibrium at the higher price level P_2 is finally given by the intersection of IS_2, LM_1, and BOP_1 at some output level Y^*, at which the aggregate demand and supply curves intersect in the top diagram of Figure 9.7.

9.4.3 *Supply side policies to achieve full employment*

Instead of the active fiscal expansion described in the previous example, suppose government policymakers decide instead to take measures to shift aggregate supply. A shift in the *AS* curve could be achieved by increasing productivity, expanding resources, or lowering supplies. All of these options are difficult to bring about in the short run. Productivity can be improved by improving technology, which requires entrepreneurship, research, and active implementation of new ideas and methods. In the late 1970s, many governments introduced so-called *supply side policies* to deregulate markets, reduce business taxes, and encourage technological competition. Expanding resources would require an increase in investment, which is also a slow, gradual process.

Policymakers could also try to induce a shift in the *AS* curve by passively waiting for labor and product markets to adjust to unemployment and excess productive capacity by lowering wages and prices. When aggregate demand is less than the economy's productive capacity, competitive producers with unused capacity or unwanted inventories may, sooner or later, cut prices in order to increase sales. Unemployed workers may accept lower wages. This passive approach, like an active supply side policy, would take the economy to a price level such as P_2 in Fig. 9.8 and a higher level of output at Y^*.

The bottom diagram in Fig. 9.8 details how the decline in the price level from P_1 to P_2 increases aggregate demand from Y_1 to Y^*. Assume again that the economy operates in a regime of fixed exchange rates, capital is immobile, and the economy's equilibrium at the initial price level P_1 and output level Y_1 is given by the intersection of IS_0, LM_0, and BOP_0. After the price decline, the *BOP* curve shifts to the right because, with a constant nominal exchange rate e and a price decline to P_3, the real exchange rate $q = e(P^*/P)$ depreciates and net exports increase. The *IS* curve shifts to the right for the same reason. The *LM* curve shifts to the right because the price decline increases the real money supply, M/P. The *BOP* and *IS* curves continue to shift to the right so long as prices continue to decline,

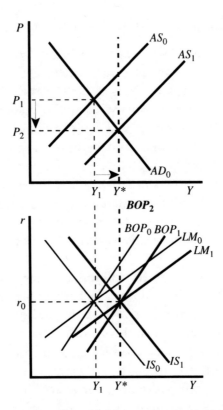

Figure 9.8   Expanding the supply side of the economy to achieve full employment.

which continues until a new equilibrium is reached at Y^*. Because the fixed exchange rate regime requires the central bank to intervene to keep the nominal exchange rate constant, the final shift in the *LM* curve reflects not only the price effect but some amount of intervention to ensure that the *LM* curve crosses the new intersection of the *BOP* and *IS* curves at the full employment. It is not clear whether the central bank needs to buy or sell the national currency in order to keep the nominal exchange rate constant; whether the nominal rate depreciates or appreciates depends on how much the increase in income Y stimulates increased purchases of imports versus how much the price decline stimulates exports and substitution of domestic goods for imports.

9.4.4 *Comparing the active and passive approaches*

In the examples above, the alternative policy approaches achieve the same gain in total output from Υ_1 to Υ^*, but little else is the same in the resulting final equilibria. Notice that in the case of the supply side policy or the passive policy of letting product and labor prices adjust to restore full employment, the interest rate remains about the same and the increase in output is largely the result of increased exports in response to a depreciation of the real exchange rate. The interest rate does not change much because the price declines both expand the real money supply and the real depreciation improves the current account, which makes it easier for the central bank to maintain a constant nominal exchange rate in the face of the real money supply growth. The constant interest rate implies that the growth in exports does not crowd out investment, as it does in the case of expansionary fiscal policy. Of course, the Schumpeter growth model reminds us that supply-side growth needs substantial and costly investments.

In the case of the expansionary fiscal policy, the interest rate rises. Hence, the increased government expenditure or reduced taxes crowd out interest-sensitive activities such as investment and the purchase of consumer durables. Furthermore, the price increase that accompanies the expansionary fiscal policy crowds out exports by appreciating the real exchange rate. Therefore, in the case of fixed exchange rates and immobile capital, a passive policy approach favors the investment and export sectors of the economy, while an active expansionary fiscal policy crowds out those same sectors in favor of government expenditures or expenditures stimulated by tax reductions.

The gain in net exports under the passive policy approach are caused by a fall in domestic prices and wages. Real income may actually decline under this scenario because in real terms the country suffers a terms of trade decline, that is, it takes more exports to acquire the same amount of imports, all other things equal. Also, there may be very substantial losses in welfare because unemployment and excess productive capacity may persist for a long time before prices and wages adjust to move the economy to Υ^* in Fig. 9.8. Explicit policies to expand the supply side of the economy also tend to take a long time to implement and may be very costly, as was pointed out in the previous chapter.

There are many other possible active policy outcomes, depending on the policies used, the exchange rate regime in effect, and the mobility of international capital flows. The questions and problems at the end of the chapter ask you to analyze some of these other possibilities. Your analysis should apply the models as in Figs. 9.7 and 9.8.

9.4.5 *Stagflation*

The Keynesian macroeconomic model, being exclusively a demand side model, cannot explain stagflation, which is the simultaneous occurrence of unemployment and inflation. The former is a function of insufficient aggregate demand in the Keynesian model, the latter is the result of excessive demand. The aggregate demand/aggregate supply model, with both a demand and a supply side, can actually explain stagflation very well.

In 1973, a group of oil exporting countries suddenly raised the price of a barrel of oil from about \$4.00 to about \$10.00. Because the price of oil had not changed much for many years while demand for energy had persistently grown during the 1950s and 1960s, the steep price hike could be maintained with just a very slight decline in oil production. For oil importing countries, the oil price hike was like a sudden negative shift in the aggregate supply curve because oil was an input in the production and transportation of most other products services. Fig. 9.9 shows that the likely outcome of such a supply shock is a simultaneous rise in prices and unemployment, a classic case of stagflation.

The 1970s were a period of high unemployment and high inflation, and policymakers struggled with how to address the situation. Note that the standard Keynesian remedy of expansionary fiscal or monetary policy, that is, a rightward shift in the aggregate demand curve, would create even higher price rises on top of already record-high price inflation caused by the supply shock. On the other hand, the passive approach was unlikely to quickly generate price declines because producers battered by higher energy costs were in no condition

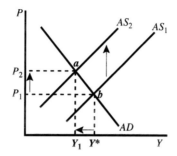

Figure 9.9 A negative supply shock and stagflation.

to cut prices to spur demand for their products, and consumers facing high energy prices were already reducing consumption of other products.

By the end of the 1970s, policymakers gradually shifted to policies to improve economic efficiency and shift the aggregate supply curve back to the right. But, despite efforts to spur technological progress and economic growth, high-income countries would not again reach the high levels of employment and economic growth they achieved during the 1950s and 1960s. Was that rapid growth the result of artificially low energy prices and an aggregate supply curve that was unrealistically low? Was the 1970s supply shock, therefore, just a correction to more realistic production costs? Some economists wondered whether stagflation was back when the prices of oil, food, and other commodities surged in 2008, just when economic activity was slowing. Because the severe global recession in 2008 only lowered commodity prices very modestly, there was fear that a recovery would quickly lead to commodity price inflation.

9.5 Macroeconomic Management in the Long Run

The introduction of the economy's supply side into our macroeconomic model seems to have made fiscal and monetary policies more difficult. An upward-sloping aggregate supply curve means that expansionary fiscal and monetary policies will inevitably be partially dissipated by inflation. But the aggregate supply curve does not necessarily slope upward when unemployment is high and expansionary macroeconomic policies are most necessary. Nor does the introduction of the supply side imply that active macroeconomic policy is no longer needed. On the contrary, the introduction of the supply side enhances the case for active macroeconomic policy to stabilize the economy's circular flow.

9.5.1 *The AS curve in a recession*

In general, the slope of the aggregate supply curve reflects the overall scarcity of resources in the economy. When most or all productive factors are already employed, the aggregate supply curve is likely to be quite steep, which means any increase in aggregate demand will generate little increased output and a lot of inflation. On the other hand, if there are many unemployed factors of production ready to be put to work, then the aggregate supply curve is likely to be quite flat. The classic Keynesian case of fixed prices describes this latter case.

Figure 9.10 shows what aggregate supply in an economy might look like. At low levels of output, many factors of production are not employed, and the aggregate supply curve will be flat. As a result, an increase in aggregate demand from AD_1 to AD_2 causes no increase in

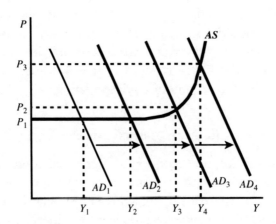

Figure 9.10   A more general aggregate supply curve.

the price level. Then as aggregate demand increases to AD_3 and output increases from Y_2 to Y_3, some factors of production become fully employed and the overall price level begins to rise from P_1 to P_2. If aggregate demand increases further to AD_4, very few unemployed factors remain after output Y_3 is surpassed, and most of the increase in aggregate demand increases the price level to P_4 while the rise in output to Y_4 is much smaller than earlier aggregate demand increases achieved.

In general, in the short run there is likely to be a tradeoff between unemployment and inflation only if the economy is near its full employment level. Note that the "sharper" is the upturn in the aggregate supply curve, the less often policymakers face the difficult choice of making such a tradeoff. That is, if factor markets stimulate additional supply without inflation until very close to full employment, then traditional Keynesian aggregate demand management can keep unemployment low without generating too much inflation. On the other hand, if factor and resource markets are controlled by cartels, such as the case of oil in the 1970s and, presumably, still today, then macroeconomic management of aggregate demand is weakened and stagflation becomes a very real possibility.

9.5.2 *Economic growth and macroeconomic management*

In the long run, the supply side of the economy is unlikely to remain constant. In the 20th century, most economies experienced economic growth, which means the aggregate supply curve gradually shifted to the right. Long-run macroeconomic management must focus on increasing aggregate demand in tandem with this gradual increase in the economy's productive capacity.

Shifts in aggregate demand or aggregate supply will, all other things equal, cause the price level to change. For example, monetary expansion, rising foreign demand for exports, or increasing government expenditures all increase aggregate demand and, in the case of an upward-sloping aggregate supply curve, cause prices to rise. On the other hand, an increase in the economy's capacity to produce output, caused by improvements in technology or new investment,

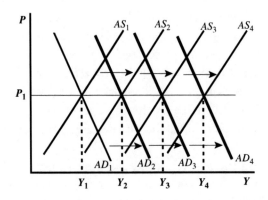

Figure 9.11   Coordinated growth of the demand and supply sides.

will shift the AS curve out and, all other things equal, cause the price level to fall.

Figure 9.11 shows how the price level can remain constant when there is economic growth. If the economy's equilibrium levels of P and Y are initially at P_1 and Y_1, respectively, and economic growth pushes the economy's AS curve continually to the right, then the price will remain unchanged only if the AD curve also shifts to the right at the exact same rate as the AS curve shifts to the right. In this case, economic growth causes Y to rise without any inflation. But, how likely is it that AD shifts out right along with the growth-induced AS curve? The answer depends on how well policymakers can keep aggregate demand in line with aggregate supply.

Policymakers do not have to do all of the shifting. The AD curve will automatically shift to the right when the AS curve shifts to the right because increasing output also increases income, and income is an important determinant of consumption, investment, and government expenditures. The relationship between output and demand is unlikely to be a neat one-for-one relationship, however. There are many determinants of consumption, investment, government expenditures, and net exports, as shown earlier, and there is no obvious reason why all those determinants will shift the aggregate supply and aggregate demand perfectly in tandem. Well administered monetary policies have proven to be useful policy tools for keeping shifts in

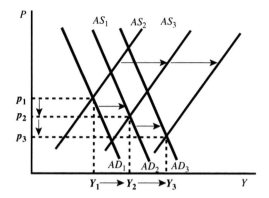

Figure 9.12 Deflation when aggregate demand grows more slowly than aggregate supply.

aggregate demand in line with shifts in aggregate supply, just as poorly administered monetary policies have been the causes of most of the worst inflations and depressions.

When monetary policy is too tight relative to aggregate demand, for example, prices will tend to fall, as illustrated in Fig. 9.12. Excessive saving in response to uncertainty about the future can depress aggregate demand and cause deflation, as can sudden rapid growth that raises income much faster than people are accustomed to spend it. The US Federal Reserve Bank's excessively deflationary monetary policies after the 1929 stock market crash and subsequent bank failures were probably the main causes of the Great Depression.

If aggregate demand expands too rapidly, inflation will result, even if there is growth in aggregate supply. Figure 9.13 illustrates this case. For example, policy makers may be very fearful of short-run unemployment so that they apply monetary or fiscal policies to expand aggregate demand that causes the long-run path of equilibria illustrated in Fig. 9.13. There are many more reasons why government policymakers might induce aggregate demand to grow more rapidly than aggregate supply. For example, governments are always pressured by their constituencies to provide for their needs and wants, many of which are not necessarily in the interest of price stability or

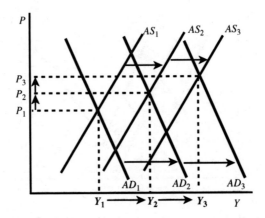

Figure 9.13   Inflationary aggregate demand management.

steady long-run growth. Also, printing money rather than using taxation to fund government expenditures is often politically convenient, but the resulting excessively expansionary monetary policy will tend to generate price increases.

In sum, the different patterns of shifts in aggregate demand and aggregate supply illustrated in Figs. 9.11 through 9.13 show that price stability depends on whether aggregate supply and aggregate demand shift in tandem. More generally, the *AD/AS* model shows that effective macroeconomic management consists of (1) creating the conditions that promote the investment and, above all, the innovation necessary to shift the aggregate supply curve consistently to the right, and (2) managing aggregate demand to maintain price stability and full employment. Note that such a policy focus on growth and full employment is compatible with the democratic principle that all members of society should participate in and enjoy the benefits of economic progress.

9.5.3 *Long-run aggregate demand and supply are related*

It is useful to once again peek at Fig. 9.1, the circular flow diagram of the economy. This diagram makes it clear that the demand and supply sides of the economy are closely related. Hence, the aggregate demand and aggregate supply curves do not move completely independently of each other. An increase in aggregate supply will increase income, which spurs aggregate demand. Also, increased aggregate demand raises profits and the need for more output, which spur the investment and innovation that shift the *AS* curve to the right. In the long run, there is an intriguing relationship between aggregate demand and economic growth that was singled out by Keynes and some other "Keynesian" economists.

Recall from Chapter 8 that investment in capital and innovative activities were fundamental to the process of economic growth. Solow (1956) showed that continual growth over long periods of time required innovation and technological progress, which Schumpeter (1912) and modern growth economists like Romer (1990) have modeled as costly and uncertain processes. Of course, Solow also showed that higher levels of output require more capital as well. Investment and innovative activities affect not only aggregate supply, however; investment and innovation are components of aggregate demand too. Harrod (1939) and Domar (1946) calculated the economy's rate of investment that would effectively keep aggregate demand and aggregate supply shifting out at the same rate so that full employment could be maintained. Their work came to be known as the *Harrod-Domar model*, and is standard material in the field of economic growth.

Harrod and Domar's separate analyses both showed that such a moving full employment equilibrium was possible, but given the assumptions that would have to be met for this to happen, it was unlikely to happen automatically as a result of individual actions alone. Suppose that in a hypothetical economy people save ten percent of their income in a certain year. Suppose also that those savings are efficiently channeled towards innovation and capital investments that raise total output in the economy by five percent over the current level for the foreseeable future (ignore depreciation for now). Therefore, next year's income will be five percent greater, but aggregate demand will be five percent larger only if all that income is spent. This will happen, for example, if the percentage of income saved remains the same and is fully channeled towards new investment and innovative projects, and all other components of aggregate demand maintain the same percentages of total income.

What if something upsets this nice pattern? Keynes (1936, Chapter 12) reasoned that the decisions to invest or innovate are not based on precise calculations of future costs and benefits, because no one has enough information with which to fully judge what the future will bring. Keynes described investment as being driven by "animal spirits", by which he meant things like sentiment, faith, and the general state of confidence in the future growth of the economy. Keynes surmised that as long as many investors' expectations are met, more investment will be forthcoming despite the lack of solid evidence supporting such decisions. But, if a large proportion of investments do not meet expectations, or what he called "convention", confidence in the economic system erodes and investment collapses.

In our simple example above, suppose the failure of the investment and innovative projects causes investors to become pessimistic, and they cancel all projects the following year. Or, as happened in 2008, suppose that the financial sector of the economy breaks down and stops lending. In such cases, investors and innovators do not employ the 10 percent of income that is saved and the aggregate demand curve shifts back by 10 percent. All other things equal, unemployment and excess capacity rise, and this further depresses aggregate demand the following year, causing unemployment and excess capacity to increase further. In short, a severe recession develops because some unforeseen change in the economic climate breaks the economy's circular flow.

Sentiment, faith, and confidence are volatile for many reasons, and there is no guarantee that all investment and innovative projects produce the expected profits each year. This is why Keynes concluded that it was the volatility of investment that caused the sudden ups and downs of economic growth. Harrod and Domar provided some rigorous calculations under a variety of assumptions to underscore Keynes' point that continual vigilance and quick action on the part of the government to adjust fiscal and monetary policies are required to keep the *AD* and *AS* curves shifting in tandem.

In sum, investment and innovation activities increase aggregate supply and, because they require the use of real resources that must be paid for, they also increase aggregate demand. However, the uncertainty of investment and innovation mean that aggregate demand and supply are unlikely to shift perfectly in tandem, nor are either aggregate demand or aggregate supply perfectly predictable. This creates a need for active macroeconomic policy. For example, if investment suddenly declines, monetary easing may be neccessary to spur new investment. And if excess capacity is so great that zero interest rates do not spur investment, expansionary fiscal policy would be needed to substitute government demand for the missing investment demand for output.

9.6 Summary and Conclusions

This chapter has put together the demand side of the economy, modeled by the Mundell–Fleming model, and the supply side of the economy, modeled by an aggregate supply function that relates output and the price level. Specific points worth emphasizing are

1. The field of macroeconomics has experienced several major paradigm shifts over the past century.
2. After gaining prominence in the 1930s, by the 1970s the Keynesian model was increasingly criticized for lacking clear microfoundations that justified its aggregate analysis.
3. Devising a logically coherent macroeconomic model based on well-defined *microfoundations* required unrealistic assumptions, such as that consumers with stable preferences maximized utility subject to income, firms maximized profits subject to stable cost functions, all economic activity occurred in efficient markets, and individuals were rational.
4. The 2008 financial crisis revealed the inaccurate assumptions behind the newer rational expectations/efficient markets macroeconomic models.
5. The Keynesian model remains useful for analyzing the economy's performance provided a supply side is added to the model.

6. Much of the disagreement between Keynesians and monetarists/ rational expectationists seems to revolve around how quickly markets clear and how well prices reflect true economic conditions and expectations.

7. Muth (1961) explicitly defined rational expectations as the mathematical expected value of all possible outcomes; Keynes' more realistically described expectations as reflecting an incomplete set of information and a less than rational analysis of those facts based on recent experience and social convention.

8. Generalizing Keynes' macroeconomic model to include more deterministic variables reveals how complex a real economy is and, therefore, how difficult accurate policy responses are.

9. Keynes' consumption function was criticized by Friedman, who suggested instead his permanent income hypothesis, but subsequent empirical evidence and models, such as Akerlof's focus on social norms, support Keynes contention that consumption depends on current income.

10. The relationship between the money supply and investment activity has been expanded since Keynes initial formulation; however, modifications such as Bernanke's focus on credit and the inclusion of innovative activity in the overall category of investment do not fundamentally alter Keynes' basic model.

11. The aggregate demand curve in the price-income plane is downward-sloping because of three hypothesized price effects: (1) *the monetary effect*, (2) *the real-balance effect*, and (3) *the foreign trade effect*.

12. When the supply side is included, fiscal or monetary policies illustrated in the Mundell-Fleming model must be adjusted.

13. Among other effects, price changes affect the *BOP* and *IS* curves because they affect the real exchange rate, eP^*/P, and they affect the *LM* curve because they affect the real money supply M/P.

14. The *AD/AS* model permits an analysis of stagflation, the problem that confused policymakers during the 1970s and eroded confidence in the Keynesian model.

15. The chapter concludes with the long-run analysis of how the growth of the supply side combines with aggregate demand management to determine long-run rates of inflation and output growth.

The aggregate demand/aggregate supply model will prove useful for analyzing the performance of the international financial system over the past century, as we will begin to do in the next chapter.

Economic thought does not remain invariant as economic conditions change. Keynes' model was a direct response to the Great Depression, and the rational expectations revolution in macroeconomics was driven by the neoliberal view of government as a burden on the economy. By the 1980s, the Great Depression had been nearly erased from economists' collective memory. The 2008 financial crisis served as a wake-up call, and, not surprisingly, Keynes suddenly became quite popular again. Economic policies across nearly all countries have a distinct Keynesian flavor to them. Terms like "fiscal stimulus" and "monetary easing" are variations on the traditional fiscal and monetary policies Keynes discussed in 1936. The *AD/AS* model can bridge many of the changes in economic thought, and we will refer to it in the upcoming chapters.

Key Terms and Concepts

Active policy approach
Coase theorem
Contingent
  commodities
Credit view
Disposable income
Efficient markets
Externalities
Fiscal policy
Foreign trade effect
Harrod-Domar model

Microfoundations
Monetarism
Monetary effect
Monetary mechanism
Monetary policy
Natural rate
Neoclassical philosophy
Nominal exchange
  rate
Open market operation
Passive policy

Permanent income
  hypothesis
Phillips curve
Rational expectations
Real balance effect
Real exchange rate
Real money supply
Stable preferences
Stagflation
Uncertainty
Wealth effect

Chapter Questions and Problems

1. Why is the aggregate demand curve downward sloping? Explain the three reasons presented in Section 9.2 why aggregate demand increases as the aggregate price level declines.

2. Figure 9.7 showed the effects of an active fiscal policy in the case of fixed exchange rates and immobile capital. Repeat the analysis, but this time suppose that government policymakers use expansionary monetary policy to achieve full employment.

3. The Mundell–Fleming open-economy macroeconomic model presented in Chapter 7 assumes that prices do not change. But when the economy pushes up against its aggregate supply constraints such an assumption is not realistic. Explain exactly how each of the curves in the Mundell–Fleming model, that is, the *IS*, *LM*, and *BOP* curves, are affected by price changes.

4. Figure 9.7 showed the effects of an active fiscal policy in the case of fixed exchange rates and immobile capital. Repeat the analysis under the assumptions of mobile capital and a floating exchange rate system.

5. Equation (9.6) presented a large number of variables that determine aggregate demand, but the text still made the statement: You can no doubt come up with more things that influence consumption, investment, government expenditures, and imports and exports of consumption, investment, and government goods and services. List and explain what explanatory variables you might add to equation (9.6).

6. Discuss the implications for short-run macroeconomic policy if Milton Friedman's permanent income hypothesis correctly describes all consumption behavior. Why do you think that the hypothesis has not held up under scrutiny and empirical evidence?

7. How rational are people? Provide as much evidence as you can find to (1) support the rational expectations hypothesis and (2) to refute the hypothesis.

8. Explain Keynes' distinction between risk and uncertainty. Also, explain why this distinction is relevant for judging John Muth's rational expectations hypothesis as he defines it.

9. Why do the neoliberal assumptions of efficient markets, rational expectations, complete financial markets, the Coase theorem, stable

preferences, and the refutation of the Phillips curve appeal to private business? Discuss.

10. Go back and review last chapter's discussion of economic growth, and then discuss how government policymakers can best shift the aggregate supply curve in response to another sudden negative supply shock such as the world experienced during the oil crisis of the 1970s. Be sure to explain why your proposals are practical in the real political, economic, and social environments governments operate in.

11. Is it necessary for a macroeconomic model to have mathematically deterministic microfoundations? Discuss. (Hint: Review the discussion of holism and scientific reductionism in Chapter 1.)

12. Friedman and Keynes hypothesized different consumption functions. Discuss why the broad embrace of the rational expectations hypothesis, which was developed after Keynes and Friedman presented their respective hypotheses, was important for switching sentiment in macroeconomics towards Friedman's permanent income hypothesis.

References

Akerlof, GA (2007). The missing motivation in macroeconomics. *American Economic Review,* 97(1), 5–36.

Arrow, K and G Debreu (1954). Existence of an equilibrium for a competitive economy. *Econometrica,* 22, 265–290.

Bernanke, B (1983). Nonmonetary effects of the financial crisis in the propagation of the great depression. *American Economic Review,* 73, 257–276.

Bernanke, B (1993). Credit in the macroeconomy. *Federal Reserve Bank of New York Quarterly Review,* Spring, 50–70.

Bourdieu, P (1984). *Distinction: A Social Critique of the Judgment of Taste.* Cambridge, MA: Harvard University Press.

Campbell, JY and N Gregory Mankiw (1989). Consumption, income, and interest rates: Reinterpreting the time series evidence. *NBER Macroeconomics Annual 1989.* Blanchard O and S Fischer (eds.), Cambridge, MA: MIT Press.

Coase, R (1960). The problem of social costs. *The Journal of Law and Economics,* 3, 1–44.

De Grauwe, P (2009). Warring economists are carried along by the crowd. *Financial Times*, 22 July.

Debreu, G (1959). *Theory of Value*. New Haven, CN: Yale University Press.

Domar, E (1946). Capital expansion, rate of growth, and employment. *Econometrica*, 14, 137–147.

Fama, E (1970). Efficient capital markets: A review of theory and empirical Work. *Journal of Finance*, 25(3), 383–417.

Frederick, S (2005). Cognitive reflection and decision making. *Journal of Economic Perspectives*, 19(4), 25–42.

Friedman, M (1953). The case for flexible exchange rates. *Essays on Positive Economics*, Friedman M (ed.), pp. 157–203. Chicago: University of Chicago Press.

Friedman, M and AJ Schwartz (1963). *A Monetary History of the United States 1867–1960*. Princeton, NJ: Princeton University Press.

Friedman, M (1957). *A Theory of the Consumption Function*. Princeton, NJ: Princeton University Press.

Friedman, M (1968). The role of monetary policy. *American Economic Review*, 58(1), 1–17.

Harrod, RF (1939). An essay in dynamic theory. *The Economic Journal*, 49, 14–33.

Le Doux, JE (1996). *The Emotional Brain: The Mysterious Underpinnings of Emotional Life*. New York: Simon and Shuster.

Lucas, RE, Jr. (1972). Expectations and the neutrality of money. *Journal of Economic Theory*, 4, 103–124.

Lucas, RE, Jr. (1973). Some international evidence on output-inflation tradeoffs. *American Economic Review*, 68, 326–334.

Kahneman, D and A Tversky (2000). *Choices, Values and Frame*. Cambridge, UK: Cambridge University Press.

Modigliani, F and R Brumberg (1954). Utility analysis and the consumption function: An interpretation of cross-section data. *Post-Keynesian Economics*. Kurihara KK (ed.). Rutgers University Press.

Muth, JF (1961). Rational expectations and the theory of price movements. *Econometrica* 29, 315–35.

Parker, J (1999). The reaction of household consumption to predictable social security taxes. *American Economic Review*, 89(4), 959–973.

Patinkin, D (1965). *Money, Interest, and Prices*. New York: Harper & Row.

Phelps, E (1968). Money–wage dynamics and labor–market equilibrium. *Journal of Political Economy*, 76(3 P. 2), 678–711.

Phillips, AW (1958). The relation between unemployment and the rate of change of money wage rates in the United Kingdom, 1861–1957. *Economica*, 25, 283–300.

Pigou, AC (1917–1918). The value of money. *Quarterly Journal of Economics*, 32.

Romer, PM (1990). Endogenous technological change. *Journal of Political Economy*, 98(5 P. 2), S71–S102.

Shiller, RJ (1997). Why do people dislike inflation? *Reducing Inflation: Motivation and Strategy*. Romer CD and DH Romer (eds.). Chicago: University of Chicago Press.

Souleles, NS (1999). The response of household consumption to income tax refunds. *American Economic Review*, 89(4), 947–958.

Weber, M (1905). *The Protestant Ethic and the Spirit of Capitalism*. London: Allen & Unwin.

Wilcox, D (1989). Social security benefits, consumption expenditure, and the life cycle hypothesis. *Journal of Political Economy*, 97(2), 988–304.

Part IV

The History of International Financial Policy

Chapter 10

Exchange Rate Crises

The over-abundance of funds, together with the difficulty of finding the most profitable employment therefore at home, has contributed greatly to the pronounced demand for and the ready absorption of large foreign issues, irrespective of quality ... While high yield on a foreign bond does not necessarily indicate inferior quality, great care must be exercised in the selection of foreign bonds, especially today, when anything foreign seems to find a ready market ... Promiscuous buying, however, is destined to prove disastrous.

(Max Winkler, 1927.[1])

In 1982, Chile's real per capita GDP fell by 18 percent after the Chilean peso lost about half its value and many heavily indebted domestic firms and banks went bankrupt.[2] Chile did not recover its 1981 per capita GDP level until 1988. Mexican per capita GDP fell by eight percent after the Mexican peso depreciated by over 50 percent relative to the US dollar in late 1994. Thailand's real per capita

---

[1] Max Winkler (1927). *The New York Tribune*, March 17.
[2] Real per capita GDP estimates are from Angus Maddison (2003).

GDP declined by nearly 14 percent when unemployment soared after a sharp devaluation of the Thai baht in 1997, and it took nearly a decade for Thailand's real per capita GDP to regain its 1996 level. The Argentine peso's collapse in 2002 similarly led to a decline in real per capita GDP of over 15 percent. The immediate cause of each of these economic crises was a sudden large change in the exchange rate following a sharp shift in the direction of international capital flows.

Economic crises such as those in Chile, Mexico, Thailand, and Argentina have diminished policy makers' enthusiasm for further opening their countries' borders to international investment. Even many economists have argued that international investment is fundamentally different from international trade in goods and services. The problem with international investment is that it can suddenly change direction, causing large shifts in the supply and demand curves for currencies and, therefore, sharp changes in exchange rates. International trade flows, on the other hand, usually change only gradually and seldom cause sudden currency depreciations. Also, foreign exchange crises almost always have very real affects on economic activity. It should not be surprising, therefore, that policy makers in countries that suffered exchange rate collapses and accompanying financial crises question whether they would not have been better off if they had prevented their firms, banks, and government agencies from borrowing so much overseas.

These questions about international investment are not new. The 1929 quote by the financial reporter Max Winkler at the start of this chapter makes it clear that the volatility of international investment flows has been a concern for a long time. The liberalization of international investment flows over the past three decades has only restored international capital flows to levels comparable to one century ago. Unfortunately, the recent exchange rate crises are also a repeat of similar crises a century ago. This chapter and the next address the question of whether the gains from international investment are really worth the risk of an exchange rate collapse and the likely decline in income that so often accompanies a large change in the exchange rate.

Chapter Goals

1. Trace the evolution of international capital flows.
2. Show that international capital flows are volatile, often subject to complete reversals when source and destination country economic conditions change.
3. Examine the case of Mexico, a country that experienced four major interruptions of foreign capital inflows between 1820 and 1994.
4. Explain the 1982 debt crisis and why it took so long before the developing country defaults were settled and capital flows resumed.
5. Detail the Brady Plan and how it satisfied the principal interest groups negotiating a settlement of the 1982 crisis.
6. Explain the important concept known as the *trilemma*.

10.1 International Capital Flows: A Historical Perspective

Large movements of capital between countries are often described as a recent phenomenon, part of today's unprecedented "globalization". Data showing that the daily volume of foreign exchange markets averages over $3 trillion per day supports the view that more money is moving between countries than ever before. But, such an impression would be very inaccurate. While it is true that international investment has grown substantially in recent years, when we go back further in history today's international investment flows do not seem so extraordinary. As a percentage of GDP, international investment was greater at the end of the 19th century than it is today in most countries.

International lending has in fact occurred for centuries, even millennia. There were strong preferences for the gold coins of certain city–states in the Middle East and the Mediterranean region well before the rise of the Roman Empire, as merchants and politically powerful people sought the safest place to store their temporary and permanent accumulations of wealth. Ancient Greek coins have been found as far to the east as India and China. As far back as the 15th century, Italian banks, such as the Medici family's banks, lent large amounts to sovereign governments throughout Europe. Later on, banks in various North Sea ports and London pioneered new financial instruments such as letters of credit and discounting of foreign receipts. By the 19th century, London was establishing itself as the world's center of international finance. The "depth" of the financial markets also grew, with the international trade in insurance, equities, bond finance, and, after the middle of the 19th century, foreign direct investment and the growth of multinational firms.

10.1.1 *Globalization in the 19th century*

International lending grew very rapidly during the 1800s, and by the end of the century reached levels that in some ways exceeded the huge international capital flows that we observe today. When measured as a proportion of GDP, for example, capital flows in many countries were much larger then than they were even during "globalization" of the 1990s. For example, over the period 1880–1914, annual capital *outflows* averaged about five percent of GDP in the United Kingdom, reaching a phenomenal nine percent in 1913. These numbers imply that the United Kingdom exported nearly half of its savings. Many British savers stored a very considerable portion of their wealth in foreign assets, either directly in the form of bonds or indirectly through loans made by their banks to foreign governments and firms. In France, outflows of savings frequently reached five and six percent of GDP, and Germany averaged capital outflows equal to two percent of its GDP over the 1880–1914 period.

The major importers of these European savings were Argentina, Australia, Canada, New Zealand, and the United States, countries populated by immigrants from Europe. Countries at the northern edge of Europe, such as Sweden and Norway, were also net importers of capital during the late 1800s. These were all rapidly growing economies where the returns to investment were high. During the 1880s, inflows of foreign savings averaged nearly ten percent of GDP in Australia, before falling to a more modest 2.5 percent during the 1890s. Of course, 2.5 percent is still very high even by 1990s and 2000s standards. Savings inflows into Canada exceeded six percent of GDP in the 1880s, averaged about 4.5 percent in the 1890s, rose to seven percent in the first decade of the 20th century, and then reached an astounding 14 percent of GDP between 1910 and 1913. As a percentage of total investment, foreign saving accounted for over one-third of total saving in New Zealand and Canada over the entire 1880–1914 period, and nearly 25 percent in Australia and Sweden. These flows of lending to what were then newly developing countries contrast sharply with more recent experience. For example, foreign savings financed less than four percent of investment in developing countries of the world during the 1980s, and even in the 1990s foreign saving only financed ten percent of investment in developing economies. Of course, today's developing countries are generally not the same countries that borrowed so heavily 100 years ago. Some of the main recipients of capital inflows were in fact colonies of the European capital exporters. It remains true, however, that in the past a higher proportion of saving flowed from wealthy to newly developing economies than is the case today. Because of the relatively high per capita income of the British economy, it was British investors who financed many of the world's railroads, electric utilities, and other infrastructure projects.

A large portion of international lending in the 1800s was in the form of bonds. London investment banks, or *investment houses* as they were referred to in those days, intermediated the sale of bonds by foreign governments and firms to British and other international savers. Records show that the London investment houses earned fees of between 1.6 and 3.9 percentage points.[3] Of course, without their services, there would have been no market. The role of the investment

---

[3] Michael Edelstein (1982).

houses included negotiating the bond's terms and promoting their sale. Sometimes the investment houses even advanced funds to the issuers of the bonds in anticipation of the sale of the bonds. The investment houses also played the important role of negotiator when defaults occurred. Large groups of diverse bondholders cannot easily negotiate with defaulters, which were often foreign governments, banks, and firms, but the investment houses could present a unified front during the negotiations. The investment houses also had clout because foreign borrowers knew they would have to deal with the investment houses if they wanted to borrow in the future. By acting as principal negotiators on behalf of bondholders, investment houses often negotiated default settlements favorable to the bondholders. The investment houses helped to expand the market for bonds because they reduced the risks for individual purchasers of foreign bonds, who had little knowledge of foreign firms and projects.

The high average annual investment flows mentioned above did not imply that capital flows were constant or steady. Actually, international capital flows during the late 1800s and early 1900s were volatile. Because Britain dominated the international financial market prior to World War I, capital flows were largely *counter-cyclical* to Britain's economic performance. When the British economy expanded and British interest rates were high, there was less incentive to invest outside the country. But, when economic growth at home slowed and interest rates fell, British savers sought the higher returns on foreign bonds.

The counter-cyclical behavior of British capital outflows was further driven by the Bank of England's management of gold flows under the rules of the gold standard. When the pound was under pressure because a booming domestic economy pulled in too many imports, the Bank would intentionally tighten credit and raise interest rates to induce capital to stay at home and keep the supply and demand for the pound compatible with the fixed gold parity of the pound. Foreign economies, therefore, experienced continual reversals of foreign capital flows, or *capital shocks*, as worldwide financial conditions changed. Some of these shocks caused exchange rates to change, which, in turn, led to defaults and economic recessions.

10.1.2 *Between the world wars*

International investment flows ceased at the start of World War I in 1914. They picked up again after World War I, but after the war London was no longer the dominant financial center for the world economy. In 1918, the United States had become the major net creditor to the rest of the world; the expense in fighting World War I had led to a very large repatriation of British savings from overseas. In fact, Britain had become a net debtor to the rest of the world, while the United States, formerly a net debtor, became the largest international creditor to the world. US investors participated as leaders in the new wave of foreign lending in the 1920s. The group of borrowers also changed in the 1920s; for the first time, governments from Eastern Europe and Asia became significant international borrowers.

With the ascendancy of the United States as the most important source of international investment funds, the counter-cyclical nature of the investment flows disappeared. International investment flows became more closely correlated with income and savings in the United States. That is, capital outflows from the United States were *pro-cyclical*. According to a recent study by researchers at the International Monetary Fund (IMF):

> This procyclicality in foreign lending was in part associated with the fact that an upswing in investment in the United States was typically accompanied by a sharp rise in domestic savings as well. In addition, the capital outflows also occurred during periods of rising commodity prices, which increased the perceived creditworthiness of the capital importing countries. On the upswing, increased creditworthiness of capital importers coincided with greater availability of capital. On the downswing, reduced capital flows combined with declining export demand, as the United States economy slowed, reinforced the spiral. To make matters more difficult for the emerging markets of the time, while the United Kingdom had financed countries that produced goods that it imported, US capital exports were directed to countries that produced goods that competed

with its exports. And, whereas the United Kingdom's policy during the period 1870–1914 was generally one of laissez-faire and free trade, the United States followed a more protectionist policy in the 1920s.[4]

These potential problems became a reality when the US economy, followed by most other developed economies, fell into an economic depression in 1930. In addition to a sharp fall in US savings, world-wide commodity prices fell sharply during what was soon referred to as the Great Depression. Export earnings of developing economies plummeted just as foreign capital outflows stopped. There were wide-spread defaults by developing country borrowers after 1930. International capital flows ceased almost entirely during the Great Depression.

10.1.3 *Defaults on foreign loans were a normal occurrence*

The defaults on foreign loans and bond servicing by developing economy firms and governments during the 1930s were not unique by any means. Large international investment flows have always been subject to occasional problems. For example, many Latin American countries defaulted in the 1820s following a borrowing binge immediately after their independence from Spain or Portugal. Even the United States defaulted on bonds in the 1830s and 1840s. Lending to Latin American governments resumed in the 1860s, followed by further defaults in the 1870s. These defaults were settled after 1880, and new bonds were issued through London and other financial centers. There were more defaults, notably by Argentina, in the 1890s, but lending resumed in the early 1900s.

Despite the difficulties, most foreign debt was serviced on schedule by borrowers. The United States, Canada, Australia, and Russia were the largest net borrowers in the 1800s and early 1900s, and the governments and firms of these countries met their debt obligations with few difficulties. Overall, despite the occasional difficulties,

---

[4] International Monetary Fund (1997). p. 238.

Eichengreen and Lindertt (1989) and Marichal (1989) present evidence showing that for British banks and investors returns on foreign lending were at least as high as domestic lending.[5]

10.1.4 *The characteristics of international lending before W.W.II*

Examination of pre-World War I capital movements reveals that:

1. Most lending took place through the exchange of bonds, with London dominating the international bond market throughout the 1800s and New York gaining prominence after World War I.
2. The holders of these bonds consisted of a widely dispersed group of private investors.
3. Flows of investment funds were subject to surges and reversals caused by economic conditions in the countries where the funds originated.
4. Defaults were not a very serious problem in terms of the amounts of money involved, but they occurred with a nagging regularity.
5. The ranks of the lenders and borrowers gradually changed over time, with the United States overtaking Britain as the major supplier of funds to the world after World War I.
6. The period came to an end in the early 1930s when the Great Depression caused most economies to shut off foreign trade and investment, and widespread defaults discouraged both lenders and borrowers.

These general characteristics of 19th century globalization provide an interesting contrast to the late 20th century phase of globalization.

10.1.5 *Case study: Mexico's many debt defaults*

During the nearly 200 years since its independence, Mexico has gone through four periods of foreign debt, default, and resolution of the

---

[5] For an interesting account of past difficulties with international investment flows, see Eichengreen and Lindert (eds.) (1989). For a historical account of inter-national investment flows specifically to Latin America, see Marichal (1989).

debt problems.[6] The first episode of foreign lending to Mexico began right after it gained its independence in 1821 in a bloody war with Spain and Spanish sympathizers in Mexico. Mexico contracted its first bond loan of £3.2 million ($16 million) through a London financial house. The Mexican government actually only received $6 million, the remainder going to discounting, withholdings for bond servicing, and commissions. Another similar bond offering was contracted in London the following year, but this time Mexico had to pledge one-third of all of its customs revenue as security for this and the previous bonds. Despite the security of supposedly linking bond repayment to customs revenues, poor administration of customs caused Mexico to suspend coupon payments on the bonds in 1827, and bondholders began a long series of negotiations with successive Mexican governments. In 1830, the Mexican government and bondholders agreed to let Mexico capitalize the interest owed through the issuance of new bonds. But, after a year Mexico stopped servicing these new bonds too.

During the Mexico–Texas war in 1836, Mexico tried to complete what is today called a debt–equity swap: In exchange for assuming some of Mexico's debt, bondholders were offered land in Texas, California, Sonora, and elsewhere. This scheme had few takers, since it was not clear that Mexico would be able to hold on to the regions where land was offered. More important was Mexico's agreement with the British government to provide restitution to British citizens whose Mexican property had been damaged during the war. This agreement altered the balance of power between Mexico and the bondholders, giving the bondholders greater leverage, but Mexico hoped it would gain greater access to foreign loans. When Mexico found itself in a war with the United States between 1846 and 1848, Mexico was unable to borrow further. French military forces invaded Mexico in 1864, allegedly to seek restitution for unpaid Mexican debts, and the country was briefly ruled by the French governor Maximilian. However, when

---

[6] This account of Mexico's history of foreign borrowing is based on Vinod K. Aggarwal (1989).

France pulled out many of its troops to meet a threat by Prussia in Europe, the Mexicans rebelled and overthrew Maximilian. The Mexican debt remained unsettled, despite continued negotiation and announced agreements.

Only with the rise to power of the dictator Porfirio Diaz in 1876 did Mexico finally settle its debts. Diaz was an autocratic and ruthless dictator who suppressed all political opposition, but he is also credited with shifting Mexico towards a modern market economy and promoting early industrialization. Because he was interested in opening the Mexican economy to trade and in attracting foreign capital and investment, Diaz immediately sought to settle the 60-year-old debt disputes with foreigners. He offered foreign holders of the bonds dating back to the 1820s a settlement under which they would recover all of their principal by 1888 and earn interest rates averaging 2.3 percent per year on the 1824 bonds and 1.1 percent on the 1825 bonds. American bankers loved Diaz.

During the 1890s, Mexico again encountered some difficulties servicing its debt, but it was able to negotiate a favorable refinancing of outstanding debt. Then, in 1901, oil was discovered, and new financing was obtained at very favorable terms.

Apparently many Mexicans did not like Porfirio Diaz as much as foreign bankers and Mexican and foreign businesspeople did, and the dictator was overthrown by a broad-based revolution in 1911. This caused a severe outflow of capital to the United States by foreign investors and some Mexican business interests. The revolutionary government sought foreign funds to counter the capital flight, and loans of $10 million were obtained from American banks in 1911 and again in 1912. However, in 1913 the United States government objected to what it interpreted as increasingly leftist political leanings of the new revolutionary government, and Washington prohibited further capital flows to Mexico.

The Mexican revolution turned into a devastating civil war, and Mexico was in no condition to service its foreign debts. Only when the revolution finally ended in 1920 did foreign bankers resume negotiations with the new revolutionary government. The Mexican government insisted on new loans as part of its agreement to resume debt service on its pre-revolutionary debt contracted mostly under Porfirio Diaz. Strong post-revolutionary nationalist sentiments in Mexico made negotiations difficult, which may have actually served to give Mexico better loan conditions. By the end of 1927, Mexico once again suspended debt service, however. A committee of bankers went to Mexico to make the best of the situation, and a very favorable agreement was reached that included the writing off of 94.5 percent of all interest arrears. However, the Mexican Congress delayed in ratifying the agreement, and in 1932 the Mexican Congress formally rejected this latest agreement. The populist President Lazaro Cardenas, who headed the government from 1934 to 1940, flatly refused to negotiate the foreign debt obligations.

Only in 1942 — with World War II underway and the United States anxious to eliminate conflicts among allies — was a final agreement reached. With the help of official US government financial assistance, Mexico was permitted to eliminate a debt of over $500 million for about $50 million in new obligations, or ten cents on the dollar. Not until the 1970s, 30 years later, would foreign bankers again begin to make significant loans to Mexico. This new lending would revive the same old ritual of lending, default, and renegotiation.

10.1.6 *Capital movements during the 1950–1980 period*

Throughout the 1930s, the World War II years, and well into the 1950s and 1960s, capital movements as a percentage of overall economic activity were very small in comparison to the late 1800s. Government-to-government loans accounted for the major part of capital flows between developed and less developed economies in the 1950s and 1960s. Private capital movements of all types were widely restricted by both capital exporting and capital importing countries. This was a period when many developing countries actively pursued import substitution policies and governments often interfered with private economic activity. Developed economies, in their concern to recover from World War II and to avoid a repeat of the 1930s depression, also thought it was in their national interest to make sure domestic saving was invested at home. By the 1960s, however, developed economies began to remove regulatory barriers to the international flow of capital. In the 1970s, lending by private banks to governments of developing countries grew rapidly. And, according to script, another series of defaults soon followed.

10.2 The 1982 Debt Crisis

Table 10.1 shows that net private capital flows to developing economies averaged over $30 billion per year over the period 1977–1982. Capital flows were closely related to the "recycling" of

Table 10.1 Capital Flows to Developing Countries (US$ Millions).

	1977–1982	1983–1989	1990–1994
All developing countries			
Total net capital inflows	30.5	8.8	104.9
Net FDI[1]	11.2	13.3	39.1
Net Portfolio Investment	−10.5	6.5	43.6
Other[2]	29.8	−11.0	22.2
Asia			
Total net capital inflows	15.8	16.7	52.1
Net FDI	2.7	5.2	23.4
Net portfolio investment	0.6	1.4	12.4
Other	12.5	10.1	16.3
Western hemisphere			
Total net capital inflows	26.3	−16.6	40.1
Net FDI	5.3	4.4	11.9
Net portfolio investment	1.6	−1.2	26.6
Other	19.4	−19.8	1.6
Other developing countries			
Total net capital inflows	−11.6	8.7	12.7
Net FDI	3.2	3.7	3.8
Net portfolio investment	−12.7	6.3	4.6
Other	−2.1	−1.3	4.3

Source: Table 1.1 from International Monetary Fund (1995). *International Capital Markets, Developments, Prospects, and Policy Issues*, Washington, DC. p. 33.

[1] Foreign direct investment is private investment by multinational firms to purchase or construct their own facilities in foreign countries.

[2] The "Other" category includes bank loans as well as foreign aid.

oil revenues from oil-producing countries to oil-importing countries. The IMF estimates that 57% of all capital flows to developing countries were in the form of bank loans, which are part of the "Other" category of Table 10.1.

10.2.1 *Oil prices and international lending*

The change in investment flows had its roots in rapid oil price rises of the early 1970s. When the Organization of Petroleum Exporting Countries (OPEC) cartel was able to sharply raise the price of oil in 1973, the trade balances of many countries were upset. The oil-producing countries suddenly found themselves in surplus, and they began accumulating large reserves of foreign assets. The oil-importing countries, of course, suddenly saw their trade balances move into the red. The OPEC countries' aggregate trade surplus rose from zero in 1972, the year before the price hikes, to a positive $60 billion in 1974, the year after the price of oil was raised from $4.00 per barrel to about $10 per barrel. Other oil-producing countries that were not members of OPEC also enjoyed increased surpluses.

The sharp changes in countries' current accounts caused great concern. Would the oil-importing countries have to limit imports? Worse, would they have to slow down their pace of economic growth in order to reduce or even reverse the growth of oil consumption? To the surprise of many, most oil-importing countries were able to continue growing because they were able to borrow enough in the world capital markets to offset the deteriorating current accounts.

The international financial system was able to "recycle" the petrodollars much more easily than most economists and policy makers had thought possible. The surge in dollars earned by oil-exporting countries caused deposits to swell at the overseas branches of the world's large commercial banks, especially those located in London and other major banking centers. This money was turned around and lent to oil importers, who used the borrowing to pay for the more expensive oil without reducing economic growth. The IMF assisted the *recycling* of petrodollars by creating a special financing facility to provide loans for the poorest developing countries. This facility was funded by money lent to the IMF by the principal oil exporting countries. There appeared to be no short-run need to adjust the economy for the higher oil prices. But, of course, many oil importing countries began to pile up debt on which interest had to be paid and which would some day have to be repaid or refinanced.

The OPEC trade surplus began to diminish after 1974 as the OPEC countries gradually increased their imports. In OPEC countries with large populations, such as Iran, Nigeria, and Venezuela, there were many pressures for governments to spend the windfall revenues from oil exports by their state-owned oil companies. The initial surge in OPEC government deposits in the world's major commercial banks, primarily those located in London, was thus followed by a gradual reduction in those same deposits. By the late 1970s the OPEC surplus was gone. But, again to the surprise of many observers, the international credit markets nevertheless remained flush with money even as the OPEC surplus dwindled.

What happened was that the central banks of most developed economies were, more often than not, expanding money supplies in response to the threat of recession triggered by the oil price supply shock. As discussed in Chapter 9, the monetary expansion in the face of adverse supply shocks led to substantial increases in inflation.

The inflationary environment caused the prices for all commodities, not just oil, to rise, which benefited many oil-importing countries. For example, Brazil saw its oil import bill triple, but its export earnings from coffee, iron ore, sugar, cotton, tobacco, and soy beans rose nearly as much. Inflation caused interest rates to rise, which was an important development since nearly all the private bank borrowing in the international financial markets was at variable interest rates that were quarterly. However, the expansionary monetary policies of the United States, Britain, and other countries kept the real interest rates very low. Inflation sometimes exceeded nominal interest rates, which meant *real* interest rates were often negative for borrowers in the late 1970s. Thus, despite the heavy international borrowing, most developing countries found that the ratio of debt service to export earnings was not growing very much, and they were able to continue borrowing to roll over existing loans while adding the substantial new loans. Some governments of oil producers, such as Ecuador, Mexico, Nigeria, and Venezuela, took advantage of the liquid financial markets to contract foreign bank loans in anticipation of future oil revenues. Given the low real interest rates and expected further rises in commodity prices, such foreign borrowing seemed to make perfect sense.

The party could not last, however. In the long run, real interest rates cannot remain negative. The situation came to a head when a second OPEC price shock occurred, raising oil prices from about $12 per barrel to over $30 per barrel in 1979. This price hike was spurred by the fall of the Shah of Iran and the subsequent political turmoil in Iran, one of the main OPEC oil producers. Initially, the price hike was easily maintained and it seemed as though it reflected true market conditions. The OPEC countries' aggregate current account surplus rose from the near zero level it had returned to in 1978, and in 1980 the joint OPEC current account surplus exceeded $100 billion. This surge in deposits in the international banking system again stimulated a massive "recycling" of petrodollars. Borrowing by developing countries expanded rapidly in 1979. During the period 1979–1981, Brazil added $16 billion, Argentina $11 billion, and Mexico $21 billion to their foreign debts. Would everything continue as before, with oil importers able to keep growing in an orgy of inflation and borrowing, fully enabled by developing countries' expansionary, and inflationary, monetary policies?

10.2.2 *The macroeconomics of international investment flows*

To answer the question at the end of the previous paragraph, let us focus first on what happens when a country's citizens, firms, or government borrow money from foreigners. By borrowing, people, firms, and government agencies in effect acquire the purchasing power with which to buy foreign goods and services. Overall, the country is able to consume and invest more than its economy produces. The term for the sum of domestic expenditures such as consumption, investment, and government purchases, in this context is *absorption*. That is, foreign borrowing (the sale of assets to foreigners) allows a country to *absorb* more goods and services than its economy produces.

For example, if the citizens, firms, and government of a country sell assets (borrow) abroad equal in value to two percent of their national product, they can "absorb" 102 percent of their national product, a net gain of two percent in welfare-enhancing consumption and/or investment. Such a net gain in current absorption implies, of course, a trade deficit equal to two percent of national product. Many developing economies in the 1970s absorbed more than they produced, which they funded by selling assets to foreigners that consisted mostly of loans by foreign private banks to developing country governments and government-owned firms and agencies. Absorption of over 100 percent of national output increases welfare beyond what the country could attain on its own, at least for as long as the country can borrow.

When countries can no longer borrow and they must pay back their outstanding loans, absorption must fall below national production. This means the country must run a trade surplus. For example, if the required payment of interest and principal over and above any new foreign borrowing, or what we call the *debt service*, is equal to two percent of GDP, then in effect two percent of national product must be transferred abroad and domestic absorption can be no more than 98 percent of national production. Thus, if foreign lending is disrupted and a country faces the sudden need to repay more than it borrows, the necessary reduction in absorption has a substantial real welfare effect.

A sudden decline in domestic consumption is not easily engineered. It can be directly brought about by a sharp reduction in government expenditures, which is effectively a contractionary fiscal policy that can push the economy into a recession with high unemployment. Or, the reversal of capital flows from a surplus inflow to a net outflow can cause a sharp decline in the exchange rate, which can lead to a *financial crisis*.

10.2.3 *Petrodollar recycling crashes in 1982*

The new surge in the recycling of petrodollars in 1979 soon proved to be different from the previous recycling episode. First of all, some central banks in developed countries had, by the end of the 1970s, begun to respond differently to the oil supply shocks. They stopped reacting to rising unemployment by increasing money supplies, as the traditional Keynesian analysis prescribes, and they began reacting to inflation by tightening money supplies, as rational expectations theory prescribes. Unfortunately, years of Keynesian policies and expectations that policymakers would continue to act like Keynesians prevented the announced tightening of monetary polices from reducing inflation without recessionary consequences. By 1980, money supplies were tight throughout the world and the US economy and others were falling into recession. The international financial markets' main source of new funds was the OPEC surplus. But that source dried up very quickly as the oil price increases did not stick in a world of tight money and rising unemployment. When the oil price fell back under $20 per barrel after reaching $36 in 1979, many OPEC countries found themselves in balance of payments difficulties. It took only two years for the huge OPEC surplus of $100 billion to move into a deficit of $10 billion.

Ironically, in early 1982, it was an oil producer, Mexico, that defaulted on its loan obligations. Mexico had borrowed heavily for a wide range of government projects in infrastructure, industry, and oil exploration, using its future oil revenues as implicit collateral. Private banks were quite willing to lend as long as money flowed to them, but when money tightened and the OPEC surplus disappeared, interest rates shot up and banks were not able to issue new loans. Mexico effectively defaulted when it informed its lenders it could not obtain enough new financing to cover its sharply higher real interest payments. Soon Brazil, Argentina, and some 30 or more developing countries in Asia, Africa, and Latin America were unable to service their debts in accordance with their loan contracts. This was the largest number of countries ever to simultaneously fail to meet their foreign debt obligations. The consequences of the end of international borrowing were devastating. The transfer of purchasing power from lenders to borrowers that had occurred throughout the 1970s suddenly ended. The indebted countries suddenly had to balance the current account by importing no more than they exported.

Table 10.2 details the less developed countries' foreign debt in 1982. Brazil had the largest foreign debt, followed by Mexico, Argentina, Korea, Venezuela, and Egypt. Table 10.2 also makes it clear, however, that the indebted countries did not all face the same debt burden. Taking the ratio of debt to GNP as a measure of "ability to pay", it appears that Costa Rica, Cote d'Ivoire, Egypt, the Sudan, Zambia, and Jamaica had accumulated the heaviest debt burdens by 1982. Another important indicator of a country's debt burden, interest payments as a percentage of GNP, indicates the proportion of domestic production that must in effect be transferred to foreigners in payment of past borrowing. For example, Costa Rican citizens' post-1982 consumption was only 85.2 percent of what it would have been if they did not have to transfer 14.8 percent of GDP to foreigners as interest payments.

Table 10.2 also shows foreign debt and interest payments as a percentage of exports, which indicates a country's ability to sustain the servicing of its foreign debt. Interest payments and eventual repayments of principal require foreign currency that must be earned by exporting goods and services. Foreign debt exceeded 400 percent of 1982 exports in Argentina, Brazil, Egypt, Morocco, and the Sudan. The rising real interest rates in the early 1980s increased interest payments to 47.1 percent of 1982 export earnings in Brazil, 43.5 percent in the Sudan, and 40.5 percent in Chile. It is difficult to see how those countries could have met their debt obligations without additional borrowing to cover the high interest payments. How much can a country reduce absorption without causing extreme hardship for its citizens? Of course, borrowing to pay interest on outstanding loans is a classic indicator of bankruptcy.

The value of the various measures of country debt burdens can be grasped by contrasting Brazil and Korea in Table 10.2. As a percentage of its national product, Korea's foreign debt was larger than Brazil's, 48.4 percent of GNP for the former as compared to 34.6 percent for

Table 10.2   Foreign Debt of 30 Selected Developing Economies in 1982.

Countries	(1) Gross debt in US$ millions	(2) Debt as a % of 1982 GNP	(3) Debt as a % of exports	(4) Interest as a percentage of 1982 GNP	(5) Interest as a percentage of exports	(6) Long-term claims of commercial banks	(7) (6)/(1)
Algeria	$17,641	34.7%	108.4%	2.9%	9.2%	$4,439	0.25
Argentina	43.634	79.0	447.8	5.9	33.3	18,104	0.42
Bolivia	3,328	101.4	348.6	3.1	10.5	901	0.27
Brazil	92,961	34.6	405.3	4.0	47.1	57,605	0.62
Chile	17,315	68.7	333.9	8.3	40.5	12,100	0.70
Colombia	10,306	16.8	145.7	1.4	12.5	3,758	0.36
Costa Rica	3,646	157.1	306.3	14.8	28.9	1,190	0.33
Côte d'Ivoire	8,945	126.7	319.6	9.8	24.7	3,487	0.39
Ecuador	7,705	64.2	273.3	8.2	34.9	3,600	0.47
Egypt	29,526	121.1	422.8	4.3	15.1	923	0.03
India	27,438	12.6	190.2	0.0	0.3	1,800	0.07
Indonesia	25,133	24.4	108.6	1.6	7.0	6,848	0.27
Jamaica	2,846	97.6	219.9	6.5	14.6	467	0.16
Korea	37,330	48.4	125.3	4.9	12.8	11,346	0.30
Malaysia	13,354	37.5	70.2	1.2	2.2	7,589	0.57
Mexico	86,081	52.0	328.0	6.0	37.8	46,666	0.54
Morocco	12,536	83.4	422.0	5.1	25.9	2,744	0.22
Nigeria	12,954	12.4	89.6	1.1	8.3	5,531	0.43
Pakistan	11,638	35.1	339.6	1.0	9.2	624	0.05

(Continued)

Table 10.2 (*Continued*)

Countries	(1) Gross debt in US$ millions	(2) Debt as a % of 1982 GNP	(3) Debt as a % of exports	(4) Interest as a percentage of 1982 GNP	(5) Interest as a percentage of exports	(6) Long-term claims of commercial banks	(7) (6)/(1)
Peru	10,712	37.8	229.1	3.7	22.2	3,061	0.29
Philippines	24,412	59.9	344.7	5.7	32.7	6,786	0.28
Sudan	7,218	101.1	823.5	5.3	43.5	1,276	0.18
Syria	6,187	43.6	241.0	0.9	4.9	0	0.00
Thailand	12,238	30.5	125.1	2.5	10.2	4,216	0.34
Turkey	19,716	36.2	238.7	3.0	19.7	4,873	0.25
Uruguay	2,647	27.9	79.7	1.7	4.8	1,276	0.48
Venezuela	32,158	32.9	145.7	1.2	5.5	14,800	0.46
Yugoslavia	19,900	30.3	126.9	2.6	11.0	12,004	0.60
Zaire	5,079	36.1	292.7	2.6	21.0	531	0.10
Zambia	3,689	99.9	332.0	5.1	17.0	132	0.04

Sources: Tables 2.1, 2.3, 2.4, 2.5, and 2.9 from Cline (1995). *International Debt Reexamined*, Washington DC: Institute for International Economics, which were in turn compiled from the World Bank's *World Debt Tables* and the International Monetary Fund's *International Financial Statistics* and *Balance of Payments Statistics Yearbooks*.

the latter. Yet, interest payments as a percentage of exports were much more burdensome for Brazil: 1982 interest payments for Korea were just 12.8 percent of exports but Brazil used nearly half of its 1982 export earnings to cover its foreign interest payments.

The reason for these differences in debt burdens was that Korea exported over four times as much of its total national production than did Brazil. But, Korea also paid a lower rate of interest on its outstanding debt than did Brazil; Brazil's higher interest rates were a sign that the banks saw Brazil's higher debt burden as increasing the risk of default. It should not be surprising that Korea had relatively little trouble in servicing its debt after the rise in interest rates in 1982. Brazil, on the other hand, defaulted on its obligations, suffered a major recession in 1982, and did not see any growth in real per capita income for the remainder of the 1980s.

The case of Egypt suggests yet another reason why debt burdens varied so much in 1982. Table 10.2 shows that Egypt had one of the highest levels of foreign debt, 121.1 percent of GNP, but its interest payments in 1982 were only 4.3 percent of GNP because foreign borrowing consisted largely of low-interest loans from foreign governments and multilateral aid agencies. The last column of Table 10.2 shows that very few of Egypt's loans were from commercial banks. When market interest rates were low in the 1970s, private bank loans seemed a bargain. But when developed country monetary policies pushed market interest rates into double digits, Egypt was lucky to be carrying mostly low-interest, subsidized debt.

10.3 Solving the 1982 Debt Crisis

In many countries, the severity of the fall in real per capita welfare after 1982 was much greater than most policy makers had expected. That was because the reduction in absorption was brought about by a sharp decline in the value of national currencies on the foreign exchange markets. This exchange rate effect not only brought about the necessary decrease in imports and eventual increase in exports, but it precipitated severe financial crises in many developing economies. As currencies depreciated, the value of the foreign debt of developing country firms, banks, and governments rose in terms of their domestic currency and their domestic income. Bankruptcies spread, especially in the banking sectors, and a financial crisis developed, which slowed investment. Economic growth turned negative, and the 1982 debt crisis turned into a long economic crisis in many developing economies. The 1982 debt crisis was the most serious breakdown of the post-World War II international financial system up to that time. Solving this global debt crisis turned out to be very difficult, not just because of the size of the debt involved, but also because of the conflicting interests of the parties involved.

10.3.1 *Default by sovereign governments*

An obvious problem with debt incurred by a sovereign government is that creditors have virtually no access to any type of collateral. Bond holders or banks in foreign countries normally find it difficult to go to court to demand payment from a foreign government. There have been times when loans to sovereign governments have been enforced with battleships and invading armies. For example, in 1902, when the government of Venezuela defaulted on its foreign debt, British, German, and Italian naval ships blockaded the country's ports until the government again began servicing its debt. Back in 1881, when the Ottoman Empire defaulted on its foreign loans, several European countries sent in commandos to seize the empire's customs houses and then helped themselves to customs revenues until the debt was paid up.[7] Remember the example earlier in this chapter of France sending Maximilian to occupy Mexico with the French army after Mexico defaulted on some loans held by French citizens. Such incidences of military intervention kill people; they are very costly, and they violate international law. However, even in the absence of military force, creditors do have some leverage over debtors. Most important, creditors can threaten to never lend again. Borrowers would then lose the capacity for using international borrowing for

---

[7] These examples of "enforcement" of loan obligations are from The Economist (2005). "A Victory By Default?" *The Economist*, 3 March 2005.

intertemporal consumption smoothing, a more efficient allocation of savings, and the diversification of wealth holdings.

Debtors also know that a large proportion of international trade is financed short-term using trade credits. Rogoff (1999, p. 31), formerly the Chief Economist at the IMF, writes: "The strongest weapon of disgruntled creditors, perhaps, is the ability to interfere with short-term credits that are the lifeblood of international trade". Rose (2002) presents evidence that the reduced access to trade credit indeed substantially reduces trade between creditor and debtor countries for as much as 15 years after a default.

10.3.2 *Solving the debt crisis*

The debt crisis of the 1980s concerned not only the debtors and creditors, however. In 1982, loans to foreign governments exceeded the capital of many major commercial banks around the world. A total default by a large number of debtor governments and firms in the indebted developing economies would have meant the failure of most of the world's largest commercial banks. The channeling of funds from savers to borrowers, known technically as financial intermediation, would have been sharply curtailed. Any disruption of financial intermediation has very real consequences for the levels of investment, and hence economic growth, in a modern market economy. This concern for the health of private banking systems around the world led developed country governments and central banks to join in the search for a solution to the "debt problem".

The debt crisis in effect became a "three-person game", with each side, foreign borrowers, lending banks, and developed country governments plus the IMF and World Bank that these governments controlled and funded, bargaining with two other interested parties. The debtor country governments attempted to negotiate a reduction in their obligations to the foreign creditor banks at the same time that they attempted to get foreign governments and international institutions like the IMF to foot part of the bill. Creditor banks also negotiated with one eye on their own governments (taxpayers) and the IMF as a source of funds to supplement the limited ability of the debtor countries to repay their foreign obligations. The governments of the high income countries whose banks had done most of the lending sought to unwind the debt without causing the banks to curtail their lending in their countries at a time when many high income countries were just emerging from recessions triggered by the tight anti-inflationary monetary policies instituted at the end of the 1970s. The difficulty of negotiating agreements among three different interest groups in many different countries dragged out the negotiations.

Among the many questions that a viable proposal would have to address to the satisfaction of all three parties were

1. How much debt should be forgiven — all, some, or none?
2. Who bears the costs of writing off debt?
3. Should all debtors enjoy debt relief or just some?
4. If just some, which debtor countries?
5. How much debt should be rescheduled as opposed to forgiven?
6. How much new lending should creditors provide to debtors?
7. Should debtors change their economic policies, and how?
8. What were the welfare costs for the citizens of debtor countries?
9. What is the role of international agencies?
10. What is the role of developed country governments?

The first question must be answered through negotiation. Obviously debtors preferred to repay less rather than more, with creditors taking the opposite view. But, all sides recognized that some debt relief is necessary because debtors simply could not meet current debt obligations. Exactly how much relief was necessary was not clear, however. In fact, depending on the economic policies adopted, debtor countries could effectively service various levels of debt.

The issue of deciding which countries merited what degree of debt reduction was difficult. Should the poorest countries enjoy the greatest reductions in debt? Or, should those countries that had adopted the most serious economic reforms enjoy the greatest forgiveness of debt? But what about those countries that had faithfully continued to service their foreign debt despite great sacrifices in terms of short-run economic welfare? At issue here were not only the solutions to past mistakes, but establishing the incentives for efficient country and bank behavior in the future.

10.3.3 *The Brady plan*

It took nearly the entire decade of the 1980s before debtor countries, banks, and developed country governments could agree on answers to the difficult questions listed above. At the very end of the decade, the United States Secretary of the Treasury Nicholas Brady introduced a framework for solving the debt crisis. The key elements of what came to be known as the Brady Plan were:

1. Countries that adopt serious economic reforms to reduce the future lending needs, such as reductions in government deficits, realistic exchange rates to avoid trade imbalances, and monetary reforms to eliminate inflation, would have their debt loads reduced.
2. The IMF would send its economists to judge and "certify" debtor countries' reform programs.
3. Creditors would write down outstanding debt to reflect the "market value" of the debt on the secondary market for sovereign debt.
4. One or more developed country governments, the IMF, or the World Bank would offer guarantees on the remaining debt so that creditors will be assured of future debt service.

The Brady Plan thus consisted of a combination of debt write-offs by the creditors, substantial policy changes to improve debt repayment by debtor governments, and subsidies by other governments and multilateral agencies in the form of loan guarantees. Problem debtors, whose debt was nearly worthless on the secondary market, in effect had almost all of their debt forgiven, while those countries that had already undertaken the reforms and sacrifices necessary to service their debt, and whose debt therefore sold for a high percent of face value on the secondary market, had relatively less debt forgiven. If this seems unjust, remember that bankruptcy proceedings often appear to reward those who behaved irresponsibly.

In 1989, Mexico became the first country to negotiate a debt relief plan along the lines of the Brady Plan. Creditors accepted a substantial reduction in expected future debt service payments, Mexico issued "Brady bonds", whose principal was backed by US Treasury notes, and the Mexican government promised IMF-mandated economic reforms designed to restore the economic growth and ensure Mexico could service its remaining foreign obligations. Among the reforms was the shift toward free trade and the negotiations for creating a North American Free Trade Area, both radical departures from the protectionist trade policies pursued by Mexico before the 1980s. The US government contributed a substantial amount of funds to help Mexico through the early stages of its economic reforms, which also included privatization of government-owned firms, liberalization of markets, and promotion of private enterprise. Many other developing countries also managed to negotiate solutions to their debt problems along the lines of the Brady Plan.[8]

10.3.4 *The controversial role of the IMF*

The IMF played an important role in implementing the Brady Plan. First of all, the IMF in its traditional role as the "central banker for central banks" was an important source of short-term credit to governments. The IMF routinely made loans available for short periods of time while the debtor countries negotiated with their creditors, for example. This gave the IMF some leverage to push the debtor countries to undertake the economic reforms deemed necessary for them to service their foreign debt and restore the economic growth. The IMF and its staff economists also served as judges of debtor countries' economic reforms.

Creditor banks faced a serious moral hazard problem: they could reach an agreement with debtor governments, under which

---

[8] In addition to Mexico, Brady bonds were issued by Argentina, Brazil, Bulgaria, Costa Rica, The Dominican Republic, Ecuador, Cote d'Ivoire, Jordan, Nigeria, Panama, Peru, the Philippines, Poland, Russia, Uruguay, Venezuela, and Vietnam.

the governments promised to institute certain economic policies that the creditors thought would be in the best interest of servicing debt, but there was no way of enforcing or even closely monitoring such agreements. The interests of the political leaders of the debtor countries were not always compatible with the economic reforms that could be expected to maximize the likelihood that outstanding debt would be serviced on schedule. Borrowers were thus likely to succumb to domestic political pressures and renege on the agreed to reforms, especially if those reforms were unpopular with the governments' key constituencies. The IMF's role as monitor of borrower economic policies was viewed by the creditor banks and their governments as a monitor of debtor countries that could reduce the likelihood that debtors would renege on their promised economic reforms. The IMF's large staff of economists were experienced at judging how well debtor governments were "stabilizing" their economies. Of course, the word "stabilization" really meant maximizing the repayment of foreign debt. Also, it was believed that because the IMF was a potential source of future financing, it would be more successful in getting the politicians to make the difficult decisions necessary to put reforms into effects.

The IMF usually insisted on economic reforms that included trade liberalization, the elimination or reduction in price distortions, the setting of a realistic foreign exchange rate, conservative monetary policies to reduce inflation, and sound fiscal policies to eliminate the government budget deficits that so often drove the inflationary money expansions. These reforms came to be known as the "Washington Consensus", in reference to the location of the IMF, the World Bank, and the US government that promoted them. These types of economic reforms were not controversial from the creditor's perspective, but they were often strenuously opposed by groups in the debtor countries. Many developing country governments had over the course of the post-World War II years established a system of trade restrictions and industrial policies that focused on the domestic market rather than international markets. Thus, a shift in policies that opened the economy to foreign competition and foreign investment, reduced subsidies, increased taxes, changed regulations, and shifted financial flows naturally upset the economic conditions that firms, consumers, and workers had been accustomed to.

The IMF was regularly depicted as a bully that sought to repay the banks with the sweat of the poor. On the other hand, because debtor governments were often lax in implementing the economic reforms demanded by creditors and the IMF, the IMF came under frequent criticism from developed country banks and politicians for not "enforcing" the agreements reached under a Brady plan. No one has yet come up with a viable alternative to handling the roles that the IMF has taken on during the various debt crises over the past decades, but the debate about the role of the IMF in the world economy remains a heated one.

10.3.5 *The countries that escaped the 1982 crisis: East Asia*

Openness to trade has been identified as one possible factor in reducing the likelihood that a country will suffer a financial crisis. Several reasons for this hypothesis have been presented. Rose (2002) suggests that open economies take greater care to avoid defaults on foreign loans and fiscal and monetary policies that might trigger capital flight because countries that depend more on trade realize that international credit is necessary for maintaining the trade flows. Rose supports his theoretical discussion with empirical evidence showing that high levels of international trade are correlated with low frequencies of sovereign debt default. Frankel and Cavallo (2004) use a variety of empirical tests to show that economies that trade more are less likely to suffer sudden reversals of capital flows or currency crashes.

Sachs (1985) showed that the East Asian economies had been less vulnerable to foreign exchange and debt crises than Latin American countries because they had much higher export-to-GDP ratios. Sachs writes: "After a decade of rapid foreign borrowing, too many of Latin America's resources were in the nonexporting sector, or abroad. When financial squeeze in the early 1980s caused banks to draw their loans, the only way that Latin countries could maintain debt servicing was through a recession and a large reduction in imports combined with debt rescheduling".[9] On the other hand, the East Asian economies, because they were already outward-oriented, found it relatively easy to expand the exports to earn more foreign exchange because they had already opened international trade channels and had a wide range of industries capable of meeting world standards and market requirements. Hence, with modest devaluations of their currencies, East Asian exports surged and the countries were able to cover their increased debt service when interest rates rose. They suffered only brief slowdowns in economic growth.

10.3.6 *Did fixed exchange rates play a role?*

One constant in the 1982 debt crisis is that all of the countries that suffered severe economic recessions after the suspension of foreign lending and defaults in 1982 had kept their exchange rates linked to one or more major currencies. These exchange rate had, over time, become unrealistic as a result of shifts in overall demand and supply of currencies in response to deviations in inflation rates, trade flows, and other economic conditions. Since most of the indebted countries held few foreign reserves with which to intervene in the foreign exchange market, the reversals in capital inflows and the loan defaults were accompanied by large depreciations of exchange rates.

Some economists have suggested that the debtor countries would have been better off letting their exchange rates float. Among other things, floating rates would have made the dangers of exchange rate depreciation clearer, and the debtor countries would most likely have accumulated less foreign debt. On the other hand, the willingness with which the world's commercial banks, which were flooded with deposits, made their loans in the late 1970s, floating exchange rates may have actually caused developing economies' currencies to appreciate, thus precipitating a even larger adjustment in 1981 or 1982. The advantages of fixed and flexible exchange rates arc still being

---

[9] Jeffrey D. Sachs (1985). p. 548.

debated today. In the remainder of this chapter, we explain why it is difficult for governments to fix exchange rates and how currency depreciations interact with other macroeconomic variables to cause severe welfare-diminishing economic declines.

10.4 The Economics of Currency Crises

The discussion of past currency crises in the previous sections have introduced you to one of the unfortunate characteristics of the international financial system: Exchange rates occasionally depreciate drastically and very suddenly. Since such exchange rate or currency crises can be very costly in terms of human welfare, it is important to understand why they occur. This section provides some useful analysis.

10.4.1 *It is difficult to fix the exchange rates*

The interest parity condition from Chapter 4 provides insight into *why* it is difficult to keep exchange rates pegged to a specific value in an open economy with large international trade and investment flows. Recall the interest parity equation

$$e_t = [(1 + r^*)/(1 + r)]^n \, E_t e_{t+n} \tag{10.1}$$

in which r and r^* are the domestic and foreign rates of return on assets, respectively, e_t is the spot exchange rate at time t, and $E_t e_{t+n}$ is the expected exchange rates n periods into the future. According to this equation, the spot exchange rates will remain the same if all variables on the right-hand side of the equation stay the same, which occurs if:

1. Expectations about future exchange rates, $E_t e_{t+n}$, do not change.
2. Returns on assets are the same at home and abroad, so that $r = r^*$.

The spot exchange rate can also remain unchanged if:

3. Policy makers are expected to adjust the domestic policies to maintain the exchange rates whenever changes in economic conditions

would otherwise shift the supply or demand curves for foreign exchange.

This latter condition requires a country's policy makers to stay attuned to exchange rates and adjust their economic policies to satisfy the interest parity condition, regardless of any other policy objectives they might have. These three conditions are very difficult to satisfy.

Despite the apparent difficulties, governments have nevertheless frequently tried to fix exchange rates. Exchange rate arrangements after World War II were usually designed to maintain the fixed exchange rates by means of central bank *intervention* in the foreign exchange markets. The Bretton Woods system kept exchange rates more or less constant among all major world currencies for 25 years between 1946 and 1971, and the European Monetary System attempted to fix the exchange rates among a group of European economies during 1979–1993. Both systems required the central banks to buy and sell foreign exchange in the foreign exchange markets to keep the supply and demand for their currencies intersecting at target exchange rates.

10.4.2 *Intervention is not a long-run tool*

Despite its apparent simplicity, intervention is not an effective tool for preventing long-run movements in exchange rates. Intervention is at most only a short-run tool. Recall from the discussion of intervention in Chapter 7 that central banks can seldom continue supplying the necessary amounts of foreign exchange for long periods of time. In the case of an overvalued currency, the central bank will eventually run out of accumulated foreign reserves with which to buy its own currency in the foreign exchange market. Foreign central banks could lend more currency, but they may not want to supply more of their currency.

Central banks do have another option for keeping the exchange rate from changing: they can change monetary policy. For example, when there is a tendency for the currency to depreciate, the central bank can try to keep the spot rate at its target level by tightening the money supply and increasing interest rates, thereby reducing the ratio $[(1 + r^*)/(1 + r)]$ in the interest parity condition so that $E_t(e_{t+n})$ translates into a lower spot rate e. Furthermore, the central bank's tighter monetary policy may convince people that there will be less inflation relative to the rest of the world, which could directly lower $E_t(e_{t+n})$.

Recall that monetary policy and foreign exchange market intervention are essentially the same thing. Conventional monetary policy appears to be a more viable long-run policy than using the central bank's limited reserves for exchange market intervention. Monetary policy is not an unlimited tool either, however. Tight monetary policy and higher interest rates slow the economic activity, reduce the tax revenues, and increases the costs of servicing debt. For example, Brazil in 1998 and Turkey in 2001 were two countries with very high levels of government debt that were judged by the markets as likely to default on their loans in the near future. In each case, an increase in interest rates to "defend the currency" actually caused the currencies to fall further in value because higher interest rates pushed government budgets further into deficit, making it even less likely that foreign debt would be serviced on schedule. Tight monetary policy and high interest rates also tend to reduce the investment and economic growth, which was expected to reduce the future competitiveness of the economy. Thus, even as a rise in domestic interest rates increases the ratio $(1 + r^*)/(1 + r)$, which would, all other things equal, lower the spot exchange rate, the expected future exchange rate $E(e_{t+n})$ could rise, leaving the net effect on the spot rate ambiguous. In sum, there may be a conflict between short-run measures to influence the exchange rate and the expectations of the long-run consequences of those short-run measures. Expectations translate the future economic events into present economic effects, thus making it harder for policy makers to use short-run intervention to influence the exchange rate.

Dominguez and Frankel (1993) examined a very large set of episodes of central bank intervention up to 1990, and they concluded that intervention *can* have an effect on exchange rates provided it is interpreted as a credible signal of a true underlying policy shift by policymakers. Sarno and Taylor (2001) re-examine the cases surveyed by Dominguez and Frankel, plus many more studies of exchange rate intervention through the end of the 20th century, and they confirm earlier conclusions: "... the evidence ... seems to us to be sufficiently strong and econometrically sound to allow us to conclude cautiously that official intervention can be effective, especially if the intervention is publicly announced and concerted and provided that it is consistent with the underlying stance in monetary and fiscal policy".[10]

While these conclusions appear to say that intervention can work, they actually confirm what the theory above suggests, namely that it is the fundamental economic policies that really determine the exchange rates, not intervention per se. Intervention can serve as a signal of government policy in a foreign exchange market where information about the future is seldom clear, and when the intervention is "concerted", meaning it is carried out simultaneously by central banks of several countries, the signal is even clearer. The evidence confirms that intervention, by itself, cannot push exchange rates toward equilibria that are incompatible with expectations.

10.4.3 *Fixed exchange rates and economic crises*

There is evidence suggesting that exchange rate volatility discourages international trade and international investment. This suggests that fixed exchange rates may be valid policy goal. The problem is that, in order to keep exchange rates from changing, policymakers may have to sacrifice other policy goals that are not compatible with the monetary and fiscal policies needed to maintain interest rates and expectations of long-run price levels that are compatible with exchange rate stability. That is, targeting a fixed exchange rate may result in the loss of macroeconomic "policy independence".

One way that a country can set its monetary and fiscal policies independently of what the interest parity condition mandates *and*

---

[10] Lucio Sarno and Mark P. Taylor (2002). p. 236.

keep the exchange rate fixed is to prohibit people from moving their wealth between assets denominated in different currencies. If savers, investors, firms, pension funds, and financial intermediaries cannot buy or sell assets across the border, then central bank intervention in the foreign exchange markets is much easier for the simple reason that not as much intervention will be required and, therefore, the money supply effects will be smaller and less likely to clash with other policy goals.

Prohibiting asset exchanges has an opportunity cost, however. This cost is equal to the lost welfare gains that would have come from allocating savings to the most productive investments, smoothing consumption, reducing risk, and expanding technology transfers for economic growth. Preventing exporters from giving foreign customers' credit or prohibiting the importers from borrowing overseas in order to finance their foreign purchases is likely to "divert" purchases to the domestic market, where credit is not restricted. Hence, placing barriers on international borrowing and lending can restrict international trade as well. In essence, barriers to financial flows reduce many forms of globalization. Policy makers concerned about exchange rate volatility therefore face a dilemma: Should they restrict financial account transactions and focus on domestic issues like employment and price stability, or should they keep the economy open and use domestic monetary and fiscal policies to keep the exchange rate steady?

10.4.4 *If policy independence is the main objective*

The dilemma described above makes it seem as though the choice for policy makers is between policy independence and globalization. That is technically correct only if a fixed exchange rate is the single overriding objective. If, on the other hand, policy independence also matters, then globalization can still be pursued if policy makers are willing to give up their quest for a fixed exchange rate and just let the exchange rate float. Floating exchange rates have their own costs, however. They add to the uncertainty that traders and investors must factor into their decisions to engage in transactions with foreigners.

The uncertainty of exchange rates may "divert" exchanges of products and assets to the domestic market and reduce the overall welfare gains from international trade and investment. The welfare losses from reduced trade and investment could be large, especially if the long-run growth effects of international trade and investment are taken into consideration. Policy makers seeking the freedom to pursue a variety of policy objectives unrelated to the exchange rate therefore face another dilemma: Should they fix exchange rates and limit their economy's contact with the global economy, or should they let the exchange rate float so that they do not have to restrict international investment?

10.4.5 *Two dilemmas equal one trilemma*

The two dilemmas discussed above imply that policy makers face a *trilemma*.[11] In the words of the international economist Maurice Obstfeld:

> A country cannot simultaneously maintain fixed exchange rates and an open capital market while pursuing a monetary policy oriented toward domestic goals. Governments may choose only two of the above. If monetary policy is geared toward domestic considerations, either capital mobility or the exchange rate target must go. If fixed exchange rates and integration into the global capital market are the primary considerata, monetary policy must be subjugated to those ends.[12]

In short, policymakers cannot simultaneously fix the exchange rate, set economic policies with only domestic goals in mind, and permit the free flow of goods and assets across national borders. For example, if policy makers opt for unrestricted investment flows between countries and a fixed exchange rate, they must align their economic policies with the rest of the world. On the other hand, if policy makers opt for fixed

---

[11] The term "trilemma" was coined by Alan Taylor and used for the first time in Maurice Obstfeld and Alan M. Taylor (1998).

[12] Maurice Obstfeld (1998). pp. 14, 15.

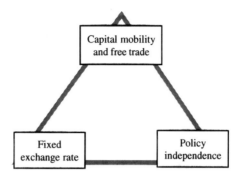

Figure 10.1 The trilemma: select any two, but not all three.

exchange rates and economic policies focused on domestic objectives, such as low inflation, high productivity growth, or increased government spending, regardless of the effects on asset returns or long-run expectations, then they cannot let people freely move their wealth across the border. In effect, the trilemma implies that policy makers must select one of the three sides of the triangle in Fig. 10.1, which means they can reach only two of the three corners.

Giving up policy independence is not always a bad choice. For example, the next chapter will detail the Argentinean 1991 currency board system, which sought to reduce the country's high rate of inflation by combining a rigid exchange rate with the liberalization of international trade and investment.

10.4.6 *Exchange rate stability and domestic political priorities*

The trilemma makes it clear how difficult it is to keep the exchange rates fixed when policy makers are faced with domestic political pressures to deal with a variety of issues and also want to participate in the global economy. Obstfeld *et al.* (2004) examine numerous historical episodes to make it clear that economic policy has been constrained by the trilemma since the classic gold standard in the last quarter of the 19th century. Governments can seldom endure the political pressures that tend to develop when domestic economic policy is restricted by the government's commitment to fix the exchange rate. Obstfeld and Rogoff (1995) observed that in the mid-1990s there were just six major economies with open capital markets that had been able to keep their currencies fixed to one of the world's major currencies for at least five years: Austria, Hong Kong, Luxembourg, the Netherlands, Saudi Arabia, and Thailand. Austria, Luxembourg, and the Netherlands were able to maintain the fixed exchange rates by keeping their economic policies closely in line with large neighboring economies, Germany in the case of Austria and the Netherlands, and Belgium in the case of Luxembourg. Hong Kong maintains a very rigid monetary policy to keep its currency pegged to the US dollar. Saudi Arabia exports huge quantities of oil that is paid for in dollars and thus finds it relatively easy to keep its currency pegged to the dollar. Obstfeld and Rogoff had difficulty explaining Thailand's ability to peg its currency to the US dollar in 1995, but by 1998 an explanation was no longer needed. Obstfeld noted in 1998, after the Thai baht had lost nearly half its value the year before, that: "The case that most puzzled us, Thailand, has dropped off the list — with a resounding crash".[13]

10.5 Summary and Conclusions

This chapter has focused on currency crises and the financial crises caused by sudden exchange rate changes.

1. Throughout the 19th century and toward the end of the 20th century, currency crises triggered by sudden sharp reversals in international capital flows have plagued the international financial system.
2. This chapter details a number of these crises, with special focus on the case of Mexico, which has suffered repeated currency crises.
3. These cases suggest that currency crises, and the follow-on financial and economic crises, are endogenous to the economic systems in place since the 19th century.

---

[13] Maurice Obstfeld (1998). p. 18.

4. Currency and financial crises have very real costs, including the loss of the gains from international trade and investment.
5. This chapter also details the 1982 currency crisis, which resulted in extended economic declines for over 40 developing countries.
6. The 1982 crisis followed a decade of heavy, and unsustainable, private bank lending to developing country governments.
7. When developed country monetary policy shifted, causing interest rates to rise sharply and commodity export prices to fall, many indebted developing economies defaulted on their debt.
8. Because of the huge amounts of money involved, negotiations after the default included not only the debtor governments and the private banks who made the loans, but also the developed country governments where the banks were located.
9. It took an entire decade to arrive at a viable compromise plan, known as the Brady Plan.
10. The 1982 currency crisis affected developing economies that had tried to maintain fixed exchange rates while contracting increasing amounts of foreign debt.
11. The conflict between (a) fixed exchange rates, (b) increased international trade and investment, and (c) macroeconomic policies aimed at domestic priorities is referred to as the trilemma: A country can pursue only two out of the three options.
12. Violations of the trilemma explain not only the 1982 debt crisis, but most of the subsequent currency crises as well.

The quote at the start of the chapter by the historian Max Winkler reminds us that over-optimism and the under-estimation of risk have been common throughout the history. The financial expert and former Chair of the Federal Reserve Bank of the United States, Volcker (1999, p. 265) writes:

> International financial crises, I might even say domestic financial crises, are built into the human genome. When we map the whole thing, we will find something there called greed and something called fear and something called hubris. That is all you need to produce international financial crises in the future.

Volcker does more than blame international financial crises on basic human nature, however. He suggests that there is something about the present economic conditions that make international financial crises more likely:

> I think we are seeing a real crisis of global capitalism. It reflects the clash of two elements. One is globalization itself, all the technology you know about better than I.... The ability to move money around the world rapidly is well known. There has not been enough emphasis on the other element in the crisis. We live in an asymmetric world.... we are dealing with very small economies.... You know, you put $30 billion of external capital into a total financial system of $100 billion, and you have a problem. A banking system that was wrong to start with will not be strong after such an influx of capital.... The inherent vulnerability of smaller countries to this kind of capital flow is a real problem, no matter how good the economic policies, no matter how good the banking system, no matter how good their accounting system.[14]

Volcker's view of the international financial system may strike some readers as too pessimistic. But Martin and Rey (2006) provide historical evidence that poor countries are more prone to financial crashes than developed economies. They write:

> While trade globalization always makes crashes less likely, financial globalization may make them more likely, especially when trade costs are high.[15]

In sum, financial crises are the result not only of basic human nature, but also of the economic system that humans have developed. Capitalism, globalization, and the current international financial system seem to combine to generate recurring financial crises.

---

[14] Paul A. Volcker (1999). p. 267.
[15] Philippe Martin and Hélène Rey (2006). p. 1631.

The agonizingly long effort to solve the 1982 debt crisis thus did not bring an end to exchange rate crises and the financial crises that flow from them. The next chapter details the many more crises that characterized the international financial system after the Brady Plan was thought to have solved the debt problem. These crises, like the 1982 crisis that slowed or stopped economic growth in most developing economies for a decade, were extremely costly in terms of human welfare. And, the concluding chapter to this textbook will highlight the 2008–2009 global financial crisis, which shows that the current international financial system does not restrict the financial crises just to developing economies.

Key Terms and Concepts

Absorption	Financial crisis	Secondary debt market
Brady Plan	Intervention	Sovereign default
Currency crisis	Investment houses	Three person game
Debt service	Petrodollars	Trilemma
Debt writeoff	Policy independence	Washington consensus
Default	Recycling petrodollars	

Chapter Questions and Problems

1. Why is exchange rate intervention not a good long-run tool for keeping the exchange rate fixed?

2. Use a diagram of the foreign exchange market to describe how central bank intervention can keep the exchange rate from changing. Explain precisely what the central bank must do if the equilibrium exchange rate is not the same as the target exchange rate and how the central bank's actions return the curves to an intersection at the target exchange rate.

3. Explain the difference or similarity between exchange rate intervention and open market operations. Then discuss the effects of each on the foreign exchange rate.

4. Review Section 10.1.5 on Mexico, and distinguish the similarities and difference between Mexico's various defaults on foreign debt. Why did

foreign banks and investors eventually resume lending after each successive default?

5. The period 1950–1970 was characterized by relatively little international borrowing by developing economies, and almost none from foreign private banks, yet economic growth was relatively rapid compared to more recent decades when foreign finance has been much greater. Does it mean there is a reverse relationship between international borrowing/lending and economic growth? Discuss whether this apparent negative correlation between economic growth and foreign borrowing represents a true economic relationship or is merely circumstantial. Why could foreign borrowing hamper growth? How could foreign borrowing enhance economic growth?

6. Use the equation that relates the spot exchange rate to the future expected exchange rate to show what it takes to keep the exchange rate fixed over time.

7. Explain precisely what we mean by the "trilemma" that policy makers face in a global economy. How might policymakers avoid the trilemma? How did the Bretton Woods system attempt to avoid the trilemma even though they explicitly sought increased international economic integration, stable exchange rates, and macroeconomic policies to avoid another Great Depression.

8. Does the trilemma explain the 1982 debt crisis? What conditions must be present for an abrupt and large change in the exchange rate to cause a major economic slowdown?

References

Aggarwal, VK (1989). Interpreting the history of mexico's external debt crises. *The International Debt Crisis in Historical Perspective*, Eichengreen B and PH Lindert (eds.). Cambridge, MA: MIT Press.

Corsetti, G, P Pesenti and N Roubini (2001). Fundamental determinants of the Asian crisis: The role of financial fragility and external imbalances. *Regional and Global Capital Flows: Macroeconomic Causes and Consequences*, Ito T and AO Krueger (eds.), pp. 11–44. Chicago: University of Chicago Press.

Dominguez, KM and JA Frankel (1993). *Does Foreign Exchange Intervention Work?* Washington, DC: Institute for International Economics.

Edelstein, M (1982). *Overseas Investment in the Age of High Imperialism: The United Kingdom, 1850–1914.* New York: Columbia University Press.

Eichengreen, B and PH Lindert (eds.) (1989). *The International Debt Crisis in Historical Perspective.* Cambridge, MA: MIT Press.

Eichengreen, B, A Rose and C Wyposz (1997). Contagious Currency Crises. *Working Paper,* March.

Flood, RP and PM Garber (1984). Collapsing exchange rate regimes: Some linear examples. *Journal of International Economics,* 17(1,2), 1–13.

Frankel, JA and EA Cavallo (2004). Does openness to trade make countries more vulnerable to sudden stops, or less? Using gravity to establish causality. *NBER Working Paper w10957,* December.

Humpage, OF and WP Osterberg (2000). Why intervention rarely works. *Economic Commentary,* Federal Reserve Bank of Cleveland, February 1.

International Monetary Fund (1997). Capital flows to emerging markets — A historical perspective. Annex VI to *International Capital Markets,* November, 1997.

Krugman, P (2000). Introduction. *Currency Crises,* Krugman P (ed.). Chicago: University of Chicago Press.

Krugman, P (1979). A model of balance-of-payment crises. *Journal of Money, Credit, and Banking,* 11(3), 311–325.

Maddison, A (2003). *The World Economy: Historical Statistics.* Paris: OECD.

Marichal, C (1989). *A Century of Debt Crises in Latin America.* Princeton, NJ: Princeton University Press.

Martin, P and H Rey (2006). Globalization and emerging markets: With or without crash? *American Economic Review,* 96(5), 1631–1651.

McKinnon, RL and H Pill (1999). Exchange-rate regimes for emerging markets: Moral hazard and international overborrowing. *Oxford Review of Economic Policy,* 15(3), 19–38.

Mendoza, EG and KA Smith (2002). Margin calls, trading costs, and asset prices in emerging markets: The financial mechanics of the 'Sudden Stop' phenomenon. *NBER Working Paper 9286.*

Mendoza, EG and KA Smith (2007). Quantitative implication of a debt–deflation theory of sudden stops and asset prices. *Journal of International Economics.*

Obstfeld, M and K Rogoff (1995). The mirage of fixed exchange rates. *Journal of Economic Perspectives,* 9(4), 73–96.

Obstfeld, M and Taylor AM (1998). The great depression as a watershed: International capital mobility over the long run. *The Defining Moment: The Great Depression and the American Economy in the Twentieth Century*, Bordo MD, CD Goldin and EN White, (eds.), pp. 353–402. Chicago: University of Chicago Press.

Obstfeld, M, JC Shambaugh and AM Taylor (2004). The trilemma in history: Tradeoffs among exchange rates, monetary policies, and capital mobility. *NBER Working Paper w10396*, March.

Obstfeld, M (1998). The global capital market: Benefactor or menace? *Journal of Economic Perspectives*, 12(4), 1–15.

Rogoff, K (1999). International institutions for reducing global financial instability. *Journal of Economics Perspectives*, 13(4), 21–42.

Rose, AK (2002). One reason countries pay their debts: Renegotiation and international trade. *NBER Working Paper No. w8853*, March.

Sachs, JD (1985). External debt and macroeconomic performance in Latin America and East Asia. *Brookings Papers on Economic Activity*, 2, 523–564.

Sarno, L and MP Taylor (2001). Official intervention in the foreign exchange market: Is it effective and, if so, how does it work? *Journal of Economic Literature*, 39(3), 839–868.

Sarno, L and MP Taylor (2002). *The Economics of Exchange Rates*. Cambridge: Cambridge University Press.

Volcker, PA (1999). A perspective on financial crises. *Rethinking the International Monetary System*, Sneddon Little J and GP Olivei, (eds.). Conference Series No. 43, Federal Reserve Bank of Boston, June 1999.

Chapter 11

More Exchange Rate Crises

How many more fiascos will it take before responsible people are finally convinced that a system of pegged exchange rates is not a satisfactory financial arrangement?

(Milton Friedman.[1])

I think the idea of a small country freely floating its exchange rate is unworkable.

(Paul Volcker.[2])

In 1990, the year the 1982 debt crisis finally ended, international capital flows to developing countries began to grow again. In fact, during the 1990–1997 period, net annual inflows of foreign capital to the developing economies was seven times as large as it was during the pre-debt crisis boom in 1973–1982. Not everything was exactly the same as before, however. One of the characteristics of international capital flows in the 1990s was that savers, investors, and banks were much more selective in where they placed their wealth. International capital flows varied according to economic conditions in developed

---

[1] Milton Friedman (1990).
[2] Paul A. Volcker (1999).

economies, and they also varied with the economic performance of borrowing countries. Other notable characteristics of 1990s international lending was that China became the largest developing country recipient of foreign capital. Ironically, these capital inflows, combined with its large trade surpluses, permitted the Chinese government to accumulate huge reserves of foreign assets.

One thing did not change in the 1990s: there were many more currency crises in many developing countries. The Brady Plan and the accompanying economic reforms did not prevent crises in Mexico in 1994, Thailand, Malaysia, Indonesia, and South Korea in 1997, Brazil in 1999, Turkey in 2000, and Russia and Argentina in 2001. These further crises involved the familiar sequence of currency depreciation, defaults, and rising unemployment and poverty.

Chapter Goals

1. Detail the major post-Brady currency crises.
2. Explain why not much more than a decade after 1982, Mexico again suffered a sharp exchange rate collapse and financial crisis.
3. Examine why the Asian tiger economies also suffered currency crises and financial crises.
4. Explain the collapse of Argentina's currency board regime.
5. Detail Brazil's 2004 tightrope walk between crisis and sustainable debt.
6. Examine Russia's currency and financial crises in 1998.
7. Explain the differences between the three generations of currency crisis models.
8. Discuss the benefits and costs of fixed and floating exchange rates.

11.1 The Post-1982 Period

The trends in international capital flows to the developing economies between 1982 and the start of the 21st century are shown in Table 11.1.

Table 11.1 Capital Flows to Developing Countries 1984–2008 (US$ billions).

	1984– 1989	1990– 1996	1998– 2000	2006	2007	2008
All developing economies						
Net private capital inflows	12.5	141.7	64.3	202.8	617.5	109.3
Net FDI	13.1	64.6	164.4	241.4	359.0	459.3
Net portfolio investment	4.4	64.0	41.4	−100.7	39.5	−155.2
Other[a]	−4.9	13.0	−141.2	62.2	219.2	−194.6
Net official flows[b]	26.5	17.4	7.1	−154.1	−100.5	−60.0
Change in reserves	−11.2	−71.3	−89.5	−751.7	−1257.8	−865.7
Current account	—	−88.7	−41.7	728.7	741.5	793.0
Africa						
Net private capital inflows	2.3	3.7	3.8	35.2	33.4	24.2
Net FDI	1.2	2.9	7.4	32.1	32.1	32.4
Net portfolio investment	−0.8	−0.2	3.8	17.6	9.9	−15.8
Other[a]	1.8	0.9	−7.3	−5.7	−8.3	7.9
Net official flows[b]	6.7	7.6	5.3	−10.0	5.0	11.1
Change in reserves	0.1	−2.2	−3.9	−54.3	−61.6	−53.8
Emerging Asia[c]						
Net private capital inflows	9.9	58.3	−13.4	31.8	164.8	127.9
Net FDI	54.5	33.3	64.0	94.3	138.5	222.6
Net portfolio investment	1.0	9.2	27.6	−107.2	11.2	−65.9
Other[a]	3.3	10.2	−105.0	44.6	15.2	−28.7
Net official flows[b]	6.7	8.0	2.4	−21.7	−36.6	−13.1
Change in reserves	−15.7	−40.2	−67.2	−372.2	−673.1	−634.3
Western hemisphere[d]						
Net private capital inflows	−0.2	46.1	58.9	10.8	107.4	58.5
Net FDI	5.3	19.1	66.6	29.1	85.8	84.3
Net portfolio investment	−0.9	32.3	13.0	−7.7	42.3	−11.2
Other[a]	−4.6	−5.3	−20.7	−10.6	−20.6	−14.7
Net official flows[b]	8.2	1.2	7.6	−17.7	1.8	11.0
Change in reserves	0.5	−18.4	2.5	−51.0	−132.4	−49.8

Sources: Table 4.9 in International Monetary Fund (1998). *World Economic Outlook and International Capital Markets, Interim Assessment*, Washington, D.C., p. 84; Table 1.2 in International Monetary Fund (2005). *World Economic Outlook and International Capital Markets, Interim Assessment*, Washington, D.C., pp. 8, 9.

[a] The "Other" category includes mostly bank loans.

[b] Includes foreign aid and other government-to-government and multilateral agency flows.

[c] All Asian economies except Japan, Korea, Singapore, and Taiwan.

[d] All western hemisphere countries except Canada and the United States.

First, note in the top section of Table 11.1 that net private capital inflows in all developing economies have varied greatly from year to year. While foreign direct investment (FDI) grew rapidly and fairly consistently, net portfolio investment fluctuated from virtually nothing during the 1980s to about $64 billion during the early 1990s, and then to negative $100 billion or more during some years of the 2000s. Similarly, the "other" category is equally volatile; this category consists mostly of bank loans. Most stunning is the recent growth of reserves in developing economies. Table 11.1 shows that in 2008, developing countries as a group accumulated net reserves of $751.7 billion, $1,257.8 billion, and $865.7 billion in 2006, 2007, and 2008, respectively. This net accumulation of reserves was partially funded by net capital inflows, but also by developing countries' rising current account balances. The lower part of Table 11.1 highlights several regions of the world; note the differences across the regions. Most of the accumulation of reserves occurred in the emerging economies of Asia. Private investment flows such as FDI and portfolio investment also differed across regions; in many years there were net inflows into some regions and net outflows from other regions.

Table 11.1 reflects another important recent trend in capital flows: investment has increasingly flowed from developing to developed countries. The President of the European Central Bank, Jean-Claude Trichet, has said: "It's not sustainable in the long-run that the emerging world would finance the industrial world...".[3] Whether such flows are "sustainable" remains an open question, but to the casual observer it certainly seems odd that investment would flow from capital-scarce countries to high-income, capital-abundant countries. In light of the crises suffered by debtor countries, however, the accumulation of foreign exchange reserves is understandable. Large reserves enable debtor countries to manage the trilemma more easily. We will return to these questions after examining the varied exchange rate crises of the 1990s and early 21st century.

---

[3] Quoted in Santiago Perez (2006). "Direction of Capital Flows Unsustainable, Trichet Says". *Wall Street Journal*, 28 January 2006.

11.2 Recent Foreign Exchange Crises

This section looks at three exchange rate crises that cover different parts of the world and economies that are seemingly very different in terms of their recent performance, government policies, and economic fundamentals. Yet, these three crises turn out to be very similar, and they had similar consequences: devastating recessions and huge welfare losses for the citizens of the countries involved.

11.2.1 *The Mexican peso crisis of 1994*

Mexico's economy had gone through a major transformation during the 1980s as policy makers shifted from protectionism to free trade, from government ownership of industry to privatization, and from rigid restrictions on inflows and outflows of foreign investment to liberalized investment. The reforms were largely the result of the devastating 1982 debt crisis, when Mexico defaulted on its foreign bank loans and was forced to shift from being a net foreign borrower to running a trade surplus in order to repay its foreign debt. Its uncompetitive and highly regulated economy was unable to respond quickly to opportunities for exporting and earning the foreign exchange necessary for servicing its foreign debt. Per capita income remained unchanged throughout the 1980s even though the country instituted the major economic reforms necessary to restore the confidence of the international investors and reverse the protectionist trade policies that had gradually undermined the incentives for investment and growth.

In the early 1990s, the Mexican economy finally began to grow again. This was taken as evidence that the Washington Consensus policies imposed by the IMF, such as the elimination of trade barriers, NAFTA, and the privatization of government assets, were producing the desired results. The government also made headway in reducing inflation by cutting monetary expansion and fixing the peso-dollar exchange rate. The government's apparent commitment to reducing inflation strengthened the value of the Mexican peso, just as the aggregate demand/aggregate supply model predicts. The reduced inflationary expectations reduced the perceived exchange rate risk associated with investing in Mexico. The good economic news encouraged foreign investors to buy Mexican stocks and bonds and it encouraged Mexican firms, banks, and government agencies to borrow overseas in order to take advantage of business opportunities and infrastructure needs in the growing economy.

Then disaster struck in 1994. That year was an important election year. In order to gain favor with voters, the Mexican government sharply increased spending and loosened monetary policy. The ruling party, the Institutional Revolutionary Party (PRI), had been in power since the 1920s, but in 1994 its hold on the presidency was tenuous. Rumors had it that the previous presidential election had required massive fraud for the PRI to maintain power, and this was expected to be a very close election. The political spending caused the economy to grow rapidly during 1994, and the PRI won the election. The rising government budget deficit and the money creation to finance the deficit undermined confidence in the government's commitment to keep the value of the peso from falling, however. In fact, even before the election it had become increasingly obvious that the government was attempting to defy the trilemma by simultaneously keeping the peso fixed to the dollar, greatly increasing spending and the money supply, all while opening the borders to trade and investment as prescribed by the new North American Free Trade Agreement (NAFTA). Many Mexican individuals and firms, as well as some foreign investors who had previously acquired Mexican assets, began exchanging peso-denominated assets for dollar-denominated assets outside the country.[4] This *capital flight* gradually grew throughout 1994, and in 1994 the Mexican central bank spent over $20 billion of its dollar reserves purchasing the many pesos being dumped on the foreign exchange market. Capital flight reached panic proportions toward the end of the year, and Mexico's reported reserves of $24 billion were nearly exhausted. In December, the government had to stop intervening in the foreign exchange market, and the peso promptly lost half its value.

---

[4] Despite criticism of foreign investors, it was mostly domestic wealth that moved out of the country first, as documented by Jeffrey A. Frankel and Sergio L. Schmukler (1996).

This collapse of the peso caused a severe slowdown in economic activity in Mexico. This fall in output surprised some prominent analysts, who expected the sharp depreciation of the peso to spur Mexican exports, increase aggregate demand, and, hence, stimulate economic growth. The problem was that the peso depreciation instantaneously bankrupted much of the Mexican banking sector. Mexican banks and manufacturers had borrowed heavily in the United States and the worldwide eurocurrency markets in order to lend to customers in Mexico anxious to invest and expand business in the growing Mexican economy. As part of its preparations for joining NAFTA and its overall economic reforms to restore growth in the Mexican economy, the government had recently deregulated banking activity. The deregulation of banking stimulated aggressive competition among banks to capture funds and attract customers for loans. Competition in banking, no doubt, can be beneficial in the long run, but the sudden deregulation left the banks unprepared. Margins were too small, and many risky loans were made by inexperienced bank personnel spurred by their managers to capture market share in the newly deregulated industry. Bank regulators were already concerned about the quality of bank assets even before the exchange rate collapse, but when the peso depreciated by 50 percent at the end of 1994, the liability side of bank balance sheets grew precipitously. Banks' foreign debt suddenly doubled in size in terms of pesos. Many of the banks' largest customers had also borrowed overseas and, therefore, also faced suddenly-larger foreign liabilities. Some of these customers defaulted on their Mexican loans as well, further weakening banks' assets. The bankrupt banks stopped lending, investment collapsed, and the economy contracted sharply. Mexico's real per capita GDP fell by nearly ten percent in 1995.

The crisis was overcome after the Mexican government quickly dealt with the failure of large numbers of domestic financial institutions and firms. A bank bailout was organized at great expense to the Mexican taxpayer, and within a year the financial sector was on firmer footing. Investment soon resumed. The loss in output in 1995 was irreversible, but by the end of 1995 the economy began slowly growing again.

There was much discussion about why Mexican banks and companies had borrowed so much overseas and left themselves vulnerable to exchange rate swings. The promise by the government to support the peso no doubt had something to do the willingness of Mexican firms to assume large foreign exchange exposure. By publicly stating that it would support the value of the peso, the government had implicitly provided domestic borrowers of dollars with a guarantee, so borrowers acted as if there was no exchange rate risk. The government's subsequent bailout in fact confirmed borrowers' expectations. This meant that future commitments by the Mexican government to fixed exchange rates could lead to an even greater disregard for exchange rate risk. This is probably why the Mexican government has let the peso float freely since 1995, a floating rate would gradually make everyone conscious of exchange rate instability. The 1994 exchange rate collapse and economic crisis had another interesting effect: In 2000, Mexican voters handed the PRI its first defeat in a presidential election in nearly 80 years. The shortsighted economic policies of the PRI in 1994 were apparently not forgotten.

11.2.2 *The Asian crisis of 1997*

The world economy was surprised in 1997 by a sudden massive outflow of money from several fast-growing East Asian economies. South Korea had been one of the very fastest growing economies of the world since 1960. It was commonly referred to as one of the *Asian tigers*, along with Hong Kong, Singapore, and Taiwan. Several other East Asian countries, Indonesia, Thailand, and Malaysia, the so-called *new Asian tigers*, had also experienced very rapid economic growth rates over the decade prior to 1997. The East Asian economies were often held up as examples of how developing economies can achieve rapid growth, and many people wondered how it was possible that economies which had done so many things right could now suffer the same type of crisis that was commonly associated with Latin American and African economies.

Indeed, the governments of most Southeast Asian countries had avoided the accumulation of large amounts of government debt, and government budgets were in balance. Inflation was not high compared to most developing economies in the 1980s. The Southeast Asian economies were *outward-oriented* and many domestic firms were actively selling in foreign markets. Thus, domestic prices in the Southeast Asian economies were not distorted and firms were not as protected from competition. Unfortunately, the fixed exchange rates were not at their long-run equilibrium levels.

The governments of most of the fast-growing Asian countries had fixed their exchange rates to the US dollar, using reserves of foreign exchange to intervene when necessary to keep the market from raising or lowering the rates. By 1997, these government-controlled exchange rates had become somewhat overvalued relative to the expected future exchange rates necessary to balance supply and demand of foreign currencies in the long run. This *overvaluation* was partly due to higher inflation rates relative to the Asian countries' principal trade partners. It was also caused by the appreciation of the US dollar relative to most other currencies after 1995, which made the East Asian countries less competitive vis-a-vis Japan, Europe, and other Asian countries; as the dollar rose in value, so did the East Asian currencies that were being fixed to the dollar by their governments. China's 1994 depreciation of its currency further contributed to the new tigers' loss of competitiveness in world markets; China produces and exports many of the same types of labor-intensive manufactures that the new tigers were exporting. Yet, the East Asian governments had committed to fixing their currencies to the US dollar, and they continued to intervene to keep the exchange rate from changing.

Gradually, as economic conditions kept changing, expectations of an eventual change in the fixed exchange rates grew stronger, and the owners of assets increasingly decided to store their wealth in assets denominated in other currencies, especially US dollars. Demand for foreign currencies thus expanded, and the supply fell. Van Wincoop and Yi (2000) report that as much as $80 billion left Indonesia, Korea, Malaysia, the Philippines, and Thailand in 1997 and 1998. The central banks of Thailand, Malaysia, Indonesia, and other East Asian economies used large amounts of their accumulated reserves of foreign exchange, which were initially quite substantial, to make up the difference between market demand and supply and keep the exchange rate from changing. However, the fixed exchange rates had to be abandoned when central banks began to run out of foreign exchange with which to supply the foreign exchange market's rising demand for dollars and yen. The national currencies fell sharply in value relative to the major currencies of the world. Just as in Mexico, the sudden rise in foreign liabilities caused bank and firm balance sheets to deteriorate, a financial crisis set in, bank lending ceased, investment stopped, and economic activity fell sharply. In 1998, real GDP fell by 13 percent in Indonesia, 11 percent in Thailand, and nearly eight percent in Malaysia.

The Indonesian, Malaysian, and Thai economies did not recover as quickly as the Mexican economy did, and five years later, in 2002, they still had not recovered their pre-1998 levels of per capita real income. Attention has focused on the apparent fragility of the banking systems in these countries. It appears that perhaps the banking systems were already weakened with large amounts of non-performing loans even before the collapse of the national currencies. Some economists, like Krueger and Yoo (2001), have suggested that the exchange rate crisis turned into a full-fledged financial crisis because of "crony capitalism".

Crony capitalism refers generally to any close relationship between private business and government policymakers. After the 1997 Asian financial crisis, the term was widely used to describe the practice under which commercial banks in South Korea, Indonesia, and Thailand were induced to channel savings to a select group of large firms, often ignoring entrepreneurs, small businesses, and other potentially more productive investment projects.

11.2.3 *The Korean chaebol*

In Korea, such directed investment went mostly to the large industrial conglomerates, or *chaebol*, which were strongly favored by the South Korean government. Chaebol such as the Hyundai, Samsung, Daewoo, LG, and SK groups, among others, were central to South Korea's goal of becoming a major industrial force in the world.

The chaebol funded little of their investment through the sale of bonds or stock. Instead, they relied on bank loans, often at very low interest rates. Loans to the chaebol required little investigation or monitoring, and so long as the large conglomerates performed reasonably well, the banks stood to make a good profit. More worrisome were the close relationships between the banks and the Chaebol conglomerates; each of the major Chaebol operated its own bank subsidiary. That is, borrowers ran some of the banks that they borrowed from, and government regulators effectively encouraged this arrangement. This was indeed a blatant case of crony capitalism.

South Korean savers had few options for storing their wealth other than the banks since the government limited the growth of alternative financial intermediaries and markets. The government also limited Koreans' ability to deposit their wealth overseas. Hence, banks did not have to pay high rates of interest to capture Koreans' savings.

The close relationship between the banks and the conglomerates was destined to cause problems because savings were not being actively channeled to the highest-return investments. By the late 1990s, it was apparent that many chaebol investment projects were unprofitable, and many Korean banks found themselves with nonperforming loans. At first, the banks rolled over the loans or even lent more to the conglomerates in the hope that the problems would go away. The situation got worse, however, because the continued flow of loans relieved the chaebol of the business pressures that might otherwise have forced them to improve their operations. More bad investments were made on top of existing unprofitable investments. Then, in 1997, following the exchange rate crises in several other Asian countries a similar exchange rate crisis developed in South Korea. The regional contagion spread to Korea because many people correctly perceived that with bank balance sheets weakened by crony capitalism, a depreciating exchange rate would prove devastating for Korea's indebted banking industry. The fear of depreciation and financial crisis soon became self-fulfilling, and foreign capital flows reversed themselves sharply in 1997.

The South Korean government had to spend substantial amounts of the taxpayers' money to restore financial sector solvency, essentially covering the discrepancies between book value of outstanding loans and the (much lower) true value of the investment projects that the loans financed. Korea's case was especially difficult because the banks' major borrowers, the chaebol, also had weak balance sheets while carrying substantial foreign debt. Hence, much of the financial restructuring involved restructuring the chaebol. Somebody must ultimately pay for the losses from costly investment projects that did not generate positive returns. The borrowers cannot pay if their projects fail. It is usually taxpayers who fill in the gaps in the financial industry's balance sheets. When a financial crisis spreads, there is also the opportunity cost of lost economic growth, which is borne in complex ways by people, firms, and public agencies throughout the economy. The financial restructuring in Indonesia, Malaysia, Thailand, and Korea has had to be much greater than the mere compensation for the exchange rate collapse, and the collapse in economic activity was greater than occurred in nearly all other recent financial crises.[5] Defiance of the trilemma is more costly when the inevitable exchange rate collapse drives a banking system with weak balance sheets into bankruptcy.

11.2.4 *The lesson that Asia should have learned from Chile's 1982 crisis*

We have examined financial crises in Mexico and East Asia. Also interesting is the 1982 crisis in Chile, a country whose government had not accumulated any foreign debt. Unlike most other LDC governments in the 1970s and early 1980s, Chile's government had reformed its fiscal system and by 1980 was generating considerable budget surpluses. A massive privatization program in the late 1970s also meant that, unlike many LDC governments, the government of Chile no longer owned many firms and utilities. The economy was

---

[5] The reasons for the exceptionally large recessions in East Asia are discussed in Robert J. Barro (2001) and Yung Chul Park and Jong-Wha Lee (2001).

largely in private hands, and the government had no need to borrow. In Chile, like East Asia in the 1990s, it was the private industrial, commercial, and financial sectors that borrowed heavily overseas.

Since the late 1970s, the Chilean government had fixed its exchange rate by using reserves to intervene in the foreign exchange markets, and it had fixed the rate at a level that resulted in large trade deficits offset by large capital inflows to private firms and banks in Chile. These capital inflows could continue so long as the world financial markets had ample funds to lend and as long as lenders had the confidence that the Chilean borrowers could service their foreign loans. When world financial markets tightened in 1982, suddenly Chilean borrowers were unable to acquire further loans or even roll over their existing loans. The decline in capital inflows meant that Chile had to spend increasing amounts of foreign reserves to keep the exchange rate from depreciating. The Chilean central bank had to supply some of the foreign currency that Chilean importers demanded in order to buy foreign goods and services and that Chilean firms and banks demanded in order to pay interest and principal on the many foreign loans they had contracted.

Reserves of foreign exchange soon ran out, and intervention in the foreign exchange markets by the Chilean central bank was no longer possible. The forces of supply and demand took over, and the Chilean peso fell in value. It suddenly took many more pesos to buy US dollars, German marks, or Japanese yen. The foreign loans, in terms of pesos, were suddenly much larger than before, and many highly-indebted firms suddenly found that their liabilities exceeded their assets. These firms had trouble repaying their domestic loans as well as their foreign loans, and the Chilean banking system found itself with many more *bad loans* than before. To make matters worse, most Chilean banks had themselves borrowed overseas at attractive interest rates and re-lent the money to domestic firms, consumers, and purchasers of homes. Of course, while these foreign obligations were in dollars or yen, their domestic loans were in pesos. After the depreciation, the banks' foreign obligations exceeded the value of the domestic peso loans even before they began adjusting the value of their outstanding loans to domestic borrowers engulfed in an economic recession.

The banking system responded by no longer making loans, and in some cases obligations to depositors could not be met. Consumption and investment decreased sharply, and the economy declined. In fact, real output fell by a whopping 15 percent in 1982, one of the biggest declines in the world that year. And, unlike the problems elsewhere in the developing world, it was not the Chilean government that had contracted the foreign loans.

Because the banks were technically bankrupt after the sharp depreciation of the peso, it took a major bailout of the banking system in 1983, at a very high cost to Chilean taxpayers, to restore bank balance sheets to where liabilities no longer exceeded assets. Once the banking sector again took up its function of smoothly channeling savings to investment projects, Chile began to grow again. In fact, Chile became one of the fastest-growing economies in the world after 1985 and its citizens today enjoy the highest per capita income in Latin America. The Asian economies that were battered by the 1997 exchange rate crisis should have learned from Chile that excessive foreign borrowing and currency imbalances on bank and business balance sheets can trigger an exchange rate crisis. Chile also showed, however, that prompt measures to restore financial health combined with other sound economic policies will restore growth fairly quickly. Alternatively, had Asian leaders studied Chile's 1982 crisis sooner, they might have shifted to more flexible exchange rates well before the panic set in.

11.2.5 *The collapse of Argentina's currency board in 2001*

Argentina has a long history of financial crises, exchange rate collapses, and defaults on foreign debt. Argentina was actually one of the ten wealthiest countries in terms of per capita real income at he start of the twentieth century, but it has suffered from inconsistent economic policies that often caused severe fiscal imbalances, high inflation, and rapidly depreciating currencies throughout the twentieth century. The most recent crisis, at the end of 2001, was the direct result of policies instituted ten years earlier. After several bouts with hyperinflation during the late 1980s, caused by the government's inability to control government expenditures and the money supply, Argentina took the extreme measure in 1991 of creating a *currency board*. A currency board is a very rigid financial arrangement that effectively eliminates the central bank as the guardian of monetary policy and limits the authorities to issuing domestic currency only when foreign currency is presented in exchange for the domestic currency at a fixed exchange rate. The currency board therefore has absolutely no discretion over monetary policy because it just mechanically creates domestic money when foreign currency is brought into the country, and it destroys domestic money when domestic money is exchanged for foreign currencies. The domestic money base is thus rigorously determined by the amount of foreign exchange that enters the country. Changes in the money base are equal to the surpluses or deficits in the balance of payments.

Currency boards date back to the British Empire, with the first one established in Mauritius in 1849. They eventually came to exist in quite a few British colonies. The end of colonialism in the 1950s and 1960s seemed to signal an end to the use of currency boards, as most newly-independent former colonies established central banks and took control of their own currencies. Recently they have reappeared in several countries, however, motivated by governments' need to establish credibility in the financial markets after long periods of inflationary monetary policies. A currency board represents a supposedly *credible* commitment to backing the national currency with foreign reserves. By law, the board is only allowed to issue domestic currency in exchange for foreign currency, which it keeps on deposit in liquid accounts at home or abroad. Proponents of currency boards say that the existence of foreign currency and foreign assets to match the money created eliminates any doubt about the currency board's ability to supply foreign exchange at the fixed exchange rate. The strict rules under which a currency board operates also implies that the domestic money supply cannot be manipulated by the government in order to cover budget deficits or to increase government revenue. This was the reason Argentina switched to the currency board; the government was perceived as incapable of running its central bank responsibly, so the switch to something as rigid as a currency board was the only way for the government to signal that political manipulation of the money supply was not going to occur again. No rational person would have believed any Argentine politician's promise that the central bank's performance would improve, no matter how sincere.

The currency board's lack of discretion over monetary policy of course has a very serious disadvantage, which is that the economy loses the benefit of letting the central bank use its monetary policy to address economic variables other than the exchange rate. The fixed exchange rate under the currency board makes the absence of monetary policy especially costly because any changes in foreign economic or financial conditions require the domestic product and factor markets to do all of the adjusting.[6]

Argentina provides a good example of both the benefits and costs of a currency board. The currency board let Argentina reduce inflation to practically zero in the 1990s, quite an accomplishment given the rate of inflation of 10,000 percent in 1990. But the Argentine economy also followed a severe stop–go pattern of growth during the 1990s. Whenever world financial markets were relatively liquid and money flowed to Argentina in the form of loans and foreign investment, Argentina's money supply expanded, its aggregate demand and aggregate supply curves both shifted out, and output grew very rapidly. But, when financial markets were threatened by economic crises in other developing economies or were just tight because of growth and financial conditions in the world's major economies, Argentina's economy turned sharply toward recession. Unemployment exceeded 15 percent in some years during the 1990s. By the late 1990s, many economists and opposition politicians argued that Argentina would be better off with a floating exchange rate and a normal central bank that could engage in discretionary monetary policy to combat unemployment.

In early 1999, the currency of Argentina's neighbor and major trading partner, Brazil, depreciated by about 50 percent. Also problematic was the fact that most of Argentina's trade was with Europe,

---

[6] For a detailed but very understandable analysis of currency boards, see John Williamson (1995).

but its currency was pegged to the US dollar. When the dollar appreciated against the European currencies, Argentina's trade balance turned sharply negative, which caused its money supply to contract under the rigid currency board system. Furthermore, while the currency board limited the amount of money in circulation, the Argentine government was spending much more than it collected in taxes and gradually built up a huge debt. While foreign borrowing served to bring foreign currency into the country to offset the negative current account's contractionary effect on the money supply, by 2001 the government's foreign debt had grown to $140 billion, the highest foreign debt of any developing economy. With Argentinean policymakers showing little inclination to reduce the government's budget deficit, foreign lenders became reluctant to lend. With a debt default in sight, Argentine citizens were in no mood to lend to their government either, and they began to worry that the government would eventually have to print money to cover its budget deficit. Argentineans feared that the currency board arrangement would be scrapped, and they began to exchange pesos for US dollars in increasing amounts.

Everyone knew that if the exchange rate changed, there would be massive bankruptcies. By late 2001 it was difficult to expect anything other than a currency collapse. The scene was set for a crisis. The International Monetary Fund's refusal to grant Argentina further emergency credit in late 2001 was taken as a clear signal that Argentina's exchange rate was not sustainable under the country's current economic policies. Panic set in. After several weeks of massive withdrawals of pesos from banks in order to exchange them for dollars, the Argentine government froze all bank accounts. The freeze was needed, the government claimed, because the banks were running out of reserves to back the peso money supply, and high unemployment precluded any further contraction of the money supply. There were riots outside the banks as savers clamored for their money in order to change it to dollars before the exchange rate collapsed. The government resigned, and the fourth temporary president in a matter of weeks, in early 2002, finally let the peso float freely. By mid-2002, it had lost three-fourths of its former value, and a financial crisis was in progress. It was estimated that real GDP declined by 15–20 percent in 2002.

The Argentinean government eventually imposed a settlement on its creditors, and by the start of 2004, the holders of nearly 75 percent of Argentina's defaulted $103 billion in government debt agreed to accept the government's offer of about thirty cents on the dollar and lengthened terms of repayment for the remaining balance. Creditors appear to have taken the offer because they expected no better offers would be forthcoming. By the beginning of 2004, the Argentinean economy had recovered most of the ground it had lost after the currency collapse in 2002. The debt settlement enabled the economy to again attract some short-term foreign capital, and the economy continued growing, at least until the 2008 global financial crisis spread around the world. As of 2010, remaining creditors were still being offered the reduced settlement terms, but many were still holding out in the hope that Argentina's government would eventually offer better term in order to restore its reputation.

11.2.6 *Common threads to the Mexican, Asian, and Argentine crises*

There are obvious parallels between the 1994 Mexican crisis, 1997 Asian crisis, and the 2001 Argentine crisis. All three countries had made economic policy reforms demanded by the IMF, such as balancing government budgets, opening the economy to foreign competition, privatizing much of the economy, and suppressing inflation with tight monetary policies. Financial account transactions were liberalized, and foreign investment had grown rapidly. Finally, all the governments committed to maintaining fixed exchange rates. That is, they had picked globalization and fixed exchange rates from the trilemma menu.

In each case, when it became apparent that underlying economic conditions and policies were not compatible with the exchange rates at which the currencies were being fixed, investors began to shift their wealth out of assets denominated in these countries' national currencies and into assets denominated in US dollars, Japanese yen, and other currencies that were expected to not lose value in the future. The shifts in wealth eventually turned into panics when it became apparent that the government was running out of reserves or politically unable to continue intervening to prevent the exchange rate from changing. Everyone became a speculator. Many importers in effect became speculators by making advance purchases of foreign goods, sometimes even making advance payments to foreign suppliers, because they feared a currency devaluation would raise the domestic price of foreign goods in the future. Exporters kept their overseas receipts parked in foreign bank accounts, awaiting the possible devaluation that would increase the amount earned from converting the foreign receipts to domestic currency. All of these things of course further increased demand for foreign exchange and reduced supply, and central banks found themselves spending reserves of foreign exchange more and more rapidly in order to bridge the growing gap between demand and supply. After losing substantial amounts of foreign reserves, the central banks gave up and let their currencies float freely according to supply and demand, as the millions of large and small speculators had expected.

11.2.7 *Why the currency crises were so costly*

The economic slowdowns in Mexico, Southeast Asia, and Argentina were so severe because the *exchange rate crises* triggered *financial crises*, which then caused severe economic recessions with high unemployment and low investment. In each case, banks had borrowed overseas in dollars and lent to domestic firms in domestic currency. Hence, exchange rate depreciation caused liabilities to suddenly rise in terms of the domestic currency. There was, therefore, a sudden deterioration of bank balance sheets; an increase in liabilities was not matched by a concurrent increase in assets. Many banks were technically bankrupt after the collapse of the exchange rate. Furthermore, many of the banks' largest customers had also borrowed overseas, and they faced similar deteriorations of their balance sheets, which translated into problem loans for the banks and a reduction in assets. Bankrupt banks cannot lend, and for this reason the financial crisis turned into a sharp slowdown in investment and any other economic activities that needed credit and financial intermediation.

Once recession slowed economic activity, more domestic loans turned sour and banks' balance sheets deteriorated further. Finally, in Asia the availability of credit from overseas also helped to create speculative bubbles in real estate markets, stock markets, and investment in general. When the sudden exchange rate collapse and recession caused the bubbles to burst, the number of bad loans faced by the already bankrupt banks increased even more. It was hard to stop the downward spiral.

An important detail to remember is that the financial crises were caused by the mismatch of liabilities and assets across currencies. Borrowers owed dollars but their assets and expected earnings were in local currency, and they had not hedged their foreign exposure. Banks, governments, and firms in Mexico, Thailand, Korea, Malaysia, and Argentina earned most of their income in domestic currency, but they had to pay foreign loan principal, interest, and dividends in US dollars and other major foreign currencies. This is a common situation when governments effectively present the fixed exchange rate as a guaranteed national policy. Of course, a country that is a net borrower cannot match the currencies of all assets and liabilities.

Most developing and small developed countries have little choice but to borrow overseas in terms of dollars or other major currencies. That is, they have to bear all of the exchange rate risk. Foreigners' unwillingness to carry the exchange rate risk may reflect their belief that the currencies in question are more likely to depreciate than to appreciate. Indicative of the difficulty for developing economies to borrow abroad in their own currencies is Colombia's attempt in 2005. It offered a 12.5 percent interest rate on the equivalent of $250 million in bonds denominated in Colombian pesos. Just two months earlier, Colombia had sold $500 million in bonds denominated in US dollars yielding 8.5 percent.[7] Colombia therefore has to pay a 3.5 percent premium to sell peso bonds instead of US dollar bonds.

---

[7] Mike Esterl (2004). "Colombia Plans Peso Offering", *Wall Street Journal*, 9 November.

It is not only the governments of poorly-managed economies that cannot borrow abroad in their own currencies. Many well-governed countries whose economies are performing well are also forced by the markets to borrow internationally in terms of one of the major world currencies. This phenomenon is often referred to as "original sin" because there is little or no evidence that countries have done anything wrong to bring this disadvantage upon themselves.[8] Contrast this situation with the United States, which, as you saw in Chapter 2, also has huge foreign net foreign debt. The US's foreign obligations are almost entirely in terms of US dollars, however. Hence, in the case of a depreciation of the dollar, there would be no change in US borrowers' dollar obligations to foreigners. There would be no financial crisis in the US; rather, it would be the foreign lenders who would suffer a financial crisis as a fall in the value of the dollar would cause their assets to suddenly lose value!

The reversals of international investment flows that triggered the exchange rate crises in Mexico, Southeast Asia, and Argentina would have been costly to human welfare even if there had been no bankruptcies and financial crises that stopped all investment and much consumer expenditure. When Mexico's citizens, firms, and government borrowed money from foreigners, for example, they were able to absorb more than their country produced. When Mexico, East Asia, and Argentina were forced to reduce their outstanding debt, however, their absorption fell below national production. A sudden shift in international investment, as happened to Mexico, East Asia, and Argentina in the cases detailed above, caused these countries to go from absorbing several percent more than they produced to absorbing several percent less than they produced. Even without a recession, a sudden reversal of international investment created by the expectation of exchange rate depreciation can indeed cause severe hardship. When a financial crisis is added to the reduction in absorption, the welfare consequences of an exchange rate collapse can clearly be devastating.

---

[8] See, for example, Barry Eichengreen and Ricardo Hausman (2002). "How to Eliminate Original Financial Sin", *Financial Times*, 22 November 2002.

11.2.8 *The recoveries*

What is surprising is that countries that default usually can begin borrowing again sooner rather than later. For example, after the government of Ecuador defaulted in 2000 and restructured its debt at a 40 percent reduction in value to creditors, it faced interest rates about five times as high as those paid by other Latin American countries. But, within two years, Ecuador was again paying the same premium it was paying before the default.[9] Nearly all of the countries discussed above have resumed borrowing.

In the case of Mexico, it took three years for the economy to bring per capita income back to its pre-crisis 1994 level. There is some indication that the bank bailout may not have truly revitalized the banking system to where it efficiently channels the economy's savings to the most dynamic sectors of the economy.[10] Nevertheless, financial stability was restored, and since 2002, Mexico's international credit rating has been "investment grade", a rare accomplishment for a developing economy. Mexico met all of its debt payments, however, albeit with some help from the Clinton administration in the US, which authorized $40 billion in loans to Mexico from a little-known stabilization fund. These loans were quickly paid back, however. By 2003, Mexico had even retired all its Brady bonds, which had been issued back in 1989 to settle the default after the 1982 crisis. In 1994 even the Mexican banking sector had recovered to where it expanded lending in real terms by nearly 25 percent over the previous year. Manuel Medina Mora, the president of the Mexican Bankers Association and head of Citibank's Latin America division, said at the start of 2005: "Two years ago, people were saying 'Why are banks not lending?' Today the question has started to be 'Are they lending too much'".[11]

---

[9] Bob Davis (2004). "Argentina Made a Bold Debt Move; Could It Backfire?" *Wall Street Journal*, 29 November.

[10] Elizabeth McQuerry (1999). "The Banking Sector Rescue in Mexico", Federal Reserve Bank of Atlanta *Economic Review*, 3rd Quarter, 1999, pp. 14, 29.

[11] Quoted in John Authers (2005). "Mexican Banks Ride a Wave of Lending", *Financial Times*, 3 March 2005.

11.3 Brazil's 2004 Tightrope Walk

In 1998 Brazil adopted an IMF-sponsored Fiscal Stabilization program. As part of this program, Brazil committed to reducing its government budget deficit, decreasing its debt-to-GDP ratio, and maintaining conservative monetary policies to keep prices steady. Six years later and after a brief crisis that led the government to let the currency float and depreciate by 50 percent in 1999, the fiscal picture looked much better, but still not good enough to avoid another crisis. In 2004, the possibility of yet another currency crisis loomed.

11.3.1 *A high government debt burden*

Toward the end of 2003, Brazil's government debt burden was still very large. Gross public-sector debt was estimated at about 80 percent of GDP, a very high ratio by IMF standards. The *net* public sector debt was considerably less, at 58 percent of GDP, but about half of the government's assets, which were used to calculate the net debt, were illiquid. Government assets included loans to public enterprises and credits committed to the Labor Assistant Fund.

One reason for the high debt-to-GDP ratio were the numerous *esceletos* (*skeletons* in the closet), which were government obligations that had been hidden from public by previous administration were now, after many years, finally brought into the visible government budgeting process. Other reasons for the growth of government debt were the high interest rates the government had to pay to service the debt, slow economic growth, and the large currency depreciation after 1998. Real interest rates (nominal interest rates adjusted for the rate of inflation) were high in Brazil, because of the conservative monetary policy to reduce inflation. In addition, perhaps as much as half of government debt was being financed using very short-term instruments like the overnight market. Slow economic growth may have been caused, in part, by Brazil's fiscal reforms designed to generate budget surpluses; these were strongly contractionary according to Keynesian analysis. The currency depreciation increased the debt burden because Brazil's foreign debt is denominated entirely in foreign currencies. At the end of 2003, 26.5 percent of Brazilian debt was denominated in US dollars. Refinetti Goldfajn and Guardia (2003) of the Central Bank of Brazil estimated that Brazil's net debt-to-GDP ratio would have been only 42 percent rather than 58 percent had no Brazilian debt been dollar-denominated.

11.3.2 *Debt dynamics*

In general, public sector debt is sustainable if the government can generate sufficient revenue to service its debt future obligations without policy changes. Of course, a government's future revenue depends on its tax rates and the rate of economic growth. The sustainability of the government's debt burden also depends on the debt-to-GDP ratio because that ratio cannot rise indefinitely.

The change in a country's real total government debt at time t, ΔD_t, is the difference between real total government debt at time t, D_t, and at time $t-1$, D_{t-1}. Specifically, that difference depends on the real interest rate at time t, r_t, and the real government *primary budget* surplus (government receipts minus non-interest expenditures) at time t, S_t, as follows:

$$\Delta D_t = D_t - D_{t1} = r_t \cdot D_{t1} - S_t \qquad (11.1)$$

Putting everything in terms of their ratio to GDP_t transforms (11.1) to

$$D_t/GDP_t = D_{t1}/GDP_t + (r_t \cdot D_{t-1})/GDP_t - S_t/GDP_t \qquad (11.2)$$

$GDP_t = (1 + g_t) \, GDP_{t-1}$, where g_t is the annual growth rate of real GDP in period t. Therefore, we can rewrite equation (11.2) as

$$D_t/GDP_t = D_{t1}/[(1 + g_t) \, GDP_{t1}] + (r_t \cdot D_{t-1})/[(1 + g_t) \, GDP_{t1}] - S_t/GDP_t \qquad (11.3)$$

By shuffling terms, this equation can be more clearly written as

$$D_t/GDP_t = [(1 + r_t)/(1 + g_t)] \, (D_{t1}/GDP_{t-1}) - S_t/GDP_t \qquad (11.4)$$

Then, if we represent the ratios of each of the variables to GDP as their lower case equivalents, we end up with

$$d_t = [(1 + r_t)/(1 + g_t)] \, d_{t-1} - s_t \tag{11.5}$$

That is, for a given primary budget surplus and initial debt burden, the debt-to-GDP ratio d_t will rise if the real interest rate on debt r_t exceeds the growth in real GDP g_t.

A simple example using equation (11.5) shows why a high debt burden is problematic. Suppose a country has a debt burden equal to 100 percent of GDP ($d_{t-1} = 1$), the primary budget is in balance ($s_t = 0$), the real interest rate $r_t = 10\%$ and GDP growth $g_t = 2\%$. Then the its public sector debt grows by

$$d_t = [(1.10)/(1.02)]1.0 = 1.078 > d_{t-1} = 1.0 \tag{11.6}$$

That is, if $d_t > d_{t-1}$ year after year, the budget deficit as a percentage of GDP grows over time and the public debt ratio is not sustainable. On the other hand, if a country has a debt burden of only 50 percent ($d_{t-1} = 0.5$), the primary budget is a positive 4 percent ($s_t = 0.04$), the real interest rate is again 10 percent, and GDP growth is still 2 percent, then public debt as a percentage of GDP shrinks, and the public sector debt *is* sustainable. Specifically

$$\begin{aligned} d_t &= [(1.10)/(1.02)].5 - .04 \\ &= .5392 - .04 = .4992 < d_{t-1} = .5 \end{aligned} \tag{11.7}$$

Now $d_t < d_{t-1}$ and the deficit as a proportion of GDP declines. In other words, the deficit is *sustainable*. Thus, the smaller the debt burden and the larger the primary budget surplus, the more likely the government debt is sustainable.

This exercise is useful for analyzing Brazil's situation in 2004. Brazil's real interest rate on government debt had exceeded the growth of real GDP in nearly every year since 1995. On average, Brazil's average annual growth rate of real GDP has been about 2 percent since the mid-1980s, and, therefore real interest rates exceeded 10 percent per year. Higgins and Humpage (2004) assumed various interest rates,

Table 11.2   Changes in Brazil's Debt-to-GDP Ratio Assuming an Initial Debt Ratio of 57.8% and Primary Budget Surplus of 4.25% and Various Alternative Assumptions About Interest Rates and GDP Growth Rates.

Real interest rate (%)	Real GDP growth rate				
	2.0%	3.0%	3.5%	4.0%	4.5%
8.0	−11.2	−18.1	−21.2	−24.2	−27.0
9.0	−4.0	−11.6	−15.1	−18.4	−21.5
10.0	4.0	−4.5	−8.4	−12.0	−15.4
11.0	12.7	3.3	−1.0	−5.0	−8.8
12.0	22.2	11.9	7.2	2.7	−1.5
13.0	32.6	21.2	16.0	11.1	6.5

Source: Table 3 from Patrick C. Higgins and Owen F. Humpage (2004). "Walking on a Fence: Brazil's Public-Sector Debt", Policy Discussion Paper, No. 6, February, 2004.

economic growth rates, and primary budget surpluses for Brazil over the subsequent ten years, 2005 through 2014, in order to see under what circumstances Brazil's debt would be sustainable and, therefore, not likely to trigger an exchange rate crisis. Beginning with Brazil's 57.8 percent debt-to-*GDP* ratio and primary budget surplus of 4.25 percent at the end of 2003, Higgins and Humpage estimated the changes in the debt-to-*GDP* ratio under various assumed combinations of annual real *GDP* growth rates and annual real interest rates. The estimated percentage point changes are given in Table 11.2. It is clear from the table that Brazil's financial situation was dangerous. Slight variations in real interest rates and real *GDP* growth rates would critically shift Brazil's debt burden from sustainable to unsustainable.

A depreciation would lower all the numbers in Table 11.2, which implies that if the Brazilian real depreciates, the debt burden rises and become more difficult to sustain, all other things equal. In other words, in the case of Brazil in 2004, the financial crisis could have easily become a self-fulfilling prophecy.

Brazil seemed to be walking on a fence between sustainable and unsustainable public debt dynamics at the start of 2004. With high real interest rates over ten percent, the debt is only sustainable if economic growth is high. But, how can the economy grow rapidly with such high real interest rates? A lowering of real interest rates would benefit growth, but lower interest rates could also cause capital out-flows to increase and capital inflows to diminish, thus causing a possible depreciation and a rise in the debt burden. The hope was that the economy would grow faster and that growth-driven increases in tax revenues would improve the primary budget surplus enough to convince creditors that the government would be less prone to print money and that, therefore, they should accept lower interest rates. If Brazilian growth would be export driven, an appreciation of the Brazilian currency would be even more likely.

In sum, Brazil's balancing act between a rising or falling debt bur-den was entirely dependent on expectations. If the international capital markets came to expect the debt burden to spiral upward in the near future, there would most certainly be a sharp outflow of money from Brazil, causing a sharp depreciation in the Brazilian real and, most likely, a debt default. But, if creditors expected Brazil's to fully service its debt, then capital would continue to flow into Brazil, interest rates would fall, growth would pick up, tax revenues would grow, and the expectation of a decline in the debt burden would be equally self-fulfilling.

Fortunately, it was the second scenario that played out in 2005. The Brazilian economy grew by over five percent in real terms, inter-est rates declined somewhat, and the primary budget surplus actually grew to 5.5 percent of *GDP* at the start of 2005.[12] Brazil continued to accumulate reserves after 2005. You might check out how the Brazilian economy is performing today in terms of growth, unem-ployment, capital inflows, and the exchange rate.

11.4 The Russian Crisis

Not all currency crises occurred in developing economies. One of the more disruptive loan defaults and currency depreciations occurred in Russia in 1997. Russia is one of the sovereign countries that emerged from the political collapse of the USSR and the Eastern European

---

[12] *The Economist* (2005). "The Dangers of Tax and Spend", *The Economist*, 3 March 2005.

governments supported by the USSR. The fall of these communist regimes was followed by a variety of schemes to "reform", or *transition*, these economies from centrally planned communist regimes to more market oriented capitalist systems. By 1997, Russia had gone through seven years of *transition* when financial disaster struck. Russia's default on its foreign debt and the collapse of the ruble, the Russian currency, had all the characteristics of the currency crises in developing economies, but Russia was clearly a very different economy. It is, therefore, worthwhile examining this currency crises to see what are the fundamental similarities between the Russian and developing country currency crises.

11.4.1 *The Russian economy before 1990*

When Joseph Stalin rose to power in the Soviet Union in the late 1920s, he focused economic policy on achieving rapid economic growth. The Soviet development model was based on state ownership of all means of production and the central planning and control of all major economic decisions. What was produced, how it was produced, and who received the income were all decided by government bureaucrats according to a national plan. Table 11.3 shows that during the 1930s, when most of the *capitalist* economies were mired in the Great Depression, the Soviet economy grew rapidly. The growth was driven by very high rates of saving and investment. Saving was not entirely voluntary, however; rather, central planners ordered

Table 11.3   Soviet Union: Growth of GNP, Inputs, and Technology, 1928–1985.

	1928–1940	1940–1950	1950–1960	1960–1970	1970–1975	1975–1980	1980–1985
GNP	5.8%	2.2%	5.7%	5.2%	3.7%	2.6%	2.0%
Capital	9.0	0.4	9.5	8.0	7.9	6.8	6.3
Combined inputs	4.0	0.6	4.0	3.7	3.7	3.0	2.5
Total factor prod.	1.7	1.6	1.6	1.5	0.0	−0.4	−0.5
GNP per unit capital	−2.9	3.4	−3.5	2.6	−3.9	−3.9	−4.0

Source: Table 1 in Gur Ofer (1987). "Soviet Economic Growth: 1928–1985", *Journal of Economic Literature* 25: 1767–1833.

consumer goods to be produced in limited amounts, leaving consumers no alternative but to save.

The numbers presented in Table 11.3 may be somewhat optimistic, as more recent information about the true value of production now shows that pre-1990 data is likely to have been overstated. Soviet output growth was still impressive nevertheless. On the other hand, even this optimistic data shows how the Soviet model of economic development was not able to generate lasting economic growth. Notice that the rates of growth declined steadily from the 1950s to the 1980s. Notice, also, what brought about the decline in output growth. First of all, the productivity of factor inputs like labor and capital declined and eventually turned negative. By the late 1970s, output was growing more slowly than inputs, which means that it was taking increasing amounts of labor, capital, and other resources to produce the same amount of output. Secondly, the return to capital fell over time. Because the growth of capital exceeded the growth of other inputs, the marginal return to capital fell. Recall from Chapter 8 that permanent economic growth requires technological progress because even the highest rates of investment will be subject to diminishing returns.

11.4.2 *Transition*

The collapse of the Soviet system in 1990 and a transition to a market economy did not lead to a quick improvement in economic growth in Russia or any of the other former Soviet Republics, as some optimistic economists predicted. To the contrary, per capita real output declined sharply. Between 1991 and 1997, output in Russia fell by 40 percent. According to Dolinskava (2002), the factors that caused the gradual slowdown of Soviet economic growth before 1990 cannot explain this more recent sharp decline in per capita output. The output collapse during the transition was far too dramatic. After 1990 there was both a steep decline in the employment of factors and a decline in the overall productivity of the factors of production still employed.

Shifting from a centrally planned and state owned economy to a private market economy cannot occur overnight. Russia's state firms struggled, and many collapsed, when the support of the central government disappeared, and new private firms were slow to emerge. Would-be entrepreneurs were discouraged by the uncertainty of the reform process, and potential profits from investing in new firms were dubious because the incomes of consumers spiraled downward with rising unemployment. Capital from the state sector was not immediately useful in the private sector. In fact, according to Dolinskaya, "part of the capital stock inherited from the socialist era is so outmoded it will never be used again and thus has to be replaced, which requires time and resources".[13]

Another reason for the slow transition from state firms to new private firms was the breakdown of production networks caused by the transition from a centrally planned economy to a market economy. Blanchard and Kremer (1997) called this breakdown of economic relations among firms *disorganization*, as there was a long delay between the collapse of traditional relations between suppliers, final manufacturers, and distributors of products and the establishment of new market relationships between private firms. The legal environment did not permit reliable contract enforcement after 1990, and this made it difficult to carry out market transactions among firms that did not know each other. Many experts in economic reform had predicted that even though unemployment was likely to grow in the short run, at least economic reform would improve the efficiency with which the employed factors were used. Through 1997, this had not yet happened in Russia, however.

11.4.3 *Signs of hope in 1997*

By 1997, Russia's sharp economic decline seemed to have come to an end, and there were solid signs of a reversal in economic fortunes. Negotiations were completed to reschedule over $80 billion in debt payments, greatly easing Russia's lingering debt burden. International trade moved into balance, inflation was brought under control, the price of oil, Russia's largest export, rose to $23 per barrel, and the

---

[13] Irina Dolinskaya (2002). p. 156.

rate of economic growth was positive for the first time since the collapse of the Soviet government. With expectations that Russia's credit rating would soon be raised, Russian banks were finally able to expand their foreign borrowing and to expand domestic lending. The Russian Central Bank was successfully keeping the exchange rate within a narrow band of 5–6 rubles per dollar. There were still serious economic problems, however. According to Chiodo and Owyang (2002), only 40 percent of workers had paying full-time jobs, the government budget deficit was still large, and low real wages were holding down consumer demand.

Then, in late 1997, the Asian currency crisis spooked the international capital markets. Foreign lenders became more cautious, and Russia's central bank had to spend $6 billion to defend the ruble against speculators betting that the slowdown in capital inflows would result in a depreciation of the ruble. Russia's President Yeltsin added to the economic uncertainty by firing his entire cabinet in early 1998. There were further speculative attacks on the ruble in early 1998, forcing the Russian central bank to raise domestic interest rates from an already high 30 percent to over 50 percent, while also spending another $1 billion in dollar reserves for foreign exchange market intervention. When the US dollar price of oil fell later in the year, the heads of several Russian oil companies demanded a devaluation to increase the ruble value of their exports. Further speculative attacks hit the ruble despite the IMF's emergency aid package of nearly $5 billion in the summer of 1998. Finally, after Russian stock, bond, and currency markets suffered further large losses in August of 1998, the government officially devalued the ruble, and when even that new rate proved difficult to defend, it let the ruble float. The ruble ended up depreciating from about 6 rubles per dollar at the start of 1998 to nearly 30 per dollar by the end of the year. Real output declined by five percent compared to 1997.

11.4.4 *Explaining the Russian crisis*

A number of factors contributed to the 1998 Russian currency crisis. The contagion of the Asian crisis helped to fuel uncertainty about the ruble in 1997. There were also fundamental economic disequilibria, most notably the government budget deficit, the uncertainty about the price of oil and export earnings, and the continued difficulties in creating private employment to replace the jobs lost by the collapse of the government owned sector of the economy. The political crisis in 1998 added to the uncertainty and probably reduced the government's credibility and, therefore, willingness to endure the austerity necessary to defend the ruble. And the translation of the ruble collapse into a financial collapse that caused further declines in output after the economy had shown some modest tendency to turn around in 1997 was similar to the financial crises triggered by currency depreciations in Mexico, Asia, and Argentina.

After 2000, Russia achieved some encouraging economic growth, driven in recent years by the sharp increase in the price of oil, which surged to above \$60 per barrel in 2006 and briefly reached \$150 in 2008. The export surge has permitted Russia to accumulate large foreign reserves, which reduces the likelihood of a speculative attack in the future. Interest rates on ruble loans have fallen to more normal levels, thus permitting investment to grow and making it less necessary for domestic investors to borrow abroad to finance their projects. Of course, it is still early to tell how Russia's dependence on resource exports will affect its economy after the 2008 global financial crisis.

11.5 Three Generations of Crisis Models

A currency crisis is the result of a sudden large outflow of capital because wealth holders want to change the currency denomination of their holdings. This might occur because investors fear that the currency will soon depreciate. A large shift in wealth from assets denominated in one currency to assets in another currency is sometimes referred to as a *speculative attack*.

The standard open-economy macroeconomic models, like the Mundell–Fleming model or the aggregate demand/aggregate supply model, cannot explain such sudden speculative attacks and currency crises. Macroeconomic models suggest gradual adjustments, but speculative attacks cause large sudden changes in key macroeconomic variables. Speculative attacks can cause recessions, inflationary episodes, and widespread defaults in the financial, industrial, commercial, and government sectors of the economy. The need to explain the symptoms and remedies of currency crises has led to the development of models that incorporate fiscal deficits, monetary policies, expectations, and financial markets. These models usually also incorporate the concept of purchasing power parity as the long-run determinant of the exchange rate. The models have been categorized into three generations, each of which focuses on certain aspects of currency crises.

11.5.1 *First generation models*

First generation models of currency crises date from the early 1980s, when it seemed that defaults on foreign debt and sudden currency crashes stemmed from the excessive accumulation of government debt and the lack of sustainability of the government budget, all brought to a sudden crisis by the drastic tightening of world financial markets.[14] Large budget deficits eventually require their *monetization* when the government can no longer tax or borrow enough to cover the debt service. The monetary expansion tends to depreciate the currency. A speculative attack occurs in these models when the central bank's store of reserves is judged to be too small relative to the perceived imbalances in the foreign accounts, and a default becomes likely. These imbalances may be long-term in nature, as in the case where current trends in foreign obligations and trade flows are projected to be unsustainable, or they may be short-term in nature, as in the case of mismatches in the currency denominations or the maturities of outstanding debt. These first generation models in effect attribute currency crises to governments' inattention to fundamentals, suggesting that the way to avoid crises is to keep fiscal policy under control and to prevent central banks from monetizing government debt. These models often lead to the conclusion that countries should reduce government expenditures, reform their tax systems,

---

[14] Two noted first-generation models are Paul Krugman (1979) and Robert P. Flood and Peter M. Garber (1984).

and establish independent central banks that have price stability as their sole purpose.

The first generation models capture perhaps the most important cause of currency crises, which is that fixed exchange rates prevented the economy from gradually changing in line with economic fundamentals, thus making an eventual crash effectively the only way that the economy would ultimately adjust to the accumulated gradual changes in fundamentals. No one disputes that fundamental economic conditions, such as the fiscal balance, monetary policy, inflation, productivity growth, etc., are important determinants of currency crises. However, the first generation models have some shortcomings. For one thing, the models hypothesize that there is some moment in time when people's expectations suddenly change and they suddenly raise the perceived probability that a default or speculative attack will occur. Yet, the models that we now classify as first-generation crisis models fail to explain the timing of such shifts in expectations. Why is it that seemingly similar conditions trigger a crisis in one country but not another? Secondly, the first generation models do not explain why currency crises often spread to neighboring countries. For example, Mexico's steep devaluation in 1994 caused the demand for many other Latin American currencies to decline sharply as well, a phenomenon that was quickly labeled the "tequila effect" in honor of Mexico's national drink. Early crisis models had nothing to say about such cross-border *contagion*.

11.5.2 *Second generation models*

After the 1994 Mexican crisis, newer crisis models sought to explain more about why and when crises occur. The newer models also sought to address the issue of *contagion* by explaining why a currency crisis in one country so often results in crises in other countries. Contagion is best described as a strong cross-country correlation between asset prices or financial flows following some macroeconomic or financial shock in one country or a small group of countries. A new generation of crisis models was developed to better capture the decisions of government officials when faced with speculative attacks on their currencies. These models came to be known as *second generation* crisis models.

Second generation models assume that governments are technically able to defend fixed exchange rates, perhaps by using politically unpopular policies such as higher interest rates, tight monetary policy, or decreased government expenditures, but policymakers may find that it is politically easier to let the exchange rates change. These models suggest that policymakers will continue to defend their currencies only for as long as the required policies are not too costly in political and economic terms, which thus permits fundamental imbalances to grow for some time, but eventually the situation leads policymakers to give up and let the currency float. At that time, because of accumulated imbalances, there is usually a rather substantial change in the exchange rate. These models' emphasis on domestic political conditions captures the political nature of the choices surrounding the trilemma. Also, differences in political conditions and systems across countries can then help to explain why similar economic conditions cause a depreciation in one country but not in another.

The second generation models also explain contagion. For example, a model by Eichengreen, Rose, and Wyposz (1997) distinguishes several channels through which a currency crisis in one country increases the probability of a crisis in other countries. First, a sharp devaluation in one country can affect other countries through changing trade flows, which alter the balance of payments accounts and the supply and demand for other currencies. A devaluation in one country can also affect other currencies purely through expectations because people recognize that the same conditions that triggered the collapse in one country also exist in other countries. Dornbusch *et al.* (2000) suggest that financial links between countries transmit currency crises by altering the availability of trade credits, reducing foreign direct investment, and discouraging other capital flows. The spread of a crisis depends on the degree of financial integration; the greater the integration, the more closely the value of assets move in tandem across countries, and the more likely a sudden change in asset values in one country will affect asset values in other countries.

The basic logic of these second generation models is that contagion is driven by changing perceptions of the political costs of the economic choices and consequences. These models do not necessarily assume irrational behavior on the part of investors and traders, even though the term "contagion" suggests some type of irrational overreaction.

11.5.3 *Third generation crisis models*

The first two generations of models do not capture another common feature of currency crises, which is that they often turn into full-fledged financial crises. Currency crises are not always followed by the freedom to pursue macroeconomic policies, as second-generation models suggest is what drove the decision to let exchange rates to float. Nor do the large changes in exchange rates that characterize currency crises necessarily bring the economy back toward a macroeconomic equilibrium. Rather, currency crises in developing economies are often followed by recession, unemployment, bankruptcies, and sharp declines in incomes. These sudden economic collapses have been called *sudden stops* in the literature.

Pioneering third-generation models by McKinnon and Pill (1999) and Corsetti *et al.* (2001) argue that implicit loan guarantees by the government or international agencies like the IMF or World Bank promote excessively risky foreign borrowing. Then, when borrowers inevitably default, capital flows reverse themselves, and governments are forced to let the exchange rate depreciate, balance sheet effects undermine the health of the economy. Specifically, currency mismatches on the balance sheets of major domestic borrowers, which may include the financial institutions themselves, cause numerous shifts from solvency to bankruptcy in the banking sector, a sharp decline in domestic investment, and an economic recession.

Third generation models show that a currency crisis can trigger a domestic economic collapse even when there are no defaults. For example, Mendoza and Smith (2002, 2007) show that the mechanics of financial markets can cause shifts in investment flows, such as when changes in asset prices trigger margin calls. Sudden stops can also be caused by trade restrictions or high trade costs. For example, Martin and Rey (2006) develop a model in which a sudden change in asset prices affects domestic demand much more when international trade is restricted.

11.5.4 *Which generation of models is most useful?*

The three generations of models suggest four factors that can cause currency crises. Growing public and private debt, changes in expectations, the condition of the financial sector, and a fixed exchange rate system can combine to cause a currency crisis followed by a financial crisis. These factors seem to be closely correlated with actual crises and the magnitude of crises. Krugman (2000) surveyed the literature and concluded that academic opinion seems to favor the second-generation "self-fulfilling" models in which expectations play a role because these models explain contagion.

On the other hand, if politics play a role, as many second-generation models assume, then changes in expectations may not be necessary to trigger a crisis. Rational political calculations may determine when a government abandons a pegged exchange rate and permits a rapid depreciation of the currency. Finally, the coexistence of currency and financial crises in most currency episodes since 1982 validates the third-generation models. Therefore, currency crises need to be analyzed from all three perspectives.

11.6 To Fix or to Float?

The discussion of foreign exchange crises in this and the previous chapters suggests that they were often caused by failed attempts by policy makers to maintain the policies necessary to keep exchange rates fixed in the face of changing economic conditions and expectations. Indeed, it is difficult to keep exchange rates from changing in "an internationally integrated world economy". It is important to note that in many cases the sudden change in the likelihood of a foreign exchange depreciation that triggers a currency depreciation and subsequent financial crises. Recall that in 1982, the main trigger of the defaults was the shift in monetary policy in the United States and other developed economies. In this light, the decision whether "to fix or to float" must take into consideration the integrated nature of the modern global economy. To avoid exchange rate crises and financial crises, it is not enough to keep one's own house in order.

11.6.1 *Advantages of floating*

In respect of the trilemma, more and more governments have chosen to let exchange rates float, even though most floats are "dirty floats" that still involve substantial amounts of official transactions and other forms of government intervention.[15] Many countries have decided that only by dropping their stated commitment to a fixed exchange rate can they simultaneously pursue economic policies to deal with their unique domestic needs and political interests while also linking their economies more closely to the dynamic global economy. Floating exchange rates also eliminate the perception that the government guarantees the fixed exchange rate, and potential borrowers and lenders are more likely to correctly assess the risks associated with international investment. The switch to floating exchange rates by governments interested in keeping their economies linked to the rest of the world calls to mind Milton Friedman's words at the start of this chapter: "How many more fiascos will it take before responsible people are finally convinced that a system of pegged exchange rates is not a satisfactory financial arrangement?"[16]

Friedman argued that countries with independent political systems will inevitably end up with economic policies that reflect domestic political pressures but conflict with the goal of maintaining a fixed exchange rate. Thus, he reasoned, in a global economy a fixed exchange rate will always fail eventually. Experience seems to support

---

[15] The continued intervention in foreign exchange markets by governments who claim to have floating exchange rates is described in Guillermo A. Calvo and Carmen M. Reinhart (2002).

[16] Milton Friedman (1992), op. cit.

Friedman's conclusion. Recall that Obstfeld and Rogoff (1995) observed that there were just six major economies with open capital markets that had been able to keep their currencies fixed to one of the world's major currencies for at least five years: Austria, Hong Kong, Luxembourg, the Netherlands, Saudi Arabia, and Thailand.

11.6.2 *Advantages of fixed exchange rates*

A fixed exchange rate still has its attractions, however. At the end of the 19th century, when exchange rates of most countries remained fixed for over thirty years under the gold standard, investment flows to the world's poorest economies were much higher than they were at the end of the 20th century.[17] At the start of this chapter there was also a quote of Paul Volcker, the former Chairman of the Federal Reserve Bank of the United States and noted financial expert: "I think the idea of a small country freely floating its exchange rate is unworkable."[18]

It is worth reading the full context of Volcker's quote. From the same source, a more complete version of Volcker's views on floating exchange rates is

> The exchange rate is a multilateral phenomenon. There are a lot of sides to it. You cannot float and have other people fixed. We cannot fix and have other people float. There has to be some coherence in the system. I do not think there is any coherence in the system now, and these people in the Asian countries are not going to be able to pick a sensible exchange rate. Conceptually, it is easy to think of Mexico with a fixed dollar rate because so much of its trade is with the United States. But what do you do if you are Thailand or Indonesia? A third of your trade is with Japan and 30 percent is with the United States and 25 percent is with Europe and 10 percent is with each other. You have nothing obvious to fix to.[19]

---

[17] See Maurice Obstfeld and Alan M. Taylor (2001) and Robert E. Lucas, Jr. (1990).
[18] Paul A. Volcker (1999). p. 268.
[19] Paul A. Volcker (1999). p. 268.

In short, floating rates are not a good idea, but what else can a country do!

Fixed exchange rates serve to discipline policy makers and prevent inflationary monetary policies. A research paper by the International Monetary Fund examined the economic performances of all member countries (most non-communist countries) over the 30-year period 1960–1990 and found that countries with floating exchange rates tended to have higher rates of inflation than countries with fixed exchange rates.[20] Specifically, over the 30-year period, countries with floating exchange rates averaged 16 percent annual inflation while countries that fixed their exchange rates averaged eight percent inflation. Recall that Argentina's replacement of its politicized central bank with a currency board was enacted to stop inflation.

11.6.3 *The advantage goes to...*

The same IMF study that found floating exchange rates were correlated with higher inflation rates also found that countries with floating exchange rates grew faster than countries with fixed exchange rates. Specifically, they found that countries with floating exchange rates had higher productivity growth, which, they argued, was partially due to the fact that the floating exchange rate countries traded more; exports grew three percentage points faster, on average, in countries with floating exchange rates. Van den Berg and Lewer (2007) surveyed hundreds of published statistical regressions relating trade and growth, and they find that, on average, economic growth is about 0.15 percent faster for every one percentage point increase in the growth of international trade. These findings are intriguing because there are other studies that have found that exchange rate risk, which should be higher under floating exchange rates, discourages trade. Perhaps the trilemma explains this dilemma because floating exchange rates are actually less disruptive of international trade and economic growth, on average, than the occasional devastating exchange rate crises that disrupt fixed exchange rate systems.

---

[20] Atish R. Ghosh *et al.* (1996).

So, when inflation is the overriding concern, a fixed exchange rate system like a currency board may be the best choice. However, if unemployment or slow economic growth are the overriding concerns, then floating exchange rates may be the appropriate exchange rate regime choice. However, one can think of many exceptions to these rules. In fact, the world has frequently shifted between fixed and floating exchange rates, and recent central bank actions and government decisions show that there is still no general consensus on the superiority of fixed or floating exchange rates.

11.7   Can Large Reserves Defeat the Trilemma?

After the 1997 exchange rate crises, many countries began building up their stocks of foreign reserves. They used central bank intervention to keep their currencies undervalued and began running persistent trade surpluses. These trade surpluses have, of course, been the flip side of the recent large US current account deficits which we discussed in Chapter 2. Some view the undervalued currencies as an attempt to boost employment and economic growth through exports. But, the extraordinary accumulation of reserves may not have been undertaken solely for stimulating exports. Given the huge costs of the recent foreign exchange crises in terms of lost economic growth, the East Asian countries may simply be accumulating reserves to protect their economies from exchange rate crises.

11.7.1   *Large reserves discourage speculation*

The massive reserves are thought to empower countries to credibly fix exchange rates, regardless of other economic policies, because potential speculators would understand that their chances of gaining from a speculative attack are greatly reduced. Aizenman and Marion (2002) show that countries that are growing fast and are well governed opt for larger reserve holdings than countries experiencing political instability or poor economic prospects. Their model illustrates that rapidly growing and well-governed countries have more to lose from a financial crisis, so they are more willing to bear the cost of accumulating reserves. Aizeman and Marion also argue that reserves serve as a signal of financial prudence for countries that are already well governed. Poorly governed countries get less of a boost to international investment from reserves because investors know that so many other things can go wrong that the reserves do little to reduce uncertainty and exchange rate risk for the country's assets.

The accumulation of large foreign exchange reserves to protect against sudden exchange rate changes also reflects the fact that exchange rate crises are not always caused by faulty policies in the countries that suffer speculative attacks on their currencies. As Frankel and Roubini (2001) point out, shifts in developed country macroeconomic policies have often been the cause of developing country financial crises. They mention, among other events, the tightening of US monetary policy as the cause of the many 1982 crises throughout the developing world. Interestingly, they also point to the easing of monetary policy in the United States and the decline in US interest rates as helping to ease the 1997 Asian crisis. To the extent that domestic policies and institutions cannot entirely prevent exchange rate crises, developing countries interested in controlling their currencies' value have little option but to run persistent trade surpluses and to accumulate large stocks of foreign currencies and assets to protect against changes in the global financial environment.

11.7.2 *Reserve accumulation may destabilize the global economy*

The accumulation of reserves may, in the long run, end up undermining exchange rate stability, however. The large reserves on the part of developing countries implies equally large increases in foreign debt in the developed economies. The United States, the country whose currency serves as the reserve currency for most countries, is the largest net debtor in the world. Eventually countries may no longer want to hold US dollars for fear that the huge US debt will cause the value of the dollar to fall. Will China, Korea, Japan, and other Asian central banks continue to accumulate US dollars and US Treasury bonds, or will these central banks diversify their reserves by acquiring euros, Swiss francs, British pounds, Japanese yen, or other foreign currencies? In early 2009, the Governor of the Bank of China, Zhou Xiaocguan, said China was studying the possibility of diversifying China's $2 trillion portfolio of official foreign assets. The history of the international financial system in the next four chapters addresses the role of the US dollar as the world's reserve currency and the likelihood that the euro or some international currency like the SDR will become the reserve currency.

11.8 Summary and Conclusions

One of the features of the international financial system is its propensity to experience exchange rate crises, which usually cause accompanying financial crises and lengthy economic depressions. On the other hand, the rapid growth of reserves in developing countries within the past ten years is a new phenomenon that may end up reducing the number of crises. Macroeconomic management, as measured by budget deficits and inflation rates, also seems to have improved in many developing economies. Of course, it is much too early to accurately assess the outcome of these shifts in recent developing country economic policies. The saying that "the more things change, the more they remain the same" may still apply.

In a more general context, the exchange rate crises over the past three decades are just the latest clashes with international finance's centuries-old nemesis, the trilemma. The next three chapters review the history of global financial systems. You will see that the trilemma has often forced countries to endure shifts in their exchange rate regimes. More important, you will see that the trilemma has been one of the most important influences in shaping recent human history.

Key Terms and Concepts

Asian tigers	Debt burden	Outward orientation
Capital flight	Dirty float	Overvaluation
Chaebol	Disorganization	Primary budget deficit
Currency contagion	Economic transition	Reserve currency
Crony capitalism	Financial crisis	Second generation crisis
Currency board	First-generation crisis	Speculative attack
Currency crisis	Monetization of debt	Sudden stop
Currency mismatch	New Asian tigers	Sustainable debt
Currency speculation	Original sin	Third generation crisis

Chapter Questions and Problems

1. Explain the key features of each of the three generations of currency crisis models. Which of the three models best describes each of the financial crises discussed in this chapter?

2. Why did the exchange rate crises turn into financial crises in Mexico and East Asia? Why did the sharp decline in the value of the national currency not trigger a boom in exports that stimulated the overall economy, as some exchange rate models suggest, but instead caused a sharp downturn in investment and economic activity? Could the financial crises have been avoided?

3. Explain how Argentina's currency board functioned. Why could the currency board system not guarantee exchange rate stability? Explain why the system failed in Argentina in 2001. Is there any way to permanently fix a country's exchange rate?

4. Discuss crony capitalism. Why did crony capitalism in Korea help to trigger a speculative attack on the won? Does crony capitalism occur in any other countries?

5. Does the United States suffer from "original sin"? Explain what the term "original sin" means in international finance, and why is it important for understanding currency crises?

6. Explain Brazil's tightrope walk between currency crisis and sustainable foreign debt. Describe exactly how it all turned out.

7. Is the accumulation of foreign reserves a cost-effective way to insure against speculative attacks and currency crises? Carefully weigh the pros and cons of accumulating large foreign exchange reserves in reaching your conclusion.

8. Recall that under the Brady Plan, debtor countries agreed to carry out a variety of economic reforms under supervision of the IMF allegedly in order to improve their ability to service their foreign debt. Despite undertaking many of the required reforms, Mexico again suffered a currency collapse and financial crisis in 1994. Did any of the economic reforms contribute to the new crisis? Hint: Review the reforms and the description of the causes of the 1994 crisis.

References

Azeman, J and N Marion (2002). The high demand for international reserves in the Far East: what is going on? *World Bank Research Observer*, 17(3), 370–400.

Barro, RJ (2001). Economic growth in East Asia before and after the financial crisis. *NBER Working Paper W8330*, June.

Barry E, A Rose and C Wyposz (1997). Contagious currency crises. *Working Paper*, March.

Blanchard, OJ and M Kremer (1997). Disorganization. *Quarterly Journal of Economics*, 112(4), 1091–1126.

Calvo, GA and CM Reinhart (2002). Fear of floating. *Quarterly Journal of Economics*, 117(2), 379–408.

Chiodo, AJ and MT Owyang (2002). A case study of a currency crisis: The Russian default of 1998. *Federal Reserve Bank of St. Louis Review*, 84(6), November/December, 7–17.

Corsetti, G, P Pesenti and N Roubini (2001). Fundamental determinants of the Asian crisis: The role of financial fragility and external imbalances. *Regional and Global Capital Flows: Macroeconomic Causes and Consequences*. T Ito and AO Krueger (eds.), pp. 11–44. Chicago: University of Chicago Press.

Dolinskaya, I (2002). Explaining Russia's output collapse. *IMF Staff Papers*, 49(2), 155–174.

Dornbusch, R, YC Park and S Claessens (2000). Contagion: Understanding how it spreads. *The World Bank Research Observer*, 15, 177–197.

Flood, RP and PM Garber (1984). Collapsing exchange rate regimes: Some linear examples. *Journal of International Economics*, 17, 1–13.

Frankel, J and N Roubini (2002). The role of industrial country policies in emerging market crises. *Financial and Currency Crises in Emerging Market Economies*, M Feldstein (ed.). Chicago, IL: University of Chicago Press.

Frankel, JA and SL Schmukler (1996). Country fund discounts and the Mexican crisis in December 1994: Did local residents turn pessimistic before international investors? *International Finance Discussion* Paper #563, Board of Governors of the Federal Reserve System, September.

Friedman, M (1992). Deja vu in currency markets. *Wall Street Journal*, 22 September.

Ghosh, AR, A-M Gulde, JD Ostry and H Wolf (1996). *Does the Exchange Rate Regime Matter for Inflation and Growth?* Washington, DC, International Monetary Fund.

Goldfajn, I and ER Guardia (2003). Fiscal rules and debt sustainability in Brazil. *Technical Notes, No. 39* (July), Central Bank of Brazil.

Higgins, PC and OF Humpage (2004). Walking on a fence: Brazil's public-sector debt. *Federal Reserve Bank of Cleveland Policy Discussion Paper*, No. 6, February.

Joshua A and N Marion (2002). Foreign exchange reserves in East Asia: Why the high demand? Federal Reserve Bank of San Francisco Economic Letter, April.

Krugman, P (1979). A model of balance of payments crises. *Journal of Money, Credit, and Banking*, 11, 311–3125.

Krugman, P (2000). Introduction. *Currency Crises*. P Krugman (ed.), p. 4. Chicago: University of Chicago Press.

Krueger, AO and J Yoo (2001). Chaebol capitalism and the currency-financial crisis in Korea. *Paper Presented at the NBER Asian Crisis Conference*, February 9.

Lucas, Jr. RE (1990). Why doesn't capital flow from rich to poor countries? *American Economic Review*, 90(3), 92–96.

Martin, P and H Rey (2006). Globalization and emerging markets: With or without crash? *American Economic Review*, 96(5), 1631–1651.

McKinnon, RL and H Pill (1999). Exchange-rate regimes for emerging markets: Moral hazard and international overborrowing. *Oxford Review of Economic Policy*, 15(3), 19–38.

Mendoza, EG and KA Smith (2002). Margin calls, trading costs, and asset prices in emerging markets: The financial mechanics of the 'Sudden Stop' phenomenon. *NBER Working Paper 9286*.

Mendoza, EG and KA Smith (2007). Quantitative implication of a debt–deflation theory of sudden stops and asset prices. *Journal of International Economics*, 61, 169–185.

Obstfeld, M and AM Taylor (2001). Globalization and capital markets. *Paper Presented at the NBER Conference Globalization in Historical Perspective*. Santa Barbara, May 4–5.

Ofer, G (1987). Soviet economic growth: 1928–1985. *Journal of Economic Literature*, 25, 1767–1833.

Park, YC and J-W Lee (2001). Recovery and sustainability in East Asia. *NBER Working Paper W8373*, July.

Van den Berg, H and JJ Lewer (2007). *International trade and Economic Growth*. Armonk. NY: M. E. Sharpe.

Van Wincoop, E and K-M Yi (2000). Asia crisis postmortem: Where did the money go and did the United States benefit? *Federal Reserve Bank of New York Economic Policy Review*, September, 51–70.

Volcker, PA (1999). A perspective on financial crises. *Rethinking the International Monetary System*. JS Little and GP Olivei (eds.). Conference Series No. 43, Federal Reserve Bank of Boston, June 1999.

Williamson, J (1995). *What Role for Currency Boards?* Washington, DC: Institute for International Economics.

Chapter 12

The International Financial System: The International Gold Standard, 1870–1914

It is the issue of 1776 over again. Our ancestors, when but three millions in number had the courage to declare their political independence of every other nation; shall we, their descendants, when we have grown to seventy millions, declare that we are less independent than our forefathers? ...instead of having a gold standard because England has, we will restore bimetallism, and then let England have bimetallism because the United States has it.

(William Jennings Bryan, July 9, 1896.[1])

Over the past four decades, exchange rates between the major currencies of the world have been allowed to fluctuate in response to the forces of demand and supply. We have become accustomed to this order, and we read the daily reports of exchange rate changes much as we read the daily stock market reports. The international monetary

---

[1] From Bryan's "Cross of Gold" speech at the 1896 Democratic Convention, Chicago. Excerpts from the speech are given in the Appendix to this chapter.

system did not always operate this way, however. There have been periods when exchange rates were held constant by a variety of institutions and rules. In fact, over the last century, we had several international financial arrangements that were very different from today's system.

For example, during the latter part of the 19th century and the beginning of the 20th century, nearly all governments followed the rules of a system called the *Gold Standard*. Under the order of the Gold Standard, the values of most currencies remained fixed to each other. Exchange rates never changed or fluctuated. World War I forced most government to suspend the rules of the Gold Standard, and after the war, exchange rates were initially left free to fluctuate. By the middle of the 1920s, however, most countries had gone back to following the rules of the Gold Standard. Less than ten years later, by the early 1930s, the rules of the Gold Standard were abandoned, as each country found it impossible to adhere to the Gold Standard's rules while also dealing with the widespread unemployment and income declines of the Great Depression.

After World War II, the *Bretton Woods* system mandated that each of the currencies of the major free market economies of the world be *pegged* to the US dollar. This system coincided with 25 years of the fastest economic growth the world has ever experienced. Nevertheless, in the early 1970s most major market economies abandoned the Bretton Woods system in favor of *floating* exchange rates. In recent decades, more and more economies moved toward more flexible exchange rates. Fixed exchange rates are not entirely out of favor, however. In 2002, 12 European Union countries formally abandoned their national currencies in favor of the ultimate fixed exchange rate: a *single currency* called the euro.

These different experiences do not seem to have brought us closer to a consensus on what would be the best exchange rate arrangement. Our present mixture of floating and manipulated exchange rates has permitted the continued growth of international trade and investment. But, as Chapters 10 and 11 described, there have been many exchange rate crises that turned into financial crises and deep

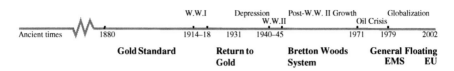

Figure 12.1 A time line of international financial orders.

economic recessions. We now wonder if there is not some better system than today's improvised mixture of exchange rate arrangements.

This is the first of four chapters that detail the history foreign exchange systems and exchange rate policies over the past 100 years. The time line in Fig. 12.1 outlines the plot of our story. This historical account will make it clear that there were advantages and disadvantages to each of the exchange rate arrangements. Some worked better than others, but all ultimately failed and were replaced. The 2008 global financial meltdown has led to urgent calls for reform of the current system. History does not reveal a clear winner.

Chapter Goals

1. Outline the development of money from ancient times to the present.
2. Explain why Britain adopted a gold standard rather than a silver standard.
3. Discuss the origins of what became the International Gold Standard.
4. Detail the "order" of the 1870–1924 International Gold Standard.
5. Explain how the system actually worked.
6. Present the interesting case of the 1896 US Presidential election, in which the Gold Standard became a populist political issue.
7. Grade the Gold Standard and position it within the trilemma.

12.1   Comparing International Monetary Arrangements

Economic historians tend to focus their attention not only on economic outcomes, but also on the incentives that caused the economic system to function as it did. In the case of the international financial system, incentives have seldom consisted of formal rules, laws, and organizational procedures like those that were explicitly set by the delegates to the 1944 Bretton Woods Conference. Most often, the incentives that guided behavior and expectations in the international financial system were little more than informal understandings among policy makers and traditions that were followed because individual governments found it to their advantage to do so or because they had no other option given their socio-political situation. Still, explicitly or implicitly, each system had its rules.

12.1.1   *The rules of the game*

The informal or formal incentives and rules that guide the monetary system are normally referred to as the international financial *order*. According to the Nobel laureate Robert Mundell:

> An *order*...is a framework of laws, conventions, regulations, and mores that establish the setting of the system and the understanding of the environment by the participants in it. A monetary order is to a monetary system somewhat like a *constitution* is to a political system.[2]

John Maynard Keynes referred to the international monetary *order* as *the rules of the game* when he described the unwritten rules that policy makers followed during the time of the Gold Standard. This latter term is still often used by financial economists.

---

[2] Robert A. Mundell (1972). p. 92.

12.1.2 *A Framework for judging the international monetary system*

In order to compare and judge the many exchange rate arrangements and other government rules, laws, and regulations that have defined the international monetary system over the centuries, we must first decide on a set of criteria for determining how well a particular monetary order enabled the international monetary system to function. Economists normally judge economic policies by how they affect human welfare. Therefore, in the case of an international monetary system, we should judge how well the economies participating in the system were able to maintain full employment in the short run and how fast they grew and raised people's standards of living in the long run.

There are, no doubt, other criteria that come to mind. For example, we might also judge the performance of the international monetary system according to how well individual economies were able to integrate into the international economy and to what extent the international monetary arrangement permitted them to engage in welfare-enhancing international trade and investment. Recall that many delegates at the Bretton Woods conference were interested in restoring international trade and investment as a specific strategy for establishing a lasting peace after the end of World War II.

The international system should also be examined for the extent to which it permits individual countries to address what they see as their particular economic, social, political, and institutional goals. For example, the macroeconomic models in Chapters 7–9 detailed how different international financial orders affect policymakers' ability to use fiscal and monetary policies to meet national economic objectives such as price stability and full employment.

Finally, some economic historians have judged the international financial system by how the gains and losses from expanding international transactions are distributed among countries and among persons within each country. Recent discussions of the merits of globalization suggest that we are still not in agreement on whether globalization is a good thing for everyone; open-economy macroeconomics suggests that the international monetary order has a lot to do with how globalization affects specific individuals and groups of individuals. Also, our financial history clearly shows that unless all countries are satisfied with the international financial order, individual governments will be more likely to adopt policies that violate the order. Hence, how well a particular order distributes the gains from globalization is critical to its long-run viability.

In this and the following three chapters, we will base our judgments of each international financial system on the following criteria:

1. Were individual economies able to maintain output levels at full employment?
2. How fast were economies able to raise their citizens' living standards?
3. Were countries able to expand international trade and investment?
4. Could governments effectively apply economic policies, such as monetary and fiscal policies, to address domestic issues?
5. Did the system encourage sound monetary policies and price stability?
6. Were the economic costs and benefits evenly spread across countries?
7. Was the system largely self-regulating or did it require active support by its members?

Each system, and the order or rules of the game that shaped that system, will be evaluated according to these seven criteria.

12.2 International Finance Before the Gold Standard

For much of human history, plunder and pillage of neighboring communities was a common method for raising one group's economic welfare. Such one-way transfers did not require the use of money, just an army sufficiently large to subdue another society. However, there is ample evidence suggesting that for thousands of years separate groups and nations have also often found it convenient to engage in voluntary and mutually-beneficial transactions. When one group's army was not large and the outcome of an invasion was in some doubt, most groups of people came to the conclusion that it would be preferable to engage in voluntary exchanges. Voluntary exchanges between nations and regions are not easy to carry out, however.

Voluntary exchanges can be carried out using barter, which is the direct exchange of one product for another. In recent millennia, intermediate commodities have been increasingly used to carry out international transactions. People have discovered that barter is a very costly method for exchanging products because every seller has to find someone who has precisely the thing the seller wants to acquire and is willing to exchange them for precisely the things the seller wants to sell, all at precisely the moment the seller wants to make the exchange. The coordination problems and costs of barter become especially onerous as economies develop and produce greater varieties of products, as exchanges are carried out over greater distances, and as people seek to store their increased wealth in safe but liquid assets. As countries develop economically, money is increasingly used to carry out transactions.

12.2.1 *The origin of money*

Thousands of years ago, people began to use scarce commodities that could serve as an intermediate *medium of exchange* and also as a *store of value*. Such commodities, or money, enabled people to exchange a much greater variety of products among a greater variety of people with wants and needs that extended over longer time horizons. When they became widely used, such commodities also served as *units of account* in which the values of the products bought and sold were valued. Commodities that simultaneously serve as medium of exchange, store of value, and unit of account are commonly referred to as *money*.

Precious metals have most often served as money because they are scarce, high in value relative to their weight, and pretty much indestructible. The benefits of using money over simple barter are so great that people resorted to using many other things as money when precious metals were not available. Some small island communities used rare seashells. In World War II prisoner of war camps, cigarettes were used as money. In war-ravaged Germany after World War II, when strict price controls were in effect and the new German monetary system had not yet been created, cigarettes, nylon stockings, and Parker fountain pens circulated as money. Today, amazingly, colorful and beautifully printed pieces of paper circulate as money.

Throughout history, regions and political states tended to develop their own moneys. The development of different moneys complicated international trade because exporting and importing products across borders came to involve not only the movement of products, but also the exchange of moneys. When money came into general use and traders crossed borders to carry out exchanges of products, foreign exchange markets naturally came into being. The manner in which foreign exchange markets operate and how different moneys are exchanged helps to define a particular *international financial system*.

12.2.2 *Ancient financial arrangements*

Silver ingots whose weight and purity were guaranteed by the state were used as money in Babylon as early as 2,000 B.C. Rare cowrie shells from islands in the Indian Ocean were used three thousand years ago from China to Africa. The first crude minted coins date back to 687 B.C. from the city-state Lydia in Asia Minor (present-day Turkey). In ancient times, the international monetary system came to consist of a variety of minted coins plus an informal network of moneychangers located in the main cities where merchants from other cities and states frequently traded goods. In some political jurisdictions, moneychangers were allowed to operate freely, in others they were restricted, and in some places they were banned. Of course, in those cities where foreign trade flourished, moneychangers must have been able to operate relatively freely; payments between merchants from different places could not have been made without them.

The rise of the Roman Empire, which brought the entire Mediterranean region under the jurisdiction of one political power, greatly advanced the use of money to carry out exchanges. The political capital of the empire, Rome, ran a considerable trade deficit with the rest of the Empire, which was covered by the inflow of tax revenues from the provinces throughout the Mediterranean region.[3] Roman taxes were required to be paid in the form of coinage, a regulation that greatly expanded the use of money throughout the economy since taxpayers had to earn coins in order to pay taxes. The eventual control of the Mediterranean region by the Romans created a large free trade area with a single currency. The Roman Empire is, therefore, an early example of a monetary union, not unlike today's euro area. However, the Roman Empire traded with many other regions of the world, such as present day India, China, and Africa. Roman coins have been found in these regions, suggesting that the Roman Empire and distant nations engaged in international trade that was facilitated by the use of money.

12.2.3 *The growing complexity of international finance*

By the late Middle Ages, certain coins came to dominate international exchanges both as a medium of exchange and as a unit of account. Especially popular for international trade were gold *florins* issued in Florence. Florins were minted in large denominations and Florentine minters rigorously preserved their coins' gold content. Florins were, therefore trusted and highly valued. Venetian *ducats* were also used throughout Europe and Asia.

In the 12th and 13th centuries the international monetary system began to take on an appearance that would be familiar to modern-day businesspeople and financial economists. The medieval fairs in the French region of Champagne established the use of "letters of fair", which were paper assets that let merchants accumulate debts and credits from one year to the next.[4] Many modern banking practices developed in the region of Lombardy, in Northern Italy. Modern banking spread to other cities such as Barcelona, Geneva, Bruges, and London. Lombard Street in the financial district of London was

---

[3] William L. Davisson and James E. Harper (1972). p. 196.
[4] Described by Rondo Cameron (1993). pp. 63–65.

named after the Italian bankers who set up offices there. Banks often developed out of what started out as depositories for precious metals and coins. These depositories began offering checking services on those deposits, and then they evolved into full-fledged lending institutions that even provided overdraft privileges to reputable customers. The earliest surviving check was drawn on the Castellani Bank of Florence in 1368; it was made out to a draper in payment for black cloth for a funeral. The use of bank drafts, or checks, proved to be more convenient than hauling coins from place to place, and international payments were soon made almost exclusively using bank checks. Money changers gradually evolved into bankers, and some banks began to exchange checks denominated in different moneys, creating commercial banking institutions that provided both loans and foreign exchange. The combination of commercial lending and foreign exchange, which, as you no doubt remember from the earlier chapters on the foreign exchange market, still characterizes the largest commercial banks today.

The use of bank drafts served as a practical way to get around the Roman Catholic Church's ban on charging interest on loans. Since bank drafts in foreign currencies involved some degree of exchange risk, the church allowed the discounting of drafts related to international trade. How much of the discounting was due to risk and how much was due to charging implicit interest was usually left unmentioned. The economic historian De Roover (1948) suggests this is an early example of how international transactions between offshore banks was used to overcome inefficient "domestic" banking regulations.

Exchange rates were clearly important even in medieval times, as evidenced by the fact that official records of exchange rates were meticulously maintained. The daily closing exchange rates from 13th century Florence in Italy and 14th century Bruges in what is today Belgium have been preserved for modern-day researchers. News of exchange rates was carried across Europe by the same couriers that regularly carried business letters, and bills of exchange, and other business and bank documents. Not until the 19th century would railroads, steamships, the telegraph, and finally the telephone accelerate the speed of communications from what it was in the 13th century.[5]

12.2.4 *Fiat money*

The arrival of *fiat money* in the form of paper money not convertible into any other commodity complicated the job of moneychangers, and it brought the potential for greater instability in the international monetary system. With paper money, the value of a currency came to depend on the value of goods that people *expected* to be able to purchase with the money, its so-called *purchasing power*, not the value of a widely-regarded value of precious metals directly incorporated in coins or into which paper was convertible. Exchange rates for fiat moneys are therefore inherently more volatile than exchange rates between moneys backed by scarce commodities with stable values, like gold or silver.

All these developments give one the impression that international finance had spread throughout Europe and the rest of the world by the beginning of the 19th century. Such an impression would be inaccurate, however. True, London and Amsterdam were important financial centers that were closely linked to many other cities in Europe and even many colonies elsewhere in the world. But much of the world, and even many parts of countries with well-developed banking centers, remained largely outside the scope of international financial activity at the start of the 19th century. That would soon change, however.

The spread of the Industrial Revolution beyond the British Isles, the acceleration of economic growth, and globalization would affect virtually all peoples' lives throughout the world by the end of the 1800s. Globalization would also spur the establishment of a new international financial system that was able to accommodate the very rapid growth of international trade and investment that characterized the 18th century. This new order linked all currencies to gold. The period when most countries adhered to this order, 1880 through

---

[5] Peter Spufford (2002). "An Encore for the Merchant of Venice", *Financial Times*, October 19/20.

1914, has come to be known as the *International Gold Standard*, or just simply the *Gold Standard*.

12.3 The Origins of the Gold Standard

The purchasing power of a currency depends on the national price level, which, as the aggregate demand/aggregate supply macroeconomic model from Chapter 9 shows, depends on the economy's capacity to produce goods and services, its long-run economic growth, aggregate demand for the economy's production, and the macroeconomic policies that influence aggregate demand. The Gold Standard that by the end of the 19th century was embraced by most of the world's governments actually had its origins in the early 19th century British Parliament's efforts to prevent inflationary monetary policy by the Bank of England. Parliamentarians were disturbed by British inflation that surged during the Napoleonic wars. This inflation was caused by the Bank of England, which functioned as Britain's central bank, when it printed large amounts of pound notes to finance the war effort. Soon the quantity of pound notes in circulation exceeded the amount of gold in the Bank's vaults, and the British government had to suspend convertibility of pound notes into gold in 1797 and, effectively, let the pound become a fiat currency.

After the war, the landowners and merchants that dominated Parliament sought to prevent future losses of purchasing power of their money by passing several acts that would effectively put Britain permanently on a gold standard. First, the *Coinage Act of 1816* authorized the government to mint gold coins in accordance with strict purity standards. In 1819, a law was passed requiring the Bank of England to make its pound notes redeemable into gold at a fixed parity rate established in the Coinage Act. Not surprisingly, with the Bank of England no longer able to print pounds without limitation, inflation came to an abrupt end. When Parliament also passed laws permitting the melting of gold coins into gold bullion as well as the free import and export of gold coins and bullion, Britain established national monetary rules that, when adopted by all countries of the world by the end of the century, would create an international financial system known as the International Gold Standard.

12.3.1 *Why Britain established a Gold Standard and not a silver standard*

It is important to recognize that the order of the Gold Standard was not in any way inevitable, even though many people today still view the Gold Standard as some sort of "natural" order for the world economy. Economic historian Barry Eichengreen in fact argues that the Gold Standard "was one of the great monetary accidents of modern times".[6] The "accident" occurred because in 1717 Sir Isaac Newton was briefly master of the British mint. One of Newton's jobs was to determine the prices that the mint would pay for gold and silver. For some reason, Newton set the price of silver relative to gold lower than the relative price of silver to gold in the rest of the world. This created a profitable arbitrage opportunity for anyone who bought silver in Britain, hauled it overseas to trade it for relatively less expensive gold, and then brought the gold back to Britain to be exchanged for the relatively cheaper silver. Such arbitragers ended up with more silver than they started out with. As a result, the British mint soon ran out of silver and ended up with only gold in its vaults. It could, therefore, only issue gold coins for circulation. So, when the British Parliament passed the Coinage Act in 1816, British coins were either made of gold or were made of other metals priced in terms of those metals' values relative to gold. Had Newton set the prices of silver and gold differently, Britain and, eventually the whole world, might have gone to a silver standard.

12.3.2 *The emergence of the International Gold Standard*

The rest of the world was not yet ready to adhere to the Gold Standard when Britain adopted it in the early 19th century. After its independence from Britain, the United States maintained a policy of *bimetallism*, which was the simultaneous circulation of both gold and silver coins. As explained below in Section 12.5, over the course of the 19th century, support for bimetallism actually grew in the

---

[6] Barry Eichengreen (1996). p. 7.

United States among farmers, who were mostly debtors. However, groups linked to the growing industrial sector gained the upper hand in US politics in the 1870s, and they favored pegging the dollar to gold and creating a stable monetary system free from inflationary tendencies. In 1873, Congress refused to authorize the unlimited minting of silver dollars, and by 1880, the US Treasury had accumulated enough gold to back the country's money supply, and make US dollars freely convertible to gold.

There was interest in a bimetallic standard in France, Belgium, Switzerland, and Italy, who in 1865 formed the *Latin Monetary Union*. Each of the four countries issued identical silver and gold coins that were a legal means of payment throughout the region.[7] But, after 1870, the tide turned in favor of a gold standard in Europe as well. In 1870, newly-unified Germany opted for the gold standard. After winning the Franco-Prussian War, Germany used the French reparations payments to buy gold. It further sold its own stocks of silver in order to purchase gold. Germany's large sales of silver and purchases of gold of course altered the relative prices of gold and silver. Then discoveries of huge silver deposits in the state of Nevada in the western United States and elsewhere further depressed the price of silver. Silver therefore began flowing to countries that had bimetallic or exclusive silver standards that guaranteed a fixed price for silver. The inflows of silver, which was converted to currency, increased the money supply and created inflation. Such a fear of inflation led the Latin Monetary Union to switch in 1878 from a bimetallic standard to making its currencies exclusively convertible into gold. With Germany and France joining Britain on the gold standard, most other European countries also began to adhere to the gold standard's order.

Despite being a result of a number of "historical accidents", such as Newton's choice of parities, the British Parliament's establishment of gold convertibility as an anti-inflationary measure, and Germany's political choice of gold over silver, after several other large economies opted for gold, most remaining countries found they had little choice

---

[7] The new euro introduced in 2002 is thus not the first attempt at creating a single currency for European countries.

but to also go on the Gold Standard. Meissner (2002) attributes such momentum toward a single worldwide system as a type of network effect; the more trade and investment partners were already on the Gold Standard, the more advantageous it became to join the club. In a related paper, López-Córdoba and Meisner (2003) in fact find that countries on the gold standard traded much more, all other things equal, than did countries with non-conforming exchange rate regimes. The Gold Standard may have improved countries' access to international capital markets because adherence to the Gold Standard rules signaled a commitment to joining the only game in town.

12.4 The International Gold Standard: 1880–1914

By 1879, most major currencies were freely convertible into gold at specific gold parities, thus establishing a truly International Gold Standard. Nearly 100 years later, the Gold Standard is often described in nostalgic terms, and some serious writers have advocated a return to the order that governments adhered to under the Gold Standard. A more serious analysis of the system has led most economists to advise against such a decision, however. To understand the arguments for and against a gold standard, one first must understand how the Gold Standard actually performed during its heyday in the late 19th century.

12.4.1 *The order of the Gold Standard*

Although there was never a formal agreement among governments, under the Gold Standard, national governments effectively adhered to the *order* or, in Keynes words, "rules of the game". Each government effectively agreed to

1. Fix an official gold price or *parity* for the national currency in terms of a fraction of an ounce of pure gold.
2. Permit the free conversion of gold into domestic money and domestic money into gold at the parity price in unlimited amounts and without exceptions.

3. Eliminate all restrictions on foreign exchange transactions and allow the import and export of gold in any quantity.

A weakness of the gold standard regime is that revenue-hungry governments may be tempted to issue more paper currency than they can back with the gold stored in their vaults. Then, if holders of paper money suspect that the government is printing too much money, they will start a "run" on gold. If people's fears are correct and there is not enough gold in the government's vaults to back the money in circulation, the government has to suspend convertibility of paper money into gold and effectively leave the gold standard. The 1880–1913 Gold Standard was thus an order built on the faith that paper money and bank accounts could always be converted to pure gold at any time without restrictions and that there would always be enough gold in the government's vaults. According to McKinnon (1993), in practice governments had to follow several other "rules of the game" in order to maintain confidence in the system:

4. Back domestic coin and currency fully with gold reserves, and link the growth of domestic money to the availability of reserves.
5. Allow the domestic price level to be determined by the world-wide supply and demand for gold.
6. If the central bank must serve as a lender of last resort in the case of short-term credit crises in the domestic banking sector, always charge interest rates well above those charged in the markets.

This latter rule was known as "Bagehot's Rule", in honor of a former director of the Bank of England who rigorously applied this rule to ensure that private banks would only borrow from the central bank when they truly faced an emergency. Bagehot's rule reduces the possibility that the central bank's role as lender of last resort will undermine the other rules requiring that the money supply remain compatible with gold supplies.

12.4.2 *The Gold Standard and exchange rates*

An interesting by-product of fixed gold parities, free convertibility, and the maintenance of credible economic policies that ensure faith in the system is that exchange rates remained unchanged. For example, the British government established free convertibility of pounds for gold at the *parity* rate of 4.24 pounds per one ounce of gold. This was the pound price of gold that the British mint paid when Britain established its gold standard in 1821. The US government offered to exchange dollars at the rate of $20.67 per ounce of gold throughout the Gold Standard period. These two parities in effect defined the exchange rate to be 4.24 pounds per 20.67 dollars, or £1.00 = $4.87. Figure 12.2 illustrates.

Because the governments of Britain and the United States were committed to converting currency to gold and gold to currency upon demand at the stated parities, the exchange rate could not differ very much from £1.00 = $4.87. Suppose, for example, that the supply curve of British pounds shifts so that it intersects the demand curve at £1.00 = $4.00, perhaps because there is a sudden surge in demand for US products in England or increased lending to US borrowers by British savers. Clearly, it would not be advantageous for English importers or the US borrowers to convert pounds to dollars at the £1.00 = $4.00 exchange rate, thus getting only 4 dollars for every pound spent. The English importers or US borrowers should, instead, buy gold with their pounds from the Bank of England at the official price of £4.24 per ounce, ship the gold to the United States

Figure 12.2 The gold parities of the pound and dollar determine their exchange rate.

and exchange it at the dollar price of gold, $20.67 per ounce, at the US Treasury in Washington. This effectively gives them $4.87 for every pound. Thus, if the exchange rate fell much below £1.00 = $4.87, gold would move from Britain to the United States.

In practice, it was not even necessary to wait for importers of goods or international borrowers to demand gold in Britain and ship it to the United States Treasury. Very little gold actually moved between countries during the Gold Standard, despite continual shifts in the supply and demand for currencies. For exchange rates to remain at their parities it was enough for people to *expect* government policy makers to follow the rules and let gold move between countries. As soon as short-run shifts in the supply and demand for foreign exchange moved equilibrium away from the gold parity exchange rate, expectations were that either gold would move or the problem would correct itself because governments would continue to adhere to the rules of the game. Thus, speculators would immediately "bet" that the gold parity rate would prevail by demanding the currency that was temporarily depreciated by selling the temporarily appreciated currency, fully expecting to capture the gains from selling high and buying low. Such speculation would immediately cause the exchange rate to return to its gold parity level. Hence, with faith in governments' commitment to the rules of the game, speculation becomes a stabilizing force.

There is some cost for shipping the gold to the United States and carrying out the foreign exchange transactions. However, by the late 1800s the reliability of steamships had lowered the cost of shipping gold across the ocean to just a few pennies per ounce. With such low arbitrage costs, this export of gold from England and sale of dollars to demand pounds became profitable when the exchange rate fell just a few pennies below the rate given by the gold parities, denoted by the dotted line labeled "gold import price" in Fig. 12.3. Since such arbitrage profit is quite straightforward when governments observe the rules of the gold standard, large sums of money are devoted to arbitrage activity as soon as the arbitrage profits exceeded the costs of shipping gold and money. Hence, the demand curve for pounds is effectively the thick "kinked" curve labeled D_A in Fig. 12.3.

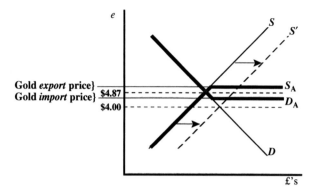

Figure 12.3   The gold points.

Similarly, if the price of pounds were to rise a few pennies above $4.87 so that it becomes profitable to use dollars to buy gold, ship it to England and exchange it for pounds, and exchange the pounds for dollars, arbitrage would make supply of pounds virtually infinite at the gold export price of foreign exchange. The gold import and export prices were often referred to as the *gold points*, the upper and lower bounds within which the exchange could fluctuate but never move beyond so long as governments maintained convertibility.

12.4.3 *Hume's specie-flow mechanism*

The arbitrage activity described here does bring up an interesting issue: Wouldn't the country supplying the gold for shipment overseas eventually run out of gold? If the supply and demand curves for pounds remain forever at the intersection of S′ and D in Fig. 12.3, then, yes, the United States Treasury will eventually run out of gold. There was a popular belief that this could not ever happen, however. Many people reasoned that as long as the rules of the game were followed, any major disequilibrium in the foreign exchange market would trigger an automatic adjustment process called the *specie flow mechanism*. *Specie* refers to precious metals, such as gold and silver coins. First described in 1752 by David Hume, the logic of the specie flow mechanism is straightforward.

If, for example, the demand for foreign exchange exceeds supply at the parity rate, and the exchange rate rises above the upper gold point in the foreign exchange market, people seeking to acquire foreign currency will instead purchase gold from the government or central bank and ship it overseas to sell to the foreign government in exchange for its currency. The resulting *flow* of gold abroad will reduce the money supply at home as money goes out of circulation and increase the money supply abroad as the foreign central bank or treasury issues money in exchange for the gold, provided, of course, that the governments in both countries follow rule 4. Hence, in the absence of offsetting monetary policies, there is a reduction in the amount of currency in the hands of the public of the country whose currency is tending to depreciate. And, when the gold is sold to other countries whose currencies are appreciating in exchange for their currency, the supply of money in the hands of its public increases. The decrease in the money supply in the deficit country will reduce prices, all other things equal, and this causes exports to increase and imports to decline. And, the increase in the money supply in the surplus country causes inflation, which reduces exports and increases imports. Thus, the gold movements cause changes in the countries' relative price levels and shift the supply and demand for currencies back to equilibrium at the fixed gold parity exchange rates. In effect, under the Gold Standard, the nominal exchange rate never changes, but because the specie flow mechanism effectively causes price levels to change the real exchange rate effectively adjusts to maintain equilibrium in the foreign exchange market.

12.4.4 *How the Gold Standard actually worked*

The Gold Standard is often depicted as functioning in strict accordance with the rules of the game as described above. That is an oversimplification, however. Central banks often engaged in discretionary monetary policy. The central banks of the major countries did usually follow Bagehot's rule, so that central bank lending did not result in monetary expansions beyond what was prudent for maintaining credibility in convertibility. But, on a year-to-year basis, governments did not make the money supply change perfectly in line with the gold stock. Nor did prices promptly move in strict accordance with the amount of currency in circulation. In the United States, year-to-year fluctuations in prices were not very closely correlated with changes in the stock of gold. Statistical studies find that changes in the gold stock "explain" very little of the changes in money growth rates during the period 1880–1913. Overall economic conditions often altered the amount of money banks lent out, the banking system's money multiplier fluctuated and prevented prices from moving in close formation with gold movements' effect on the monetary base.

Another reason that exchange rates were not immediately influenced by fluctuations in money supplies and price levels is that capital movements between countries in the late 1800s and early 1900s were very large. Especially important were the large flows of capital from Great Britain to the newly settled economies of the world, such as the United States, Australia, Canada, and Argentina. Railroads, electric power plants, harbor facilities, mines, and a great variety of other capital projects in these countries were financed with British money. Capital flows from the United States and the major European economies also played a role, and they were often channeled through London. These capital flows, which were large relative to overall economic activity compared to capital flows in today's global economy, were easily able to offset trade deficits. Confidence in the Gold Standard also meant that only very small changes in interest rates were needed to generate the capital necessary to keep supply and demand for currencies in equilibrium at the gold parities.

Central banks, especially the Bank of England, routinely manipulated interest rates in order to influence international capital flows. If money became tight because trade deficits were causing gold to flow out of the country, the Bank of England would raise interest rates, and capital would flow in from abroad, thereby keeping the total supply and demand for foreign exchange in balance even as the trade balance moved into deficit or surplus. The dominance of the London financial markets in mediating international transactions and the management of the Bank of England combined to let investment flows, rather than price changes, do most of the *short-run* adjusting during the Gold Standard's 35 year reign.

The Gold Standard period was also characterized by cooperation between governments in dealing with exchange rate pressures. According to the financial historian Barry Eichengreen:

> The dilemma for central banks and governments became whether to provide only as much credit as was consistent with the gold-standard statutes or to supply the additional liquidity expected of a lender of last resort. That this dilemma did not bring the gold-standard edifice tumbling down was attributable to luck and to political conditions that allowed for international solidarity in times of crisis.[8]

For example, in 1890 the British merchant bank Baring Brothers became insolvent as a result of extensive defaults on its loans to the government of Argentina.[9] Investors questioned whether the Bank of England had enough resources to both serve as a lender of last resort to Barings and defend the pound's convertibility. Despite raising interest rates sharply, large amounts of gold were being sent overseas. The supply of gold at the Bank of England was dwindling, and the situation became desperate. Would the anchor of the gold standard have to suspend convertibility? Bank of England officials were able to quickly arrange a loan of gold from the Bank of France and the Russian State Bank. An overnight emergency shipment from Paris permitted the Bank of England to continue selling gold, and soon the panic subsided when it became apparent that the Bank of England would not run out of gold. Speculators soon returned their gold to London and the Bank of England repaid its debts to the foreign central banks.

---

[8] Barry Eichengreen (1996). op. cit., p. 8.

[9] Yes, Baring Brothers is the same bank that ran into trouble in the early 1990s when one of its foreign exchange traders ran up huge losses; it was recently bailed out and acquired by the Dutch banking group ING.

12.4.5 *In the long term, the rules were followed*

The widespread confidence in the Gold Standard, which largely eliminated exchange rate risk and made people willing to shift large
amounts of their wealth across borders, was dependent on the continued expectation that governments would follow the order of the
Gold Standard in the long run. Indeed, despite the variability in
money supplies from one year to the next, in the very long run prices
did roughly respond to the supply of gold. As McCloskey and Zecher
(1984) show, purchasing power parity was effectively maintained over
the Gold Standard period. Because exchange rates remained fixed, the
persistence of purchasing power parity implies that the price levels of
individual countries, in the long run, moved in tandem with all other
countries' price levels.

The average world price level also reflected the worldwide supply
of gold. Until 1890, prices around the world gradually declined as
economic activity expanded more rapidly than the gold-based world
money supply. By the mid-1890s, however, the development of the
potassium cyanide process for extracting gold from ore and a series of
major gold discoveries in Alaska, South Africa, Russia, and elsewhere
began expanding the money supply more rapidly than overall economic activity. Prices trended consistently upward between 1895 and
1914. Over the entire period of the Gold Standard, 1870–1914,
prices ended about where they started. There were substantial year-
to-year fluctuations in prices, but there was no hint of the type of high
inflation as we have observed in the latter half of the twentieth century. Figure 12.4 shows the price levels in the United States and
Canada. You can clearly see the long decline until 1896, followed by
a gradual increase until 1914.

There is considerable debate about whether the persistent deflation
between 1870 and 1895 was harmful to human welfare. Bordo *et al.*
(2004) show that the 19th century deflation was not "bad", although
most people at the time, and most historians subsequently, viewed it in
a negative light. They show that the deflation during the Gold Standard
was essentially a combination of rapid growth of aggregate supply that
exceeded the somewhat slower, but still rapid, growth of aggregate

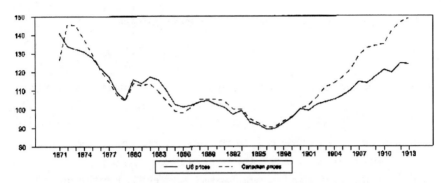

Figure 12.4   Price changes in the United States and Canada, 1871–1913.
Source: Bordo *et al.* (2004).

demand. Bordo *et al.* contend that deflation is bad only if it is the result of declining aggregate demand that exceeds the decline in aggregate supply, as during the Great Depression, for example.

The period from 1880 to 1914 was one of rapid economic growth fueled by scientific discoveries and technological advances. This meant real wages consistently rose, and even in years of declining prices, nominal wages did not decline as rapidly as prices. According to Thomas Dernberg:

> Adjustment in such an environment of growth is far easier and less painful than in a stationary or stagnant one. For example, with productivity and real wages growing rapidly, adjustment to a payments deficit could be achieved by a barely noticeable slowdown in the rate of wage increase rather than by the need to lower the absolute wage level, which would be required in the absence of growth in labor productivity.[10]

Indeed, the world economy had never grown as rapidly as it did during the 1870–1913 Gold Standard period. Furthermore, technological progress was also unprecedented. Electricity, the telephone,

---

[10] Thomas F. Dernberg (1989). p. 377.

the horseless carriage, the airplane, the record player, central heating, the refrigerator, and successful mass vaccinations against disease were just a few of the many revolutionary new products introduced to the world. Not all parts of the world enjoyed rapid improvements in living standards, however. The world was still divided into various global empires, and much of the benefits from technological progress and the industrial revolution accrued to the imperial powers, not the colonies. However, most descriptions of the Gold Standard period were written in Europe and North America, and it was the perceived success in those nations that gave the Gold Standard a mystique that persisted well into the 20th century, even though careful analysis reveals a less flattering picture.

12.4.6 *Evaluating the international Gold Standard*

The Gold Standard was a qualified success. Economic growth and globalization were unprecedented. World merchandise exports tripled in real terms between 1880 and 1914. It is impossible to say with complete certainty that it was the Gold Standard that caused the unprecedented economic growth of nations, however. It could also have been the case that good economic conditions allowed the Gold Standard to operate successfully. What is certain, however, is that the Gold Standard was not a serious impediment to globalization and economic growth in the major economies of Europe and North America. Overall, prices were fairly stable; there were certainly none

Report Card: The Gold Standard

1. Stability/employment	Fail
2. Economic growth	Marginal pass
3. Globalization	Pass
4. Policy independence	Fail
5. Price stability	Pass
6. Mutually beneficial	Fail
7. Self regulating	Marginal pass

of the episodes of rapid inflation that had characterized the pre-Gold Standard period. Late in the 20th century, rising inflation would lead some economists to call for a return to the Gold Standard.

The Gold Standard did not satisfy the first, fourth, and sixth criteria of success for monetary orders, however. The rigid rules of the Gold Standard often caused financial panics and severe ups and downs in economic activity in many countries. National governments had little freedom to adjust monetary policies. The order of the Gold Standard mandated that central banks keep the money supply in line with gold stocks to maintain convertibility. Whether all countries gained from the Gold Standard is difficult to say. Economic growth rose in much of the world, but the variation in growth rates was very large. Some countries raised the standard of living of their citizens by multiples of 2, 3, or even more, but many parts of the world saw only modest gains. Countries like China and India experienced no gains in real per capita income at all. The manipulation of interest rates by the Bank of England to balance Britain's payments caused international capital flows to vary from year to year, and the fluctuations in investment flows occasionally caused liquidity problems and defaults on foreign loans in Latin America and Asia.

Finally, criteria two and seven were only partially met. Economic growth in many underdeveloped economies, especially colonized economies, did not enjoy consistent rises in living standards. The Gold Standard may not be directly to blame for the colonial structures imposed on the world. However, the counter-cyclical capital flows under the Gold Standard also played a role in preventing the spread of wealth generated by the industrial revolution to all parts of the world. Secondly, the Gold Standard did not prove to be as automatic and self-correcting as Hume's specie-flow mechanism suggests. It took constant adjustments by the Bank of England and other central banks to maintain credibility and prevent suspensions of convertibility, but the costs of central bank activity were certainly not high relative to the growing levels of GDP throughout the period.

In terms of the trilemma, which we discussed in the previous chapter and illustrate here in Fig. 12.5, the Gold Standard effectively implied the choice of capital mobility and a fixed exchange rate over

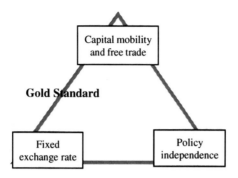

Figure 12.5 The trilemma under the International Gold Standard.

policy independence. The exchange rates of all the major currencies of the world remained unchanged for over 35 years, and international trade and investment grew rapidly, if erratically. The Gold Standard period was clearly a period of rapid growth and globalization. But individual governments had no power to carry out long-run monetary and fiscal policies in response to domestic economic conditions. Of course, not all governments were interested in using macroeconomic policies at that time in history. Political opposition to a government-run central bank meant the United States did not even have a central bank to conduct monetary policy until 1913, the last year the international financial system operated under the Gold Standard order.

12.4.7 *International investment in the late 19th century*

In the 1800s, international lending grew very rapidly and, by the end of the 1800s, reached levels that in some ways exceeded the huge international capital flows that we observe today. When measured as a proportion of GDP, capital flows in many countries were much larger then than they were even during globalization of the 1990s. For example, over the period 1880–1914, annual capital *outflows* averaged about five percent of GDP for the United Kingdom, nearly half of its total savings. Capital outflows from Britain reached a phenomenal nine percent in 1913. Outflows of savings frequently reached five and six percent of GDP in France. Germany averaged capital outflows equal to two percent of its GDP over the same 1880–1914 period.

Outflows of savings from one country of course imply inflows elsewhere in the world. The major importers of savings in the world in the late nineteenth century were the countries newly populated with European immigrants, such as Australia, Canada, Argentina, the United States, and New Zealand. These were all rapidly growing economies, and returns to investment there were high. During the 1880s, inflows of foreign savings averaged nearly ten percent of GDP in Australia, before falling to a more modest 2.5 percent during the 1890s. Of course, 2.5 percent is still very high even by the standards of the 1990s. Savings inflows into Canada exceeded six percent of GDP in the 1880s, averaged about 4.5 percent in the 1890s, rose to seven percent in the first decade of the twentieth century, and reached an astounding 14 percent of GDP between 1910 and 1913. As a percentage of total investment, foreign saving accounted for nearly 35 percent of total saving in New Zealand and Canada over the entire 1880–1914 period, and nearly 25 percent in Australia. In contrast, foreign savings financed less than four percent of all investment in developing countries of the world during the 1980s, and even in the 1990s foreign saving only financed 10 percent of investment in developing economies in Latin America, Africa, and Asia.

A large portion of international lending in the 1800s was in the form of bonds. Most often it was British investment banks, or *investment houses* as they were commonly referred to in London, who intermediated the sale of bonds by foreign governments and firms to domestic savers. According to evidence gathered by Edelstein (1982), London investment houses earned hefty fees of between 1.6 and 3.9 percentage points. This is not to say that the banks provided no service; without the banks there would have been few international capital flows. The services provided by the investment houses included negotiating the bonds' terms and promoting their sale. Sometimes the investment houses advanced funds to the issuers of the bonds in anticipation of the sale of the bonds.

The investment houses were also an important factor when defaults occurred; because large groups of diverse bondholders cannot negotiate as easily with defaulters as a single bank or small group of private banks. The investment houses usually acted as principal negotiators on behalf of the bondholders, and given the near-monopoly that the investment houses held in the international capital markets, negotiations often led to default settlements favorable to the bondholders. The investment houses also helped to spread the risk for individual purchasers of foreign bonds, who had no knowledge of foreign firms and projects. In any case, because of the London investment houses and the relatively high level of wealth accumulated in Britain, British investors financed many of the world's railroads, electric utilities, and other infrastructure projects.

The high average values for the investment flows mentioned above obscure the volatility of international capital flows during the late 1800s and early 1900s. That volatility of course had much to do with Britain's monetary policies, which, as pointed out earlier, fluctuated in response to the Bank of England's management of Britain's balance of payments.

12.4.8 *Around the world with British pounds*

As a final note in this description of the Gold Standard, we refer to Jules Verne's famous novel, *Around the World in Eighty Days*. This novel provides some interesting insights into the extent of globalization in the late 1800s. As the novel's hero, Phileas Fogg, noted when he bet he could circumvent the globe in 80 days, the world indeed was getting much smaller. "Smaller" also meant "more integrated", because Mr. Fogg was able to use pound notes wherever he went. You may recall, if you have read the novel or seen the equally famous movie with David Niven as Fogg, that Fogg's faithful servant, Paspertous, carried a large carpetbag full of pound notes, which were used to buy train tickets, meals, and even a hot air balloon in different countries around the world. It did not seem to matter what country they were in, the pound notes were readily accepted. This was not an oversight on the part of Verne; he was correctly describing the world during the Gold Standard. British pounds were accepted everywhere, and it was quite possible to travel around the world with pounds.

The international financial system became tightly integrated during the Gold Standard. With London at the center, international banking and financial trading spread to all corners of the world. Obstfeld and Taylor (2004, pp. 23, 24) describe the period as follows:

> Finance also advanced through the development of a broader array of private debt and equity instruments, through the expansion of insurance activities, and through international trade in government bonds. By 1900, the key currencies and instruments were known everywhere and formed the basis for an expanding world commercial network, whose rise was equally meteoric. Bills of exchange, bond finance, equity issues, foreign direct investments, and many other types of transaction were by then quite common among the core countries, and among a growing number of nations at the periphery.

This is not to say that financial markets were as deep in terms of variety of instruments as they are today, but their capacity for moving investment around the world was without a doubt unprecedented. In fact, international investment flows subsided after World War I, and they would not regain similar levels relative to world GDP until the 1990s.

12.5 The United States and the International Gold Standard

The International Gold Standard seems to have enjoyed broad support by the world's governments. Nevertheless, it would be inaccurate to say that there was no opposition to the Gold Standard and its rules of the game. In fact, there was strong political opposition to the gold standard in the United States, at least until the turn of the century. The opposition was partially driven by the active lobbying for bimetallism by the Nevada silver mining industry, as might be expected. But there was a more fundamental political battle being waged in the United States during the latter half of the 19th century. This battle was between industrial/financial interests and the farm sector, which consisted of millions of individual farmers. These two sectors' diverging economic interests often came to the surface in political debates between the Republican Party and the so-called Populist wing of the Democratic Party. The Populists enjoyed their greatest support in the Midwestern farm states. The Republicans were strong in the industrial states of the Great Lakes region and the Northeastern states where both industry and the biggest banks were headquartered. The Populists were against the gold standard, which they saw, correctly according to Fig. 12.5, as the cause of gradual deflation that often made life difficult for debtors, which is what most farmers were most of the time. Farmers routinely financed the purchase of land, equipment, and the seeding of their crops.

Under the gold standard, the US money supply could only expand as rapidly as the amount of gold in the government vaults increased. The United States economy grew rapidly in the late 1800s because of rapid immigration, large investments, and rapid technological progress. The supply of gold did not keep up with the expansion of real GDP, and therefore prices more often than not declined between the late 1860s and 1890. The gradual decline in prices meant that even if nominal interest rates were close to zero, real interest rates were high. High interest rates favored creditors at the expense of debtors. Because Midwestern farmers borrowed to finance their crops, real interest rates were a major determinant of their real income.

The United States had no central bank in the latter half of the 19th century, and it therefore did not have an institutional structure to carry out an active monetary policy. Until the Federal Reserve Bank was established in 1913, the amount of money in circulation in the US was effectively a function of how much paper currency was printed by the US. Treasury and how much the banking system multiplied the portion of the printed money that was deposited in the banking system. In the latter half of the 19th century, the money supply was very volatile as cyclical variations in economic activity were aggravated by the banking system's role in expanding the money supply. Bank runs were frequent occurrences, and financial panics periodically generated recessions and bouts of high unemployment and sharp price declines for farm products.

The ups and downs of economic activity plus the secular decline in prices began to foment discontent with the Gold Standard and the rules of the game that effectively dictated a passive but tight monetary policy. Most people vaguely grasped the economics of the Gold Standard, but populist politicians took it on as a major issue in the country's political debate. Most often, opponents to the Gold Standard promoted the alternative of bimetallism, which meant basing the money supply on the combined stocks of gold and silver. The perception was that with more commodities backing money, there would be more money in circulation and, therefore, prices would be higher and real interest rates lower. There were some gaps in the logic of the bimetallists, but in principal their linkage of money supplies and prices was correct, as Friedman and Schwartz (1963) pointed out a century later.[11] No politician used the issue of gold better than William Jennings Bryan from Nebraska. Bryan was a Populist politician who overwhelmed the Democratic Party Convention with his "Cross of Gold" speech and gained the Democratic Party's nomination to run against William McKinley, the pro-gold standard Republican candidate, in the 1896 presidential election.[12]

Bryan had been given little chance of winning the nomination at the Democratic convention in Chicago in the summer of 1896. Several other pro-silver candidates were ahead of him in the party pecking order, and a number of Democratic Party leaders from industrial states openly supported maintaining the Gold Standard. When other potential candidates faltered in gaining enough support to win majority support at the convention, however, Bryan saw his chance. He became a sensation with a speech that still stands as one of the

---

[11] See also: Milton Friedman (1990).

[12] The material in this sections draws on Ranjit Dighe (2002, Hugh Rockoff (1990), Quentin Taylor (2005), and François Velde (2002a, 2002b).

most emotional and stirring political speeches in American history. Bryan's 1896 Convention speech was in some ways typical populist rhetoric:

> There are two ideas of government. There are those who believe that, if you will only legislate to make the well-to-do prosperous, their prosperity will leak through on those below. The Democratic idea, however, has been that if you legislate to make the masses prosperous, their prosperity will find its way up through every class which rests upon them.

But Bryan went well beyond the standard populist message. He explicitly pitted "hard-working" rural America against the elites of the cities:

> You come to us and tell us that the great cities are in favor of the gold standard; we reply that the great cities rest upon our broad and fertile prairies. Burn down your cities and leave our farms, and your cities will spring up again as if by magic; but destroy our farms and the grass will grow in the streets of every city in the country.

And Bryan exploited nationalism by depicting the gold standard being imposed on the United States by foreigners:

> It is the issue of 1776 over again. Our ancestors, when but three millions in number had the courage to declare their political independence of every other nation; shall we, their descendants, when we have grown to seventy millions, declare that we are less independent than our forefathers? Having behind us the producing masses of this nation and the world, supported by the commercial interests, the laboring interests and the toilers everywhere, we will answer their demand for a gold standard by saying to them: You shall not press down upon the brow of labor this crown of thorns, you shall not crucify mankind upon a cross of gold.

As Bryan concluded the speech with his arms spread as if he was being crucified, the convention burst into a long enthusiastic applause. The politician from Nebraska won the nomination shortly thereafter. For those of you interested in politics, more of Bryan's speech is in the Appendix to this chapter.

Bryan nearly became President of the United States in 1896, losing the election by just a few percentage points despite being out-spent by McKinley 30 to 1. A number of prominent Democrats had even openly opposed Bryan's anti-gold campaign, and most of the country's major newspapers actively supported McKinley. Bryan nev-ertheless received 47 percent of the popular vote to McKinley's 51 percent. Bryan's voter support surprised many pundits at the time, much as it had surprised everyone when the lesser known populist came away with the Democratic Party nomination.

After 1896 the gold issue lost its urgency, largely because the supply of gold began to increase rapidly following discoveries of gold in Alaska, Russia, and South Africa. A gradual inflation replaced the gradual deflation from before 1890, and by 1913, the year before World War I ended the Gold Standard, the overall price level had risen back to its 1870 level. Bryan again ran for President in 1900, but without the emotional issue of gold, he lost by a much greater margin.

The important aspect of Bryan's near win in 1896 is that the United States, in fact, came very close to electing a President who almost certainly would have taken the US off the Gold Standard. The importance of Bryan's challenge to the established regime was evidenced in the financial markets in late 1896, where a mini-panic briefly sent interest rates soaring and severely disrupted financial transactions. What the consequences of the United States aband-oning the gold standard would have been makes for interesting speculation.

Friedman (1990) used a monetarist model to estimate what the world would have looked like under the assumption that the United States continued to freely mint silver dollars after 1873 at the pre-Civil War silver content instead of adopting the Gold Standard. He concluded that the world price level would have been more stable than the 25 years of deflation followed by 20 years of inflation under the Gold Standard. Velde (2002) uses a different model to estimate the consequences of the US not adopting the Gold Standard after 1873, and he concludes that:

> The US would have remained a bimetallic country for twenty years, and its price level (indeed, price levels around the world) would have been more stable. However, abandonment of silver by other countries would have ultimately forced the US off bimetallism and onto silver standard, where it would have been alone with China. The sharp depreciation of silver in the early 20th century would have induced considerable inflation. In short, the stability of the price level in the 1870s and 1880s would have been paid with higher inflation in the 1890s.[13]

Velde extends his counterfactual construction in another interesting direction to ask whether it would have made sense for other countries to stay on silver or bimetallic standards if the US had maintained its bimetallic standard. He finds that if several large silver countries had not adopted the Gold Standard, then the price of silver would not have fallen as much, inflation would have been lower, and the US could have maintained its bimetallic standard up to World War I without great economic difficulties.

12.6 The Suspension of the International Gold Standard

When World War I broke out in 1914, many countries promptly suspended convertibility. In fact, virtually all countries would effectively abandon convertibility within the first year of the war. Many economic historians thus set 1914 as the end of the Gold Standard. It is true that the order would be revived after the war, but it would not prove to be a successful revival, as the next chapter will detail.

---

[13] François Velde (2002).

In many ways, the period 1870–1914 is a unique period of human history for a number of reasons. Never had the world economy grown as fast, never had global trade, investment, and immigration grown as fast, and never had technology progressed as rapidly. At the same time in part because of the colonial regimes and the capitalist economic system European nations imposed on much of the world, never before had income and wealth been so unevenly distributed among the world's people The mechanics of the Gold Standard and the uneven benefits from international investment no doubt worsened the distribution of the world's income.

The world had changed in many ways when World War I broke out. In fact, World War I itself was a result of the complex social and political changes that occurred during the period when the Gold Standard order was in effect. The Gold Standard seemed to have provided some order to a period in which the world experienced incredible economic, political, and social change. Perhaps that accounts for the Gold Standard's image as a source of stability. A careful reading history does not support that positive image, as pointed out in this chapter. The Gold Standard could not prevent, and many argue that it actually caused, the continual financial panics, debt defaults, and economic recessions that were a hallmark of the 1879–1913 Gold Standard period. Still, the major powers of the world were intent on restoring the Gold Standard after World War I. The next chapter describes this ill-fated return to the order of the Gold Standard in the 1920s.

Key Terms and Concepts

Bagehot's rule	Gold parity	Rules of the game
Bimetallism	Gold points	Seignorage
Coinage Act of 1816	Gold standard	Specie flow mechanism
Convertibility	Investment houses	Store of value
Fiat money	Latin Monetary Union	Unit of account
Financial order	Medium of exchange	

Chapter Questions and Problems

1. Describe the gold standard, its origins, its success, and its eventual demise. Provide an overall evaluation of the gold standard as a financial order, and explain why it could, or could not, work today.

2. How was the trilemma dealt with under the Gold Standard? Does the Trilemma help to explain why the Gold Standard was not considered to be a viable international financial order at Bretton Woods? Discuss.

3. One of the unwritten rules under the order of the Gold Standard was that governments would return to convertibility under the old gold parity as soon as possible in the case of an emergency that required the temporary suspension of convertibility. Why was this rule important to the continued maintenance of fixed exchange rates during the wars, political crises, and other brief interruptions of convertibility during the gold standard? Was the rule adhered to after the end of World War I?

4. After reading about the Gold Standard, William Jennings Bryan's emotional speech, write an essay analyzing what might have happened if William Jennings Bryan had won the 1896 election in the United States? Most likely, Jennings would have taken the US off the Gold Standard, but perhaps your understanding of international finance and macroeconomics lets you see other possible outcomes. Be creative and enjoy this opportunity to write an alternative history of the world, but be sure to give your alternative history a solid economic and financial foundation.

5. The chapter provides a Report Card on the 1880–1913 Gold Standard. Provide a second opinion and explain why you agree or disagree with the Report Card.

6. Explain the specie flow mechanism and how it was expected to operate under the rules of the game of the Gold Standard.

7. Define the gold points, and then explain what they implied for exchange rates during the Gold Standard period.

8. Explain why Great Britain ended up with a gold standard and not a silver standard. Provide an alternative set of gold and silver prices that might have resulted in Britain adopting the silver standard.

9. Why did major events like wars lead governments to suspend convertibility? What should such suspensions have suggested about the Gold Standard's long-term viability?

10. Explain in detail why exchange rates remained essentially fixed when all countries adhere to the Gold Standard's effective rules of the game as described in this chapter. Detail the role of each of the rules and how suspension of any of those rules can cut exchange rates lose.

References

Bordo, M, JL Lane and A Redish (2004). Good versus bad deflation: Lessons from the gold standard era. *NBER Working Paper No. w10329*, February.

Cameron, R (1993). *A Concise Economic History of the World: From Paleolithic Times to the Present*, 2nd ed., pp. 63–65. New York: Oxford University Press.

Davies, G (1996). *A History of Money*, rev. ed. Cardiff: University of Wales Press.

Davisson, WL and JE Harper (1972). *European Economic History, Volume I, The Ancient World*. New York: Appleton-Century-Crofts.

Dernberg, TF (1989). *Global Macroeconomics*. New York: Harper & Row.

De Roover, R (1948). *Money, Banking and Credit in Medieval Bruges*. Cambridge, MA: The Medieval Academy of America.

Dighe, RS (ed.) (2002). *The Historian's Wizard of Oz*. Westport, CN: Praeger.

Edelstein, M (1982). *Overseas Investment in the Age of High Imperialism: The United Kingdom, 1850–1914*. New York: Columbia University Press.

Eichengreen, B (1996). *Globalizing Capital: A History of the International Monetary System*. Princeton, NJ: Princeton University Press.

Friedman, M (1990). Bimetallism revisited. *Journal of Economic Perspectives*, 4(4), 85–104.

Friedman, M and AJ Schwartz (1963). *A Monetary History of the United States 1867–1960*. Princeton, NJ: Princeton University Press.

López-Córdoba, E and C Meisner (2003). Exchange rate regimes and international trade: Evidence from the classical gold standard era. *The American Economic Review*, 93(1), 344–353.

McCloskey, DN and JR Zecher (1984). The success of purchasing power parity: Historical evidence and its implications for macroeconomics. *A Retrospective on the Classical Gold Standard, 1880–1913*, Bordo MD. and AJ Schwartz (eds.). Chicago: University of Chicago Press.

McKinnon, RI (1993). The rules of the game: International money in historical perspective. *Journal of Economic Literature*, 31(1), 1–44.

Meisner, CM (2002). A new world order: Explaining the emergence of the classical gold standard. *NBER Working Paper No. w9233*, September.

Mundell, RA (1972). The future of the international financial system. *Bretton Woods Revisited*. Acheson, ALK, LK Chant and MFJ Prachowny (eds.). Toronto: University of Toronto Press.

Mundell, RA (2000). A reconsideration of the twentieth century. *American Economic Review*, 90(3), 327–340.

Obstfeld, M and AM Taylor (2004). *Global Capital Markets, Integration, Crisis, and Growth*. Cambridge: Cambridge University Press.

Rockoff, H (1990). The 'Wizard of Oz' as a monetary allegory. *Journal of Political Economy*, 98(4), 739–760.

Taylor, QP (2005). Money and politics in the land of Oz. *The Independent Review*, 9(3), 413–426.

Velde, FR (2002a). Following the yellow brick road: How the United States adopted the gold standard. *Federal Reserve Bank of Chicago Economic Perspectives*, 2Q, 42–58.

Velde, F (2002b). The crime of 1873: Back to the scene. *Federal Reserve Bank of Chicago working paper WP 2002–29*.

Appendix

Excerpts from William Jennings Bryan's "cross of gold" speech, Chicago: 9 July 1896

[Note: This speech was given during the 1896 Democratic National Convention. It was Bryan's contribution to a planned convention-wide debate over monetary policy. A moderately well known delegate before he gave the speech, this emotional speech immediately made Bryan a candidate for the Party nomination for President. When none of the established party leaders could muster a majority among the delegates during early votes, sentiment switched to Bryan. After several other candidates dropped out of the running, Bryan gained a majority of the votes to become the Democratic/Progressive Party candidate for US President.

This speech is not included here because of its accurate economic analysis. Rather, it is included to give you some understanding of the political sentiments driving political debate in the United States 100 years ago. Bryan used patriotism, religion, and divisive claims of the moral superiority of farmers over urban bankers and industrialists to appeal to Midwestern delegates at the Convention. Note that he even criticizes "trickle-down economics" and takes the side of the debtor over the creditor. It was a blatantly political speech. It is not clear whether Bryan really cared or fully understood how bimetallism would work if it were actually instituted; rather he saw gold as a convenient symbol that raised the emotions of the electorate during an era when income differences had grown larger, unemployment was high, and farm foreclosures by banks occurred frequently. The fact that Bryan came so close to winning the election serves as a strong reminder of how difficult it is to maintain a rigid rules-based economic system when that system generates economic and social pressures that politicians can easily exploit.]

Mr. Chairman and Gentlemen of the Convention:

I would be presumptuous, indeed, to present myself against the distinguished gentlemen to whom you have listened if this were a mere measuring of abilities; but this is not a contest between persons. The humblest citizen in all the land, when clad in the armor of a righteous cause, is stronger than all the hosts of error. I come to speak to you in defence of a cause as holy as the cause of liberty — the cause of humanity.

    ...

Never before in the history of this country has there been witnessed such a contest as that through which we have just passed. Never before in the history of American politics has a great issue been fought out as this issue has been, by the voters of a great party. On the fourth of March, 1895, a few Democrats, most of them members of Congress, issued an address to the Democrats of the nation, asserting that the money question was the paramount issue of the hour; declaring that a majority of the Democratic party had the right to control the action of the party on this paramount issue; and concluding with the request that the believers in the free coinage of silver in the Democratic party should organize, take charge of, and control the policy of the Democratic party. Three months later, at Memphis, an organization was perfected, and the silver Democrats went forth openly and courageously proclaiming their belief, and declaring that, if successful, they would crystallize into a platform the declaration which they had made. Then began the conflict. With a zeal approaching the zeal which inspired the Crusaders who followed Peter the Hermit, our silver Democrats went forth from victory unto victory until they are now assembled, not to discuss, not to debate, but to enter up the judgment already rendered by the plain people of this country. In this contest brother has been arrayed against brother, father against son. The warmest ties of love, acquaintance, and association have been disregarded; old leaders have been cast aside when they have refused to give expression to the sentiments of those whom they would lead, and new leaders have sprung up to give direction to this cause of truth. Thus has the contest been waged, and we have assembled here under as binding and solemn instructions as were ever imposed upon representatives of the people.

...

The gentleman who preceded me [ex-Governor Russell] spoke of the state of Massachusetts; let me assure him that not one present in all this Convention entertains the least hostility to the people of the state of Massachusetts, but we stand here representing people who are the equals, before the law, of the greatest citizens in the state of Massachusetts. When you [turning to the gold delegates] come before us and tell us that we are about to disturb your business interests, we reply that you have disturbed our business interests by your course.

We say to you that you have made the definition of a business man too limited in its application. The man who is employed for wages is as much a business man as his employer; the attorney in a country town is as much a business man as the corporation counsel in a great metropolis; the merchant at the cross-roads store is as much a business man as the merchant of New York; the farmer who goes forth in the morning and toils all day, who begins in spring and toils all summer, and who by the application of brain and muscle to the natural resources of the country creates wealth, is as much a business man as the man who goes upon the Board of Trade and bets upon the price of grain; the miners who go down a thousand feet into the earth, or climb two thousand feet upon the cliffs, and bring forth from their hiding places the precious metals to be poured into the channels of trade are as much businessmen as the few financial magnates who, in a back room, corner the money of the world. We come to speak of this broader class of business men.

Ah, my friends, we say not one word against those who live upon the Atlantic Coast, but the hardy pioneers who have braved all the dangers of the wilderness, who have made the desert to blossom as the rose — the pioneers away out there [pointing to the West], who rear their children near to Nature's heart, where they can mingle their voices with the voices of the birds — out there where they have erected schoolhouses for the education of their young, churches where they praise their creator, and cemeteries where rest the ashes of their dead — these people, we say, are as deserving of the consideration of our party as any people in this country. It is for these that we speak. We do not come as aggressors. Our war is not a war of conquest; we are fighting in the defence of our homes, our families, and posterity. We have petitioned, and our petitions have been scorned; we have entreated, and our entreaties have been disregarded; we have begged, and they have mocked when our calamity came. We beg no longer; we entreat no more; we petition no more. We defy them!

The gentleman from Wisconsin has said that he fears a Robespierre. My friends, in this land of the free you need not fear that a tyrant will spring up from among the people. What we need is an Andrew Jackson to stand, as Jackson stood, against the encroachments of organized wealth.

...

They say that we are opposing national bank currency; it is true. If you will read what Thomas Benton said, you will find he said that, in searching history, he could find but one parallel to Andrew Jackson; that was Cicero, who destroyed the conspiracy of Catiline and saved Rome. Benton said that Cicero only did for Rome what Jackson did for us when he destroyed the bank conspiracy and saved America. We say in our platform that we believe that the right to coin and issue money is a function of government. We believe it. We believe that it is a part of sovereignty, and can no more with safety be delegated to private individuals than we could afford to delegate to private individuals the power to make penal statutes or levy taxes. Mr. Jefferson, who was once regarded as good Democratic authority, seems to have differed in opinion from the gentleman who has addressed us on the part of the minority. Those who are opposed to this proposition tell us that the issue of paper money is a function of the bank, and that the government ought to go out of the banking business. I stand with Jefferson rather than with them, and tell them, as he did that the issue of money is a function of government, and that the banks ought to go out of the governing business.

...

Let me call your attention to two or three important things. The gentleman from New York says that he will propose an amendment to the platform providing that the proposed change in our monetary system shall not affect contracts already made. Let me remind you that there is no intention of affecting those contracts which, according to present laws, are made payable in gold; but if he means to say that we cannot change our monetary system without protecting those who have loaned money before the change was made, I desire to ask him where, in law or in morals, he can find justification for not protecting the debtors when the act of 1873 was passed, if he now insists that we must protect the creditors.

...

And now, my friends, let me come to the paramount issue. If they ask us why it is that we say more on the money question than we say upon the tariff question, I reply that, if protection has slain its thousands, the gold standard has slain its tens of thousands. If they ask us why we do not embody in our platform all the things that we believe in, we reply that when we have restored the money of the Constitution all other necessary reforms will be possible; but that until this is done there is no other reform that can be accomplished.

...

Mr. Carlisle [President Grover Cleveland's Treasury Secretary, who had earlier come out in favor of bimetallism] said in 1878 that this was a struggle between "the idle holders of idle capital" and "the struggling masses, who produce the wealth and pay the taxes of the country"; and, my friends, the question we are to decide is: Upon which side will the Democratic party fight; upon the side of "the idle holders of idle capital" or upon the side of "the struggling masses"? That is the question which the party must answer first, and then it must be answered by each individual hereafter. The sympathies of the Democratic party, as shown by the platform, are on the side of the struggling masses who have ever been the foundation of the Democratic party. There are two ideas of government. There are those who believe that, if you will only legislate to make the well-to-do prosperous, their prosperity will leak through on those below. The Democratic idea, however, has been that if you legislate to make the masses prosperous, their prosperity will find its way up through every class which rests upon them.

You come to us and tell us that the great cities are in favor of the gold standard; we reply that the great cities rest upon our broad and fertile prairies. Burn down your cities and leave our farms, and your cities will spring up again as if by magic; but destroy our farms and the grass will grow in the streets of every city in the country.

My friends, we declare that this nation is able to legislate for its own people on every question, without waiting for the aid or consent of any other nation on earth; and upon that issue we expect to carry every state in the Union. I shall not slander the inhabitants of the fair state of Massachusetts nor the inhabitants of the state of New York by saying that, when they are confronted with the proposition, they will declare that this nation is not able to attend to its own business. It is the issue of 1776 over again. Our ancestors, when but three millions in number had the courage to declare their political independence of every other nation; shall we, their descendants, when we have grown to seventy millions, declare that we are less independent than our forefathers?

No, my friends, that will never be the verdict of our people. Therefore, we care not upon what lines the battle is fought. If they say bimetallism is good, but that we cannot have it until other nations help us, we reply that, instead of having a gold standard because England has, we will restore bimetallism, and then let England have bimetallism because the United States has it. If they dare to come out in the open field and defend the gold standard as a good thing, we will fight them to the uttermost. Having behind us the producing masses of this nation and the world, supported by the commercial interests, the laboring interests and the toilers everywhere, we will answer their demand for a gold standard by saying to them: You shall not press down upon the brow of labor this crown of thorns, you shall not crucify mankind upon a cross of gold.

Chapter 13

The Tumultuous Interwar Period: 1918–1940

A closer look reveals that the economic repercussions of a stock market crash depend less on the severity of the crash than on the response of economic policymakers, particularly central bankers. After the 1929 crash, the Federal Reserve mistakenly focused its policies on preserving the gold value of the dollar rather than stabilizing the domestic economy.

(Ben Bernanke, 2000.[1])

The world went through an extraordinary period of economic and social change during the 19th century. Economic growth and technological progress were unprecedented, and most people in the world's major economies experienced huge changes in the way they lived and worked. The 19th century also saw an unprecedented globalization of economic activity. Jules Verne's novel *Around the World in 80 Days*, with its steamships, railroads, telegraph messages, hot air balloons, modern banking services and travel agencies at every stop,

---

[1] Ben Bernanke (2000). "A Crash Course for Central Bankers", *Foreign Policy*, September–October.

and the widespread use of British pound throughout the world, epitomizes the times. Equally illustrative is John Maynard Keynes' famous description of life in London just before the outbreak of World War I:

> What an extraordinary episode in the economic progress of man that age was which came to an end in August, 1914. The greater part of the population, it is true, worked hard and lived at a low standard of comfort, yet were, to all appearances, reasonably contented with this lot. But escape was possible, for any man of capacity or character at all exceeding the average, into the middle and upper classes, for whom life offered, at a low cost and with the least trouble, conveniences, comforts, and amenities beyond the compass of the richest and most powerful monarchs of other ages. The inhabitant of London could order by telephone, sipping his morning tea in bed, the various products of the whole earth, in such quantity as he might see fit, and reasonably expect their early delivery upon his doorstep; he could at the same moment and by the same means adventure his wealth in the natural resources and new enterprises of any quarter of the world, and share, without exertion or even trouble, in their prospective fruits and advantages; or he could decide to couple the security of his fortunes with the good faith of the townspeople of any substantial municipality in any continent that fancy or information might recommend.... . But, most important of all, he regarded this state of affairs as normal, certain, and permanent, except in the direction of further improvement, and any deviation from it as aberrant, scandalous, and avoidable.[2]

This global society and its international economy came to an end in 1914. This chapter covers the attempts to restore the Gold Standard in the post-World War I economic and political environment.

---

[2] John Maynard Keynes (1920). pp. 11, 12.

Chapter Goals

1. Describe the economic and political environment that existed at the close of World War I.
2. Detail how the Versailles Treaty contributed to political conflict.
3. Discuss why and how the Gold Standard was restored, and why it was ultimately abandoned for good.
4. Discuss the slow economic recovery in Europe after World War I, especially in Germany.
5. Explain how the rules of the gold standard and the fact that the gold standard was really a "gold-reserve standard" quickly transformed the US financial crisis into a global depression.
6. Discuss efforts in the 1930s to replace the gold standard and restore some degree of order to the international financial system.

13.1 Back to Normal After World War I?

Like all wars, World War I was deadly. Even though the war was fought almost exclusively in Europe, millions of soldiers from non-European countries and colonies participated and died in the conflict. The historian Margaret MacMillan points out that the war's toll was largely human. "Away from the battlefields, Europe still looked much the same. The great cities remained, the railway lines were more or less intact, ports still functioned".[3] But the psychological effects of the huge loss of human life during the "Great War" came at a time when the human psyche already had to deal with unprecedented changes in the economic, social, and political structures of the world.

After the war, world leaders declared their intention to establish a lasting peace, and they met for six-months in Paris to achieve that goal. The leaders of most countries sought to return to the pre-war

---

[3] Margaret MacMillan (2001). pp. xxv–xxvi.

economic environment described by Keynes. It is safe to say that most leaders, save those of the new communist regime in Russia and those in Europe's overseas colonies, also believed a return to the gold standard was necessary. The "normal, certain, and permanent" state as described by Keynes could not be brought back, however. New political forces emerged after the war; Russia threw out its feudal society in favor of communism, and many countries in Europe and Latin America turned to fascism when the pre-World War I order could not be revived. In many countries, the advance of democracy pushed governments to pay more attention to the interests of broader segments of their populations, and this made a return to the gold standard more difficult in many industrial countries.

13.1.1 *The costs of the war*

The cost of the "World War", as World War I was then called, was staggering when compared with earlier wars. Nearly all governments stopped redeeming their currencies for gold because they had no other option than to print money to finance the war. All countries involved in the war suffered severe economic upheaval that would not be easy to set right after the war. Entire industries had been converted to wartime production, and the well-established international trade patterns had been completely disrupted. The cost of the post-war recovery was grossly underestimated by most policymakers. Unfortunately, that turned out to be the least serious mistake by the world's leaders at the close of the war.

Policymakers' biggest failure was their inability to see that the world had changed in fundamental ways. These changes had been brewing well before World War I broke out. The rapid economic growth and the extraordinary technological progress achieved during the decades before the war had changed not only the way the global economy worked, but the political and social environments within which policymakers had to operate had also changed. The most obvious evidence of the changing economic, political, and social conditions was World War I itself. The outbreak of World War I was not just some random disturbance that just happened to interrupt the globalized world described by Keynes. The war itself was caused by economic, political, and social forces that were not well understood, or even perceived, by policymakers and their constituencies. People were not prepared for the serious conflicts created by the rapid economic and political changes. Again, Keynes provides an insightful interpretation of pre-war attitudes:

> The projects and politics of militarism and imperialism, of racial and cultural rivalries, of monopolies, restrictions, and exclusion, which were to play the serpent to this paradise, were little more than the amusements of his daily newspaper, and appeared to exercise almost no influence at all on the ordinary course of social and economic life....[4]

Animosities had been growing well before the war because of imperial rivalries, especially between the early colonial powers like Britain, France, and the Netherlands, and the latecomers to imperialism like Germany and Italy. The formation of political and military alliances did not help either. Individual countries feared being isolated, so they rushed to join either the Central Powers, which included Germany, Austria–Hungary, Romania, and the Ottoman Empire, or the Triple Entente of Britain, France, and Russia. Then, throw in ethnic tensions within many of the larger countries, growing nationalism, militarism, an aggressive press that often fanned the flames of nationalism and cultural conflict, and rapid technological advances in weaponry that inflated assessments of likely military victories, and the world was clearly poised for war. It only took an assassination of an Austrian Duke by a group of Serbian-sponsored terrorists to set the spark.

The unexpectedly-long four-year war did not sort things out. To the contrary, the new political and economic environments that remained after the war would actually bring many of the underlying political and economic conflicts further out in the open. The same conflicts that sparked the war severely hampered efforts by the world's leaders to restore order to the world. Unfortunately, the extent of the

---

[4] John Maynard Keynes (1920). p. 12.

fundamental changes that economic progress had brought was not fully grasped by the world's leaders. The failure of the post-World War I order was not the result of a lack of effort to deal with the pressing issues; it was more a case of the rate of change in human society outpacing humans' ability to comprehend their changing economic and social environments.

13.1.2 *Reviving the gold standard under changed circumstances*

An early casualty of World War I was the gold standard. When hostilities began in August 1914, most countries suspended convertibility of their currencies into gold. The needs of war resulted in widespread deficit spending that was often financed by printing money. The resulting inflation as well as the distorted trade patterns caused by the hostilities left governments no option other than to abandon the rules of the gold standard. Winning the war became everyone's first priority; concerns about convertibility and price stability were no longer important.

When World War I ended in 1918, foreign exchange markets expected the gold standard to be quickly reinstated. According to the financial economist Leland Yeager:

> Towards the end of the war speculation centered on belief that exchange rates would soon return to "normal". At the time of the armistice, the rates of the Netherlands, Spain, the United States, Great Britain and the Empire, Japan, France, Sweden, Argentina, Brazil, and Italy diverged remarkably little from the prewar pattern, considering the circumstances.[5]

However, a quick return to the gold standard was not possible. For one thing, the United States had stayed on the gold standard; because it had supplied large amounts of arms, food, raw materials, and many other goods to the belligerents, it had run very large trade surpluses and accumulated large amounts of gold. Furthermore, the war years

---

[5] Leland B. Yeager (1976). p. 311.

were inflationary. The US Federal Reserve Bank converted the inflows of gold to money as the rules of the game mandated. Inflation ensued, and US prices doubled during the war. Most other countries, no longer bound by the gold standard, had printed money to finance their war efforts and, therefore, also suffered high rates of inflation. Because inflation had increased all countries' price levels, in 1919 there was not enough gold in the world to back all of the currency in circulation if the old gold parities were applied. Furthermore, since everyone's rates of inflation were different, the pre-war gold parity exchange rates did not reflect post-war purchasing power parities.

Most countries actually let exchange rates float freely during the years immediately after World War I. But, most policy makers began to prepare for the world's return to the gold standard at the old gold parities. For example, the newly-created central bank of the United States, the Federal Reserve Bank, tightened monetary policy and engineered a massive deflation in 1920–1922. Prices fell by nearly 20 percent between 1920 and 1922. Unemployment also surged, however, and after 1921 the Federal Reserve opted to just maintain price stability rather than try to push prices down any further. Other countries, most notably Britain, also instituted deflationary monetary policy in order to return to the gold standard under the old gold parities.

The deflationary policies adopted by Britain's leadership were harshly criticized by John Maynard Keynes. In his 1923 *Tract on Monetary Reform*, Keynes argued that the tight monetary policies required to restore the real value of gold relative to the world's money supplies under the old gold parities would cause a continual recession. The cost in terms of unemployment, falling investment, and lost output would be too great, he claimed. He instead suggested that countries wanting to return to the gold standard should set new parities in line with existing gold reserves, which meant they only had to maintain price stability at the higher price levels instead of first having to deflate prices. If the price of gold had been raised as Keynes suggested, there again would have been enough gold to back the money in circulation, and lengthy recessions to drive down prices would not have been necessary. Why this was not done remains something of a mystery. Had the rules of the Gold Standard become an unalterable element of a culture that people equated with modern civilization rather than just an international financial arrangement?

13.1.3 *The Treaty of Versailles*

The post-World War I period cannot be understood without taking note of the Paris Peace Conference in 1919. President Woodrow Wilson of the United States, the Prime Ministers of France and Britain, Georges Clemenceau and David Lloyd George, and nearly all other world leaders led large delegations of diplomats, economists, bankers, and lawyers to Paris to negotiate a new world order that would establish permanent peace. For six months, these leaders lived in Paris and participated in the daily negotiations. Effectively, the world's governments operated from Paris for half a year! Agreement was reached on the creation of the League of Nations, an international body that would deal with international issues and conflicts. The Conference also created the International Labour Organisation, which today falls under the auspices of the United Nations. The Conference redrew the world political map, with old countries broken up and new countries created. The Austria-Hungarian Empire was split into Austria, Hungary, Czechoslovakia, Romania, and Yugoslavia. Poland, Lithuania, Latvia, and Estonia were created out of former Russian territory. The Middle East was completely reorganized, with Turkey, Syria, Iraq, Palestine, and other countries created out of the former Ottoman Empire. Also, the Conference negotiated a set of treaties that defined the terms of surrender of Germany, Austria, Hungary, Bulgaria, and Ottoman Turkey.

The Treaty between the Allied countries and Germany was signed in June of 1919 in the Paris suburb of Versailles. This Treaty and the others signed with the other countries that fought on the side of Germany determined that Germany and its allies should compensate Britain, France, and its allies for their war losses. Losses due to Germany alone were assessed at $30 billion at 1920 prices, which was slightly more than double Germany's annual GDP at that time.[6] A rigorous time schedule for payment was laid down.

---

[6] Based on data from Angus Maddison (1991).

Although he is well known for his dominant role in shaping the Bretton Woods Agreement, John Maynard Keynes was also a member of the British delegation to the Paris Conference as chief Treasury advisor. He became disillusioned by the negotiations, and when he returned to his academic position at the University of Cambridge, he wrote a book critical of the Paris Conference. In his 1920 book entitled The Economic Consequences of the Peace, Keynes warned:

> If the European Civil War is to end with France and Italy abusing their momentary victorious power to destroy Germany and Austria-Hungary now prostrate, they invite their own destruction also....[7]

The governments of France, Britain, and Italy were probably not interested in destroying their enemies, although some individual leaders may have had revenge on their minds. Rather, countries such as France and Britain saw the reparations payments as a convenient source of revenue for their own debt repayments to the United States. The Allies had borrowed heavily from the United States to purchase arms and food, and the US viewed the loans as commercial transactions that could not be canceled or renegotiated. It was, therefore, not a coincidence that the reparations payments from Germany and its allies stipulated in the Treaty of Versailles were about equal to the war-time foreign borrowing by Britain, France, Italy, and other Allied countries. Short-run fiscal expediency seems to have triumphed over the facts and justice.

Regardless of their justification, the German reparations payments posed a serious practical problem: How were tax payments by German citizens to their government in German marks to be converted to dollars so British and French governments could repay their US loans? Several things had to happen for this scheme work:

1. The German government would have to increase taxes or borrow from its citizens in order to cover its foreign reparations payments.

---

[7] John Maynard Keynes (1920).

2. Germany would have to run a large current account surplus with the allied countries in order to earn the British pounds, French francs, and Italian lira needed to pay war reparations.
3. The allied countries would have to run current account surpluses with the United States in order to retire their debts with US lenders.

Political conditions in Germany, the Allied European countries, and the United States prevented things from unfolding in this required manner, however.

Reparations are effectively transfers, which appear in the current account of the balance of payments. Therefore, barring large private investment inflows, Germany would have to offset these transfers to Britain, France, and others with a trade surplus. The German government also ended up running large budget deficits in order to pay the reparations. These budget deficits were at first financed by domestic borrowing, but when doubts arose over the German government's ability to ever pay back its growing debt, German citizens and banks were no longer willing to purchase their government's bonds. At that point, the German government was forced to print money to cover its budget deficit, and accelerating inflation was the predictable result. The faster prices rose, the more money the government had to print to cover its expenditures. By 1922, prices were rising by several thousand percent per month. Many of Germany's allies, such as Austria, Hungary, Poland, and Bulgaria, similarly generated *hyperinflation*, which is inflation of more than 100 percent, as they struggled to pay for reparations payments.

An aid package by the United States and Britain, known as the *Dawes Plan*, provided Germany with loans with which it could meet its reparations payments. Germany's 1924 budget reform increased taxes and reduced expenditures, and inflationary monetary expansion was ended. Private lending also resumed, and Germany was in fact able to borrow enough to more or less cover its balance of payments deficit for much of the remainder of the 1920s. But it was not able to consistently run surpluses to "earn" the foreign currencies by running trade surpluses. High unemployment caused by deflationary policies deemed neccessary to restore the gold standard led to political pressure for Allied countries to increasingly restrict imports. That is, the countries who demanded the reparations payments effectively continued to prevent Germany from running a current account surplus with which to finance its reparations payments. In the end, the "victors" were able to collect only a small fraction of the reparations specified in the Treaty of Versailles. The United States eventually canceled remaining debts of its allies, but the damage had been done.

13.1.4 *Isolationism in the United States*

The second link in the intricate trade pattern that would be necessary for the world economy to handle the post-World War I reparations and debt repayments also failed: The United States refused to permit imports from its former allies to increase and to tolerate the trade deficit that would permit its allies to repay their debts. The US instead raised tariffs after World War I. US industry, which had expanded rapidly during World War I, felt vulnerable to foreign competition after the war. It clamored for protection, and the new Republican administration that took office in 1921 immediately set out to oblige its business constituency by passing protectionist legislation. The *Fordney-McCumber Tariff* of 1922 doubled average US tariff rates.

But higher tariffs were just one reflection of the sharp isolationist turn by the United States after World War I. The US Congress refused to ratify participation in the League of Nations after World War I. This new international body was one of President Woodrow Wilson's "Fourteen Points" that he presented to the Paris Conference. After the Conference, Wilson traveled by train across the United States promoting ratification of the Treaty of Versailles and participation in the League of Nations, but he could not muster enough support. The Congress insisted that a number of "reservations" be added to the Treaty. When Wilson's health deteriorated and he returned to Washington at the insistence of his wife, doctor, and close advisors late in 1919, no one took up the fight for ratification. The Congress simply did not act. Then, in 1920, American voters effectively rejected Wilson's plan by voting for the

Republican candidate Warren Harding in 1920. Harding actively campaigned against participation in the League of Nations or any other international organization.

Perhaps the clearest sign of its isolationist national mood was the US reversal of its long-standing policy of open immigration. In 1921, Congress passed the *Emergency Quota Act*, which set strict limits on immigration for the first time in US history. This act was followed by the blatantly racist *Japanese Exclusion Act of 1924*, which banned all immigration from one specific country and severely strained US relations with Japan. The shift in immigration policy was completed some months later with the passing of the *Immigration Act of 1924*. This latter act limited immigration from any particular country to two percent of the number of descendants of immigrants of that nationality residing in the United States back in 1890. The racist quotas appealed to the many Americans who feared that the recent immigration from Southern and Eastern Europe was upsetting the country's culture. Legislators apparently thought that the racial mix of 1890 more accurately represented the "traditional" ethnic makeup of the United States than the racial/ethnic mix reported in the 1920 census.

One of the most damaging economic policy decisions by the United States after World War I was its infamous Smoot-Hawley Tariff. After the 1929 stock market crash and the sudden slowdown in economic activity, lobbying for protection grew stronger. As industry after industry clamored for protection, Senators and Representatives participated in a classic example of "logrolling", which is the process in which individual members of Congress agree to support each other's local interests. New tariffs protecting specific industries in each Congressional district soon added up to the highest average overall tariff ever enacted by the United States.

The bill that emerged from Senator Smoot's committee in the Senate and Hawley's committee in the House of Representatives immediately caused a trade war that engulfed much of the world. Faced with unemployment and calls for protection at home, few countries accepted the increased US tariffs without retaliation. Most major trading countries imposed equal or more severe tariff increases.

Some countries that had closely followed the bill through the Congress raised tariffs even before the Smoot-Hawley tariffs took effect.

The consequences of the Smoot-Hawley tariffs and other countries' retaliation were that by 1931 world trade volume had fallen by more than 50 percent from its 1929 levels. As Kindleberger's (1973) account of the Great Depression revealed, by 1933 world trade had fallen by about 70 percent. In the United States and elsewhere, the new protectionism created no additional jobs because, even though import-competing industries benefited from the protection, foreign retaliation caused exports to decline. All other things equal, real income fell because, effectively, foreign protectionism reduced the size of each country's most competitive and efficient industries while expanding its least competitive industries slowly, if at all, given the recessionary environment. The Smoot-Hawley tariff, and the trade war it instigated, were partially responsible for turning a serious recession into a decade-long depression.

13.1.5 *Senator Reed Smoot, the proud protectionist*

Looking back with perfect hindsight, one wonders how the United States could have been so blind to the damage its protectionism was causing. However, domestic politics often plays out in ways that are shortsighted from an international perspective. In most countries, trade policy tends to be shaped by domestic political forces. The isolationist mood in the United States during the 1920s removed international concerns from most political discussions.

Senator Reed Smoot of the state of Utah entered Congress in 1903, when the exceptionally high *Dingley Tariff* of 1897 was still in force. When Smoot was appointed by the Senate leadership to the Senate Finance Committee in 1908, he actively sought more high tariffs, especially on sugar and wool, two major Utah products that competed with imports. When the Democrat Woodrow Wilson became president and the Democratic Party gained majorities in both houses of Congress in 1912, they sharply reduced tariffs. Republicans like Smoot never forgave President Wilson for those tariff cuts, so when the Republicans returned to national power in 1920 they quickly reintroduced laws raising tariffs. Not surprisingly, the 1923 the Fordney-McCumber Tariff included higher tariffs on Cuban sugar, a direct competitor with Utah's beet sugar industry. When Smoot became the Chairman of the Senate Finance Committee in the late 1920s, he pushed for even higher tariff rates.

In 1929, Smoot's Senate Finance Committee started the logrolling process, described earlier, that eventually led to the Smoot-Hawley Tariff of 1930. Even though the United States, as a creditor nation, could only be paid the interest and principal due from the rest of the world if it ran a trade deficit, Republican President Hoover signed the bill. The Smoot-Hawley bill immediately boosted average import tariffs by 53 percent, the highest in American history. Smoot never acknowledged the negative consequences of his legislation. In fact, in the depths of the depression in 1933 he argued that the rate might not be high enough. In his memoirs, the "great protectionist", as he was known to his supporters, claimed the 1930 tariff as his "proudest achievement".[8]

13.2 The Gold Standard and the Great Depression

Protectionism was just one factor that turned the 1929 stock market crash into the Great Depression. The main cause of the Great Depression was the ill-fated partial return to the gold standard. The monetary policies mandated by the Gold Standard's rules of the game worsened the recession and turned the loss of wealth after the US stock market crash into a financial crisis. The Gold Standard's rules of the game also caused the U.S. recession to quickly spread to the rest of the world.

13.2.1 *Economic recovery under the rules of the game*

Most countries struggled to restore convertibility to gold during the 1920s, but by 1926 most of the major economics of the world

---

[8] This account is taken from James B. Allen (1977) and Mary Beth Norton *et al.* (1990).

claimed to again be "on the gold standard". As described earlier, the return to the gold standard did not come easy. Most European countries remained in recession with high levels of unemployment as monetary and fiscal policies were designed to deflate price levels and effectively expand the monetary value of national gold stocks. As a result, the post-World War I international financial system turned out different than the pre-war Gold Standard.

Many countries failed to rigorously follow the "rules of the game" because domestic political pressures did not permit them to do so. The constant pressure of unemployment and slow growth often led governments to reverse their policies and expand money supplies. The incompatibility of money expansion and full convertibility forced countries to limit free convertibility. Also, many countries held foreign currencies instead of gold, allegedly under the justification that the foreign reserves were backed by gold. This practice effectively created a gold-exchange standard rather than a gold standard. This was a type of *fractional reserve* monetary system, some called it a *gold-reserve system*, because countries held other countries' gold-backed currencies as reserves rather than holding actual gold. This practice increased the world money supply relative to the gold base, a convenient result given the difficulties of deflating prices to the point where money supplies were fully backed by gold. However, it also meant that changes in the gold stock would multiply changes in the money supply, thus amplifying economic disturbances.

Obstfeld and Taylor (2002) compared interest rates on government foreign debt during the classic Gold Standard period 1870–1913 and during the inter-war return to the gold standard between 1925 and 1931. During the former period, interest rates on loans to countries that adhered to the gold standard were 40 to 60 basis points lower, all other things equal, than for loans to countries whose currencies were not convertible to gold. During the latter period, however, for many countries the announced adherence to the gold standard did not result in lower interest rates. In other words, countries' commitments to gold convertibility were not as credible as their pre-World War I commitments to full convertibility to gold.

13.2.2 *The importance of US international lending*

US loans helped to finance German reparations payments for a time and even enabled Germany to restore limited convertibility to gold in 1926. But, US capital flows overseas reversed themselves towards the end of the 1920s, when a booming stock market and high interest rates in the US pulled money back home. Then interest rates rose in 1928 because the Federal Reserve Bank tightened monetary policy in response to what it saw as a developing stock price bubble. Under the rules of the gold standard, the struggling democratic Weimar government in Germany had to let the money supply contract as money flowed back to the United States and the German balance of payments went into deficit once again. Price levels declined, and unemployment rose. The deflation raised debtors' real liabilities, which increased bankruptcies and loan defaults. The financial crisis caused German economic activity to collapse.[9] Then when the US economy slowed after the 1929 stock market crash, German exports declined, driving the German economy further into its deep recession. One German politician who exploited the deteriorating economic condition was the leader of the small National Socialist Party, Adolph Hitler. When economic times are difficult, people often follow those who offer seemingly easy solutions.

13.2.3 *Spreading the economic misery*

When the Great Depression spread from country to country, political pressures for expansionary monetary and fiscal policies overwhelmed the desire to hold on to the gold standard and its fixed exchange rate. Austria's largest bank, the Vienna Kreditanstalt, collapsed in May 1931. A full-fledged banking panic spread into Germany and Hungary and eventually forced the United Kingdom off the gold standard. One by one, nearly all other countries suspended convertibility and effectively abandoned the gold standard.

---

[9] Barry Eichengreen (1996).

According to Robert Mundell: "Had the price of gold been raised in the late 1920's, or, alternatively, had the major central banks pursued policies of price stability instead of adhering to the gold standard, there would have been no Great Depression....[10] The economic historian Eichengreen (1992, 1996) similarly attributes the perverse behavior of central banks around the world in the face of economic recession to the need to follow the rules of the gold standard. He claims that the fixed exchange rates and the specie flow mechanism caused the US recession that followed the 1929 US stock market crash to be quickly transmitted to other economies. The rules of the Gold Standard mandated that central banks facing declining exports to the US contract their money supplies in order to maintain convertibility and fixed exchange rates. The 1930 US recession was primarily due to the US Federal Reserve Bank's contractionary monetary policies after the stock market crash. The Smoot-Hawley tariff in 1930, discussed above, reduced US imports and induced monetary contractions in other countries when their exports declined. Table 13.1 shows how drastically exports fell after 1929. The declines in foreign exchange earnings from exports declined because both the volume and the prices of exports declined. In 1932, exports were little more than one third of their value in 1929.

Table 13.1   World Merchandise Exports: 1919–1934.

Years	Export value (US$ billions)	Value index (1929 = 100)	Export volume (1929 = 100)
1929	32.7	100	100
1930	26.2	80	93
1931	18.6	57	86
1932	12.6	38	73
1933	14.8	45	75
1934	18.6	58	78

Source: Maddison (1995).

---

[10] Robert Mundell (2000). p. 331.

13.2.4 *The consequences of the economics*

The high unemployment and stagnant incomes led to the rise of new political leadership in many countries. Some of those new leaders offered false solutions. It is important to return to Robert Mundell's quote in the previous section; the complete quote ends as follows:

> Had the price of gold been raised ... there would have been no Great Depression, no Nazi revolution, and no World War II.[11]

Adolph Hitler exploited a dismal economy to gain control in Germany; Benito Mussolini earlier had done the same in Italy, and in several Latin American countries fascist-leaning military leaders came to power during the Great Depression. And according to the international economist Richard Cooper:

> What is less well known is the influence of the Smoot-Hawley Tariff and the sharp down-turn in world economic activity in undermining the position of internationally minded officials and politicians in Japan, in favor of an imperialistic nationalism which led to the Japanese invasion of Manchuria in late 1931, the real beginning of the Second World War.[12]

In 2001, Japan's prime minister Junichiro Koizumi, in a surprisingly blunt discussion on Japan's role in World War II, echoed Richard Cooper's assessment: "Why did Japan go to war? It was because it was isolated from the international world".[13] The irresponsible Smoot-Hawley Tariff obviously does not justify Japan's turn towards militarism, but the case reminds us that protectionism can have some dire consequences. A shift in one country's trade policies alters the economic situation in other countries, and economic changes can upset social and political balances in unexpected and unfortunate ways.

---

[11] Robert Mundell (2000). p. 331.

[12] Richard N. Cooper (1992). p. 2123.

[13] Quoted in Robert L. Bartley (2001). "China II — The Lessons From Rising Japan", *The Wall Street Journal*, 14 May.

It may seem somewhat of a stretch to argue that the international financial order was the cause of the Depression, the Nazi atrocities, and World War II, as Mundell argues. On the other hand, the Bretton Woods Conference in 1944 suggests that the leaders of the Allied nations were clearly convinced that the international financial order was indeed a very important determinant of world peace and economic well-being.

13.2.5 *The Gold Standard mentalité as cause of the Great Depression*

The economic historians Barry Eichengreen and Peter Temin contend that the fundamental cause of the Great Depression was that the Gold Standard had become an "ideology". This ideological status led policymakers to continue following the "rules of the game" well after it should have become obvious that the consequences of rigid monetary policies were causing economic devastation:

> The constraints of the gold standard system hamstrung countries as they struggled to adapt during the 1920s to changes in the world economy. And the ideology, mentalité and rhetoric of the gold standard led policy makers to take action that only accentuated economic distress in the 1930s. Central bankers continued to kick the world economy while it was down until it lost consciousness".[14]

By *mentalité* Eichengreen and Temin mean "the mind set of policy makers, which shaped their notions of the possible". They go on to explain:

> Historians have pondered why policy makers failed to counteract the Depression and why the actions they took in fact aggravated its severity. The recent literature shows that they saw no other option, given the international system they confronted and the ideological lens [model] though which they viewed it.[15]

---

[14] Barry Eichengreen and Peter Temin (1997). pp. 1, 2.
[15] Barry Eichengreen and Peter Temin (1997). p. 5.

That is, despite the clear adverse effects of their policies, policymakers remained confident that their model would prevail and that the policies it pointed to would prove effective for overcoming the difficulties their economies faced. The rules of the game mandated that they respond to balance of payments deficits and gold losses by restricting credit and deflating the economy until balance was restored.

Other new factors were at work to depress economic activity. Labor markets had become more rigid because of the growth of labor unions and the management of labor by personnel departments of the oligopolistic corporations that dominated most industries. Kindleberger (1973) has suggested that the failure of the gold standard to function properly was due to the loss of London as the center of the international monetary system, with New York not willing to assume London's role. But, Kindleberger's view is just another version of the predominant mentalité, because his concern was that the gold standard was not being properly managed, not that there was a problem with the gold standard.

Keynes' suggestion that the deflationary problems might have been avoided had countries returned to gold at more realistic parities was more helpful, but while such a policy would have limited the damage of deflation in the late 1920s, realistic parities would not have eliminated the perceived need for sharp reductions in wages and prices once the Great Depression struck. Of course, in the 1930s Keynes was arguing for a completely new macroeconomic policy approach that included active government fiscal and monetary policies to increase aggregate demand. But such policies would have to wait as long as the politicians in power had the gold standard mentalité. Again according to Eichengreen and Temin: "Policies were perverse because they were designed to preserve the gold standard, not employment".[16] The rationale for this approach was the belief that maintaining the gold standard was the best solution to solving the unemployment problem.

So convinced were many central bankers, economists, and others of this approach, that they would later suggest that it was the abandonment

---

[16] Barry Eichengreen and Peter Temin (1997). p. 19.

of the gold standard that caused the Great Depression! US President Hoover referred to the gold standard as "little short of a sacred formula".[17] When the US commitment to the gold standard came into question in 1931 after Britain abandoned the gold standard, the US Federal Reserve Bank signaled its commitment to the gold standard by raising interest rates. This contractionary policy in the midst of rapid economic decline was "inept" according to Milton Friedman and Anna Schwartz. "The Federal Reserve System reacted vigorously and promptly to the external drain. On October 9, the Federal Reserve Bank of New York raised its discount rate to 1.5 percent and on October, to 3.5 percent — the sharpest rise within so brief a period in the whole history of the System, before or since...".[18] The gold standard mentalité thus drove the US economy deeper into its depression.

13.2.6 *The end of gold*

The British government was among the first to abandon their commitment to exchange British currency for gold at a fixed rate in the fall of 1931. This event was met with disbelief and criticism in Britain and elsewhere. Jackson E. Reynolds, President of the First National Bank of New York, equated the decision to "the end of the world". Tom Johnson, parliamentary secretary for Scotland, famously exclaimed "Nobody told us we could do that!" The Bank of England was unable to let go of its gold standard mentalite:

> It hesitated to reduce interest rates after devaluation in order to avoid inflation. Inflation! In the most deflationary setting the world has ever known, when prices in all industrial countries were falling about 10 percent a year. It was, in an observer's trenchant words, 'to cry, Fire, Fire, in Noah's flood'.[19]

---

[17] Quoted in Harris Gaylord Warren (1959). p. 280.

[18] Milton Friedman and Anna Schwartz (1963). p. 317.

[19] Barry Eichengreen and Peter Temin (1997). pp. 30, 31.

The United States did not abandon gold convertibility until 1933, after elections brought Franklin D. Roosevelt into the White House and Democrats gained large majorities in both houses of Congress. Switzerland, France, and the Netherlands stayed with the gold standard for several more years.

Most countries defended gold convertibility by trying to increase their holdings of gold and reducing the share of foreign exchange in their reserves. Global monetary reserves fell to 11 percent by the end of 1931, down from 37 percent three years earlier. The 1920s gold-exchange standard, under which reserves of one or more of the major currencies were often substituted for actual gold in many countries, was effectively abandoned in favor of a pure gold-based system, which central bankers felt would better enable them to maintain credibility. This flight to the safety of real gold ended up sharply reducing money supplies just when the world's economies were falling deeper and deeper into recession. The contractionary monetary policies to defend convertibility caused widespread financial instability. Deflation increased real outstanding debt, and retrenchments and defaults further reduced aggregate demand.

How much better off would countries have been if they had abandoned the gold standard sooner? Bordo *et al.* (2006) use a macroeconomic model to estimate that if Switzerland had devalued with Britain in 1931, Swiss real GDP would have been 18 percent higher in 1935. Even if Switzerland had waited to devalue its franc with the US dollar in 1933, they estimate that its 1935 real GDP would still have been 15 percent higher.

13.3 A New Order

Eichengreen and Temin conclude that the gold Standard had become an ideology, not unlike mercantilism in the 17th and 18th centuries, communism and capitalism in the 20th century, and neoliberalism at the start of the 21st century:

> The world economy, most observers agree, is endowed with powerful self-correcting tendencies. When activity turns down, its inner

workings provide a tendency for it to bounce back. Only sustained bad policies can drive the world economy so far off this path that it loses its capacity to recover. And only a hegemonic ideology can convince leaders to persist in such counterproductive policies.[20]

It seems to take a change in leadership to change an ideology. In the United States, President Hoover was defeated at the polls by Franklin D. Roosevelt, who during his campaign stated: "The sound internal economic situation of a nation is a greater factor in its well-being than the price of its currency".[21] These words are reminiscent of what Adam Smith wrote in his Wealth of Nations when he explained that mercantilism's goal of accumulating gold by means of trade surpluses is detrimental to human welfare, the true measure of economic success. Western European governments also changed leadership, which then took their countries off the gold standard and introduced alternative economic policies to deal with the Depression.

13.3.1 *Brazil's unintended "Keynesian" recovery*

At the beginning of the Great Depression, Latin America's largest economy, Brazil, was a typical exporter of primary products, such as cotton, sugar, and, above all, coffee. The prices of primary products fell precipitously in the early 1930s as the Great Depression reduced demand around the world. Brazil's terms of trade, the ratio of export prices to import prices, fell by about 50 percent in 1933. That is, Brazil's exports of coffee and other primary products only purchased half as many real imports as in 1929. Fortunately for Brazil, it had never been a strict adherent to the gold standard's rules of the game, and it certainly did not feel bound by them in 1930. With few gold reserves or reserve currencies on hand to prevent a depreciation, Brazil let its currency depreciate sharply in 1930.

---

[20] Barry Eichengreen and Peter Temin (1997). pp. 37, 38.

[21] Quoted from Edgar B. Nixon (1969). *Franklin D. Roosevelt and Foreign Affairs*, January 1933–February 1934, Vol. I, Cambridge, MA: Harvard University Press. p. 269.

The depreciation of Brazil's currency kept Brazil's dwindling international trade in balance by making imports much more expensive relative to domestic products. Exactly as exchange rate theory predicts, the rise in the prices of imports relative to domestic products led Brazilian consumers to substitute domestic goods for foreign goods. It suddenly became economical to produce many products in Brazil that had previously been imported from abroad. Brazil's failure to adhere to the gold standard before the Great Depression had actually prevented it from contracting much foreign debt; foreign lenders did not trust countries that were not disciplined enough to follow the rules of the game! In 1930, this lack of foreign debt allowed Brazil to avoid the severe financial crisis that would accompany similar currency depreciations later in the 20th century, 1982 for example, when Brazil would hold large amounts of foreign debt.

Even more ironic was how special interest politics in Brazil led the government to unintentionally implement the stimulative fiscal and monetary policies that Keynes would some years later prescribe for an economy caught in a depression. Coffee producers were a very powerful political force in Brazil, so when coffee prices fell sharply, the Brazilian government responded with huge subsidies to maintain coffee producers' domestic currency incomes despite the fall in international coffee prices. To add insult to the injury of the dominant economic ideology, the Brazilian government increased the domestic money supply in order to finance the huge coffee subsidies. Politically, the printing of money was much more convenient than raising taxes or borrowing from domestic sources, and international borrowing was out of the question during the depression years.

Brazil, therefore, effectively conducted exactly the expansionary monetary and fiscal policies as John Maynard Keynes advocated as the solution to the depression in his *The General Theory of Employment, Interest and Money*. While Keynes urged government policymakers to explicitly enact stimulative fiscal and monetary policies to increase domestic demand and reduce the high unemployment that plagued so many countries during the Great Depression, Brazil stumbled into exactly those policies with its politically motivated coffee subsidies and convenient money expansion. In the words of the Brazilian economic historian Celso Furtado:

> It is therefore quite clear that the recovery of the Brazilian economy which took place from 1933 onward was not caused by any external factor but by the pump-priming policy unconsciously adopted in Brazil as a by-product of the protection of coffee interests.[22]

Furtado is not entirely correct when he writes "not caused by external factors", however. The sharp depreciation of the Brazilian currency following the collapse of commodity prices was very helpful because it caused most of the increase in domestic demand to be directed at domestic producers rather than the suddenly very expensive imports, thus enhancing the stimulative effect of the expansionary macroeconomic policies. If the rest of the world had not held on to the gold standard for a while longer, the Brazilian currency may not have fallen as much in value relative to the world's other currencies, and its accidental economic stimulus would not have been as strong.

By 1933, industrial production in Brazil had recovered its 1929 level, unlike the performance in many developed economies. 1933 marked the deepest point of the Depression in most countries of the world. By 1937, Brazil's industrial production was 50 percent greater than it was in 1929, and overall real GDP was 20 percent greater in 1937 compared to 1929, quite a feat during the 1930s. Not being bound by the mentalité of the Gold Standard was clearly an advantage in the 1930s.

13.3.2 *Reversing the financial chaos*

The Gold Standard and the Smoot-Hawley tariff were not the only causes of the worldwide Great Depression. After World War I, the international financial system was also hampered by the lack of international cooperation. Before the war, there was often cooperation

---

[22] Celso Furtado (1963). p. 212.

between central banks; recall how several European central banks helped out the Bank of England when Argentina's loan default in 1890 triggered the Baring crisis and reduced Britain's gold reserves to dangerously low levels. After the war, however, the onerous Treaty of Versailles, the difficulties with Germany's reparations payments, the refusal of the United States to participate in international institutions like the League of Nations, and, eventually, the Smoot-Hawley tariff and widespread retaliation combined to contaminate the international political environment. When the Credit-Anstalt crisis struck Vienna in May of 1931 and Austria sought foreign help, the French demanded that Austria first renounce its intention of forming a customs union with Germany. When the crisis spread to Germany, Britain and France agreed to help only if Germany agreed to stop insisting on a renegotiation of reparations payments and ceased construction of battleships.

But as the Great Depression spread over the world, some politicians grasped for possible solutions. In 1933, at the depth of the Great Depression, a World Monetary Conference was organized in London in the hope that a cooperative effort to restore prosperity might succeed where unilateral attempts had clearly failed. Discussions centered around restoring the gold standard, reducing tariffs and other barriers to trade, and setting rules for improving the international coordination of economic policies. The conference failed to reach a consensus, however, largely because new leaders in most countries had become leery of restoring the gold standard but did not yet have well defined ideas about what international financial order should replace the Gold Standard.

13.3.3 *Individual country actions to restore order*

After countries abandoned convertibility in the 1930s, governments actively intervened in the foreign exchange markets. This intervention was mostly unilateral and not subject to any type of international coordination of policies. Ragnar Nurkse (1944) described the situation as follows:

> ...freely fluctuating exchange rates were far from common in those years. Exchange rates changed indeed; but the changes were usually

controlled. For considerable periods at a time, rates were "pegged" or kept within certain limits of variation.[23]

Governments of smaller countries often intervened to keep their currencies aligned with the major currencies, the US dollar and the British pound.

Many countries also established what came to be called *exchange rate stabilization funds*, which were really governmental agencies located in the finance ministry or central bank and authorized to use accumulated foreign exchange reserves to intervene in the foreign exchange market. These funds were officially designated to smooth out seasonal and speculative fluctuations in exchange rate, as most governments were reluctant to just let currencies float freely in the volatile economic environment of the Great Depression. Many governments quickly began using the *stabilization* funds to actively *undervalue* their currencies in order to give their exporters an advantage in international markets. In the deflationary environment of the Great Depression, flooding the foreign exchange market with domestic currency to drive down its value did not clash with domestic economic goals; to the contrary, such an increase in the money supply was desirable on its own. In addition, excessive depreciations were a form of Keynesian expansionary macroeconomic policy that boosted exports and, therefore, aggregate demand. The problem with such "competitive devaluations" was that they caused retaliation in kind by other countries, however, just like the Smoot-Hawley Tariff in 1930 led other countries to impose retaliatory tariffs. There were calls for coordination among countries to stabilize exchange rates at "realistic" levels.

It is not correct to conclude, as some economic historians have, that flexible exchange rates were the cause of exchange rate instability during the 1930s. Exchange rates were not, in fact, flexible. Governments routinely intervened in the foreign exchange markets, often directly by restricting international trade, international credit, and international investment. Yeager (1976) suggests that the correct "lesson" from the 1930s is that "flexible management of exchange

---

[23] Ragnar Nurkse (1944). pp. 8, 9.

rates by uncoordinated national action seems to work badly".[24] But how can flexible management be coordinated?

Exchange rate policies were just one of the many types of policies that governments debated during the Depression. The shift towards "Keynesian" macroeconomic policies became more pronounced as the economic difficulties of the Great Depression gradually forced the replacement of old political leaders with new leaders that were not handicapped by the gold standard mentalité. When President Franklin D. Roosevelt took office in 1933, he immediately set a new policy course. He eventually adopted Keynesian policies, abandoned the gold standard, sought to revive international trade, and began discussions with close allies to seek international agreement on a new international financial order. Roosevelt also experimented with many other policies to address the social and economic pressures of the Great Depression, and not all of these policies worked as hoped. But his administration's focus on international economic issues is now seen as very appropriate and necessary. Roosevelt pushed the *Reciprocal Trade Agreements Act* through the Congress in 1934, which gave him the power to negotiate trade agreements to reverse the high Smoot-Hawley Tariff and foreign retaliatory tariffs. The Roosevelt Administration also negotiated the Tripartite Agreement in 1936, which marked the definitive end to the gold standard.

13.3.4 *International cooperation: the Tripartite Agreement*

Governments had to decide whether to definitively abandon the gold standard or just adopt temporary policies to stimulate economic activity so that they could, eventually, return to the gold standard. Those governments no longer interested in returning to the gold standard still faced the problem of dealing with the exchange rate instability caused by competitive devaluations and other poorly-managed interventions in the foreign exchange market. Economists debated two possible solutions to the problem of exchange rate instability: (1) international

---

[24] Leland Yeager (1976). Chapter 18.

cooperation or (2) floating exchange rates free of government intervention. The governments of the major economies were, mostly,
reluctant to accept the idea of completely freely floating exchange rates,
especially since markets could easily again be manipulated by governments to boost domestic aggregate demand at the expense of others
countries' aggregate demand. Hence, the first approach was seen as the
only solution. That was the thinking behind the *Tripartite Monetary
Agreement*, negotiated by the United States, Great Britain, and France
in 1936.

Under the Tripartite Agreement, the United States, Great Britain,
and France decided to fix exchange rates between their currencies. The
Tripartite Agreement did not envision a return to the gold standard;
rather, it mandated continual central bank intervention in the foreign
exchange markets to keep exchange rates at or near their agreed-to levels. In light of the recent experience at the start of the Great
Depression, the designers of the Tripartite Agreement insisted on
keeping their fixed exchange rate system more flexible than the Gold
Standard. They, therefore, added the provision that the target rates
could be changed under certain circumstances, such as sharply rising
unemployment. Such a system of fixed, but adjustable, exchange rates
is usually referred to as a system of *pegged* exchange rates.

By the time the Tripartite Monetary Agreement went into effect
in 1936, the world was hopelessly divided into conflicting political
camps. There was little hope of extending the agreement to more
countries, or of using the agreement as a step toward a different
broader agreement that many countries could embrace. It would take
another World War before further cooperation among countries
would be sought. But when the time was ripe, at Bretton Woods, the
Tripartite Monetary Agreement would serve as a model for a worldwide financial order.

13.4 Assessing the Gold Standard During the Interwar Period

There really are not many good things to say about the international financial system between the two World Wars. High levels of

unemployment plagued many economies during the 1920s and all major economies during the Great Depression, which was caused by the stubborn adherence to the gold standard order. It took military expansions and another world war to finally eliminate unemployment in the United States, Germany, the United Kingdom, and most other major economies.

The Report Card: Interwar Period

1. Stability/employment	Fail
2. Economic growth	Fail
3. Globalization	Fail
4. Policy independence	Fail
5. Price stability	?
6. Mutually beneficial	Fail

In addition to the basic economic performance variables, the protectionist policies of the United States and retaliatory measures by most other countries greatly reduced international trade. This, combined with the complete cessation of international lending and borrowing, effectively destroyed globalization. The world separated into isolated economic spheres defined by ideologies rather than comparative advantage or common economic interests. Prices were fairly stable during the 1920s but then they mostly fell during the 1930s. It is not clear that price stability is a positive outcome when it comes at the cost of unemployment, stagnation, and declining world trade. Finally, the gold standard and its fixed exchange rates caused the US recession to be quickly transmitted to all other economies, and the chaotic abandonment of the gold standard then made any constructive international cooperation difficult. The international financial system did not bring home a very good report card during the interwar period.

13.4.1 *The trilemma between the wars*

The inter-war period saw economic policy come to the forefront of political debate. This had already occurred in the United States before World War I, when William Jennings Bryan almost won the 1896 presidential election by linking people's perceived economic difficulties to the Gold Standard. During the interwar period, in most developed economies "the trilemma was the issue at the very center of events".[25] In a way, it was the trilemma that ultimately forced the "ideology of the gold standard" to give way to the more popular macroeconomic focus on employment and price stability. More fundamentally, it was the rise of democracy, organized labor, and the increased popularity of socialism that shifted political pressures and made policymakers more uncomfortable with the lack of policy independence under the rules of the game of the gold standard.

Economic policies varied greatly during the interwar period, and it is impossible to generalize across all countries. Figure 13.1 presents a general picture of how the trilemma was dealt with between 1920 and the end of the 1930s. Immediately after the war, many countries had few gold reserves. Countries had also experienced different inflation rates that had driven the traditional gold parities far away from their purchasing power parity equilibria. A quick return to the Gold Standard was impossible; instead, the world operated with what were managed floating exchange rates. In the meantime, policymakers fell back on traditional policies that they believed would put their economies in a position to go back on the Gold Standard.

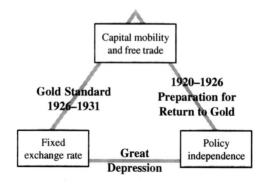

Figure 13.1　The trilemma between the world wars.

---

[25] As described by Maurice Obstfeld, Jay C. Shambaugh, and Alan M. Taylor (2004).

After nearly eight years of struggling to deflate prices and accumulate reserves, in 1926 the major economies of the world declared their currencies were again convertible to gold. As a sign of success, exchange rates remained fixed after 1926 until the early 1930s. However, after the Great Depression spread across the globe, and the gold standard's rules of the game seemed to facilitate the spread of the depression, more and more countries abandoned the gold standard in favor of greater policy independence. New leadership in many countries was committed to paying attention to unemployment rates and not exchange rates.

After they abandoned gold convertibility, policymakers usually did not opt for floating exchange rates, however. Rather, they generally selected the combination of managed exchange rates and domestic policy independence from among the trilemma's three options. They effectively accepted the collapse of international trade and investment, the third corner of the trilemma, as the result of global economic and political forces beyond their immediate control.

Key Terms and Concepts

Competitive devaluation	League of Nations	Retaliatory tariff
Dawes Plan	Managed exchange rates	Smoot-Hawley Tariff
Gold reserve system	Neoliberalism	Tripartate Agreement
Gold Standard	Paris Conference	Versailles Treaty
Great Depression	Pegged exchange rates	War reparations

Chapter Questions and Problems

1. One of the rules under the order of the Gold Standard was that governments would return to convertibility under the old gold parity as soon as possible in the case of an emergency that required the temporary suspension of convertibility. Why was this rule important to the continued maintenance of fixed exchange rates during the wars, political crises, and other brief interruptions of convertibility during the gold standard? Was this rule applied after World War I?

2. What role did the Trilemma play in the success and eventual failure of the Gold Standard? Does the Trilemma help to explain why the Gold Standard has never been restored since its final collapse in the 1930s? Why or why not?

3. What are the lessons from the interwar period? Given what we know now, what should have been done differently? Did things have to work out so badly?

4. Explain precisely how the transfers required for the war reparations mandated by the Versailles Treaty could have been carried out.

5. Why do you suppose the United States, Britain, France, and other countries blocked imports after they signed the Versailles Treaty, which effectively required them to permit other countries to export to them in order to pay debt and/or reparations? Do these inconsistent policies make sense?

6. Describe the Gold Standard order, and then explain how that order helped to spread the recession from one country to another after the 1929 US stock market crash. (Hint: Use a macroeconomic model to illustrate precisely how a tightening of monetary policy in one country affected aggregate demand and the BOP curve in other countries.)

7. Use an open-economy macroeconomic model, such as the Mundell–Fleming model or the AD/AS model that incorporates the Mundell–Fleming model, to illustrate how an intentional devaluation of the currency affects the level of domestic output and employment in the domestic and foreign economies. (Hint: Recall how the exchange rate affects the BOP and IS curves, shift those curves in accordance with a devaluation, and then, under specific assumptions on the exchange rate regime and capital mobility, determine how the economy adjusts to its new equilibrium level of output.)

References

Allen, JB (1977). The great protectionist: Sen. Reed Smoot of Utah. *Utah Historical Quarterly*, 45.

Bernanke, B (2000). A crash course for central bankers. *Foreign Policy*, September.

Bordo, M, T Helbing and H James (2006). Swiss exchange rate policy in the 1930s: Was the delay in devaluation too high a price to pay for conservatism? *NBER Working Paper w12491*, August.

Cooper, RN (1992). Fettered to gold? Economic policy in the interwar period. *Journal of Economic Literature*, 30(4), 2120–2128.

Eichengreen, B (1992). Fettered to gold? Economic policy in the interwar period. *Journal of Economic Literature*, 30(4).

Eichengreen, B (1996). *Globalizing Capital: A History of the International Monetary System*. Princeton, NJ: Princeton University Press.

Eichengreen, B and P Temin (1997). *The Gold Standard and the Great Depression*. NBER Working Paper No. 6060.

Friedman, M and A Schwartz (1963). *A Monetary History of the United States*, 1867–1960. Princeton, NJ: Princeton University Press.

Furtado, C (1963). *The Economic Growth of Brazil, A Survey from Colonial Times to Modern Times*. Berkeley: University of California Press.

Hetzel, RL (2002). German monetary history in the first half of the twentieth century. *Economic Quarterly*, Federal Reserve Bank of Richmond, 88(1), 1–35.

Keynes, JM (1920). *The Economic Consequences of the Peace*. London: Harcourt, Brace and Howe, Inc.

Keynes, JM (1923). *A Tract on Monetary Reform*. London: MacMillan.

Kindleberger, CP (1973). *The World Depression, 1929–1939*. London: Allen Lane Penguin Press.

MacMillan, M (2001). *Paris 1919*. New York: Random House.

Maddison, A (1991). *Dynamic Forces in Capitalist Development, A Long-Run Comparative View*. New York: Oxford University Press.

Maddison, A (1995). *Monitoring the World Economy*, 1820–1992. Paris: OECD.

Mundell, RA (2000). A reconsideration of the twentieth century. *American Economic Review*, 90(3), 327–340.

Norton, MB *et al.* (1990). *A People and a Nation*, Boston: Houghton Miflin.

Nurkse, R (1944). *International Currency Experience*. Geneva: League of Nations.

Obstfeld, M and AM Taylor (2002). *Sovereign risk, credibility and the gold standard: 1870–1913 versus 1925–1931*. NBER Working Paper 9345, November.

Obstfeld, M, JC Shambaugh and AM Taylor (2004). Monetary sovereignty, exchange rates, and capital controls: The trilemma in the interwar period. *NBER Working Paper No. w10393*, March.

Warren, HG (1959). *Herbert Hoover and the Great Depression*. New York: Oxford University Press.

Yeager, LB (1976). *International Monetary Relations: Theory, History, and Policy*, 2nd ed. New York: Harper & Row.

Chapter 14

Bretton Woods to the Present

Experience is the name we give to past mistakes, reform that which we give to future ones.

(Henry Wallach, 1972)

The world financial system took on a very different look after World War II. A completely new international financial order was deliberately constructed by the governments of the Allied countries. The formal process of rebuilding the international financial system began at the Bretton Woods Conference in 1944, and continued at a string of meetings during the years immediately following the war. The delegates at Bretton Woods sought to correct for what they thought were fatal weaknesses of the interwar financial order. Clearly on the delegates' minds were the draconian Treaty of Versailles, the ill-fated attempt to return to the Gold Standard, German reparations payments, the trade war triggered by the US Smoot-Hawley tariff, the beggar-thy-neighbor competitive devaluations, the enormous cost of the Great Depression, and, of course, World War II.

This chapter details the Bretton Woods Conference and analyzes the performance of the world economy since the Bretton Woods order was put into effect. Of specific interest are the additional measures required to recover from the war, the evolution of the Bretton Woods system and its eventual collapse, and the complex mixture of national institutions and policies that shape our international financial system today.

The past 65 years contain many examples of humanity's capacity to think abstractly and formulate positive responses to complex problems. But, the post-World War II period also reveals humanity's ever-present tendency to fall back on narrow, short-sighted analysis. The 2008 financial crisis is just the latest example of humanity's failure to consistently carry through with the holistic thinking that prevailed in Bretton Woods and the aftermath of World War II. By detailing the events at Bretton Woods and the subsequent evolution of the international financial system, this chapter lays the basis for analyzing the future.

Chapter Goals

1. Describe the events at Bretton Woods in July, 1944.
2. Detail the Bretton Woods financial order and the system that evolved.
3. Explain the strengths and weaknesses of the Bretton Woods financial system.
4. Describe the Marshall Plan and examine its role within the Bretton Woods international financial order.
5. Describe the events leading up to the collapse of the Bretton Woods system.
6. Explain the collapse of the Bretton Woods system from the perspective of the trilemma.
7. Describe the evolution of the international financial system since the Bretton Woods order was abandoned.
8. Evaluate the Bretton Woods system and contrasts it to the current mixture of national economic strategies and exchange rate policies.

14.1 The Extraordinary Bretton Woods Conference

In July of 1944, while the Second World War was still raging and just weeks after the invasion of Normandie by the Allied forces, economic policy makers, monetary authorities, and economists from all the Allied countries met in the United States to establish the order that would guide the post-World War II international system. The meeting was held at the Mount Washington Hotel in Bretton Woods, a tiny hamlet in the White Mountains of northern New Hampshire in the United States.

14.1.1 *The motivation for Bretton Woods*

The motivations for the *Bretton Woods Conference* were obvious: The Great Depression and the unmistakable trends toward political and economic isolation during the interwar years had contributed to the rise of the fascist regimes in Germany, Japan, and elsewhere. Adolf Hitler was able to exploit Germany's economic problems and Germans' resentment over the unfair terms of the Treaty of Versailles to gain enough votes for his National Socialists to lead the German government. The "glorious isolation" of the United States following World War I, when the leading economy of the world withdrew from participating in post-World War I agreements and institutions, was not helpful either. The United States culminated its retreat into isolation by starting a trade war in 1930 with the enactment of its infamous Smoot-Hawley tariffs. The breakdown of world trade that followed when other countries retaliated against the US trade restrictions by increasing their own tariffs was a major factor in turning the recession of 1930 into the Great Depression. Perhaps most instrumental in driving the world into the Great Depression was the post-World War I consensus to restore the pre-war Gold Standard. When protecting a currency's gold parity took precedence over countering the collapse in aggregate demand following the US financial crisis, an economic depression became inevitable.

The stated purpose of the Bretton Woods conference was to design a world economic order that would minimize economic conflict, encourage the macroeconomic policies necessary to maintain full employment and generate economic growth, and restore international trade between countries. By eliminating the underlying economic causes of the Great Depression and increasing economically-beneficial international interdependence, it was believed that a third world war would be less likely. Arguably, the Bretton Woods conference was one of the most enlightened events in human history. How many instances can you recall from history where, while a war was still in progress and its outcome still in doubt, some of the combatants began to seriously think about how to restore economic well-being for the citizens of the countries on *both* sides of the conflict? The Bretton Woods conference resulted in the winners of a war creating an economic environment intended to not just help themselves recover from the war, but also to help the losers recover and become part of a peaceful, closely integrated world economy.

14.1.2 *Designing the institutions to shape the world economy*

The conferees in Bretton Woods faced difficult choices. Should the gold standard be restored? Should exchange rates be permitted to float? Should new international institutions be created to manage the world economy? The world had just gone through the Great Depression, and there was not much consensus on what the best economic system was. The inter-war period showed that the gold standard would not work if incorrect gold parities were set and if the specie flow mechanism did not quickly restore balance of payments equilibria; countries would simply be forced off the gold standard at the first sign of trouble, as happened during the Great Depression. But, there was little support for a regime of floating exchange rates. The heads of the US and British delegations thought floating exchange rates would be too volatile, create too much uncertainty for exporters and importers, and thus hamper the all-important goal of restoring international trade and economic growth in what was already an uncertain post-World War II economic environment.

One difficult issue that had to be dealt with was how to reconcile the desire of the heads of the US and British delegations to give national governments a degree of autonomy to pursue macroeconomic policies to promote full employment with the desire to keep exchange rates fixed. There was clearly a trilemma here. How can the world pursue policy independence, fixed exchange rates, and increased international trade at the same time? The head of the US delegation, Harry Dexter White, and the head of the British delegation, John Maynard Keynes, were both "Keynesians" who wanted to focus economic policies on maintaining full employment. Recall from the previous chapter that Keynes had been a critic of the return to a gold standard at pre-war gold parities. White and Keynes also understood very well how the rules of the gold standard had spread the recession in the United States in 1930 quickly to the rest of the world. They further understood that favoring policies to maintain gold parities over policies to boost aggregate demand had turned recessions into a decade-long Great Depression. White had been a proponent of "Keynesian" policies such as expansionary monetary policy and fiscal policy to combat the recession in the early 1930s. As Chief Economist in the US. Treasury Department under the Franklin Roosevelt administration, White had actively advocated for policies that clashed directly with the deflationary monetary policies called for under a gold standard.

White and Keynes worked well together before, during, and after the Bretton woods Conference, but they did differ on several issues. Keynes sought to create a financial system in which Britain and the United States would jointly lead. White, on the other hand, wanted a system that was technically multilateral but which, in practice, would permit the United States and the US dollar to dominate. Since the US economy was far and away the largest and wealthiest economy in the world, there was little doubt that the United States would effectively lead an international financial system that did not explicitly give other countries specific powers.

It was White who had promoted the Bretton Woods Conference over the previous practice of holding smaller meetings because he thought presence of additional nations would help counterbalance the obvious influence of Keynes and the British. White used the participation of the delegations from Canada, India, France, and the Latin American countries to shape the final agreement. In the end, Keynes had a great influence on the conference, but the final agreement was very close to what White had sought. The Bretton Woods system would be a multilateral arrangement with the United States at the center.

White's role in shaping a pro-US agreement at Bretton Woods has often been minimized by claiming US dominance was inevitable given the United States economic power and its leadership in the war effort. Such arguments ignore White's abilities and the respect he held among international economists and financial experts. White was the chief international economist at the US Department of the Treasury after all, and he held a PhD in economics from Harvard, where he studied under several noted international economists. Also indicative of his stature was the fact that Treasury Secretary Morgenthau gave White ample independence and authority to lead the US delegation. White was able to establish what was very much his own vision of a multilateral financial system that would avoid the disastrous divisions that followed World War I.[1]

14.1.3 *The details of the Bretton Woods order*

The delegates at Bretton Woods opted for an eclectic system that included elements of the gold standard, many remnants of the earlier Tripartite Agreement, and a strong respect for the Keynesian view that macroeconomic policy should be focused on preventing unemployment. It was agreed that:

1. The value of the dollar will be set at \$35 per ounce of gold.
2. The general public will not be allowed to convert dollars into gold; only central banks can trade dollars for gold or gold for dollars.
3. Each country will peg its currency in terms of gold, and thus indirectly in terms of the dollar.
4. The pegs will be kept within plus or minus one percent of their stated parity through intervention in the foreign exchange market by the central banks of each country.

---

[1] This paragraph draws heavily from James M. Boughton (2002).

5. The dollar pegs can be changed only in the case of a fundamental balance of payments disequilibrium.

6. The *International Monetary Fund* (IMF) will serve as a central bank for central bankers by holding stocks of different currencies that could be borrowed by national central banks if needed to support exchange rates.

7. Countries will contribute capital to the IMF according to the shares agreed to at Bretton Woods, which were set roughly in proportion to the relative size of each country's economy.

8. The IMF will maintain a staff of economists to monitor the economies and advise member governments on macroeconomic policy, as well as to rule on whether exchange rate dis-equilibria are serious ("fundamental") enough to justify changes in the pegged exchange rate instead of other macroeconomic policy adjustments.

9. *The International Bank for Reconstruction and Development*, commonly known as the *World Bank*, will provide long-term financing to governments for rebuilding after the war and assist developing economies.

10. The *International Trade Organization* will coordinate negotiations to reduce trade barriers and enforce international trade rules.

Note that the Bretton Woods system would resemble the gold standard only in that the exchange rate would be nearly fixed. The link to gold was only indirect, and it was intended to enhance confidence among those who still regarded the Gold Standard as a source of stability. Under the Bretton Woods system, gold really only served as a unit of account in which the values of individual currencies would be stated. The permanence of the fixed exchange rates really depended on whether macroeconomic policies were compatible with the pegged exchange rates and whether the central banks had enough dollars to intervene in the foreign exchange market.

The Bretton Woods order reflected the consensus of the economists present at the conference that a fixed exchange rate was necessary in order to stimulate the growth of world trade. The cost of protectionism in the early 1930s was still very clear in the minds of the delegates. Many economists feared that floating exchange rates might prove to be too unstable, thereby imposing high costs and uncertainty on exporters and importers. A document by the Swedish economist Nurkse (1944), published to coincide with the Bretton Woods Conference, claimed that the interwar experience with floating exchange rates proved that floating rates were unstable and detrimental to international trade.

Several studies showing that floating exchange rates were not detrimental to international trade were also available to the delegates. For example, Haberler (1933) had argued that flexible exchange rates would have prevented the transmission of booms and busts from one country to another as occurred at the start of the Great Depression. Studies by Angell (1933), Harris (1936), and the United States Tariff Commission (1933) had concluded that countries with floating or frequently-changed exchange rates did not contract as rapidly as trade by countries who maintained fixed gold parities. This evidence had little influence on discussions at Bretton Woods, however, because it conflicted with the Keynesian view of macroeconomic policy that dominated the Bretton Woods Conference in the persona of Keynes and White.[2]

John Maynard Keynes and Harry Dexter White wanted fixed exchange rates, but with a twist. The key feature of the financial order they advocated was that exchange rates were to be *pegged* rather than permanently fixed. Recall from the previous chapter that John Maynard Keynes blamed tight monetary policies to lower prices and enable Britain to restore its traditional gold parity for the pound for the high unemployment and economic stagnation in the 1920s. Keynes insisted that exchange rates be alterable in the case of a *fundamental disequilibrium*, which he defined as an exchange rate that was not compatible with the monetary and fiscal policies necessary for maintaining full employment in each national economy. Countries were to be permitted to *devalue* or *revalue* their currencies (change their peg) if the balance

---

[2] See Micahel D. Bordo and Harold James (2001) for a discussion of this intellectual conflict.

of payments remains out of balance over a long period of time. With the Great Depression still fresh on their minds, most delegates at the Bretton Woods system agreed with Keynes and White that a country suffering serious unemployment should not have its policy options restricted by the need to maintain a fixed exchange rate.

14.1.4 *Capital controls*

One area where White and Keynes disagreed was on whether the financial account transactions should be freed. The trilemma suggested that the stated goal of policy independence is not compatible with pegged exchange rates and the desire to expand trade among countries. Keynes recognized the power of the trilemma when he argued ahead of the Bretton Woods Conference "that control of capital movements, both inward and outward, should be a permanent feature of the post-war system".[3] That is, globalization must be restricted in order to have fixed exchange rates and policy independence. However, the United States delegation stuck to the position that countries should have the option of keeping their capital market open to foreigners. They were strongly influenced by the private US banking industry, which considered the clearing of international payments as their natural business. White prevailed, and no explicit controls on capital were to be required of countries. On the other hand, Keynes' opposition to eventual liberalization of all capital movements kept any explicit mention of liberalizing capital flows out of the final agreement. The following clause was included in the Bretton Woods Agreement:

> No member shall, without the approval of the Fund, impose restrictions on the making of payments and transfer for current international transactions.

It was everyone's understanding at the time of Bretton Woods that what were called *current transactions* included normal trade credit, but not other capital movements. Hence, the Bretton Woods agreement

---

[3] John Maynard Keynes (1943). p. 31.

stated that international trade and the direct financing of trade was not to be restricted by means of controls on foreign exchange transactions. Countries were free to regulate, or not, capital inflows and outflows.

The capital controls Keynes advocated implied that international trade would not be entirely unencumbered either. In 1943, Keynes had proposed a clearing union through which all international payments would pass. As part of that arrangement, Keynes suggested a system of fines to force countries to keep their current accounts in balance so that capital movements would not be required to offset current account imbalances. Countries with persistent deficits would be charged increasingly large fines for borrowing from the clearinghouse, and surplus countries would have their net foreign exchange earnings confiscated unless they took effective measures to reduce their surplus. The US opposed Keynes' plan at Bretton Woods, allegedly because it would restrict free trade.

Interestingly, after the war it was the United States that opposed the creation of the International Trade Organization as mandated in the Bretton Woods Agreement. The US felt that the ITO would undermine US sovereignty. Instead, the United States supported the General Agreement on Tariffs and Trade (GATT), which was simply a treaty that specified the rules under which countries would conduct international trade. Only fifty years later, in 1994, would the United States finally agree to establish a permanent organization where trade disputes could be arbitrated, the World Trade Organization (WTO). These observations make it clear, once again, that countries' actions and behavior at international meetings are not always consistent, due, no doubt, to the complex political forces that influence government behavior.

14.2 The Early Years of Bretton Woods

The international financial system that actually came into being and then evolved after the end of World War II was close to, but not exactly, the system envisioned by the Bretton Woods Agreement. First of all, it took some effort to restore the world economy after the end of World War II. The destruction and the political vacuum left by the war meant that the Bretton Woods principles would have to be introduced gradually.

14.2.1 *The Marshall Plan*

It is not possible to discuss the post-war recovery in the late 1940s without recognizing the importance of the *Marshall Plan*. On 5 June 1947, Secretary of State (and the former US Army Chief of Staff during World War II) George C. Marshall spoke at Harvard University and outlined what would become known as the Marshall Plan. Europe, still devastated by the war, had just survived one of the worst winters on record. The devastated European economies had little to sell abroad to earn dollars to pay for needed imports. Something had to be done to deal with the humanitarian crisis. There was also the threat of a westward spread of communism. The political leaders of the United States were still quite aware of how fascist leaders exploited poor economic conditions to rise to power in Europe before the war.

General George Marshall had served as Army Chief of Staff from 1939 through 1945, so he had overseen the massive worldwide military operation during World War II. He was not afraid of complexity, and he shunned simplistic or short-sighted solutions. He recognized that Europe needed money to restore its financial systems, pay for urgently needed imports for its ruined economies, and to boost aggregate demand and spur private economic activity. Under the Marshall Plan, the United States offered up to $20 billion (close to $200 billion in 2009 dollars) for relief, but only if the European nations would coordinate a rational plan on how they would use the aid. The Marshall Plan effectively forced European countries to not only cooperate, but to act as a single economic unit within a European administrative organization. Marshall also offered aid to the Soviet Union and Eastern Europe, but Stalin denounced the program as a "capitalist" trick and refused to participate. Ironically, the Russian rejection actually made passage of the measure through the US Congress easier.

Much of the money provided under the Marshall Plan was used to buy goods from the United States, so the aid did not significantly affect the US balance of payments. By 1953, the United States had provided $13 billion for European projects, and the European economy was beginning to grow; growth would soon become very rapid. Moreover, the Plan included West Germany, which was thus reintegrated into the European community. (The aid was all economic; it did not include military aid until after the Korean War.)

Interestingly, the establishment of a European administration of the Marshall Plan led to the Schuman Plan for European economic integration, which in turn led to the European Coal and Iron Community and the European Common Market. In many ways, the Marshall Plan satisfied both those who wanted US foreign policy to be generous and idealistic and those who demanded realpolitik; it helped feed the starving and shelter the homeless, and at the same time stopped the spread of communism and put the European economy back on its feet. A recent historical account of the Marshall Plan by Behrman (2007) refers to the Marshall Plan as "The Most Noble Adventure".

14.2.2 *The Marshall Plan in Germany*

While the Marshall Plan certainly played a very important role in enabling the German economy to recover from the war, Germany's own decisions on how to reform its economy were also instrumental in creating the conditions for its subsequent economic recovery. Even since the rise to power of Adolf Hitler in 1933, Germany had administered an elaborate system of price controls. These price controls had enabled Hitler to spend on rearmament and many major infrastructure projects by printing money without causing inflation. This system of price controls had been maintained by the occupying American, British, French, and Russian forces after the war. Even after the United States administration in Germany introduced a currency reform for Germany, the US occupying administration was reluctant to abandon price controls.

The post-war currency reform consisted of the creation of a smaller quantity of new Deutschmarks (DM) to replace the large quantity of old Hitler-era reichsmarks in circulation. This currency exchange would greatly reduce the perceived savings of many people because the clearly over-valued reichsmarks were to be exchanged for DMs at the rate of ten to one. There was a fear that, even with the exchange of fewer DMs for the large accumulated stock of old reichsmarks, inflation would still result if price controls were eliminated because of the limited supply of goods and services in the devastated economy. General Clay, the Allied Commander for Germany, had therefore favored maintaining price controls after the currency reform.

To widespread disbelief, the German economist Ludwig Erhard, who had been put in charge of the American-British Bizonal Economic Administration by the US authorities, unilaterally suspended all price controls the day after the currency reform went into effect even though, technically only General Clay had the authority to make such a decision. The historian Smyser (1999, p. 77) describes the tense meeting between Clay and Erhard the day after the reform:

> Clay called in Erhard to lecture him. He told Erhard that US experts had warned that his policies would fail. Erhard, puffing on his ever-present cigar, replied laconically: "My experts tell me the same thing". Clay, who had long since learned to distrust experts, thereupon backed Erhard to the hilt.

The suspension of rationing quickly eliminated shortages of products, and before the end of the 1940s, the German economy was growing. Erhard's free market reforms on top of the Marshall Plan's funding proved to be the key to what came to be called the German economic miracle.[4]

When Joseph Stalin and the Soviet government decided to not participate in the Marshall Plan and the German currency reform, they effectively decided to split Germany into two parts, West Germany and East Germany, and Europe into Western Europe and Eastern Europe. This split of Europe would make it very clear how

---

[4] For a monetary view of the German recovery, see Robert L. Hetzel (2002).

important the Marshall Plan was in fostering economic recovery in Europe. While East Germany languished, the West German economy grew quickly to become the second largest economy in the world and the leading economy of Europe. The DM became the dominant European currency, and by the end of the Bretton Woods era, it would compete with the US dollar as a major international currency in the international financial system.

14.2.3 *The US dollar assumes a special role*

The Bretton Woods Agreement formally gave all currencies having equal standing, with each of them valued in terms of gold. In practice, however, the Bretton Woods system functioned as a "*fixed-rate dollar standard*". The United States and its currency, the dollar, assumed a special role in the actual system that arose. Pegging exchange rates requires central bank intervention in the foreign exchange market, but not every central bank needs to actively intervene. Recall from Chapter Three that if there is triangular arbitrage across all n currencies, then there are only $n-1$ fundamental exchange rates. Therefore, in a world with n countries and currencies, all exchange rates can be kept fixed if $n-1$ of the central banks actively intervene to keep their currency pegged to the nth currency. As the Bretton Woods system came into operation, the practice was for all central banks except the US central bank to intervene. The United States, as the nth country, remained passive and effectively did not have an active exchange rate policy. It was reponsible for determining the supply of the nth currency and indirectly, the supplies of all the other currencies pegged to the dollar.

While being the nth country relieved the United States of any obligation to intervene in the foreign exchange markets, it did give the United States another unique responsibility. With all other countries pegging their currencies to the dollar and the dollar effectively taking the role that gold assumed under the gold standard, the United States effectively determined worldwide monetary policy. Recall how under the Gold Standard, the supply of gold relative to worldwide economic growth determined world price levels. When the supply of gold grew more slowly than the world economy grew between 1870 and 1895, price levels declined. When William Jennings Brian protested against the "cross of gold", he was protesting deflation. Then, after discoveries of gold in Alaska, Russia, South Africa, and elsewhere, the gold supply grew more rapidly than economic activity and prices rose until the beginning of World War I. Now, with all currencies pegged to the dollar, it was the supply of dollars that effectively determined the world's money supply. During the 1950s, most countries did not object to US monetary policy. Later, during the 1960s, US economic policy and its management of what was effectively the international reserve currency would become an issue.

The potential problems associated with one country's currency serving as the international reserve currency had led Keynes to propose the creation of a separate international reserve currency, called the *Bancor*, to be managed by the International Monetary Fund. Envisioning its future role as provider of international reserves, and the advantages associated with that role, the US delegation opposed any discussion of the Bancor at Bretton Woods.

14.2.4 *The performance of the Bretton Woods system*

The Bretton Woods system worked well during the 1950s. There were two small devaluations of the French franc in 1957 and 1958, but otherwise the pegged exchange rates came under little pressure. World trade started growing rapidly after 1950, and many of the countries that had been destroyed by the war recovered impressively. West Germany and Japan were the big economic success stories of the decade; their rapid economic recoveries were often referred to as "economic miracles". It appears as though the designers of the Bretton Woods system had been right: A pegged exchange rate, adjustable under extreme circumstances, would help create an economic climate appropriate for rapid economic growth. The system was not really tested in the 1950s, however.

The trilemma, which is the conflict between policy independence, increased trade, and fixed exchange rates, was not applicable before 1960. Most countries were willing to follow US economic policy, current accounts were small as world trade was still just recovering from the protectionism of the 1930s, and financial account transactions were tightly controlled by most countries. The United States carried out a non-inflationary monetary policy that was not far out of line with what other countries would themselves have selected. And, with foreign exchange transactions related mostly to still-modest levels of international trade, not international investment, the required intervention to maintain exchange rate pegs was not very large even when other countries' monetary and fiscal policies differed somewhat from those necessary to match US policies.

14.2.5   *The world economy outgrows the Bretton Woods system*

With economic growth at all-time highs and the growth of trade twice as fast as economic growth, current account transactions also grew very rapidly. In 1958, most European governments abolished the myriad of permits and restrictions that had governed all foreign exchange transactions since the end of World War II and made their currencies freely convertible to dollars. Free "convertibility" meant that people and businesses no longer had to report every foreign exchange transaction and they could exchange currencies without restriction for normal current account and many financial account transactions. The foreign exchange markets grew rapidly, and the larger the foreign exchange markets, the greater the amounts of intervention necessary by central banks in order to maintain pegged exchange rates in the face of shifts in supply and demand. You might reason that foreign exchange market intervention should not pose a major problem so long as shifts in supply and demand for foreign exchange consist of random disturbances with a mean of zero. Random shifts in imports and exports are not so benign when foreign exchange markets are large, however. Recall from Chapter 7 that when a central bank buys foreign exchange in order to prevent its currency from appreciating, it simultaneously supplies more of its own currency, increasing the supply of money. Thus, as the amount of intervention grows, it tends to cause undesirable fluctuations in a

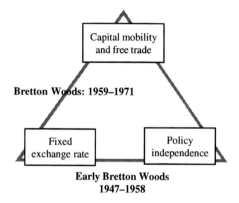

Figure 14.1 The Bretton Woods system and the trilemma.

country's money supply and, therefore, undesirable changes in price levels, interest rates, employment, and growth. By the late 1960s and early 1970s, daily interventions of over one billion dollars were sometimes required to keep exchange rates within their one percent margins of their pegs. Central bankers increasingly complained that their domestic monetary policies were being determined by the foreign exchange market, not their mandated macroeconomic goals of price stability, full employment, and economic growth.

Figure 14.1 shows the two phases of the Bretton Woods system. During the early years, 1947–1958, central banks had quite a bit of independence to set policies because most countries restricted international investment flows and even international trade was tightly regulated in many countries. After 1958, the freeing of international transactions from the burdensome bureaucratic controls that had prevailed since the end of World War II meant that the trilemma came into play and central banks increasingly had to focus on exchange rates rather than domestic economic conditions.

The size of the interventions necessary to keep exchange rates from changing was only part of the problem. A divergence of policies and economic goals on the part of several major economies drove the equilibrium exchange rates away from the pegged rates in the 1960s. The United States had relatively expansionary fiscal policies in the

1960s after tax cuts, increased expenditures for the Vietnam War, and expanded social programs under President Johnson's War on Poverty programs. The Federal Reserve's policy of targeting interest rates rather than price levels to guide monetary policy further gave the overall US macroeconomic policies a strong inflationary bias. Interest rates normally tend to rise when the economy is expanding and to fall when economic activity is weakening; therefore, a policy of interest rate targeting meant that during the 1960s, when expansionary fiscal policies were already pushing the economy close to its productive capacity and interest rates rose, interest rate targeting effectively expanded the money supply and created a combination of expansionary fiscal and monetary policies that pushed the economy to the right of its long-run supply curve.

US inflation began to exceed that of Germany, Switzerland, and other European countries, thus violating purchasing power parity. This divergence of price levels caused demand for dollar to fall in the foreign exchange market and supply of dollars to rise. With this market pressure tending to depreciate the value of the dollar, the German central bank had to intervene by buying dollars and supplying marks. This, of course, increased the German money supply and led to claims that the United States was "exporting inflation" to other countries. Germany was in effect being forced into an undesirable monetary policy by expansionary US monetary policy. When, in the late 1960s the trade balance of the United States turned somewhat negative for the first time since the end of World War II, people began to move their wealth into non-dollar assets for fear of an eventual devaluation of the dollar. Even more intervention was required.

Triffin (1960) alerted the world that for the US dollar to serve as the world's reserve currency, the US would have to run balance of payments deficits so that other countries could accumulate dollars. The amount of reserves needed in a world with growing international trade and investment flows required US deficits that would, paradoxically, undermine confidence in the US dollar as a reserve currency. The "Triffin paradox" was even more troubling when it became apparent that the amount of dollars needed in the world would eventually exceed the amount of gold available to back those dollars at the

Bretton Woods parity of $35 per ounce. When, later in the 1960s, the French central bank began exchanging its accumulated dollars for gold, as the Bretton Woods Agreement allowed, the reserve role of the dollar was increasingly seen as unsustainable.

14.2.6 *The collapse of the Bretton Woods system*

Nixon acted in accordance to the spirit of Bretton Woods Articles that permitted exchange-rate flexibility; the US government duly informed the International Monetary Fund of the decision. The dollar devaluation violated the unwritten rules of the game of the fixed-rate dollar standard, however. The United States was not supposed to interfere in the foreign exchange markets because its currency served as the numeraire by which all other currencies were valued. But because Nixon also suspended the convertibility of the dollar to gold, albeit a convertibility permitted only for foreign central banks, he further broke with the Bretton Woods rules of the game. While designed to stem the speculation against the dollar, the US actions served only to increase it.

Germany, the Netherlands, Switzerland, and several other European governments reacted to the speculation against the dollar by suspending their central bank intervention in the foreign exchange markets and effectively letting their currencies float. Without the central bank intervention, the US dollar quickly lost value. As expected, the German mark, the Swiss franc, the Dutch guilder, and numerous other currencies all rose in value relative to the dollar. World leaders were not yet willing to embrace floating exchange rates, however. Throughout 1971 there were active negotiations among the governments of the United States, Japan, and the European countries, with the intent of modifying the Bretton Woods Agreement so that the basic system could continue to function. In December 1971, in a meeting at the Smithsonian Institution in Washington, finance ministers of the major Western economies agreed to return to fixed exchange rates, albeit without any link to gold and at new pegs that reflected the changes in market exchange rates during the brief 5-month floating period. It was also agreed that the US dollar would not be convertible to gold and that currencies would be permitted to fluctuate within a band of plus or minus 2.25 percent of the "pegged" exchange rate. Hence, the basic structure of pegged exchange rates was to be maintained but there would be added flexibility. President Nixon described the *Smithsonian Agreement* as "the most significant monetary agreement in the history of the world".[5] By early 1973 the US dollar was under speculative attack again, however, with record sales of dollars for marks, francs, guilders, and other currencies expected to appreciate against the dollar if the currencies were again cut lose from intervention.

The US did not fundamentally alter its monetary and fiscal policies after the Smithsonian meeting. The US government was much too concerned with ending the Vietnam War and preventing a looming recession in the 1972 election year. Switzerland was so overwhelmed by inflowing dollars that it began requiring negative interest rates on foreign-owned bank deposits, but even that measure did not stem the demand for Swiss francs. The continued inflow of foreign money had serious inflationary consequences, and in early 1973 Swiss authorities decided to stop intervening and let the franc float upward. Then people, firms, and financial institutions began to switch their wealth to the still-pegged German mark, Dutch guilder, and Japanese yen, and other currencies that were viewed as undervalued relative to the dollar.

In February of 1973, the United States announced that the dollar would be devalued by 10 percent against other major currencies. There was no clear evidence that the dollar was overvalued by exactly that amount, but it seemed like a convenient number. At first, the foreign exchange markets reacted by pushing the value of the dollar back up, probably the result of demand for dollars by profit-taking speculators who had earlier moved out of dollars. But a month later, the dollar was already sinking below its new peg. On 11, March Germany, France, Belgium, the Netherlands, and Denmark simply floated their currencies, and soon most other central banks also stopped intervening in the foreign exchange market. The dollar has been floating ever

---

[5] Quoted in Eichengreen (1996). p. 133.

since. In terms of the trilemma, policy makers effectively opted for capital mobility and policy independence in 1973. They abandoned their attempts to balance globalization, pegged rates, and policy independence. Pegged rates were sacrificed.

14.2.7 *Evaluating the Bretton Woods system*

Many writers have judged the Bretton Woods system harshly. Admittedly, it did eventually fail. But, in a broader sense the system was successful. Its collapse was actually caused by successfully achieving the idealistic goals of the Bretton Woods delegates. Recall that the purpose of the Bretton Woods Conference was to establish an international financial order that would help to reverse economic isolation and promote economic growth of all countries, thereby hopefully avoiding the unemployment and economic stagnation that could cause another wave of dictators and wars. The Bretton Woods order had enabled the world to accomplish those goals beyond most people's expectations. Economic growth reached unprecedented rates during the 1950s and 1960s. Never had world real per capita income risen as fast as it did during these two decades. Unemployment rates were generally low as the growing economies of the world created new jobs in record numbers. The business cycle exhibited some noticeable ups and downs in many market economies, especially in the United States and the United Kingdom.

The Bretton Woods seems to have been less than successful in some other respects, however. As a fixed exchange rate arrangement,

The Report Card — Bretton Woods Period

1. Stability/employment	Pass?
2. Economic growth	Pass
3. Globalization	Pass
4. Policy independence	Fail
5. Price stability	Fail?
6. Mutually beneficial	Fail?

it severely limited governments' ability to carry out economic policies, especially after international trade and investment began to expand rapidly. Also, inflation in the United States became a serious concern in the 1960s and early 1970s. Finally, the Bretton Woods system required the constant monitoring by central banks and government policy makers. Keeping exchange rates fixed in a globalized economy required increasing levels of cooperation and planning among countries, something that political leaders of the major countries were not always interested in.

14.3 After Bretton Woods

When the Bretton Woods system was unable to solve the trilemma, it was abandoned for floating exchange rates. That is not to say that floating rates were explicitly the choice of policy makers around the world. It was more a matter of any lack of consensus on what to do; floating exchange rates were the default mode when no other specific measures were taken.

14.3.1 *Meetings, but no agreement*

In 1973 and 1974, there were meetings of officials from the finance ministries and central banks of the major economies convened under the auspices of the C-20 (The Committee of Twenty). The meetings attempted to establish a system with more flexibility for individual countries to pursue their national policies while maintaining exchange rate stability. The meetings were reported to have been leaning toward a more symmetric system in which the dollar did not play such a central role. But, as described by Williamson (1977) in his appropriately entitled book, *The Failure of World Monetary Reform, 1971–1974*, the C-20 meetings came to naught. The mindset, or perhaps we should use Eichengreen and Temin's (1977) term *mentalité*, had not yet adjusted to the realities of the 1970s, and the search for a revised Bretton Woods system that could combine stable exchange rates in an increasingly global economy was doomed by the lack of consensus or willingness to coordinate policy among countries.

Several major countries still sought to maintain a system of pegged exchange rates. France, among others, sought agreement for a system under which countries would be subject to strict fiscal and monetary rules. The French also sought to limit the United States' privilege of being able to finance its external liabilities in dollars, which the French argued relieved the United States from the international market discipline that all other countries faced. The United States objected to that plan, and instead offered to accept the responsibility of stabilizing exchange rates within wide bands. At the Rambouillet Summit in 1975, countries agreed to work toward a "stable system" of exchange rates, but not a "system of stable exchange rates", as the French had wanted. Finally, in 1978 countries agreed on the *Second Amendment* to the original Bretton Woods *Articles of Agreement*, which officially legalized the floating exchange rates that had been a fact since 1973. The *Second Amendment* did require countries to maintain stable economic policies in order to minimize exchange rate volatility. Finally, the IMF was authorized to monitor and critique countries' economic policies on a continual basis. The rapidly changing international economic conditions in the 1970s, which included oil price shocks, rising inflation in many countries, and slowing economic growth would quickly lead countries to ignore the terms of this agreement at their convenience.

In summary, without any agreement on a revised or new international financial system in 1973, the world effectively switched to floating exchange rates. Some central bankers who had longed for policy independence, and economists such as Milton Friedman, who had long advocated floating exchange rates, were comfortable with a switch to floating exchange rates. Others were apprehensive. As it turns out, the floating system did not sink, but the waters were very choppy.

14.3.2 *Surprising volatility*

Many proponents of flexible exchange rate had suggested that freely floating exchange rates would be more stable than pegged exchange rates. It was reasoned that, so long as long-run expectations were

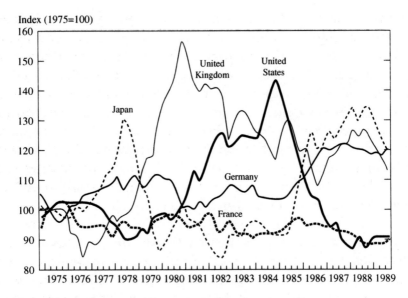

Figure 14.2   The volatility of real exchange rates during the 1970s.

stable, arbitragers and speculators would smooth out short-term fluctuations. In fact, exchange rates fluctuated wildly after 1973. For example, the dollar fell from 3.65 German marks per dollar in 1970 to 2.28 marks in 1979, a 38 percent decline. Such a change means it took 50 percent more dollars to buy the same amount of marks in 1979 than it did in 1970. Then, from 1979 to 1985 the dollar recovered all of its value lost relative to the mark since 1973, but by 1989 it again fell to less than it was worth in 1979. Of course, with the high rates of inflation in many countries during the 1970s, one needs to ask whether these changes in bilateral nominal exchange rates greatly overstated the changes in real effective exchange rates. However, Fig. 14.2 makes it clear that real effective exchange rates for the world's major currencies also fluctuated widely beginning in 1974.

14.3.3 *The Plaza and Louvre Accords*

The US dollar's gradual fall in value relative to most other major currencies came to an end in 1979. With inflation reaching 15 percent per year, the chairman of the Federal Reserve Bank, Paul Volcker, applied the brakes to monetary policy. The dollar appreciated by 28 percent in real terms between 1980 and 1982. The expansionary fiscal policy of the Reagan administration, which consisted of tax cuts and sharply increased defense expenditures in 1981, combined with the tight monetary policy to raise real interest rates in the United States to over 13 percent. This tightening, you may recall from Chapter 10, was one of the decisive factors in the 1982 Debt Crisis in many developing economies. The high real interest rates strengthened the US dollar as foreign money was used to buy US assets.

The difference between foreign interest rates and US interest rates peaked in early 1984. But, when the interest rate differential began declining in 1984, the dollar kept on rising anyway, confirming that exchange rates do not always respond to fundamentals as economists' models suggest they should. The dollar finally peaked a year later, in February of 1985. It then began a steady decline that continued for over two years.

The dominant story about the turnaround of the dollar in 1985 involves the secret meeting of finance ministers and central bankers of France, West Germany, Japan, the United Kingdom, and the United States in the Plaza Hotel in New York in September of 1985. Only at the close of that meeting was a public announcement made and a formal agreement presented to the press. As part of that agreement, the United States agreed to cut the government deficit, Japan promised to expand its monetary policy and to push forward stalled reform of its financial sector, and West Germany agreed cut taxes. There was also agreement on the need for concerted intervention in the foreign exchange markets to bring currencies into alignment with economic fundamentals. According to paragraph 18 of the agreement that came to be known as the *Plaza Accord*:

> The Ministers and Governors agreed that exchange rates should play
> a role in adjusting external imbalances. In order to do this, exchange
> rates should better reflect fundamental economic conditions than
> has been the case. They believe that agreed policy actions must be

implemented and reinforced to improve the fundamentals further, and that in view of the present and prospective changes in fundamentals, some further orderly appreciation of the main non-dollar currencies against the dollar is desirable. They stand ready to cooperate more closely to encourage this when to do so would be helpful.

By the end of 1987, the dollar had fallen by 54 percent against the German mark and the Japanese yen from its peak in February, 1985. It is not clear that the Plaza Accord, as the agreement became known, was the cause of the currency realignment, however.

The dollar had actually begun falling in value in February of 1985, and it had already declined sharply by the time of the Plaza meeting in September of 1985. Nevertheless, the Plaza Accord is important because it illustrated that the leading economies were willing to cooperate and even alter their policies in the interest of exchange rate stability. Not all the policy changes were actually made; as so often happens, domestic politics intervened between the time of the accord and the actual implementation of the promised fiscal policy shifts and regulatory changes. But, enough of the countries adhered to enough of their commitments so that, when the accord was combined with the clear coordination of exchange rate intervention by the five central banks, market expectations shifted substantially and foreign exchange markets continued to drive down the value of the dollar as hoped.

The plunge of the dollar after February 1985 began raising fears that the dollar would fall too far. Another meeting was held in 1987 at the Louvre Museum in Paris, after which the US was called on to further tighten its fiscal policy and Japan agreed to further loosen the monetary policy, among other things. The Louvre Accord also called for concerted exchange rate intervention by all central banks. The dollar recovered some of its real value relative to other currencies, but, again, it is not clear that the Louvre Accord was the motivating factor. In any case, the post-Louvre appreciation of the dollar was small. The US followed through on some of the promises it made in the Plaza and Louvre Accords most notably by enacting a large tax reform to reduce the budget deficit in 1986. But, by the early 1990s, had the reverted back to its traditional policy of benign neglect, preferring to let the markets (and other governments) determine the value of the dollar. Indicative of US policy in the early 1990s was President George Bush's answer to a question about the dollar: "Once in a while, I think about those things, but not much".[6]

14.3.4 *Do floating exchange rates decrease international trade?*

Despite the fears of the delegates at the Bretton Woods conference, there is no evidence that floating exchange rates have depressed world trade and investment. Many studies covering the period after 1973 when trade volumes were expanding and exchange rates were floating have concluded that the volume of international trade would not have grown any faster if exchange rates had still been pegged instead of floating.[7] International investment has also grown especially rapidly since the 1970s. However, Esquivel and Larraín (2002) find statistical evidence suggesting that exchange rate volatility may reduce international trade and investment in developing economies. In general, however, forward foreign exchange markets and other forms of hedging seem to have been able to protect traders from the uncertainty of floating exchange rates. Floating exchange rates have not discouraged long-term investors either.

14.3.5 *Evaluating the post-Bretton Woods period*

Most of the report card's goals were not consistently met by the Post-Bretton Woods international financial system. Unemployment reached high levels in many countries during at least some of the period, and economic growth slowed markedly in many countries compared to the Bretton Woods period. Exchange rate volatility

---

[6] Quoted in Randall Henning (1994).

[7] See, for example, Phillippe Bacchetta and Eric van Wincoop (1998). M. D. McKenzie (1999), and S. Wei (1996).

seems to have played a role in the many currency crises that occurred during the post-1973 period. These currency crises, which have been accompanied by financial crises and deep recessions in most developing economies, underscore the lack of stability in output and employment that has plagued many countries after the collapse of the Bretton woods system.

The Report Card — Post Bretton Woods Period

1. Stability/employment	Fail
2. Economic growth	Mixed
3. Globalization	Pass
4. Policy independence	Pass?
5. Price stability	Fail
6. Mutually beneficial	Fail?

Many developed economies experienced rising unemployment, especially in Europe, during the 1970s and 1980s. The growth miracles in Germany and Japan came to a complete end as these economies performed poorly during the 1990s. After the dismal 1970s, the US economy enjoyed relative stability and modest economic growth during the 1980s into the early 2000s. Globalization may have been partially responsible for the sharp rise in income inequality that resulted in the top ten percent of US income earners capturing nearly all of the growth in income between 1980 and 2007. The US economy exhibited rapid growth and technological progress in the 1990s, although Kouparitsas (2005) shows that recent US technological progress was merely back on its post-1960 trend, not above trend as some "new economy" enthusiasts have suggested.

Economic growth slowed in most developed, and most developing countries in Africa and Latin America, compared to the 1947–1973 period. The variability in growth rates across countries greatly increased as well, as there were some outliers that did manage to achieve rapid growth in those two regions. Of course, a number of East Asian economies grew at unprecedented rates during the post-Bretton Woods period. China and India, the two most populated countries in the world with over one-third of the world's population between them, accelerated their economic growth.

The post-1973 period has a mixed record with respect to inflation. Inflation exploded in both developed and developing economies during the 1970s as many countries loosened monetary policies. Developed countries revised their policies, and they brought inflation under control. However, developing countries experienced even worse inflationary episodes after the 1982 debt crisis, especially Latin America. In the 1990s and early 2000s, however, inflation has been subdued in nearly all of the world's economies. This experience makes it clear that floating exchange rates accommodate inflation, in large part because floating rates give governments the freedom to establish whatever macroeconomic policies they want. But, floating exchange rates do not necessarily result in higher inflation. While floating rates effectively eliminate a source of price discipline for central banks, there is nothing about floating exchange rates that *prevents* central banks from keeping inflation in check.

When it comes to the issue of policy independence, floating rates do seem to permit the major economies to carry out macroeconomic policies more independently. At the same time, the increased levels of globalization may introduce other mechanisms through which policymakers are restricted in their policy choices. With international trade and investment so prominent in most economies, the shifts in trade and investment flows caused by exchange rate adjustments have many real effects on aggregate demand, employment, interest rates, investment, and many other real economic variables. These real effects may again "force" policymakers to change their policies in ways they had not anticipated or desired. In 2009, for example, some economists suggested that even the United States has become so dependent on foreign capital flows that it might have to take measures to increase household saving and reduce fiscal deficits if it is to avoid a sudden reversal of savings inflows. This suggests that in today's world, in which supply chains and financial markets are global in nature and organization, national governments no longer have the choices of the trilemma.

14.4 The Bretton Woods Institutions

An important legacy of the Bretton Woods system are the so-called *Bretton Woods institutions*. The first is the International Monetary Fund, IMF for short, which the Bretton Woods Conference designed to function as the central banks' central banker. The IMF would provide assistance in keeping exchange rates pegged, and its economics staff would provide advice and approval of countries macroeconomic policies. The second was the International Bank for Reconstruction and Development, or the World Bank, which was to provide financing to help nations rebuild after World War II and to help channel money to developing economies that were not able to borrow through the private international financial markets.

These institutions were set up with funds provided by the signatories to the Bretton Woods agreement, each paying in proportion to its share of world GDP. Since the United States' GDP was equal to about 25 percent of world GDP at the end of World War II, it contributed about 25 percent of the initial capital of the IMF and World Bank. The influence of member countries on how the institutions operate is proportional to countries' contributions to the institutions' capital. Initially, the United States, had about 25 percent of the votes on the Executive Boards of the IMF and the World Bank. Both of these institutions survived the end of the Bretton Woods financial order and continue to operate. In early 2009, the governments of the major economies of the world agreed to provide additional financing to the IMF so that it can play a more aggressive role in dealing with the aftermath of the 2008 financial crash.

US influence in the IMF and World Bank has been somewhat reduced over the years, but in 2000 the US still contributed 17.6 percent of the IMF's capital. The next largest contributors are Japan, Germany, France, and the United Kingdom, all shares between 5 and 6.5 percent of the IMF's capital. Since major decisions by those institutions require an 85 percent supermajority, the US still holds effective veto power. Several nations have been pushing for a change in the rules to strip the US of its veto power and to allocate votes more equitably among countries. The rapidly growing BRIC economies (Brazil,

Russia, India, and China) have pushed hard for more influence in the IMF and World Bank, and although the US, Europe, and Japan are resisting changes to the voting structure, the Bretton Woods institutions will no doubt change in the near future.

The IMF and World Bank have proven to be able to adapt to changing circumstances. The roles of the IMF and the World Bank changed after the fall of the Bretton Woods system in the early 1970s. With many currencies floating, the IMF is no longer as often called on to provide countries with foreign exchange with which to intervene in the foreign exchange markets in support of pegged exchange rates. And, with World War II a distant memory, the World Bank's role in financing post-war reconstruction has long since elapsed. The World Bank now lends exclusively to low-income developing economies, especially those that have trouble accessing private financial markets. In line with the initial intentions of the Bretton Woods delegates, the two institutions have continued to promote globalization and economic growth.

The IMF and the World bank are today concerned with two main problems of globalization, which are (1) the volatility of international investment flows and (2) the poor growth performances of so many developing countries. The IMF's main activities over the past two decades have been to assist countries in avoiding exchange rate crises and, when that fails, helping countries recover from exchange rate crises and financial crises. The World Bank finances long-term infrastructure and social projects to promote economic growth, such as education, transportation facilities, communications, and electricity generators. The IMF's emergency lending when countries face sudden shifts in international investment flows is usually closely linked to a set of policy changes that the IMF deems to be necessary for countries to solve the fundamental imbalances that caused the shifts in international investment flows. The IMF often insists on policies that reduce government budget deficits, tightly restrict monetary expansion, reduce government interference in the economy, privatize government assets, and rationalize tax systems. The World Bank also makes its loans conditional on governments' changes in economic policies.

The IMF and World Bank are often depicted as US-dominated institutions that dictate economic policies to borrowers for the benefit of lenders in general and the United States in particular. The truth of the matter is much more complex. The IMF generally attempts to find the quickest and least costly solution to exchange rate crises, and such solutions necessarily require that fundamental economic problems be dealt with. Such policy changes usually have short-run costs for certain people and groups, which almost guarantees that the IMF will be criticized by someone, no matter what it proposes. Similarly, the World Bank's development projects are explicitly designed to bring change, not maintain the status quo.

On the other hand, the World Bank and the IMF are suspected of pushing policies that favor the interests of the United States, its business sector, and the global financial industry. As described in Chapter 10, the IMF was a strong proponent of a set of economic policies that are known as the "Washington consensus". Now, the Bretton Woods institutions will evolve further in a global economy where the BRIC nations will have more economic and political power.

14.5 Summary and Conclusions

Figure 14.3 summarizes the detailed discussion of this chapter. Over the past 100 years, many different international financial orders were tried. The world has wavered between fixed exchange rates and

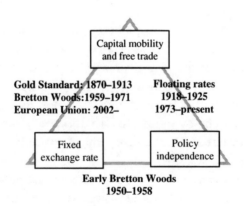

Figure 14.3   Summary of the Trilemma since 1870.

floating exchange rates, and there have been many variations and combinations of those two extremes. Today we have a complex mixture of national orders, including fixed exchange rates, both clean and dirty floating exchange rates, currency boards, and a full currency union among European economies.

Among the specific points and historical highlights brought out in this chapter are:

1. The Bretton Woods order was, in effect, a recognition of the many policy failures during the inter-war years.
2. The new Bretton Woods order was a pragmatic mixture of rules and guidelines that would create an international financial system to accommodate economic recovery and integration of national economies into a global economic system.
3. The Bretton Woods order consisted of

   a. Pegging the dollar at $35 per ounce of gold.
   b. Banning gold sales to the public; only central banks would exchange gold.
   c. Creating a system of pegged exchange rates that remained constant except in the case of a fundamental disequilibrium.
   d. Central bank intervention using dollars and other currency reserves to keep exchange rates with one percent of their pegs.
   e. The International Monetary Fund.
   f. The World Bank.

4. The Bretton Woods Agreement also foresaw an International Trade Organization, but that did not come to pass due to US sovereignty concerns.
5. While the Bretton Woods order provided the rules and institutions, the US Marchall Plan provided the stimulus for European economic recovery.
6. The Bretton Woods system functioned from 1947 through the early 1970s, a period of unprecedented economic growth in nearly all countries that were part of the system.

7. Ultimately, the trilemma was violated when countries diverged in their economic policies; notable was the divergence of inflation between the US and Germany.

8. After 1973, exchange rates among the major currencies were allowed to float.

9. The post-Bretton Woods system has permitted globalization to progress, but in terms of other measures of human progress, the report card is not as impressive as the 1947–1971 Bretton Woods period.

10. The current decentralized international financial system continues to evolve as individual nations and groups of nations modify their economic policies and their economies grow at diverse rates.

Recent discussions over the long-run role of the US dollar, the governance structures of the IMF and World Bank, and the roles of rapidly growing economies such as China and India point to further changes in the international financial system. The central role of the dollar and the dominance of the United States in international institutions will be increasingly questioned.

The different orders chosen by governments reflect alternative ways of dealing with the trilemma. During the 1990s, a number of countries shifted from fixed exchange rates to more flexible rates. Members of the European Union, on the other hand, opted for a single currency, effectively surrendering national policy independence. Some countries have found some other creative solutions, such as currency boards or adopting the currency of another country. In 2000 Ecuador and El Salvador abolished their own currencies and made the US dollar the national currency, closing their central banks and letting the US Federal Reserve Bank and international financial transactions determine their monetary supplies.

The post-World War II period, which includes the Bretton woods system and the post-Bretton Woods system, is characterized by historically high inflation. Figure 14.4, taken from a recent report by the Federal Reserve Bank, shows price levels in England, France,

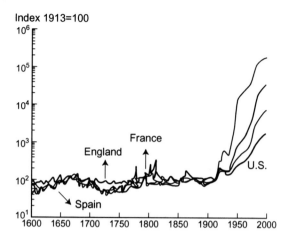

Figure 14.4 Inflation in England, France, Spain, and the United States, 1600–2000.

Spain, and the United States from 1600 through the present. Prices fluctuated but did not exhibit any discernable trend for over 300 years. Then after World War I and on through the Bretton Woods period, prices rose consistently. Policy autonomy and fiat moneys seem to have enabled inflationary monetary policies (or is the causality in the other direction?). Only toward the end of the 20th century did inflation slow, suggesting central banks were beginning to reign in their printing presses. The 21st century will reveal whether policymakers can learn to use monetary policy effectively to stabilize economic activity without succumbing to the temptation to print too much money and push aggregate demand out faster than aggregate supply.

On a final note, this review of the post-Bretton Woods period gives us a mixed picture of successes and failures. Before we criticize the recent financial order for failing to meet the objectives by which we judge international financial systems, we should keep in mind that the international financial system has had to deal with a large number of shocks and very substantial change in overall economic circumstances. During the 1970s, the growing world economy began to run into the scarcity of key natural resources, such as oil, on which the 20th century economy had been built. Policymakers were not prepared to deal with such supply shocks. Also, the past three decades have seen the emergence of a large number of new economic powers, including East Asia, China, Brazil, Mexico, and now India. The Soviet Union collapsed under its own inefficiency, and a whole group of new independent countries became integral parts of the global economy. The US economy, which has been the center of the Bretton Woods and post-Bretton Woods systems, is showing serious signs of weakness. The emitter of the world's reserve currency has an extremely low savings rates, slow productivity growth, increasing income inequality that threatens its social cohesion, and aggressive military policies that undermine international cooperation. Many members of the European Union now use a single currency, the euro, managed by a regional central bank, the European Central Bank, but by 2010, this amazing experiment was showing severe signs of stress. Globalization has progressed in many other fundamental ways, the most important of which has been the expansion of multinational corporations. The growth of MNEs has effectively brought into existence a parallel institutional structure that strongly influences international trade, international investment, and international finance. On top of all these changes, there are two billion more people in the world today than there were thirty years ago.

Recall that the original Gold Standard could not survive the broad economic, social, and political changes of the early 20th century. With all these recent changes, it is hard to imagine that a gold standard or a global system of pegged exchange rates could have survived. Pragmatists contend that today's eclectic mixture of floating exchange rates, dirty floats, pegs, and regional currencies is the only possible response by policymakers to the uncertain economic environment they face. On the other hand, the 2008 global financial crisis and the first worldwide decline in output since World War II, in 2009, suggest that the current system is flawed. Do we need another Bretton Woods Conference?

Key Terms and Concepts

Bancor
Bretton Woods
BRIC nations
Committee of 20
Current account
Devaluation
European Union
Free convertibility
Financial account
Fundamental
  disequilibrium
Fixed-rate dollar
  standard

General Agreement in
  Tariffs and Trade
  (GATT)
Gold standard
International Bank for
  Reconstruction and
  Development
International
  Monetary Fund
International Trade
  Org.
Louvre Accord
Marshall Plan

Pegged exchange rate
Plaza Accord
Revaluation
Smithsonian
  Agreement
Triffin paradox
World Bank
World Trade Org.

Chapter Questions and Problems

1. Detail the Bretton Woods order and the system that operated between 1947 and 1971. Why did it eventually collapse?
2. Using the criteria developed in Chapter 12 (the report card), judge the performance of the Bretton Woods system and the system that came into being after the Bretton Woods order was abandoned.
3. Explain precisely how the Bretton Woods system and the post-Bretton Woods system dealt with the *trilemma*. Which system was more successful?
4. Explain how nations dealt with the *trilemma* under the Bretton Woods system of pegged exchange rates during the periods 1946–1958 and 1958–1971. Specifically, begin by defining the *trilemma*, and then relate the Bretton Woods system's "rules of the game" to the changing economic circumstances and choices that the *trilemma* forced nations to make.
5. Explain the circumstances preceding the Plaza Accord. What do you see as the significance of the accord? Was it successful?
6. Is a system of fixed exchange rates a realistic option in the current global economy? Discuss the various advantages of a fixed exchange rate system

along with the various advantages, and then carefully weigh the advantages and disadvantages.

7. Review the purpose of the Bretton Woods Conference (You might review Chapter 1 as well as the discussion in this chapter), and then discuss whether the goals of the conference were met. Granted, the Bretton Woods system ultimately collapsed, but did it still accomplish enough to be considered a success? Would a different monetary system have worked better?

8. The world has gone through several different international financial orders over the past 100 years. Explain how each one came into being, why that particular order seemed to be a good set of rules at the time, and why the order eventually ran into difficulties and was superseded by another order.

9. Was the Bretton Woods Conference necessary? Was it as important as historians often suggest? What might the world have been like if there had been no preparations for the end of World War II?

10. Investigate the two Bretton Woods institutions, the World Bank and the IMF. Do they need to be reformed or replaced? Or can they function effectively as they are now organized?

References

Angell, JW (1933). Exchange depreciation, foreign trade and national welfare. *Proceedings of the Academy of Political Science,* 15, 290–291.

Bacchetta, P and E van Wincoop (1998). Does exchange rate stability increase trade and capital flows? *Working Paper.* New York Federal Reserve Bank.

Behrman, G (2007). *The Most Noble Adventure.* New York: Free Press.

Bordo, MD and H James (2001). Haberler versus Nurkse: The case for floating exchange rates as an alternative to Bretton Woods? The Adam Klug Memorial Lecture. *NBER Working Paper No. 8545,* October.

Boughton, JM (2002). Why White, not Keynes? Inventing the postwar international monetary system. *IMF Working Paper WP/02/52,* March.

Eichengreen, B (1996). *Globalizing Capital: A History of the International Monetary System.* Princeton, NJ: Princeton University Press.

Haberler, G (1937). *Prosperity and Depression: A Theoretical Analysis of Cyclical Movements.* London: George Allen and Unwin.

Harris, S (1936). *Exchange Depreciation, Cambridge, MA*: Harvard University Press.

Hening, R (1994). *Currencies and Politics in the United States, Germany and Japan.* Washington. DC: Institute for International Economics.

Hetzel, RL (2002). German monetary history in the first half of the twentieth century. Federal Reserve Bank of Richmond *Economic Quarterly*, 88(1), 1–35.

Higgins, B (1993). Was the ERM crisis inevitable? *Federal Reserve Bank of Kansas City Economic Review*, 4th Quarter, 1993, 27–40.

Kevin, D (2001). The emergence of fiat money: A reconsideration. *Cato Journal*, 20(3), 467–476.

Keynes, JM (1943). Proposals for an international clearing union. *The International Monetary Fund, 1945–1965, Vol. III, Documents.* Washington, DC [1969].

Kouparitsas, MA (2005). Is there evidence of the new economy in US GDP data? *Federal Reserve Bank of Chicago Economic Perspectives*, 29(1), 12–29.

Leland BY (1976). *International Monetary Relations: Theory, History, and Policy*, 2nd Ed. New York: Harper & Row.

McKenzie, MD (1999). The impact of exchange rate volatility on international trade flows. *Journal of Economic Surveys*, 13(1), 71–106.

McKinnon, RI (1993). The rules of the game: International money in historical perspective. *Journal of Economic Literature*, 31(1), 1–44.

McKinnon, RI (1997). EMU as a device for collective fiscal retrenchment *American Economic Review*, 87(2), 227–229.

Meltzer, AH (1999). What's wrong with the IMF? What would be better? *Independent Review*, 4(2), 201–215.

Milton, F (1953). The case for flexible exchange rates. *Essays in Positive Economics.* M Friedman (ed.). pp. 157–203. Chicago: University of Chicago Press.

Mundell, RA (1997). Currency areas, common currencies, and EMU. *American Economic Review*, 87(2), 214–216.

Nurkse, R (1944). *International Currency Experience.* Geneva: League of Nations.

Obstfeld, M (1997). Europe's gamble. *Brookings Papers on Economic Activity*, 28(1), 241–317.

Raymond FM (2000). Bretton Woods — original intentions, current problems. *Contemporary Economic Policy*, 18(4), 404–414.

Rose, AK and E Van Wincoop (2001). National money as a barrier to international trade: The real case for currency union. *American Economic Review*, 91(2), 386–390.

Smyser, WR (1999). *From Yalta to Berlin: The Cold War Struggle over Germany.* New York: St. Martin's Press.

Sneddon LJ and GP Olivei (1999). Rethinking the international monetary system: An overview. *New England Economic Review*, Federal Reserve Bank of Boston, November/December, 3–24; downloadable from www.bos.frb.org.

Triffin, R (1960). *Gold and the Dollar Crisis.* New Haven: Yale University Press.

United States Tariff Commission (1933). *Depreciated Exchange*, Report No. 44, second series, Washington, DC: US Government Printing Office.

Wallach, HC (1972). The monetary crisis of 1971 — The lessons to be learned. Per Jacobsson Lecture.

Wei, S (1996). Intra-national versus international trade: How stubborn are nations in global integration? *NBER Working Paper 5531.*

Williamson, J (1977). *The Failure of World Monetary Reform, 1971–1974.* London: Thomas Nelson and Sons.

Appendix

Secretary of State George C. Marshall's June 5, 1947 speech at the Harvard University Graduation ceremony, outlining what was to become the Marshall Plan

I need not tell you gentlemen that the world situation is very serious. That must be apparent to all intelligent people. I think one difficulty is that the problem is one of such enormous complexity that the very mass of facts presented to the public by press and radio make it exceedingly difficult for the man in the street to reach a clear appraisement of the situation. Furthermore, the people of this country are distant from the troubled areas of the earth and it is hard for them to comprehend the plight and consequent reaction of the long-suffering peoples, and the effect of those reactions on their governments in connection with our efforts to promote peace in the world.

In considering the requirements for the rehabilitation of Europe the physical loss of life, the visible destruction of cities, factories, mines, and railroads was correctly estimated, but it has become obvious during recent months that this visible destruction was probably less serious than the dislocation of the entire fabric of European economy. For the past 10 years conditions have been highly abnormal. The feverish maintenance of the war effort engulfed all aspects of national economics. Machinery has fallen into disrepair or is entirely obsolete. Under the arbitrary and destructive Nazi rule, virtually every possible enterprise was geared into the German war machine. Long-standing commercial ties, private institutions, banks, insurance companies and shipping companies disappeared, through the loss of capital, absorption through nationalization or by simple destruction. In many countries, confidence in the local currency has been severely shaken. The breakdown of the business structure of Europe during the war was complete. Recovery has been seriously retarded by the fact that two years after the close of hostilities a peace settlement with Germany and Austria has not been agreed upon. But even given a more prompt solution of these difficult problems, the rehabilitation of the economic structure of Europe quite evidently will require a much longer time and greater effort than had been foreseen.

There is a phase of this matter which is both interesting and serious. The farmer has always produced the foodstuffs to exchange with the city dweller for the other necessities of life. This division of labor is the basis of modern civilization. At the present time it is threatened with breakdown. The town and city industries are not producing adequate goods to exchange with the food-producing farmer. Raw materials and fuel are in short supply. Machinery is lacking or worn out. The farmer or the peasant cannot find the goods for sale which he desires to purchase. So the sale of his farm produce for money which he cannot use seems to him unprofitable transaction. He, therefore, has withdrawn many fields from crop cultivation and is using them for grazing. He feeds more grain to stock and finds for himself and his family an ample supply of food, however short he may be on clothing and the other ordinary gadgets of civilization. Meanwhile people in the cities are short of food and fuel. So the governments are forced to use their foreign money and credits to procure these necessities abroad. This process exhausts funds which are urgently needed for reconstruction. Thus a very serious situation is rapidly developing which bodes no good for the world. The modern system of the division of labor upon which the exchange of products is based is in danger of breaking down.

The truth of the matter is that Europe's requirements for the next three or four years of foreign food and other essential products — principally from America — are so much greater than her present ability to pay that she must have substantial additional help, or face economic, social, and political deterioration of a very grave character.

The remedy lies in breaking the vicious circle and restoring the confidence of the European people in the economic future of their own countries and of Europe as a whole. The manufacturer and the farmer throughout wide areas must be able and willing to exchange their products for currencies the continuing value of which is not open to question.

Aside from the demoralizing effect on the world at large and the possibilities of disturbances arising as a result of the desperation of the people concerned, the consequences to the economy of the United States should be apparent to all. It is logical that the United States should do whatever it is able to do to assist in the return of normal economic health in the world, without which there can be no political stability and no assured peace. Our policy is directed not against any country or doctrine but against hunger, poverty, desperation, and chaos. Its purpose should be the revival of working economy in the world so as to permit the emergence of political and social conditions in which free institutions can exist. Such assistance, I am convinced, must not be on a piecemeal basis as various crises develop. Any assistance that this Government may render in the future should provide a cure rather than a mere palliative. Any government that is willing to assist in the task of recovery will find full cooperation, I am sure, on the part of the United States Government. Any government which maneuvers to block the recovery of other countries cannot expect help from us. Furthermore, governments, political parties, or groups which seek to perpetuate human misery in order to profit therefrom politically or otherwise will encounter the opposition of the United States.

It is already evident that, before the United States Government can proceed much further in its efforts to alleviate the situation and help start the European world on its way to recovery, there must be some agreement among the countries of Europe as to the requirements of the situation and the part those countries themselves will take in order to give proper effect to whatever action might be undertaken by this Government. It would be neither fitting nor efficacious for this Government to undertake to draw up unilaterally a program designed to place Europe on its feet economically. This is the business of the Europeans. The initiative, I think, must come from Europe. The role of this country should consist of friendly aid in the drafting of a European program so far as it may be practical for us to do so. The program should be a joint one, agreed to by a number, if not all European nations.

An essential part of any successful action on the part of the United States is an understanding on the part of the people of America of the character of the problem and the remedies to be applied. Political passion and prejudice should have no part. With foresight, and a willingness on the part of our people to face up to the vast responsibilities which history has clearly placed upon our country, the difficulties I have outlined can and will be overcome.

Source: Congressional Record, 30 June 1947.

Chapter 15

The Euro and the European Union

So much of barbarism, however, still remains in the transactions of most civilized nations, that almost all independent countries choose to assert their nationality by having, to their own inconvenience and that of their neighbors, a peculiar currency of their own.[1]

(John Stuart Mill, 1894)

It hardly appears within the realm of political feasibility that national currencies would ever be abandoned in favor of any other arrangement.[2]

(Robert Mundell, 1961)

When the Bretton Woods system collapsed in 1973, many Europeans were not happy about the prospect of having to deal with floating exchange rates. Volatile exchange rates during the 1970s and 1980s, illustrated in Fig. 14.5 in the previous chapter, were very costly to Europe because the volume of trade between the European countries had grown to be very large. Small European economies, such as Belgium, the Netherlands, and Luxembourg, export over half of their

---

[1] John Stuart Mill (1894). *Principles of Political Economy*, Vol. 2, New York, p. 176.
[2] Robet Mundell (1968). p. 177.

output and import over half of the products they consume. Even the larger European countries export and import at least one quarter of their production and consumption, about twice as much as a percentage of GDP as the average country. Hence, floating exchange rates added risk to a large proportion of all transactions in the European economies.

While European policymakers realized it would be impossible to keep their exchange rates fixed in terms of the US dollar, the Japanese yen, or other major world currencies, they nevertheless felt it would be advantageous and possible to at least peg the exchange rates among the European currencies. This chapter discusses Europe's attempts to fix its exchange rates after the fall of Bretton Woods and its subsequent creation of a single regional currency, the euro.

Chapter Goals

1. Describe Europe's international financial policies after the fall of Bretton Woods.
2. Detail the history of the EMS and explain why it ultimately failed to stabilize European exchange rates.
3. Describe the movement toward a single currency.
4. Detail the procedures for switching to the euro.
5. Explain the concept of an optimum currency area (OCA).
6. Examine whether Europe is now, or can soon be, an OCA.
7. Place the recent movement to a single currency within the context of post-World War II economic integration in Europe.
8. Fill in the euro area's first report card: A pass through 2007, but watch out for the trilemma after the 2008 financial crisis.

15.1 Seeking Exchange Rate Stability After Bretton Woods

The Bretton Woods system was the second fixed exchange rate order to fail during the 20th century. The first order, the Gold Standard, in fact failed twice, first in 1914 when it was confronted with World War I, and then in the 1930s when the world fell into an economic depression. The shift to floating exchange rates was not greeted as an improvement over pegged rates by many government officials and businesses in Europe, and there was support in many European countries for renewed efforts to restore the Bretton Woods system after 1973.

15.1.1 *The snake in the tunnel*

When the 1971 Smithsonian Agreement permitted exchange rates to fluctuate more widely within a band of 2.25% to each side of the pegged rate, compared to the previous rule of 1% to each side of the peg, European countries coincidentally agreed to keep their mutual exchange rates within 1.125% of their pegs. The tighter fluctuations among European currencies, while the whole group of currencies varied by plus or minus 2.25% against the rest of the world's currencies, was called the "snake in the tunnel". After the abandonment of the Bretton Woods order in 1973, five European countries, Belgium, Denmark, Germany, the Netherlands, and Luxembourg, agreed to continue to maintain the "snake's" 1.125% margins vis a vis each other's currencies. This arrangement was successful because each of the smaller countries in the group coordinated its monetary policies with those of Germany.

15.1.2 *The EMS: a mini-Bretton Woods*

In 1979, the above five "snake" countries plus France and Italy, all members of the European Community, established a formal system of fixed exchange rates called the European Monetary System (EMS). They agreed to float as a group against all other currencies and peg the exchange rates between their currencies within narrow bands using central bank intervention. They recognized the difficulty of maintaining fixed exchange rates among all currencies, especially among large economies with different economic policies, and they did not attempt to extend their arrangement to countries outside Europe. The EMS grew in size when Great Britain, Spain, Portugal, Denmark, and Austria joined later in the 1980s.

The EMS functioned similarly to the Bretton Woods system. Each country agreed to intervene in the foreign exchange markets to keep their currencies within 2.5 percent of each currency's pegged exchange rate. For example, the central banks of Germany and the Netherlands intervened in the foreign exchange markets to maintain the guilder/mark exchange rate within 2.5 percent of an agreed value, but they let the mark and guilder float freely against the US dollar or the Japanese yen. Each country's central bank would maintain supplies of other European currencies in order to intervene in the foreign exchange markets if necessary. In recognition of the trilemma, the European countries participating in the EMS also agreed to coordinate economic policies so that the underlying supply and demand curves for foreign exchange would intersect at or near the targeted exchange rates.

Table 15.1 shows how frequently the pegs were changed for each of the participating currencies. With some of the countries changing pegs almost yearly in the early 1980s, it is quite a stretch to say that the EMS functioned as a fixed exchange rate arrangement. Beginning in 1987, the participating countries increased efforts to synchronize policies, and the pegged exchange rates remained unchanged for the next five years. Then, to many people's surprise, in 1992 speculative attacks on the British pound and Italian lira caused those countries to leave the EMS. The following year, there was further speculation against several other European currencies, and the EMS was suspended.

15.1.3 *The incompatibility of economic policies, again*

The EMS was the third fixed exchange rate system to collapse during the twentieth century. The cause of the collapse of the EMS was the sudden incompatibility of economic policies and the fixed exchange rates after the fall of the Berlin Wall in 1989. When West Germany absorbed East Germany, it was faced with the problem of how to unify the monetary systems of the two countries. West Germany had to exchange West German marks for the East German marks held by the former citizens of East Germany. But at what rate? Officially, East Germany had always maintained that one East German mark was

Table 15.1   Percentage Changes in the Effective EMS Exchange Rates.

Date	BLF	DK	DM	ESC	FFR	IL	IP	DG	PTA	UKP
9-24-79	—	-2.86	+2.0	*	—	—	—	—	*	*
11-30-79	—	-4.76	—	*	—	—	—	—	*	*
3-23-81	—	—	—	*	—	-6.0	—	—	*	*
10-5-81	—	—	+5.5	*	-3.0	-3.0	—	+5.5	*	*
2-22-82	-8.5	-3.0	—	*	—	—	—	—	*	*
6-14-82	—	—	+4.25	*	-5.75	-2.75	—	+4.25	*	*
3-21-83	+1.5	+2.5	+5.5	*	-2.5	-2.5	-3.5	+3.5	*	*
7-22-85	+2.0	+2.0	+2.0	*	+2.0	-6.0	+2.0	+2.0	*	*
4-7-86	+1.0	+1.0	+3.0	*	-3.0	—	—	+3.0	*	*
8-4-86	—	—	—	*	—	—	-8.0	—	*	*
1-12-87	+2.0	—	+3.0	*	—	—	—	+3.0	*	*
Five years of stability										
9-13-92	—	—	—	—	—	-7.0	—	—	—	—
9-17-92	—	—	—	—	—	*	—	—	-5.0	*
11-23-92	—	—	—	-6.0	—	*	—	-6.0	*	*
2-1-93	—	—	—	—	—	*	-10.0	—	—	*
5-14-93	—	—	—	-6.5	—	*	—	—	-8.0	*

Source: From Table 2 in Higgins (1993). Was the ERM crisis inevitable? Federal Reserve Bank of Kansas City *Economic Review*, 4th Quarter, 31.
* Not part of the EMS at the time.
— No change.

BLF: Belgian franc; DK: Danish Kroner; DM: German mark; ESC: Portuguese escudo; FFR: French franc; IL: Italian lira; IP: Irish pound; DG: Dutch guilder; PTA: Spanish peseta; UKP: British pound.

equal to one West German mark, but the real purchasing power of the East German mark in East Germany was much lower than the West German mark in West Germany. In fact, in the black market, the West German mark traded for as much as five East German marks. Therefore, if West German authorities had wanted to keep the real money supply unchanged, they should have exchanged West German marks for East German marks at somewhere near the purchasing power parity exchange rate between the two currencies. Instead, the West German government decided to exchange a large portion of East German marks at the official but inaccurate one-to-one exchange rate. This implied a large one-time subsidy by West Germans to East Germans. It was also a large increase in the real money supply of the unified Germany.

The reasons for the one-to-one exchange were political and cultural, not economic. Perhaps West Germany's politicians thought this would help the political unification of the two countries. Or, perhaps, they correctly sensed the need to extend aid to the economically depressed regions that made up East Germany. In any case, the surge in the German money supply, if unchecked, would have caused inflation to rise sharply in the unified Germany. The German central bank promptly tightened monetary policy to prevent an inflationary outburst. Interest rates rose sharply, and this in turn caused an equally sharp increase in demand for German assets and a corresponding increase in demand for the marks to acquire the assets. The foreign exchange market intervention necessary to keep the mark from appreciating would undo the German central bank's efforts to prevent inflation, of course. By shifting large amounts of wealth into mark assets, speculators effectively bet that the West German central bank would not intervene to prevent the mark from appreciating.

At first, central banks intervened actively to discourage speculation. Reportedly, the German central bank spent about 100 billion German marks to buy francs, krone, pounds, pesetas, and other currencies. The French central bank spent $55 billion to defend the franc. But the required intervention to counter the massive speculative flows was simply too large to sustain, and the central banks eventually gave up and let the currencies float. This episode is perhaps the clearest example of the failure of central bank intervention to maintain pegged exchange rates when broad-based market sentiment for a change is strong.

15.1.4 *Seeking a more durable alternative to the EMS*

The EMS experience once again brought out the trilemma. It proved impossible to fix exchange rates as the EMS did, liberalize international trade and capital flows as the European Community did, and pursue independent domestic economic policies as Germany did after unification. European countries were faced with either accepting floating exchange rates, restricting international transactions, or giving up policy independence. In 1992, the European Community opted for fixed exchange rates and open borders.

The 1992 *Maastricht Treaty* stipulated that the European countries completely liberalize trade, investment, and immigration among the 15 European economies. To confront the trilemma, the twelve also agreed to work toward the introduction of a *single currency* for all of Europe managed by a single central bank. A single currency replacing the separate national currencies of each of the member countries effectively implies permanently fixed exchange rates between the currencies. The European Community changed its name to European Union to signify its intent to establish a complete economic union in which goods and services were freely traded, people and capital could cross borders without restrictions, and a single monetary policy would apply to all member countries.

15.1.5 *Establishing the monetary union*

At a meeting in Madrid in December of 1995, the European Union, recently expanded to 15 members, reiterated its intent to create a single currency. The new currency would be called the *euro* and be denoted by the symbol €. European governments agreed to a three-step procedure for moving toward a single currency. First, a set of specific economic goals were set, and these goals would have to be met by a country before it could become part of the single currency area. These goals were related to a country's monetary policy and fiscal policy:

1. The currency's exchange rate must have remained within a tight band for two years.
2. Inflation must be less than 1.5 percent above the average inflation rate of the three European countries with the lowest inflation.
3. Interest rates on openly traded government bonds must be less than two percentage points above the average rates for the three European countries with the lowest rates.
4. The government budget deficit must be less than three percent of GDP.
5. Total government debt must be less than 60 percent of GDP.

At a meeting in May of 1998, the European Union looked at the economic data and officially announced that of the 15 member countries, only Greece had failed to make "satisfactory progress" toward meeting the criteria for joining the euro system. Notice in Table 15.2, however, that a number of countries did not yet actually meet the criteria; "satisfactory progress" was apparently a very subjective standard. Nor did all the 15 countries want to join the scheme. Of the 15 members of the EU, Denmark, Sweden, and Britain opted to keep their own currencies and not join the single currency area. These countries may yet join, of course, although none have yet indicated they are interested in joining.

On 1 January 1999, the eleven approved and willing countries permanently fixed their exchange rates relative to each other and ceded all monetary policy to the new European Central Bank (ECB). Greece was later deemed to have come into compliance with the stated guidelines and joined in 2000. During this initial phase of monetary unification, each national currency continued to circulate but its supply was managed by the ECB. This transitional phase came to an end between January 1 and 1 March 2002, when the national currencies were all exchanged for euros at the exchange rates set in

Table 15.2 Where European Economies Stood in Mid-1998.

EMU criteria	Interest rates less than 7.7% of GDP	Inflation rate 3.2% of GDP	Govt. debt 60% of GDP	Govt. deficit 3.0% of GDP
Austria	5.5	1.5	64.7	2.3
Belgium	5.7	1.3	118.1	1.7
Britain	7.0	2.3	53.0	0.6
Denmark	6.2	2.1	59.5	−1.1
Finland	5.9	2.0	53.6	−0.3
France	5.3	1.0	58.1	2.9
Germany	5.6	1.7	61.2	2.5
Greece	9.8	4.5	107.7	2.2
Ireland	6.2	3.3	59.5	−1.1
Italy	6.7	2.1	118.1	2.5
Luxembourg	5.6	1.6	7.1	−1.0
Netherlands	5.5	2.3	70.2	1.6
Portugal	6.2	2.2	60.0	2.2
Spain	6.3	2.2	67.4	2.2
Sweden	6.3	1.5	74.1	−0.5

1999. The euro became the official currency of Austria, Belgium, Finland, France, Germany, Greece, Ireland, Italy, Luxemburg, the Netherlands, Portugal, and Spain.

15.2 History of the European Union

Europe's decision to pursue a monetary union with the euro as its single currency can only be understood in the context of Europe's post-World War II political and economic reorganization. The euro is really just one component of a much larger set of policies aimed at promoting unity, pursued by a group of post-World War II leaders intent on creating a political and economic environment that would once and for all end Europe's tendency for war. The reasons for European leaders' focus on building a new political and economic environment in Europe were obvious. European countries had continually fought each other for centuries, and the two World Wars of the 20th Century were the most devastating of all of

Europe's wars. Both World Wars began as conflicts among European nations. In many ways, the euro is the end result of the goals of the Bretton Woods Conference. Recall that the delegates of the Bretton Woods Conference had openly stated their desire to create a new economic order that could avoid further wars and economic recessions. While the Bretton Woods international financial order ultimately failed, Europe's leaders, and their electorates, did not abandon the goals of Bretton Woods. Attempts to maintain fixed exchange rates among the European currencies after 1973 reflected the consensus for pegged exchange rates at the Bretton Woods Conference.

The establishment of the European Union has transformed Europe into a more peaceful region. The pursuit of European political unification grew out of the Bretton Woods Conference and the Marshall Plan. The recent adoption of the euro by 16 European countries must be seen as part of the political process of European unification, like the establishment of a European Parliament, and not just as a decision based on the merits of permanently fixed exchange rates.

15.2.1 *The early stages of European economic integration*

The idea of a politically united Europe was not entirely a late 20th Century development. Since the Middle Ages, emperors and kings had on may occasions attempted to unite Europe through conquest. This propensity for Europe's nations to go to war led the 19th Century French novelist Victor Hugo to advocate a peaceful "United States of Europe" guided by the humanistic ideals of the Enlightenment. Unfortunately, throughout the 19th Century and the first half of the 20th Century, European countries ignored Hugo's idea and continued to wage war on each other, often for reasons that baffle historians. At the end of World War II, however, the leaders of several European countries acknowledged their electorates' fatigue with war and began a serious process to fundamentally change the economic and political environment of Western Europe.

Between 1945 and 1950, Germany's Konrad Adenauer, Britain's Winston Churchill, Italy's Alcide de Gasperi, and France's Robert Schuman, among many others, openly called for closer cooperation among European governments. This interest in a more united Europe came at the same time that the Marshall Plan established a European bureaucracy to administer the distribution of US financial assistance, as discussed in the previous chapter. In fact, under the Marshall plan, one of the conditions for receiving aid was a country's promise to pursue an integrated European market for goods and services. In the spirit of Bretton Woods, trade was seen as a practical route towards maintaining peace in Europe and facilitating economic recovery.

In 1950, the French Foreign Affairs Minister Robert Schuman and his fellow French statesman Jean Monet proposed the creation of the *European Coal and Steel Community* (*ECSC*). This was to be a multinational authority for governing the production and distribution of coal and steel in France, West Germany, Italy, and the Benelux countries of Belgium, the Netherlands, and Luxembourg. Under a treaty signed in Paris in 1950, these six countries agreed to eliminate all tariffs and quotas on the trade in coal and steel among themselves. They also agreed to establish a regional authority with executive powers, an assembly consisting of delegates from the individual countries, a council of ministers to safeguard the countries' national interests, and a court of justice to settle disputes. One of the goals of the ECSC was to monitor German industry and to put a crucial part of that country's industry under the control of a supranational body. There was concern among some leaders in the former Allied countries that an economic recovery of German industry would enable Germany to rearm for yet another war. This concern conflicted with the stated goal at the Bretton Woods Conference of creating the conditions in which all countries on both sides of the war could recover from the war and enjoy economic prosperity. Monet and Schuman, and other European leaders, felt that the creation of regional institutions like the ECSC could prevent Germany from using its industrial recovery for military purposes. In practice, the ECSC turned out to be the first of many steps toward European cooperation and economic integration culminating with today's European Union and the introduction of the euro.

The six members of the *European Coal* and *Steel Community* signed two more agreements in 1957, the first establishing the *European Atomic Energy Community* (Euratom) and the second, the *Treaty of Rome*, establishing the *European Economic Community* (EEC). The *Treaty of Rome* called for the elimination of all restrictions on trade between the member states. *The Treaty* also mandated that the members of the EEC set common external tariffs; that is, the members would have to agree to a common trade policy. Technically, therefore, the EEC was planning to become a *customs union*. *The Treaty* also included long term goals that would eventually remove distortions to business competition throughout the region, create a common agricultural policy, and permit the free movement to labor and capital among member countries. Meeting these goals would make the EEC a full fledged common market and move it toward becoming an *economic union*.

Figure 15.1 illustrates the five levels of economic integration. They range from a simple preferential trade area, in which members

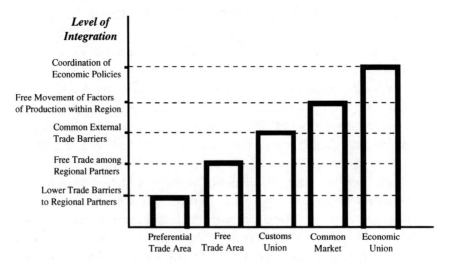

Figure 15.1   The levels of regional economic integration.

apply lower tariffs but not necessarily zero tariffs, on each others' products, to complete economic union, in which member countries effectively erase their mutual borders and coordinate their economic policies.

There was more to the Treaty of Rome than the creation of a common market, however. Article 2 of the Treaty of Rome set much broader aims for the EEC:

> ...to promote throughout the Community a harmonious develop-
> ment of economic activities, a continuous and balanced expansion,
> an increase in stability, an accelerated raising of the standard of living
> and closer relations between the States belonging to it.

To achieve these goals, not only would borders have to be opened to the flow of goods, services, people, and capital, but there would have to be broad cooperation among governments. Most important, national governments would have to surrender a considerable degree of national sovereignty. To underscore their willingness to support a regional governance structure, the EEC members authorized the creation of a European Parliament, whose members would be elected by the voters in each country. The Parliament would exercise oversight of the operation of the EEC. To the surprise of many observers, European countries proceeded not only to meet the goals set out in the Treaty of Rome, but over the remainder of the 20th Century these countries' leaders set, and met, even loftier goals.

In 1967, the members of the EEC established a more formal governance structure. First, they created the *European Commission*, which was to be made up of representatives appointed by each member country. The commission served as the executive branch of the EEC and. later, the European Union. One representative member of the Commission is selected by the countries as the President of the European Union, who has the authority to speak for the European Union at international meetings and organizations. Second, they created the *Council of Ministers*, which more closely approximates a legislative branch that directly represents the governments of the member states within the European Union. The Council consists of sitting ministers from member states, and its makeup varies depending on the issues under discussion. For example, when economic issues are on the agenda, the Council will likely be made up of the Ministers of Economy or similar positions in member country governments. Most decisions of the Council are by consensus, but sometimes votes are taken, with each minister's vote weighed by a formula that partially reflects each country's relative population size. The highest level of the Council is the *European Council*, which consists of the heads of each national government. Every six months a different country's minister serves as Chair of the European Council; the Chair has considerable influence in setting the legislative agenda of the Council of Ministers.

The desire for free trade in Europe was not limited to the six countries that founded the EEC. In 1960, seven other Western European countries negotiated a more modest free trade area. The Stockholm Convention established the *European Free Trade Area* (EFTA) among Austria, Denmark, Norway, Portugal, Sweden, Switzerland, and the United Kingdom. Finland joined in 1961. EFTA eliminated trade restrictions among its member countries, but the agreement did not address the more ambitious goals of the EEC. EFTA was seen by some of its members as a temporary step toward eventual membership to the EEC and its higher level of economic integration. Others preferred to limit the level of integration to free trade because they were not willing to give up their autonomy in setting trade policies toward countries outside EFTA or they were not willing to pursue higher levels of cooperation with other countries because of the loss of policy autonomy and national sovereignty.

15.2.2 *The growth and maturization of the EEC*

The customs union foreseen in the Treaty of Rome became a reality on 1 July 1968, when the last remaining tariffs between the six countries were removed, ten years after the Treaty of Rome. Common external trade policies were also negotiated and implemented during the 1960s. The long term goal of a Common Agricultural Policy (CAP) was also achieved during the 1960s, and the CAP remains a major feature of European cooperation. Countries outside the

European Union see the CAP's agricultural subsidies and import restrictions as a protectionist trade policy, however. The EEC was enlarged in 1973, when Denmark, Ireland and the United Kingdom joined. This enlargement had been blocked by the French government throughout the 1960s because then-President, Charles De Gaulle, was afraid that the United Kingdom would tilt the EEC away from the French — German axis and reduce French cultural and economic influence. It took the resignation of De Gaulle in 1968 to open the EEC to British membership. Because Ireland and Denmark were close trade partners with the United Kingdom, they naturally followed Britain into the EEC in 1973.

In the early 1970s, European leaders began to seriously think about expanding the EEC to include a monetary union. At about this time, the Bretton Woods system had collapsed, and there was great instability in the world's money markets. The introduction of the European Monetary System (EMS) in 1979 was an attempt to stabilize exchange rates, and the EMS encouraged Community member states to cooperate in setting economic and monetary policies. Complicating matters, however, was the further expansion of the EEC to include Greece in 1981 and Spain and Portugal in 1986. This made it all the more urgent to introduce "structural" programs such as the first Integrated Mediterranean Programs (IMP), aimed at reducing the economic development gap between the 12 member states.

By the 1970s, the EEC began assuming a more active and prominent international role. The EEC signed a series of agreements with most of its former colonies in Africa, the Caribbean and the Pacific dealing with foreign aid and the lowering of European trade barriers (Loméé I, II, III and IV, 1975–1989). The EEC also continued to expand its membership, with Austria, Finland, and Sweden in 1995. The Norwegian government had also negotiated accession to the European Union, but before Norway formally joined the EEC, the Norwegian electorate voted in a referendum to not join the European Union. Norway remains in EFTA but outside the European Union today, and it represents one of the few setbacks for the proponents of European economic unification after World War II.

In 1985, the EEC took a major step toward higher levels of European economic integration with the publication of an ambitious "White Paper" written by a group headed by the European Commission President Jacques Delors. The paper emphasized that the expanding Community had the potential to become a single market serving more than 300 million consumers. The White Paper also pointed out this potential was still held back by many obstacles: "queues at border crossings; technical barriers to trade; closed markets for public contracts…" The cost of this inefficiency — the "cost of non-Europe" as the White Paper called it — was estimated at around 200 billion euros per year. To the surprise of many commentators, the 12 member states reacted positively to the White Paper and, in 1986, signed the *Single European Act*. This act set out a precise timetable of 275 specific steps, or actions, necessary for moving Europe to a full *common market* by 1993. As Fig. 15.1 shows, a common market implies not only the free movement of goods and services, but also the free movement of labor and capital.

In 1991, the EEC member states went much further and negotiated the Maastricht Treaty, which set the ambitious goal of monetary union by 1999. The EEC changed its name to the European Union (EU). The Maastricht Treaty also established European citizenship, a Common Foreign and Security Policy (CFSP), and arrangements for internal security. Today, the European Union negotiates as a single participant in the World Trade Organization, the International Monetary fund, and other international organizations. The *Amsterdam Treaty* in 1997 formalized European rules on citizenship, standardized employment laws and regulations across the member countries, harmonized some social policies across countries, and further improved the organization of a common European trade policy vis a vis the rest of the world. The Amsterdam Treaty gave the European Union many new powers and responsibilities over individual European nations.

15.2.3 *Recent expansion*

The political and economic environment of Europe changed dramatically with the fall of the Berlin Wall in 1989. Germany was reunified, and the other former communist countries of central and eastern Europe broke away from Soviet control. Soon after Austria, Finland, and Sweden joined the ambitious EU, another 12 states applied for membership. The European Union received applications from the former Soviet-controlled eastern European countries, Bulgaria, the Czech Republic, Hungary, Poland, Romania and Slovakia, three Baltic states that had once been part of the Soviet Union, Estonia, Latvia and Lithuania, one of the republics of the former Yugoslavia, Slovenia, and two Mediterranean island countries, Cyprus and Malta. The early supporters of the European Coal and Steel Community in 1950 would no doubt have been surprised by how far European economic and political integration had proceeded when negotiations were completed in December of 2002 for 10 of the applicants to join the European Union, thus bringing membership to 25 states. These ten members officially became part of the EU in 2004. In 2007, Romania and Bulgaria were admitted to the European Union.

Further expansion of the EU may be forthcoming, and discussions are underway with Turkey. However, many politicians in Europe have spoken out against continuing accession discussions with Turkey. Other Eastern European countries such as Ukraine, Belarus, and Moldova, and former Yugoslavian states such as Serbia, Bosnia, and Croatia are also seen as likely future members of the EU. One former Yugoslavian state, Slovenia, was already admitted in 2004.

Agreement has also been reached to integrate the economies of the few remaining members of the European Free Trade Area (EFTA) into the EU. The EFTA members, which now comprise only Iceland, Liechtenstein, Norway, and Switzerland, continue to oppose full EU membership and the loss of national sovereignty that EU membership would imply. However, three of the four EFTA members have agreed to negotiate a new organization that encompasses both the EU and EFTA: *The European Economic Area* (EEA). Switzerland's voters rejected membership in the EEA, apparently because they feared the EEA implied too much of a loss of sovereignty for the oldest independent democracy in the world. The EEA mandates not only free trade among the EU and three countries of EFTA: Iceland, Norway, and Liechtenstein, but also the free movement of goods, services, capital, and persons, although it does not involve the setting of common trade policy towards outside countries. The EEA thus has many of the characteristics of a common market and a customs union. It is clearly not an economic union, however, since it explicitly does not obligate the EFTA members to adhere to the EU's Common Agricultural Policy, its Common Fisheries Policy, its common Foreign and Security Policy, or its Justice and Home Affairs Policy. And, the EEA is not a monetary union. Despite its rejection of the EEA, Switzerland continues as a member of EFTA and thus trades freely with the other EFTA and EU countries.

15.2.4 *A European constitution*

From the start, the European Economic Community was intended to promote the political integration of Europe and as well as its economic integration. In 2001, the European Council authorized a *Convention on the Future of Europe* to prepare a *European Constitution*. Former French President Valéry Giscard d'Estaing was appointed Chairman of the Convention. While the European Monetary Union was to be the culmination of European economic integration, the European Constitution would definitively establish the political unification of Europe. The Constitution was to define the scope of national governments within the new European governing structure. The European Constitution would, effectively, codify the extent to which national sovereignty had been given up to the new European institutions. Needless to say, this was a hugely controversial exercise.

The *Convention on the Future of Europe* completed its work on the draft European Constitution in 2003, and later that year an intergovernmental conference drew up a new treaty embodying the Constitution. The member nations of the European Union began the process of ratifying the Constitution in 2004. After a number of countries ratified the new treaty, the process came to a sudden halt when in 2005 voters in France and the Netherlands rejected the treaty in national referendums. The "no" vote in the Netherlands was especially surprising because voters in that country had always strongly supported European integration. The Constitution is now on hold;

further ratification votes in other member countries are unlikely. Further political unification may yet happen, but in 2005 the political process towards a unified Europe had clearly slowed.

15.3 Optimum Currency Areas

The euro's role in solidifying the economic integration of Europe was brought into question in 2010 when a number of European governments faced serious problems funding their governments debt. It is clear that the 2008–2009 recession caused debt to rise sharply, but in order to understand why the debt threatened the viability of the single currency, it is useful to begin with Robert Mundell's (1961) concept of *optimum currency areas.*

An optimum currency area (OCA) is a region just large enough so that the circulation of a single currency maximizes the difference between the gains from not having to exchange currencies when carrying out transactions within the area and the losses from having to design a single monetary policy to address the region's employment, growth, and price stability. The larger a single currency area is, the greater the gains from not having to exchange currencies are, but the blunter a tool monetary policy becomes. In the case of the European Union, the single currency eliminates about half of the foreign exchange transactions importers, exporters, and international investors would have to carry out if each of the members of the eurozone still had national currencies. But when it was faced with pockets of high unemployment across the 6 countries, the European Central Bank could only focus its monetary policy on "average" EU unemployment. An EU economist recently commented when asked about such an "average" policy approach: "Since no country is average, you've ensured that every country has the wrong monetary policy all the time".[3] Individual European countries with very high unemployment could only increase government spending, and debt. An obvious question is, therefore, whether the EU is an optimum currency area

---

[3] Quoted in Christopher Rhoads (2003). "The 'Average' Interest Rate In Euro Zone Helps No One", *Wall Street Journal,* 19 May 2003.

that maximizes the gains from having a single currency relative to the losses in monetary policy effectiveness.

15.3.1 *Mundell's examples*

A single currency area consists of a central bank with money-creation powers and a legal framework that makes the single currency the exclusive legal tender within the area. In his classic article, Robert Mundell first presents the case of two separate currency areas that correspond to two nations, A and B. He also assumes that the two nations' central banks intervene in the foreign exchange market to fix the exchange rate between the two currencies. He then assumes that world product demand shifts from country A to country B. If prices are sluggish in both countries and labor cannot move from A to B, the shift in product demand will cause unemployment in A and inflationary pressure in B. In the short run, if capital is mobile (as would be the case for most countries today) each country's exchange rate intervention would result in monetary policies that make matters worse! To prevent depreciation, country A's central bank would have to buy its currency, thus shrinking its money supply and worsening its unemployment. Country B's central bank would sell its currency to prevent appreciation, thus fueling inflation further.

There are two ways in which this unfortunate scenario can be avoided. First, countries A and B could let the exchange rate float. With freely floating exchange rates and sluggish prices, the nominal depreciation of A's currency relative to B's will alter the real exchange rate and balance both countries' international payments. The depreciation of A's exchange rate will mitigate the unemployment in A by boosting exports and reducing imports, and it will mitigate the inflation problem in B by increasing imports and decreasing export demand. Because they do not have to worry about fixing the exchange rate, the two countries can also use active monetary policies to address unemployment and inflation. They can let the exchange rate do all the necessary adjustment to keep international payments in balance. On the other hand, even if the exchange rate is pegged, unemployment and inflation can be avoided in A and

B, respectively, if prices adjust quickly and labor can move from one country to the other. If prices quickly decline in A and they rise in B, then the real exchange rate effectively changes in much the same way as in the example of flexible exchange rates. Furthermore, if labor can move easily from A to B, unemployment will also be reduced in A and inflation avoided in B. In sum, in the case of external demand shocks to a national economy, full employment and price stability can be maintained in the case where prices are sluggish and factor movements are restricted if exchange rates are free to change. And, in the case of fixed exchange rates, these macroeconomic goals can be met if prices are flexible and/or factors move quickly from one country to another.

In explaining his concept of the optimum currency area, Mundell also highlights the case where A and B are regions within the same country and, therefore, within the same national currency area. In this case, a shift in world demand from A to B is more problematic because the exchange rate is effectively fixed and there is only one central bank to conduct monetary policy. One monetary policy cannot address both unemployment in the country's region A and inflation in region B. Of course, if markets adjust quickly when supply and demand curves shift, overall price levels in regions A and B will also adjust to prevent unemployment in A and excess demand in B. Alternatively, if labor moves from region A to region B, unemployment and inflation will also be reduced.

If prices, wages, and labor do not move quickly, the central bank cannot satisfy both policy goals. In this case, there is an advantage to having separate currencies in regions A and B so that the exchange rate between the two currencies can adjust to maintain balance while the two central banks address unemployment and inflation in A and B, respectively. In this case, Mundell would describe each of the two regions A and B as candidates for optimum currency areas. The country with the two separate regions is clearly not an optimum currency area. In general, an optimum currency area can be larger than a nation or smaller than a nation. Its size depends on the flexibility of prices and the geographic mobility of factors of production like labor.

15.3.2 *The costs of multiple currencies*

Taking these examples to their logical conclusion suggests that if there is price inflexibility or costs to moving factors between regions, then the best approach to minimizing unemployment and keeping prices stable would be separate regional currencies linked by floating exchange rates. We have not yet considered the costs of increasing the number of currencies, however. As John Stuart Mill implied in his quote at the start of the chapter, there are costs to increasing the number of currencies. Among the most obvious costs of increasing the number of currencies in the world are:

- The costs of exchanging currencies in foreign exchange markets.
- Greater exchange rate risk and increased costs of hedging foreign exchange rate exposure.
- Reduced efficiency in foreign exchange markets as each of the separate markets becomes thinner.
- The need to operate more central banks and monetary authorities to conduct separate monetary policies.
- Greater difficulty to evaluate relative prices of products, factors, and assets denominated in different currencies.
- The need to hold more currencies for transactions purposes.

With more currencies, there are more foreign exchange markets. Recall from Chapter 3 that in the case of n different currencies there are $[n(n - 1)]/2$ different foreign exchange markets. With the world's 200 currencies, there are therefore 19,900 exchange rates. If, for example, we split every country into two separate currency areas, there will be 400 different currencies, or 79,800 foreign exchange markets. Many of those markets would no doubt fail to operate, and many currencies would be indirectly traded through vehicle currencies. However, with the number of fundamental exchange rates doubled, the total number of foreign exchange markets would clearly have to increase. The individual markets would therefore be thinner in terms of volume. Transactions would be cleared less often during the day, the accuracy of the exchange rates would decline, and the ability of individual traders or small groups of speculators to move prices would increase.

The other costs of increasing the number of currencies are straightforward. More currencies imply that more exchanges of products, factors, and assets involve the exchange of currencies. Hence, there is increased exchange rate exposure that either adds to risk or requires costly hedging strategies. More currencies also imply operating more central banks and monetary authorities. The advantage of being able to fine tune monetary policy to fit a small, integrated region sounds attractive, but in the real world central banks are costly. Economists and bankers must be employed to make the difficult monetary policy decisions in each currency area. Finally, remember that prices play a central role in guiding economic activities throughout an economy. The use of different currencies with continually changing exchange rates makes price signals much less clear. As the number of different currencies increases and fluctuating exchange rates muddy the price signals, transactions will not be efficient and total welfare generated in the economy will be reduced.

15.3.3 *The optimum number of currencies*

The optimum amount of currencies is found when the marginal gains in the accuracy and effectiveness of macroeconomic policies from increasing the number of currencies equals the marginal costs to society of having to deal with more currencies. For a given degree of price flexibility and labor mobility, the marginal gains from more accurate macroeconomic policies decline as more and more currencies are added. The marginal costs of increasing the number of currencies rise as more and more transactions require currency exchanges. Figure 15.2 illustrates how to find an economy's optimum number of currencies. Specifically, in this figure, the particular marginal gains and costs from increasing the number of currency areas in this economy lead to the conclusion that the optimum number of currencies is N.

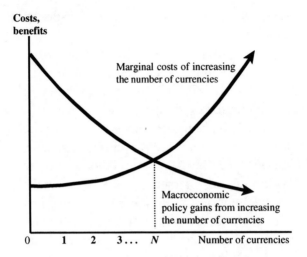

Figure 15.2   The optimum number of currencies.

The optimum number of currencies changes if either the effectiveness of monetary policy or the costs of dealing with multiple currencies change. For example, if prices react, or are adjusted, more quickly to economic shocks, the need for monetary policy will diminish. Similarly, if the mobility of labor between regions of the economy increases because transportation and communications improve, monetary policy is not as necessary to keep employment and inflation at their target levels. If markets adjust automatically or labor moves relatively quickly from one region to another, monetary policy is no longer as necessary for maintaining macroeconomic stability. As Fig. 15.3 shows, increased market efficiency, greater mobility of labor and other factors, and greater mobility of investment implies a downward shift in the macroeconomic policy gains curve, and the optimum number of currencies is reduced.

The optimum number of currencies would also be reduced if, all other things equal, the cost of dealing with multiple currencies rises. This would be the obvious result of economic growth and the accompanying increase in economic transactions. Also, if barriers to inter-regional trade are eliminated and asset exchanges across regions expand because of financial deregulation, more costly exchanges of currencies will have to be carried out and more foreign exchange

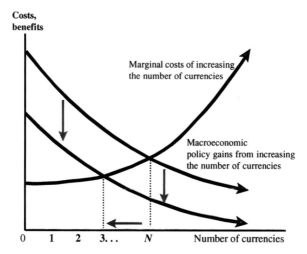

Figure 15.3 The optimum number of currencies after an increase in labor mobility.

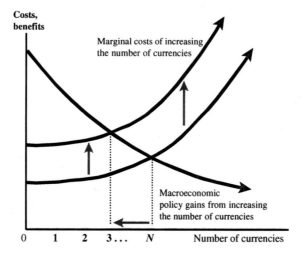

Figure 15.4 The optimum number of currencies after a decline in monetary policy effectiveness.

exposures have to be hedged. Figure 15.4 illustrates this case of a rise in the cost of multiple currencies curve. The higher the marginal cost of increasing the number of currencies, the lower the number of optimum currency areas.

15.3.4 *The criteria for an optimum currency area (OCA)*

Based on Mundell's work, economists generally look at four criteria to determine whether a region or group of regions/countries constitute an optimum currency area: (1) regions should be exposed to similar sources of economic disturbance, they should have *common shocks*; (2) the relative importance of these shocks across regions should be similar, or what economists would describe as *symmetric shocks*; (3) regions should have similar responses to common shocks; and (4) if regions are subject to region-specific economic disturbances, or what economists call *idiosyncratic shocks*, they need to be capable of quick adjustment.

With these criteria in mind, is the euro zone in Europe an optimum currency area? An area size of the euro area, which covers 16 different countries from Finland to Greece and from Ireland to Italy is likely to have both common, or *symmetric*, shocks and shocks that are particular to just some of the countries or even just regions of countries. Also, it is unlikely that each of the 16 economies react to the shocks in a similar manner. Finally, it is well-known that Europe's product and labor markets may not react to dissipate shocks quickly. Labor mobility is hampered by language and cultural barriers to the movement of people between countries, and, as of 2010, there are still explicit barriers to the movement of people between the most recent EU member states and the origin 12 EU members. Europe may some day become an OCA, but it probably is not yet an OCA. In sum, while the growth of trade and investment has increased the cost of maintaining individual currencies, the cost of losing monetary policy autonomy is still high because asymmetric shocks cannot be easily dissipated through price changes and labor movements.

15.3.5 *Is the United States an OCA?*

The United States is often held up as an example of an OCA. One could view each of the 50 states as potential currency areas. Kouparitsas (2001) investigated whether the United States is an optimum currency.

He answers this question using the same set of criteria used to evaluate the European Union above. Using data for 1969–2002, Kouparitsas finds that:

1. The main influence on regional activity appears to be a common shock to income.
2. With the exception of Plains states and Southwest states, US regions have similar responses to common shocks.
3. There is a great deal of variation in the share of income fluctuations explained by region specific shocks.
4. Impulse response functions suggest that regions adjust quickly to region specific disturbances, with most of the adjustment to these shocks occurring in the first year after the shock.

Kouparistas therefore concludes that the United States is indeed close to an OCA. Clearly, Europe has not reached the levels of economic integration, market efficiency, and labor mobility of the United States. If the United States is close to an OCA, Europe clearly must still have some way to go to become an OCA. The next section provides a closer examination of the euro area.

15.4 Evaluating the European Union

At a European Council meeting in Lisbon in March 2000, additional reforms of the European Union's institutions were discussed. A number of European leaders were seriously concerned about reports that Europe was falling behind the United States in terms of technology and economic growth, and they used the Lisbon meeting to propose strategies for making the EU economies more competitive and innovative. Since 2000, European economies did not lag behind the US in growth or employment, but it is not clear that the "Lisbon strategy" of opening up the European economics to more competition, encouraging innovation and business investment, and modernizing Europe's education systems played much of a role. In fact, the Lisbon strategy was not enacted by most countries.

Table 15.3   Unemployment Rates in the 27 EU Countries (All Figures Percentages in March 2009).

Austria*	4.8	Germany*	7.5	The Netherlands*	3.4
Belgium*	7.9	Greece*	9.5	Poland	8.2
Bulgaria	6.8	Hungary	10.0	Portugal*	9.6
Cyprus	5.3	Ireland*	11.9	Romania	6.9
Czech Rep.	6.7	Italy*	7.8	Slovakia	12.0
Denmark	6.0	Latvia	17.1	Slovenia*	5.9
Estonia	13.8	Lithuania	13.7	Spain*	18.0
Finland*	8.2	Luxembourg*	5.4	Sweden	8.3
France*	9.5	Malta	6.9	United Kingdom	7.6

* Members of the euro area.

Concern for whether the EU is an OCA grew as the economic recession worsened following the 2008 global financial crisis. Unemployment grew substantially after the crisis, but it grew at very different rates across the 16 EU countries that had adopted the euro. Table 15.3 shows European unemployment rates in March of 2009.

A 2005 European Union report listed what part of the Lisbon Strategy had already been accomplished:

1. The national public contract markets have been opened up, thanks to tougher rules requiring transparent procedures and proper checks for public supply and works contracts.
2. Disparities between national tax systems have been ironed out by certain common rules on indirect taxation, value added tax (VAT) and excise duties.
3. The money markets and financial services markets have been liberalized.
4. Steps have been taken to harmonize national laws on safety and pollution, and more generally EU countries have agreed to recognize the equivalence of each other's laws and certification systems.
5. Obstacles hindering the free movement of persons have been removed: passport checks at most of the EU's internal borders

have been abolished, and professional qualifications are mutually recognized by the EU countries.

6.   Company law has been harmonized.

7.   Member states have brought their national laws on intellectual and industrial property rights (trade marks and patents) into line with one another.

In 2005 the European Union also recognized that freedom of movement for people in Europe was still "far from complete" and that competition was still lacking in the service sectors of most member countries. The report goes on to say: "The single market is certainly up and running, but it is still very much a 'work in progress' with constant room for improvement". Recent work to complete the single market has focused on service sectors that, in some countries, have long been the preserve of national service providers. Opening them up to competition should help create jobs and strengthen Europe's economy. The 2009 recession and surge in unemployment will severely test the euro.

15.4.1   *Trade effects of the EMU*

Many studies have looked at the effects of the EMU on trade between the EMU members. Perhaps most often cited is the statistical analysis by Rose and van Wincoop (2001), who find that international trade greatly expands among countries adopting a common currency.[4] They conclude:

> Currency union reduces trade barriers associated with national borders, leading to substantial increases in both trade and welfare. That is, a national currency seems to be a significant barrier to trade. Reducing these barriers through currency unions like EMU or dollarization in the Americas will thus result in increased international trade. Our empirical work indicates that this effect may be large, in excess of 50 percent for EMU.

---

[4] Andrew K. Rose and Eric van Wincoop (2001). p. 390.

Frankel and Rose (2002) look at all countries in the world, and they estimate that belonging to a currency union triples trade with currency union partners, all other things equal. Tenreyro and Barro (2003) use a different statistical procedure but reach the same conclusion as Frankel and Rose.

By 2004, there had been 34 studies that investigated the effect of a currency union on trade. The currency unions studied consisted mostly of groups of countries that used other countries' currencies; for example, Liechstenstein uses the Swiss franc and El Salvador uses the US dollar as its currency. Rose (2004) looks at all of these studies to pick out their consistent conclusions in what he calls a "meta-analysis" that combines the statistical results of each of these studies. He concludes that the results may have been biased by "publication bias"; studies that reported a strongly significant and positive relationship between a currency union and trade were more likely to be published than papers that reported insignificant results. Perhaps the enthusiasm for monetary union biased editors and the economists doing the studies. Nevertheless, Rose summarizes the whole set of results as reasonably solid evidence that (1) a currency union definitely increases trade among the countries that share a currency over and above what trade would be in the absence of the common currency, and (2) the increase in trade probably is somewhere between 30 and 90 percent. However, given the broad range of results that cannot be linked to specific sample sizes or statistical methods, we should not accept these conclusions without reservations. And, because some of the studies that Rose compiled examined common currency areas other than the euro area, the conclusions above may not accurately represent the precise positive effect of a currency union on EU trade.

15.4.2 *Are business cycles synchronized with a single currency area?*

Frankel and Rose (1998) concluded that increased trade between countries is associated with more synchronized business cycles. Therefore, if the EMU increases trade among European countries, and the increased trade, in turn, reduces asymmetric shocks across the

EMU countries, then the costs associated with losing monetary autonomy may not be as large. It is not clear that the EMU will reduce asymmetric shocks, however. In another empirical study of the effects of a common currency, Tenreyro and Barro (2003) found that currency unions tend to decrease the synchronization of macroeconomic shocks throughout the currency area. They suggest this effect might be due to the increased specialization that accompanies the expansion of trade. Hence, it is not clear whether a currency union provides its own impetus for reducing the need for independent monetary policy or not. For now, this remains an open question.

15.4.3 *Inflationary or unemployment bias?*

If Europe is not yet an optimum currency area, then it clearly faces another problem. When there are simultaneously areas of high unemployment and areas of high inflation within the region, the single European Central Bank must decide which problem to address with its monetary policy. Focusing on "average" EU inflation and unemployment is not obviously the correct approach. Recall the comment on an "average policy" above: "Since no country is average, you've ensured that every country has the wrong monetary policy all the time".[5] In his article on optimum currency areas, Robert Mundell suggested that a focus on unemployment will bias monetary policy toward inflation. This does not seem to have happened in Europe, however. The European Central Bank (ECB) has maintained the strict anti-inflation bias of its model, the German Bundesbank, and the first two ECB Directors have done everything possible to establish a strong anti-inflation reputation for the ECB. It is interesting to note that, before the 2008 financial crisis, unemployment rates were somewhat lower in the countries that did not join the euro, such as the United Kingdom and Sweden, than in the average eurozone country. On the other hand, unemployment was also much lower in Ireland, which did adopt the euro, which suggests other factors may have been at play.

---

[5] Christopher Rhoads (2003). op. cit.

15.4.4 *Factor mobility*

Blanchard and Giavazzi (2002) examined capital mobility among the member countries of the European Union, and they found a clear rise in capital mobility. Specifically, they found that correlations between domestic saving and investment had declined sharply, and individual countries were running larger financial account deficits and surpluses. This increased capital mobility has exposed one of the potential vulnerabilities of a monetary union, which is the so-called "free rider" problem.

Because individual countries in the EU have some freedom to set their own fiscal policies, even after numerous agreements to harmonize taxes and government expenditures, the 16 euro countries' national governments run very different fiscal balances. When countries have their own currencies, interest rates in each country will tend reflect the fiscal discipline of each government. But with a single currency, the interest rate on euro bonds converges to a regional average. According to two *Financial Times* writers:

> Indeed, bond investors' complacency may be fuelling the fiscal problem, since it is reducing pressure on countries with bigger deficits to cut their debt. So is the behaviour of the European Central Bank, which treats all eurozone debt equally in its daily monetary operations. This means that an investor can post Greek bonds as collateral, for example, and get German bonds in return. This reinforces the convergence of yields and further reduces the market pressure on governments to reform.[6]

How serious is this danger that the ECB is subsidizing the countries with weaker fiscal responsibilities?

The European Union allegedly addressed the free rider problem with its set of criteria for joining the euro area, as detailed in Section 1 of this chapter. And, shortly after the introduction of the euro, a

---

[6] George Parker and John Thornhill (2005). "An Unhappy Union: Why Europe Is in Danger of Becoming Hollow At the Core", *Financial Times*, 27 April 2005.

Stability and Growth Pact was negotiated, which extended the accession criteria into a more detailed set of rules of fiscal behavior. However, these rules did not cover all the ways in which governments can free ride. For example, they can alter labor regulations, welfare payments, industry subsidies, corporate profits taxes, environmental regulations, and infrastructure to encourage investment and trade flows. More important, however, was the almost immediate abandonment of the *Stability and Growth Pact* that had officially extended the accession criteria into a set of ongoing rules of behavior. When several of the largest members of the EU, notably France and Germany, missed some of the main targets in March of 2005, the European Council agreed that circumstances justified the flouting of the rules. This effective abandonment of the Stability Pact puts the long-term stability of the euro in doubt.

At the same time labor mobility is not enough to mitigate the fiscal policy discrepancies. There are cultural barriers and language barriers that keep people from moving to other European countries even when per capita incomes and employment opportunities differ greatly. The barriers to labor movement appear to extend beyond just the usual difficulties of adopting to new cultures and institutions encountered by all people moving to other countries. European governments have put in place specific rules about labor migration from the 12 new member nations to the 15 existing members of the European Union. The popularity of the campaign against the "Polish plumber" in 2004 by right-wing political parties in France highlight the latent resistance to further integration in Europe.

The lack of labor mobility makes it more difficult for the EU to maintain full employment throughout the 12-country region. The single central bank can only address regional goals, but as pointed out earlier, "average" goals do little to solve local economic problems. Hence, monetary policy cannot address regional problems. But fiscal policy may not be able to address local problems either.

First of all, there are not the large automatic stabilizers that characterize US fiscal policy within its "monetary union". Because US government expenditures account for 20 percent of US GDP, automatic adjustments in income tax collections, profits taxes, and other tax collections on the revenue side and on the expenditure side, unemployment insurance payments, food stamps, medicaid programs, and other social safety net programs quickly respond to regional differences in employment and inflation. Differences in economic performance thus trigger shifts in payments flows between regions that automatically serve to reduce the differences in economic activity. In Europe, however, EU taxes and expenditures are less than two percent of GDP. Furthermore, EU taxes and payments are often fairly rigidly defined, thus leaving little room for adjustment in response to shifts in economic condition. The trilemma thus led European countries to flout the rules of the *Stability and Growth Pact.*

A more serious problem is the growth of budget deficits and government debt after the 2008–2009 recession. With the high debt burdens, national governments no longer have the room to deficit spend and stimulate economic activity.

15.4.5 *A first report card for 2001–2007*

Report Card: The Euro 2001–2007

1. Employment	Needs improvement
2. Economic growth	Marginal Pass
3. Globalization	Pass
4. Policy independence	Fail
5. Price stability	Pass
6. Mutually beneficial	Incomplete

For the first year after 2001, the euro seemed to perform very well. The European currency appreciated strongly against the US dollar. Still, it is not possible to reach a definitive conclusion on whether the euro has been a positive development for the 16 countries that have adopted it in place of their own national currencies. Even over the 2000–2007 period, before the 2008 global financial crisis caused the entire global economy to contract, the report card for the euro is mixed. Some of the euro countries continued to experience relatively high levels of unemployment, although most were able to reduce unemployment rates. Economic growth was relatively good compared to the previous two decades. The euro economies grew substantially faster than Japan, and they also grew faster than the United States. The common currency seems to have caused trade among euro countries to grow rapidly on top of already very high levels of regional trade. However, the common currency may have diverted trade from countries outside the currency union. As for independence, there is no doubt that the euro severely limits national governments' ability to engage in macroeconomic policy. The national central banks were replaced by the ECB, and the *Stability and Growth Pact* limits countries' fiscal policies. Price stability was a success in the euro area as the ECB has focused on preventing inflation. Finally, the euro has a mixed record on spreading the costs and benefits of a common currency. Growth rates and unemployment rates vary considerable across euro area.

There is interest on the part of other European Union members to join the euro area. Slovenia, and Slovakia, Malta and Cyprus qualified for euro area membership in 2006, which raised the euro area to 16 members. But then the 2008 financial crisis and the first global decline in GDP since World War II put a strain on the euro area.

15.4.6 *The euro after the 2008 financial crisis*

The eurozone economies did not all decline in tandem after 2007. Ireland, for example, experienced a decline in GDP of close to ten percent in 2009, while French GDP fell by little more than one percent. The European Central Bank took a fairly conservative approach to the threatening economic decline, and it was largely left to individual governments to deal with the financial crisis and the subsequent ensuing economic recession. With each country selecting different combinations of direct interventions in the banking system and fiscal stimulus, this was a more difficult test for the euro area than its founders anticipated so early in its life. More worrisome was the sharp deterioration of the government budgets of many EU members.

Greece was considered the most difficult case in 2010. Its public debt was growing by about 20 percent from an already extremely high 112 percent of GDP in 2009. Section 11.2.1, where we analyzed Brazil's precarious debt situation in 2003, provides a convenient formula with which to analyze Greece's situation in 2010. Specifically, the change in Greece's total accumulated government debt as a percentage of GDP in 2010, d_{2010}, depends on Greece's total government debt as a percentage of GDP in 2009, d_{2009}, the real interest rate that the government must pay on its accumulated debt in 2010, r_{2010}, the growth of GDP between 2009 and 2010, g_{2010}, and the real government *primary budget* surplus (government receipts minus non-interest expenditures) as a percentage of GDP in 2010, s_{2010}, as follows:

$$d_t = [(1 + r_{2010})/(1 + g_{2010})] \, d_{2009} - s_{2010} \qquad (15.1)$$

This formula specifically differentiates between how much new debt is due to the government's current expenditures and tax receipts and how much is due to the need to pay interest on accumulated debt from earlier years. The ratio of government debt to GDP will rise when $d_t > d_{t-i}$. This is more likely to happen when, all other things equal, the real interest rate exceeds the growth in real GDP and when the primary budget surplus is negative.

In the case of Greece in 2010, $r = 6.5\%$, $g = -2\%$, $d_{2009} = 113\%$, and $s = -12.5\%$. The ratio of Greece's government debt to GDP in 2010 was expected to be:

$$d_t = [(1.065)/(.98)] \, 1.13 - (-0.125) = 1.35 \qquad (15.2)$$

This increase in Greece's debt to GDP ratio from 113% to about 135% is an increase of about 20 percent. A similar interest rate, growth rate, and primary budget deficit through next year would cause the debt ratio to grow by close to 20 percent again, to about 155% of GDP. Clearly, this path was not sustainable, and the reluctance on the part of lenders to keep lending to the Greek government in 2010 was understandable. The high 6.5% interest rate on Greek debt in early 2010, about three percentage points above what the German and Dutch governments paid on euro borrowing, reflected lenders' fears about Greece's ability to avoid default or currency depreciation. The interest rate paid by Greece by April of 2010 exceeded 10%.

The governments of the other euro countries urged Greek authorities to take strong measures to reduce, and ultimately eliminate, the primary budget deficit. This would require both tax increases and expenditure reductions, and there was immediate strong opposition by labor groups, government employees, retirees, and others who feared they would bear large consequences from government fiscal adjustments. A goal of reducing the primary budget deficit from 12.5% to 7.5% was agreed to, but even such unpopular expenditure reductions and/or tax increases would not stop the debt ratio from rising further:

$$d_t = [(1.065)/(.98)] \, 1.13 \, (-0.075) = 1.30 \qquad (15.2)$$

This is still a 15 percent rise in the debt ratio. Obviously, the Greek government would have to commit to not just cutting the budget deficit, but it would have to turn the primary budget surplus positive, much like Brazil was forced to do in the case discussed in Chapter 11. For even this strategy to work, however, lenders would have to be willing to continue lending at favorable interest rates until the Greek debt ratio eventually began falling. Guarantees on Greek loans were promised by the other EU governments, and direct lending by the IMF was being negotiated in April of 2010 to comfort the market.

The alternative, which is that Greece abandon the euro and reissue its national currency at a sharply depreciated exchange rate to the euro in purchasing power parity terms, would have devastating short-run effects in Greece and throughout the EU. Depending on how Greek debt was denominated, in euros or a new national currency that would likely depreciate rapidly, either Greek borrowers would suffer huge rises in debt or lenders would suffer huge losses. Defaults by borrowers in Greece and lenders in other EU countries would be likely. Since the lenders to the Greek government consisted mostly of European banks, other European governments would have to go through yet another bailout to avoid serious disruption of banking systems still reeling from the 2008 financial collapse.

In early 2010, negotiations were held between Greece, other EU governments, and the IMF for massive loans to cover the Greek government deficit and permit Greece to continue with the euro. The EU's largest economy, Germany, hesitated to provide Greece with loans, and it simply refused to participate in a bailout, an option many economists argued would be inevitable if the euro area was to be preserved with its current 16 members. Portugal and Spain were having similar difficulties in borrowing to cover their governments' budget deficits. There was the usual political bluster about Greece's "irresponsible" government spending, but Krugman (2010) points out that the budget deficits of all the problem countries had been quite manageable just three years earlier. Clearly, it was the global financial panic, which originated in the U.S., and the subsequent economic recession, that led to Greece's immediate problems. More fundamentally, the problem was the single currency: a permanently fixed exchange rate limits a country's response to high unemployment to fiscal stimulus. But, as Greece found out, if government debt grows too large, further borrowing is no longer possible. In this case, the government is left with no macroeconomic policy with which to increase employment. Of course, the trilemma suggests another option, which is to let the exchange float and use monetary policy. But that means countries like Greece must abandon the euro.

In May of 2010, Greece agreed to make very substantial cuts in government expenditures and raise taxes in order to reduce its primary budget deficit to less than 3 percent of GDP by 2014. On the other side, EU government and the IMF agreed to provide up to €120 billion over four years. There were strikes and protests by government employees, and it was not certain that the Greek government would be able to comply with its agreement. At the same time, Greek economic growth estimates were adjusted downward to a negative 4 percent for 2010 as government budget cuts took their macroeconomic effect. At the time this was being written, it was not clear whether Greece would be able to begin reducing its debt ratio, restore confidence for lenders, and stay on the euro.

15.5 Summary and Conclusions

The financial history of the Europe after World War II is fascinating. A region torn by war for centuries suddenly manages to form an economic union! Individual European nations give up substantial sovereignty in order to fully integrate their economies and establish a regional governance structure that includes a European Central Bank and a European Parliament with taxation and redistributive powers. Laws and regulations are harmonized. Most stunning to neutral observers, perhaps, is Europe's willingness to abandon that most national of all symbols, their national money. At the start of the 21st century, 12 European nations exchanged their marks, francs, guilders, lira, and pesetas for a single currency called the euro. By 2010, four more countries had joined the euro area.

In discussing the euro, this chapter brought out the following major concepts, ideas, historical facts, and lessons:

1. After the fall of Bretton Woods, Europe's commitment to regional economic integration led it to seek regional systems for stabilizing exchange rates among its currencies.
2. Trade among the European Union members was too large to tolerate the wild swings in exchange rates that characterized the post-Bretton Woods period.
3. First, Europe created the European Monetary System (EMS), which operated like a mini-Bretton Woods.
4. The EMS gradually grew to include all of the members of the European community, but the trilemma caused it to fail when political priorities caused national economic policies to diverge.
5. Europe's long-term commitment to regional unity prevailed, however, and new ways were sought to establish exchange rate stability in the region.
6. In early 1992, the Maastricht Treaty formalized the movement towards a single currency.

7. In 1993, the European Union became a full-fledged common market, with free movement of products, labor and capital.
8. The criteria for adopting the euro include limits on interest rates, budget deficits, and government debt.
9. On 1 January 1999, the currencies of 11 European Union members were permanently fixed to the new unit of account, the euro, with the European Central Bank managing the supplies of each currency.
10. In January and February 2002, after three years of permanently-fixed exchange rates, national currencies were retired and replaced by the euro at the fixed rates that prevailed since 1999.
11. By 2010, 16 EU countries had abandoned their national currencies in favor of the euro, but the severe economic recession put on hold other countries plans to join the single currency area.

The lessons from Europe's experience with pegging exchange rates and finally moving to a single currency is that the quest for fixed exchange rates is difficult. Each step towards fixed exchange rates came with the usual cost of losing policy autonomy. The trilemma was always in play because Europe's attempts to fix exchange rates coincided with the opening of Europe's mutual borders to free trade and unrestricted capital movements with the establishment of the European Economic Community and, later, the European Union. Before the euro came into being in 1999, Europe's attempts to permanently fix the exchange rates between its currencies all eventually failed. The question facing the European Union today is whether the introduction of the euro will finally prove to be a lasting solution to Europe's aversion to floating exchange rates.

The euro is a major historical event. That a continent destroyed by the biggest war ever just 65 years ago could achieve such a degree of economic, political, and social integration undoubtedly constitutes one of history's greatest achievements. The euro is not yet a guaranteed success, however. First of all, not all members of the European Community have adopted the euro. The most obvious absence from the euro zone is the United Kingdom. Sweden and Denmark seem equally unenthusiastic about joining the euro area at this time. Most of the 12 new members that joined EU after 2002 have yet to satisfy the criteria for membership in the euro area. In addition, the difficulty that several members were having in 2010 in dealing with high unemployment and the large budget deficits needed to stimulate their economies during the severe economic recession seemed to discourage further expansion of the euro area.

Also worrisome is the lack of restraints on individual countries' fiscal policies. In 2005, five of the 12 euro area countries had fiscal deficits exceeding three percent of GDP. Greece's fiscal deficit exceeded six percent of GDP. Worse yet, it now appears that Greece has been misstating its accounts for years, and it may not have actually qualified for entry into the euro zone in 2000.[7] Feldstein (2005) singles out the cause of these deficits:

> ...the European institutional structure with a centralized monetary policy but decentralized fiscal policies creates a very strong bias toward large chronic fiscal deficits and rising ratios of debt to GDP. An effective political agreement among the Eurozone countries is needed to prevent those deficits.

Feldstein's suggested "political agreement" has not progressed very well. In fact, in 2005, the European Council effectively suspended enforcement of the *Stability and Growth Pact's* limits on national fiscal deficits for euro countries. With the global recession after the 2008 financial crisis, the fiscal deficits of most European countries have grown larger, and more countries are in violation of the guidelines for participation in the euro area. In dealing with the Greek crisis described above, European governments were clearly struggling to redesign its EU institutions to handle a broad economic recession spread unevenly across its region.

There have also been some setbacks in creating new institutional structures for the region. The implementation of so-called "Lisbon agenda" has been very slow. At the 2000 Lisbon Conference, all the EU

---

[7] John W. Miller (2004). "Greece's Missteps Put EU Statistics in Doubt", *Wall Street Journal*, 24 September 2004.

heads of state agreed to actively pursue measures to increase competition and technological progress in Europe. Thus far, much of the substance of the agreement has not yet been carried out. The "Services Directive" that was supposed to liberalize trade in services throughout the European Union ended up passing but in a very watered-down version. Ministers to the European Parliament mustered a majority for approval only after more than 200 amendments were added to the original plan. Many amendments create exceptions to free trade in services. Governments will now have leeway to restrict services providers on the grounds of public policy, national security, environmental regulations, and public health issues. Small businesses in many countries were disappointed by the elimination of the "country-of-origin" principle from the final version of the bill. This provision would have permitted small firms and individual service providers to operate in all 27 member nations of the EU under the rules and laws of their home countries. The costs for small firms to deal with the multiple regulations, rules, licensing procedures, and other paperwork in other countries are often prohibitive. On the other hand, elimination of the rule would, most likely, have resulted in a substantial amount of "gaming" national regulations by basing service businesses in those countries with the most lax regulations and oversight.

Another setback was the failure of voters in France and the Netherlands to ratify the draft EU Constitution in 2005. In 2009, elections for the European Parliament revolved around the future of the European Union, with many candidates campaigning on platforms that sought either a slowdown in further expansion of centralized EU governance or membership. After admitting Bulgaria and Romania in 2007 and bringing the membership up to 27, there is now strong opposition to further expansion of the membership. Nevertheless, the EU is in negotiations with "candidate countries" Croatia, Turkey, and the former Yugoslav Republic Macedonia. The EU classifies as "potential candidate countries" Albania and the former Yugoslav republics of Bosnia and Herzegovina, Montenegro, and Kosovo.

In sum, the European Union and the euro are major accomplishments. They are a tribute to the post-World War II European leaders who sought to forever change the economic, political, and social landscape of Europe. Realistically, many difficult decisions remain to be made, and it will be a challenge to continue making the difficult decisions within an organization of 27, or more, nations. Remember, however, that in the case of the EU, the skeptics repeatedly have been proven wrong.

A more holistic way to look at the European Union and the euro is from the perspective of national sovereignty. Recall from Chapter 1 Seabright's (2004) benefits and dangers from dealing with strangers. In the modern world, sovereignty is seen from the national perspective, which is why people debate "foreign policy". In a modern world, nations are dependent on, and responsible to, other nations. The Bretton Woods Conference put the world on a path to greater economic integration by encouraging economic development in general and international trade in particular. Europe has now opted for an economic union, which takes interdependence into the political sphere.

John McClintock (2009) argues that the surrender of national sovereignty is not just an option that will prove economically beneficial, but it is an absolute necessity for humanity's ability to meet its greatest challenges. The modern world's greatest challenges, including global warming, nuclear proliferation, economic inequality, the concentration of economic power in the hands of multinational corporations, financial instability, and the corruption of national government by corporate interest groups, are all global in nature. International cooperation and the creation of global institutions are essential for dealing with these complex global problems. To date, the world has taken some steps to create international institutions. But as of 2010, the United Nations remains the only real attempt at global governance, and it has not been very effective. McClintock argues that the widespread resistance to surrendering national sovereignty could be more easily overcome if international economic and political integration begins with regional groups of countries such as the European Union. Overwhelming global problems will only induce countries to cede sovereignty quickly if there are good relations among the countries involved. McClintock explicitly argues that the EU is well positioned to tackle bigger global problems because its regional structure of governance already includes a real transfer of sovereignty from nations to a multinational institution. It thus serves as a model, which others can emulate and achieve greater economic and political integration of the world's nations. The difficulties faced by Greece in 2010, and the slow response by the EU's members throw some doubt on McClintock's optimism about the EU as a global role model. Note also that negotiations on how to assist Greece in 2010 eventually required bringing in the IMF. This suggests that global institutions still have not moved very far since those amazing three weeks in July of 1944.

Perhaps we have made too much of the euro. Perhaps it is nothing more than another phase in the ever-evolving ups and downs of the international financial system. Still, if we contemplate the 65 years since Bretton Woods, the transformation of Europe into a peaceful and integrated economic and political entity consisting of nations that confronted each other in two world wars and, more recently, a Cold War, it is difficult to *not* see the European Union and the euro as very large accomplishments.

Key Terms and Concepts

Accession criteria
Amsterdam Treaty
Common Agricultural
    Policy
Common market
Council of Ministers
Customs union
Delors White Paper
Economic
    integration
Economic union
Euratom
Euro
European Central
    Bank

European Coal and
    Steel Community
European Commission
European Council
European Economic
    Area
European Economic
    Community
European Free Trade
    Area
European Monetary
    System
European Parliament
European Union
Free rider problem

Free trade area
Lisbon strategy
Maastricht Treaty
Optimum currency
    area
Preferential trade
    area
Single currency
Snake in the tunnel
Stability & Growth
    Pact
Stockholm
    Convention
Symmetric shocks
Treaty of Rome

Chapter Questions and Problems

1. Explain the metaphor "snake in the tunnel", which described the exchange rate system in Europe after the 1971 Smithsonian Agreement.

2. Describe in detail the differences between a preferential free trade area, a free trade area, a customs union, a common market, and an economic union. Illustrate the differences by applying the terms to the phases of European economic integration from 1950 to the present.

3. One of the early regional policies of the European Economic Community was the Common Agricultural Policy (CAP). Explain the CAP and why there is opposition to it within and outside the EU.

4. Explain European citizenship as it is currently defined.

5. Define an optimum currency area. (Hint: Use the diagram in this chapter, explain what each of the two curves stands for, and what determines the equilibrium in the model.)

6. Is the EU an optimum currency area? Discuss.

7. What, precisely, determines the levels of the curves in Fig. 15.2, and what causes them to shift? Relate your discussion to specific changes in the institutions and economic development of the EU.

8. Write a brief essay on why members of the European Union opted to create a single currency. Discuss the events that led up to the decision, and describe how the trilemma influenced the rules under which countries were permitted to join the system.

9. The textbook writes:

   "In his classic article, Robert Mundell first presents the case of two separate currency areas that correspond to two nations, A and B. He also assumes that the two nations' central banks intervene in the foreign exchange market to fix the exchange rate between the two currencies. He then assumes that world product demand shifts from country A to country B. If prices are sluggish in both countries and labor cannot move from A to B, the shift in product demand will cause unemployment in A and inflationary pressure in B. In the short run, if capital is mobile (as would be the case for most countries today) each country's exchange rate intervention would result in monetary policies that make matters worse!"

Use an open-economy model or a combination of open-economy models to explain exactly what is written above.

10. How would you go about determining the optimal number of currencies in the world? In a region like Europe? Within a country like the United States? Describe your approach to the issue, and use your analytical framework to compare the appropriateness of single-currency areas like Europe and the United States.

References

Blanchard, O and F Giavazzi (2002). Current account deficits in the euro area. The end of the Feldstein Horioka puzzle? *Massachusetts Institute of Technology Working Paper 03–05*, September 17.

Feldstein, M (2005). The euro and the stability pact. *NBER Working Paper w11249*, March.

Frankel, J and A Rose (1998). The endogeneity of the optimum currency area criteria. *Economic Journal*, 108(449), 1009–1025.

Frankel, J and A Rose (2002). An estimate of the effect of common currencies on trade and income. *Quarterly Journal of Economics*, 116(2), 437–466.

Krugman, P (2010). The Euro Trap. *New York Times*, 30.

Kouparitsas, MA (2001). Is the United States an optimum currency area? An empirical analysis of regional business cycles. *Federal Reserve Bank of Chicago Working Paper WP2001-22*.

McClintock, J (2009). *The Uniting of Nations: An Essay on Global Governance*, 3rd Ed. Brussels: Peter Lang.

Mill, JS (1894). *Principles of Political Economy*, Vol. 2, New York.

Mundell, RA (1968). *International Economics*. New York: The MacMillan Company.

Mundell, RA (1961). A theory of optimum currency areas. *American Economic Review*, 51(4), 657–665.

Rose, AK (2004). A meta-analysis of the effect of common currencies on international trade. *NBER Working Paper w10373*, March.

Rose, AK and E van Wincoop (2001). National money as a barrier to international trade: The real case for currency union. *American Economic Review*, 91(2), 386–390.

Tenreyro, S and RJ Barro (2003). Economic effects of currency unions. *NBER Working Paper No. w9435*, January.

Part V

International Financial Issues

Chapter 16

Foreign Direct Investment and Multinational Enterprises

Traditionally investment has followed trade. But trade is increasingly becoming dependent on investment.

(Peter Drucker, 1987)

In the early 2000s, the US city of Holland, Michigan, was steadily losing industrial jobs. Several industrial plants closed, among them a factory owned by the French operator of water systems, Vivendi. Then, in 2004, the German multinational firm Siemens bought the local Holland factory shut down by the French operator and began manufacturing similar wastewater equipment.[1] Vivendi closed the plant because it had excess production capacity; the firm used the plant only to supply its own water systems around the world. In fact, Vivendi prohibited the plant from supplying equipment to water utilities operated by Vivendi's competitors. Siemens, on the other hand had a different business strategy for the plant; it supplied its dealers in over 190 countries around the world. Four years later, the factory had twice as many workers as it employed under Vivendi.

---

[1] This case is described in Peter S. Goodman (2008). "When Foreigners Buy Factories: 2 Towns, 2 Outcomes", *New York Times*, April 7.

675

Some 50 miles to the north of Holland, the town of Greenville, Michigan lost 2,700 jobs in 2006 when the Swedish firm Electrolux shifted refrigerator manufacturing from the Greenville plant to Mexico. That was a huge loss for a town of only 8,000 inhabitants. Despite the devastating departure of Electrolux, the governor of Michigan, Jennifer Granholm, actively sought to attract another foreign firm to Greenville. "Pursuing international investment is one strategy to get jobs", she said. In the modern global economy, it is increasingly seen as the only strategy.

This chapter examines foreign direct investment (FDI), the investment flows that build multinational business enterprises (MNEs). FDI is often the largest line in the financial account of a modern country's balance of payments.

Chapter Goals

1. Define foreign direct investment (FDI) and distinguish it from other categories of international investment.
2. Detail the recent growth of FDI and multinational enterprises (MNEs).
3. Present a brief history of MNEs.
4. Discuss the reasons for the growth of FDI and MNEs.
5. Discuss economic, political, and social problems associated with MNEs.
6. Examine the role of FDI and MNEs in transferring technology across borders.
7. Discuss the role of MNEs in the global economy, as well as the implications for the process of international economic integration.

16.1 Foreign Direct Investment

FDI is defined more generally as the acquisition of foreign assets over which the purchaser has a substantial degree of control. For example, included under the heading of foreign direct investment in the standard balance of payments accounts are everything from the cross-border payments to acquire ownership of at least ten percent of the voting stock to the payments needed to construct a fully owned and operated foreign manufacturing plant.

16.1.1 *Peculiarities of FDI*

FDI is fundamentally different from the purchase of many other types of financial assets, such as buying 100 shares in a foreign firm, buying a bond, or making a bank loan. FDI involves active participation in the management and financial monitoring of the foreign investment.[2] There are some advantages to direct ownership and control of foreign businesses; indeed there must be substantial advantages because FDI has become very large in recent years. FDI also seems to bring greater international technology transfers than other forms of international investment, perhaps because it facilitates the types of human contact necessary to transfer knowledge and methods. Finally, FDI is closely related to international trade. In the early 2000s close to 90 percent of US imports and exports involved a multinational enterprise on at least one end of the transaction. In short, the global economy is being fundamentally reshaped by the growth of foreign direct investment and the multinational enterprises the FDI creates.

FDI includes building new factories overseas, expanding foreign marketing and distribution organizations, and acquiring controlling interests in existing firms overseas. This latter form of FDI is referred to as *mergers and acquisitions (M&A)*; the first two items are examples of *greenfield investments* because they involve the establishment of new businesses and production facilities. In recent years, net international investment flows have become very large. In 2000, they were the largest category of international investment flows. Along with the growth of financial markets across the world, FDI is largely a

---

[2] See Richard Caves (1996) or Robert E. Lipsey (2001) for a discussion of the various definitions of FDI and MNEs. The ten percent rule is standard in the literature.

20th century phenomenon that has shaped the globalization of economic activity. FDI continues to grow at the start of the 21st century.

16.1.2 *Growth of FDI*

During the 1960s, FDI accounted for about 6 percent of all international investment. In 1990, FDI accounted for about 20 percent of all international investment, and by the 2000s it often accounted for more than 30 percent of cross-border capital movements. During the 1990s and 2000s, FDI grew at a rate about three times as fast as overall investment worldwide.[3] According to the United Nations, the accumulated stock of FDI has grown from about $3.2 trillion in 1990 to well over $10 trillion in 2005. In real terms, this amounts to a doubling of total FDI in 15 years. Over $1.25 trillion was added in 2000 alone, the year when FDI reached its all-time one-year high. In 2006, there were about 160,000 foreign affiliates belonging to almost 60,000 MNEs operating throughout the world.[4]

Table 16.1 provides some details. Note that FDI to developing countries has grown much faster, from $21 billion to over $1 trillion, than overall FDI, but developed economies still host over 90 percent of all FDI. Note also that FDI in service industries accounts for the greater part of total FDI. The popular image of FDI as moving manufacturing plants to low-wage countries is not accurate.

16.1.3 *FDI creates MNEs*

By extending a business organization across borders, foreign direct investment effectively creates *multinational enterprises*. A *multinational enterprise* (MNE) is a firm that manages and owns production and distribution facilities in more than one country. Hence, by definition, multinational firms carry out all of the world's *foreign direct investment*, which is defined as the purchase of controlling interest in

---

[3] *The Economist* (1997). "A Worldbeater, Inc", November 22.

[4] *UNCTAD* (2007). Annex Table A.1.5.

Table 16.1 Estimated World FDI Stock, by Sector and Industry: 1990 and 2005 (US$ Billions).

	1990			2005		
	MDCs	LDCs	World	MDCs	LDCs	World
1. *Primary*	161.5	2.2	163.8	584.1	35.4	618.6
Agriculture, forestry, and fishing	5.2	0.3	5.6	4.3	1.6	5.9
Mining, quarrying, petroleum	156.3	1.9	158.2	577.4	33.8	610.2
2. *Manufacturing*	793.6	6.4	800.0	2,655.3	117.4	2,774.3
Food, beverages, tobacco	75.6	0.4	76.0	298.8	2.5	301.4
Textiles, clothing, leather	19.6	0.2	19.7	132.2	3.2	135.5
Wood and wood products	21.5	0.0	21.6	81.7	2.1	83.8
Publishing, printing, recorded media	2.3	—	2.3	15.6	0.0	15.7
Coke, oil refining, nuclear products	39.3	—	19.3	35.7	0.0	35.7
Chemicals	150.9	0.8	151.7	560.0	3.6	564.5
Rubber and plastic products	14.5	0.1	14.6	33.7	2.2	35.9
Non-metallic mineral products	13.1	0.2	13.3	35.3	0.8	36.2
Metal products	66.4	0.9	66.4	266.3	1.5	268.1
Machinery and equipment	42.0	0.0	42.1	108.9	0.5	109.5
Electrical and electronic equipment	97.5	1.0	98.5	240.6	9.0	149.6
Precision instruments	13.5	—	13.5	50.8	0.3	51.0
Motor vehicles, transport equipment	60.3	0.0	60.3	427.4	1.3	428.7
Other Manufacturing and unspecified	177.1	3.5	181.6	368.3	90.3	458.7

(*Continued*)

Table 16.1 (*Continued*)

	1990			2005		
	MDCs	LDCs	World	MDCs	LDCs	World
3. *Services*	834.9	11.6	846.6	6,264.0	830.7	7,095.6
Electricity, gas, water	9.6	—	9.6	96.5	6.8	103.7
Construction	18.2	0.2	18.4	73.1	8.7	81.1
Trade	139.9	1.9	141.8	631.1	107.2	738.4
Hotels and restaurants	7.1	—	7.1	96.2	8.6	104.8
Transport, storage, communications	39.8	0.5	40.3	557.4	53.6	611.2
Finance	400.0	7.2	407.2	2,208.9	176.7	2,385.8
Real estate sales	—	—	—	1.7	—	1.7
Business activities	55.1	1.3	56.4	2,127.2	454.3	2,582.1
Public administration and defense	—	—	—	4.0	—	4.0
Education	0.4	—	0.4	0.4	—	0.4
Health and social services	0.9	—	0.9	1.2	—	1.2
Community, social services	3.4	—	3.4	19.5	1.7	21.2
Other services and unspecified	160.5	0.5	161.0	448.5	13.1	461.6
Total	1,794.2	20.9	1,815.2	9,570.4	1,005.1	10,577.1

Source: UNCTAD (2007). *World Investment Report 2007.* New York: United Nations Conference on Trade and Development. Annex Table A.1.11.

foreign firms or foreign real assets. The presence of MNEs also implies that international trade is carried out not only between different firms located in different countries, but often between different branches of the same firm located in different countries. Such trade is called *intra-firm trade.* The fact that the same management now often controls both the exporter in one country and the importer in another country does not neccessarily alter our conclusions about the gains from trade. In fact, multinational enterprises seem to be able to better exploit comparative advantage and economies of scale. MNEs flourish because in the complex global economy internal transactions across borders are easier to carry out than market transactions between separate firms.

16.1.4 *Vertical and horizontal FDI*

FDI can be *vertical* or *horizontal*. Vertical FDI occurs when an MNE builds or acquires foreign facilities that fit into one stage of the supply chain that is not served by other corporate facilities elsewhere. An example of a vertical foreign direct investment is Ford's engine plant in Brazil, which supplies engine blocks to Ford assembly plants in Brazil, Europe, and the United States, where they are finished into complete engines and assembled into finished automobiles. Similarly, Toyota's wholesale organizations located in nearly every country of the world are vertically related to its manufacturing plants located in just a few countries.

Horizontal FDI, on the other hand, consists of MNE investments that duplicate facilities and operations that the company already owns in other countries. The huge French retailer Carrefour, for example, operates distribution centers and chains of retail stores in a number of countries, and its investment in distribution, warehousing, and retail facilities is similar in every country. Ford and Toyota operate automobile assembly plants in a number of countries, and often similar or even identical cars are produced in several different countries at plants that are near duplicates of each other.

MNE investments across developed economies are more often horizontal investments, and MNE activity in developing countries more often serves to vertically integrate the supply chain. For example, Shatz and Venables (2000) estimate that less than four percent of production by European affiliates of US MNEs is sent back to the United States market, but 18 percent of US affiliate production in developing economies is exported to the United States. US affiliates in Mexico send over 40 percent of their output to the United States. Shatz and Venables also confirm Brainard's (1997) earlier finding that the spread of an MNE's production is more likely to be horizontal the higher are transport costs and trade barriers and the lower are scale economies at the plant level. Vertical investment is driven by factor cost differences, the principal determinant of comparative advantage. This seems to be a restatement of an often-noted pattern of international trade: Factor endowments tend to drive trade between developed and developing countries and increasing returns to scale more often determine trade between developed countries.

Caves (1996) urges caution in modeling FDI. His extensive research leads him to conclude that classifications such as vertical and horizontal are fuzzy. Horizontal foreign subsidiaries of MNEs manufacturing similar products in different countries often also export or import products from subsidiaries in other countries. In effect, differences in comparative advantages, transactions costs, transportation costs, tariffs and quotas, and market size across countries and industries lead MNEs to engage in a variety of investment projects throughout the world, some horizontal, some vertical.

16.1.5 *The history of MNEs*

Business firms have spread their operations across borders for centuries. In fact, some 2,500 years ago Sumerian merchants stationed employees abroad to sell goods or receive foreign products to be sent back home. By 1600, private companies began setting up permanent operations in colonial regions protected by their governments' armies and navies. Wilkins (1970) describes the 1606 settlement at Jamestown, the first British colony in what is today the state of Virginia in the United States, as effectively a direct foreign investment by the British-base Virginia Company. Many other colonial enterprises could be classified as foreign direct investments, although the lines between private and government were often blurred. It was not until the 19th century that the modern multinational enterprise began to take shape.

The Singer Company's building of a sewing machine factory in Scotland in the late 1860s is often given as the earliest example of the modern MNE. The I. M. Singer Company was formed in 1851 after Isaac Singer perfected the bobbin, the technological breakthrough that made mechanical sewing possible. After setting up manufacturing in Elizabeth, New Jersey, Singer offered exclusive territories within the US to local independent salespeople. Singer took a different approach to foreign markets, however; in 1855, Singer authorized a French company to manufacture its sewing machines in France for a royalty of 15 percent. Neither of these arrangements proved to be profitable, however. The independent salespeople did not sell as much as Singer's own sales staff, and the French firm was found to be under-reporting how many machines it manufactured in France. Singer therefore switched to expanding its own sales organizations domestically and overseas, supplied from its New Jersey factory. By 1861, Singer had sales offices with its own employees in Glasgow and London.

After the Civil War, US sales grew very rapidly, and Singer had trouble supplying the British market. Rather than expand its New Jersey manufacturing capacity, Singer decided in 1867 to open a factory in Glasgow, Scotland, thus becoming a truly multinational manufacturer. By the end of the 19th century, Singer operated sales organizations, retail stores, distribution centers, or factories in over 100 countries.[5]

In 1914, nearly three-fourths of US-owned assets abroad were direct investments. This was not the case for other countries; recall from earlier discussions of international investment that British investors preferred portfolio investments (mostly bonds) to direct foreign investments. Early in the 20th century, when the United States was still a net debtor to the rest of the world overall, its foreign direct investments greatly exceeded foreigners' direct investments in the United States. As recently as 1960, half of the world's accumulated stock of FDI was owned by US-based corporations.

Table 16.2 lists the 25 largest non-financial MNEs, ranked by the value of their overseas assets in 2006. In recent years, foreign firms have caught up to the United States in terms of FDI. Japanese, British, Dutch, French, Swiss, and German MNEs have become household brands throughout the world. Japan's Toyota is as well known as Ford of the US, British Petroleum is as well known as Exxon-Mobil, and Switzerland's Nestle's is as prominent in supermarkets as Coca Cola.

---

[5] Isaac Singer had another motivation for setting up a factory in Scotland: he was being prosecuted for bigamy in the United States, and he found it convenient to move to Scotland with one of his wives.

Table 16.2   The World's Largest Non-financial MNEs, Ranked by Assets: 2007 (Millions of US$s and Number of Employees).

Corporation	Home	Industry	Assets		Sales		Employees	
			Foreign	Total	Foreign	Total	Foreign	Total
1 General Electric	U.S.	Electrical	420.3	795.3	86.5	172.7	168,112	327,000
2 Vodafone Group	U.K.	Communications	230.6	254.9	60.3	71.1	62,008	72,375
3 Royal Dutch/Shell	U.K./Neth.	Petroleum	196.8	269.5	207.3	355.8	86,000	104,000
4 British Petroleum	U.K.	Petroleum	185.3	236.1	223.2	284.4	80,600	97,600
5 ExxonMobil	U.S.	Petroleum	174.7	242.1	269.2	390.3	50,904	80,800
6 Toyota Motor	Japan	Motor Vehicles	153.4	284.7	145.8	230.6	121,775	316,121
7 Total	France	Petroleum	143.8	167.1	177.8	233.7	59,146	96,442
8 Electricite de Fr.	France	Electric Utility	128.9	274.0	40.3	87.8	16,971	154,033
9 Ford Motor Co.	U.S.	Motor Vehicles	127.9	276.5	91.6	172.5	134,734	246,000
10 E.ON	Germany	Electricty, gas	123.4	202.1	41.4	101.2	53,344	90,758
11 ArcelorMittal	Luxembourg	Metals, steel	119.5	133.6	105.2	105.2	244,872	311,000
12 Telefonica S.A.	Spain	Telecom.	107.6	155.9	52.1	83.1	192,127	245,427
13 Volkswagen	Germany	Motor Vehicles	104.4	214.0	120.8	160.3	153,388	328,594
14 Conoco-Phillips	U.S.	Petroleum	103.5	177.8	56.0	187.4	14,591	32,600
15 Siemems AG	Germany	Electrical	103.1	134.8	74.9	106.7	272,000	398,000

(*Continued*)

Table 16.2 (*Continued*)

Corporation	Home	Industry	Assets		Sales		Employees	
			Foreign	Total	Foreign	Total	Foreign	Total
16 Daimler Chrysler	Germany/US	Autos	100.5	198.9	113.1	146.3	105,703	272,384
17 Chevron	U.S.	Petroleum	97.5	148.8	120.1	214.1	34,000	65,000
18 France Telecom	France	Communications	97.0	149.0	37.0	78.0	81,159	187,331
19 Duetsche Telecom	Ger.	Communications	96.0	177.6	46.8	92.0	92,488	241,426
20 Suez	France	Gas, Water	90.7	116.5	52.3	69.9	82,070	149,131
21 BMW AG	Germany	Motor Vehicles	84.4	131.0	64.9	82.5	27,376	107,539
22 Hutchinson W.	Hong Kong	Diversified	83.4	102.4	33.3	39.6	190,428	230,000
23 Honda Motor Co.	Japan	Motor Vehicles	83.2	110.7	87.3	105.3	158,962	178,960
24 Eni Group	Italy	Petroleum	78.4	149.4	73.5	128.5	39,319	75,862
25 Eads	Neth/Ger/French	Aircraft	75.1	111.1	52.5	57.6	72,471	116,493

Source: UNCTAD (2007). *World Investment Report 2009*, New York: United Nations Conference on Trade and Development., Annex Table A.1.19.

After 1960, foreign MNEs began to direct increasing amounts of FDI towards the U.S. In 2000, for example, foreigners' new FDI in the U.S. was $267.7 billion, nearly twice as much as U.S. FDI abroad of $152.4 billion.[6] Worldwide, in 2000 U.S. MNEs owned less than one-fourth of he world's total accumulated stock of FDI, compared to about half 40 years earlier. Note, however, that this rising share of foreign MNEs did not occur because U.S. MNEs reduced their overseas investment. Rather, U.S. MNEs continued to invest overseas, but because FDI by foreign MNEs rose so much faster, the U.S. share of the global stock of FDI declined. As shown in Table 16.3, by 2006 the U.S. share of the world stock of FD had declined to less than 20 percent (S2,384/12,474).

Table 16.3 also reveals another change from FDI in the past, namely the growth of MNEs from emerging economies. In 2006, nearly 15 percent of the accumulated stock of FDI was owned by MNEs based in developing countries.[7] Among such developing country FDI are the purchases of IBM's personal computer business by the Chinese firm Lenovo, Ford's Jaguar division by the Indian firm Tata, and growth of Mexico's Cemex into the world's leading producer of cement.

16.1.6 *MNEs and international trade*

Not only do MNEs account for an increasing share of the world's production, but they also account for most of the world's exports and imports. Already in the 1980s, a study on the role of MNEs in US foreign trade revealed that of the total US exports of $212.2 billion in 1982, $203.4 billion (95.9 percent of the total) were made by US MNE's (72.2 percent of total exports) and affiliates of foreign MNE's (23.7 percent). At the same time, US and foreign MNEs in the United States imported 77 percent of all goods imported into the United States. The data also highlighted the fact that a substantial portion of exports and imports were intrafirm trade. Specifically, the data showed that of total exports of $212.2 billion, $46.6 billion were

---

[6] Harlan W. King (2001). Maria Borga and Raymond J. Mataloni, Jr. (2001).

[7] Robert E. Lipsey (2001).

Table 16.3 FDI Stocks and Annual Flows by Region and Country, 2006[a] (US$s Millions).

	Inward stock	Outward stock	Inward flow	Outward flow
World	$11,998,838	$12,474,261	$1,305,852	$1,215,789
European Union	5,717,202	7,107,823	530,976	572,440
France	782,825	1,080,204	81,076	115,036
Germany	502,376	1,005,078	42,870	79,427
Italy	294,790	375,756	39,159	42,035
The Netherlands	451,491	652,633	4,371	22,692
The United Kingdom	1,136,265	1,486,950	139,543	79,457
Other Europe	282,873	679,158	35,414	96,258
North America	2,174,274	2,833,039	244,435	261,857
Canada	385,187	449,035	69,041	45,243
United States	1,789,087	2,384,004	175,394	216,614
Other developed economies	562,377	769,337	46,675	92,155
Australia	26,173	226,764	24,022	22,347
Japan	107,633	449,567	6,506	50,266
Africa	315,128	60,012	35,544	8,186
South Africa	77,038	43,499	323	6,674
Latin America	908,575	387,944	83,753	49,132
Argentina	58,604	24,047	4,809	2,008
Brazil	221,914	87,049	18,782	28,202
Chile	80,732	26,787	7,952	2,876
Mexico	228,601	35,144	19,037	5,758
Venezuela	45,398	11,559	543	2,089
West Asia	242,603	42,973	59,902	14,053
East Asia	1,191,291	923,403	125,774	74,099
China	1,061,588	752,304	112,350	59,589
South Korea	70,974	46,760	4,950	7,129
Taiwan	50,386	113,910	7,424	7,399
South Asia	72,862	14,198	22,274	9,820
India	50,680	12,964	16,881	9,676
South-East Asia	420,192	171,396	51,483	19,095
Malaysia	53,575	27,830	6,060	6,041
Singapore	210,089	117,580	24,207	8,626
Thailand	68,058	5,608	9,751	790
Former USSR	280,756	160,479	42,934	18,126
Kazakhstan	32,476	0	6,143	412
Russia	197,682	156,824	28,732	17,979

[a]The figures for inflows do not exactly match outflows because the estimates are based on different data compiled by different countries; the discrepancy is an indication of the inaccuracy of investment data, as discussed in chapter 2.

Source: UNCTAD (2007). *World Investment Report 2007*, New York: United Nations Conference on Trade and Development., Annex Tables B.1 and B.2.

by US MNE's to their foreign affiliates and $20.2 billion were by US affiliates of foreign MNE's to their own firms' home-country operations. That is, 31.5 percent of all US goods exports were intrafirm transfers. For imports the situation was similar: 36.6 percent of all US goods imports were intrafirm transfers.

More recent studies suggest that MNEs role in international trade has not diminished since the detailed study of the 1980s.[8] It is safe to say that that MNEs today are involved in at least 75 percent of all international trade.

MNEs seem to locate their production very much in accordance with the law of comparative advantage. MNEs have increasingly moved labor intensive production to low-wage countries, while many of the same firms export capital intensive and technology intensive products from the more developed economies. In many cases, MNEs produce high technology components in developed economies and export them to their overseas plants for the labor-intensive process of final assembly.

16.1.7 *MNEs and the spread of technology*

MNEs carry out most of the world's private R&D, and MNEs, therefore, control much of the world's industrial technologies. MNEs, by their international nature, play a major role in the dissemination of technology throughout the world. The spread of knowledge and technology constitutes an inherently difficult communications process. The communication of complex ideas, methods, and techniques comprises a complex learning process based on a variety of personal contacts, learning processes, and hands-on experiences.

The reason why the spread of technology across borders is of great concern to countries around the globe is that the *creation* of new technology and knowledge is highly concentrated geographically. According to Blomström and Kokko (1996), "over four fifths of

---

[8] See, for example, William J. Zeile (1997).

the global stock of FDI originates from the half dozen home countries that dominate the world's research and technology: the United States, the United Kingdom, Japan, Germany, Switzerland, and the Netherlands". Later in this chapter, we examine the evidence on technological transfers by MNEs.

16.1.8 *MNEs are controversial*

Because MNEs promote international specialization and trade, they are also intimately involved in the reallocation of employment across borders. The traditional "jobs argument", namely, that MNEs eliminate jobs in one country and add jobs in another, is inaccurate. With proper macroeconomic policies, all countries can maintain full employment even when trade alters the mix of jobs performed in individual countries. However, it is quite true that increased international trade and investment alters the *types* of jobs that people occupy in an economy, and it also affects the wages they earn. There are distributional effects associated with these changes in the location of production, as factor payments to capital, resources, and the different types of labor tend to change. According to Rangan and Lawrence (1999), "it appears that firms with operations in several countries are both willing and able to switch the location of their production in response to changes in cost differentials".[9]

The employment effects of FDI and the shift in world production that such investment implies is not the only controversial aspect of MNEs. There are many reasons why MNEs are so often depicted as detrimental to human well-being. Labor organizations argue that shifting production abroad weakens labor's bargaining power. The international mobility of capital also reduces governments' power to tax capital. If MNEs are indeed highly responsive to cost differences, attempts to increase corporate taxes will cause outflows of FDI. It would become impossible to redistribute income from capital to poor and unemployed workers.

---

[9] Subramanian Rangan and Robert Z. Lawrence (1999). pp. 6, 7.

These concerns will remain a major focus of political debate in most countries of the world. We need to continue improving our understanding of the role of MNEs in our global economy so that their role can be properly assessed and appropriate polices can be designed.

16.1.9 *A final note on FDI data*

Not all FDI is recorded in the balance of payments. MNEs often obtain local financing to acquire foreign assets or they use accumulated profits from their foreign operations, in which case their acquisition does not involve international payments. Nor does FDI necessarily imply investment in the normal economic sense, namely the creation of new productive capital. What is termed FDI often involves only the acquisition of firms in already existing another country. That is, a large portion of FDI consists of mergers or acquisitions (M&A), not *green-field investments*, which are new facilities and business organizations built from scratch. However, what is certain is that FDI extends a business organization across borders. The analysis of FDI must, therefore, concentrate on how the spread of control of a business organization across borders affects economic outcomes and specifically, the economic variables that are important to human well being.

16.2 The Theory of Multinational Enterprises and FDI

The growth of MNEs in the 20th century and their dominance in international trade and investment has brought forth many explanations. The literature on multinational enterprises suggests that there is no one single driving force behind their unrelenting growth during the past century. There are, in fact, many reasons for the growth of MNEs.

16.2.1 *Internalizing transactions costs*

If a business firm finds it is less costly to *internalize* transactions than to engage in arms-length transactions with other firms, managers will elect to allocate resources *administratively* rather than using market transactions. In his textbook on multinational enterprises, Caves (1998) describes these decisions as follows:

> The Darwinian tradition holds that the most profitable pattern of enterprise organization should ultimately prevail: Where more profit results from placing plants under a common administrative control, multiplant enterprises will predominate, and single-plant firms will merge or go out of business. In order to explain the existence and prevalence of MNEs, we require models that predict where the multiplant firm enjoys advantages from displacing the arm's-length market and where it does not. In fact, the prevalence of multiplant (multinational) enterprises varies greatly from sector to sector and from country to country.[10]

Thus, if a firm believes that it can best exploit its unique assets, talents, technology, and reputations in other national markets by extending its own organization to those locations, then it will opt to become an MNE.

Firms exploit their accumulated knowledge by operating in several countries because knowledge is very difficult to trade in markets. The licensing of technology to foreign firms is one such way to increase earnings from knowledge, but for practical reasons licensing is limited to well-defined designs and procedures. Many types of knowledge or know-how are not easily transferable. Know-how is often unique to the firms that developed it or built up the experience that gradually produced the know-how. It may be impossible to transfer know-how and techniques to others who have not endured a similar learning period. Thus, these firms must establish overseas units to apply their in-house know-how and reap the economic rewards of their proprietary technology.

The increased use of international *outsourcing*, which is the purchase of parts and components from other manufacturers,

---

[10] Richard E. Caves (1996). op. cit., pp. 1, 2.

shows that modern communications have reduced the costs of completing some types of transactions that in the past were internalized. So far, the growth of outsourcing has not slowed the growth of FDI, however. Up until the 2008 global economic slowdown, globalization was progressing in the form of both MNE growth and outsourcing.

Outsourcing is restricted by the so-called *hold-up problem*. Outside suppliers are obviously reluctant to make large investments in capacity and technology to supply specialized products to a specific firm. Long-term supplier contracts can help to mitigate this problem, but it may not be possible to write and enforce complete contracts that cover all contingencies. In fact, a purchasing firm has a real incentive to induce a supplier to make substantial investment in building capacity and know-how for supplying specialized products, and then to "renegotiate" the terms of the contract once the supplier is locked into this new supplier capacity. In fact, it has become commonplace for outsourcing firms to "squeeze" their suppliers for lower prices. Clearly, suppliers are leery of opening themselves to such pressure, and they can strengthen their hand by *holding up* their investments until the outsourcing firm agrees to contractual terms more favorable to the supplier. Or, the supplier may insist that the outsourcing firm provide the technology, machinery, or other assets so as to even out the eventual bargaining positions. The outsourcing firm may then decide to bring the production in house, where it can control the investment.

16.2.2 *Economies of scale*

Firms may become more efficient at a certain tasks the larger their operations become, and therefore a single firm spread throughout the world may be able to produce more efficiently than independent firms located in each of the countries of the world. Certain tasks such as research, product development, central administration, marketing design, and product design are the same no matter how many products are sold. A firm already in possession of a product design or a large research facility would be at a competitive advantage vis-à-vis a smaller local firm that must start from scratch to develop a product.

16.2.3 *Keeping core competencies in house*

Outsourcing is a simple concept: Firms should concentrate on what they do best and acquire from other firms the services, inputs, and goods that they cannot themselves produce as cheaply as others can. In short, outsourcing is the straightforward application of the principle of comparative advantage. By specializing and exchanging, firms lower their costs and improve their productivity. The basic concept of outsourcing is that core competencies provide the firm with the greatest profit margins because it is those activities where the firm is most unique and faces the least direct competition. The overall profit margin of a firm that focuses only on core competencies will be greater, all other things equal, than that of a firm that performs and invests in the capacity to perform many tasks, including those for which there are many competitors.

Of all US firms listed on organized stock exchanges, the proportion operating in a single industry rose from 38 percent in 1979 to 58 percent in 1988.[11] The divesting of businesses by companies continued through the 1990s. Berger and Ofek (1995) found that, on average, diversified companies were valued at a discount of 13 to 15 percent to the imputed value of their parts. Others have disputed whether such a discount exists, however, and research continues. Nevertheless, management consultants such as McKinsey & Company continue to advocate focusing on "core competencies" by divesting unrelated businesses and outsourcing production and services related to the form's core competencies but which can be supplied more cheaply by others.

FDI is a logical extension of a core competencies strategy. Rather than let other firms in other countries gain part of the profits from the

---

[11] Simon London (2005). "The Importance of Choosing the Right Track", *Financial Times*, January 17.

firm's core competencies, FDI enables the firm to extend its organization globally in order to keep all the core activities in house.

16.2.4 *Exploiting reputations*

Many firms have built up considerable reputations over the years, and often the only way to exploit those reputations in other markets is to actually set up operations in those markets. Licensing a foreign firm to produce a product may not transfer that reputation effectively if local consumers know that the product is not really produced by the true originator of the product. Successful MNEs are often those firms that have established strong reputations and brands. The importance of reputation and brand recognition tends to favor large firms, which can devote more resources to establishing their brands in the market.

There are many examples of how reputations have been damaged by outsourcing or licensing to foreign firms in foreign markets. For example, The British firm Rouwntree, a maker of high-quality chocolates and confectionaries, decided it could better exploit its reputation in the protected market of South Africa by licensing to a local firm; exports had become prohibitively expensive with the imposition of tariffs by the South African government. Problems arose, however, when the South African licensee began to reduce costs, and quality, in the hope that Rouwntree's international reputation would still permit the firm to charge premium prices in the closed South African market. After some years, Rouwntree noticed a serious loss of reputation that even hit its other foreign markets, and it decided to acquire majority interest in the South African licensee in order to reestablish control over the manufacturing process.[12]

16.2.5 *Jumping trade barriers*

If firms have reputations, know-how, fixed product development costs that can be profitably exploited in foreign markets, then trade barriers

---

[12] This case is mentioned in Giorgio Barba Navaretti and Anthony J. Venables (2004). pp. 38, 39.

can lead them to invest in factories to manufacture their products behind the tariff and quota walls that block imports. For example, when developing countries applied protectionist import substitution policies after World War II, MNEs were often the ones who took advantage of the protection to establish local production. Local firms seldom had the know-how to operate plants in industries such as automobiles, chemicals, and electronics. MNEs came to dominate local manufacturing in developing countries such as Brazil, Mexico, and Argentina.

Trade barriers also stimulated FDI activity in the European Union after the region established common tariffs vis-a-vis the rest of the world but permitted the free flow of goods within the region. There was *trade diversion* in the form of replacing imports from countries outside the EU to new industries established within the EU by the former outside exporters.

16.2.6 *Avoiding taxes and regulations*

MNEs are often accused of evading environmental and labor regulation by moving production overseas. Since firms seek to minimize costs, there should be little doubt that they would prefer environmental and labor regulations to impose as few costs as possible, all other things equal. All other things are never equal, of course, and the countries with the most lax environmental and labor laws are not necessarily the least expensive manufacturing sites; labor productivity may be low, government services may be poor, and other necessary inputs may be expensive. Nevertheless, differences in regulation and taxation may make certain business activities more profitable in some countries than others.

MNEs may have a competitive advantage over national firms because they can manipulate transfer prices on goods and services traded among branches in different countries. For example, if a country places high tariffs on imports, the MNE may try to set low transfer prices on the components imported from foreign affiliates. Similarly, if a country levies high corporate income taxes compared to other countries in which the MNE operates, it will try to set transfer prices on the products exported to its foreign affiliates on the low side so that the subsidiary in the high tax country earns less profit and subsidiaries in low tax countries earn higher profits. Total taxes paid by the MNE across all countries are thus lower.

16.2.7 *Hedging exchange rate exposure*

As discussed at length in Chapter 5, exporters and importers face exchange rate risk. By spreading its production and marketing operations across countries to balance expenses and revenue in each currency, an MNE can reduce its exposure to foreign exchange fluctuations. If production costs are recorded in the same currency as sales revenues, only profits, the difference between the two, varies with the exchange rate. Unlike unhedged exposure to currency mismatches across assets and liabilities, the profit residual can never reverse sign.

16.2.8 *MNE as a diversified portfolio*

Multinational firms, with operations in many countries, provide an alternative to a diversified portfolio of assets; the returns to stock in an MNE reflect the returns to the firm's assets located in many different economies. Stock or bonds issued by MNEs are an alternative to an internationally diversified investment portfolio. Thus, an MNE may be able to finance its investments at more favorable rates than a purely national firm because it offers the purchaser of its stock and bonds less risk. The lower cost of financing leads to the growth of MNEs over national firms and more national firms expanding overseas and becoming MNEs.

Recent flows of capital to the so-called *emerging markets*, or developing economies, suggest that MNEs indeed are better able to deal with the difficulties of financing investment in economies where financial systems and institutions to enforce contracts are not as well developed. For example, net portfolio flows to emerging markets showed no growth trend during the 1990s and early 2000s, and the net inflows went almost entirely to Asia. FDI, on the other hand, expanded rapidly during the 1990s and early 2000s.

16.2.9 *Diversifying business risk*

The expansion of a business organization across political borders, oceans, and continents may end up diversifying away some business risk. When a firm is dependent on the market in just one country, its fortunes rise and fall with that market. The diversification motive may be especially strong for firms from developing countries and helps to explain the growth of MNEs from developing countries. For example, the Brazilian steel firm Gerdau suffered from the large swings in the Brazilian economy after the 1982 debt crisis. It therefore began to diversify its holding by acquiring steel firms in neighboring countries as well as in developed economies. In 1985, Gerdau acquired a small steel company in Uruguay, and in 1989 it acquired a Canadian steel firm. Then it acquired firms in Chile and Argentina in the 1990s, and in 1999 it acquired the US firm Ameristeel and its four US mills. After its Ameristeel acquisition, Gerdau was able to reduce its financing costs by 20 percent.[13] Cai and Warnock (2004) find strong evidence that the stock values of MNEs are higher, all other things equal, which they attribute to MNEs' inherent reduction in business risk.

16.2.10 *Reducing competition*

The spread of MNEs is usually described as an increase in global competition, as a greater number of firms from a variety of countries compete in the many individual national markets formerly dominated by a few domestic firms. That was often indeed the case in the early stages of FDI and growth of MNEs. However, we are now observing FDI fueling a worldwide consolidation of industries into a sharply reduced number of global MNEs. The automobile industry, the financial industry, and the food processing industry are examples of rapid consolidation across borders.

---

[13] Raymond Colitt (2000). "Breaking from the Traditional Brazilian Mould", *Financial Times*, September 12.

16.2.11   *Enhancing innovative success*

As discussed in Chapter 8, Joseph Schumpeter described the aggressive technological competition between large corporations. It is to be expected, therefore, that firms organize themselves, at least in part, to maximize their performance as innovators. Archibugi and Michie (1995) hypothesize that the aggressive search for innovation has led MNEs to increasingly invest in overseas research facilities. Blanc and Sierra (1999) provide an interesting rationale for the globalization of innovation, which is that innovation is a process that is subject to large economies of scale but also very dependent on outside ideas.

On the one hand, research and development activities are best carried out by concentrating them in a single location where researchers interact often and can draw on a variety of talents and resources. We often observe R&D activities concentrated at research centers, and we commonly see research activity concentrated in specific geographic regions like Silicon Valley. On the other hand, new knowledge and technology follows a combinatoric process in which old knowledge and technologies are combined to form new ideas, which means innovation needs access to existing knowledge and ideas. A Schumpeterian competitor, therefore, seeks an optimal combination of centralization (internal proximity) and dispersion (external proximity) of research activity.

The MNE has more options than a purely domestic firm in reaching the most efficient compromise between external and internal proximity in organizing its R&D activity. According to Blanc and Sierra: "MNFs increasingly tend to develop international intra-firm networks to exploit the 'locationally differentiated potential' of foreign centres of excellence".[14]

16.2.12   *Summarizing the reasons for the growth of MNEs*

The many explanations for the growth of MNEs are not mutually exclusive; several may apply to each case of FDI. For example, the large

---

[14] Hélène Blanc and Cristophe Sierra (1999). p. 203.

inflow of FDI to Ireland over the past two decades has been driven by the desire to jump over the European Union's trade barriers, to take advantage of Ireland's low corporate taxes, and to exploit Ireland's particular comparative advantages for production within the European Union. Overall, many factors have combined to make MNEs the dominant form of business organization in the global economy.

While the causes of MNEs are apparent, the implications of FDI and MNEs for the global economy and human welfare are the subject of much professional research and public discussion. We have already mentioned the role of MNEs in expanding trade and shifting employment across borders. We have also touched on FDI's role in disseminating technology. Opponents of globalization point to social upheaval from the destruction of traditional agriculture, the standardization of products, the exploitation of labor, and the reduction in the role of government from corporate "regulatory and taxation shopping". For more criticism of MNEs, one needs only to access one of the very many websites devoted to discussing globalization and global corporations.

16.3 Why Doesn't Capital Flow from Rich to Poor Countries?

Lucas (1990) asked the interesting question in the title of this section: "Why doesn't capital flow from rich to poor countries?" After all, poor countries have much less capital than rich countries, and, all other things equal, the marginal return to capital should be much higher in poor countries than in rich countries. Yet, most international investment occurs between high-income countries, not between rich and poor countries.

16.3.1 *FDI is different*

Prasad *et al.* (2007) examined capital flows from high-income to low-income countries, using a database covering 59 developing countries over the period 1970–2004. They found that:

> Over the period 1970–2004, as well as over shorter periods, the net amount of foreign capital flowing to relatively high growth

developing countries has been smaller than that flowing to the medium- and low-growth groups. During 2000–2004, the pattern is truly perverse, with China, India, high-growth and medium-growth countries all *exporting* significant amounts of capital.[15]

When Prasad *et al.* separate out FDI from other investment flows, however, the Lucas paradox largely disappears. The fastest-growing group of non-industrial countries received the most FDI over the entire period of 1970–2004. The paradox does not entirely disappear, however. During 2000–2004, substantial amounts of FDI flowed from low-income to high-income countries. China, which is still a relatively poor country, has exported capital despite its still low per capita income and phenomenal rates of economic growth.

To examine whether the entire set of capital flows is positively correlated with economic growth, Prasad, Rajan, and Subramanian test the relationship between current account deficits and economic growth. According to traditional economic theory, a rapidly growing country should be a net borrower and run a current account deficit. The authors write that

> We conducted thorough statistical analysis, ... accounting for various other factors that could be driving growth, and examined the robustness of the results in a number of ways. For instance, we looked at the correlation just for the period 1985–1997. This was in some sense the heyday of recent global integration, with rising capital flows and a relatively tranquil period in international financial markets (barring the Mexican Tequila Crisis). This should have been the period when the benefits of capital inflows shone forth. In most cases, however, the association between current account balances and growth remains positive for nonindustrial countries (the correlation is zero in the remaining cases). In no case do we find the negative relationship predicted by economic theory.[16]

---

[15] Prasad *et al.* (2007). p. 18.

[16] op. cit. p. 18.

The main variable that seems to be driving the surprising results is that rapidly growing economies save much more than slow-growing economies. Economic growth seems to stimulate the very savings it needs, so rapidly growing developing economies are not short of capital at all. An alternative explanation Prasad *et al.* offer is that a reliance on foreign capital has long-run costs and possible adverse consequences for the receiving economy. For example, large capital inflows may cause exchange rate appreciation, which reduces exports and increases imports, thus holding back industrial development.

Lucas (1990) examined several possible explanations for the lack of foreign investment in countries where capital is scarce: (1) technology is not as advanced in low-income economies, (2) people have more human capital as well as physical capital in the rich countries, and human capital is complementary to physical capital, (3) intertemporal transactions between countries are risky because long-term contracts cannot be effectively enforced, and (4) there are explicit restrictions on international investment. The first two explanations suggest that the slope of the production function is not really steeper in developing countries; the latter two explanations suggest that even if the return to capital *is* higher in developing countries, international investment is in some way prevented from responding to the incentive of higher returns. Lucas suggested policies that increase education and increase human capital, eliminate barriers to capital flows, and improve the legal institutions to regulate and enforce long-term contracts so that intertemporal transactions can be carried out with less risk.

16.3.2 *What is the role of FDI in transferring technology?*

Many economists have focused on FDI as a channel for transferring technology. One of the frequent findings of this literature is that FDI tends to have especially large technology spillovers. According to Moran (1998):

> Local subsidiaries exhibit an integration effect when they become part of the parents' strategy to maintain a competitive position in world markets that provides more rapid upgrading of management,

technology, and quality control than any other form of transfer. Thus, they create a dynamic link to the global frontier of best practices, most advanced technologies, and most sophisticated operational techniques in an industry. Simultaneously, they generate direct and indirect spillovers and externalities for domestic suppliers. FDI that creates a proprietary network of suppliers introduces a powerful interaction between parents and subsidiaries and between subsidiaries and host countries.[17]

This description of the growth effects of international investment provides an explanation for the fact that many developing countries are eager to attract FDI.

The growth economist Romer (193, p. 548) provides another reason why FDI may offer the best channel for technology transfers: "Access to ideas that are available in the rest of the world can come partly through unimpeded flows of the capital goods that are produced in the industrialized nations of the world.... But for the poorest developing nations, letting multinational firms profit from the international transmission of ideas is the quickest and most reliable way to reduce the idea gaps that keep them poor".

Technology transfers are costly. Even when knowledge and technology are available, there are still costs associated with the learning process and/or the adaptation of the technology to a new economic and business environment. In his ground-breaking study, Teece (1977) estimated the costs of technology transfers across countries in the chemicals, petroleum refining, and machinery industries. He found that, on average, the cost of adopting foreign technologies was equal to 19 percent of total project costs. Mansfield *et al.* (1981) also found the costs of adopting existing technologies to be substantial. For 48 product introductions in the chemical, drug, electronics, and machinery industries in the United States, they estimated cost of imitation to be about 65 percent of the total cost of innovation. The costs of imitation may be greater in developing countries.

---

[17] Theodore H. Moran (1998). p. 158.

Teece (1977) and David (1992) emphasized that most technology transfers between industrial plants require person-to-person contacts, follow-up information, training sessions, and many other repeated communications. Relevant here is Polanyi's (1958) description of most knowledge as "tacit" and thus requiring that it be passed on "by example from master to apprentice".[18] If you have ever tried to put together a disassembled foreign-made product using instructions poorly translated from a foreign language, you can imagine how difficult it would be to assemble an entire factory using nothing more than written instructions from abroad and then to operate the factory on the basis of written instructions alone. Actual technology transfers seldom occur exclusively in the form of precise blueprints. This means that the transfer of technology will tend to follow the patterns of international investment, and that countries must have the resources necessary to learn, adopt, and apply technologies from other countries. Research has increasingly focused on human capital and institutions as the critical elements for technology adoption. Clearly, an MNE enjoys an advantage in transferring technology because its organization already has people that understand the technology.

Borensztein *et al.* (1998) tested the relationship between FDI on economic growth using data on FDI flows from developed economies to 69 developing economies during the 1980s and 1990s. In agreement with the above paragraph, they found that FDI contributed more to growth in developing economies than domestic investment. They also found that FDI was associated with faster growth rates of output only if a country surpassed a certain threshold level of human capital. Their conclusion directly supports one of Lucas' suggestions for increasing investment flows to developing economies.

16.3.3 *What do we really know about technology transfers?*

The result that FDI is correlated with the growth of output does not directly prove that FDI causes technology transfers. But, it is very

---

[18] Polanyi (1958). p. 53.

difficult to measure the geographic spread of technology. Krugman (1991) went so far as to suggest that there may not be much that economists can say about technology flows because "they leave no paper trail by which they may be measured and tracked, and there is nothing to prevent the theorist from assuming anything about them that she likes".[19] Krugman may have been a bit too pessimistic, however. Innovative researchers *have* found some paper trails.

One popular strategy for uncovering the flow of technology and ideas has been to examine patent data. Patent applications require an explicit listing of prior ideas and discoveries on which the new idea is based, and in many countries patent applications require that the country of origin of the prior patents and ideas be listed as well. Hence, patent applications provide a paper trail of where knowledge came from. A shortcoming of patent data is that it captures only a small portion of all innovative activity that occurs in an economy. Most new knowledge is not patented. Also, some patented knowledge moves only after patents have run out; hence, there is a long lag between the creation of an idea and the time it spills over to other industries and countries. Nor do patents accurately reflect the importance of each innovation. Finally, patent data is of little help in tracing technology transfers within MNEs, since a patent held by an MNE tells us nothing about where the firm actually applies a technology.

Many researchers have sought other data that more accurately capture the actual creation and application of what we broadly define as technology. Most OECD countries collect data on R&D activity within their borders, and a few developing countries also compile such data. A common approach has been to statistically test the relationship between measured R&D activity in one country and measures of productivity growth in other countries. Standard national accounts data can be used to calculate total factor productivity or the productivity of individual factors of production. In some countries, data has been compiled that permits researchers to calculate R&D activity and productivity in individual manufacturing sectors. Such detailed industry information also permits the analysis of technology

---

[19] Paul Krugman (1991). pp. 53, 54.

spillovers between sectors of the economy, between firms within sectors, and across borders.

Published data on R&D activity clearly does not capture all innovative activity that occurs in a country, however. Keller (2004) points out that data on expenditures on R&D activity measures "primarily resources spent towards innovation, and not those resources spent on imitation and technology adoption. Technology investment of middle income and poor countries can therefore typically not be analyzed using R&D data".[20]

Clearly, we need more primary data on the value of innovation and the exact inputs into the innovative process across industries and countries. An interesting case study by Felipe *et al.* (2000) on Intel's factory in Costa Rica is a good example of such a detailed analysis. But, such studies have been very rare because they are very costly. Also, few firms willingly provide information on their operations to individual researchers. In the meantime, researchers have worked with the data available to them. The benefits of FDI and MNEs remain open to question, therefore.

16.4 Some Final Comments on Multinational Enterprises

In this last section, we briefly review some additional characteristics of FDI and the MNEs that FDI creates and expands. Specifically, this section examines the volatility of FDI flows compared to other forms of international investment, FDI's relationship to international trade, the clash between MNEs and individual nations, and the consequences of the growing economic and political dominance of what are effectively undemocratic, autocratic organizations.

16.4.1 *Is FDI less volatile than other capital flows?*

FDI is often touted as the least volatile form of international investment. You no doubt recall from the discussion on financial crises in

---

[20] Wolfgang Keller (2004). p. 757.

developing countries from Chapters 10 and 11 that many of these crises were triggered by sudden shifts in international flows of capital. For example, the 1982 debt crisis that affected so many developing economies was caused by a sudden stop in bank lending when monetary policy was tightened in the United States and other developed economies. The more recent crises in Asia, Mexico, Russia, Argentina, and other developing countries saw reversals of private portfolio flows. FDI, it is argued, is more stable because it cannot be as quickly reversed as bank lending and portfolio investments; FDI involves the acquisition of assets that are not so easily bought and sold. Also, FDI implies an extension of business organizations across borders. It is difficult to quickly change a business organization, its supply channels, and its marketing channels.

This image of FDI as a stable form of international investment may not be entirely accurate, however. While it is difficult to reverse FDI flows entirely because it takes time to dispose of real assets like factories or sell the ownership in firms, inflows of new FDI can certainly fall to zero very suddenly. The sudden cessation of the customary inflows can trigger an exchange rate crisis just as easily as a sudden departure of foreign capital, especially if the country was receiving large inflows of FDI and had been running a large current account deficit. Also, FDI may be more mobile than many policymakers suspect. In a study of foreign-owned plants in Indonesia, Bernard and Sjöholm (2003) find that, controlling for plant size, in the case of an economic slowdown "foreign-owned plants are 20 percent more likely to close than domestically-owned plants".[21]

Another concern about FDI is that at the time of an economic crisis well-funded foreign firms can acquire assets in a country at what Krugman (1998) labeled "fire-sale prices". Then, once the crisis has passed and exchange rates recover, foreign firms end up earning extremely high rates of return on their investments. Finally, FDI implies control of assets, and well-endowed MNEs can use such control to drive local firms out of the local market. This latter fear has always been present, especially in developing countries that were once

---

[21] Andrew B. Bernard and Fredrik Sjöholm (2003). p. 12.

colonies of countries where most of the world's major MNEs are based.

16.4.2 *FDI and global economic integration*

The growth of FDI and MNEs may be contributing to the increased synchronization of economic fluctuations across countries. Desai and Foley (2004) examine the rates of return and investment rates of MNEs in different countries, and they find that the rates of return and investment rates between overseas affiliates and their parent firms are highly correlated. Thus, when they extend their business organizations across borders, MNEs effectively create significant economic linkages that reduce economies' independence and facilitate the international transmission of economic shocks.

MNEs are also likely to transmit economic shocks from one country to another. Just think about what motivates MNEs to extend their business organizations across borders. Recall that MNEs have an advantage because they have access to overseas financing that purely domestic firms do not have. This implies that foreign financial conditions will tend to be reflected in a domestic affiliate's investment behavior. Furthermore, the advantage that MNEs have in spreading technology implies that new investment reflects overseas product developments and introductions. Also, the vertical FDI that characterizes many MNE investments in developing economies links output in those countries closely to demand in other countries. This latter linkage helped spread the 2008 recession quickly from one country to another as international trade fell sharply.

16.4.3 *Drucker's hypothesis*

The well-known management guru, Peter Drucker, predicted some 20 years ago that the growth of FDI would increasingly replace international trade as the driving force of globalization. Today, MNEs are responsible not just for an increasing share of international investment, but they dominate world trade. They also increasingly directly and indirectly drive international migration, either by moving personnel between parts of the company or altering labor market conditions as they shift production between countries. This intimate relationship between FDI, trade, and the movement of people obviously changes the reaction of trade to changes in the exchange rate. What a nation imports is as much determined by where MNEs have decided to locate their factories as by the exchange rate. Since most automobiles produced in the US are made up of foreign components that exceed 25 percent of the total value of the final product, a fall in the value of the dollar may stimulate some increase in domestic production that replaces imports of competing foreign products, but the combination of a lower dollar and a high percentage of imported components prevents the value of imports from falling very much. The international aircraft industry provides another example, as described in a *New York Times* article:

> Aircraft engines and engine parts, a category that has experienced a 24 percent increase in imports in the latest 12 months, are also affected by global sourcing, but in a more complex way. General Electric in the United States and Snecma of France, for example, jointly manufacture the jet engine for Boeing's 737 and Airbus's 320. G.E. makes the "hot section" at its plant in Cincinnati, while Snecma manufactures the giant fans in France. They ship these components to each other and each partner does the final assembly of the engines for its customers. In addition, G.E. makes smaller jet engines for the commuter planes that Bombadier makes in Canada and Embraer in Brazil. These are exported to those countries, but 24 percent of the value of the engines is composed of components imported from Japan. The upshot is that exports of engines and engine parts are rising, but so are imports.[22]

---

[22] Louis Uchitelle (2005). "Made in the USA. (Excepts for the Parts)", *New York Times*, April 8.

If Drucker is correct and investment, not trade, drives the global economy, exchange rates will have little impact and trade imbalances will be depend largely on FDI decisions made by the Directors and CEOs of MNEs.

The growth in the importance of international investment represents a challenge to international economists. Drucker (1987) therefore warns of a new era for the global economy:

> We ... have no theory for an international economy that is fueled by world investment rather than by world trade. As a result, we do not understand the world economy and cannot predict its behavior or anticipate its trends".

16.4.4 *MNEs and policy independence*

FDI is intimately mixed up with the disruptive processes of economic growth, such as the shifting of jobs across borders, the stagnation of workers' wages in many developed economies, and the volatile prices of commodities. After presenting evidence that MNEs significantly boost exports and economic growth in a host country, Lipsey (2002, p. 60) nevertheless notes:

> The association of FDI with more trade and faster growth would not necessarily please critics of multinationals. Trade links reduce the freedom of action of a country's government domestically, if not that of its people. Fast growth involves disruptions and the destruction of the value of old techniques of production and old skills. Those who value stability over economic progress will not be convinced of the worth of the gifts brought by foreign involvement. That is especially true if the gains are captured by small elements of the population or if no effort is made to soften the impact of the inevitable losses.

Critics of MNEs have not only questioned whether the economic growth MNEs may bring is worth the economic and social disruption. They also question whether FDI really brings true improvements in human welfare. The high costs of attracting FDI by means of tax benefits and other assorted subsidies must, obviously, be based on solid evidence of positive externalities and long-run growth in true human well-being. A survey of the economics and finance literature suggests the depiction of MNEs and FDI is not always fully holistic in the sense that all of the economic, social, and environmental consequences of the spread of multinational business organizations are taken into consideration.

16.4.5 *MNEs and national sovereignty*

The extension of business organizations across borders also threatens the concept of nationhood. Which country does an MNE have allegiance to? Today's large MNEs are normally owned by stockholders in many countries, they operate in many countries, their managers are nationals from many different countries, they have employees from many different countries, and their customers are spread across the globe. What is such a firm's true nationality? This lack of nationality scares some people. For example, when IBM sold its PC business to the Chinese computer firm Lenovo, there was an outcry because the Chinese government held a stake in Lenovo. A Congressman from the United States noted that IBM was a supplier of computers to the US government: "Why would the US government be reliant on a Chinese company whose major shareholder is the Chinese government? That in itself sends a chill up and down the spines of members of Congress".[23] Also, how many people remember that, during the US invasion and occupation of Iraq, one of the biggest war contractors, the US firm Halliburton, shifted its headquarters offshore to Dubai on the Persian Gulf?

A more important question, perhaps, is: Who does the MNE owe allegiance to? Only the stockholders? The employees as well? The customers? The growing concentration of economic activity within fewer and fewer increasingly large multinational business and financial

---

[23] Quoted in Charles Forelle (2005). "Sale of IBM Unit to Chinese Firm Faces US Review", *Wall Street Journal*, January 28.

firms, does not seem to be consistent with the notion that private business naturally maximizes the welfare of all people. Indeed, MNEs can stabilize trade and investment flows, they can facilitate the spread of technology, and they can integrate the world's economies to an extent that the participants in the Bretton Woods Conference could only dream would be possible. On the other hand, there are severe dangers associated with the concentration of immense economic power in the hands of largely unaccountable business organizations with compliant employees indoctrinated to believe in their employer's benevolence but managed by people facing incentives designed to appeal directly to personal greed. An examination of the root causes of the 2008 financial crisis makes it clear that many national firms do not hesitate to take actions that diminish the welfare of their fellow citizens. Why would we, therefore, expect foreign firms to behave in a manner that optimizes the well-being of people in their host countries?

16.4.6 *A dramatic example of the impact of foreign direct investment*

To counter the image of private business firms as the essential foundation of the modern global economy, we briefly look at Joseph Conrad's short novel, *Heart of Darkness*. This is a tale, written at the close of the 19th century, about an English captain hired by a colonial enterprise to navigate a riverboat to an ivory trading post deep in the Belgian Congo. The local manager of this outpost was named Kurtz, who is described by Conrad as not only "an emissary of pity, and science, and progress", but also an egotistical tyrant: "'my ivory, my station, my river, my —' everything belonged to him". Conrad also noted that "Kurtz had been educated partly in England... His mother was half-English, his father was half-French. All Europe contributed to making Kurtz...".[24]

Especially interesting is the English captain's description of a company report that Kurtz had written. The following passage, which

---

[24] Joseph Conrad (1899 [2003]). p. 92.

consists of the captain repeating and describing the lofty language of the report, is especially relevant:

> 'By the simple exercise of our will we can exert a power for the good practically unbounded', etc. From that point he soared and took me with him. The peroration was magnificent, though difficult to remember, you know. It gave me the notion of an exotic Immensity ruled by an august Benevolence. It made me tingle with enthusiasm. This was the unbounded power of eloquence — of words — of burning noble words. There were no practical hints to interrupt the magic current of phrases, unless a kind of note at the foot of the last page, scrawled evidently much later, in an unsteady hand, may be regarded as the exposition of a method. It was very simple, and at the end of that moving appeal to every altruistic sentiment it blazed at you, luminous and terrifying, like a flash of lightning in a serene sky: 'Exterminate all the brutes!'[25]

In short, stated good intentions do not prevent bad behavior on the part of MNE personnel. This is especially true when the day-to-day struggles weigh heavy on the individuals in charge of carrying out the firm's fundamental objective of making money. The colonial system and the colonial businesses that exploited foreign workers and resources were the aim of Conrad's criticism. Today, the world faces the extraordinary economic power and political influence of MNEs that transcend nations and shape the lives of people throughout the world. MNEs are not managed all that differently from the colonial enterprises of the past, with their self-righteous mission statements, strong profit motives, inconsistent employee incentives, and autocratic top-down management structures.

MNEs dominate business in most countries today. More importantly, because they spread technology, shape consumer demand, and employ an increasing share of the world's labor, MNEs shape human societies. Through perpetual lobbying, constant threats of

---

[25] Joseph Conrad (1899 [2003]). p. 92.

shifting jobs and investment to other political jurisdictions, and through their effective control of the entertainment firms that now run most of the world's news media, MNEs have gained great political power, not unlike the colonial era private enterprise described by Conrad. MNEs have the power to exterminate those they see as brutes, so to speak. Ominously, some of today's MNEs are run by modern-day Kurtz's.

16.5 Summary and Conclusions

This chapter focused on foreign direct investment (FDI) and the multinational enterprises (MNEs) that FDI effectively creates. Among the specific points brought out were

1. MNEs are created by FDI.
2. FDI is one of the largest categories of international capital movements.
3. Most FDI, over 90 percent, still occurs between developed economies.
4. MNEs have existed for centuries in various forms, but they came into prominence during the 20th century.
5. Today's MNEs have many nationalities; some are owned by shareh from many different countries and thus, operate as truly international business organizations
6. MNEs grew because they have a number of distinct advantages over other forms of business organization; specifically, MNEs may be better able to:

   a. Internalize transactions that are difficult to carry out externally.
   b. Exploit economies of scale by spreading their organizations across borders.
   c. Exploit and protect the core competencies.
   d. Exploit reputations across borders.
   e. Jump trade barriers by operating as "domestic" businesses in other countries.

    f. Exploit differences in taxes and regulations across countries.

    g. Hedge exchange rate exposure.

    h. Diversify business risks across borders.

    i. Reduce financing costs because they are diversified.

    j. Enhance innovative success through better access to foreign ideas and resources.

7. MNEs may contribute positively to a country's economic growth by facilitating the international flow of technology, and it may do so better than other forms of international investment.

8. Peter Drucker, the well-known business educator, hypothesizes that MNEs are altering international trade patterns in ways not yet analyzed by traditional trade theory.

9. MNEs create international organizations that may undermine the traditional political division of the world into nations.

10. FDI and the MNEs it creates can have many benefits, such as faster technological progress and increased specialization and trade, but there are likely to be costs in the form of economic and social disruption and the growing influence of what are inherently undemocratic and autocratic organizations structured to benefit those who control them.

FDI has played a central role in expanding globalization over the past half century by extending the private corporations that produce and distribute most of the world's goods and services. MNEs account for a large share of investment and innovation in most countries. They also employ an increasing share of the world's population, carry out most private research, and dominate the channels of information either through their ownership or their advertising expenditures.

    The international financial system can only be understood if we recognize the dominant role of MNEs in nearly all categories of the balance of payments. We have not yet touched on yet another way in which MNEs impact the international financial system: the private financial industry also increasingly consists of MNEs. In the next chapter, we examine the MNEs that dominate the international financial industry.

Key Terms and Concepts

Colonialism

Core competencies

Corporate citizenship

Emerging markets

Fire-sale asset
  prices

Flow of FDI

Foreign direct
  investment

Greenfield investment

Hold-up by supplier

Horizontal FDI

Internal transactions

Intra-firm trade

Mergers and
  acquisitions

Multinational
  enterprises

Outsourcing

Risk diversification

Stock of FDI

Tacit knowledge

Technology transfers

Trade diversion

Vertical FDI ·

Chapter Questions and Problems

1. Explain why multinational enterprises have grown to become so dominant in nearly all of the world's economies? (Hint: Discuss the unique
   advantages of an international business organization over other forms of
   business organization.)

2. The focus on core competencies seems to mandate both a downsizing of a
   firm and the expansion of the firm overseas. Is this a contradiction? (Hint:
   Discuss the concept of core competencies and then show how spreading a
   business across borders expands the gains from its core competencies.)

3. Explain how an MNE can circumvent taxes and government regulations.
   Does this give MNEs an advantage over purely national firms? Discuss.

4. From a human welfare perspective, explain the advantages of MNEs and
   the disadvantages of the growth of MNEs. Overall, are MNEs a good
   thing for human societies, or are they detrimental?

5. What effect does FDI and the MNEs it creates have on international trade?
   Discuss. (Hint: Draw on both traditional trade theory and the principle of
   comparative advantage, as well as Peter Drucker's ideas in Section 16.4.3.

6. What would be the effect of an international agreement among governments to enforce a strict set of anti-trust laws forbidding cross-border
   mergers and acquisitions that reduce the number of competitors in the
   global market?

7. Does an MNE's pursuit of profit ensure its behavior and actions benefit
   humanity? Discuss.

8. Why are MNEs more criticized than domestic businesses? Why might the priorities of an MNE clash with national interests more often? Discuss.

9. Answer Robert Lucas' question: Why doesn't capital flow from rich countries to poor countries?

10. Explain why purchasing the stock of an MNE may be less risky than purchasing shares of the local firm? (Hint: Discuss portfolio diversification and show how an MNE is effectively a diversified portfolio.)

11. At the end of this chapter, MNEs are compared to colonial enterprises that operated at the end of the 19th century. Colonial enterprise were often private firms that benefited from government protection and control of foreign countries. Is this a fair comparison? Discuss. (Hint: Don't hesitate to criticize the textbook; the conclusion of the chapter was very strong and intended to stimulate discussion of a controversial issue.)

References

Altshuler, R, H Grubert and TS Newlon (1998). Has US investment abroad become more sensitive to tax rates? *NBER Paper W6383*, January.

Archibugi, D and J Michie (1995). The globalization of technology: A new taxonomy. *Cambridge Journal of Economics*, 19, 121–140.

Barba, NG and AJ Venables (2004). *Multinational Firms in the World Economy*. Princeton, NJ: Princeton University Press.

Bernard, AB and F Sjöholm (2003). Foreign owners and plant survival. *NBER Working Paper 10039*, October.

Berger, P and E Ofek (1995). Diversification's impact on firm value. *Journal of Financial Economics*, 37, 39–65.

Blanc, H and C Sierra (1999). The internationalization of R&D by multinationals: A trade-off between external and internal proximity. *Cambridge Journal of Economics*, 23, 187–206.

Blomström, M and A Kokko (1996). The impact of foreign investment on host countries: A review of the empirical evidence. *Working Paper*, December.

Borensztein, E, JD Gregorio and JW Lee (1998). How does foreign direct investment affect economic growth? *Journal of International Economics*, 45, 115–135.

Borga, M and RJ Mataloni, Jr. (2001). Direct investment positions for 2000, country and industry detail. *Survey of Current Business,* 91(7), 16–29.

Brainard, SL (1997). An empirical assessment of the proximity-concentration trade-off between multinational sales and trade. *American Economic Review,* 87(4), 520–544.

Cai, F and FE Warnock (2004). International diversification at home and abroad. Board of Governors of the Federal Reserve System, *Discussion Paper 793,* February.

Caves, RE (1996). *Multinational Enterprise and Economic Analysis.* Cambridge, UK: Cambridge University Press.

Conrad, J (1899 [2003]). *Heart of Darkness.* New York: Barnes and Noble Classics.

David, P (1992). Knowledge, property, and the systems dynamics of technological change. *Proceedings of the World Bank Annual Conference on Development Economics.* L Summers and A Shah (eds.), pp. 215–248.

Drucker, PF (1987). From world trade to world investment. *Wall Street Journal,* May 26.

Gresik, TA (2001). The taxing task of taxing multinationals. *Journal of Economic Literature,* 39(3), 800–838.

Hipple, FS (1990). The measurement of international trade related to multinational companies. *American Economic Review,* 80(5), 1263–1270.

Keller, W (1992). International technology diffusion. *Journal of Economic Literature,* 42(3), 752–785.

King, HW (2001). The international investment position of the United States at yearend 2000. *Survey of Current Business,* 90(7), 7–15.

Krugman, P (1991). *Geography and Trade.* Cambridge, MA: MIT Press.

Lipsey, RE (2001). Foreign direct investment and the operations of multinational firms: Concepts, history, and data. *NBER Working Paper 8665,* December.

Lipsey, RE (2002). Home and host country effects of FDI. *NBER Working Paper 9293,* October.

Lucas, RE, Jr. (1990). Why doesn't capital flow from rich to poor countries? *American Economic Review,* 80(2), 92–96.

Mansfield, E, M Schwartz and S Wagner (1981). Imitation costs and patents: An empirical study. *Economic Journal,* 91, 907–923.

Moran, TH (1998). *Foreign Direct Investment and Development.* Washington, DC: Institute for International Economics.

Polanyi, M (1958). *Personal Knowledge: Towards a Post Critical Philosophy.* London: Routledge.

Prasad, E, R Rajan and A Subramanian (2007). The paradox of capital. *Finance & Development,* 44(1).

Rangan, S and RZ Lawrence (1999). *A Prism on Globalization, Corporate Responses to the Dollar.* Washington, DC: Brookings Institution Press.

Romer, P (1993). Idea gaps and object gaps in economic development. *Journal of Monetary Economics,* 32, 543–573.

Shatz, HJ and AJ Venables (2000). The geography of international investment. *The Oxford Handbook of Economic Geography.* GL Clark, M Feldman and MS Gertler, (eds.). Oxford, UK: Oxford University Press.

Teece, DJ (1977). Technology transfer by multinational firms: The resource cost of transferring technological know-how. *Economic Journal,* 77(1), 49–57.

UNCTAD (2007). *World Investment Report 2007.* New York: United Nations Conference on Trade and Development.

Wilkins, M (1970). *The Emergence of Multinational Enterprise: American Business Abroad from the Colonial Era to 1914.* Cambridge, MA: Harvard University Press.

Zeile, WJ (1997). US intrafirm trade in goods. *Survey of Current Business,* 87(2).

Chapter 17

International Investment, International Banking, and International Financial Markets

Judge to bank robber Willie Sutton: "Mr. Sutton, why do you rob banks?"

Willie Sutton: "Because that's where the money is".

International investment has reached unprecedented levels. Never before have people owned so many assets outside their own countries. The flip side of that cross-border ownership is obviously also true: Never before have people, firms, and governments owed so much to banks, stockholders, lenders, and owners in other countries. It is not only the size of foreign asset ownership that makes today's globalization unprecedented; the variety and complexity of international asset holdings also distinguishes today's international investment from international investment during previous episodes of globalization. Today's international investment is much "deeper" than ever before, where "deeper" means that international finance consists of many more types of financial institutions, assets, and markets.

The globalization of banking and financial services, plus the development of alternative financial markets, has created multinational financial firms that do business in many different countries and spread their ownership across many countries. This emergence of multinational financial enterprises has facilitated the movement of money across borders, but it has also created new problems. In 2009, the financial crisis laid bare the downside of recent financial innovation and the mergers of private financial enterprises. While it was often described by economists and policy makers as one of the great achievements of the modern global economy, the international financial industry is now soberly regarded as the party responsible for plunging the global economy into what may become the worst slump since the Great Depression. This chapter examines the development of international banking and international financial markets, with special attention given to the devastating failures of the global financial industry.

Chapter Goals

1. Describe the recent trends in the global financial industry.
2. Describe the history of the eurocurrency markets.
3. Explain the economic role of the financial sector and its place in the circular flow of economic activity.
4. Explain the inherent weaknesses and inevitable failures of financial markets and financial intermediaries.
5. Discuss financial innovation and its role in the 2008 global financial crisis.
6. Present Islamic finance as an alternative institutional framework for the financial sector.
7. Contrast financial markets and financial intermediaries.
8. Discuss the growth of bond and stock markets, and their roles in the international financial system.

17.1 The Rapid Growth and Diversification of International Investment

Bank lending accounts for a major share of international flows of capital. You may recall from the discussion of the 1982 debt crisis that during the 1970s bank lending accounted for most of the financial flows to developing countries. By the early 2000s, portfolio investment and foreign direct investment have grown to be larger than international bank lending. This shift in international investment towards *financial markets* and away from *financial intermediaries* like banks has occurred not only in the more developed economies of the world; even in many developing economies there has been a gradual shift to stock markets, bond markets, and overnight money markets. Banks have responded by consolidating and expanding into investment banking, brokerage, and other financial services.

17.1.1 *Shifts in the ranks of the financial MNEs*

Table 17.1 shows the 25 most global financial multinational enterprises in 2008. This ranking is based on UNCTAD's *Spread Index*, which is calculated as the square root of the ratio of foreign affiliates to all affiliates, multiplied by the number of host countries. Many of the banks that are part of these large financial MNEs have been internationally active for decades or even centuries. Some of these corporate conglomerates started out as insurance companies. Almost all became larger and more global through mergers and acquisitions. For example, the Royal Bank of Scotland (RBS) briefly became the world's largest financial MNE in 2007 after acquiring ABN Amro, a Dutch Bank that was also among the largest financial MNEs. In 2009, RBS failed and was taken over by the British government; its acquisition, ABN Amro, was handed over to the Dutch government. Others on the top 25 list, including Citigroup, BNP Paribas, UBS, ING, AIG, Credit Suisse, Fortis, and Dexia were also in various states of insolvency, government takeover, or forced consolidation in early 2009. Future rankings will, no doubt, be very different from what you see in Table 17.1.

Table 17.1 The 25 Most Global Financial MNEs, Ranked by UNCTAD's Spread Index[a] (2008, millions of US$s).

| Financial MNE | Home | (Billions US$) | | Affiliates | | | |
		Assets	Employees	Total	Foreign	Ratio	Countries
1. Citigroup Inc.	U.S.	1,938.5	322,000	1,020	723	71	75
2. Alianz	Germany	1,367.1	182,865	823	612	74	52
3. ABN Amro	Netherlands	954.0	69,747	945	704	74	48
4. Generali Group	Italy	549.3	84,063	396	342	86	41
5. HSBC	U.K	2,527.5	331,458	1,048	683	65	54
6. Societe Generale	France	1,616.6	160,430	526	345	66	53
7. Zurich Financial	Switzerland	327.9	57,609	393	383	98	34
8. UBS AG	Switzerland	1,926.2	77,783	465	432	93	35
9. Unicredit Group	Italy	1,495.9	174,519	1,111	1,052	95	34
10. Axa	France	963.4	109,304	575	464	81	39
11. BNP Paribas	France	2,969.3	173,188	664	423	64	48
12. Deutsche Bank	Germany	3,150.8	80,456	934	713	76	36
13. AIG	U.S.	860.4	116,000	612	356	58	45
14. Credit Suisse	Switzerland	1,118.9	47,800	299	252	84	31
15. Swiss Re	Switzerland	229,328	11,560	180	173	96	26

(*Continued*)

Table 17.1 (*Continued*)

Financial MNE	Home	(Billions US$) Assets	Employees	Affiliates Total	Foreign	Ratio	Countries
16. Dexia	Belgium	931.4	28,099	275	231	84	26
17. Credit Agricole SA	France	2,365.1	88,933	420	234	56	39
18. Natixis	France	795.1	22,096	313	162	52	38
19. ING Groep NV	Netherlands	1,905.1	124,661	1,114	555	50	38
20. Banco Santander	Spain	1,501.6	170,961	424	267	63	30
21. KBC Groupe SA	Belgium	508.3	59,510	346	265	77	22
22. Bank of Nova Scotia	Canada	416.4	69,049	85	62	73	23
23. Barclays PLC	U.K	3,001.4	151,500	604	235	39	41
24. Fortis NV	Belgium/Neth.	132.9	10,374	352	240	68	23
25. Royal Bank of Canada	Canada	593.8	73,323	188	160	85	18

[a] UNCTAD's Geographical Spread Index consists of the square root of the ratio of foreign affiliates to all affiliates, multiplied by the number of host countries.

Source: UNCTAD (2009), *World Investment Report 2009*, New York: United Nations Conference on Trade and Development, Annex Table A. 1.15.

17.1.2 *A financial sector in turmoil*

The ranking of financial firms for 2008 in Table 17.1 reflects the global economy at the start of the financial crisis that began in late 2007 and became a global recession in 2008 and 2009. At the time of this writing, in 2010, many of the financial giants listed have been taken over by governments, accepted large ownership stakes by governments, or merged into other financial firms. The shift towards large global firms that provide many financial services has not been successful. The global financial industry came to be dominated by conglomerates that were "too big to fail". Hence, governments throughout the world have intervened in these financial MNEs, allegedly to keep the global financial sector intact.

This chapter will summarize the recent history of international banking and it will discuss what went wrong with international banking and the international financial markets. Despite growing ever larger in the circular flow of the global economy, banks and other financial markets failed to provide a sustainable financial sector to support continued economic growth and globalization.

17.2 The Eurocurrency Markets

International banks and international financial markets differ from purely domestic banks and markets in that they have to operate in a variety of institutional and regulatory environments that differ quite a bit from one country to another. By an institutional environment we mean the rules, regulations, traditions, and competitive environment that determine how banks carry out their roles as intermediaries between savers and investors and how financial markets operate. International banking has learned to operate between all of these national institutional environments. In many ways, it has learned to take advantage of the many institutional differences; international banking effectively operates outside the jurisdiction of any single country's banking authorities in what effectively has become an unregulated business environment. Nothing illustrates the growth of international banking better than the emergence of the *eurocurrency* markets.

Eurocurrency is money deposited in banks located in countries other than those where the currency was issued, for example, US dollar deposits in a London bank. The network of banks that takes deposits and lends in foreign currencies is called the eurocurrency market. Because they deal in foreign currencies, the eurocurrency markets are controlled only indirectly by the various national banking authorities of the countries where they operate. There are many places around the globe where banks provide financial services denominated in many different currencies. You can borrow Japanese yen in New York and open a yen account in Singapore. You can also deposit dollars in the Bahamas and borrow British pounds in the Grand Cayman Islands.

17.2.1 Origins of the eurocurrency markets

In the 1950s, London banks were gradually losing their position in international banking, largely because Britain no longer had a large empire and the British pound was no longer the dominant world currency. London banks had gained their international reputations when Britain was the world's principal trader and investor, especially during the 1800s. But, while British banks were still active in financing international trade after World War II, the rise of the US dollar as the international currency gave US banks a great advantage in providing trade finance to the global banking market. London banks suddenly grasped a unique opportunity in 1956.

In that year, the British government feared that foreign speculators and governments opposed to its involvement in the Israeli–French–British attack on Egypt, known as the Suez crisis, would sell pounds and put downward pressure on the exchange rate. British authorities therefore prohibited British banks from lending pounds overseas; their rationale was that if foreigners had no pounds, they could not sell them on the foreign exchange markets. This effectively forced London banks out of the international banking market altogether, which was a devastating prospect for these once-proud international bankers already facing a gradual erosion of their international business to US banks.

Several London banks reacted to the British government's ban on foreign lending by taking dollar deposits at very attractive rates and lending in dollars instead, a business strategy that the British government had no objection to. To many bankers' surprise, their dollar business quickly grew. Some prospective borrowers and depositors of dollars rather liked the opportunity of doing business in London rather than in the US. One such customer was the Soviet Union, which engaged in a limited amount of foreign trade and was forced to receive and make payments in dollars, the currency of its Cold War adversary, the United States. The Soviet Union was not very comfortable depositing money in the United States, even for a short while, because their deposits could easily be confiscated by a hostile US government. Hence, when London banks began accepting dollar deposits, the Soviet Union was an eager customer. The USSR even opened its own London branch of the Moscow Narodny Bank to hold its dollar deposits.

The British government realized that the dollar business was an opportunity to revive London as the world's leading banking center. In effect, the British government recognized that the Bretton Woods system made the US dollar the world's dominant currency, and it aggressively sought to make London the center of international dollar intermediation. British authorities provided explicit incentives for banks to do *eurodollar* business. The government exempted banks dealing with foreign customers in dollars from bank taxes, minimum reserve requirements, and most other forms of regulation and control. Eurodollar banks could therefore pay above-market rates on deposits and charge below-market rates on loans to reputable and trusted customers. Soon, many foreign banks set up branches in London to take advantage of the deregulated environment and the vast pool of banking talent working in London.

These overseas loans and deposits of dollars were a completely new development. Never before had it been possible to do business with a bank in a currency other than the one that circulated in the country where the bank was located. Now it was possible to borrow and deposit dollars in a unique unregulated environment outside the United States.

The US government inadvertently helped to expand the eurodollar market in the 1960s when it restricted international lending from the US in an effort to prop up the dollar exchange rate. US firms that wanted to invest overseas could no longer borrow in the US and export the money, so they borrowed on the eurodollar market instead. The higher deposit rates meant that US exporters found it more advantageous to deposit their overseas earnings in London than to bring the money back to the United States, where it would earn lower interest rates. More deposits meant the London banks had more dollars to lend, and thus the eurodollar market grew rapidly.

Soon other currencies began to be accepted by London banks, and other countries began to permit their banks to lend and accept deposits in foreign currencies. We now refer to this *offshore* banking market as the *eurocurrency market*, for some reason the *euro* portion of the term *eurodollar* stuck, even though banks in many financial centers around the world are now permitted by their governments to accept deposits and offer loans in foreign currencies, but the word *currency* replaced *dollar* to reflect the expansion of the market to include many currencies. The US government eventually caved in to competitive forces, and rather than seeing all international banking activity going offshore, it began permitting banks in the United States to deal in foreign banking under more favorable conditions. As a result, New York has been able to remain a major international banking center in terms of volume. Among the largest international banking centers are the traditional banking centers like London, New York, Paris, Frankfurt, and Zurich. Tokyo, Hong Kong, Sydney, and Singapore have also become important financial centers as economic activity shifted to Asia during the latter half of the 20th century. Eurocurrency centers have also arisen in Dubai, the Grand Cayman Islands, Aruba, Bermuda, Panama, and other "exotic" places as international banks and their customers sought to escape even the reduced regulations in the major banking centers.

17.2.2 *Offshore banking centers*

An interesting characteristics of the eurocurrency market is the growth of banks in exotic places like the Aruba, Bahamas, Bermuda,

Curacao, the Cayman Islands, the Isle of Man, and Panama. There are dozens of small countries that have banking sectors completely out of proportion to their own economies and that cater largely to international customers.

These *offshore banking centers* generally offer their customers lower costs and higher returns because governments in these locations tax financial services less than other governments do. Regulatory requirements also tend to be less onerous and compliance less costly, and supervision also tends to be less frequent and less invasive. Many of these offshore bank centers offer greater bank secrecy for their customers. Switzerland is best known for enforcing strict *bank secrecy*, which prohibits banks from revealing any information about their customers' banking activities to anyone, including the government. Bank secrecy protects bank customers, but it also prevents governments and the courts from uncovering tax evasion, business fraud, and other illegal activities. These banks are often accused of *money laundering*, which refers to the process of exchanging tainted money for new money that cannot be linked to the source of the tainted money.

After the World Trade Center attack in New York by political/religious terrorists in 2001, efforts to control the funding of international criminal activities further singled out the offshore banking centers as likely conduits for such funding. More recently, the European Union and the United States have pressured Switzerland, Luxembourg, and the smaller offshore banking centers to reveal the identities of their depositors so that they can be monitored for tax evasion. The 2008 financial crisis has further amplified calls for more regulation of offshore banking centers, especially as it became apparent that some of the illegal and fraudulent excesses relied on bank secrecy in Caribbean and other offshore banking centers. A major shift in Swiss banking policy may have been signaled in early 2009 when the Swiss bank UBS settled a criminal case with the US Department of Justice, under which UBS agreed to disclose the names of nearly 300 US clients suspected of tax evasion in the United States. The US Dept. of Justice continued to seek access to the accounts of another 52,000 Americans suspected of using Swiss banks to hide income from the

US tax authorities.[1] In early 2010, however, a Swiss court ruled that the Swiss government must stop forcing private Swiss banks to cooperate with foreign governments.

17.2.3 *Financial Innovation*

Eurocurrency markets and offshore banking centers are forms of *financial innovation*. The term *financial innovation* generally refers to the new financial institutions and new financial instruments. But in a broader sense, the consolidation of financial services into ever larger conglomerates and the spread of these banking and financial MNEs across borders constitutes the most significant form of financial innovation. The international financial industry has changed drastically over the past 25 years.

It is still an open question whether financial innovation has improved the performance of the world's economies or whether the growth of the financial sector in the economic circular flows has really benefited anyone other than the financial sectors. The global financial collapse in 2008 suggests that financial innovation has hindered rather than enhanced the financial sector's ability to carry out its fundamental roles in the economy. The next section discusses the fundamental roles that the financial sector plays in a modern economy.

17.3 The Economic Role of the Financial Sector

Economist and Nobel laureate Hicks (1969) wrote that the Industrial Revolution would not have happened without the concurrent development of financial markets. According to Hicks, the Industrial Revolution was characterized by a sharp rise in the use of machinery and other capital goods, and thus large investment in fixed real assets was required in order to realize the Industrial Revolution's gains in productive efficiency. Such investment required the mobilization of large amounts of saving, which would have been impossible without

---

[1] Haig Simonian (2009). Swiss Meet US Government over Defence of Bank Secrecy", *Financial Times*, March 2.

the creation of liquid financial assets. Hicks' analysis concluded that the development of the financial sector and financial markets was a key determinant of economic growth over the past 200 years.

There are also many examples of the financial sector's failure to perform its function of efficiently allocating savings to investment and innovation. In general, the decision to *save* does not automatically result in *investment* and *innovation*. Saving is the act of *not consuming* and storing wealth for future use, but investing involves using real resources to *create new capital* or to *develop new technology*. The incentives that influence saving are not the same as those that motivate investment. And the incentives that stimulate innovation are different again. Also, people motivated to save are, in general, not the same people who are motivated to carry out investment and innovative activities. It is the financial sector's job, therefore, to channel funds made available by savers to those who can carry out the most productive investment projects. This is not an easy task.

17.3.1 *Failure is a constant in the financial sector*

The 1997 financial crisis in Asia, discussed in Chapter 11, was in large part the result of poorly performing banks. The biased allocation of loans to favored industries by banks, often because the banks belonged to the same conglomerates that owned the industries, had already diluted the quality of bank assets in South Korea, Indonesia, Malaysia, and Thailand, among other countries. There were reports that some major banks were already bordering on insolvency in 1997. External financial pressures thus easily pushed the financial system in these countries into bankruptcy, causing the 1997 financial crisis and recession.

The collapse of the Mexican economy in 1995, when per capita output fell so sharply that it took five years before 1994 standards of living were regained, was also due in large part to the fragility of the Mexican financial sector, which had leveraged itself through excessive foreign borrowing. On top of the decline in per capita income, the cost to Mexican taxpayers to cover losses from bad loans by the nation's commercial banks amounted to about 15 percent of annual GDP.

The Russian financial crisis was preceded by the theft of billions of US dollars worth of savings from the banking system and "laundered" through assorted foreign bank accounts and businesses.

Fraud, incompetent management, and inefficient allocation by financial sectors are not unique to developing or Eastern European transition economies, of course. The failures of savings and loan banks in the United States in the 1980s required a massive government injection of capital to restore the failed banks' balance sheets. In total, this government intervention cost US taxpayers over $200 billion at the time. And in 2008, world financial markets were rocked by a new wave of bank failures, failures of derivatives markets, and even the failure of insurance companies. The 2009 crisis was not confined to just one sector of the financial sector or to one country. Governments in the United States, Europe, Japan, and elsewhere were forced to respond with massive injections of public funds totaling several trillion dollars, although at this writing, it is not clear how much will be repaid and recovered from asset sales. The "deeper development" of the global financial sector meant that the failures extended beyond just banks, and globalization meant that the crisis quickly spread throughout the world.

These examples suffice to make the point that the financial sector of both developing and developed economies can fail to carry out its function of allocating savings to society's most deserving and necessary investment and innovative projects. After explaining the idealized model of the market for loanable funds below, the next major section discusses why financial markets do not deliver the outcome suggested in the model.

17.3.2 *A Model of the financial sector*

Savers are individuals, households, firms, or governments who do not use all of their current income to acquire consumption goods but instead carry their income over to later periods. Investors are those who seek to create productive capital. It is very unlikely that each saver also has investment opportunities that can exactly absorb desired saving in any given period of time. Many savers do not have the managerial ability, the foresight, the technical know-how, the entrepreneurial zeal, or the knowledge to invest their savings themselves. On the other hand, those with the best ideas for productive investments often do not possess the savings necessary to carry out their projects. This mismatch of people who wish to save and people who wish to invest establishes the need for financial markets and financial intermediaries through which savers and investors can exchange current purchasing power for future purchasing power.

In order to illustrate the source of demand for savings, suppose that an individual can invest in several different projects. One opportunity might bring an expected return of, say, 25 percent; that is, by investing $1,000 in this project, the investor will receive $250 per year in output or money. There is another opportunity that offers 20 percent on an investment of $2,000, another that offers 15 percent on an investment of $2,500, one that offers 12.5 percent on an investment of $2,000, a fifth that offers 7.5 percent on $500, a sixth that offers five percent, and so forth. How many of these projects that the individual invests in depend on the interest rate at which he or she can borrow and lend. For example, suppose that it is possible to borrow or lend at an interest rate of ten percent. The investor can profitably invest in projects 1 through 4 by borrowing a total of $7,500. The net gain is the difference between the total returns of the investments and the cost of borrowing, the area beneath the 10 percent interest rate line for each investment, or the areas a, b, c, and d. in Fig. 17.1.

The market rate of interest also defines the opportunity cost of funds. If, for example, our investor has $15,000 in accumulated wealth, he or she will still only invest in the first four productive projects with returns above ten percent and lend the remaining $7,500 to others at the market interest rate of ten percent. Investing in the fifth and sixth projects would not be worthwhile because the opportunity cost of the ten percent return available elsewhere exceeds the projects' returns of 7.5 and 5 percent, respectively. Our investor would do better by channeling the $7,500 to the other investors with projects whose returns exceed ten percent.

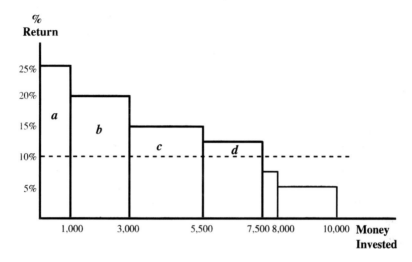

Figure 17.1   The marginal efficiency of investment.

17.3.3 *Extending the analysis to the whole economy*

The individual behavior illustrated in Fig. 17.1 needs to be modified if we look at the capital market of an entire economy. Instead of an individual investor/borrower facing a given market rate of interest at which a seemingly infinite amount of wealth can be lent or borrowed, the total demand for savings will be the sum of all the individual investors' projects. Total demand for savings can be represented by a smooth downward-sloping curve instead of the step-wise pattern in Fig. 17.2.

As shown in Fig. 17.2, equilibrium in the financial market is at the intersection of the demand-for-funds curve, D, and the supply-of-savings curve, S. The area under D represents the total returns to the economy's investment projects. The supply curve of saving reflects people's opportunity cost of foregone consumption, and the upward-sloping supply of savings curve in Fig. 17.2 implies that the interest must rise to induce people to save more.

Equilibrium in Fig. 17.2 occurs at the market rate of interest of ten percent, and total investment is I. Investors receive returns equal to the height of the demand-for-loanable-funds curve, while they

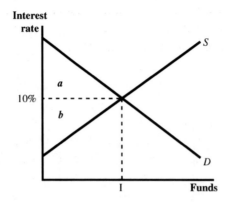

Figure 17.2   A more general model of demand and supply of loanable funds.

must pay ten percent for borrowed funds; they earn a surplus equal to the area *a*. Similarly, savers earn a surplus over and above their perceived value of foregone consumption equal to the area *b*. According to this model, *intertemporal* trade is clearly beneficial to both lenders and borrowers.

The financial sector is unlikely to generate the simple outcome illustrated in Fig. 17.2, however. The model implicitly assumes that lenders and borrowers are all acting on full information about the counterparties, that there is no risk of default or fraud, and that everyone is certain that things will turn out as expected. The model also assumes that the financial market operates at no cost to the lenders and borrowers. In the real world, none of these assumptions are accurate.

17.4 Market Failures in the Financial Sector

Financial markets often fail to complete what would be mutually-beneficial intertemporal exchanges. Among the reasons for such *market failures* are (1) *financial repression* by governments or bank collusion, and (2) the unique characteristics of intertemporal markets that make it inherently difficult to complete welfare-enhancing intertemporal transactions even when there are no government restrictions on such transactions. Financial repression consists of the regulations, taxation, and legal codes that restrict how the financial sector channels savings to investors. We will deal with the second set of sources of market failure in the next section and return to financial repression later in the chapter.

17.4.1 *Default*

Intertemporal trades involve the exchange of something today for something else at a later time. A fundamental problem inherent in any intertemporal trade is that one party to the agreement has incentives to accept a payment or good now and then not deliver on the future obligation. If a *default* on an agreed-to future payment or future delivery of a good or service is likely, the party that incurs the earlier cost will not enter into such a transaction. Note that the transaction would be beneficial to both parties if they could somehow commit to carrying out fully the terms of the intertemporal transaction. Such intertemporal market failures can be overcome, as evidenced by the fact that many intertemporal transactions *are* routinely carried out. Most societies have established procedures to prevent people from reneging on intertemporal agreements, such as the threat of compensatory payments, fines, confiscation of goods or wealth, or even imprisonment to force people to honor intertemporal agreements and contracts.

17.4.2 *Case study: contract enforcement in Taiwan*

Taiwan is one of the four *Asian tigers* that achieved phenomenal rates of economic growth over the past four decades. Unlike another Asian tiger, South Korea, which actively promoted the creation of large industrial conglomerates (known as *chaebol*), the Taiwanese economy has been characterized by the rapid growth of large numbers of small firms. Many of these small firms have successfully grown to become major exporters of manufactured goods. How were the entrepreneurs that founded these many small businesses financed? The Taiwanese financial sector must have performed the task of channeling savings to productive investors quite well.

Over the decades that Taiwan achieved its rapid economic growth, the financial sector functioned as a strange mix of tightly regulated banks and largely unregulated "curb" lenders. The term "curb" is often used to refer to less formal financial markets because the earliest informal lenders often operated on the curb in front of formal regulated banks. Banks have been government-owned in Taiwan, and they have been run in a very bureaucratic fashion. The banks took few risks and dealt mostly with well-established borrowers that had sufficient collateral to cover their loans. The low interest-rate ceiling imposed by the government caused demand for credit to exceed supply, and the already risk-averse bureaucrats became even more prone to lend only to the most secure borrowers. Entrepreneurs with good ideas but little collateral had to find their financing elsewhere. It is estimated that small and medium firms financed up to 65 percent of their investment internally through family sources and retained earnings. Many other investment projects were financed through curb markets.

Lenders in Taiwan's informal markets were often businesses that did have access to credit from government-owned banks. For example, large firms that had investments in plant and equipment that could serve as collateral could obtain a low-interest loan from a government bank, which they used to extend credit to smaller suppliers and customers. But, why would large firms accept the risks of default by small and medium firms? This *dual* system of finance functioned because in 1955 the government supported the curb market with a critical piece of legislation, the *Negotiable Instruments Law*:

> Transactions between upstream suppliers and downstream manufacturers, for example, were generally conducted with 30- and 45-day postdated checks made out for an amount equal to the principal plus interest for the agreed time period. These checks could then be discounted by the supplier through curb market brokers. Because trade credit was so important for doing business in Taiwan ... the government intervened to secure the postdated check market.[2]

---

[2] Tyler S. Biggs (1991). p. 182.

By strictly enforcing the law that made bouncing a postdated check a serious crime, the government in effect made the curb market for trade financing viable.

Taiwan's dual financial sector of formal banks and informal curb markets is giving way today to a more sophisticated multi-layered financial industry. This is only natural as the Taiwanese economy develops. Nevertheless, Taiwan offers an example of how a limited financial sector can be reinforced by small changes in government institutions to become a much more efficient channel for savings to reach the most productive investment projects.

17.4.3 *Enforceable contracts do not solve all market failures*

There is a more difficult problem inherent to intertemporal trade that has nothing to do with theft and dishonesty: A borrower responsible for a future payment or producer committed to a future delivery of some good or service may simply be unable to make the required payment or delivery despite every intention to honor the contract. Perhaps the investment project for which an entrepreneur borrowed other people's savings does not generate the expected earnings. Maybe economic conditions in the economy change unexpectedly, causing expected earnings to fall short of what is needed to meet the future obligation. Perhaps the future obligation requires more hard work, effort, or sacrifice than was thought necessary when borrower took on the obligation for future payment or delivery of some service. Intertemporal trades therefore involve uncertainty and risk even when informal or explicit legal institutions deal effectively with intentional defaults on future obligations.

The risk inherent in intertemporal trades may prevent some welfare-enhancing trades from being concluded for the simple reason that lenders may be *risk-averse*. On the margin, individual risk-averse lenders will prefer to lend to the project with the more certain payoff even if the expected payoff of the more certain project is less than the expected payoff of the less certain project. From society's perspective, it would be preferable to undertake the projects with the highest expected payoffs because society's risk is spread across a large number of projects. But, any single potential lender will clearly have to take into consideration the specific risks of each project.

The way to get individual investors to allocate their savings in a way that maximizes the returns for society as a whole is to reduce individual lenders' risks to the level that society faces. This is where *financial intermediaries,* such as banks, mutual funds, or pension funds, come in. These intermediaries can reduce risk to individual savers by *pooling* savings among a diverse set of investment projects. Banks, for example, pool the savings of their many depositors by lending to a variety of projects. Mutual funds provide savers with the opportunity to hold a share of a diversified portfolio of stocks or bonds even though they contribute only a small amount of money to the fund. The benefits for economic growth are obvious: while individual savers would not risk all of their wealth on a single risky but promising entrepreneur, financial intermediaries eliminate risk to individual savers by making pooled savings available to many risky entrepreneurs with potentially high-return projects.

17.4.4 *Asymmetric information and adverse selection*

Even with financial intermediaries that pool risks, there is still the problem that savers, and their intermediaries, have only incomplete information with which to assess the likelihood that a borrower will default on future obligations. One problem is that borrowers usually know more about an investment project and their ability to repay than do lenders. That is, information is said to be *asymmetric.* Asymmetric information can result in *adverse selection,* which causes various market failures. Adverse selection may cause markets to inefficiently allocate savings to investment projects, and it is likely "repress" the market and reduce the amount of savings channeled to investment and innovations.

To illustrate the problem of asymmetric information and adverse selection, suppose two apparently equal people walk into a bank and claim to have $1,000 projects that promise an average return of 20 percent. Should the bank indiscriminately give each of them the requested funds if the going interest rate is ten percent? Or, should the bank refuse one or the other request for a loan? Your answer will depend on the risk associated with each project, of course. Suppose that the first prospective borrower's project is guaranteed to yield a 20 percent return no matter what happens. But the second borrower's expected 20 percent return is the average of two equally likely outcomes, one with a 140 percent return but the other resulting in the complete loss of the entire investment. There is thus a 50 percent chance that the borrower ends up with $2,400 and a 50 percent chance that the borrower loses everything. On average, the borrower ends up with $1,200, indeed a 20 percent return on the $1,000 investment. The bank sees the situation very differently: in the case of the 140 percent, it still gets only $1,100 back, its original $1,000 plus the 10 percent interest rate charged on the loan. The borrower gets to keep $2,400 − $1,100 = $1,300. In case of total failure, on the other hand, the lender loses $1,000 but the borrower ends up with no more or less than she started out with. The borrower expects to earn $650, or ($1,300 + $0)/2. But, for the bank the expected outcome is highly negative, the average of a ten percent or $100 gain and a $1,000 loss. Thus, the bank should only lend to the first prospective borrower.

How does the bank know what the true nature of the prospective borrowers' projects is? What if the second borrowers lies and claims to have project like the first borrower's? Banks in fact make it their business to find out as much as possible about borrowers, their projects, their abilities to manage projects, and their reliability in meeting obligations. But, the lack of complete information means banks always face some default risk.

But there is also an *adverse selection* problem: Prospective borrowers like the second one are more likely to seek loans for the simple reason that, from their perspective, they will gain more than borrowers with more certain projects like that of the first borrower. Thus, like the insurance company selling flood insurance, banks will find that the riskiest borrowers are likely to be the most frequent seekers of loans! The bank could of course raise interest rates in an attempt to be certain of covering the potential losses from giving loans to too many risky borrowers. But, this may actually make the situation even worse because if interest rates rise above 20 percent, *only* risky borrowers like the second one will request loans. So, how can the bank profitably lend?

Stiglitz and Weiss (1981) show that in such as case it is optimal for a bank to randomly *ration* loans at an interest rate below the rate that clears the market because a higher interest rate would cause more losses from adversely selected borrowers than a lender gains from the higher interest rate. But, because loan demand exceeds the bank's supply of loanable funds when it arbitrarily rations loans, society suffers the loss of potentially beneficial intertemporal trades. That is, the intertemporal market fails to complete all potentially welfare-improving transactions.

17.4.5 *One more problem: moral hazard*

Another problem that hinders financial transactions is *moral hazard*, which refers to the likelihood that once borrowers have acquired a loan, they will behave differently than they would without the loan. The insurance industry of course deals with this problem all the time. For example, a person with fire insurance may feel less of a need to buy a fire alarm than the person without insurance; hence, a fire becomes more likely when insurance is in place. Similarly, a firm may take more risks after acquiring a large loan because, after all, it is not so much theirs as other people's money they are risking.

Lenders therefore have to monitor the activities of borrowers. Banks require progress reports on projects for which they lend money, bank officials may schedule periodic meetings with borrowers, and in many countries bank officials even sit on the boards of directors of firms who are major borrowers. Venture capital firms also take very active roles in the operations of the projects and companies in which they invest. Lenders must find ways to make sure that borrowers do not use money borrowed for a new warehouse to build a beach house instead or that a loan earmarked for research and development is not used to buy a Porsche for the firm's owner.

17.4.6 *Government regulation to solve the information problem*

Information asymmetries point to a role for government policy. In a developed economy such as the United States, the *Securities and Exchange Commission* (SEC), one of the government agencies that oversee financial markets, requires firms that issue stock or bonds to provide financial information to prospective buyers. Similarly, in most countries the government agencies that supervise banks require financial statements be public so that depositors and other holders of bank liabilities can judge the bank's ability to meet its obligations. Government-mandated information can thus overcome, at least in part, the asymmetric information problem and permit financial transactions to be completed where they otherwise would fail.

Despite the United States' reputation for having a very well-developed financial market, the recent global financial collapse started because of a fundamental US regulatory failure. US investment banks created and sold worldwide large numbers of securities backed by mortgages issued by loan officers at banks and mortgage loan firms throughout the United States. These securities enabled banks to effectively finance domestic real estate lending in the global securities market. While this was initially hailed as a sign of how globalization improved the efficiency of the financial sector, the realization in 2007 that these mortgage-backed securities were not worth what everyone thought they were ended up undermining the balance sheets of virtually all financial firms across the globe, an informational failure caused by poor regulation and oversight.

It is now clear that there was extensive fraud at various levels of management, obscured by the complexity of the financial transactions and ignored by those who falsely believed that US regulators were on top of the situation. Of special interest is the failure of the ratings agencies, the private firms who, for a fee, perform analysis of securities and institutions and issue a rating of the risk and financial worth. These private agencies rated securities backed by large pools of mortgages as safe, even though the mortgages were issued to risky borrowers during a real estate bubble. Investigations show that the ratings firms were clearly biased by the fact that they were paid for the ratings by the very investment banks who sold the securities.

Some economists have argued that it is the business of banks and other financial intermediaries to acquire the information necessary to complete intertemporal transactions, and that government interference is, therefore, not necessary. In practice, however, even if they could acquire the necessary information, intermediaries have insufficient incentive to do so because the information that they acquire quickly becomes a public good. For example, suppose that a bank devotes a large amount of resources to investigate the viability of a borrower's project, and it then decides to grant a loan to the borrower. Other banks and investors can then use the bank's decision to help them decide whether to lend to that firm, buy its stock, or buy its bonds. They effectively use the first bank's hard-found information free of charge. In fact, the other intermediaries, because they would not have to incur the costs of investigating the borrower, could offer intermediation services at a lower price and take business away from the first bank. The first bank may, therefore, decide to not devote resources to information gathering and, instead, wait for other banks to reveal information. If all intermediaries behave in this fashion, society as a whole will spend too little on gathering information, and savings will not be as efficiently allocated to investment and innovative projects.

17.4.7 *Collateral: another role for government*

There are other subtle roles for the government to play in enhancing the financial sector's ability to channel savings to investment projects. The government can establish and enforce property rights, and with well-defined property rights, borrowers can pledge their property as *collateral* to secure a loan. Collateral can substitute for the costly acquisition of information and continued monitoring by lenders. If the borrower defaults, property pledged as collateral will compensate the lender. Collateral also sends a strong signal that the borrower really intends to repay the loan, because a default leads to the loss of collateral property worth as much or more than the repayment of the loan. Collateral thus overcomes the information asymmetry between borrower and lender, and it lowers the cost of financial intermediation.

Collateral for loans is normally classified as either *personal property*, which consists of tangible things, such as real estate, structures, inventory, equipment, livestock, and tools, or intangibles, such as accounts receivable and contracts to supply future goods or services. In international banking and other types of international lending, collateral is further complicated by the fact that the transaction crosses cultural and legal lines. That is, a lender located in one country may not have sufficient legal status in the country where the borrower resides. A foreign depositor in a bank that refuses to honor a withdrawal request may have no legal recourse if the bank has its nation's laws on its side. For example, in the United States, a foreign depositor who is suspected of engaging in the drug trafficking or who is found to be on a list of designated terrorists may not be permitted to withdraw bank deposits. Even if the charges are untrue, such depositors will have great difficulty ever recovering their US bank deposits. On the other hand, a US bank may have difficulty recovering its loan to a foreign borrower when the borrower's country does not recognize collateral or its legal system does not consistently enforce contracts.

Also problematic is lending to sovereign foreign governments, or what is simply called *sovereign lending*. How does a private bank in, say, Japan collect a loan to the government of Zimbabwe that it refuses to repay? The courts in Zimbabwe are unlikely to rule against their government. The bank could go to court in its own country, Japan, and seek authorization to confiscate assets in Japan owned by the government of Zimbabwe. Diplomatic agreements prevent confiscation of the Embassy of Zimbabwe in Japan, and Zimbabwe probably has few other assets in Japan. Holders of sovereign debt have actually received court approval for confiscating the airplanes of foreign government-owned airlines when they land in third countries or the bank accounts of foreign governments in third countries. But, in general, sovereign debt is lost if the borrower defaults.

17.4.8 *Financial intermediaries also have bad incentives*

When savers entrust banks and hedge funds with their money, will the banks and funds invest the money with the best interest of the savers in mind? An individual profit-maximizing bank can be tempted to invest in excessively risky assets in order to maximize the expected difference between earnings and the costs of capturing funds from savers. If the excessively risky assets work out, then the bank owners enjoy high profits. If they do not work out, then the bank folds and it is the depositors who suffer most of the losses. The fear of bank failure has led many countries to provide depositors with *deposit insurance*, which compensates depositors if a bank fails. But such insurance creates adverse selection because, just as in the case of the more risky borrower in the example earlier, the banks with the riskier projects will tend to expend more effort to seek deposits or simply offer higher interest rates, knowing that insured depositors will not care how the bank invests their deposits.

The so-called "savings & loan" crisis in the United States in the 1980s exemplifies these perverse incentives. The US deregulated its savings banks in the early 1980s, and after decades of limits in the interest rates they paid depositors and limiting their loans to financing the purchase of homes, the savings banks were freed to set their interest rates and to make commercial loans. They immediately began to compete for funds by offering higher interest rates on deposits, and they began offering commercial loans even though they lacked the expertise to properly assess the risks. In more than a few cases, unethical businesspeople (thieves) acquired savings banks specifically to capture funds from savers protected by government deposit insurance and to channel those savings directly to offshore bank accounts.

17.5 Portfolio Investment

In most developed countries, and in an increasing number of developing economies, we see an increasing variety of financial markets and intermediaries functioning simultaneously. The complexity of financial intermediation, especially the problems of moral hazard, adverse selection, asymmetric information, fraud, and contract enforcement, explains this variety. For example, relatively inexpensive financial markets such as bond and stock markets can exchange the stocks and bonds of well-known corporation whose value can be easily judged by most savers. But, small unknown firms rely more on banks, which have traditionally been set up to devote resources to investigating and monitoring small business firms and their projects. Financial intermediaries such as banks, pension funds, mutual funds, and insurance companies are good at pooling risk, something that individual savers cannot easily do by themselves. Thus, stock and bond markets will normally coexist with banks, pension funds, and insurance companies in what we broadly term the financial sector of the economy. The more developed the financial sector, the greater the variety of financial markets and intermediaries.

The development of stock and bond markets in many countries has enabled the growth of what we call international portfolio investment, the cross-border trade in assets like stocks and bonds by savers seeking to diversify and reduce the overall risk of their wealth. In this section, we briefly examine portfolio investment in the international economy.

17.5.1 *Defining portfolio investment*

Portfolio investment consists of purchases and sales of securities, such as bonds and stocks, in amounts that do not imply any direct management control or influence on the businesses issuing the securities. International portfolio investment includes a foreign investor buying 100 shares in Ford Motor Company or a $10,000 bond issued by the US Treasury. It would also include a US mutual fund specializing in green investments buying several thousand shares in the Danish windmill manufacturer Vestas or a pension fund buying a wide variety of foreign stocks across many different countries and industries in order to reduce its portfolio's overall risk.

For the years in the early 2000s, portfolio investment was either the largest or second largest category of international investment, as individual investors, mutual funds, and pension funds have diversified their portfolios to include foreign stocks and bonds. The prominence of international portfolio investment is a very recent phenomenon, however. International portfolio investment was negligible before 1980.

17.5.2 *International equity markets*

You can appreciate the globalization of stock, or "equity", trading by looking in *The Wall Street Journal* or the *Financial Times,* two of the world's leading business newspapers. On 2 March 2009, for example, the *Financial Times* showed the stock indexes covering stock exchanges in 62 different countries in its "Global Equity Markets" section. Stock market activity is highly concentrated, and the New York Stock Exchange still traded nearly half of the world's stocks in terms of their value. The New York Stock Exchange's dominance reflects the historical leadership of the US in developing equity markets as well as the current trend toward consolidation of stock markets. The stock of over 400 non-US corporations are traded in New York, so the capitalized value of the companies whose stocks are traded on the New York Stock Exchange includes the values of many foreign MNEs. It is simply more efficient to trade more stocks on fewer markets.

Also important for the future volume of international portfolio investment is the trend toward 24-h trading through affiliations between stock markets around the globe. When stock markets in different countries across the globe join forces, they can essentially maintain active trading around the clock. For example, a merger between the New York, Paris, and Singapore exchanges, plus a slight extension of hours, would cover the entire 24-h day. Or, if the same stocks are listed on more than several exchanges in different parts of the world, trading could also be continuously maintained. The growth of stock exchanges and, consequently, the growth of international equity investment is very dependent on improved communications and the availability of information.

The advantages of size and geographic spread have hampered small stock exchanges in developing economies. With small volumes and trading stocks in companies that are not well known outside their home markets, volume at many developing country stock exchanges has remained small, despite the enthusiasm with which stock markets were launched over the past several decades. In order to attract buyers, larger corporations from developing economies have increasingly listed their stocks on exchanges in developed countries. Many foreign stocks are traded on the New York Stock Exchange and the Nasdaq in the United States, for example. Because stock exchanges in developed economies are generally perceived as operating under more rigorous regulatory requirements for information and public disclosure for the companies they list than do the exchanges in most developing economies, buyers of stock prefer to buy foreign equity that is traded on the major exchanges. Of course, the apparent lack of oversight and accounting rigor that triggered the 2008 financial collapse in the United States and Britain suggests such respect for developed country financial supervision was misplaced. But with limited options, wealth looks at relative safety, and wealth still tends to flow to the bond and stock markets in the most developed economies, as evidenced by the continued strength of the US dollar even after the financial collapse caused by the irresponsible derivatives trading by US financial conglomerates.

17.5.3 *ADRs make foreign stock look like a domestic asset*

An important innovation has made it easier for foreign firms to trade stock on stock markets in the financial centers of the world. For example, when British Petroleum (BP) completed its $55 billion acquisition of Amoco Corp. in 1998, Amoco's US stockholders were not given stock in BP; rather, they were given *American Depository Receipts*, or ADRs, which are receipts for actual BP stock deposited in a bank. The BP ADRs were traded on the New York Stock Exchange, unlike the actual BP stock, which was issued in the United Kingdom and traded on the London Stock Exchange. The advantage of ADRs for the American stockholders is that they are valued in US dollars, and they pay out dividends in US dollars even though the underlying BP stock is valued in British pounds and pays dividends in British pounds.

At the end of 2000, it was estimated that US investors owned about $1.7 trillion in foreign equities. About 42 percent of these equities were in the form of ADRs, issued on the stock of corporations from 38 different countries. Foreign corporations find the arrangement attractive because American investors' greater willingness to acquire ADRs effectively lowers their financing costs. American investors enjoy the convenience of transacting exclusively in dollars and avoiding the often-higher transactions costs of acquiring foreign equities on foreign exchanges. An added benefit is that foreign issuers of ADRs are required to satisfy the US reporting requirements and disclosure rules that US investors are familiar with in order to have their ADRs listed on US exchanges.

17.5.4 *The globalization of over-the-counter financial markets*

Stock and bond markets are not the only national financial markets that have been "globalized" by the participation of increasing numbers of foreign investors. The countries that have led the way in financial innovation have also led the way in opening their markets to foreign investors. Therefore, when US banks began creating collateralized debt obligations (CDOs) made up of bundles of mortgages and other types of debt, they immediately marketed them to buyers throughout the world. Similarly, the credit default swaps used to insure the CDOs were also marketed throughout the world. New types of financial instruments like CDOs and CDSs have been marketed through over-the-counter markets operated by banks, investment banks, and other financial firms. Because the market makers are large international private financial firms that operated in many countries, the trade was immediately global in nature.

Financial deregulation in most major economies made such over-the-counter markets possible, but their lack of transparency has turned out to be a major problem. When, in 2008, financial markets froze because of the declining prices of CDOs it proved difficult to determine who owned how many of those assets. Many of the CDOs were held off the balance sheets of the banks and other financial firms in what are known as "conduits", or independent entities created explicitly to hold such assets. Yet, the banks and other financial firms were still obligated to meet the obligations of the assets in the conduits. This lack of transparency contributed to a sharp slowdown in interbank lending because no one could judge the financial health of borrowers.

17.5.5 *Then, in 2008, a global collapse!*

Before 2008, this section of the book might have been concluded with the following summary:

> The financial sector of the economy consists of a variety of institutions, including commercial banks, investment banks, stock markets, bond markets, insurance firms, and pension funds. These financial markets and intermediaries facilitate the flow of savings to investment projects despite the different motivations, abilities, needs, and knowledge of savers and investors. Risk is reduced by the liquidity of financial markets and the pooling of assets and liabilities by specialized intermediaries. Risk is further reduced by the specialization in gathering information by financial intermediaries. Today's financial markets and intermediaries permit a saver who merely wants to save some money "for a rainy day" to earn an attractive return from participating in a long-term industrial project located half way around the world. And the creative entrepreneur with a new idea does not also have to be lucky enough to have rich parents willing to lend her money in order to carry out a profitable investment project.[3]

After 2008, however, the reality of the global financial meltdown makes such a conclusion much too optimistic.

By 2009, bank lending had diminished, government bailouts of banks and other financial institutions throughout the world summed to several trillion dollars, and international institutions such as the International Monetary Fund and regional development banks were being called on to resume lending to developing countries in place of the sharply diminished private flows. For the first

---

[3] The author admits that this was, in fact, the summary in an earlier version of this manuscript.

time since World War II, the total world economy was on track to contract in 2009. With short-term interest rates in the United States, Japan, and the United Kingdom approaching zero, the average saver was happy to just maintain her nominal wealth, quietly hoping that the growing debts of her government will not undermine the government's obligation to insure her savings account or trigger future inflation that destroys the real purchasing power of her savings.

Clearly, the financial sectors of the world's economies have not performed their task of efficiently channeling savings to society's most advantageous investments. Holistically, the financial sector has played a very disruptive role in the world's economic system and society. Since the financial sector operates within the rules and norms of the international financial order, some political leaders and many economists have called for reform of the international financial system. Others have urged that all financial instruments be traded openly on centralized exchanges that enforce some degree of uniformity and basic standards.

International portfolio investment in particular has often been accused of fomenting economic instability in the global economy. Because financial markets increase the liquidity of assets like stocks, bonds, insurance, and many derivatives, these liquid assets can be quickly bought and sold in response to perceived or expected changes in prices or economic conditions. The immediate globalization of the financial contraction triggered by faulty mortgage-backed CDOs issued in the United States has, therefore, renewed calls for greater regulation and restrictions on the international trade in assets.

The final, chapter of this book addresses the issue of reform. The last section of this chapter prepares the way by describing another model of finance that is popular in some parts of the world. As the shortcomings of the current dominant financial model have become all to clear, it is useful to remind ourselves that there are other ways of doing things. The current "Western" model of banking and financial markets should certainly be open to revision.

17.6 Changing Institutions: The Growth of Islamic Finance

The globalization of international banking and financial markets is often assumed to cause financial sectors to become more similar across countries. Indeed, the growth of multinational financial enterprises, the opening of stock and bond markets in many countries, and the liberalization of banking have made many financial products more similar. However, one interesting phenomenon runs counter to this trend: The growth of Islamic, or sharia-compliant, finance.

17.6.1 *What is Islamic finance?*

Islamic principles have been interpreted by many scholars as prohibiting the charging of predetermined, guaranteed interest rates. It is interesting to investigate how this prohibition is dealt with by financial institutions that practice the category of finance that is generally referred to as *Islamic finance*.[4] There are also a number of stock funds based in non-Islamic countries that invest only in companies that comply with Islamic principles, including one operated by the United States financial firm Citigroup and another by Germany's Commerzbank AG.[5] The belief that predetermined and guaranteed rates of interest go against Islamic principles is based on the prophet Mohammad's prohibition of *riba*, or "an excess;" the charging of a fixed rate of interest is said to be the type of *riba* that the prophet had in mind. Many Muslims believe that social justice requires borrowers and lenders to share rewards as well as losses, which will not be the case if one participant in an intertemporal transaction has to pay interest regardless of the success or failure of the project for which the money was borrowed. Thus, savings accounts that pay a predetermined rate

---

[4] For an introduction to Islamic finance; see, Zamir Iqbal (1997) or Timur Kuran (1995).

[5] Sara Calian (1999). "German Bank Plans Islamic Stock Fund", *The Wall Street Journal*, December 1, 1999; Sathnam Sanghera (1999). "FTSE to Launch Islamic Indices", *Financial Times*, November 15, 1999.

of interest are not allowed, but mutual funds in stocks that pay dividends according to company performance are acceptable.

In some ways, Islamic finance is not different from the way financial markets work in most parts of the world. Islamic finance seeks to efficiently allocate savings to the highest-return projects since that would be the preference of both lenders and borrowers. Clearly, lenders are highly motivated to carefully examine potential projects and to monitor the management of the projects as well, since their earnings depend on the future income of the borrower. But, there is a conflict with regard to the risk of potential ventures, with lenders preferring less risk and borrowers preferring more risky ventures because it is not their money that is at risk. Moral hazard and adverse selection could prevent mutually beneficial transactions from being carried out. These problems are no different from traditional Western finance, of course. But where the conflict over risk is different is that Islamic finance does not permit one party to an intertemporal exchange to carry more or all the risk. Islamic banks thus cannot provide the Western banks' service of converting short term deposits into long-term loans.

17.6.2 *Sharing risk under sharia law*

The recent expansion of Islamic mutual funds that invest in stocks, commodities, or leasing contracts suggests that these funds' have not been severely constrained in providing liquidity while still meeting Islamic finance rules. The "securitization" of investments has permitted the pooling of risk while still, in principle, following Islamic law.

Interestingly, the equal sharing of risk can prevent some of the instability that has plagued Western financial sectors because savers and investors are more likely to share the same concerns and interests. The closer synchronization of payoff periods and holding periods also reduces the chance that financial institutions suffer cash flow problems and default on their short-run obligations.

The sharing of profits and losses by lenders and borrowers is actually quite appropriate for financing new entrepreneurs. After all, the venture capital funds that have been so important in promoting new enterprises in the United States behave in much the same way as

Islamic finance requires: if a new entrepreneur fails, the venture capital fund writes the project off, but if the venture succeeds, the lender takes a large portion of the profits. For ventures that have a high probability of failure, but which pay handsome rewards in the case of success, the standard fixed-interest loan is not very attractive: the lender suffers the loss of most if not all the principal if the project fails, but gains only the stated interest return while the entrepreneur captures most of the large gain in the case of success. This may be why banks traditionally favor well-established firms and individuals for loans over riskier entrepreneurs with new projects. Just as the venture capital firm, the Islamic financial institution may be more likely to favor riskier but potentially highly-profitable projects because it will share the profits and losses.

Islamic banks face a serious adverse selection problem, however. Kuran (1995), in his assessment of Islamic finance, finds that most Islamic banks have gone to great lengths to charge fees that are in most ways very similar to interest rates; under five percent of loans made by Egyptian Islamic banks are reported to have been true risk-sharing arrangements. The reason Islamic banks effectively charge fixed interest rates is they fear "that industrialists with high expected returns will borrow from conventional banks (to maximize their returns in the likely event of success), while those with low expected returns will favor profit and loss sharing (to minimize their losses in the likely event of failure)".[6] Risk sharing therefore implies an ever-higher effective interest rate, which drives away the less risky borrowers, as suggested by Stiglitz and Weiss (1981).

There are other problems that Islamic finance has not been able to solve. The most important one is the apparent barriers it imposes on transactions between Muslims and non-Muslims. Because most of the world does not follow Islamic finance rules and principles, international investment by Islamic financial institutions is difficult. In fact, many countries where Islam is the dominant religion, do not have financial sectors that uniformly practice Islamic finance. Islamic banks are thus faced with deciding whether they can lend to firms that

---

[6] Timur Kuran (1995). p. 162.

also carry some conventional debt, and Islamic stock funds must decide whether they can include stock in companies that have issued conventional fixed-interest bonds. Compounding these problems is the fact that religious principles are not consistently interpreted or applied in different Islamic countries. Finally, there is the interesting question of how Islamic finance handles government borrowing: How do savers "share risk" with the government? Overall, the Western model of finance has not dealt with the sharing of risk very effectively either, as has become all too clear in recent years. All forms of financing thus struggle with risk and how to share the consequences of unforeseen changes in circumstances.

17.6.3 *The future of Islamic finance*

There is obviously a role for Islamic finance in countries where religion plays a strong role in governing people's behavior. Islamic financial institutions have devised many new assets that permit some mutually beneficial intertemporal exchanges that are necessary for economic growth and yet still fall within the accepted rules of Islam.

The global financial meltdown in 2008–2009 could either stimulate or hamper the growth of Islamic finance. The slowdown in investment, trade, and economic activity in general will slow all forms of banking, including Islamic banking. On the other hand, the obvious failures of Western finance could lead more savers, investors, and governments to look at Islamic finance as an alternative. The more equal sharing of risks under sharia-compliant financial rules, as well as the need for greater transparency under such arrangements, are features that the complex and sometimes-fraudulent Western financial system may be forced by regulators to adopt in the future.

In 2009, the shift towards sharia-compliant financial activity continued, albeit at a modest pace. Despite official support, Indonesia's sharia banking industry still accounted for less than two percent of the Indonesian banking industry's total assets. In Malaysia, on the other hand, sharia-compliant banks held 17 percent of total bank sector assets.[7] In early 2009, as the global financial markets froze, the Indonesian government sold $462 million in sharia bonds to retail investors.

17.7 Summary and Conclusions

This chapter focused on the financial sector of the economy. The main points made include

1. Large private financial multinational firms have come to dominate the financial sectors of many of the world's economies.
2. These financial MNEs arose after financial deregulation in many countries permitted their entry or their acquisition of local banks and financial firms.
3. The spread of the financial MNEs has accelerated the international integration of banking and financial markets.
4. The eurocurrency markets, initiated in London in the mid-1950s, helped to create the integrated banking and financial sector that so quickly spread the "toxic" mortgage-backed securities throughout the world.
5. Offshore banking centers led many traditional financial centers to deregulate as well.
6. The fundamental function of an economy's financial sector is to channel savings to its most productive applications, as the simple model described in Section 17.3 illustrates.
7. A second function of the financial sector is to reduce risk to individual savers to where their risks are similar to those of the aggregate economy.
8. Intertemporal markets are prone to failure for many reasons:
   a. Risk of default from fraud.
   b. The adverse selection problem that makes the average borrower more risky than the average member of society.

---

[7] John Aglionby (2009). "Indonesian Bond Success Bodes Well", *Financial Times*, 2 March.

     c. The moral hazard problem that leads borrowers to change their behavior after they have secured a loan.

     d. Information asymmetries that create risks for lenders.

9. Government regulation and oversight can mitigate some of these problems by requiring information, verifying information, limiting detrimental behaviors, enforcing contracts, and supporting collateral.

10. Borrowers are not the only sources of market failure in the financial sector: financial intermediaries and markets themselves can discourage both lenders and borrowers from using them.

11. Financial sectors have become "deeper" in most countries over the past half-century, as evidence by the growth of stock and bond markets.

12. There is a danger to financial deepening, however, as evidenced by the creation of securitized debt obligations and credit default swaps, whose defaults combined to sink the global economy into recession in 2008.

13. The financial deepening has also been characterized by the growth of over-the-counter markets, which are inherently secretive, non-transparent, expensive, and exclusive; risk is impossible to calculate.

14. The chapter concludes with a discussion of Islamic finance, which is becoming more common not only in the Middle East, but in some major financial centers as well.

15. Islamic is differentiated from traditional Western models of finance by the requirement that risk be equally shared between lender and borrower.

This discussion of the financial sector completes our examination of the components of the international financial system as well as the overall system that links these components. The historical account of the system shows that it has achieved both successes and helped to generate economic and social catastrophes. Just during the post-World War II period, the world has experienced impressive growth in material welfare in most countries. However, the international financial system has also featured recurring episodes of instability, financial crises, irregular financial flows between countries, the development of unsustainable payments imbalances between countries, and, in 2009, an actual decline in global output and income. In 2008, fraud, poor regulation, greed, and structural failures led to the creation of "toxic assets" in the United States, the financial market often described as the "deepest" and most developed. These toxic assets quickly caused havoc throughout the integrated global financial sector. To date, it is unclear how this global crisis will work itself out and how the international financial sector will be reformed to avoid such global financial disasters. Efforts to reform the international financial system have, as of mid-2010, progressed slowly. In the face of strong opposition from the private financial industry, it has proven difficult for policy makers to agree on how to make the international financial system better serve humanity. International meetings have continued. Hopefully, there will have been progress by the time you read these words.

The next chapter concludes with a detailed analysis of the financial crisis of 2008 and the state of the international system in its aftermath. We also contemplate a trip back to Bretton Woods.

Key Terms and Concepts

Adverse selection
American Depository
  Receipts
Asymmetric information
Bank intermediation
Bank secrecy
Collateral
Collateralized debt
  obligations
Conduit
Contract enforcement
Credit default swaps
Curb money market
Default
Deposit insurance

Eurocurrency
Eurodollars
Financial deepening
Financial
  intermediary
Financial innovation
Financial market
Intermediation
Intertemporal
  exSchange
Islamic finance
Marginal efficiency
Market failure
Moral hazard
Offshore finance

Offshore banking
Over-the-counter mkt.
Overnight market
Portfolio investment
Riba
Risk pooling
Risk aversion
SEC
Securitization
Sharia law
Sovereign lending
Tangible asset
Venture capital

Chapter Questions and Problems

1. The British economist and Nobel laureate, John Hicks, states flatly that the Industrial Revolution would have been impossible without the concurrent development of financial markets. Explain why the financial sector might play such a critical role in Industrial Revolution.

2. Explain the point made by Stiglitz and Weiss (1981), namely that it can actually be optimal for a bank to *ration* loans at an interest rate below the rate that clears the market. What specific market failure does rationing attempt to mitigate?

3. Use a diagram such as in Fig. 17.2 to show how intermediation costs reduce the amount of intertemporal transactions that are completed. (Hint: With intermediation costs, the market does not clear at a single interest rate that applies to both borrower and lender; rather, intermediation costs drive a wedge between the return to the lender and the interest rate that the borrower pays.)

4. Explain why Islamic finance might be more appropriate for directing funding toward new entrepreneurs than the traditional fixed-interest loans given by banks in most countries of the world. Base your explanation on the example of a banker facing a prospective entrepreneur with a project costing $100 that has a 75% chance of earning a 200% return on investment and a 25% chance of losing all the money invested. Would you give the loan at, say, 10% interest? What if you could split the actual return evenly with the entrepreneur?

5. Discuss the advantages and disadvantages of Islamic finance, making specific references to the traditional banking problems of risk, adverse selection, and moral hazard.

6. Think of a "bad" investment? Describe it and discuss whether it could have been avoided.

7. Why are home equity and car loans easier to get than small business loans?

8. The case study on Taiwan describes how post-dated checks became a common form of financing for small businesses outside of the formal banking system. Investigate how post-dated checks create a form of financing and describe how such a system worked in Taiwan and how it could work in other countries whose financial sectors serve large firms fairly well but do not deal with small businesses.

References

Biggs, TS (1991). Heterogeneous firms and efficient financial intermediation in Taiwan. *Markets in Developing Countries.* M Roemer and C Jones (eds.). San Francisco: ICS Press.

Kuran, T (1995). Islamic economics and the islamic subeconomy. *Journal of Economic Literature* 9(4), 155–173.

Stiglitz, J and A Weiss (1981). Credit rationing in markets with imperfect information. *American Economic Review,* 71(3), 393–410.

Zamir, I (1997). Islamic financial system. *Finance & Development,* 34(2), 42–45.

Chapter 18

The 2008 Financial Collapse and Recession: Is It Time for a New Bretton Woods Conference?

Once instability is understood as a theoretical possibility, then we are in a position to design appropriate interventions to constrain it.

(Hyman Minsky, 1982, p. xii)

Modern communications, profit-driven financial innovation, and the persistent dismantling of national financial regulations and government oversight have radically changed the international financial system. The effects of the latter, deregulation, were especially potent. Even when individual countries attempted to maintain their regulations and oversight, the fact that some countries disabled substantial parts of their financial regulatory structures made it difficult for any country to maintain control of its financial sector. Modern communications and the financial industry's innovations driven by its relentless quest for short-term profits made a mockery of the fragmented and often-weak political institutions that were supposed to protect the broader economic and social interests.

Today's international financial order is very different from the one created at Bretton Woods in 1944. The international financial system during the Bretton Woods era (1947–1971) was characterized by

761

controls on cross-border financial transactions and pervasive regulation and oversight of the financial sector in each national economy. Even the United States, which at Bretton Woods argued for liberalizing both financial and current account transactions, tightly regulated its banks and financial markets. After 50 years of active lobbying by the financial industry and the fading of the Great Depression from humanity's collective memory, the regulations were gradually eliminated or evaded under what can best be described as policies of regulatory neglect. Right on cue, this lax regulatory structure bred the massive 2008 financial crisis. This chapter, therefore, asks whether governments need to again take a more active role in the international financial system. Is it time for a new meeting in Bretton Woods?

Chapter Goals

1. Describe the events leading up to the 2008 global financial industry.
2. Pinpoint the many regulatory and oversight failures that enabled the irresponsible and unethical behavior in the US financial industry.
3. Explain credit default swaps (CDSs), collateralized debt obligations (CDOs), and securitization, which were the innovations that triggered the 2008 crisis.
4. Explain Hyman Minsky's financial instability hypothesis, and examine its relevance for the 2008 global financial crisis.
5. Discuss the Keynesian foundation of Minsky's hypothesis.
6. Review the principal suggestions for reforming the international financial order.
7. Is it time for a new Bretton Woods Conference?

18.1 A Picture of the 2008 Crisis

The Dutch financial conglomerate, ING Group, decided in 2000 to enter the US retail banking market. Entering the US market with a traditional bank would have required ING to build a physical presence in the form of bank offices and branch banks. Many foreign banks entered the US market acquiring or merging with existing banks. Royal Bank of Scotland had just taken over Citizens Financial Group in the United States, which after its subsequent takeover of Charter One Bank had quickly become the eighth largest bank in the United States.[1] Deregulation of the banking sector and disregard for anti-trust laws eliminated virtually all barriers to such acquisitions and mergers in the US. Domestic banks like Citibank, Wells Fargo, and Bank of America have similarly used mergers and acquisitions to spread throughout much of the United States. Still, acquisitions of other banks take a long time and a lot of money. ING had a different business plan that bypassed the investment in bricks and mortar or the cost of acquiring other banks: it decided to set up an Internet banking firm called ING Direct.

ING promoted its Internet bank by means of aggressive advertising and by offering attractive interest rates on both its deposits and loans. The Internet bank was made viable by offering only a standard savings account, a limited number of certificates of deposit, standard real estate loans, car loans, and a limited number of other standard products. "We're positioned more like Wal-Mart", said Arkadi Kuhlmann, ING Direct's president in 2000. "We shouldn't forget that 80 per cent of people live on main street, not Wall Street".[2] Perhaps people appreciated the simplicity of ING's offerings; 20 years of financial liberalization in the United States had created a very complex array of financial products and great variations in interest rates and prices. ING's Internet business grew very fast.

There are some more complex details behind ING's rapid rise in the US banking market. For example, in order to operate as an Internet bank, remaining banking regulations in the United States still required ING to set up some physical presence. ING Direct thus opened several small banks that doubled as coffee shops. Customers could make deposits or take out a home loan while enjoying a double latte.

---

[1] John Lanchester (2009). "It's Finished", *London Review of Books*, 28 May.

[2] Noreen O'Leary (2000). "ING Makes a Colourful US Debut", *Financial Times*, 9/10 September.

In order to operate in the US, ING Direct also had to incorporate in the US. Not surprisingly, ING Direct incorporated in Delaware, which has long been the state that offered the least expensive and least intrusive corporate regulations. ING also found it convenient to incorporate as a savings bank, which would subject it to less supervision and oversight than if it incorporated as a commercial bank. Under Delaware banking laws, however, savings banks were required to hold a large percentage of their assets in the form of housing and real estate loans. Since ING did not have the brick and mortar physical presence nor the in-house expertise to originate mortgages as fast as its sharp marketing department attracted deposits, ING Direct met the Delaware rules by investing in collateralized debt obligations (CDOs) backed by mortgages originated by other banks and bundled together into marketable securities.

CDOs were one of the highly-touted financial innovations of the past ten years. CDOs permitted banks to originate loans and, rather than holding the loans as assets until their maturity, they could "structure" the loans into CDOs and sell them on the international market for securities. Specifically, saving banks and commercial banks made mortgage loans, auto loans, credit card debt, and consumer loans, which they then bundled together in securities and, with the intermediation of one of the large financial conglomerates or investment banks, sold to investors, pension funds, mutual funds, and other banks throughout the world.

The CDOs were not simple bundles, however. To make these securities more profitable for the sellers, the bundles of mortgages, auto loans, credit card debt, etc. were split into separate "tranches," each of which would receive payment from the whole bundle of underlying loans in a pre-determined order. The top tranche of the CDO offered purchasers a relatively low interest rate but placed them at the front of the line in getting paid from the returns on the whole bundle of assets. The purchasers of the other tranches would be paid only after the higher tranches were paid. The bottom tranche would be paid its relatively high stated interest rate only after all the other tranches were paid. The lower tranches were referred to as "toxic waste" or just "toxic assets". The tranches were carefully "structured" to include the mixture of assets that met the minimum requirements for a specific rating from one of the major ratings agencies, such as Standard and Poor's, Fitch, or Moody's. The top tranche was typically rated AAA because analysts and professional ratings agencies judged it to be virtually impossible for the whole asset bundle to not generate enough income to pay the relatively low interest rates for the top tranche.

Of course, the top tranche was made as large as possible because AAA tranches of the CDOs sold at the highest price. Thus, at the time of issue the tranche was very close to the size where adding any more assets from the full set of underlying assets to the upper tranche would cause it to lose its AAA rating. These AAA tranches actually were quite large during the optimistic early 2000s. The market for CDOs made up of subprime mortgages provides a good example. As their name suggests, subprime mortgages are home loans made to people who, because of their low income or past record of default, were considered risky borrowers. But, despite the risk of subprime mortgages, Greenlaw *et al.* (2008) examined data from the bond rating firm Moody's and found that the AAA-rated top tranche of subprime mortgage CDOs issued during 2005–2007 included about 80 percent of all such mortgages. Hence, if more than 20 percent of the subprime borrowers stopped servicing their debt, the AAA rated top tranche would no longer earn full returns. Under normal circumstances, the probability of this happening may indeed have been small, but these were not normal circumstances. First of all, many of the subprime mortgages had enticed borrowers with exceptionally easy "introductory" interest charges for the first two or three years, which would then rise to a much higher rate for the remainder of mortgage. And by 2004, US housing prices were clearly in a bubble, and it was likely that prices would fall below the value of the mortgage loan in the future. In either case, defaults were likely in the future, and the AAA rating was clearly inaccurate and perhaps even corrupt.[3]

---

[3] There is vast evidence of bias by the ratings agencies, which are paid directly by the firms issuing the securities. See, for example, Roger Lowenstein (2009). "Triple-A Failure", *New York Times Magazine*, 27 April.

ING, like many other purchasers of mortgage backed CDOs, felt fairly safe, even given the potential for default, because it protected itself by purchasing default insurance. Specifically, it purchased credit default swaps (CDSs) covering the payments on the tranches of CDOs it acquired. CDSs were options that paid out the full value of the CDO in the case of default. These instruments were increasingly used not only by purchasers of CDOs, but by purchasers of all kinds of financial assets as well as hedge funds, speculators, and plain old gamblers who did not own any CDOs but just wanted to place a bet that the CDOs would default in the future.

It may seem strange that people and groups would "insure" a CDO they did not own, but that is exactly what happened in the CDS market. Note that the purchase of a CDS by someone or some hedge fund that did not actually own a CDO is as if you purchased a fire insurance policy on your neighbor's house. Then if your neighbor's house burns down, you receive a windfall equal to the value of the house without the actual loss of the house (your neighbor loses the house). If you question the use of CDSs purely for making bets on events in which the purchaser has no direct interest, you are not alone. The over-the-counter CDS market is another example of what John Maynard Keynes alluded to when he described how the daily transactions in the stock market had little to do with the alleged purpose of spurring real business investment by providing liquidity to purchasers of corporate stocks.

It is estimated that, by 2007, over $50 trillion in credit default swaps had been contracted by investors, hedge funds, banks, and other assorted gamblers throughout the global financial industry. The CDS were offered by insurance firms, banks, and other financial groups willing to assume risk in return for a premium payment. One of the largest sellers of credit default swaps for the CDOs was the American insurance firm A.I.G.

When ING purchased the highly rated top tranches of mortgage CDOs in order to satisfy the rules for savings banks, and it duly insured its investment with a CDS, it no doubt felt its investments were secure. Unfortunately, when the housing bubble in the US burst, these tranches were shown to be more risky than their AAA ratings suggested, and their ratings were subsequently downgraded. Since ING was required to hold specific percentages of their assets in the form of safe AAA assets, when the CDOs were downgraded it had to sell them and acquire other safer assets. Many other holders of CDOs were in the same position, and the prices of the CDOs plummeted with the panic selling. Holders of these assets, including ING Direct, lost billions of dollars from their balance sheets. When the CDOs were revalued to their new post-crash market prices, ING's US subsidiary was technically insolvent.

In early 2009, the firm was being supported by a cash injection of billions of euros by the Dutch government. Taxpayers in Holland were effectively helping pay the high interest rates that ING had offered its American on-line depositors! So it goes in the current global financial system. Financial markets are global, banks are global, and financial failures in one country almost immediately have global consequences.

18.2 Deregulation and Innovation

Since the 2008 financial crisis originated in the United States, many analysts blamed the crisis specifically on the dismantling of US banking and financial regulations. Among the regulations recently eliminated were the "firewalls" to separate different banking and financial businesses. These regulatory limits had been instituted during the Great Depression in response to the risky financial behavior that was seen as having contributed to the sharp decline in lending and investment after the stock market crash in 1929.

18.2.1 *The Glass-Steagall Act*

The 1933 Glass-Steagall Act set strict rules for what each type of financial firm could, and could not, do. Savings banks were limited to taking deposits and making mortgages, commercial banks were limited to making business and consumer loans, and investment banks, which took greater risks, were not permitted to solicit deposits from the general public. These rules were intended to prevent a financial institution from directing the savings deposited by people who wanted safe retirement accounts toward risky speculative investments. If the risky investments fail, then the savers deposits are underfunded.

Glass-Steagall was overturned in 1999, however, after years of strong lobbying by the financial industry. Senator Phil Gramm, the top recipient of campaign contributions from commercial banks between 1989 and 2002, sponsored the 1999 legislation. Gramm's law received strong support from President Clinton and his Treasury Secretary Lawrence Summers, who is now chief economic advisor in the Obama administration.[4] Said Summers at the time:

> Today Congress voted to update the rules that have governed financial services since the Great Depression and replace them with a system for the 21st century.[5]

After 1999, financial conglomerates were permitted to engage in all types of financial activities. They could lend the savings of depositors seeking low-risk certificates of deposit to high-risk hedge funds. Reserves set aside by insurance companies to cover risks for fire and life insurance were effectively mixed with the reserves backing the credit default swaps that insured financial derivatives like CDOs or just countered the bets of those who gambled on their failure.

Not everyone thought it was a good idea to abolish Glass-Steagall. Senator Byron Dorgan of North Dakota said on the day in 1999 the Great Depression era law was overturned: "I think we will look back in 10 years' time and say we should not have done this but we did because we forgot the lessons of the past, and that that which is true in the 1930s is true in 2010".[6] Dorgan was off by just a couple of years.

---

[4] *The Guardian* (2009). "Twenty-Five People at the Heart of the Meltdown", *The Guardian*, 26 January.

[5] Quoted in Stephen Labaton (1999). "Congress Passes Wide-Ranging Bill Easing Bank Laws", *New York Times*, November 5.

[6] Quoted in Labaton (1999). op. cit.

18.2.2 *Globalization and financial deregulation*

Some viewed the 1999 repeal of the Glass-Steagall Act as nothing more than a long-overdue recognition of the fact that the fire walls had already been breached by the globalization of banking and financial enterprises. Because the world's major banks and financial firms operated in many countries, they routinely "shopped around" for the regulatory structure that let them do what they wanted. If, for example, a US bank was not permitted to underwrite bond issues, then perhaps its London or Frankfurt branch could do it under the regulations of the United Kingdom or Germany. In this global environment, it helped little if one country maintained strict firewalls while other countries did not. The globalization of banking was, in fact, used as an argument for eliminating all remaining limits on financial firms. "If we don't pass this bill, we could find London or Frankfurt or years down the road Shanghai becoming the financial capital of the world," said Senator Charles Schumer before the decisive final Senate vote on abolishing Glass-Steagall in 1999.[7]

A tragic example of how globalization effectively disabled existing national financial regulation is the case of A.I.G., the American insurance giant. A.I.G. found it more convenient to open a London office to sell credit default swaps (CDS) covering the upper tranches of those mortgage CDOs issued in the United States. In London, A.I.G.'s Financial Products division was not covered by any requirements for reserves as long as its models showed reserves were not necessary. A.I.G.'s London office then used a financial model that showed there was absolutely no risk that the upper tranches of the mortgage-backed CDOs would default, and A.I.G.'s management apparently agreed that reserves were not necessary to cover the risk of default on the hundreds of billions of dollars of CDOs A.I.G. ended up insuring.[8]

---

[7] Quoted in Labaton (1999). op. cit.

[8] This information on A.I.G. is from Gretchen Morgenson (2008). "Behind Insurer's Crisis, Blind Eye to a Web of Risk", *New York Times*, 28 September; Bloomberg News (2009). "Britain Investigates A.I.G. Unit in London", reported in *New York Times*, 13 February; and Cyrus Sanati (2009). "As Regulator Watched, A.I.G. Unit Piled on Risk", *New York Times*, 5 March.

Of course, A.I.G.'s customers thought there was risk, because they paid billions of dollars in premiums for the CDSs. Nevertheless, A.I.G.'s London office booked the premiums as pure profit. A.I.G. earned hundreds of millions of dollars in profit per year on this new insurance business to supplement its rather staid traditional insurance business conducted by the remaining 99 percent of the firm. So impressed was A.I.G.'s management with the 400 employees in its London office that it paid each one of them more than $1 million per year in bonuses, or about one-third of the premiums collected on the CDSs. The CEO of AIG, of course, also increased his own bonuses as the company's profits rose. The manager of A.I.G. Financial Products in London, Joseph Cassano, earned £280 ($400) million over the 2000–2008 period. He stated in 2007:

> It is hard for us, without being flippant, to even see a scenario within any kind of realm of reason that would see us losing one dollar in any of those transactions.[9]

When the CDOs proved to be risky after all, and A.I.G. was called on to pay out on the losses, there were no reserves to cover the losses. By early 2009, the US government had channeled over $180 billion to A.I.G. to keep the large insurance firm solvent so that its life insurance, fire insurance, auto insurance, and other insurance businesses could continue to operate. A.I.G. was deemed to be too important for the US economy to let it fail and suddenly leave people and businesses uninsured.

18.2.3 *The great monetary expansion*

The financial innovations and expansion of the financial industry discussed above took place in an extremely accommodative monetary policy environment. Since the 1980s, the US Federal Reserve Bank had kept monetary policy exceptionally lose. After the 1991 recession, the Federal Reserve accelerated money growth. Despite

---

[9] Quoted in Gretchen Morgenson (2008). op. cit.

concerns that its continued expansionary monetary policy would cause inflation to rise, US price levels remained surprisingly stable throughout the 1990s. Then Chair of the Federal Reserve, Alan Greenspan explained that inflation was subdued, allegedly because of the rapid growth in technology during the 1990s, especially information technology, but certainly also because of the price-moderating effects of massive imports of manufactured goods from low-cost countries like China. However, the monetary expansion did fuel a stock market bubble.

The stock market bubble burst in 2000, and the US economy slowed further after the 11 September 2001 terrorist attacks. The US Federal Reserve Bank responded by again increasing the money supply and, over a two-year period, consistently lowering the discount rate from five percent to just one percent. Surprisingly, this monetary expansion again did not generate inflation in the United States and other developed economies. Again, rapid growth of imports from China and other low-wage economies, plus increasing legal and illegal immigration, kept wages low or even declining during the economic recovery in the United States, Britain, Ireland, and elsewhere.

The lack of general inflation was surprising when we consider that the expansionary Federal Reserve monetary policy was magnified by the securitization of debt. But the expansion of the money supply ended up flowing into sectors where securitization was most common, such as housing, auto loans, and credit card debt. Therefore, while imports kept most consumer product prices stable, the rapid growth of the global market for "securitized" and "structured" financial products, like tranches of CDOs, did cause a massive housing price bubble in the United States. Housing cannot be imported, unlike autos and consumer appliances. And, securitization let banks issue many more mortgages than they could have supported with only the money they captured through deposits at their bank. Securitization also encouraged banks to permit their loan officers to issue mortgages with little concern for borrowers' ability to service the debt. The banks quickly bundled the mortgages into CDOs and sold them on to others. Some reasoned that as long as housing prices kept rising, borrowers could always sell their houses at a profit if they ran into trouble servicing their debt. But the housing bubble had already lifted prices to unsustainable levels.

According to one news report: "the nation's mortgage system was set up to promote and encourage outright fraud in order to close a loan — and everyone, from brokers to loan officers to Wall Street, looked the other way".[10] Everyone seemed to profit, the bank officers who received bonuses for originating the mortgages, the real estate brokers who earned commissions on the ever-higher house prices, the Wall Street financial executives who earned bonuses for creating CDOs and the CDSs to insure the CDOs, and the growing number of employees working in the booming financial centers of the world. Regulators and the banks themselves should have become suspicious when loan officers openly began to refer to the subprime mortgage market as "the liar's market".[11] Both lenders and borrowers did not tell the truth about the terms of the loans or the ability to pay. But as long as the global markets absorbed the securities, the mortgage lenders continued to make loans, bundle them up into new securities that could be sold on to other investors and banks throughout the world, and earn more fees and bonuses. The banks used the revenue from selling the CDOs to make yet more loans and bundle them into still more CDOs. In short, rather than spreading risk and permanently increasing home ownership, the system was really a sham to pad the current incomes of bankers and financial executives at the long-run expense of taxpayers, duped investors, pensioners, stockholders, and foreclosed homeowners.

18.2.4 *From financial crisis to recession*

The financial expansion came to an end when the housing price bubble popped in 2006 and the securitized mortgages, often bundled together with other securities, had to be downgraded to reflect their diminished value. Like ING Group described above, many banks and

---

[10] Mary Kane (2008). "How Fraud Fueled the Mortgage Crisis", *The Washington Independent*, 1 May.

[11] Mary Kane (2008). op. cit.

other financial institutions scrambled to shore up their balance sheets and avoid violating regulatory guidelines. The market for securitized bundles of mortgages and other debt quickly dried up, sharply reducing financing for housing and other loans. Borrowing costs rose, and building and investment activity slowed sharply.

As construction activity fell sharply and bank lending slowed, the United States fell into recession in late 2007. More important, this collapse of lending in the United States was repeated in many other countries around the globe. For example, when ING Direct in the United States became insolvent, ING in Europe also stopped lending. Other countries, most notably Ireland, Spain, and the United Kingdom, also experienced housing booms and housing price bubbles until the world markets for CDOs dried up in 2007, even though the European Central Bank had not driven the housing bubble like the US Federal Reserve had. This suggests that the financial innovations of securitization and their insurance through credit default swaps were the real culprit in causing the global financial collapse.

Financial innovation is to blame for the global recession for another reason: the complexity of the CDOs and CDSs plus the fact that they were sold in secretive over-the-counter markets made it impossible to calculate risk. Lenders could not trust borrower's balance sheets because they did not know what assets backed the CDOs, who held those CDOs, and who held and backed the CDSs that insured the CDOs. Instead of lending, financial sectors in economies exposed to US CDOs "fled to safety" by holding cash or government bonds.

The recession spread throughout the world very quickly. Even countries that were not directly affected by the financial crisis were eventually affected by declining international trade. For example, US consumers quickly stopped buying foreign autos and other products when their economy slowed. Immigrants in the United States and Europe stopped sending remittances back home. Hence, many emerging economies also slowed or stagnated. In sum, deregulation and questionable banking practices in the United States triggered a global financial crisis and recession. In 2009, real world GDP shrank for the first time since World War II.

18.2.5 *Fiscal stimulus and financial reform*

The policy response to the financial crash and economic recession has consisted of (a) fiscal stimuli such as increased government spending and cuts in taxes, (b) very accommodative monetary policies, (c) direct infusions of cash into the banking system in order to keep banks afloat, and (d) initiating discussions on how to change the regulations and government agencies responsible for overseeing the financial sector. The first is intended to minimize the depth of the recession and prevent unemployment from growing further. Monetary policy was expansionary enough to drive interest rates on short-term United States Treasury bonds close to zero. It is safe to say that no central bank anywhere dared to repeat the contractionary monetary policies after 1929 when the Gold Standard mindset still prevailed. The third set of measures amounted to trillions of dollars lent to private banks or used to purchase government ownership in private banks. Such "bailouts were deemed necessary because the major banks in each country were "too big to fail". It was argued that there would be no economic recovery unless banks resumed their normal lending activity, and they could not do that if they were bank-rupt. It was hoped that most of the government funds used to prop up the banks would eventually be recovered when banks' assets recovered their previous values and when government stakes in the banks could be sold back to private investors.

There were international meetings among government officials and central bank officials on how to restructure the regulatory struc-tures to ensure there would be no recurrence of financial crises such as the one that triggered this recession. At the time of this writing, in early 2010, there had been no substantial reform of the international financial system. Political debates instead focused on reform in each particular country, where active lobbying by the financial industry was often successful in limiting the agenda to measures that would not severely change the parameters within which the industry had been operating. The next section explains why, without reforming the current deregulated, profit-motivated, innovation-driven, and increas-ingly concentrated private financial industry, a recurrence of the 2008 collapse is inevitable.

18.3 Minsky's Financial Instability Hypothesis

The 2008 economic recession seemed to take the world by surprise. Up to 2007, the world was mesmerized by the extraordinarily high economic growth rates for China and India, which together account for one-third of the world's population. Economic growth rates were positive almost everywhere else, and several other emerging economies were doing well. The US economy, the largest in the world, exhibited several unsustainable trends, including large and growing trade deficits, very low saving rates, continued government deficits, and growing foreign debt. But, it was widely believed that the United States would be able to handle these unsustainable imbalances. The US financial industry was considered by most economists to be the world's most efficient, and the persistent rises in asset values and corporate profits, which we now know were themselves unsustainable, were seen by many economists as a sign of the strength and resiliency of the US economy.

What was perhaps most surprising about the 2008 recession was that economists largely failed to anticipate it. Somehow, the mainstream economic paradigm was not useful for detecting the inherently unsustainable trends or the precarious state of the financial sector. Interestingly, we see today a sudden revival of John Maynard Keynes, and indeed his macroeconomic analysis provides the insight necessary to explain what went wrong in the US and global economies. Another "Keynesian" economist, Hyman Minsky (1982), built on Keynes' ideas to develop a lucid analytical model that explains how, and why, the housing bubble in the US generated a major global recession. Minsky's *financial instability hypothesis* also explains why the world was surprised by the 2008 financial crisis.

18.3.1 *The three categories of finance*

The stability of the financial system depends on how investment is financed. Every investment project is "financed", implicitly or explicitly, because it is an intertemporal project involving up-front payments and future returns. Minsky identifies three broad categories of investment finance: *hedge finance, speculative finance,* and *Ponzi finance.* An investment project's financing is characterized as hedge financing if the project's cash flow is sufficient to meet all debt payment obligations. That is, the cash flow from the project covers not only all the required interest or dividend payments, but the cash flow also suffices to pay off the debt by the scheduled due dates.

Speculative finance characterizes those businesses and projects that can cover all of their interest and dividend payments out of cash flows and some, but not all, of the scheduled principal repayments. Speculative projects are financially sound in that they meet their interest, dividend, or expected profit payments, but it will be necessary to "roll over" some of the debt when it comes due. That is, cash flow only partially reduces the debt incurred in financing the project before it comes due. Many new projects, newly formed businesses, and innovative activities are speculative in nature, and while such projects individually are not a concern for the health of the financial system, if a large proportion of an economy's investment projects are financed this way the financial system could become unstable if credit suddenly becomes less plentiful or financial markets freeze. For example, many of the debt crises in developing economies over the past three decades were due to sudden changes in exchange rates and/or reversals of international lending, which caused viable speculative businesses to suddenly become ventures whose cash flows from operations were not sufficient to meet even interest or dividend payments, much less cut into the outstanding debt. Minsky called these *Ponzi ventures* because, in the tradition of Ponzi schemes, they must borrow just to meet normal day to day payments and expenses.

According to Minsky, the precise mix of hedge, speculative, and Ponzi financing determines whether an economy has a stable or unstable financial system. If most financing arrangements in the economy are hedge financing, and there are few cases of Ponzi financing, then the financial system will be relatively stable and unlikely to generate panics and widespread economic distress. After all, modern financial systems can handle risk and predictable rates of default. It takes a very substantial shift in economic circumstances to convert hedge financing into speculative financing or Ponzi financing. On the other hand, if speculative and Ponzi financing are prominent throughout the economy, then even a modest change in actual or perceived economic conditions can trigger a sudden rise in defaults that the financial industry cannot cover from its reserves and accumulated capital. In the latter case, the financial sector will become defensive, stop lending, and cause an economic recession.

Fundamentally, it is the job of the financial sector, its auditors and regulators, and macroeconomic policymakers to prevent the growth of speculative and Ponzi financing. For example, bank regulators can set reserve requirements and loan terms. Auditors often conduct *stress tests* on financial institutions' balance sheets to determine whether a change in economic circumstances could cause a dangerous shift in investments from hedge investments to speculative and Ponzi investments. Macroeconomic policies, of course, are supposed to prevent the types of shifts in overall economic conditions that would substantially alter firms' and banks' balance sheets.

18.3.2 *Minsky's second theorem*

Minsky used his analysis of the conditions in which financial crises develop to conclude that every prolonged period of economic growth, if left to run its course, will end with a financial collapse. The *second theorem* of his financial instability hypothesis states:

> Over periods of prolonged prosperity, the predominant form of financing tends to shift from hedge to speculative and even to Ponzi postures, and, therefore, the financial system gradually becomes unstable.

In short, a capitalist system in which investment is enabled by borrowing and lending through a private financial system is characterized by boom periods followed by economic collapses. Good economic times contain the roots of their own end. In Minsky's words: "Stability — or tranquility — in a world with...capitalist financial institutions is destabilizing".[12]

---

[12] Hyman P. Minsky (1982). p. 101.

Economic conditions inevitably change because an economy is complex and the process of economic growth is precarious. Constant growth requires that research and investment remain consistently successful in increasing production and efficiency. Innovation and the quest for new knowledge is, unfortunately, not a predictable and consistent process. Hence, growth will fluctuate, and economic conditions will change. In Minsky's framework, such inevitable changes in economic circumstances will make the financial system less stable and, eventually, cause financial instability and economic collapse.

But, Minsky's Second Theorem is based on more than just the inevitability of economic shocks or that "stuff will happen". Investment in new capital and innovation is itself precarious because it is based on expectations, not firm facts. When it comes to the future, we have few facts or fundamentals to go by. Minsky describes a prolonged period of growth as a period during which investors and innovators repeatedly find their hopes and expectations validated in the form of profits and cash flow sufficient to cover financial obligations, which makes both lenders and investors/innovators comfortable to continue doing what they did. Investment and innovation will only occur if there is a reasonable expectation that returns exceed financing costs, or that the investment and innovative projects are hedge projects or, at worst, speculative ventures.

Minsky is thoroughly Keynesian when he points out that the continued growth that generates the profits that validate investors' expectation will only continue as long as the investors keep aggregate demand growing by continuing to invest. According to Minsky, "if the short run equilibrium implicit in the state of long run expectations is attained and then sustained, a 'stable' or a 'tranquil' behavior of the economy will result".[13] But, note that this situation is an inherently precarious one. If for some reason profits do not materialize, and expectations are not confirmed, speculative financing effectively becomes Ponzi financing, lenders are less likely to continue lending, investment may stop, aggregate demand declines, which in turn causes further reductions in investment, and the economy spirals into recession.

---

[13] Hyman P. Minsky (1982). p. 100.

18.3.3 *Keynes' description of long-term expectations*

Minsky draws on Keynes' (1936) brilliant Chapter 12 on expectations. As we have earlier discussed in Chapters 4 and 9 when disputing
the rational expectations hypothesis, Keynes argued that the future
cannot be predicted using standard concepts of risk because we do
not know the true distributions of possible future economic outcomes. Keynes argued that when we face the future, we face
uncertainty, not risk. Uncertainty describes the common situation
where we cannot put any probabilities on the possible outcomes.

According to Keynes, investors and innovators must reach a decision on whether to invest, and lenders must decide whether to lend,
even though their "knowledge of the factors which will govern the
yield of an investment some years hence is usually very slight and
often negligible".[14] The difficulty in predicting the distant future into
which investment and innovative projects must be projected makes it
unlikely that a "stable" economy will persist. Sooner or later, expectations will not be met, and either lenders or borrowers will pull back.
Then economic growth will slow, disappointing more investors and
their lenders, and a downward economic spiral develops.

Keynes (1936, Chapter 12) argued that the volatility of the market depends on confidence and convention. The latter term refers to
our understanding of how things will pan out; think of convention
as a popular model. People remain confident, and prone to engage
in investment and innovative activities with uncertain outcomes as
long as outcomes from our investments and innovations are in accordance with out model, or what we have come to view as "normal."

Minsky argues that the likelihood that expectations will not be
met becomes more likely the longer growth is sustained:

> Such a stable or tranquil state of the economy, if sustained for a
> while, will feed back and affect long term expectations about
> the performance of the economy. This will affect views of the
> uncertainties involved which, in turn, will affect asset values and
> permissible liability structures.[15]

---

[14] John Maynard Keynes (1936[1964]). p. 149.
[15] Minsky (1982). op. cit.

That is, an acceleration in economic growth is initially seen as a pleasant surprise, and investors react cautiously at first by not increasing investment immediately. But the longer growth is sustained, the more investors and lenders begin to view the growth as normal. Soon they forget the recessions in the more distant past, or they convince themselves that the world is now in some way different, and they ratchet up their expectations. Investment thus increases, which increases aggregate demand and economic growth and effectively makes the higher expectations self-fulfilling. This process of rising expectations may continue for some time, but as expectations rise, the likelihood of not meeting those expectations also rises.

Keynes (1936) emphasized the tendency for investors, and lenders, to focus on the near past rather than the distant past in shaping their view of the future. His reasoning was quite accurate and has been validated by recent psychological research. Psychologists have found that people discount the past, just as they tend to discount the future, relative to today. Keynes observed: "It is reasonable ... to be guided to a considerable degree by the facts about which we feel somewhat confident, even though they may be less decisively relevant to the issue than other facts about which our knowledge is vague and scanty".[16] Thus, we use our recent experience to project the future. Hence, the longer economic growth continues, the more we expect it to continue because the last recession or financial collapse is farther and farther in the past, and the less we prepare for a possible slowdown in growth. Expectations thus become ever more optimistic the longer the good times last.

18.3.4 *The separation of finance and investment*

The stability of economic growth is further diminished by the fact that a modern complex economy uses a separate financial sector, such as banks and financial markets, to channel savings to investment and keep the flows of income (aggregate supply) compatible with consumption and investment (aggregate demand). Recall the circular

---

[16] John Maynard Keynes (1936). p. 148.

flow diagram from Chapter 2 and the role of the financial sector in balancing all the savings and borrowing flows from the other economic units. The creation of financial intermediaries and markets, separate from savers and investors, was the main source of instability in a modern capitalist economy according to Keynes.

To explain this point, Keynes (1936, p. 150) first describes the environment in which investment and innovative activities occurred before the development of modern financial systems:

> In former times, when enterprises were mainly owned by those who undertook them or by their friends and associates, investment depended on a sufficient supply of individuals of sanguine temperament and constructive impulses who embarked on business as a way of life, not relying on a precise calculation of prospective profit.... Decisions to invest in private business of the old fashioned type were, however, decisions largely irrevocable, not only for the community as a whole, but also for the individual.

With the development of securities markets, investment decisions have become revocable, however, at least for the individual. Keynes (1936, p. 150) writes:

> It is as though a farmer, having tapped his barometer after breakfast, could decide to remove his capital from the farming business between 10 and 11 in the morning and reconsider whether he should return to it later in the week. The daily revaluations of the Stock Exchange, though they are primarily made to facilitate transfers of old investments between one individual and another, inevitably exert a decisive influence on the rate of current investment. For there is no sense in building up a new enterprise at a cost greater than that at which similar existing enterprise can be purchased; whilst there is an inducement to spend on a new project what may seem an extravagant sum, if it can be floated off on the Stock Exchange at an immediate profit.

Investment is not revocable for the community, of course. After they are built, a factory, bridge, or machine continue to exist even if their ownership or market value change. Keynes saw the fact that financial markets make investments "liquid" for the individual, but keep them "fixed" for the community, as the major source of instability in the economy. Short-term prices and returns in financial markets end up influencing what are, fundamentally, long-term decisions by lenders and borrowers.

Keynes (1936, p. 153) goes even further to argue that short-term asset prices on financial markets bear little connection to the long-term views of investors:

> As a result of the gradual increase in the proportion of the equity in the community's aggregate capital investment which is owned by persons who do not manage and have no special knowledge of the circumstances, either actual or prospective, of the business in question, the element of real knowledge in the valuation of investments by those who own them or contemplate purchasing them has seriously declined.

Surely, this observation is even more relevant today, when many more people buy and sell stock, bonds, foreign exchange, and many other financial assets and derivatives. If the focus of financial markets is short-term gains, rather than long-term returns to investment projects, the allocation savings to investment will not be efficient:

> When the capital development of a country becomes a by-product of the activities of a casino, the job is likely to be ill-done.[17]

Keynes suggested that financial markets would function better if they were taxed, so that short-term transactions would not so easily interfere with long-run purchases and sales of assets.

This is precisely the idea that Minsky later drew on to argue that as long as expectations are validated, people keep borrowing, lending, investing, innovating, and, thereby, increasing aggregate demand in line with the economy's growth of output.

---

[17] Keynes (1936). op. cit., p. 159.

18.3.5 *Back to the 2008 financial collapse*

As mentioned above, eventually something happens to undermine rising expectations and economic boom. For example, Minsky argued that the inevitable financial collapse is often triggered by contractionary monetary policies imposed by the authorities to combat common outcomes of prolonged economic booms, such as inflation or trade deficits. If the central bank, for example, decides to tighten monetary policy to slow price rises, then the rise in interest rates will push some projects from hedge financing to speculative financing and, even worse, some speculative financing to Ponzi financing. Consequently, businesses with cash flow shortfalls are forced to sell assets, and the resulting collapse of asset values triggers even more shifts from hedge financing to speculative financing or Ponzi financing, which then forces more asset sales, asset prices decline further, and so on, until a full-fledged financial crisis sets in. Fearful of the financial state of borrowers, banks stop lending, and a lengthy recession may ensue.

In the case of sub-prime mortgages issued in the United States during the early 2000s, interest rate payments were often programmed to increase after the first few years of payments. Specifically, low-income home buyers were lured into signing mortgage agreements that offered special low interest rates for the first two or three years of the mortgage, after which rates would rise to much higher levels normally associated with relatively risky "sub-prime" mortgages. Therefore, when the higher interest rates kick in, the holders of such mortgages were in effect automatically switched from what they thought was hedge financing to speculative financing, or worse, from speculative financing to Ponzi financing. In 2007, the housing bubble included by easy money engineered by the Federal Reserve Bank popped. As housing prices suddenly fell steeply, the market for securitized mortgage-back CDOs dried up because of rising default rates. Many borrowers were in the state of speculative financing or Ponzi financing, and they saw no reason to continue to service even part of their debt because the declining housing price meant they were obligated to pay more for their house than it was worth on the market. As prices fell further defaults also rose further, and the CDOs into which the mortgages had been bundled were downgraded. And so the world ended up with a financial crisis, government bailouts of the financial intermediaries, and a deep recession.

18.3.6 *Keynes, Minsky, and rational expectations*

Looking back now, it should have been obvious that in the early 2000s US housing prices were rising well above sustainable levels and likely to fall before too long. It should have been clear that the programmed rises in mortgage interest rates would trigger defaults if housing prices declined. And, it should have been anticipated that the CDOs built on sub-prime mortgages did not accurately price in these eventualities. The real question is why these likely events were not foreseen before they occurred.

Recall from Chapter 9 that Muth (1961) and Lucas (1972) argued people use all available knowledge and information to, on average, accurately anticipate future events. They described such unbiased and fully informed anticipation of future events as *rational expectations*. The concept of rational expectations underlies the efficient markets hypothesis, which predicts that the consensus back in the early 2000s should have been that the housing bubble would pop. Therefore, rational bank managers would have refrained from making the subprime (liars') loans, home seekers would not have taken on loans they would not be able to pay back, financial groups would not have bought the derivative securities based in these loans, and construction firms would have refrained from building the houses that would not be paid for. Minsky's reply to this prediction is that few people anticipate the end of a long period of prosperity.

Keynes' description of how investors set expectations clearly conflicts with the rational expectations hypothesis that underlies modern macroeconomic and financial analysis. We have earlier explained that Keynes in 1936 rejected the assumption that Muth and Lucas made, namely that people's expectations are a rational calculation of the mathematical expectation of probable outcomes. His exact words are worth repeating:

> The actual results of an investment over a long term of years very seldom agree with the initial expectations. Nor can we rationalise our behaviour by arguing that to a man in a state of ignorance errors in either direction are equally probable, so that there remains a mean actuarial expectation based on equi-probabilities. For it can easily be shown that the assumption of arithmetically equal probabilities based on a state of ignorance leads to absurdities .... our existing knowledge does not provide a sufficient basis for a calculated mathematical expectation.[18]

The recent financial crisis clearly validates Keynes' suggestion that the recent past disproportionately determines our expectations. In fact, many of the risk models used in the financial industry, such as those that led Joseph Cassano of A.I.G.'s London Financial Products Division to claim that he did not "see a scenario within any kind of realm of reason that would see us losing one dollar", were estimated using data going back as few as five years. The financial models would have predicted more accurately if their parameters had been estimated taking into consideration the Great Depression from 70 years ago. But that is not how people, even those really smart people who were paid very high salaries, actually set their expectations of an unknown future or, apparently, how they estimate their sophisticated financial models.

18.3.7 *Some further observations on the 2008 financial crisis*

Minsky's framework explains the 2008 financial collapse very well. But the collapse was also driven by outright fraud and corruption.

---

[18] John Maynard Keynes (1936[1964]). p. 152.

Evidence on the way subprime mortgages were marketed and administered, the way ratings of the CDO tranches were determined, the inaccurate financial models used to justify business decisions, and the politics driving the deregulation of the global financial industry suggests many people acted unethically. It is impossible to believe that no one, neither the regulators, policymakers, CEOs, news reporters, nor all the employees in the financial industry saw the dangers. Time will tell how much evidence of misbehavior comes to light. It is this author's view that the legitimization of short-term profit as the sole driver of financial decisions lowered business ethics, and deregulation provided ample room for the chicanery to grow.

Now that the world economy, for the first time since World War II, contracted in 2009, policymakers are faced with the challenge of dealing with the economic consequences of the financial collapse. Furthermore, they are challenged to take measures to prevent similar collapses in the future. But, what can policymakers do? How can government and governmental agencies reduce the economic damage, shorten the duration of the economic recession, and speed economic recovery?

As of April 2009, most developed country governments had instituted various types of fiscal stimulus measures, loosened monetary policy, and intervened directly in the financial sector to sanitize balance sheets and maintain financial functions deemed critical for the economy. There were an assortment of direct bank takeovers by government in European countries, and numerous "bailouts" of banks in the form of loans, temporary exchanges of public cash for questionable assets on the banks' books, and nationalizations. In the United States alone, the eventual cost of government assistance and interventions in the private financial industry would likely end up costing US taxpayers about $1.9 trillion according to the IMF.[19] However, by mid-2010, in only a few countries had there been

---

[19] As reported in Krishna Guha (2009). "US Taxpayer Face Bill f $1,900bn, Fears IMF", *Financial Times*, 30 April.

changes in the way the financial industry is being managed. Returning to our case study of ING, for example, in April 2009, the new CEO of ING, Jan Hommen, announced that ING would be split into separate banking and insurance firms, while many marginal businesses would be sold off.[20] Hommen had taken over as CEO in early 2009 at the insistence of the Dutch government, which had injected €10 billion into the firm in late 2008 and offered further guarantees on ING assets in early 2009. It is "back to basics", said Hommen. In reference to the earlier discussion of ING Direct, ING still views its US subsidiary to be a successful, or potentially successful, business in the future. ING Direct will be moved to the separate banking division of ING, however, while the firm deals with its €28 billion illiquid portfolio of mortgage-backed securities. In the United States, most of the private financial firms that received public money continue to operate much as they did before the crisis. Executive compensation at US banks and financial conglomerates was reported rising again in 2009.

More critical to long-term economic health is the willingness of the world's leaders to rethink all the rules that govern the international financial system. There is growing consensus that the international financial system is too critical to a modern economic system to entrust to unregulated financial markets and private financial firms driven largely by short-run profits and employee bonuses. There are too many perverse incentives that tempt CEOs of financial firms, fund managers, loan officers, ratings officers, and all the other human managers of financial enterprises to take excessive risks and engage in fraudulent and unethical behavior. It is time for global negotiations, perhaps another Bretton Woods conference. But, unlike the 1944 conference, when the world economy needed to be reintegrated, today we need to simplify and re-regulate financial activity to enable our internationally integrated financial system to operate safely and effectively.

---

[20] Michael Steen (2009). "New ING Chief to Sell Off Up to €8bn in Assets", *Financial Times*, Saturday, 11 April.

18.4 Reforming the International Financial System

It is an exaggeration to compare 2009 to July 1944, when the Bretton Woods Conference was held. As ominous as the 2008 recession and its aftermath may turn out to have been, it cannot match the devastation of World War II and the Great Depression. Still, new economic measures are again called for, especially now that it is clear that 2009 will be the first year since World War II that world economic output actually shrinks. But what should those measures be?

The measures that economists and other interested groups have suggested fall into three categories: (a) immediate macroeconomic responses to stop the decline in economic activity and rise in unemployment, (b) changes in the rules and regulations to prevent a repeat of the sub-prime mortgage fiasco and financial crisis, and (c) reform of the international financial system to deal with a variety of serious imbalances in trade and investment flows, income distribution, debt, environmental sustainability, and the control of international institutions that developed over the past several decades. This section discusses these issues.

18.4.1 *Dealing with the 2008 recession*

Standard macroeconomic analysis suggests that monetary and/or fiscal policy can be applied to deal with the sudden increases in unemployment in most of the world's economies. Either policy will shift the aggregate demand curve so that it intersects with the aggregate supply curve at the full employment level of output. However, in the case of a severe financial crisis, the money mechanism may not work. An increase in the money supply may not induce banks to lend more and financial markets to expand.

Keynes (1936) wrote that a critical component of a policy package aimed at ending a financial crisis is to restore the state of confidence of the "speculative investor". But Keynes also pointed out that merely creating the conditions under which prospective investors are willing to borrow and invest again is, by itself, not enough to end a financial crisis because

...we must also take account of the other facet of the state of confidence, namely, the confidence of the lending institutions towards those who seek to borrow from them, sometimes described as the state of credit. But whereas the weakening of either is enough to cause a collapse, recovery requires the revival of both.[21]

At the depth of a recession caused by a financial crisis, when aggregate demand is likely well below the economy's full employment capacity and many prospective borrowers are in a precarious financial state, monetary policy may not have much immediate effect on aggregate demand because no one wants to borrow, and lenders are afraid to lend even if there are willing borrowers. It takes time to restore the confidence of both investors and lenders.

In 2008, many governments, and their central banks, began to assist banks in cleaning up their balance sheets by lending them cash and government bonds in exchange for "toxic" US securities. Central banks also engaged in much routine monetary expansion, injecting great amounts of money into the banking system through open market operations. These policies had little immediate effect, however, and throughout 2008 and 2009, unemployment continued to grow.

Keynes (1936) explained that during a deep recession, the economy is stuck in a *liquidity trap*. Figure 18.1 presents a Mundell–Fleming diagram to illustrate the liquidity trap. Note that an increase in the money supply, which shifts the LM curve to the right to LM', does not change the economy's equilibrium at Y'. This happens because the LM curve is horizontal at the low interest rate r^*; if the LM curve was the typical continuously upward-sloping curve from Chapter 7, a shift to the right would have resulted in a new equilibrium at a lower interest rate and higher level of output, and thus a higher level of aggregate demand. Clearly, the interest rate cannot fall below zero percent because people and banks can always hold cash at zero percent rather than "pay" a negative interest rate to deposit or lend money. But Keynes reasoned that the interest rate will stop falling before it reaches zero percent because no one will acquire

---

[21] John Maynard Keynes (1936[1964]). p. 158.

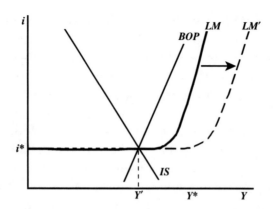

Figure 18.1   The Keynesian liquidity trap: Increasing the money supply has no effect on Y.

long-term assets with very low positive interest rate for fear of capital losses when the interest rate goes back up in the future. Hence, a liquidity trap develops once interest rates are very low, and no amount of monetary expansion will lower interest rates further to stimulate additional investment. And if the equilibrium in the Mundell–Fleming model does not shift, then neither does the aggregate demand curve in the *AD/AS* model.

In 2008, many economies were stuck in liquidity traps. For example, in the United States, the Federal Reserve Bank expanded the money supply to where short-term interest rates approached zero percent; even long-term rates fell to under two percent at one point. But, lending and investment did not increase at all. The collapse of the market for securitized products and the still-shaky balance sheets of most financial institutions made the liquidity trap even harder to work out of. Since monetary policy was unlikely to work in the short run, and the massive infusions of government money to clean up bank balance sheets were having little effect on lending, policymakers were left with only fiscal policy to resuscitate the economy.

The US government provided a fiscal stimulus in early 2008, when the recession was first becoming apparent, and a much larger fiscal expansion was enacted in early 2009. Other countries have been slower to follow the United States, and this became one of the early areas of disagreement among world leaders on how to deal with the global recession. Fiscal expansion to increase demand for the economy's goods and services is some mixture of tax cuts and a wide variety of new government expenditures, and in either case, the government's budget goes deeper into deficit. In 2008, many of the world's governments already carried high levels of debt, which added to the fear that aggressive fiscal stimuli would increase the likelihood of future inflation. Interestingly, the Chinese government, which was unburdened by debt, enacted a very large fiscal expansion in 2008–2009. As consequence the Chinese economy resumed its rapid growth in 2009.

18.4.2 *Restoring financial regulation and oversight*

Since the 2008 economic crisis became obvious, discussions have focused on the failure of national regulatory agencies to notice, much less prevent, the risky activities of the private financial industry. The activities of A.I.G.'s London office, detailed above, are but one example of the aggressive pursuit of profit by any means possible practiced by private global financial firms. After considerable debate within its ranks, the European Union agreed to present five specific proposals for a 15 November, 2008, summit on reforming the international financial system:

1. Supervisory panels for all large private international financial firms.
2. Stronger risk control mechanisms, such as reserve requirements and diversification requirements, for all private international financial firms.
3. Strict codes of conduct on risk-taking behavior in the financial industry.
4. Tighter rules for credit ratings firms.
5. Harmonization of accounting definitions to improve international coordination of regulatory requirements.

Even Jean-Claude Juncker, prime minister of Luxembourg, a country that has exploited global financial deregulation and innovation to build a large financial industry, openly blamed the global financial crisis on a "deregulatory frenzy".[22]

In late 2008, the US financial industry was lobbying hard to limit regulatory changes. It was only a month after JP Morgan, Chase, Goldman Sachs, Citigroup, and Bank of America accepted billions in government assistance that they created a lobbying group, the CDS Dealers Consortium, to fight against any increased regulation of derivatives trading, for example. By mid-2009, no regulatory changes had yet been put in place in the United States. In some European countries, on the other hand, re-regulation of the financial industry was more a priority of policymakers. But not all EU countries have changed the rules for their banks. Britain has taken a different position from Germany and France when it comes to regulation and institutional changes. Britain is anxious to protect London's prominence in the global financial markets, of course, and new regulations that limit financial industry growth would severely impact London.

Lanchester (2009) explains the reluctance of the US and British governments to expand regulation as follows:

> The Anglo-Saxon economies [Britain and the US] have had decades of boom mixed with what now seem, in retrospect, smallish periods of downturn. During that they/we have shamelessly lectured the rest of the world on how they should be running their economies. We've gloated at the French fear of debt, laughed at the Germans' 19th-century emphasis on manufacturing, told the Japanese that they can't expect to get over their 'lost decade' until they kill their zombie banks, and so on. It's embarrassing to be in worse condition than all of them.

Lanchester suggests that instituting new regulations on British and American banks or breaking up "too-big-to-fail" conglomerates "would mean that the Anglo-Saxon model of capitalism had failed".[23]

---

[22] Tony Barber (2008). "EU Calls for Tighter Financial Controls", *Financial Times*, 5 November.

[23] John Lanchester (2009).

Differences in national regulatory policies are problematic; in fact, they constitute a problem that, by itself, merits an international conference of the scope of Bretton Woods. The global nature of the financial industry means that internationally coordinated reform is urgently needed, not a diverse set of national regulatory agencies with incompatible mandates. The ability of financial firms to move between political jurisdictions in effect makes the most lax national regulatory structure the world's regulatory structure.

18.4.3 *Reforming the international financial system*

Even before the 2008 financial crisis, there had been talk of reforming the international financial order. Since the Bretton Woods system was created in 1944, there have been many formal meetings to introduce modifications in the order. For example, the Smithsonian Agreement introduced some marginal changes in an attempt to keep the basic Bretton Woods order intact. Later, in the 1980s, there were the Plaza and Louvre Accords, each of which brought together a small number of leading economies to introduce specific economic policy shifts in the hope they would stabilize currency values and reduce the growing balance of payments imbalances that were developing. There have, of course, been frequent "summits" of world leaders at which economic issues are discussed, and central bank executives meet informally on a regular basis. But there has been nothing equivalent in scope to the Bretton Woods Conference.

One of the obvious failures of the international financial system since the Bretton Woods order was abandoned in the early 1970s has been the exchange rate instability and the repeated financial crises. These crises have, almost always, caused severe economic recessions in the countries affected, some lasting for years. The 1982 debt crises throughout the developing world stopped economic growth in Africa for several decades and Latin America for a full decade. This crisis effectively put the neoliberal paradigm, which included the policies justified by the rational expectations and efficient markets hypotheses, at the center of IMF and World Bank programs. The collapse of the Soviet Union in 1989 seemed to leave Western capitalism as the only remaining option. Embracing free markets, free trade, unfettered international financial transactions, and the spread of multinational corporations did not bring financial stability, however.

Chapters 10 and 11 detailed the many exchange rate crises that turned into serious financial crises and steep economic downturns throughout the 1990s and into the early 2000s, such as the 1994 crisis in Mexico, the 1997 Asian crisis, the 1998 Brazilian crisis, and the 2001 Argentinean crisis. These crises brought into question the neo-liberal economic paradigm, although mainstream economists with their first generation crisis models (Chapter 11) more often than not attributed the crises to failures of governments to institute policies compatible with the favored neo-liberal paradigm. More damaging to the neo-liberal consensus was the dismal economic performance of the Eastern European and the former U.S.S.R. republics after the fall of communism. The neo-liberal policies did not bring economic growth; to the contrary, the former communist states experienced drastic economic declines. It proved impossible to quickly install efficient free market regimes in place of the former centrally planned communist regimes.

In the late 1990s, as various financial crises developed, there were frequent calls for a new Bretton Woods conference in order to build new institutions to deal with the changed global economic conditions. Eichengreen and Portes (1995), Sachs (1995), and Krueger (2001) called for discussions to create an international sovereign bankruptcy court. Banking CEO Kaufman (1998) advocated the creation of a global financial regulatory agency to coordinate the activities of the fragmented network of national sregulatory agencies. Former currency speculator and billionaire Soros (1998) advocated the creation of an international deposit insurance corporation, such as those operated in many developed economies to protect small consumer bank deposits. There were also repeated calls for reforming the existing international institutions such as the World Bank, the IMF, and the Bank for International Settlements (BIS).

Little came of these suggestions, however, even as financial crises continued to plague the international financial system. Many East Asian countries took matters into their own hands and accelerated the accumulation of foreign reserves by undervaluing their currencies and generating huge trade surpluses. The rationale for such reserve accumulation was that with billions of dollars and other foreign currencies on hand, speculators would be discouraged from attacking a currency. These Asian trade surpluses became the flip side of the large current account deficits of developed economies such as the United States and the United Kingdom and their accumulation of foreign debt. In the case of the United States, which issues the dollars that are used as international reserves by most countries, the growing foreign debt brought back the Triffin paradox of the 1960s: Would countries accumulate as reserves a currency that was likely to depreciate in the future? Would the US current account deficits really bring stability to the international financial system, as the East Asian countries apparently expected?

Perhaps it was the false impression that financial crises only occur in developing economies and countries transitioning from communism to capitalism that prevented serious reform of the international financial order. History provides ample evidence that financial crises are caused by many different economic and political shifts, including sudden reversals of international investment flows and foreign trade, declines in aggregate demand, and bubbles in domestic and international asset markets. More important, no country is immune to financial crises, as the 2008 crisis so rudely reminded us. The events since 2008 also make it clear that a financial crisis originating in the private financial industry based in a developed country closely integrated into the financial sectors of all the world's major economies is much more devastating than any of the recent crises in developing or emerging economies. The fraudulent creation of financial derivatives in the United States based on housing and stock market bubbles, enabled, ironically, by the glut of public and private saving from East Asian and other developing countries building up reserves to protect them against crises, has now, in 2009, brought bank lending and global economic activity to a stop.

18.4.4 *Some new proposals*

Nobel laureate Stiglitz (2009) argues for a strong global response to the economic downturn. National responses are inevitably less accurate and weaker than what is needed because they do not take their effects on other countries into consideration. A case in point are the fiscal stimuli, which are often criticized because a portion of the increase in aggregate demand "spills over" into other countries and weakens the domestic benefits. When every country takes such a view, argues Stiglits, the sum of fiscal stimulus measures are likely to be too small to address the global slowdown. Stiglitz also points out that the 2008 recession was caused by developed countries' regulatory and institutional failures, not the usual alleged failures of developing country institutions. "In the United States a financial crisis transformed itself into a global economic crisis; in many developing countries the economic downturn is creating a financial crisis", writes Stiglitz.

Stiglitz chaired a United Nations Commission that was given the task to prepare an interim report on what went wrong in 2008 and how to prevent another similar economic crisis from developing. The report was presented at the G20 meeting that brought together the leaders of the world's 20 largest economies in London in June 2009. The United Nations Commission recommended that a new international financial regulatory regime recognize that

1. The 2008 crisis was caused by too much deregulation.
2. Self-regulation will not suffice.
3. Regulation must deal with the negative externalities of financial failures across borders.
4. Transparency alone will not always eliminate the failures of complex financial markets and products; some financial activities must simply be prohibited.
5. Incentives in the private financial industry encourage excessive risk-taking and prevent accurate risk assessment.
6. Individual incentives in the industry further encourage risky strategic choices.

7. Financial firms have grown too big, making government bailouts more likely and, thus, giving those firms an incentive to take on excessive risk.
8. Regulation should be comprehensive in order to avoid a "race to the bottom".
9. If a race to the bottom develops, countries must be permitted to take defensive measures to protect their regulatory structures from "deregulatory competition".
10. Regulation has to be comprehensive across all financial firms and products.

These recommendations were straightforward, given what we have learned about the events, but the politically powerful private financial industry has lobbied very hard to get these recommendations off the table.

The United Nations Commission also addressed the concerns of developing nations by recommending that the G20 nations agree to:

1. Strong fiscal stimulus policies in developed countries.
2. Additional funding for developing countries to stimulate their economies.
3. More funding in the form of grants, rather than loans, to avoid creating more long-run debt.
4. Devote one percent of their stimulus packages to funding projects and programs in developing countries.
5. Give the developing economies more freedom to carry out diverse economic policies that diverge from the mainstream consensus.
6. Reduce protectionism that restricts developing country exports.
7. Further opening of markets to developing countries' exports.
8. Eliminate agricultural subsidies that distort international trade.

Developing countries fear, justifiably, that developed countries facing deep recessions will quickly forget their earlier promises for increased development aid and the opening their markets. In fact, a number of the stimulus packages enacted by developed economies contain "buy domestic" clauses for recipients of the stimulus funds.

The Bank for International Settlements, which brings together the heads of the world's central banks on a regular basis, also set forth a number of recommendations for reform before the G20 meeting.[24] Specifically, the BIS recommended that international regulations be adopted that

1. Limit the over-the-counter markets and interbank transactions in favor of open exchanges.
2. Require financial institutions that pose a greater risk to the financial system to hold proportionately larger reserves.
3. Establish a hierarchical list of financial products in terms of their risk, with markets for each level of products restricted to those customers that can handle the risk and complexities.

The BIS report also scolded national governments for their indiscriminate bailouts of private financial firms, which it feared would actually increase moral hazard in the future because government interventions have consolidated the financial industry into even fewer but larger financial conglomerates.

There have been many more proposals by individual economists, the financial industry, pundits, and private and public organizations and agencies. Eventually some consensus will develop. The specific consensus that develops will, in large part, be reflected in the models that are used to analyze and explain the causes of the crisis and the consequences of proposed new regulations and institutions. Which model should be used?

18.5 Back to Keynes

It was mentioned earlier that economists were, for the most part, surprised by the severity of the 2008 financial crisis and subsequent global economic recession. Their models had not predicted these results.

---

[24] Chris Giles (2009). "BIS Calls for Wide Global Financial Reforms", *Financial Times*, 30 June.

Recall from Chapter 9 that macroeconomics had come to embrace the neoliberal paradigm built around a rigorous set of microfoundations that explained macroeconomic outcomes. Among the microfoundations of aggregate economic outcomes was Fama's (1970) model of efficient markets that built all available information into asset prices, Friedman's (1953) hypothesis that speculation always stabilizes financial markets, the Coase (1960) theorem that eliminated the problem of externalities, Lucas (1972, 1973) and Muth's (1961) rational expectations hypothesis, and an almost blind faith in the efficiency of markets to channel not only goods and services, but also financial assets to their most valuable applications. Underlying the whole paradigm is Arrow and Debreu (1954) and Debreu's (1959) elaborate general equilibrium models that included competitive markets in *contingent commodities*. These markets, combined with the microfoundations just described and other convenient assumptions such as stable and separable individual preferences and stable and separable production and cost functions, would effectively eliminate uncertainty and, therefore, permit the economy to maximize human welfare under all circumstances.

The 2008 financial crisis and the global recession that followed have pealed away any remaining covers of the truth, which is that the whole neoliberal theoretical construct is a fantasy. Many sober economists now ask themselves: How did mainstream economics end up with a macroeconomic paradigm that denies the possibility of instability and crises? Clearly, a model based on assumptions of rational expectations, efficient markets, stabilizing speculation, completely subservient business managers, stable preferences, and fully insurable risk cannot explain a financial crisis and economic collapse. It is time to return to the Keynesian model, albeit with a supply side attached, because it can handle disequilibria and instability. Recall Hyman Minsky's quote at the start of this chapter: "Once instability is understood as a theoretical possibility, then we are in a position to design appropriate interventions to constrain it".[25]

---

[25] Hyman Minsky (1982, p. xii).

18.5.1   *Why Keynes got it right*

Taking culture, social norms, and evolved human neurological and psychological behavior into consideration, which Keynes implicitly did, views of the Keynesian and neoliberal, or New Classical, macroeconomic models change drastically. The Keynesian model's assumption of fixed prices no longer seems so unrealistic, and the neo-liberal hypotheses of rational expectations and ubiquitous efficient markets seem quite unrealistic. That is, despite neo-liberal (sometimes called New Classical) macroeconomics' emphasis on microfoundations, it is Keynes who had the individual and business motivations right. Recall the discussion in Chapter 9 on how mainstream economists' quest for mathematically tractable systems led them to adopt unrealistic assumptions. Keynes, unconstrained by mathematics but aided by a keen understanding of humanity, could focus on being realistic.

Akerlof (2007, p. 31) summarizes the state of macroeconomic knowledge:

> The New Classical research program was correct in viewing models of the early Keynesians as too primitive. They had not been sufficiently attentive to the role of human intent in choices regarding consumption, investment, wages, and prices. But that research program itself has failed to appreciate the extent to which the Keynesians' views of macroeconomics were also reflective of reality, since they were based on experience and observation.

Research from many fields of science and social science supports Keynes much more than the neoliberal paradigm.

18.5.2   *Social norms*

Akerlof (2007) points out that human societies have established norms and institutions to help guide behavior within complex social and economic environments. These norms and institutions complement humans' emotional and cognitive capacities to enable us to survive successfully in our complex global society. But they do not cause us to behave rationally in accordance with Muth's definition of rationality.

Norms may cause wages and prices to be sticky, just as the Keynesian model assumes is the case. According to Akerlof (2007, p. 27), "evidence suggests that wage earners and customers have views on what wages and prices *should* be. The reflection of such views in utility functions produce trade-offs between inflation and unemployment". In support of Akerlof's focus on social norms, Shiller (1997) found that almost exactly half of those surveyed agreed that they would be more satisfied if their nominal wage rose, even if prices rose just as much. Customers similarly have been found to have specific feelings about nominal price changes, not just real prices. Customers are more likely, for example, to begin looking for alternative suppliers when nominal prices rise along with inflation than when nominal prices stay the same under no inflation. In both cases, real prices are unchanged, but unlike what the rational expectations hypothesis suggests, human behavior is different in the two cases.

18.5.3 *Further research in psychology and neuroscience*

Research from neuroscience substantially undermines the rational expectations hypothesis because the latter effectively assumes that all decisions are made in the prefrontal cortex of the human brain. Neuroscience shows that it is impossible for humans to decide everything with that section of their brains; other automatic and instinctive brain functions often impose their will, and the cognitive portion has a very limited capacity. According to LeDoux (1996), "the wiring of the brain at this point in our evolutionary history is such that connections from the emotional systems to the cognitive systems are stronger than connections from the cognitive systems to the emotional systems". Emotion stimulates quick action, and it also serves to redirect cognitive processes to make decisions important for dealing with changing circumstances. The human brain reacts strongly to immediate threats and sudden changes in our environment, but it often ignores or postpones reactions to subtle and small shifts in our natural or social environments. Sudden changes in perceptions often result in large changes in behavior, while more gradual changes usually alter human behavior very little, even if those gradual changes eventually add up to major changes in humans' natural or social environment.

Experiments in the field of behavioral economics show that humans often make cognitive mistakes. Specific evidence is presented by Frederick (2005), who reports the results from asking various samples of people questions that they should be able to answer using a moderate amount of cognitive reasoning but which also tend to solicit response from all of the brain's processes. Frederick finds that people routinely miss the obvious answers.

Another very important finding for the accuracy of the rational expectations hypothesis is the finding that the cognitive portion of the brain can only handle a limited amount of information at one time. Even the most intelligent people must concentrate on one problem, or at most just a few problems, in order to effectively apply their prefrontal cortexes efficiently toward finding solutions.

The psychologists Kahneman and Tversky (2000) documented a very important finding for international finance, namely people's apparent risk aversion, or more precisely, loss aversion. They found that people seldom take an even bet. Rather, people normally require a substantial expected premium over a certain outcome before they select the uncertain outcome over the certain one. One such experiment asked people whether they preferred $2 given to them on the spot to an even chance of gaining $0 or $10 in a coin throw to be held on the other side of the room. The majority of those asked, took the $2 even though the expected value of the even bet is $5. This human reaction clearly does not reflect the cognitive part of the brain at work. From an evolutionary perspective, of course, these results make perfect sense. When life was much less secure than it is today for most people in high income countries, one misstep implied death and the end of the line for the embodied genes. Hence, the human brain evolved to prefer a secure outcome over an uncertain set of outcomes that included many real improvements but also a possibility of a really bad outcome.

Kahneman and Tversky (2000) have also noted that people disproportionately value their current status quo over other possibilities. Specifically, people value the object A that they have over the object B that they do not possess, but when they find themselves in possession of object B while object A belongs to someone else, a surprising number of people then claim to prefer the object B to object A. Kahneman and Tversky refer to this phenomenon as the "endowment effect". This effect implies that people are loss averse, that they will fight harder to hold on to what they have than to acquire something new, and that they need an extra inducement to get them to abandon their status quo and pursue a new situation. This endowment effect is observed in many animal species in the form of territoriality. Many animals fight much harder to keep their claimed territory than they fight to capture another's territory.

The finding that people have specialized brain functions that are invoked in specific situations conflicts with the neo-liberal model of economics, which assumes that people have a stable set of preferences. Human preferences are not stable if people behave differently in different circumstances. Equally disruptive of standard economic models is the observed non-linear relationship between neural signals and human actions. In some cases, small changes in circumstance can cause a very large change in human behavior. In other cases large changes in human circumstances may leave people surprisingly unresponsive. Also, humans are more attuned to *changes* in stimuli rather than the *levels* of stimuli. People's sensitivity to changing circumstances helps to explain why the evaluation of a risky gamble depends on one's reference point. More recent circumstances, rather than distant past or future expected circumstances, influence our brains' interpretation of an outcome as a gain or a loss.

In sum, there is overwhelming evidence from other fields such as psychology, sociology, neuroscience, and behavioral economics, as well from the field of economics itself, that shows that Muth's assumption of rational expectations is unrealistic, that markets are not, and cannot be, efficient, that people's preferences change with the circumstances they are in and the culture they relate to, that cost functions depend critically on culture, norms, and institutions, and that, most importantly, systems are not simple linear sums of their components. Much of this evidence does support the Keynesian model and its policy prescriptions. The finding that humans' embrace of the status quo and social norms makes prices rigid and that human cognitive capabilities do not meet the requirements for Muth's definition of rationality strengthens the case for active macroeconomic policy and weakens the case for passive policy. Humanity must, therefore, pay more attention to our governments and institutions. There is no system of efficient markets or, failing those, a cadre of benevolent corporate CEOs, that will, in the absence of a competent government, automatically or unselfishly provide us with a stable and welfare-maximizing economy.

18.6 Summary and Conclusions

The first chapter began on the train to Bretton Woods on a warm night on the last day of June, 1944. This chapter ends with the suggestion that the world's financial policymakers may want to pack their suitcases for another trip to Bretton Woods. The Mount Washington Hotel in Bretton Woods is still open. A new conference wing was opened last year, and the entire hotel was refurbished in early 20th century decor. Of course, not everyone agrees that we need another multilateral conference to change the international financial system, and some countries may prefer a new location to reflect changes in the world order.

18.6.1 *Summary*

This last chapter tried to show why the current system is not stable:

1. The near complete freedom financial firms have to operate, combined with the globalization of the financial industry, has led to excessive risk taking, lack of transparency, market manipulation, fraud, and financial innovation that adds only to profits but nothing to economic efficiency.
2. Still relying on the general acceptance of the neo-liberal economic paradigm by policymakers and its aggressive lobbying, the

financial industry hopes to avoid renewed regulation despite having caused the 2008 financial crisis and subsequent global economic recession.

3. The world's leaders have addressed the 2008 recession through (1) fiscal expansion to stop the downward spiral in output, (2) government subsidies, nationalizations, and asset purchases to help financial firms resume normal lending, (3) some reform of regulatory and oversight structures, and (4) discussion on reforming the international financial system that accommodated the crisis and then quickly spread the recession throughout the world.

The chapter also discussed Hyman Minsky's financial instability hypothesis, which is based on Keynes' (1936) discussion of expectations and financial markets:

1. Financial crises are caused by shifts in the proportions of financial arrangements between hedge, speculative, and Ponzi financing.

2. A financial crisis becomes almost inevitable the longer good economic conditions persist because people raise their expectations of future profits and, therefore, their willingness to undertake investment and innovative projects.

3. An extended economic boom causes financing to more often become speculative in nature as investors and lenders become more confident about future economic prospects, but this means there will be more Ponzi financing when, eventually, economic conditions return to their long-run path.

4. The only way to keep financing from becoming more risky is to regulate the financial sector.

5. When regulation actually works to prevent crises for many decades, it actually becomes politically easier for the financial industry to convince the governments to eliminate its regulations and oversight structure.

As Minsky predicted, after financial deregulation in most of the major economies of the world, the world found itself rudely awakened by a financial crisis in 2008. In 2010, people had figured out what caused the crisis, but there was little consensus on how to deal with it:

1. How much emphasis should be placed on reviving aggregate demand?
2. What needs to be done to restore the financial system to where it can perform its basic function of channeling savings to society's most welfare-enhancing investment and innovative projects?
3. What should be done to prevent a recurrence of the crisis?
4. Do we need to redesign the international financial order?

There were many proposals for reform. This chapter briefly presented a very arbitrary selection. By the time you read this book, there will surely have been many more proposals and counterproposals presented.

Since some of the proposals will be to either do nothing or to at least wait for less turbulent times to act so that new mistakes can be avoided, it is useful to heed Wolf's (2009) reminder that one of the most successful reform episodes, Bretton Woods, took place during World War II and no assurance that the Great Depression had been firmly put to rest. "If they could fight a war and redesign the global economy at the same time, so can we fight a crisis and redesign global institutions simultaneously".[26]

18.6.2 *The legacy of Keynes*

In addition to a possible return to Bretton Woods, this chapter also discussed a "return to Keynesianism". We are today in the midst of yet another paradigm shift in economics, a common occurrence when there is a major economic disruption. At the time of this writing, there is a renewed interest in the writings of Keynes and his macroeconomic model. We need to be very careful to emphasize the true contributions of Keynes, not only the simplified model his followers

---

[26] Martin Wolf (2008). "Why Agreeing a New Bretton Woods Is Vital and So Hard", *Financial Times*, 5 November.

put in their textbooks. Hopefully, this textbook did Keynes full justice, especially in the case of his insightful explanations of expectations and financial markets.

John Maynard Keynes was a prominent figure at Bretton Woods, but in the end it was the US delegation that got its way most often. The Bretton Woods system put the US dollar at its center, a position that it still enjoys today. Having the dollar function as the world's reserve currency gives the US privileges, such as the ability to run current repeated account deficits and to borrow in dollars. The dollar was challenged in the 1960s, but despite being cut lose from gold, it has maintained its status as the premier reserve currency. The instability of the international financial system and the repeated financial crises actually induced more countries to accumulate dollars, thus permitting the United States to run huge current account deficits and to consume much more than it produced year after year during the 1980s, 1990s, and 2000s. This era may have come to an end in 2009, but it is not at all clear how the international financial system will change.

It is interesting to think about what a new Bretton Woods Conference would look like at this point in financial history. The United States is more in the position of Great Britain at the original Bretton Woods Conference, since it is the most recent owner of the world's reserve currency. On the other hand, while the British pound had already lost its position to the US dollar in 1944, the demise of the dollar has not yet occurred. It may not occur for a long time. China and Russia, among other countries, have urged that a new reserve currency be created; countries that have accumulated large amounts of dollars, like China, Korea, Japan, and Taiwan, are justifiably concerned about the future value of their investment in dollars. China owns over $2 trillion! If the United States had to borrow overseas in something other than dollars, it would be exposed to exchange risk, and to avoid instability it might be forced to reduce its current account deficit. Its consumption would have to fall in order to generate more internal savings, which is not an attractive policy for an economy mired in recession.

Clearly, the US delegation at a new Bretton Woods conference would resist the creation of such an international reserve. But does the United States still have the clout to prevent such a change? Of course, China and others could simply begin accumulating other currencies as reserves, which they certainly have the option to do under today's order. But they would, most likely, devalue their accumulated dollar reserves if their shift to another reserve currency drives down the value of the dollar.

Before the original Bretton Woods Conference, Keynes had suggested creating an international reserve currency, the Bancor, so that no one national currency would serve as reserve currency. Keynes suggested the Bancor should be managed by a world central bank, like the IMF. 65 years later at the G20 conference in July 2009, world leaders approved the idea of creating additional special drawing rights (SDRs), which are similar to Keynes' Bancor, to be administered by the IMF and honored as payment by all countries. These additional SDRs are to be used by developing and other countries facing difficulties in financing fiscal stimulus programs during the 2008–2009 recession. Still, the US dollar and dollar assets continue to be accumulated by China, Japan, and other trade surplus countries.

It is interesting to think of who would make up the national delegations if we held a new Bretton Woods Conference. Who would be the leading characters? For the US delegation, the Treasury Secretary Timothy Geithner would perhaps play the role of Harry Dexter White. Or would he take a less active role, as Henry Morgenthau did, and let the chief economist in the Obama administration, Larry Summers, run the show. More personally, who would play the role of Keynes, the elder statesman and the undisputed leading economist of his time? Is there such a personality alive today? If there were, would he be invited to take a prominent seat at the table of a new Bretton Woods Conference?

Predicting the future is always hazardous. For this reason, we will leave many of these questions without answers for now. Hopefully, the textbook has provided you with a sufficiently holistic view of the international financial system so that you can correctly interpret the future and the answers it will provide.

Key Terms and Concepts

Asset bubble	Glass-Steagall Act	Securitization
Collateralized debt	Hedge financing	Speculative financing
Conduits	Housing bubble	Stock market bubble
Credit default swaps	Liquidity trap	Stress tests
Default insurance	Ponzi financing	Sub-prime mortgage
Endowment effect	Roll over	Toxic assets
Financial instability	Ratings firms	Tranches
hypoth.		

Chapter Questions and Problems

1. Do you think it is fair that the taxpayers of one country bail out a bank with customers in other countries? Discuss.
2. The US insurance firm A.I.G. operated under regulations that permitted it to issue insurance without increasing reserves if it had a credible model showing that there was no risk it would have to pay out on credit default swaps on the more highly rated tranches of collateralized debt obligations. Does this make sense? Discuss.
3. Discuss the various causes of financial crises. How can they be prevented? How should the international financial system be reformed to reduce the chances that a financial sector in one or more countries is forced to curtail lending?
4. Does the globalization of financial services imply that regulation and oversight should be conducted by international institutions rather than national institutions, as is currently the case? Discuss.
5. Review the circumstances that led to the growth of collateralized debt obligations built on sub-prime housing loans (mortgages). Do you think the behavior of the borrowers, the loan officers, the bank mangers, the bank stockholders, the ratings agencies, the real estate agents, the bank regulators and supervisors, the bank auditors, and anyone else involved was ethical? Were the mistakes "honest" mistakes, or were they understood by those involved? Discuss.

6. Does the financial industry need more regulation? Why or why not?

7. Do we need another Bretton Woods Conference? If yes, what should the agenda be? If no, then how should the recent financial failures be addressed?

8. In this chapter, a case is made for restoring the Keynesian model to the forefront of macroeconomic analysis, largely because the alternative neoliberal models of rational expectations, efficient markets, and stable underlying preference and cost functions failed so miserably in missing the 2008 economic crisis. But can the open-economy *AD/AS* model with its Keynesian demand side analyze all prospective macroeconomic issues accurately? Discuss. (Hint: Select one or more possible macroeconomic problems, such as inflation from a rapid economic recovery after 2009, a major health catastrophe such as the swine flu, or a reversal in the recovery due to the lack of a second wave of fiscal stimulus, and use the model to explain the consequences.)

9. Explain the Keynesian liquidity trap. How does the existence of a liquidity trap limit policymakers' options for dealing with high unemployment?

10. Speculate on how likely it is that the EU's five suggestions for dealing with the global financial crisis will be carried out. What could block their implementation?

11. Does recent research in psychology, experimental economics, and neuroscience undermine the hypotheses of the neo-liberal paradigm and confirm the accuracy of the Keynesian macroeconomic model? Explain why or why not. (Do not be afraid to defend the neo-liberal paradigm and dispute the Keynesion model if your conclusions differ from those of the author)

References

Akerlof, GA (2007). The missing motivation in macroeconomics. *American Economic Review*, 97(1), 5–36.

Arrow, K and G Debreu (1954). Existence of an equilibrium for a competitive economy. *Econometrica*, 22, 265–290.

Eichengreen, B and R Portes (1995). *Crisis? What Crisis? Orderly Workouts for Sovereign Debtors*. London: Centre for Economic Policy Research.

Coase, R (1960). The problem of social costs. *The Journal of Law and Economics*, 3.

Debreu, G (1959). *Theory of Value*. New Haven, CN: Yale University Press.

Fama, E (1970). Efficient capital markets: A review of theory and empirical work. *Journal of Finance*, 25(3), 383–417.

Frederick, S (2005). Cognitive reflection and decision making. *Journal of Economic Perspectives*, 19(4), 25–42.

Friedman, M (1953). The case for flexible exchange rates. *Essays on Positive Economics*. M Friedman (ed.), pp. 157–203. Chicago: University of Chicago Press.

Greenlaw, D, J Hatzins, A Kashyap and YS Shin (2008). Leveraged losses: Lessons from the mortgage market meltdown. *Proceedings of the US Monetary Policy Forum*, New York, 29 February.

Kahneman, D and A Tversky (2000). *Choices, Values and Frame*. Cambridge, UK: Cambridge University Press.

Kaufman, H (1998). Preventing the next global financial crisis. *Washington Post*, January 28.

Keynes, JM (1936[1964]). *The General Theory of Employment, Interest, and Money*. New York: Harcourt Brace Jovanovich.

Krueger, A (2001). International financial architecture for 2002: A new approach to sovereign debt restructuring. Address at the National Economists' Club, American Enterprise Institute, Washington, DC: November 26.

Lanchester, J (2009). It's finished. *London Review of Books*, 31(10), 28 May.

Le Doux, JE (1996). *The Emotional Brain: The Mysterious Underpinnings of Emotional Life*. New York: Simon and Shuster.

Levine, R (1997). Financial development and economic growth: Views and agenda. *Journal of Economic Literature*, 35(2), 688–726.

Lucas, RE, Jr. (1972). Expectations and the neutrality of money. *Journal of Economic Theory*, 4, 103–24.

Lucas, RE, Jr. (1973). Some international evidence on output-inflation tradeoffs. *American Economic Review*, 68, 326–334.

Minsky, HP (1982). *Can "It" Happen Again?* Armonk, NY: M. E. Sharpe, Inc.

Muth, JF (1961). Rational expectations and the theory of price movements. *Econometrica*, 29, 315–335.

North, DC and RP Thomas (1973). *The Rise of the Western World; A New Economic History*. Cambridge: Cambridge University Press.

Simonian, H (2009). Swiss meet US government over defence of bank secrecy. *Financial Times*, March 2.

Shiller, RJ (1997). Why do people dislike inflation? *Reducing Inflation: Motivation and Strategy*. CD Romer and DH Romer (eds.). Chicago: University of Chicago Press.

Soros, G (1998). *The Crisis of Global Capitalism*. New York: Public Affairs Press.

Stiglitz, J (2009). A global recovery for a global recession. *The Nation*, June 24.

Stiglitz, J and A Weiss (1981). Credit rationing in markets with imperfect information. *American Economic Review*, 71, 393–410.

UNCTAD (2007). *World Investment Report 2007*. New York: United Nations Conference on Trade and Development.

Index